OXFORD MONOGRAPHS
IN INTERNATIONAL LAW

Coastal State Jurisdiction over Living Resources in the Exclusive Economic Zone

OXFORD MONOGRAPHS IN INTERNATIONAL LAW

The aim of this series is to publish important and original pieces of research on all aspects of international law. Topics that are given particular prominence are those which, while of interest to the academic lawyer, also have important bearing on issues which touch the actual conduct of international relations. Nonetheless the series is wide in scope and includes monographs on the history and philosophical foundations of international law.

RECENT TITLES IN THE SERIES

International Law and Corporate Actors in Deep Seabed Mining
Joanna Dingwall

The Concept of an International Organization in International Law
Lorenzo Gasbarri

Necessity and Proportionality and the Right of Self-Defence in International Law
Chris O'Meara

Neutrality in Contemporary International Law
James Upcher

Geographical Change and the Law of the Sea
Kate Purcell

Coastal State Jurisdiction over Living Resources in the Exclusive Economic Zone

CAMILLE GOODMAN

OXFORD
UNIVERSITY PRESS

OXFORD
UNIVERSITY PRESS

Great Clarendon Street, Oxford, OX2 6DP,
United Kingdom

Oxford University Press is a department of the University of Oxford.
It furthers the University's objective of excellence in research, scholarship,
and education by publishing worldwide. Oxford is a registered trade mark of
Oxford University Press in the UK and in certain other countries

First Edition published in 2021

Impression: 1

Published in the United States of America by Oxford University Press
198 Madison Avenue, New York, NY 10016, United States of America

British Library Cataloguing in Publication Data

Data available

Library of Congress Control Number: 2021942854

ISBN 978–0–19–289684–1

DOI: 10.1093/oso/9780192896841.001.0001

Printed and bound by
CPI Group (UK) Ltd, Croydon, CR0 4YY

General Editors' Preface

One of the innovations of the 1982 Law of the Sea Convention (LOSC) is the establishment of the 200-mile exclusive economic zone (EEZ) in which coastal States enjoy exclusive sovereign rights over, inter alia, the living resources of the zone. Uptake by coastal States in proclaiming this new zone was both swift and widespread, which is unsurprising given that over 70 per cent of the world's commercially exploited fish stocks are found within 200 miles of the coast. Equally notorious is the ambiguous nature of the EEZ provisions contained in Part V of LOSC, which generated significant contemporaneous analysis, with subsequent treatises analysing various aspects of living resource exploitation and management. Yet—as Camille Goodman herself encountered in government legal practice when asked to advise on questions regarding the extent of coastal State jurisdiction in the zone—the answers are not always to be found in a literature where several of the major monographs predate the entry into force of LOSC. This gap was the inspiration for her undertaking a PhD on the subject at the Australian National University, from which this splendid monograph arises.

Drawing upon several decades of practice by a wide range of States in the implementation of the 'painful ambiguities and existing possibilities'[1] contained in the provisions of Part V of LOSC, *Coastal State Jurisdiction over Living Resources in the Exclusive Economic Zone* adopts an inductive approach to analysing the nature and extent of coastal State jurisdiction over living resources in the EEZ. It adds to the existing scholarship a much-needed contemporary analysis of the extent of such jurisdiction and provides a useful framework within which to understand contemporary, and potentially to resolve future, jurisdictional issues. Within this framework, each chapter sets out the relevant LOSC provisions, highlights where they are ambiguous or unclear and leave room for interpretation, and discusses any relevant case law and national legislation. The purpose is not to provide a rigid formula, which is neither realistic nor desirable given continuing changes in the circumstances in which States exercise jurisdiction over living resources, ranging from technological change to the climate emergency. Rather, it is to identify the contemporary extent of coastal State jurisdiction over living resources in the EEZ, to discern the general principles informing the nature of coastal State jurisdiction, and to elucidate the broader nature of that jurisdiction as 'flexible but functional', with the dominant characteristic of the EEZ regime remaining the substantial discretion enjoyed by the coastal State.

[1] Philip Allott, 'Power Sharing in the Law of the Sea' (1983) 77 AJIL 1, 8.

Coastal State Jurisdiction over Living Resources in the Exclusive Economic Zone is a valuable addition to the literature to which any practitioner, policy maker, legal advisor and academic in the law of the sea will turn. General international lawyers too will find much of interest here in the discussion of the nature and extent of prescriptive and enforcement jurisdiction in the EEZ and of the interplay of treaty law and practice.

CR, RO'K
Oxford and Milan
August 2021

Acknowledgements

I am extremely grateful to the institutions and individuals whose support has enabled me to write this book, and to conduct the doctoral research on which it is based. First and foremost, I would like to acknowledge the support of the Australian Government Attorney-General's Department through the Sir Roland Wilson Foundation Scholarship Program at the Australian National University (ANU). This Program enables members of the Australian Public Service to undertake academic research, encourages the development and deepening of links between academia and public policy, and acknowledges the importance of academic research to ensuring high quality, evidence-based policymaking. Of course, the views expressed in this book are mine alone, and do not reflect those of the Attorney-General's Department or the Australian Government. I am also very grateful to have received the support of the ANU College of Law throughout this process, first as a doctoral student and subsequently as a Visiting Fellow.

Writing a book (or undertaking a PhD) is something that you do alone, but that doesn't mean it is lonely. I am extremely fortunate to have been surrounded by a wide and wonderful group of people—both in Australia and overseas—who have provided advice and encouragement, generously shared their knowledge and expertise, and given me confidence and inspiration over the course of my research and writing. While it is not possible to mention all these people individually, I must thank my doctoral supervisor Professor Donald Rothwell and adviser Associate Professor Sarah Heathcote. I would also like to sincerely acknowledge and thank my colleagues (past and present) in the Office of International Law at the Attorney-General's Department, the ANU College of Law and the Australian National Centre for Ocean Resources and Security, as well as the 'virtual network' of overseas colleagues developed during my PhD and all those others with whom I have worked on fisheries and law of the sea issues over the years—in Australia, the western and central Pacific, and beyond. I am very grateful for all that you have taught me, and I hope you find this work interesting and useful.

Preface

This book is based on a PhD thesis awarded by the Australian National University in 2019. It reflects the law as it stood, to the best of the author's knowledge, on 31 December 2020, although it has been possible to incorporate some subsequent developments in legislation or litigation. Parts of Chapter 2 (and in particular Section 2.3) have previously been published in a substantially similar form as Camille Goodman 'Rights, Obligations, Prohibitions: A Practical Guide to Understanding Judicial Decisions on Coastal State Jurisdiction over Living Resources in the Exclusive Economic Zone' (2018) 33 IJMCL 558.

Due to the volume of State practice cited in this book, abbreviated titles for national legislation are used in the footnotes and Tables, and full titles are provided in the Table of Legislation. Much of this legislation can be found in the FAOLEX Database, available at <http://www.fao.org/faolex/country-profiles/en/>. Where possible, English-language sources or official translations of foreign language sources were used. Where these were not available, foreign language sources were translated using translation software. Where there was doubt about the meaning or effect of primary or secondary legislation, confirmation of its practical effect was sought through additional sources, including policy documents, judicial decisions, diplomatic acts correspondence, public statements by Government ministers or relevant officials, press releases, and news reports.

In quoted material, some spellings have been regularized for consistency with the general text. Summaries of foreign language material were prepared by the author.

The maps in this book were prepared by Dr Dražen Tutić. They were made with Natural Earth raster and vector map data, available at <http://naturalearthdata.com>, and using Flanders Marine Institute Maritime Boundaries Geodatabase: *Maritime Boundaries and Exclusive Economic Zones* (200NM) (Version 11, 2019), available at <http://www.marineregions.org/>. The data was verified through additional sources including the United Nations Food and Agriculture Organisation (FAO) Regional Fishery Bodies Map Viewer, available at <http://www.fao.org/figis/geoserver/factsheets/rfbs.html>.

All website addresses were accurate on the date of access indicated and were archived online on that date at <http://archive.org/web/> where they will remain accessible in their original form even if the original website is altered or removed.

Table of Contents

List of Figures

List of Tables

Table of Cases

Note on tables: *For the benefit of digital users, table entries that span two pages (e.g., 52–53) may, on occasion, appear on only one of those pages.*

INTERNATIONAL CASES AND AWARDS

DOMESTIC CASES

Table of Agreements and Arrangements

1978

1982

1992

1993

1994

1995

2001

2002

2003

2004

2006

2007

2008

2009

2010

2011

2012

2013

2014

2016

2019

Table of Legislation

This Table refers to laws and regulations as amended and in force at 31 December 2020, except where otherwise indicated.

Egypt

Equatorial Guinea

Eritrea

Gabon

Gambia

Ghana

Guinea

Guinea-Bissau

Kenya

Liberia

Libya

Madagascar

Mauritania

List of Abbreviations

Advances in MarBiol	*Advances in Marine Biology*
AFZ	Australian Fishing Zone
AIS	Automatic information system
AJIL	*American Journal of International Law*
ALC	Automatic location communicator
ALJ	*Australian Law Journal*
AnnFrDroitIntl	*Annuaire français de droit international*
Ant&SthnOcean L&Pol OccPap	*Antarctic and Southern Ocean Law and Policy Occasional Papers*
APacJOceanL&Pol	*Asia Pacific Journal of Ocean Law and Policy*
Asian JIntlL	*Asian Journal of International Law*
AUD	Australian dollars
AustJMar&OceanAff	*Australian Journal of Maritime and Ocean Affairs*
AustYBIL	*Australian Yearbook of International Law*
BerkleyJIntlL	*Berkley Journal of International Law*
BIOT	British Indian Ocean Territory
BrazilJIntlLaw	*Brazilian Journal of International Law*
BYIL	*British Yearbook of International Law*
CalWIntlLJ	*California Western International Law Journal*
CARICOM	Caribbean Community
CaseWResJIntlL	*Case Western Reserve Journal of International Law*
CCAMLR	Commission for the Conservation of Antarctic Marine Living Resources
CCCFP	*2011 Agreement Establishing the Caribbean Community Common Fisheries Policy*
China Oceans LRev	*China Oceans Law Review*
ChineseJIntlL	*Chinese Journal of International Law*
CHOGM	Commonwealth Heads of Government Meeting
CLCS	Commission on the Limits of the Continental Shelf
CPPS	Permanent Commission of the South Pacific
CRFM	Caribbean Regional Fisheries Mechanism
CUP	Cambridge University Press
DeakinLRev	*Deakin Law Review*
DOALOS	Division of Oceans Affairs and the Law of the Sea
EEZ	Exclusive economic zone
EJIL	*European Journal of International Law*
ELQ	*Ecology Law Quarterly*
Env&Planning LJ	*Environment and Planning Law Journal*
EU	European Union

FAO	Food and Agriculture Organization
FAO Code of Conduct	*1995 Code of Conduct for Responsible Fisheries*
FAO Voluntary Guidelines	*2014 Voluntary Guidelines for Flag State Performance*
FCWC	Fisheries Committee for the West Central Gulf of Guinea
FCWC MRA Convention	*2013 Convention on Minimum Requirements for Access to the Fishery Resources of the Area of the Fisheries Committee for the West Central Gulf of Guinea (FCWC)*
FFA	Forum Fisheries Agency
FFA Harmonized MTCs	*1990 Harmonized Minimum Terms and Conditions for Access by Fishing Vessels*
Fish&Fisheries	*Fish and Fisheries*
GeoIntlEnvtlLRev	*Georgetown International Environmental Law Review*
GoettingenJIntlLaw	*Goettingen Journal of International Law*
GWashIntlLRev	*George Washington International Law Review*
GYIL	*German Yearbook of International Law*
HarvLRev	*Harvard Law Review*
ICJ	International Court of Justice
ICLQ	*International and Comparative Law Quarterly*
IJECL	*International Journal of Estuarine and Coastal Law*
IJMCL	*International Journal of Marine and Coastal Law*
ILC	International Law Commission
ILR	*International Law Reports*
IMO	International Maritime Organization
IntlJMarAff&Fish	*International Journal of Maritime Affairs and Fisheries*
IntlLSt	*International Law Studies*
IntSt	*International Studies*
IOTC	Indian Ocean Tuna Commission
IPOA-IUU	*2001 International Plan of Action to Prevent, Deter and Eliminate Illegal, Unreported and Unregulated Fishing*
ITLOS	International Tribunal for the Law of the Sea
IUU	*Illegal, unreported, and unregulated (fishing)*
JIntlWildlifeL&Pol	*Journal of International Wildlife Law and Policy*
JMarL&Com	*Journal of Maritime Law and Commerce*
JTransnatLawPol	*Journal of Transnational Law and Policy*
Law&Env	*Law and the Environment*
LJIL	*Leiden Journal of International Law*
LOSC	*1982 United Nations Convention on the Law of the Sea*
LQR	*Law Quarterly Review*
MarPol	*Marine Policy*
MarPolManagement	*Maritime Policy Management*
MarSafety&SecLJ	*Maritime Safety and Security Law Journal*
MaxPlanckYrbkUNL	*Max Planck Yearbook of United Nations Law*
MCS	Monitoring, control, and surveillance
MelbJIntlLaw	*Melbourne Journal of International Law*
MPA	Marine protected area

MTC	Minimum terms and conditions
MUP	Manchester University Press
NAFO	North Atlantic Fisheries Organization
NEAFC	North East Atlantic Fisheries Commission
NGO	Non-governmental organization
Niue Treaty Subsidiary Agreement	*2012 Agreement on Strengthening the Implementation of the Niue Treaty on Fisheries Surveillance and Law Enforcement in the South Pacific Region*
NYIL	*Netherlands Yearbook of International Law*
NYUJIntlL&Pol	*NYU Journal of International Law and Politics*
NZD	New Zealand dollars
Ocean&CoastMan	*Ocean and Coastal Management*
OceanYB	*Ocean Yearbook*
ODIL	*Ocean Development and International Law*
OECS	Organization of Eastern Caribbean States
OLDEPESCA	Latin American Organization for Fisheries Development
OrLRev	*Oregon Law Review*
OSPESCA	Central American Fisheries and Aquaculture Organization
OtLR	*Otago Law Review*
OUP	Oxford University Press
PacRim L&PolJ	*Pacific Rim Law and Policy Journal*
PCIJ	Permanent Court of International Justice
PLOS ONE	*PLOS ONE*
PNA	Parties to the Nauru Agreement
PNG	Papua New Guinea
Port State Measures Agreement	*2009 Agreement on Port State Measures to Prevent, Deter and Eliminate Illegal, Unreported and Unregulated Fishing*
ProcAnnMtg (ASIL)	*Proceedings of the Annual Meeting (American Society of International Law)*
RdC	*Recueil des Cours*
RECIEL	*Review of European, Comparative and International Environmental Law*
RFMO	Regional fisheries management organization
RPOA-IUU	*2007 Regional Plan of Action to Promote Responsible Fishing Practices including Combating Illegal, Unreported and Unregulated Fishing in the Region*
SAAT	Southern and Antarctic Territories (France)
SADC	South African Development Community
SADC Protocol	*2001 South African Development Community Protocol on Fisheries*
SanDiegoLRev	*San Diego Law Review*
SGSSI	South Georgia and the South Sandwich Islands

SIOFA	*Southern Indian Ocean Fisheries Agreement*
SRFC	Sub-Regional Fisheries Commission
SRFC MCA Convention	*2012 Convention on the Determination of the Minimal Conditions for Access and Exploitation of Marine Resources within the Maritime Areas under the Jurisdiction of the Member States of the Sub-Regional Fisheries Commission (SRFC)*
StanEnvLJ	*Stanford Environmental Law Journal*
SWIOFC	South West Indian Ocean Fisheries Commission
SWIOFC MTCs	*2019 Guidelines for Minimum Terms and Conditions (MTC) for Foreign Fisheries Access in the South West Indian Ocean Fisheries Commission (SWIOFC) Region*
TulMarLJ	*Tulane Maritime Law Journal*
UAE	United Arab Emirates
UN	United Nations
UNCLOS I	First United Nations Conference on the Law of the Sea
UNCLOS II	Second United Nations Conference on the Law of the Sea
UNCLOS III	Third United Nations Conference on the Law of the Sea
UNFSA	*1995 Agreement for the Implementation of the Provisions of the United Nations Convention on the Law of the Sea of 10 December 1982 relating to the Conservation and Management of Straddling Fish Stocks and Highly Migratory Fish Stocks*
UNGA	United Nations General Assembly
UNSC	United Nations Security Council
UNSWLJ	*University of New South Wales Law Journal*
USD	United States dollars
UWALRev	*University of Western Australia Law Review*
VaJIntlL	*Virginia Journal of International Law*
VCLT	*1969 Vienna Convention on the Law of Treaties*
VDS	Vessel Day Scheme
VHF	Very high frequency (radio)
VMS	Vessel monitoring system
VUWellLRev	*Victoria University of Wellington Law Review*
Waseda GlobalFor	*Waseda Global Forum*
WCPFC	Western and Central Pacific Fisheries Commission
WTrRev	*World Trade Review*
YaleLJ	*Yale Law Journal*
YJIL	*Yale Journal of International Law*

1
Introduction

Encompassing one-third of the world's ocean space and the vast majority of its commercially exploitable resources, the 200 nautical mile exclusive economic zone (EEZ) affects 'more interests of more States'[1] than any other aspect of the 1982 *United Nations Convention on the Law of the Sea* (LOSC).[2] Since the EEZ is beyond the territory—and the territorial sovereignty—of any State, understanding the extent to which States have both the freedom to act and the authority to regulate in this zone is crucial, but complex. Although the LOSC delineates the rights and duties of coastal and other States over specific activities and resources within the EEZ, there remains a good deal of uncertainty about the extent and limit of that jurisdiction—particularly with respect to the regime for living resources. Under Part V of the LOSC, coastal States have 'sovereign rights' to explore and exploit, conserve and manage the living resources of the EEZ, and may take measures to ensure compliance with laws and regulations adopted in the exercise of such rights. However, the nature and extent of these sovereign rights—and the way in which coastal States may employ them—is not well understood, and coastal States have employed innovative approaches to the exercise of this jurisdiction.

This book examines coastal State jurisdiction over living resources in the EEZ under the framework established by the LOSC. This examination has two objectives: first, to articulate the substantive *extent* of coastal State jurisdiction over living resources in the EEZ under the relevant provisions of the LOSC; and second, to formulate a broader statement about the underlying *nature* of that jurisdiction. These objectives inform and influence each other: discerning the general principles that inform the nature of coastal State jurisdiction is crucial to determining its substantive extent; and determining the practical extent of the authority that is exercised on the basis of such jurisdiction can help to reveal its underlying nature. Nonetheless, they also require the examination of different issues: understanding the nature of coastal State jurisdiction requires consideration of the general framework and principles that underpin the legal regime for the EEZ at a theoretical and systemic level, while articulating the extent of coastal State jurisdiction necessarily involves examining the way in which the framework and principles are interpreted and applied as a matter of practice.

[1] Barbara Kwiatkowska, *The 200 Mile Exclusive Economic Zone in the New Law of the Sea* (Martinus Nijhoff 1989) xxiii–iv.
[2] (Opened for signature 10 December 1982, entered into force 16 November 1994) 1833 UNTS 3.

Coastal State Jurisdiction over Living Resources in the Exclusive Economic Zone. Camille Goodman, Oxford University Press.
 DOI: 10.1093/oso/9780192896841.003.0001

This examination is framed and focused by the unique context of the EEZ. Despite then being a novel and untested concept, the EEZ was recognized by the International Court of Justice (ICJ) as part of 'modern international law' before the LOSC was even signed.[3] And yet, four decades later, there is still significant ambiguity about the *sui generis* jurisdictional regime that applies in this important zone; it is not based on the territorial sea regime of sovereignty, nor the high seas regime of freedom, but reflects a carefully negotiated compromise intended to balance the *inclusive* interests of the international community with the *exclusive* interests of coastal States. While the framework established in Part V of the LOSC outlines the basic rights and obligations of coastal States with respect to the living resources of the EEZ, the open-ended and highly qualified nature of these rights and obligations—together with their general exclusion from compulsory dispute settlement—makes it difficult to determine the practical extent of the coastal State's jurisdiction in this regard. As Gavouneli has observed, the drafting of the LOSC 'has left even the International Tribunal for the Law of the Sea at a loss to identify the exact powers of States in the [EEZ]'.[4]

The circumstances under which coastal States exercise jurisdiction over living resources in the EEZ have changed significantly since the adoption of the LOSC, and will continue to do so. The global population—and the associated demand for protein from fishery resources—has increased rapidly.[5] Technology and infrastructure is constantly developing, providing new tools and techniques for use by illegal operators and enforcement authorities alike. Illegal, unreported, and unregulated (IUU) fishing has become a global issue,[6] and is commonly acknowledged to have links to other forms of criminal activity, such as drug trafficking, people smuggling, and slavery. There is pressure from communities, consumers, and civil society to increase regulation and implement higher standards in relation to social and environmental issues—from labour exploitation on fishing vessels to the expansion of no-take marine protected areas. The changing climate is affecting the marine environment and altering the distribution and abundance of living marine resources, producing new challenges and opportunities, and potentially leading to new conflicts.

In this context of existing ambiguity and continuing change, State practice has played a crucial role in interpreting and implementing the LOSC framework for living resources in the EEZ. To that effect—and in keeping with the historical

[3] *Continental Shelf (Tunisia v Libyan Arab Jamahiriya) (Judgment)* (1982) ICJ Rep 18 [100] (*Tunisia v Libya*).

[4] Maria Gavouneli, *Functional Jurisdiction in the Law of the Sea* (Martinus Nijhoff 2007) 7.

[5] Between 1961 and 2017, global food fish consumption increased by 3.1 per cent annually (almost twice the rate of population growth of 1.6 per cent): United Nations (UN) Food and Agriculture Organization (FAO), *The State of World Fisheries and Aquaculture 2020: Sustainability in Action* (FAO 2020) 3.

[6] Eliminating IUU fishing is one of the targets of UN Sustainable Development Goal 14. See 'The Future We Want' UNGA Res 66/288 (27 July 2012) UN Doc A/RES/66/288 [170].

importance of State practice in the development of the law of sea—this book takes an inductive approach, reviewing and analysing State practice in order to articulate and underpin a contemporary statement about the nature and extent of coastal State jurisdiction over living resources in the EEZ. The footnotes, figures, and tables in the book convey the depth of practice that substantiates the contemporary extent of coastal State jurisdiction with respect to specific issues. They also provide content and context to complement the doctrine and jurisprudence, which are drawn on and distilled to suggest a broader formulation encompassing the underlying—and ongoing—nature of coastal State jurisdiction over living resources in the EEZ. This may help to resolve new or different jurisdictional questions in a way that ensures that the EEZ regime continues to appropriately 'balance' all relevant interests under changing circumstances.

This Chapter examines two foundational issues necessary to anchor this law of the sea inquiry firmly within the doctrinal and methodological context of general international law. First, it outlines the role and effect of the international law concept of 'jurisdiction', and its role and application in the law of the sea in general, and the EEZ in particular (Section 1.1). Second, it considers the legal effect of State practice on both treaty law and customary international law in the context of the law of the sea (Section 1.2). It concludes by outlining the approach and structure of the book (Section 1.3).

1.1 Jurisdiction and the Law of the Sea

To properly examine the nature and extent of coastal State jurisdiction over living resources in the EEZ, it is necessary to start by clarifying the role and effect of the 'abstract concept'[7] of jurisdiction. Jurisdiction refers to the authority of a State to 'make, apply, and enforce rules of conduct upon persons'.[8] It sits at the very heart of the international legal order, and underpins the peaceful coexistence of sovereign States by providing a framework for the lawful exercise of regulatory authority.[9] In a world of nearly 200 independent sovereign States, each seeking to regulate the natural and legal persons, property and activity which may affect their territory, population, security, or economic interests, this framework is of vital importance to avoiding 'rancour and chaos'.[10]

[7] Cedric Ryngaert, *Jurisdiction in International Law* (2nd ed, OUP 2015) 1.

[8] Christopher Staker, 'Jurisdiction' in Malcolm Evans (ed), *International Law* (4th ed, OUP 2014) 309.

[9] Alex Mills, 'Rethinking Jurisdiction in International Law' (2014) 84(1) BYIL 187, 188.

[10] Rosalyn Higgins, 'International Trade Law and the Avoidance, Containment and Resolution of Disputes' (1991-V) 230 RdC 9, 89.

1.1.1 The General Law of Jurisdiction

The concept of jurisdiction is rooted in the same principles as the State itself; it is an incident of sovereignty, exercisable by a State in relation to its defined territory and permanent population.[11] The starting point for jurisdiction under international law is thus territorial; in general a State may exercise both prescriptive and enforcement jurisdiction[12] with respect to any person and any activity within its territory.[13] The territorial nature of jurisdiction was underlined in the 1927 *Lotus* case, in which the Permanent Court of International Justice (PCIJ) held, as to enforcement jurisdiction, that: 'The first and foremost restriction imposed by international law upon a State is that—failing the existence of a permissive rule to the contrary—it may not exercise its power in any form in the territory of another State. In this sense jurisdiction is certainly territorial; it cannot be exercised by a State outside its territory except by virtue of a permissive rule derived from international custom or from a convention.'[14]

On this basis, in relation to the exercise of *enforcement* jurisdiction, the majority judgment distinguished clearly between *extraterritorial* jurisdiction (which the Court found was generally prohibited in the absence of a specific permissive rule), and *territorial* jurisdiction, which the Court found was generally permitted unless limited by prohibitive rules. In contrast, the Court found that States may exercise *prescriptive* jurisdiction extraterritorially unless there is a prohibition. Having drawn this distinction between the extent of prescriptive and enforcement jurisdiction on the basis of territoriality, the Court concluded that '[a]ll that can be required of a State is that it should not overstep the limits which international law places upon its jurisdiction; within these limits, its title to exercise jurisdiction rests in its sovereignty.'[15]

Unfortunately, as a result of the Court's *obiter* statements that '[r]estrictions upon the independence of States cannot therefore be presumed'[16] and that international law leaves to States 'a wide measure of discretion which is only limited in certain cases by prohibitive rules',[17] the *Lotus* case is often cited as authority for the position that, by virtue of their sovereignty, States can take whatever action

[11] FA Mann, 'The Doctrine of Jurisdiction in International Law' (1964-I) 111 RdC 1, 30.

[12] Prescriptive jurisdiction refers to the jurisdiction to prescribe—to apply laws and regulations to the activities, relations, or status of persons or their interests. Enforcement jurisdiction refers to the jurisdiction to enforce—to compel compliance or punish non-compliance, whether through executive, administrative, police, or judicial power. On the categories of jurisdiction, see generally Ryngaert, *Jurisdiction in International Law* (n 7) 9–16; American Law Institute, *Restatement (Fourth) of the Foreign Relations Law of the United States* (2018) §401.

[13] FA Mann, 'The Doctrine of International Jurisdiction Revisited After Twenty Years' (1984-III) 186 RdC 9, 20.

[14] *Case of the SS 'Lotus' (France v Turkey)* (1927) Series A(10) PCIJ Rep 18–19 (*Lotus*).

[15] Ibid.

[16] Ibid 18.

[17] Ibid 19.

they please provided it is not prohibited by international law (the so-called '*Lotus* principle').[18] On this basis, the *Lotus* case has been widely criticized as outdated,[19] overly positivist,[20] and the 'high water mark of *laissez-faire* in international relations'.[21] However, a careful reading of the judgment reveals this to be an overly broad interpretation, which fails to take account of its full content or context;[22] a better view is that the Court's dictum in *Lotus* cannot reasonably be read any higher than indicating that, once it has been determined that there is no express prohibition, a State may exercise *prescriptive* jurisdiction with respect to persons, property, and acts outside its territory, provided that it does not *enforce* such jurisdiction extraterritorially.[23] Even on this reading, however, the *Lotus* judgment has remained contentious.[24]

At the heart of this contention is the characterization of the relationship between sovereignty and jurisdiction. The starting point for both sovereignty and jurisdiction is territoriality—since States have sovereignty over their territory, they have the right to prescribe the laws for public order within that territory, and those laws apply to everyone within that territory.[25] However, this does not equate to unrestrained freedom: in a system of multiple co-existent sovereigns, there are inherent limits on the freedom of action of each State. This was clearly described in Judge Shahabudeen's dissenting opinion in the *Nuclear Weapons Advisory Opinion*:

> The existence of a number of sovereignties side by side places limits on the freedom of each State to act as if the others did not exist. These limits define an objective structural framework within which sovereignty must necessarily exist; the framework, and its defining limits, are implicit in the reference in '*Lotus*' to

[18] Gerald Fitzmaurice, 'The Law and Procedure of the International Court of Justice, 1951–54: General Principles and Sources of Law' (1953) 30 BYIL 1, 16–17.

[19] Higgins, 'International Trade Law' (n 10) 114.

[20] JL Brierly, 'The "Lotus" Case' (1928) 44 LQR 154, 155.

[21] *Arrest Warrant of 11 April 2000 (Democratic Republic of the Congo v Belgium)* (Judgment) (2002) ICJ Rep 3 (Sep Op Higgins, Kooijmans, and Buergenthal) 79 (*Arrest Warrant*).

[22] See, eg, Ole Spiermann, '"Lotus" and the Double Structure of International Legal Argument' in Laurence Boisson de Chazournes and Philippe Sands (eds), *The International Court of Justice and Nuclear Weapons* (CUP 1999) 141–2; Staker, 'Jurisdiction' (n 8) 313–14; An Hertogen, 'Letting Lotus Bloom' (2015) 26(4) EJIL 901, 903; Douglas Guilfoyle, 'SS Lotus' in Eirik Bjorge and Cameron Miles (eds), *Landmark Cases in Public International Law* (Hart 2017) 107.

[23] *Arrest Warrant* (Diss Op van den Wyngaert) 167–8.

[24] For example, in a controversial 2019 decision, the International Tribunal for the Law of the Sea (ITLOS) found that the principle of exclusive flag State jurisdiction prohibits the exercise of both enforcement *and* prescriptive jurisdiction over the 'lawful activities' of foreign-flagged vessels on the high seas: *MV 'Norstar' (Panama v Italy)* (Judgment) (2018–2019) ITLOS Rep 7 [224]–[225] (*Norstar*). This was opposed in a strongly worded joint dissent, which stated that nothing in the LOSC, treaties, custom, or State practice altogether excludes the exercise of prescriptive criminal jurisdiction with respect to activities on the high seas, and cited *Lotus*: ibid (Joint Diss Op Cot, Pawlak, Yanai, Hoffmann, Kolodkin, Lijnzaad, and Treves) [19] and [36]. The ongoing effect of this decision is yet to be seen: no reasoning was given, the intended effect of the reference to 'lawful activities' is not clear, and it appears contrary to existing law and practice. However, it was cited in *obiter* in *The 'Enrica Lexie' Incident (Italy v India)* [2020] PCA Case 2015-28 [527] (*Enrica Lexie*).

[25] Staker, 'Jurisdiction' (n 8) 316.

> 'co-existing independent communities' .... Thus, however far-reaching may be the rights conferred by sovereignty, those rights cannot extend beyond the framework within which sovereignty itself exists.[26]

Unfortunately, the majority judgment in *Lotus* did not explicitly set out this notion of limitation or restraint—but it is implicit in the Court's general observation regarding the nature of the international system, and its statement that rules of international law are established in order to 'regulate the relations between co-existing independent communities' and achieve common aims.[27] Accordingly, *Lotus* can reasonably be understood as supporting the proposition that States have a wide discretion—not an unlimited freedom—to exercise jurisdiction within their territory in respect of events occurring outside it, provided there is no prohibition under international law (whether due to an explicit rule prohibiting the exercise of jurisdiction in a specific instance, or the implicit limitation on any exercise of jurisdiction which would infringe the sovereignty of another State).

Regardless of which approach is taken to the interpretation of *Lotus*, in reality (and in customary international law), State practice has given rise to a hybrid approach that is neither truly prohibitive nor truly permissive, but 'restrictive'.[28] While States do not routinely justify exercises of extraterritorial jurisdiction by reference to *specific* permissive rules, neither do they assert an unlimited freedom of action absent specific prohibition. Instead, States rely on broad, classical principles reflecting aspects of sovereignty such as territoriality and nationality to justify the extraterritorial exercise of prescriptive jurisdiction. In theory, this 'restrictive' approach to jurisdiction requires States to found any assertions of extraterritorial authority in one of the accepted bases of jurisdiction. These include, with differing levels of acceptance: (i) jurisdiction in relation to activities abroad which have effects within the territory of the State (the 'subjective-territoriality' and 'objective-territoriality' principles, the 'effects doctrine' and the 'protective principle'); (ii) jurisdiction in relation to nationals abroad (the 'nationality' and 'passive personality' principles); and (iii) jurisdiction in relation to issues of common concern to the community of nations (the 'universality' principle).[29] In practice, however, there is no conventional or customary consensus on the actual extent of jurisdiction that may be exercised on the basis of these principles.

[26] *Legality of the Threat or Use of Nuclear Weapons* (Advisory Opinion) (1996) ICJ Rep 226 (Diss Op Shahabuddeen) 393 (*Nuclear Weapons Advisory Opinion*).

[27] *Lotus* 18. See *Nuclear Weapons Advisory Opinion* (Diss Op Shahabuddeen) 393; Staker, 'Jurisdiction' (n 8) 314–5; Hertogen, 'Letting Lotus Bloom' (n 22) 903.

[28] James R Crawford, *Brownlie's Principles of Public International Law* (8th ed, OUP 2012) 457; Ryngaert, *Jurisdiction in International Law* (n 7) 29.

[29] See Higgins, 'International Trade Law' (n 10) 89–90; Crawford, *Brownlie's Principles of Public International Law* (n 28) 462–3; Staker, 'Jurisdiction' (n 8) 316–23; American Law Institute, *Restatement (Fourth)* (n 12) §§407–13.

While public international law does not prescribe hard and fast limits on the exercise of jurisdiction, it does 'postulate the existence of limits' and 'involve for every State an obligation to exercise moderation and restraint'.[30] This obligation of restraint is embodied in the generally accepted rule that any exercise of extraterritorial jurisdiction must be based on a 'reasonable connection' between the State and the factual situation it is seeking to regulate.[31] Accordingly, jurisdiction can be understood as a unilateral assertion of entitlement, legitimized by legally relevant contact (or a 'reasonable connection') with the facts, which may be exercised with a wide measure of discretion in the absence of a prohibition. However, since jurisdiction is not a 'monolithic or one-size-fits-all concept' but appears in different forms,[32] what constitutes a 'reasonable connection' has to be determined 'in light of the substantive standards which have emerged in the various areas of international practice'.[33]

In this regard, the concept of allocating jurisdiction has become a common feature in multilateral treaty regimes—in particular, those addressing issues of common concern to the international community (such as international criminal law and terrorism) and those developed to regulate the exercise of jurisdiction in areas that necessarily transcend territory and territorial boundaries (such as activities at sea, in the air, in outer space and in Antarctica). By establishing a framework for ascertaining the State or States that may exercise jurisdiction in relation to a particular situation, these treaties seek to codify the situations that will legitimately give rise to a 'relevant connection', generally founded in one of the classic jurisdictional principles—in particular, subjective and objective territoriality, nationality, passive personality, and universality.[34]

The growth of treaty-based jurisdictional obligations has also given rise to acceptance that jurisdiction is not just a matter of 'right' but also a question of 'duty'.[35] The jurisdictional 'duties' established in treaties range from:

- the relatively straightforward situations in which traditional jurisdictional rights are converted to duties in respect of which national jurisdiction must be either exercised or forfeited—such as obligations requiring States to exercise

[30] *Barcelona Traction (Belgium v Spain)* (Judgment) (1970) ICJ Rep 3 (Sep Op Fitzmaurice) [70].
[31] See, eg, Crawford, *Brownlie's Principles of Public International Law* (n 28) 457; Mann, 'The Doctrine of International Jurisdiction Revisited' (n 13) 28; American Law Insitute *Restatement (Fourth)* (n 12) §407 Comment (c).
[32] Bruno Simma and Andreas T Muller, 'Exercise and Limits of Jurisdiction' in James R Crawford and Martti Koskenniemi (eds), *The Cambridge Companion to International Law* (CUP 2012) 147.
[33] Andrea Bianchi, 'Reply to Professor Maier' in Karl M Meessen (ed), *Extraterritorial Jurisdiction in Theory and Practice* (Kluwer Law International 1996) 90.
[34] These principles are not 'categories of jurisdiction specifically recognized by international law', but simply provide evidence of a reasonable connection between the State and the conduct in question: Crawford, *Brownlie's Principles of Public International Law* (n 28) 477.
[35] Mills, 'Rethinking Jurisdiction' (n 9) 211–12.

jurisdiction on the basis of the (traditionally discretionary) grounds of territory and nationality in relation to certain categories of offence; to

- the assignment of responsibilities as a corollary of jurisdictional rights in substantive areas of international law—such as the 'due regard' rule established in Articles 56(2) and 58(2) of the LOSC, pursuant to which the sovereign rights of coastal States and the navigational freedoms of flag States in the EEZ are subject to corresponding duties; and
- the creation of rights that give rise to jurisdictional duties in respect of (and potentially even toward) individuals—such as the obligations of treatment of foreign nationals under international investment law, and the rights of access to justice afforded individuals under international human rights law.

Accordingly, jurisdiction should no longer be conceived of merely as a 'ceiling', regulating the maximum limits of State power, but in many circumstances as a 'floor', establishing the minimum standards of jurisdiction necessary to satisfy international obligations.[36] In light of this 'mixture of discretionary, mandatory and prohibitive elements',[37] jurisdiction can be viewed as a continuum of prohibitions, rights, and obligations pursuant to which a State may be *obliged*, *authorized but not required*, or *prohibited* from exercising jurisdiction in relation to a person or activity.[38]

1.1.2 Jurisdiction in the Law of the Sea

In areas that are beyond the territory—and the territorial jurisdiction—of any State, jurisdiction is necessarily *extra*territorial, and the traditional (territorially based) forms of jurisdiction are not directly applicable.[39] Jurisdiction at sea is underpinned by an inherent tension between claims of national sovereignty or jurisdiction over the ocean space, and the traditional principle of freedom of the seas, and the history of the law of the sea has been described as 'a search for coherent rules to regulate the projection of State authority over the oceans'.[40] This search has

[36] Ibid 209–10.

[37] Ibid 212–13.

[38] Cedric Ryngaert, 'Jurisdiction: Towards a Reasonableness Test' in Malcolm Langford et al (eds), *Global Justice, State Duties. The extraterritorial scope of economic, social and cultural rights in international law* (CUP 2013) 210–11.

[39] All waters on the landward side of the baseline from which the territorial sea is measured are within the territory of the coastal State and subject to its territorial jurisdiction. The territorial sea and archipelagic waters are subject to the sovereignty of the coastal State but are subject to the regime of innocent passage—and thus the right of access by foreign vessels. While the EEZ is derived from territory (as an entitlement generated from the coastline), it is beyond the territory and territorial jurisdiction of the coastal State.

[40] Tim Stephens and Donald R Rothwell, 'The LOSC Framework for Maritime Jurisdiction and Enforcement 30 Years On' (2012) 27 IJMCL 701, 701–2.

been a long one; the history of the law of the sea is replete with assertions of every degree of sovereignty and freedom, from *mare clausum* to *mare liberum* and back again,[41] in line with the interests of the dominant powers of the time.[42]

In the first half of the twentieth century, recognizing the resource potential of the oceans and drawing on developments in technology and scientific research, States sought to extend their influence over and occupation of the ocean. Expanded assertions of jurisdiction by coastal States, such as the 1945 *Truman Proclamation* on the natural resources of the continental shelf[43] and the 1952 *Santiago Declaration on the Maritime Zone*,[44] prompted fears of 'creeping jurisdiction' and the 'territorialization' of the oceans,[45] and highlighted the need to develop a set of global rules for the uniform allocation of jurisdiction at sea. The First United Nations Conference on the Law of the Sea in 1958 (UNCLOS I) proved inadequate; while it resulted in four conventions,[46] they did not adequately address key issues including the breadth of the territorial sea and the extent of exclusive fishing rights. The Second United Nations Conference on the Law of the Sea in 1960 (UNCLOS II) also failed to resolve these issues.[47] States chose to ratify only certain of the 1958 conventions and continued to expand their jurisdictional assertions over resources of the water

[41] These terms, which translate from Latin as 'closed sea' and 'open sea', entered the law of the sea lexicon after they were used as the titles of works on these topics by Hugo Grotius (1609) and John Selden (1635).

[42] DP O'Connell, *The International Law of the Sea, Vol I* (OUP 1982) 1.

[43] United States, *Proclamation No 2667* 'Policy of the United States With Respect to the Natural Resources of the Subsoil and Sea Bed of the Continental Shelf', 28 September 1945, 10 FR 12303.

[44] Chile, Ecuador and Peru, *Declaration on the Maritime Zone* (signed 18 August 1952) 1006 UNTS 325.

[45] Bernard H Oxman, 'The Territorial Temptation: A Siren Song at Sea' (2006) 100 AJIL 830, 832. The term 'creeping jurisdiction' generally refers to expanded assertions of jurisdiction by coastal States. It was originally used in relation to geographic expansions of jurisdiction over the continental shelf and the patrimonial sea or EEZ: see LDM Nelson, 'The Patrimonial Sea' (1973) 22 ICLQ 668, 682–3; Erik Franckx, 'The 200-Mile Limit: Between Creeping Jurisdiction and Creeping Common Heritage?' (2007) 39 GWashIntlLRev 467, 476–81. Since the adoption of the LOSC, it has been used in relation to the increasing range of activities sought to be regulated within areas under national jurisdiction, as well as the assertion of jurisdiction beyond the EEZ: see, eg, John A Knauss, 'Creeping Jurisdiction and Customary International Law' (1985) 15(2) ODIL 209; Wayne S Ball, 'The Old Grey Mare, National Enclosure of the Oceans' (1996) 27 ODIL 97, 103; Sam Bateman, Donald R Rothwell and David Van der Zwaag, 'Navigational Rights and Freedoms in the New Millennium: Dealing with 20th Century Controversies and 21st Century Challenges' in Donald R Rothwell and Sam Bateman (eds), *Navigational Rights and Freedoms of the New Law of the Sea* (Kluwer Law International 2000) 323–5.

[46] UNCLOS I concluded with the adoption of four conventions (collectively, the 1958 Conventions): the *Convention on the Territorial Sea and the Contiguous Zone* (1958 Convention on the Territorial Sea) (opened for signature 29 April 1958, entered into force 10 September 1964) 516 UNTS 206; the *Convention on the High Seas* (1958 Convention on the High Seas) (opened for signature 29 April 1958, entered into force 30 September 1962) 450 UNTS 11; the *Convention on Fishing and Conservation of the Living Resources of the High Seas* (opened for signature 29 April 1958, entered into force 20 March 1966) 559 UNTS 285; and the *Convention on the Continental Shelf* (1958 Convention on the Continental Shelf) (opened for signature 29 April 1958, entered into force 10 June 1964) 499 UNTS 311.

[47] UNCLOS II failed to adopt any proposal on the key questions before it (the breadth of the territorial sea and fishery limits). See DW Bowett, 'The Second United Nations Conference on the Law of Sea' (1960) 9 ICLQ 415, 432.

column, seabed, and subsoil. Against a growing backdrop of concern about the creeping jurisdiction of coastal States,[48] the Third United Nations Conference on the Law of the Sea (UNCLOS III), held between 1973 and 1982, culminated in the successful adoption of the LOSC, which established a comprehensive framework for the allocation of jurisdiction at sea. Developed in order to settle 'all issues relating to the law of the sea' and establish 'a legal order for the seas and oceans',[49] the LOSC embodies a purposeful allocation of jurisdiction over all activities in the maritime space and regulates 'in greater or lesser detail, almost every possible activity on, in, under and over the sea'.[50] In essence, it is a treaty-based system for the allocation of jurisdiction amongst States in the maritime space, beyond the land territory of any State.

Like jurisdiction under general international law, the exercise of jurisdiction under the law of the sea can be understood as a unilateral assertion of entitlement, legitimized by a reasonable connection with the facts, which may be exercised with a wide measure of discretion in the absence of a prohibition. In theory, the jurisdictional framework set out in the LOSC is derived from the traditional bases of jurisdiction under general international law. For example, coastal State authority is derived from territorial jurisdiction, flag State jurisdiction reflects nationality, and the general jurisdiction over piracy and slavery is founded in the principle of universality.[51] In practice, however, the nature and exercise of jurisdiction in the law of the sea raises different—or additional—considerations to jurisdiction under general international law, for which the traditional bases of jurisdiction cannot provide adequate support. Since jurisdiction at sea is commonly extraterritorial, concurrent, and related to a question of 'common goods', it involves a complex balance of interests and requires consideration of both rights and obligations. So while the traditional elements of territoriality, nationality, and universality can be identified in the LOSC framework, they have been adapted and intertwined with other 'functionally' based rights and responsibilities.[52]

In order to find an enduring balance between the competing interests of all States and establish a comprehensive, stable, and predictable framework for the law of the sea, the jurisdictional framework established in the LOSC is underpinned by two key concepts: spatial jurisdiction, pursuant to which the ocean space is divided into different zones within which basic jurisdictional rules apply; and functional jurisdiction, which allocates regulatory powers by reference to specific subject

[48] Franckx, 'The 200-mile Limit' (n 45) 476–80.

[49] LOSC, Preamble.

[50] Robin R Churchill, 'The 1982 United Nations Convention on the Law of the Sea' in Donald R Rothwell et al (eds), *The Oxford Handbook of the Law of the Sea* (OUP 2015) 24.

[51] Gavouneli, *Functional Jurisdiction* (n 4) 7.

[52] Ivan Shearer, 'Problems of Jurisdiction and Law Enforcement Against Delinquent Vessels' (1986) 35 ICLQ 320, 343.

matters or functions (such as fisheries, energy generation, or marine environmental protection). These two concepts enable jurisdiction to be defined both geographically and substantively,[53] and allow a range of jurisdictional rights, duties, and prohibitions to be allocated between coastal States, flag States, and port States under the LOSC in a highly flexible and selective manner.

The LOSC framework also anticipates and addresses some of the unresolved tensions that arise in respect of jurisdiction under general international law. For example, the LOSC specifically prescribes the issues, activities, and situations that will give rise to a 'relevant connection' for the purpose of exercising jurisdiction and specifies both the particular *rights* that may be exercised by each State in the various zones into which the sea is divided, as well as a range of *responsibilities* that each State must fulfil concomitant with the exercise of those rights. This approach—under which jurisdiction exists simultaneously as a minimum duty and a maximum right—reflects the compromise that is embodied in the heart of the LOSC in order to balance the interests of coastal States, flag States, and the international community as a whole. It reaches its maximum expression in the 'revolutionary compromise'[54] between the interests of coastal States and other States in the *sui generis* regime for the EEZ established in Part V of the LOSC.

1.1.3 Coastal State Jurisdiction in the EEZ

The establishment of the 200 nautical mile EEZ, in which the coastal State has 'sovereign rights' over living resources, was the largest transfer of resources to national jurisdiction in history.[55] While this acquisition of 'sovereign rights' presented enormous economic and development opportunities for coastal States, it also presented them with significant challenges: how to fulfill the responsibility to conserve and manage the fishery resources of the EEZ, design and adopt policies to maximize the returns from those resources; regulate the activities of foreign fishing vessels in the EEZ; and enforce their jurisdiction as coastal States. Of course, it also presented significant challenges for other States, particularly those wanting to ensure continued access to—and optimum utilization of—marine resources in order to maintain domestic industries and satisfy the constantly increasing demand for fish for human consumption, protect the rights of land-locked and geographically disadvantaged States, and ensure the freedom of navigation.

[53] Oxman, 'The Territorial Temptation' (n 45) 835.
[54] Gemma Andreone, 'The Exclusive Economic Zone' in Donald R Rothwell et al (eds), *The Oxford Handbook of the Law of the Sea* (OUP 2015) 161.
[55] Gunnar Kullenberg, 'The Exclusive Economic Zone: Some Perspectives' (1999) 42(9) Ocean&CoastMan 849, 849.

These conflicting interests were accommodated through a number of carefully negotiated compromises embedded in Part V of the LOSC, intended to ensure an enduring 'balance' between the interests of all States in the EEZ. Thus, while coastal States have 'sovereign rights' with respect to the exploration, exploitation, conservation, and management of the living resources in the EEZ,[56] and the right to take such enforcement measures as may be necessary to ensure compliance with their laws and regulations in this regard,[57] the exercise of these rights is qualified by a wide range of duties and limitations.[58] Non-coastal States retain the freedoms of 'navigation and overflight and of the laying of submarine cables and pipelines, and other internationally lawful uses of the sea related to these freedoms', but only in so far as they are not incompatible with Part V, and provided they are exercised with 'due regard to the rights and duties of the coastal State'.[59] While this provides a 'common denominator for the divergent interests of all States' with respect to the EEZ,[60] the significant discretion and ambiguity inherent in this framework—together with the gaps created by changes in practice and developments in technology and society—has given rise to a range of new questions and 'user conflicts' that have challenged its interpretation and implementation.

For example, in the age of modern industrial fishing, where fishing vessels operate in conjunction with transhipment, refuelling, and resupply vessels that allow them to stay at sea for months at a time, what types of vessels and activities may be regulated on the basis of the coastal State's sovereign rights over living resources in the EEZ? In the face of global acknowledgement of the problem of IUU fishing, what is the coastal State's jurisdiction over foreign fishing vessels exercising—or claiming to exercise—the freedom of navigation through the EEZ? What sort of enforcement measures are 'necessary' and 'reasonable' to deal with these challenges, and to what extent can modern technologies be relied on in taking such measures? These practical questions about the *extent* of coastal State jurisdiction give rise to broader, more systemic issues about the *nature* of that jurisdiction. Has the EEZ regime had the intended effect of freezing the creeping expansion of coastal State authority, and providing stability and predictability in the exercise of jurisdiction at sea? Does it enable inclusive and exclusive interests to be balanced appropriately over time and under changing circumstances? Is the open-ended and discretionary approach of the EEZ regime unclear and overly ambiguous, or is it a workable, flexible way to fill the gaps and resolve the tensions inherent in the LOSC framework?

[56] LOSC, art 56(1).
[57] Ibid art 73(1).
[58] Ibid arts 61–4 and 73(2)–(4).
[59] Ibid art 58.
[60] Helmut Tuerk, *Reflections on the Contemporary Law of the Sea* (Martinus Nijhoff 2012) 3.

1.2 State Practice and the Law of the Sea

In order to answer these questions, this book undertakes a widespread examination of State practice, which seeks to establish the extent to which a coastal State may subject foreign vessels, persons, or property to its law on the basis of its rights with respect to resources in the EEZ, without giving another State valid grounds for objecting that it lacks capacity to take such action, or that such action infringes another State's rights under the law of the sea. This Section describes the conceptual framework that underlies this examination. It outlines the way in which the rules of international law—several of which are unsettled as a matter of general international law—apply in the unique context of the law of the sea, explains how these rules are used to evaluate the legal effect of State practice under treaty law and customary international law, and sets out the parameters used to determine the State practice examined in this book.

1.2.1 The Relevant Rules of International Law

The law of the sea is part of the general corpus of international law, generated and governed by the sources set out in the *Statute of the International Court of Justice*—in particular, customary international law and treaties.[61] While the history of the law of the sea is based on centuries of State practice giving rise to customary law, the LOSC put the law of the sea on a conventional footing, providing a treaty-based framework to settle 'all issues relating to the law of the sea', and establish a legal order which would consider the inter-related problems of ocean space 'as a whole'.[62] In order to ensure the widest possible acceptance of this framework, all substantive provisions were adopted by consensus and it was understood that the LOSC was a 'package deal' containing a series of inter-related compromises in which the acceptance of certain provisions was conditional upon the inclusion of others, creating an integrated and indivisible linkage between many of the Articles.[63]

Accordingly, the provisions of the LOSC cannot be applied selectively; it is not possible for States to pick what they like and to disregard what they do not like, and rights cannot be claimed without the acceptance of correlative duties.[64] This approach is reinforced by the prohibition on reservations in Article 309 and the

[61] Annex to the *Charter of the United Nations* (opened for signature 26 June 1945, entered into force 24 October 1945) 1 UNTS XVI, art 38(1).

[62] LOSC Preamble [1] and [3].

[63] See Hugo Caminos and Michael R Molitor, 'Progressive Development of International Law and the Package Deal' (1985) 79(4) AJIL 871; William E Butler, 'Custom, Treaty, State Practice and the 1982 Convention' (1987) 81 ProcAnnMtg (ASIL) 84; Rudolf Bernhardt, 'Custom and Treaty in the Law of the Sea' (1987) 205 RdC 255.

[64] Tommy Koh, 'A Constitution for the Oceans' in *Official Text of the United Nations Convention on the Law of the Sea with Annexes and Indexes* (UN 1983) xxxiv.

compulsory dispute settlement system in Part XV. This 'package' is widely ratified: at the time of writing, there were 168 Parties to the LOSC.[65] For those 168 Parties, the vast majority of activities at sea are governed by the treaty-based framework established in the LOSC, which is interpreted pursuant to the general rules of treaty interpretation codified by Articles 31 and 32 of the *Vienna Convention on the Law of Treaties* (VCLT)[66] and supplemented, where necessary, by other rules of international law.[67]

However, custom still plays a significant role in the law of the sea. Custom governs the rights and obligations of States that are not Party to the LOSC and applies for all States in relation to issues that are not covered in the LOSC. And significant portions of the LOSC constitute custom—including existing rules of custom codified in the LOSC, rules that crystallized into custom during the negotiation and adoption of the LOSC, and rules that were not customary at the time the LOSC was adopted but have since acquired that status. Accordingly, significant aspects of the LOSC—including the EEZ—have been recognized as reflecting custom.[68] However, it is not always clear exactly which aspects of the LOSC are customary and which are not. In this regard, there are two particular difficulties.

First, in order to give rise to a new rule of custom, treaty provisions must be of a 'fundamentally norm-creating character such as could be regarded as forming the basis of a general rule of law'.[69] This raises questions about whether some of the highly discretionary provisions in the LOSC can give rise to rules of custom, or whether they simply constitute guidelines that States can apply, taking into account their individual circumstances.[70] Second, the unique 'package deal' of the LOSC raises significant questions about the extent to which rights and obligations that were originally constituted in the form of correlative treaty provisions can be 'disjunctively' considered as treaty-generated custom without leading to an unbalanced customary international law.[71] On this basis, it has been suggested that the compromise entered into in the LOSC has altered the application of the treaty-custom relationship, and that the LOSC thus constitutes an 'indivisible package of inter-related compromises' in which support cannot generally be found for the exercise of customary rights.[72] In practice, however, given the significant portions

[65] <un.org/Depts/los/reference_files/chronological_lists_of_ratifications.htm> accessed 11 February 2021.

[66] (Opened for signature 23 May 1969, entered into force 27 January 1980) 1155 UNTS 331.

[67] The LOSC remains part of general international law, and the obligations of its Parties include requirements of general international law. See, eg, LOSC Preamble [8] and art 293(1).

[68] See, eg, J Ashley Roach, 'Today's Customary International Law of the Sea' (2014) 45(3) ODIL 239.

[69] *North Sea Continental Shelf Cases (Germany v Denmark; Germany v Netherlands)* (Judgment) (1969) ICJ Rep 3 [72] (*North Sea Continental Shelf Cases*).

[70] Kwiatkowska, *The 200 Mile EEZ* (n 1) 93.

[71] Yoram Dinstein, 'The Interaction between Customary International Law and Treaties' (2007) 322 RdC 243, 373.

[72] Caminos and Molitor, 'Progressive Development of International Law' (n 63) 885. Similarly, Butler, 'Custom, Treaty, State Practice and the 1982 Convention' (n 63) 86–7.

of the LOSC that have already been recognized as custom, the effect of the compromise could perhaps more realistically be understood as a requirement to ensure that in the transformation from treaty to custom, rights formulated in the LOSC are not 'used and invoked in an excessive way while duties are neglected', or that 'unilateral State interests are to a large extent recognized while community interests are forgotten.'[73]

This combination of conventional and customary rules gives rise to some significant complexities in assessing the legal significance of State practice in the law of the sea—in particular, whether it constitutes 'State practice' from which customary international law is derived, or 'subsequent practice' giving rise to an agreement regarding the interpretation of a treaty within the meaning of Article 31(3)(b) of the VCLT. As the International Law Commission (ILC) has identified, subsequent practice under Article 31(3)(b) of the VCLT requires 'a common understanding regarding the interpretation of the treaty which the parties are aware of and accept'.[74] In this respect, subsequent practice embodies an implied or tacit agreement between the Parties in relation to the interpretation of a conventional rule that already exists—it does not establish a new rule.[75] It is thus consensual in nature, and is underpinned by a previously expressed intention to be bound; provided that the Parties understand and are aware that the practice relates to the interpretation of the treaty, and are acting in application of the treaty (or are 'motivated by' the treaty), no additional subjective element is required.[76]

In contrast, a customary rule requires not only practice but *opinio juris*, in the sense that the State is engaging in the practice because it is permitted, required, or prohibited by customary international law, rather than as a matter of consensual interpretation of a treaty obligation.[77] Accordingly, in order to produce a customary rule in relation to the law of the sea, it is necessary to show that the practice is accompanied by *opinio juris* to the effect that the right or obligation in question is required or permitted by an independent rule of international law—not by the LOSC. Thus, in order to properly evaluate the consequences—or legal effect—of State practice in relation to activities at sea, it is important to distinguish between

[73] Bernhardt, 'Custom and Treaty in the Law of the Sea' (n 63) 279. Similarly, O'Connell, *The International Law of the Sea, Vol 1* (n 42) 49.

[74] ILC, 'Text of the Draft Conclusions on Subsequent Agreements and Subsequent Practice in Relation to the Interpretation of Treaties', *Report of the International Law Commission on the Work of its 68th Session (2 May–10 June and 4 July–12 August 2016)* UN Doc A/71/10) 120 (Draft Conclusion 10(1)).

[75] Katharina Berner, *Subsequent Agreements and Subsequent Practice in Domestic Courts* (Springer 2017) 124.

[76] ILC, 'Draft Conclusions on Subsequent Agreements and Practice' (n 74) 158 (Commentary to Draft Conclusion 6(1)). The standard for determining motivation depends on the context, and on the character of the treaty or of a specific provision. For example, in the context of the establishment of a maritime boundary, there must be 'compelling evidence' of tacit agreement: *Territorial and Maritime Disputes between Nicaragua and Honduras in the Caribbean Sea (Nicaragua v Honduras)* (Judgment) (2007) ICJ Reports 659 [253].

[77] *North Sea Continental Shelf Cases* [77].

subsequent practice by Parties in the application of the LOSC (the legal effect of which relates to the LOSC), and State practice that relates to a rule of customary international law.

1.2.2 Subsequent Practice in the Application of the LOSC under Treaty Law

The potential legal effects of subsequent practice in the application of the LOSC can be considered as a spectrum, ranging from basic implementation to interpretation, modification, and, ultimately, inconsistency or breach.[78] At one end of the spectrum, subsequent practice may simply be undertaken in implementation of the LOSC, consistent with a good faith interpretation in light of object and purpose, pursuant to Article 31(1) and (2) of the VCLT. This has no particular legal impact, other than to confirm the 'ordinary meaning' of the provision,[79] or as a supplementary means of interpretation under Article 32 of the VCLT.[80]

Further along the spectrum, subsequent practice (and subsequent agreement)[81] can contribute to confirming, clarifying, or supplementing the operation or application of the LOSC through an authentic interpretation under Article 31(3)(a) and (b) of the VCLT. In order to have this effect, the practice must be sufficient to 'establish the agreement of the Parties' regarding the interpretation of the treaty. While this does not require 'abundant practice' by all Parties,[82] the practice should be 'consistent rather than haphazard', should have 'occurred with a certain frequency', and 'will have been acquiesced in by the other Parties; and no other Party will have raised an objection.'[83] Some of the literature and jurisprudence refers to a

[78] See Giovanni Distefano, 'La Pratique Subséquente des États Parties à un Traité' (1994) 40 AnnFrDroitIntl 41.

[79] ILC, 'Draft Conclusions on Subsequent Agreements and Practice' (n 74) 166 (Commentary to Draft Conclusion 7(1)).

[80] Ibid 129 (Commentary to Draft Conclusion 4(3)).

[81] Since there are no particular requirements regarding the form of the agreement under art 31(3)(a), the distinction between subsequent agreement under art 31(3)(a) and subsequent practice under art 31(3)(b) can be extremely fluid and difficult to draw: Irina Buga, *Modification of Treaties by Subsequent Practice* (OUP 2018) 53. The only distinguishing characteristic is that a 'subsequent agreement' must be 'reached' and therefore presupposes 'a single common act by the Parties by which they manifest their common understanding regarding the interpretation of the treaty': ILC, 'Draft Conclusions on Subsequent Agreements and Practice' (n 74) 138–40 (Commentary to Draft Conclusion 4(1)). Since in many cases subsequent practice and subsequent agreement coincide and cannot be distinguished—and the legal effect under art 31(3) is the same—this book generally uses the term 'subsequent practice' to encompass the means of interpretation referred to in both art 31(3)(a) and (b).

[82] Richard Gardiner, *Treaty Interpretation* (2nd ed, OUP 2015) 270.

[83] Mark E Villiger, *Commentary on the 1969 Vienna Convention on the Law of Treaties* (Martinus Nijhoff 2009) 431. See, eg, the *Virginia G* case, in which ITLOS' interpretation of the extent of coastal State jurisdiction over the bunkering of foreign fishing vessels referred to the national legislation of 'several States', and noted that 'there is no manifest objection to such legislation and that it is, in general, complied with': *MV 'Virginia G' (Panama v Guinea-Bissau)* (Judgment) (2014) ITLOS Rep 4 [218] (*Virginia G*). See also, on the absence of reaction as subsequent practice, *Dispute between Argentina and Chile concerning the Beagle Channel, Award of 18 February 1977* XXI RIAA 53 [169(a)].

requirement that the practice be 'concordant, common and consistent'.[84] While this formula may be useful for determining the weight of practice in a particular case, the ILC notes that it is not sufficiently well established to articulate a minimum threshold and has the risk of being overly prescriptive. Accordingly, the ILC suggests that the weight of subsequent practice varies according to the way in which it demonstrates the understanding of the Parties.[85] In addition, while the practice must be 'in the application of the treaty', it is not limited to conduct specifically referable to the particular provision of the treaty in issue,[86] nor does it require positive action—in some circumstances, consistent *absence* of action where such action might have been expected can indicate interpretative agreement.[87] Importantly, however, subsequent practice is not the sole determinant of authentic interpretation; it is applied together with the other rules of interpretation in Articles 31 and 32 of the VCLT in a 'single combined operation',[88] in which appropriate emphasis is placed on the various means of interpretation in order to determine the proper meaning of the treaty.[89]

Even further along the spectrum of legal effects, subsequent practice can result in the tacit modification or amendment of the LOSC—such as by updating the meaning of a term, supplementing a provision with a novel element or direction, or even altering the content of a right or obligation.[90] However, the legal basis giving rise to this outcome is more controversial: while the process of tacit modification by subsequent practice has been widely acknowledged,[91] it is not clear whether it constitutes a form of interpretation by subsequent practice under Article 31(3) of the VCLT,[92] or a modification of the treaty pursuant to the general rule on amendment in Article 39,[93] or whether modification by subsequent practice is a rule

[84] See, eg, *Japan: Alcoholic Beverages II–Appellate Body Report* (4 October 1996) WT/DS8/AB/R, WT/DS10/AB/R, and WT/DS11/AB/R, 12–13 (*Japan: Alcoholic Beverages II*); Ian Sinclair, *The Vienna Convention on the Law of Treaties* (2nd ed, MUP 1984) 137.

[85] ILC, 'Draft Conclusions on Subsequent Agreements and Practice' (n 74) 190–1 (Commentary to Draft Conclusion 9).

[86] Gardiner, *Treaty Interpretation* (n 82) 261.

[87] Ibid 262–4.

[88] ILC, 'Draft Conclusions on Subsequent Agreements and Practice' (n 74) 130–1 (Draft Conclusion 2(5) and associated Commentary).

[89] Berner, *Subsequent Agreements and Subsequent Practice* (n 75) 127.

[90] There are several commonly cited examples of tacit modification of the LOSC by subsequent agreement and subsequent practice, including: the Part XI Agreement; the 'one-time deferment' of the first election of judges to ITLOS; the postponement of the first election of members of the Commission on the Limits of the Continental Shelf (CLCS); and the extension of the time limit for coastal States to lodge submissions concerning the outer limits of the continental shelf.

[91] Irina Buga, 'Between Stability and Change in the Law of the Sea Convention: Subsequent Practice, Treaty Modification and Regime Interaction' in Donald R Rothwell et al (eds), *The Oxford Handbook of the Law of the Sea* (OUP 2015) 50–5 fns 22–5.

[92] The ILC's Draft Conclusions contend that 'the possibility of amending or modifying a treaty by subsequent practice has not generally been recognized', but do not exclude the possibility that such modification may occur on the basis of art 39 of the VCLT: ILC, 'Draft Conclusions on Subsequent Agreements and Practice' (n 74) 173 (Draft Conclusion 7(3)).

[93] Art 39 of the VCLT provides that a treaty may be amended by agreement between the Parties. The term 'agreement' does not imply any particular level of formality, and '[a]n amending agreement may

of customary international law that sits outside the VCLT.[94] In addition, it is extremely difficult to distinguish interpretation from modification—particularly given the reluctance of States to recognize that practice amounts to anything more than interpretation[95]—and as the ILC has observed, both States and international courts 'prefer to make every effort to conceive of an agreed subsequent practice of the parties as an effort to interpret the treaty in a particular way', and 'accord States parties a rather wide scope for the interpretation of a treaty by way of a subsequent agreement', that may even go beyond the ordinary meaning of the terms of the treaty.[96]

Finally, at the far end of the spectrum of legal effects, subsequent practice could constitute a breach of the LOSC, which may ultimately lead to the institution of legal proceedings by another Party under Part XV, or give rise to liability for an internationally wrongful act under the laws of State responsibility.[97]

1.2.3 State Practice relating to Customary International Law

A similar spectrum of potential legal effects exists in the context of customary international law. Practice can simply reflect the application of an existing and acknowledged customary rule. To the extent that it departs from such a rule, it may—if it is sufficiently widespread, representative, and consistent, and accompanied by the requisite *opinio juris*—generate a new rule of customary international law.[98] Alternatively, it may be inconsistent with existing customary rules. However, in the context of the law of the sea, this evaluation is complicated by the need to consider whether—or in relation to what issues—the practice of particular States is referable to customary international law, as distinct from the LOSC.

Strictly speaking, since the practice of the 168 Parties to the LOSC in respect of issues addressed by the Convention is presumably undertaken in the application of treaty-based rights and obligations, it cannot legitimately be inferred to relate to a rule of customary international law.[99] Of course, the practice of the twenty-nine

take whatever form the parties to the original treaty may choose': ILC, *Yearbook of the International Law Commission (1966) Vol II*, UN Doc A/CN/SER.A/1966.Add.1 232–3.

[94] ILC, 'Draft Conclusions on Subsequent Agreements and Practice' (n 74) 175 (Commentary to Draft Conclusion 7(3)).

[95] Buga, 'Between Stability and Change in the LOSC' (n 91) 51.

[96] ILC, 'Draft Conclusions on Subsequent Agreements and Practice' (n 74) 174–5 and 180 (Commentary on Draft Conclusion 7(3)).

[97] *Articles on the Responsibility of States for Internationally Wrongful Acts* annexed to UNGA Res 56/83 (12 December 2001) Un Doc A/Res/56/83.

[98] ILC, 'Text of the Draft Conclusions on the Identification of Customary International Law', *Report of the International Law Commission on the Work of its 68th Session (2 May–10 June and 4 July–12 August 2016)* UN Doc A/71/10, 76 (Draft Conclusions 2 and 8(1)).

[99] *North Sea Continental Shelf Cases* [76].

States that are *not* Party to the LOSC[100] is directly relevant to the establishment of custom—but since only fourteen of these are coastal States, the amount of practice generated in this manner is limited.[101] This trend is only likely to continue, since for every additional State that becomes Party to the LOSC, there are fewer States whose practice remains relevant to the determination of custom.

If taken to its logical conclusion, this would result in a situation—commonly referred to as 'Baxter's paradox'—where, since 'little or no customary international practice is generated by the non-Parties, it becomes virtually impossible to determine whether the treaty has passed into customary international law', or what the customary law would be in the absence of the treaty.[102] While this result is arrived at by application of the basic rules of consent to norms in international law, it is 'at least counter-intuitive, perhaps even contradictory, certainly contrary to practice', and in the extensive literature on treaties, no one has been able to resolve it.[103] In practice, however, the relationship between treaty and custom is more flexible than Baxter's paradox suggests, and various conceptual approaches or 'legal fictions' can be applied in order to address—if not resolve—it.

With respect to the law of the sea, if there is no alternative rule in play and the rule in the LOSC has not attracted criticism from third States,[104] it is arguable that the LOSC rule should be considered to reflect a general practice accepted as law, applying equally to Parties and non-Parties.[105] In this respect, widespread participation in the LOSC could be considered to generate a presumption of *opinio juris* leading to the formation of a customary rule.[106] Alternatively, it could be argued that the Parties to the LOSC believe in the independently obligatory character of their actions, such that their practice—even if carried out on the basis of the LOSC—could be considered relevant to establishing an independent rule of customary international law.[107] Pursuant to these approaches, regardless of the

[100] This figure is calculated by subtracting the number of UN member States that are Party to the LOSC (164) from the overall number of UN member States (193). There are a further four Parties to the LOSC who are *not* formally UN member States (the Cook Islands, Niue, the European Union (EU), and the State of Palestine).

[101] Of course, the practice of land-locked States is relevant to both the interpretation of the LOSC and customary rules on the law of the sea, and some land-locked States have significant fleets. However, relevantly for the practice examined in this book, the FAO's fishery statistics do not report any marine capture fisheries by vessels flagged to land-locked countries between 2009 and 2018: FAO, *Yearbook of Fishery and Aquaculture Statistics 2018* (FAO 2020).

[102] RR Baxter, 'Treaties and Custom' (1970-I) 129 RdC 27, 96.

[103] James Crawford, 'Chance, Order, Change: The Course of International Law' (2013) 365 RdC 27, 91.

[104] On the significance of silence—or failure to react—where a response may be expected in the context of customary law, see *Sovereignty over Pedra Branca/Pulau Batu Puteh, Middle Rocks and South Ledge (Malaysia v Singapore)* (Judgment) (2008) ICJ Rep 12 [121]. See also ILC, 'Draft Conclusions on the Identification of Custom' (n 98) 99 (Draft Conclusion 10(3)).

[105] For discussion on this issue in respect of LOSC art 76, see Crawford, 'Chance, Order, Change' (n 103) 103.

[106] See ibid 109; Robert Kolb, *The Law of Treaties* (Edward Elgar 2016) 264.

[107] See Villiger, *Commentary on the 1969 VCLT* (n 83) 7.

presumption or belief employed in respect of the practice of Parties to the LOSC, there is an important role for the practice and *opinio juris* of non-Parties—whether in supporting the existence of the rule, rebutting the presumption so as to prevent its establishment, or persistently opposing its application to themselves.[108] It is also important to ensure that custom develops in a balanced way that maintains the integrity of the integrated, indivisible 'package' of correlative rights and obligations established in the LOSC—and in this respect, the stability of the package deal lies to a significant extent in the hands of the Parties to LOSC in *not* acquiescing to the creation of customary norms that would undermine it.[109]

Since it is clear that practice in respect of the LOSC can contribute to the formation (or non-formation) of custom, the remaining question is: to what extent can custom modify the LOSC? The principle underlying this complex question is unresolved as a matter of general international law. Some commentators accept that, since custom and treaties are sources of equal value at international law, supervening custom can clarify ambiguities, fill gaps and even modify or terminate a treaty—particularly if it cannot realistically be amended through formal channels.[110] To the extent that such modification is considered possible, the role that custom can play is limited by the scope of the treaty provision in question, the nature and context of the treaty itself, and the will of the parties.[111] However, other commentators conclude that 'if a treaty contains specific rules then, so long as it is in force it derogates from whatever new customary rule emerges as a result of consensus.'[112]

In the general context of the law of the sea, the possibility of modification through supervening custom is more widely accepted, particularly in light of the way that developments in customary international law affected the 1958 Convention on the High Seas.[113] Some have expressed doubt about the extent to which such

[108] *Fisheries Jurisdiction (United Kingdom v Norway)* (Judgment) (1951) ICJ Rep 116, 131. See also ILC, 'Draft Conclusions on the Identification of Custom' (n 98) 112 (Draft Conclusion 15). In this context there are some well-known 'persistent objectors' amongst the non-Parties to the LOSC (including in particular Colombia, El Salvador, Venezuela, and Turkey) who oppose any general recognition of the LOSC as custom.

[109] Caminos and Molitor, 'Progressive Development of International Law' (n 63) 889.

[110] See, eg, Michael Akehurst, 'The Hierarchy of the Sources of International Law' (1975) 47 BYIL 273, 275; Nancy Kontou, *The Termination and Revision of Treaties in the Light of New Customary International Law* (OUP 1994); Mark E Villiger, *Customary International Law and Treaties* (2nd ed, Kluwer Law International 1997) 195–200; Irina Buga, *Modification of Treaties by Subsequent Practice* (n 81) 213–5 and 366–7. See also *South China Sea Arbitration (Philippines v China)* [2016] PCA Case 2013-19 [274] (*South China Sea Arbitration*).

[111] Kontou, *The Termination and Revision of Treaties* (n 110) 18.

[112] O'Connell, *The International Law of the Sea, Vol I* (n 42) 47. See also Marcelo Kohen and Sarah Heathcote, '1969 Vienna Convention: Article 42 (Validity and Continuance in Force of Treaties)' in Olivier Corten and Pierre Klein (eds), *The Vienna Convention on the Law of Treaties: A Commentary, Vol II* (OUP 2011) 1025.

[113] See, eg, Robin R Churchill, 'The Impact of State Practice on the Jurisdictional Framework Contained in the LOS Convention' in Alex G Oude Elferink (ed), *Stability and Change in the Law of the Sea: The Role of the LOS Convention* (Koninklijke Brill NV 2005) 95–6. See also Kontou's detailed review of the impact of new customary international law regarding fishery limits on a range of previously concluded fisheries agreements: Kontou, *The Termination and Revision of Treaties* (n 110) 38–71.

modification is possible in the case of the LOSC[114] in light of its 'in-built' mechanisms for change,[115] which include: provisions allowing for the incorporation of externally agreed standards (such as those adopted by the International Maritime Organization in relation to maritime safety and marine environmental protection) and the application of other rules of general international law;[116] a formal amendment procedure;[117] and institutions that provide a vehicle for continuous improvement and change.[118] In any case, since the LOSC has near-universal membership and establishes a broad framework intended to cover all matters relating to the law of the sea, it is more likely that modifications will occur through subsequent practice of the Parties as a matter of treaty law, rather than through supervening custom.

1.3 Approach and Outline of the Book

Since the type and degree of practice required to establish the status of conventional and customary international law rules can vary widely, this book adopts an inductive approach, gathering the material of the law as it is revealed in the practice of States and applying the legal rules outlined in Section 1.2 to establish its legal effect. In order to provide the most comprehensive analysis possible, every effort has been made to ensure that the *degree* of practice examined is widespread and representative, and the *type* of practice examined is relevant and consistent (in the sense of being comparable).

This book examines practice from 134 of the 150 coastal State members of the UN,[119] as well as: the two self-governing territories that have ratified the LOSC pursuant to Article 305(1)(e);[120] nine overseas regions, territories, and non-self-governing territories whose fisheries legislation is independent from that of the metropolitan territory;[121] and the fishing entity of Chinese Taipei. It also examines relevant practice of the European Union (EU) which has the capacity, as a manifestation of its unique legal order, to prescribe fisheries law for all its member States,

[114] Churchill, 'The Impact of State Practice' (n 113) 97.

[115] Buga, 'Between Stability and Change in the LOSC' (n 91) 66.

[116] See n 67 and associated text.

[117] Arts 312 and 313 provide a mechanism for formal amendment of the LOSC, although there is very little prospect of it being used.

[118] These include the International Seabed Authority established in art 156, the CLCS established in Annex II, and the Meeting of States Parties convened under art 319(2)(e).

[119] These figures do not include the EU or the State of Palestine, which are permanent observers to the UN and not member States.

[120] Cook Islands and Niue.

[121] New Zealand's non-self-governing territory of Tokelau; the French 'outermost region' of Mayotte and the French overseas territories of New Caledonia and the Southern and Antarctic Territories (SAAT); and overseas territories of the United Kingdom including the Falkland Islands, Montserrat, Pitcairn Islands, South Georgia and the South Sandwich Islands (SGSSI), and Turks and Caicos Islands.

including with respect to fishing by foreign vessels in EU waters.[122] The coastal States whose practice is examined (and omitted) in this book are listed in Table 1.1. In order to organize the material clearly and consistently throughout the book, represent the geographic breadth of practice, and demonstrate any regional trends, the list is organized by UN Regional Group. As Table 1.1 shows, this book examines practice from all major coastal and fishing States, developed and developing States, States from all regions and legal traditions, and Parties and non-Parties to the LOSC.

Since States exercise their powers in different ways, State practice takes many forms and—as discussed in this Section—its legal relevance varies depending on the rule and context in question. In the context of the law of the sea, the extra-territorial exercise of jurisdiction over actors and activities relies overwhelmingly on legislation, rules, and regulations adopted by States to give effect to their rights and regulations in the ocean space—from the establishment of maritime zones to the regulation of vessels and aircraft, use of resources, and conduct of scientific research. Accordingly, this book examines State practice primarily by reference to national legislation relating to the regulation of living resources, supplemented by additional sources including policy documents, judicial decisions, diplomatic acts and correspondence, public statements, press releases, and news reports, which help to confirm how laws and regulations are interpreted and implemented 'beyond the statute books'. Account is also taken of the obligations assumed by each State under—and activities undertaken pursuant to—binding and non-binding global, regional, and bilateral agreements and arrangements.

It is important to acknowledge the limitations and challenges inherent in this approach. Since national legislation is drawn up to address the conditions, issues, and objectives faced by each coastal State in its own EEZ, the presence (or absence) of regulation on certain issues or in certain forms is not necessarily indicative of the coastal State's view on their legality or otherwise. Since constitutional, legislative, and administrative practices vary between countries, relevant issues may be addressed in other ways—or in other legislation—not examined in this book. In practice, there are often gaps between law and policy—and between prescription and enforcement—which make it important to examine not only the 'law as written', but the way in which laws and policies are implemented and enforced. And while every effort has been made to collect reliable and current versions of primary source material, and to translate and interpret it correctly, in some cases

[122] As described in the EU's Declaration of Competence under art 5(1) of Annex IX of the LOSC, EU member States have transferred to the European Community exclusive competence in relation to the conservation and management of living resources, both in areas under national jurisdiction and on the high seas. Accordingly, the practice of EU member States in matters relating to the conservation and management of living marine resources is considered by reference to EU regulations, rather than the national legislation of member States. However, since member States retain competence in respect of the exercise of jurisdiction over vessels and the enforcement of penal and administrative sanctions, those matters are examined by reference to the national legislation of each EU member State.

Table 1.1 Coastal States examined and omitted in this book

African Group
Coastal States examined: Algeria, Angola, Benin, Cameroon, Cape Verde, Comoros, Republic of Congo, Cote d'Ivoire, Djibouti, Egypt, Equatorial Guinea, Eritrea, Gabon, Gambia, Ghana, Guinea, Guinea-Bissau, Kenya, Liberia, Libya, Madagascar, Mauritania, Mauritius, Morocco, Mozambique, Namibia, Nigeria, Sao Tome and Principe, Senegal, Seychelles, Sierra Leone, Somalia, South Africa, Tanzania, Togo, Tunisia. **Coastal States not examined:** Democratic Republic of Congo, Sudan.
Asia-Pacific Group
Coastal States examined: Bahrain, Bangladesh, Brunei, Cambodia, China, Chinese Taipei, Cook Islands, Cyprus, Fiji, India, Indonesia, Iran, Japan, Kiribati, Korea, Kuwait, Malaysia, Maldives, Marshall Islands, Micronesia, Myanmar, Nauru, Niue, Oman, Pakistan, Palau, Papua New Guinea, Philippines, Qatar, Samoa, Solomon Islands, Sri Lanka, Thailand, Timor-Leste, Tonga, Tuvalu, United Arab Emirates, Vanuatu, Vietnam, Yemen. **Coastal States not examined:** Democratic People's Republic of Korea, Iraq, Jordan, Lebanon, Saudi Arabia, Singapore, Syria.
Eastern Europe Group
Coastal States examined: Albania, Bulgaria, Croatia, Estonia, Latvia, Lithuania, Montenegro, Poland, Romania, Russia, Slovenia **Coastal States not examined:** Bosnia and Herzegovina, Georgia, Ukraine.
Latin American Group
Coastal States examined: Antigua and Barbuda, Argentina, Bahamas, Barbados, Belize, Brazil, Chile, Colombia, Costa Rica, Cuba, Dominica, Dominican Republic, Ecuador, El Salvador, Grenada, Guatemala, Guyana, Honduras, Jamaica, Mexico, Nicaragua, Panama, Peru, Saint Kitts and Nevis, Saint Lucia, Saint Vincent and the Grenadines, Trinidad and Tobago, Uruguay, Venezuela. **Coastal States not examined:** Haiti, Suriname.
Western Europe and Others Group
Coastal States examined: Australia, Belgium, Canada, Denmark, Finland, France and Mayotte, New Caledonia and the Southern and Antarctic Territories (SAAT), Germany, Greece, Iceland, Ireland, Italy, Malta, Netherlands, New Zealand (NZ) and Tokelau, Norway, Portugal, Spain, Sweden, Turkey, United Kingdom (UK) and Falkland Islands, Montserrat, Pitcairn Islands, South Georgia and South Sandwich Islands (SGSSI), and Turks and Caicos Islands, United States of America (United States). **Coastal States not examined:** Israel, Monaco.

Notes

a. All the coastal States listed in Table 1.1 are Party to the LOSC, except:

(i) seven States that have signed but not ratified the LOSC (Cambodia, Colombia, the Democratic People's Republic of Korea, El Salvador, Iran, Libya, the United Arab Emirates), and
(ii) seven States that have neither signed nor ratified the LOSC (Eritrea, Israel, Peru, Syria, Turkey, the United States of America, and Venezuela).

b. In matters relating to the conservation and management of living marine resources, the practice of EU member States is examined by reference to EU regulations. The EU member States whose practice is examined are: Cyprus (Asia-Pacific Group); Bulgaria, Croatia, Estonia, Latvia, Lithuania, Poland, Romania, Slovenia (Eastern Europe Group); Belgium, Denmark, Finland, France, Germany, Greece, Ireland, Italy, Malta, Netherlands, Portugal, Spain, Sweden (Western Europe and Others Group).

it may be superseded or incomplete, or subject to errors in translation or interpretation. Accordingly, this book includes summaries of and pinpoints to relevant provisions of coastal State legislation, for which full references are provided in the Table of Legislation.

With these doctrinal and methodological issues established, Chapter 2 commences by describing the basic legal framework for the regulation of living resources in the EEZ, as it is established in the LOSC and other international instruments. It looks beyond the rights and obligations on the face of the LOSC and establishes the 'continuum' of coastal State jurisdiction, setting out clearly what they *must, may*, and *must not* do in exercising their sovereign rights over living resources in the EEZ by reference to the broader, normative principles that constrain and enable the actions of coastal States in the EEZ. The book then turns to consider the substantive extent of coastal State jurisdiction from a range of different perspectives, which enable examination of the key legal issues relating to coastal State jurisdiction over living resources in the EEZ. While each Chapter considers the relevant provisions of the LOSC and the way they have been interpreted in the jurisprudence and literature, the primary focus is on how coastal States have given effect to the LOSC in practice, and the legal effects of this practice—in particular, the extent to which it implements, interprets, modifies, or is inconsistent with the rules established in the LOSC or (where relevant) customary international law.

Chapter 3 considers the type of 'fishing activities' and 'fishing vessels' that may be regulated by the coastal State on the basis of its sovereign rights over living resources in the EEZ under Article 56(1) of the LOSC. Chapter 4 explores the extent and expression of the prescriptive jurisdiction that may be exercised by the coastal State with respect to foreign vessels fishing under licence in the EEZ, on the basis of its sovereign rights over living resources under Articles 61 and 62 of the LOSC. Chapter 5 examines the extent to which—and the manner in which—jurisdiction may be exercised by the coastal State over unlicensed foreign fishing vessels in transit and exercising the freedom of navigation through the EEZ, pursuant to Articles 56 and 73. Chapter 6 investigates issues associated with the coastal State's enforcement of laws and regulations within the EEZ on the basis of its sovereign rights over living resources and its enforcement jurisdiction under Article 73. Chapter 7 extends the enquiry to the circumstances under which—and the way in which—enforcement powers may be exercised by the coastal State over foreign fishing vessels beyond the EEZ following a hot pursuit under Article 111.

Finally, Chapter 8 returns to broader questions of the nature and extent of coastal State jurisdiction in the EEZ. It draws on and distils the law and practice examined throughout the book in order to identify both the contemporary 'extent' of coastal State jurisdiction over living resources in the EEZ and the underlying 'nature' of that jurisdiction in a way that may help to provide a more predictable framework to understand and resolve current and future jurisdictional issues, and maintain the balance of interests at the heart of the jurisdictional regime for the EEZ.

2

The Framework for Coastal State Jurisdiction over Fishing in the EEZ

With the adoption of the United Nations Convention on the Law of the Sea (LOSC) and the concept of the 200 nautical mile exclusive economic zone (EEZ), a 'revolutionary compromise' was struck between the rights of coastal States and the freedoms of other States under the law of the sea.[1] Pursuant to the jurisdictional framework for the EEZ set out in Part V of the LOSC, the coastal State has 'sovereign rights' under Article 56(1) to explore and exploit, conserve and manage the natural resources of the EEZ, while other States enjoy the freedoms of navigation, overflight, laying of cables and pipelines, and other internationally lawful uses of the sea related to these freedoms under Article 58(1). However, given the varied and constantly evolving activities taking place at sea, it is not always clear whether an activity in the EEZ falls within the coastal State's sovereign rights and jurisdiction under Article 56, or the freedoms of other States under Article 58.

The LOSC contains a number of mechanisms designed to maintain an appropriate balance between these rights and freedoms. These include a general obligation of 'due regard' which applies to the activities of all States in the EEZ, and a number of specific 'duties' for both coastal States and other States in—or in relation to—the EEZ. The LOSC also safeguards against excessive assertions of coastal State jurisdiction over the living resources of the EEZ by limiting the exercise of enforcement powers. However, since these rights and duties are commonly expressed using general or aspirational terms such as 'due regard' or 'seek to cooperate', or accompanied by qualifiers such as 'reasonable', 'necessary', or 'appropriate', the LOSC framework does not provide clear guidance on how and where to strike the balance between the rights of coastal States and the freedoms of other States.[2]

In practice, this balance is struck initially by coastal States asserting rights and assuming duties over living resources in the EEZ in their implementation of the LOSC. But given the ambiguity inherent in the compromise—and the possibility for coastal State jurisdiction to 'creep' further than it should—there is also an important role for international courts and tribunals in reviewing the innovations

[1] Gemma Andreone, 'The Exclusive Economic Zone' in Donald R Rothwell et al (eds), *The Oxford Handbook of the Law of the Sea* (OUP 2015) 161.

[2] James Harrison, 'Safeguards Against Excessive Enforcement Measures in the Exclusive Economic Zone—Law and Practice' in Henrik Ringbom (ed), *Jurisdiction over Ships: Post-UNCLOS Developments in the Law of the Sea* (Brill Nijhoff 2015) 218.

Coastal State Jurisdiction over Living Resources in the Exclusive Economic Zone. Camille Goodman, Oxford University Press.
 DOI: 10.1093/oso/9780192896841.003.0002

and interpretations offered by coastal States and clarifying the meaning of relevant provisions.[3] Due to the limitations on compulsory jurisdiction under the LOSC dispute settlement framework, international courts and tribunals have had little opportunity to *directly* consider the legality of particular forms of coastal State jurisdiction over living resources in the EEZ. Nonetheless, a growing body of jurisprudence is developing on this issue through *indirect* consideration in cases involving prompt release, marine environmental protection, the exercise of advisory jurisdiction, and jurisdiction over artificial installations and non-living resources.

This Chapter outlines and analyses the legal framework for the regulation of living resources in the EEZ established in the LOSC and other instruments. It considers the basic rights and duties described in the LOSC and the gaps and ambiguities in the framework (Section 2.1) and the effect of the various binding and non-binding instruments that have subsequently been adopted (Section 2.2). It also looks beyond the basic list of rights and duties set out on the face of these instruments in order to identify the broader, normative principles and approaches identified in the jurisprudence, and provide clear guidance on what coastal States *must*, *may*, and *may not* do in exercising their jurisdiction in the EEZ (Section 2.3).[4]

2.1 The LOSC Framework

The EEZ is an 'experiment in functionalism',[5] underpinned by the constant search for balance between the diverse interests at play: between the exclusive rights of the coastal State, inclusive freedoms of other States and interests of the international community as a whole; between the coastal State's sovereign rights to exploit living resources and its duties of conservation and sustainable use; between the enforcement of coastal State regulations and the freedom of foreign-flagged vessels; and between the rights and interests of coastal States, and those of land-locked and geographically disadvantaged States. In order to manage these competing interests, Part V of the LOSC establishes a broad framework within which all States are required to respect and accommodate the rights and legitimate uses of other States in the EEZ.

As described in Article 55 of the LOSC, the EEZ is subject to a 'specific legal regime', characterized by a selected combination of rights, freedoms, and obligations, allocated between coastal States and other States. The basic parameters of this regime are established through Article 56, which specifies the selected matters

[3] Ibid.

[4] Parts of this Chapter (and in particular the content of Section 2.3) have previously been published in a substantially similar form. See Camille Goodman, 'Rights, Obligations, Prohibitions: A Practical Guide to Understanding Judicial Decisions on Coastal State Jurisdiction over Living Resources in the Exclusive Economic Zone' (2018) 33 IJMCL 558.

[5] David Joseph Attard, *The Exclusive Economic Zone in International Law* (Clarendon Press 1987) 66.

over which the coastal State has sovereign rights or jurisdiction, Article 58, which preserves the rights and freedoms of other States, and Article 59, which provides a method for resolving conflicts in cases where the LOSC has not attributed rights or jurisdiction to either the coastal State or to other States. This is complemented by a number of specific provisions that set out rights and detailed obligations with respect to the conservation and utilization of living resources (Articles 61 and 62), cooperation regarding particular stocks and species (Articles 63 to 67), and the enforcement of fisheries regulations (Articles 73 and 111).

2.1.1 Coastal State Rights and Duties

Pursuant to Article 56(1)(a), the coastal State has sovereign rights for the purpose of exploring and exploiting, conserving and managing all living resources of the EEZ, except for sedentary species associated with the seabed and subsoil, which are regulated by the continental shelf provisions in Part VI of the LOSC. The coastal State's sovereign rights are plenary and exclusive; they ensure that the coastal State has the sole prerogative and final authority over any decisions regarding the conservation and use of the living resources of the EEZ.[6] However, the coastal State's discretion is not unlimited. The principal restraint is Article 56(2), which plays an important role in balancing the rights, jurisdiction, and duties of the coastal State with those of other States by providing that, in exercising its rights and performing its duties in the EEZ, the coastal State 'shall have due regard to the rights and duties of other States and shall act in a manner compatible with the provisions of this Convention'.[7]

The rights and duties of other States, set out in Article 58 are 'essentially concerned with international communications and are those high seas freedoms that have survived the demands of coastal States'.[8] As Article 58(2) clarifies, these high seas freedoms are not imported into the EEZ in an unmodified fashion, but only in so far as they are compatible with the other provisions of Part V.[9] Article 58(3)

[6] See Francisco Orrego Vicuna, *The Exclusive Economic Zone* (CUP 1989) 50–1; William T Burke, *The New International Law of Fisheries* (Clarendon Press 1994) 39–40. In contrast to the 'exclusive jurisdiction' over artificial islands, installations, and structures in art 60(1), and 'exclusive' rights to living resources on the continental shelf in art 77(2), the term 'exclusive' is not used with respect to the coastal State's sovereign rights over living resources in Part V. Proelss suggests that this may be to reflect the possibility of access by other States pursuant to arts 62(2), 69, or 70: Alexander Proelss, 'Article 56' in Alexander Proelss (ed), *United Nations Convention on the Law of the Sea: A Commentary* (CH Beck 2017) 424. In any case, notwithstanding this omission, the coastal State's sovereign rights should nonetheless be regarded as being generally exclusive.

[7] Satya Nandan and Shabtai Rosenne (eds), *United Nations Convention on the Law of the Sea 1982: A Commentary, Vol II* (Martinus Nijhoff 1993) 543.

[8] RR Churchill and AV Lowe, *The Law of the Sea* (3rd ed, MUP 1999) 170.

[9] Alexander Proelss, 'Article 58' in Alexander Proelss (ed), *United Nations Convention on the Law of the Sea: A Commentary* (CH Beck 2017) 446.

confirms the reciprocal nature of the due regard rule established in Article 56(2), by requiring that when exercising their rights and duties in the EEZ, States 'shall have due regard to the rights and duties of the coastal State, and shall comply with the laws adopted by the coastal State' in accordance with the LOSC. There is a slight but significant asymmetry between the specific rights, duties, and jurisdiction established in Articles 56(2) and 58(3): while coastal States must act 'in a manner compatible with' the LOSC, other States must 'comply with the laws and regulations adopted by the coastal State'. However, the duty to have due regard is identical, reflecting the general relationship of legal equality between States.[10]

Between them, Articles 56 and 58 deal extensively—but not exhaustively—with the rights and obligations of coastal States and other States in the EEZ.[11] Accordingly, should a conflict arise in respect of unattributed rights or jurisdiction, Article 59 directs that it be resolved on the basis of equity and in light of all the relevant circumstances, taking into account the respective importance of the interests involved to the parties and to the international community as a whole.[12] This combination of jurisdictional rules is intended to establish a *sui generis* regime, characterized by the functional jurisdiction of the coastal State and the freedoms of other States. In practice, however, it is an 'imperfect compromise between competing interests',[13] which has resulted in significant ambiguity regarding the sovereign rights and jurisdiction of coastal States, and the rights and duties of other States in the EEZ.

2.1.2 Conservation and Utilization of Living Resources

The sovereign rights of the coastal State under Article 56(1) are complemented by a more detailed regime of rights and duties for conservation and utilization of living resources in the EEZ. Article 61, which concerns the conservation of living resources, requires the coastal State to 'determine the allowable catch of the living resources' of the EEZ and adopt the conservation and management measures necessary to ensure that they are not endangered by over-exploitation.[14] The nature and extent of the 'obligation' to determine an allowable catch is unclear: although the coastal State's responsibility to determine the allowable catch has been confirmed in the jurisprudence,[15] it is not always feasible or appropriate to do

[10] Julia Gaunce, 'On the Interpretation of the General Duty of "Due Regard"' (2018) 32 OceanYB 27, 36.

[11] Donald R Rothwell and Tim Stephens, *The International Law of the Sea* (2nd ed, Hart 2016) 90.

[12] On the issue of art 59 and residual rights, see nn 149–56 and Section 3.1.3.

[13] Tim Stephens and Donald R Rothwell, 'The LOSC Framework for Maritime Jurisdiction and Enforcement 30 Years On' (2012) 27 IJMCL 701, 702.

[14] LOSC art 61(2).

[15] *Request for an Advisory Opinion Submitted by the Sub-Regional Fisheries Commission* (Advisory Opinion) (2015) ITLOS Rep 4 [96] and [104] (*SRFC Advisory Opinion*).

so.[16] In practice, while States generally determine a total allowable catch for stocks which are at or close to their maximum sustainable limit, there is no consistency regarding the establishment of a total allowable catch for all—or even all commercially significant—stocks.[17] In fulfilling these obligations, the coastal State is required to take into account the best scientific evidence available[18] and the effects on associated or dependent species,[19] and to exchange data and information relevant to the conservation of fish stocks through relevant organizations.[20] While the coastal State is also directed to maintain or restore stocks at a level that can produce the 'maximum sustainable yield',[21] there are so many qualifications on this obligation as to give the coastal State almost complete discretion in this regard.[22]

Article 62, which addresses the utilization of living resources, is directed primarily at determining the circumstances under which other States may access living resources in the coastal State's EEZ. To promote the overall objective of optimum utilization,[23] the coastal State is required to determine its own capacity to harvest the allowable catch,[24] and to take various steps to enable other States to access the surplus. This includes: setting the terms and conditions on which foreign nationals may access the resources;[25] negotiating agreements or other arrangements for access which reflect those terms and conditions;[26] and giving 'due notice' of conservation and management regulations.[27] While the coastal State is required to promote the objective of 'optimum utilization' of the living resources in the EEZ, since this term is not defined in the LOSC and is expressed to be 'without prejudice to Article 61', the 'optimum' level of utilization may be less than full or maximum biological or economic utilization, and the coastal State may set conservative levels for exploitation if justified by conservation principles.[28] In giving other States access to the surplus, the coastal State is required to have 'particular regard' to the provisions of Articles 69 and 70 (relating to the rights of land-locked

[16] Shigeru Oda, 'Fisheries under the United Nations Convention on the Law of the Sea' (1983) 77 AJIL 739, 743; Barbara Kwiatkowska, *The 200 Mile Exclusive Economic Zone in the New Law of the Sea* (Martinus Nijhoff 1989) 49.

[17] Marion Markowski, *The International Law of EEZ Fisheries* (Europa Law 2010) 109–12.

[18] LOSC art 61(2).

[19] Ibid art 61(4).

[20] Ibid art 61(5).

[21] Ibid art 61(3).

[22] Ibid. The obligation to maintain or restore populations at levels which can produce the maximum sustainable yield is 'qualified by relevant environmental and economic factors, including the economic needs of fishing communities and the special requirements of developing States, and taking into account fishing patterns, the interdependence of stocks and any generally recommended minimum standards, whether subregional, regional or global'.

[23] LOSC art 62(1).

[24] Ibid art 62(2).

[25] Ibid art 62(4).

[26] Ibid art 62(2).

[27] Ibid art 62(5).

[28] Donna R Christie, 'The Conservation and Management of Stocks Located Solely Within the Exclusive Economic Zone' in Ellen Hey (ed), *Developments in International Fisheries Law* (Kluwer 1999) 398.

and geographically disadvantaged States),[29] and 'take into account' the requirements of developing States and the need to minimize economic dislocation in States whose nationals have habitually fished in the zone or contributed to the research and identification of stocks.[30] However, since the coastal State may take into account 'all relevant factors' in granting access, including its own economic and other national interests,[31] any 'right' of access by other States (including landlocked and geographically disadvantaged States) is subject to the almost complete discretion of the coastal State.

While access to the surplus is framed primarily by reference to foreign *States*, Article 62(4) also refers to the application of coastal State regulations to foreign *nationals*, providing that 'nationals of other States fishing in the [EEZ]' must comply with the conservation measures, terms, and conditions established in the laws and regulations of the coastal State. This has given rise to significant uncertainty about the extent of the coastal State's discretion; in particular, what is the permissible scope of the laws and regulations that may be applied under Article 62(4), to whom may they be applied, and how? Do such regulations apply to all foreign nationals, or only to those from States or on vessels accessing the surplus under Article 62(2)? And who is the 'ultimate regulatory target' of Article 62(4)—does it create responsibilities with which other States must comply pursuant to Article 58(3) or establish direct obligations for private foreign actors (legal or natural persons) engaging in fishing activities in the EEZ?[32] These difficult questions about the coastal State's ability to apply its laws and regulations to foreign vessels and nationals under different circumstances will be explored in more detail in Chapters 3, 4, and 5.

While the coastal State's sovereign rights over living resources described in Article 56(1) constitute customary international law,[33] the more detailed obligations contained in Articles 61 and 62 do not.[34] As Kwiatkowska observes, many of the criteria and practical methods set out in these Articles for determining the extent of the coastal State's rights and duties regarding the conservation and utilization of living resources are a source of technical guidance, but do not constitute norm-creating principles capable of generating customary international law.[35]

29 LOSC art 62(2).
30 Ibid art 62(3).
31 Ibid.
32 See *SRFC Advisory Opinion* (Sep Op Paik) [14].
33 Proelss notes that the customary international law status of art 56 as a whole cannot be answered in general terms because the scope of the coastal State's jurisdiction requires consideration of other rights, duties, and principles established by the LOSC, as clarified in art 56(1)(b) and (c). However, there is general agreement on the customary status of the broad areas of jurisdiction established in art 56(1) and the obligation of due regard in art 56(2): Proelss, 'Article 56' (n 6) 421.
34 See, eg, Edward Duncan Brown, *The International Law of the Sea: Vol 1* (Dartmouth 1994) 225; Gemma Andreone and Giuseppe Cataldi, 'Sui Generis Zones' in David Attard, Malgosia Fitzmaurice, and Norman A Martinez Gutierrez (eds), *The IMLI Manual on International Maritime Law: Vol I—The Law of the Sea* (OUP 2014) 222.
35 Kwiatkowska, *The 200 Mile EEZ* (n 16) 47, citing the rule in *North Sea Continental Shelf Cases* [72].

Most of the obligations in these Articles include non-exhaustive and highly discretionary elements, and are qualified by power modifiers such as 'take into account' or 'without prejudice to', which render them 'incapable of implying any legal obligation on the part of a coastal state or rights on the part of third state'.[36] While the broad obligations of conservation and optimum utilization can be described as principles of customary international law,[37] in practice coastal States follow their own approach to implementing these obligations, including with respect to setting the allowable catch, allocating access, and enacting conservation and management measures for living resources.[38] In particular, since the obligation to establish a total allowable catch is more apparent than real,[39] 'the references to declaring a surplus and allowing foreign access are obligations whose content is left to the discretion of the coastal State.'[40]

The breadth and discretionary nature of the coastal State's rights—and the difficulty in establishing the extent of its obligations—with respect to living resources in the EEZ is further reinforced by their specific exclusion from the compulsory dispute settlement framework in Part XV of the LOSC. Disputes regarding the interpretation or application of the LOSC with regard to 'fisheries' are subject to compulsory dispute settlement in accordance with Section 2 of Part XV. However, Article 297(3)(a) makes an exception for disputes relating to the coastal State's 'sovereign rights with respect to living resources in the EEZ or their exercise', including with respect to the discretionary powers for determining the allowable catch, the coastal State's harvesting capacity, the allocation of surpluses to other States, and the terms and conditions established in conservation and management laws and regulations. The effect of this provision is to negate any coastal State obligation to submit to compulsory settlement any dispute about its sovereign rights over living resources, or their exercise or non-exercise.

Of course, if a coastal State's refusal to do anything regarding the establishment of an allowable catch, or determination or allocation of a surplus, is 'arbitrary', it can be required to submit to compulsory conciliation under Article 297(3)(b), but any resulting recommendations are not binding. And while Article 300 provides that States must fulfil their LOSC obligations in good faith and not exercise their rights, jurisdiction, and freedoms in a manner that would constitute an abuse of rights, the exceptions set out in Article 297(3)(a) suggest that the coastal State's

[36] Kwiatkowska, *The 200 Mile EEZ* (n 16) 90. Kwiatkowska argues that these detailed provisions are in the nature of guidelines for the implementation of the principle of optimum utilization: ibid 48. Similarly, Christie observes that the LOSC standards for coastal State conservation and utilization of fisheries in the EEZ are 'largely ambiguous, incredibly flexible and virtually unenforceable': Donna R Christie, 'It Don't Come EEZ: The Failure and Future of Coastal State Fisheries Management' (2004) 14 JTransnatLawPol 1, 34.

[37] Kwiatkowska, *The 200 Mile EEZ* (n 16) 91–2.

[38] Andreone and Cataldi, 'Sui Generis Zones' (n 34) 222.

[39] See the discussion in nn 15–17 and associated text.

[40] Burke, *The New International Law of Fisheries* (n 6) 44–5.

refusal to exercise its discretion in these matters does not constitute an abuse of rights.[41] In addition, Article 298(1)(b) permits a State to exempt itself from compulsory dispute settlement with respect to disputes concerning law enforcement activities in regard to the exercise of sovereign rights or jurisdiction excluded from the jurisdiction of a court or tribunal under Article 297(3).

2.1.3 Cooperation regarding Shared Stocks

The coastal State's comprehensive 'zonal' jurisdiction over living resources in the EEZ is complemented by a 'species' approach,[42] with specific provisions directed at the conservation and management of a range of shared stocks,[43] including transboundary and straddling stocks (Article 63), highly migratory species (Article 64), marine mammals (Article 65), anadromous stocks (Article 66), and catadromous species (Article 67). Since the distribution of these stocks and species extends beyond the EEZ of a single coastal State, their conservation and optimum utilization cannot be realized through the unilateral action of the coastal State but requires cooperation. The LOSC formulates very general principles establishing a basic duty to cooperate, which employ subtle variations in substance and expression to reflect the coastal State's sovereign rights over living resources within the EEZ.

With respect to transboundary stocks, Article 63(1) provides that the relevant coastal States must 'seek to agree', directly or through appropriate subregional or regional organizations, on the measures necessary to ensure the 'conservation and development' of such stocks, without prejudice to the other provisions of Part V—with the effect that both (or all) coastal States retain their coastal State rights under Articles 56, 61, and 62. With respect to straddling stocks, Article 63(2) provides that coastal States and States fishing on the high seas must 'seek to agree', directly or through appropriate subregional or regional organizations, on measures necessary for the 'conservation' of these stocks—but only in 'the adjacent area' of high seas, and not in the EEZ, where the coastal State's sovereign rights prevail.[44]

[41] William T Burke, '1982 Convention on the Law of the Sea Provisions on Conditions of Access to Fisheries Subject to National Jurisdiction' (1984) 63 OrLRev 73, 91.

[42] Burke, *The New International Law of Fisheries* (n 6) 40.

[43] While the term 'shared stocks' is not found in the LOSC, it is used by the United Nations (UN) Food and Agriculture Organization (FAO) as a collective term for: 'transboundary' stocks (which cross the EEZ boundaries of two or more coastal States); 'straddling' stocks (which occur both in the EEZ and on the adjacent high seas); highly migratory species (listed in Annex I of the LOSC); and discrete high seas fish stocks (found exclusively on the high seas): GR Munro and A Van Houtte, 'The Conservation and Management of Shared Fish Stocks: Legal and Economic Aspects' *FAO Fisheries Technical Paper 67* (FAO 2004) 3.

[44] The duty described in art 63 for coastal States to cooperate in the conservation and development of straddling and transboundary stocks is an emerging principle of customary international law: Kwiatkowska, *The 200 Mile EEZ* (n 16) 79–80; Guifang Xue, *China and International Fisheries Law and Policy* (Martinus Nijhoff 2005) 27.

With respect to highly migratory species, Article 64(1) provides that coastal States and other States must cooperate with a view to 'ensuring conservation and promoting the objective of optimum utilization' of such species throughout the region, both within the EEZ and on the high seas. In contrast to transboundary and straddling stocks, Article 64 requires States to take a multilateral approach to the governance of highly migratory species throughout their range, in both the high seas and the EEZ. However, notwithstanding the more peremptory wording of Article 64(1) ('shall cooperate' rather than 'seek to agree'), Article 64(2) makes clear that the regime for highly migratory species does not derogate from the sovereign rights of the coastal State within the EEZ but applies 'in addition to' the other provisions of Part V.

The special interests of the coastal State are also recognized with respect to marine mammals,[45] anadromous stocks (which spawn in the freshwater rivers of a coastal State and later migrate to the high seas),[46] and catadromous species (which reproduce at sea before migrating to the rivers and lakes of a coastal State where they spend the majority of their lives).[47] Marine mammals and anadromous stocks are exempt from the obligation of 'optimum utilization',[48] and since fishing for anadromous stocks and catadromous species on the high seas is generally prohibited,[49] the coastal State's duty to cooperate with respect to such stocks and species is limited.[50]

While the 'duty to cooperate' established in Articles 63 and 64 is additional to the general rights and duties of the coastal State under Articles 61 and 62, its overall effect is to confirm the primacy of coastal State rights with respect to the management of living resources in the EEZ. This is because 'management' is excluded from the ambit of cooperation, which only includes 'conservation', 'development', and—in respect of highly migratory species only—'optimum utilization'.[51] The LOSC

[45] LOSC art 65.

[46] Ibid art 66.

[47] Ibid art 67.

[48] Art 65 allows the coastal State to prohibit, limit or regulate the exploitation of marine mammals more strictly than provided for elsewhere in Part V, and requires States to cooperate with a view to their 'conservation' (and does not mention 'utilization'). Art 66 requires the State in whose rivers anadromous stocks originate to ensure their conservation by adopting 'appropriate regulatory measures' for the EEZ but does not require the establishment of allowable catches or the allocation of surplus.

[49] Art 66(3) prohibits fishing for anadromous stocks on the high seas unless this would result in economic dislocation for a State other than the State of origin, in which case it may be agreed on terms and conditions that give due regard to the conservation requirements and needs of the State of origin. Art 67(2) prohibits high seas fishing for catadromous species in all circumstances.

[50] Art 66(4) provides that if anadromous stocks should migrate into or through the EEZ of another State, that State must 'cooperate' with the State of origin regarding their conservation and management. Art 67(3) provides that the management and harvesting of catadromous species which migrate through the EEZ of another State must be 'regulated by agreement' between that State and the State in whose waters they spend the greater part of their life cycle. In contrast, art 65 requires States (not just coastal States) to 'cooperate with a view to the conservation of marine mammals'.

[51] William M Sutherland, 'Management, Conservation, and Cooperation in EEZ Fishing: The Law of the Sea Convention and the South Pacific Forum Fisheries Agency' (1987) 18 ODIL 613, 621. In contrast, art 118 of the LOSC provides that 'States shall cooperate with each other in the conservation *and management* of living resources in the areas of the high seas' (emphasis added).

does not provide any guidance about the allocation of straddling or highly migratory species as between the EEZ and the high seas. Article 116 provides simply that the freedom of fishing on the high seas is 'subject to' the rights, duties, and interests of coastal States under Articles 63 and 64 to 67.[52] This provision seems to indicate that the preferential rights of coastal States with respect to living resources extend (beyond the EEZ) to affect the high seas, at least in so far as distant water fishing nations may not unilaterally adopt measures for high seas fishing of such species without fulfilling the duty to cooperate with relevant coastal States.[53] Moreover, if a distant water fishing nation requires access to the waters of a coastal State (or coastal States) in a region in order to provide sufficient fishing opportunities for its fleet, the coastal States concerned can make that access subject to conditions regarding the conduct of high seas fishing.[54]

2.1.4 Coastal State Enforcement Powers

Even the most extensive prescriptive powers in the world are of little practical consequence without enforcement jurisdiction to ensure their effectiveness. Article 73(1) provides that in the exercise of its sovereign rights over the living resources of the EEZ, the coastal State has the right to 'take such measures, including boarding, inspection, arrest and judicial proceedings, as may be necessary to ensure compliance with the laws and regulations adopted by it in conformity with [the LOSC]'. In addition, under Article 111 the coastal State has the right to continue hot pursuit beyond the EEZ in order to take enforcement measures with respect to violations of fisheries regulations committed within the zone.

At first blush, these provisions may appear to create a potentially unbalanced set of coastal State powers—particularly since disputes concerning law enforcement activities in regard to the exercise of sovereign rights can be excluded from compulsory settlement by virtue of Article 298(1)(b). According to Judge Oda, as presented in Article 73(1): 'the mode of exercise of jurisdiction is no different from that exercised by the coastal State within its territorial sea and, so far as the development of the natural resources of the sea is concerned, its competence in the [EEZ] is equivalent to that it enjoys in the territorial sea.'[55] However, like the coastal State's prescriptive rights over living resources under Article 56(1), this enforcement jurisdiction is not unlimited.

[52] Tore Henriksen and Alf Håkon Hoel, 'Determining Allocation: From Paper to Practice in the Distribution of Fishing Rights Between Countries Determining Allocation' (2011) 42 ODIL 66, 70.

[53] Barbara Kwiatkowska, 'The High Seas Fisheries Regime: At a Point of No Return?' (1993) 8 IJMCL 327, 330. This point is reinforced by the prohibition on high seas fishing for anadromous and catadromous species under arts 66 and 67.

[54] William T Burke, 'Highly Migratory Species in the New Law of the Sea' (1984) 14 ODIL 273, 285–6.

[55] *Tunisia v Libya* (Diss Op Oda) [124].

First, the seemingly broad authority described in Article 73(1) is limited to actions that are 'necessary' to ensure compliance with the coastal State's laws and regulations.[56] Second, the coastal State's enforcement jurisdiction is qualified by the requirement in Article 73(2) that arrested vessels and their crews be promptly released on the posting of a 'reasonable bond or other security'.[57] Third, Article 73(3) limits the coastal State's discretion regarding the types of penalties that may be imposed for fisheries violations in the EEZ, by precluding imprisonment for foreign fishermen (unless otherwise agreed with the State concerned) as well as any form of corporal punishment. And fourth, underpinning all of this are the important questions of whether the coastal State's measures have been prescribed 'in conformity with' the LOSC as required by Article 73(1), and which vessels and activities can be subject to coastal State enforcement jurisdiction.

In addition, in conducting fisheries enforcement activities, coastal States must comply with the requirements of Articles 224 and 225. Article 225 provides that enforcement measures against foreign vessels must be undertaken with due regard for the safety of navigation, and the protection of the marine environment.[58] Article 224 specifies that enforcement powers may only be exercised against foreign vessels 'by officials or by warships, military aircraft or other ships or aircraft clearly marked and identifiable as being on government service and authorized to that effect.' While Article 224 is only expressed to apply to enforcement activities under Part XII of the LOSC, its requirements have been found to apply to the conduct of enforcement activities under Article 73(1) as a matter of general international law,[59] and similar requirements also apply to the conduct of hot pursuit under Article 111(5).

The implementation of these provisions through the conduct of enforcement activities by coastal States—and challenges to the legality of such activities by flag States—has brought to light the significant uncertainties and ambiguities inherent in the LOSC framework. These include, in particular: the difficult question of what enforcement measures are 'necessary' to ensure compliance with coastal State laws and regulations; the extent to which general international law can or should affect the interpretation of the LOSC provisions; the role of international courts and tribunals in reviewing the actions of coastal States; and the way in which the delicate

56 While the term 'necessary' does not set an objective standard, if the threshold for 'necessity' under this provision is set too high it would impede the coastal State's ability to fulfil its obligations to effectively conserve and manage the living resources of the EEZ: James Harrison, 'Article 73' in Alexander Proelss (ed), *United Nations Convention on the Law of the Sea: A Commentary* (CH Beck 2017) 558. On the issue of what is 'necessary' in the context of coastal State enforcement jurisdiction, see Section 6.1.

57 On the issue of what may properly constitute a 'bond' under art 73(2), see Section 6.3.1.

58 LOSC art 225. Since this provision refers to the exercise of enforcement powers 'under the [LOSC]', it applies to all enforcement activities, including fisheries enforcement: Harrison, 'Safeguards Against Excessive Enforcement' (n 2) 228.

59 *Virginia G* [342]. On the formalities for exercising enforcement powers under art 73, see further Section 6.2.3.2.

'balance of interests' established in the LOSC is maintained. These questions are examined in detail in Chapters 6 and 7.

2.1.5 Protection and Preservation of the Marine Environment

While Part V is the primary source of coastal State rights and duties under the LOSC, Article 56(1)(c) provides that, in the EEZ, the coastal State also has 'other rights and duties provided for in [the LOSC]'. These include the obligations in Part XII of the LOSC regarding the protection and preservation of the marine environment that apply to all States, in all areas, including the EEZ. Article 192 establishes the fundamental obligation to 'protect and preserve the marine environment', which is elevated above the coastal State's sovereign rights to exploit its natural resources by Article 193, which provides that such rights must be exercised in accordance with the State's duty to protect and preserve the marine environment.[60] While the bulk of Article 194 is directed specifically at measures to prevent marine pollution, it also has a bearing on the conservation and management of living resources, since Article 194(5) requires States to take the measures necessary to 'protect and preserve rare or fragile ecosystems as well as the habitat of depleted, threatened or endangered species and other forms of marine life.' These provisions extend the conservation duty set out in Part V by providing a more widely framed obligation to protect the marine environment (including marine habitat and biodiversity), rather than the more limited notion of conserving the living marine resources of the EEZ.[61] They have been applied to significant effect in a number of recent decisions by international courts and tribunals.[62]

2.2 The Effect of Post-LOSC Instruments

Since the LOSC was adopted nearly forty years ago, the international community has made a concerted effort to clarify and strengthen the framework for fisheries within and beyond the EEZ, by adopting a wide range of binding and non-binding instruments. While the majority of these instruments are focused predominantly on the obligations of flag States and the governance of shared stocks and high seas fisheries (in particular, the 1993 *Agreement to Promote Compliance with International Conservation and Management Measures by Vessels on the High Seas* (Compliance Agreement)),[63] several have played an important role in developing

[60] Rothwell and Stephens, *The International Law of the Sea* (n 11) 90.

[61] Michaela Young, 'Then and Now: Reappraising Freedom of the Seas in Modern Law of the Sea' (2016) 47 ODIL 165, 168. While Young makes this point in respect of high seas fishing, given the general application of arts 192 and 194 it must apply equally to fishing in the EEZ.

[62] See nn 127–134 and associated text.

[63] (Opened for signature 24 November 1993, entered into force 24 April 2003) 2221 UNTS 91.

the framework for coastal State jurisdiction over living resources in the EEZ. First, through the strengthened conservation and management concepts adopted in the 1995 *Agreement for the Implementation of the Provisions of the United Nations Convention on the Law of the Sea of 10 December 1982 relating to the Conservation and Management of Straddling Fish Stocks and Highly Migratory Fish Stocks* (UNFSA)[64] and the 1995 *Code of Conduct for Responsible Fisheries* (FAO Code of Conduct).[65] Second, through the concept of illegal, unreported, and unregulated (IUU) fishing described in the 2001 *International Plan of Action to Prevent, Deter and Eliminate Illegal, Unreported and Unregulated Fishing* (IPOA-IUU)[66] and further applied in the 2009 *Agreement on Port State Measures to Prevent, Deter and Eliminate Illegal, Unreported and Unregulated Fishing* (Port State Measures Agreement)[67] and by regional fisheries management organizations (RFMOs).

2.2.1 Strengthened Conservation and Management Concepts

While the UNFSA only applies to straddling and highly migratory fish stocks in areas 'beyond national jurisdiction',[68] Article 3 establishes three important exceptions to this rule: the general principles established in Article 5 apply *mutatis mutandis* to the conservation and management of such stocks within 'areas under national jurisdiction';[69] and the provisions of Article 6 (relating to the precautionary approach) and Article 7 (governing compatibility) also apply 'within areas under national jurisdiction'.[70] These strengthened conservation and management concepts are a significant advance on the LOSC principles,[71] and have had an important effect on coastal State rights and responsibilities over living resources in the EEZ.

Article 5 of the UNFSA raises the overall standard of coastal State responsibility for conservation and management of living resources—replacing the discretion of the LOSC provisions ('take into account' and 'consider') with obligations ('shall' adopt, ensure, and protect).[72] In line with its underlying objective of ensuring the long-term conservation and sustainable use of straddling and highly migratory fish stocks through the effective implementation of the LOSC,[73] Article 5 of the UNFSA also strengthens the coastal State's obligations of conservation and

[64] (Opened for signature 4 December 1995, entered into force 11 December 2001) 2167 UNTS 88.
[65] (Adopted 31 October 1995).
[66] (Adopted 2 March 2001).
[67] (Opened for signature 22 November 2009, entered into force 5 June 2016) UNTS I-54133.
[68] UNFSA art 3(1).
[69] Ibid art 3(2).
[70] Ibid art 3(1).
[71] William Edeson, 'Closing the Gap: The Role of "Soft" International Instruments to Control Fishing' (1999) 20 AustYBIL 83, 89.
[72] Christie, 'The Conservation and Management of EEZ Stocks' (n 28) 413.
[73] UNFSA art 2.

optimum utilization by specifying a number of general principles to be applied by States 'in giving effect to their duty to cooperate in accordance with the [LOSC]'.[74] In addition to restating obligations from Articles 61 and 62 of the LOSC, it establishes new or elaborated requirements relating to the implementation of an 'ecosystem approach' to the conservation and management of fishery resources. While there is no formal legal definition of an 'ecosystem approach', it can be understood as recognizing that, since fisheries have a direct impact on the ecosystem, which is also impacted by other human activities, they need to be managed with recognition of the interconnections between the component parts of the overall ecosystem.[75] Accordingly, an ecosystem approach to fisheries conservation and management requires the protection of associated or dependent species; the assessment of the impacts of fishing and other human activities on living resources; the minimization of pollution, waste and discards, and the use of selective fishing gear; the protection of biodiversity; and the provision of complete and accurate data concerning fishing activities.

In addition, the UNFSA requires States to apply the precautionary approach, which had not been conceptualized at the time the LOSC was negotiated but emerged in domestic and regional instruments on the protection of the environment in the mid-1980s, and achieved prominence in Principle 15 of the 1992 Rio Declaration.[76] It has since been included in virtually every treaty and declaration relating to the conservation of fisheries resources and the protection of the marine environment.[77] Pursuant to Articles 3, 5(e), and 6 of the UNFSA, States are required to apply the precautionary approach widely to the conservation, management, and exploitation of straddling and highly migratory fish stocks both within areas of national jurisdiction and on the high seas, in order to protect living marine resources and preserve the marine environment. Article 6 provides detailed guidance for applying this approach, according to which States must be cautious when information is uncertain, unreliable, or inadequate and may not use the absence of adequate scientific information as a reason for postponing or failing to take conservation and management measures. Practical steps to give effect to these requirements are further elaborated in Annex II of the UNFSA, which contains guidelines for the development and application of stock-specific precautionary reference points and management strategies to maintain or restore living resources at levels consistent with such reference points.

[74] Ibid art 5.

[75] See SM Garcia et al, 'The Ecosystem Approach to Fisheries: Issues, Terminology, Principles, Institutional Foundations, Implementation and Outlook' *FAO Fisheries Technical Paper 443* (FAO 2003) 5–6.

[76] 'Rio Declaration on Environment and Development', *Report of the United Nations Conference on Environment and Development* (Rio de Janeiro, Brazil, 3–14 June 1992) A/CONF.151/26/Rev.1 (Vol 1) 3.

[77] Xue, *China and International Fisheries* (n 44) 50 fn 50.

Article 7 of the UNFSA clarifies the content of the duty to cooperate, requiring States to ensure that the conservation and management measures adopted for the EEZ and those adopted for the high seas are 'compatible', in order to ensure the conservation and management of straddling and highly migratory stocks in their entirety. While the issues to be taken into account in determining compatible conservation and management measures reflect the interests of both coastal States and States fishing on the high seas, the overall balance of the provision gives the coastal State 'decisive influence', including with respect to the level of fishing on the high seas.[78] For example, measures established for the high seas must not 'undermine the effectiveness' of measures established by coastal States for the EEZ,[79] and account must be taken of the distribution of the stocks, including the extent to which they occur and are fished in areas under national jurisdiction.[80]

Of course, any treaty is only binding on its parties, so while the UNFSA is now widely ratified,[81] it is still important to consider whether these provisions have achieved customary status. In this regard, it is worth noting that since 2003, the Sustainable Fisheries Resolution adopted annually by the United Nations General Assembly (UNGA) has included a paragraph that 'calls on all States, directly or through [RFMOs] and arrangements, to apply widely, in accordance with international law and the Code, the precautionary approach and ecosystem approaches to the conservation, management and exploitation of fish stocks, and also calls upon States parties to the [UNFSA] to implement fully the provisions of article 6 of the Agreement as a matter of priority'.[82]

Not only does the UNGA's unambiguous call to 'all States' (not just 'Parties') indicate collective support for these important conservation and management concepts,[83] but it suggests that they should be applied to all fish stocks, not just straddling and highly migratory stocks—although the detailed guidelines for implementing the precautionary approach, set out in Article 6 of the UNFSA, do not yet appear to have been similarly recognized. Nor has the principle of

[78] Henriksen and Hoel, 'Determining Allocation' (n 52) 73. This provision reflects a significant compromise reached during the UNFSA negotiations between coastal States, who proposed that States fishing for straddling and highly migratory stocks must take all measures necessary to 'give effect to the special interest and responsibility of the coastal State' in respect of those resources on the high seas, and distant water fishing States who regarded this proposal as a renewed attack on the freedom of fishing: M Hayashi, 'The Straddling and Highly Migratory Fish Stocks Agreement' in Ellen Hey (ed), *Developments in International Fisheries Law* (Kluwer 1999) 62–3.

[79] UNFSA art 7(2)(a). Opinion on the effect of this provision is divided. While some view it as giving the coastal State superior rights, others consider that the difference in wording between art 7(2)(a) ('not undermine the effectiveness' of coastal State measures) and art 7(2)(b) ('take into account' measures adopted for the high seas) is not relevant: see Alex G Oude Elferink, 'The Determination of Compatible Conservation and Management Measures for Straddling and Highly Migratory Fish Stocks' in JA Frowein and R Wolfrum (eds), MaxPlanckYrbkUNL, Vol 5 (Kluwer 2001) 564–5 fn 27.

[80] UNFSA art 7(2)(d) and (e).

[81] At 31 December 2020, the UNFSA had ninety-one Parties.

[82] See UNGA Res 75/89 (8 December 2020) UN Doc A/75/89 [16].

[83] James Harrison, *Making the Law of the Sea* (CUP 2011) 109–10.

compatibility received the same level of collective support.[84] While the concept of compatibility is reflected in many of the more recently adopted constituent instruments of RFMOs, the variety of ways in which it is expressed and implemented indicate that the compromise in Article 7 of the UNFSA is not yet a generally accepted formula, particularly with respect to the relationship between the measures adopted by the coastal State for areas under national jurisdiction, and the measures established for the high seas.[85]

These concepts are further reinforced in the FAO Code of Conduct, a globally applicable instrument that provides principles and standards for the conservation, management, and development of all fisheries in all maritime zones.[86] While not legally binding, it is intended to be interpreted and applied consistently with the key conventions and in light of relevant declarations and other international instruments.[87] The FAO Code of Conduct reinforces and elaborates on the strengthened conservation and management concepts set out in Articles 5, 6, and 7 of the UNFSA. It provides additional detail on general fisheries management principles and the ecosystem approach,[88] gives specific guidance on the application and implementation of the precautionary approach,[89] and notes the requirement for compatibility between conservation and management measures adopted for the high seas and the EEZ.[90]

2.2.2 Illegal, Unreported, and Unregulated Fishing

The other important post-LOSC development affecting coastal State jurisdiction is the concept of IUU fishing, which is universally agreed to be 'one of the greatest threats to fish stocks and marine ecosystems and continues to have serious and major implications for the conservation and management of ocean resources, as well as the food security and the economies of many States'.[91] While the concept of

[84] To date, the principle of compatibility has not been referred to in any of the UNGA Sustainable Fisheries Resolutions.

[85] See Oude Elferink, 'The Determination of Compatible Measures' (n 79) 583–91 and 605.

[86] FAO Code of Conduct art 1.

[87] Ibid arts 1 and 3. Some commentators conclude that the FAO Code of Conduct has acquired the status of customary international law: see Maria Gavouneli, *Functional Jurisdiction in the Law of the Sea* (Martinus Nijhoff 2007) 108. However, given its drafting history and use of hortatory language it seems unlikely to have the potentially norm-creating character required to generate new rules of customary international law: Harrison, *Making the Law of the Sea* (n 83) 218.

[88] FAO Code of Conduct arts 6, 7, and 8.

[89] Ibid art 7.5.

[90] Ibid art 7.3.2. The FAO Code of Conduct extends the principle of compatibility beyond straddling and highly migratory stocks to all shared stocks. Consistent with UNGA and RFMO practice described above, it does not replicate the detailed guidance on the implementation of the compatibility principle, but simply states that compatibility 'should be achieved in a manner consistent with the rights, competences and interests of the States concerned'.

[91] UNGA Res 75/89 [79].

IUU fishing does not appear *in* the LOSC, it can be said to have appeared largely *because* of the LOSC, since the framework established in the LOSC (the extension of coastal State rights to the EEZ, and consequent displacement of foreign fleets from vast areas that had previously been high seas), and the gaps in that framework (including the ineffective nature of the 'genuine link' requirement and the limitations on the exercise of enforcement jurisdiction) contributed to the development of a political, economic, and legal environment conducive to the emergence of IUU fishing.[92]

IUU fishing is a broad concept that encompasses a suite of fishing and related activities undertaken with the aim of avoiding regulation, whether on the high seas, in areas regulated by RFMOs, or in the EEZs of coastal States.[93] This is reflected in the descriptive definition (or 'explanation')[94] of IUU fishing in paragraph 3 of the IPOA-IUU, which is framed around three key aspects of illicit conduct—'illegal' fishing, 'unreported' fishing,[95] and 'unregulated' fishing—categorized according to where that conduct takes place (in waters under the jurisdiction of a coastal State, in areas under the competence of an RFMO, or in unregulated areas of high seas).[96] The IPOA-IUU is designed to provide all States with 'comprehensive, transparent and effective measures' by which to act in order to prevent, deter and eliminate IUU fishing practices,[97] which commonly include activities such as fishing without or in contravention of an authorization, contravening the conservation and management measures of a coastal State or RFMO, or failing to report or misreporting catch.

The root cause of IUU fishing is the lack of effective flag State control, which allows vessels to engage in a wide range of illegal activities with impunity. Given the difficulty of securing flag State responsibility for the activities of their vessels in the EEZs of other States,[98] coastal States—particularly developing coastal States—face enormous challenges in addressing IUU fishing by foreign vessels in their EEZs, which provide the most lucrative opportunities for IUU fishing because they

[92] See Rachel Baird, 'Illegal, Unreported and Unregulated Fishing: An Analysis of the Legal, Economic and Historical Factors Relevant to Its Development and Persistence' (2004) 5 MelbJIntlLaw 299.

[93] Ibid 300.

[94] Jens T Theilen, 'What's in a Name? The Illegality of Illegal, Unreported and Unregulated Fishing' (2013) 28 IJMCL 533, 534.

[95] As has been widely observed, 'unreported' fishing activities are in fact merely a sub-category of 'illegal' fishing activities. See Ibid 541; Baird, 'Illegal, Unreported and Unregulated Fishing' (n 92) 302.

[96] Ibid 301.

[97] IPOA-IUU [8].

[98] Prior to the 2015 *SRFC Advisory Opinion*, the prevailing view was that flag State obligations to combat illegal fishing in the EEZs of other States could not be read into any provisions of the LOSC: Valentin Schatz, 'Combating Illegal Fishing in the Exclusive Economic Zone—Flag State Obligations in the Context of the Primary Responsibility of the Coastal State' (2016) 7(2) GoettingenJIntlLaw 383, 399. The *SRFC Advisory Opinion* concluded that flag States *do* have a responsibility to ensure that vessels flying their flag do not conduct IUU fishing activities within the EEZs of coastal States, but liability only arises if the flag State fails to exercise due diligence. Moreover, the primary responsibility to prevent, deter and eliminate IUU fishing in the EEZ rests with the coastal State: *SRFC Advisory Opinion* [106].

contain the vast majority of the world's marine fishery resources.[99] The necessity of effective coastal State measures to combat IUU fishing is recognized in paragraph 51 of the IPOA-IUU (the only of the post-LOSC instruments to specifically and substantively address coastal State rights and duties), which provides that, in the exercise of its sovereign rights to explore, exploit, conserve, and manage living marine resources, each coastal State 'should implement measures to prevent, deter and eliminate IUU fishing in the EEZ'.[100] It also provides a list of suggested measures that the coastal State should consider taking to give effect to this objective, which include:

- measures for effective monitoring, control, and surveillance of fishing activities;[101]
- measures to ensure that no vessel undertakes fishing activities in the coastal State's EEZ without a valid authorization to fish issued by that coastal State;[102]
- measures to ensure that at-sea transhipment and processing of fish and fish products in coastal State waters are authorized by the coastal State, or conducted in conformity with appropriate regulations;[103] and
- measures to regulate access to the fisheries of the EEZ in a way that will help to prevent, deter, and eliminate IUU fishing.[104]

This list of measures not only contributes to the interpretation of the coastal State's duties to conserve and manage the living resources of the EEZ but confirms the practical extent of the rights that are necessary in order to give effect to such duties and is thus an important contribution to elaborating the content of coastal State jurisdiction under the LOSC and customary international law.

While the IPOA-IUU is not legally binding,[105] it has had an enormous influence. The importance of preventing, deterring, and eliminating IUU fishing has been

[99] An estimated 95 per cent of marine capture fisheries take place in waters under national jurisdiction: 'Agenda 21', *Report of the United Nations Conference on Environment and Development* (Rio de Janeiro, Brazil, 3–14 June 1992) A/CONF.151/26/Rev.1 (Vol 1) 257 [17.70].

[100] IPOA-IUU [51]. The Compliance Agreement does not contain any provisions relating to coastal State rights and duties. The UNFSA contains specific provisions relating to the duties of the flag State (art 18), enforcement by the flag State (art 19), and measures that may be taken by port States (art 23) but does not address coastal State rights and duties, except in the context of the duty to cooperate in conservation and management. Similarly, the FAO Code of Conduct contains specific provisions relating to flag and port State rights and duties, but only refers to coastal States in the context of integrating fisheries into coastal area management (art 10). The Port State Measures Agreement relates to the duties of port States (based on port State jurisdiction over vessels in port, not coastal State jurisdiction over vessels in the EEZ) and flag States (art 20).

[101] IPOA-IUU [51.1].

[102] Ibid [51.3].

[103] Ibid [51.6].

[104] Ibid [51.7].

[105] The IPOA-IUU is a voluntary instrument elaborated within the framework of the FAO Code of Conduct as a 'further commitment by all States to implement the Code of Conduct': ibid [4] and [7]. In many respects, the IPOA-IUU can be considered to constitute an authentic interpretation of the LOSC under art 31(3)(a) and (b) of the Vienna Convention on the Law of Treaties (VCLT).

subject to repeated calls for action in decisions and resolutions from the UNGA,[106] the FAO,[107] and other global[108] and regional bodies.[109] A wide range of additional instruments and approaches have been adopted to address IUU fishing, including not only strengthened standards for flag State responsibility,[110] but measures for collective action (such as 'IUU vessel lists' and catch documentation schemes in RFMOs) and the use of port and market State measures (such as the Port State Measures Agreement). The definition of IUU fishing in paragraph 3 of the IPOA-IUU has been incorporated (directly or by reference) into binding instruments ratified by both flag and coastal States from all over the world, including the constituent instruments and conservation and management measures of RFMOs, and in a global legally binding mechanism (the Port State Measures Agreement).[111] In short, underpinned by wide-ranging support and an inter-laced set of hard and soft law instruments, the concept of IUU fishing has contributed significantly to the emergence of a less traditional, more integrated approach to the conservation and management of global fisheries, and to the development of a more comprehensive understanding of coastal State rights and duties.

2.3 The 'Continuum' of Coastal State Jurisdiction

As established in the *Lotus* case,[112] States have a wide discretion—not an unlimited right—to exercise jurisdiction within their territory in respect of events occurring outside it, provided there is no express or implicit prohibition. The lawful limits of this jurisdiction are established by a flexible and differentiated continuum constrained by minimum *duties* and maximum *prohibitions*. Similarly, States have discretion to exercise jurisdiction at sea within the limits of lawfulness established explicitly and implicitly in the LOSC and in customary international law. Accordingly, the permissible extent of coastal State jurisdiction over living

[106] This issue is regularly addressed in the annual UNGA Sustainable Fisheries Resolutions, which include language calling on all States 'urgently to take all steps necessary to implement' the IPOA-IUU. See, eg, UNGA Res 75/89 (n 82) [79] and generally to [108].

[107] See, eg, FAO, 'Report of the Thirty-Third Session of the Committee on Fisheries, Rome, 9–13 July 2018' *FAO Fisheries and Aquaculture Report 1249* (FAO 2019) [47]–[59].

[108] See, eg, 'Decision X/29 Marine and Coastal Biodiversity', *Report of the Tenth Meeting of the Conference of the Parties to the Convention on Biological Diversity* (Nagoya, Japan, 29 October 2010) UNEP/CBD/COP/10/27 229 [13(g)]; 'The Future We Want', UNGA Res 66/288 (27 July 2012) UN Doc A/RES/66/288 [170].

[109] See, eg: in the Asia-Pacific, the *Regional Plan of Action (RPOA) to Promote Responsible Fishing Practices Including Combating IUU Fishing in the Region* (adopted 5 May 2007 in Bali, Indonesia); in the Caribbean, the *Castries (St Lucia) Declaration on Illegal, Unreported and Unregulated Fishing* (adopted 28 July 2010 at Castries, St Lucia).

[110] Such as those in the Compliance Agreement, the UNFSA, the FAO Code of Conduct, the Port State Measures Agreement, and the FAO *Voluntary Guidelines for Flag State Performance* (FAO Voluntary Guidelines for Flag State Performance) (adopted 12 June 2014).

[111] Port State Measures Agreement art 3(3) and (1)(e).

[112] *Lotus* 18–19.

resources in the EEZ is found on that part of the continuum that falls *between* the minimum duties and maximum prohibitions.

In order to establish the basic continuum of coastal State jurisdiction over living resources in the EEZ, it is necessary to look not only at the list of rights and duties set out in the LOSC, but to examine the broader, normative principles and approaches identified in the jurisprudence of international courts and tribunals to understand what coastal States *must, may*, and *may not* do in the exercise of their jurisdiction in the EEZ. After confirming the basic rights and duties of coastal States by reference to the caselaw, this Section looks beyond the face of the LOSC and identifies the key obligations, rights, and prohibitions identified in the jurisprudence, in order to provide a clear guide as to what coastal States must, may, and may not do in the exercise of their jurisdiction in the EEZ.

2.3.1 The Basic Rights and Duties of Coastal States

The 2015 *SRFC Advisory Opinion* afforded the International Tribunal for the Law of the Sea (ITLOS) an opportunity to clarify the interpretation of the basic rights and duties of coastal States with respect to living resources in the EEZ. While the Request was directed principally to the obligations of flag States in relation to the conduct of IUU fishing, the Tribunal started by addressing a number of issues relating to coastal States. It confirmed that responsibility for the conservation and management of living resources in the EEZ rests with the coastal State,[113] which must adopt conservation and management measures for all living resources in the EEZ.[114] Such measures must be based on the best scientific evidence available, and when such evidence is insufficient, the coastal State must apply the precautionary approach in order to ensure that the living resources in the EEZ are not endangered by over-exploitation.[115] The coastal State is responsible for setting the allowable catch, and is required to give other States access to any surplus through agreements or arrangements.[116]

To meet these responsibilities, the coastal State is required to adopt the 'necessary' laws and regulations, including enforcement procedures, which must be consistent with the LOSC.[117] The coastal State may take such measures 'as may be necessary' to ensure compliance with these laws and regulations, including boarding, inspection, arrest, and judicial proceedings.[118] Thus, ITLOS concluded: 'in light of the special rights and responsibilities given to the coastal State

[113] *SRFC Advisory Opinion* [104].
[114] Ibid [96].
[115] Ibid [208].
[116] Ibid [104].
[117] Ibid.
[118] Ibid [105].

in the [EEZ] under the Convention, the primary responsibility for taking the necessary measures to prevent, deter and eliminate IUU fishing rests with the coastal State.'[119]

The Tribunal was specifically asked to consider the rights and obligations of coastal States in ensuring the sustainable management of shared stocks.[120] The Tribunal found that the coastal State is obliged to ensure the sustainable management of shared stocks while they occur in the EEZ.[121] It highlighted the key aspects of the LOSC provisions relating to shared stocks, including obligations to: 'cooperate' in ensuring that the maintenance of shared stocks is not endangered by over-exploitation under Article 61(2); 'seek to agree' on measures necessary to ensure the conservation and development of shared stocks under Article 63(1); and 'cooperate' with a view to ensuring conservation and promoting the objective of optimum utilization of highly migratory species in the EEZ under Article 64(1), in which regard the measures taken should be 'compatible' with those established by the relevant RFMO throughout the region.[122] In order to comply with this obligation, coastal States must ensure that conservation and management measures for these resources meet the various requirements set out in Article 61.[123] The Tribunal stated that the requirements to 'seek to agree' under Article 63(1) and to 'cooperate' under Article 64(1) are due diligence obligations, which require meaningful, good faith consultation by all States concerned.[124]

The Tribunal specifically noted that 'although the [LOSC] approaches the issue of conservation and management of living resources from the perspective of obligations of the coastal State, these obligations entail corresponding rights.'[125] Unfortunately, the Tribunal did not elaborate on the relationship between these rights and obligations, or how they 'correspond' to one another, which, as Judge Paik touched upon in his separate opinion, is at the core of the legal difficulties in this area.[126] However, as explored below, some guidance on the general approach to be taken to this question can be found by considering the broader approaches taken in the jurisprudence and the literature regarding what coastal States *must*, *may*, and *must not* do in exercising their rights and fulfilling their obligations under conventional and customary international law.

The jurisprudence also provides guidance on basic coastal State rights and obligations relating to the protection and preservation of the marine environment,

[119] Ibid [106].

[120] The question posed in the Request concerned 'shared stocks and stocks of common interest, especially the small pelagic species and tuna', which the Tribunal interpreted as equating to the stocks addressed in arts 63 and 64 of the LOSC: ibid [183]–[204].

[121] Ibid [207].

[122] Ibid [207]–[209].

[123] Ibid [208]–[209].

[124] Ibid [210]. On due diligence obligations, see Section 2.3.2.2.

[125] Ibid [205].

[126] Ibid (Sep Op Paik) [31].

and confirms that: the marine environmental protection obligations in Part XII of the LOSC apply to all States in all maritime areas, both within and beyond national jurisdiction;[127] the conservation of living resources is an element in the protection and preservation of the marine environment;[128] and the obligations in Articles 192 and 194 of the LOSC are of a due diligence nature, relating not only to activities directly taken by the State and its organs, but also to ensuring that, to the extent possible, activities within the State's jurisdiction and control do not harm the marine environment.[129] In this regard, as the *Chagos Arbitration* Tribunal confirmed, Article 194 is not limited to measures aimed strictly at controlling pollution, but extends to measures focused primarily on conservation and the preservation of ecosystems.[130]

This reasoning was adopted and extended in the *South China Sea Arbitration*, in which the Arbitral Tribunal found that Article 192 is informed by three categories of norms: the corpus of international law relating to the environment; the other provisions of Part XII (including Article 194); and specific obligations set out in other international agreements, as provided in Article 237 of the LOSC.[131] In this regard, the Tribunal found that the *Convention on International Trade in Endangered Species of Wild Fauna and Flora*,[132] which is the subject of nearly universal adherence, forms part of the general corpus of international law that informs the interpretation of Articles 192 and 194(5), and that accordingly: 'the general obligation to "protect and preserve the marine environment" in Article 192 includes a due diligence obligation to prevent the harvesting of species that are recognized internationally as being at risk of extinction and requiring international protection.'[133]

The *South China Sea Arbitration* Tribunal went on to extend the application of Article 192 even further—beyond preventing the direct harvesting of species threatened with extinction, to 'the prevention of harms that would affect depleted, threatened, or endangered species indirectly through the destruction of their habitat'.[134] While this decision concerned the exercise of flag State jurisdiction rather than coastal State jurisdiction, since the general obligations in Part XII of the LOSC apply to all States in all areas, it must be considered to affect flag States and coastal States in equal measure.

[127] *SRFC Advisory Opinion* [120]; *South China Sea Arbitration* [940].

[128] *Southern Bluefin Tuna (New Zealand v Japan; Australia v Japan)* (Provisional Measures Order, Order of 27 August 1999) (1999) ITLOS Rep 280 [70]; *SRFC Advisory Opinion* [216].

[129] See *SRFC Advisory Opinion* [118]–[136]; *South China Sea Arbitration* [944].

[130] *Chagos Marine Protected Area (Republic of Mauritius vs United Kingdom of Great Britain and Northern Ireland)* [2015] PCA Case 2011-3 [538] (*Chagos Arbitration*).

[131] *South China Sea Arbitration* [941]–[942].

[132] (Opened for signature 3 March 1973, entered into force 1 July 1975) 993 UNTS 243.

[133] *South China Sea Arbitration* [956].

[134] Ibid [959].

2.3.2 The Obligations of Coastal States: Things they Must Do

By reviewing the jurisprudence and associated commentary, it is possible to clearly discern three key things that coastal States must take into account in regulating the living resources of the EEZ: the rule of due regard, the rule of due diligence, and the applicable rules of general international law.

2.3.2.1 The Rule of Due Regard

The primary restraint on coastal State jurisdiction in the EEZ is the rule of due regard—a substantive obligation under Article 56(2) of the LOSC that permeates almost every facet of the coastal State's jurisdiction and has received attention in a variety of contexts and decisions. Due regard is generally agreed to be a positive obligation that requires more than simply 'non-interference'.[135] It is an obligation of conduct (not result), and is procedural in nature, meaning that its performance may require concrete action to be taken.[136] Beyond this, the substantive content of the obligation has been somewhat clouded by judicial comparisons to a number of similar, yet different, provisions in the LOSC.[137] For example, the due regard obligation in Article 56(2) has been equated with the requirement of 'all possible consideration' from Article 110,[138] combined with the obligation to protect and preserve the marine environment in Articles 192 and 194,[139] and found to be equivalent to the of good faith required by Article 2(3) in the context of the territorial sea.[140]

The most comprehensive statement on the substance of the due regard obligation in Article 56(2) is in the *Chagos Arbitration*, which found (with regard to the obligations of the United Kingdom as a coastal State) that:

> the ordinary meaning of 'due regard' calls for the United Kingdom to have *such regard for the rights of Mauritius as is called for by the circumstances and by the nature of those rights*. The Tribunal declines to find in this formulation any universal rule of conduct. The [LOSC] does not impose a uniform obligation to avoid any impairment of Mauritius' rights; nor does it uniformly permit the United Kingdom to proceed as it wishes, merely noting such rights. Rather, the extent of the regard required by the [LOSC] *will depend upon the nature of the rights held by Mauritius, their importance, the extent of the anticipated impairment, the nature and importance of the activities contemplated by the United Kingdom, and*

[135] Shotaro Hamamoto, 'The Genesis of the "Due Regard" Obligations in the United Nations Convention on the Law of the Sea' (2019) 34 IJMCL 7, 24.

[136] Mathias Forteau, 'The Legal Nature and Content of "Due Regard" Obligations in Recent International Case Law' (2019) 34 IJMCL 25, 32.

[137] Ibid 37–8.

[138] *Virginia G* [347]–[349].

[139] *SRFC Advisory Opinion* [216].

[140] *Chagos Arbitration* [520].

> *the availability of alternative approaches.* In the majority of cases, this assessment *will necessarily involve at least some consultation* with the rights-holding State.[141]

While the *Chagos Arbitration* related to the declaration of a marine protected area, this is a very clear summary of the considerations that must be taken into account by the coastal State in exercising jurisdiction in the EEZ, and the issues highlighted in this decision are likely to be equally relevant in relation to the regulation of living marine resources.[142] Accordingly, fulfilment of the due regard obligation can be understood to require consideration of all the circumstances of the case and the nature of the rights concerned, the extent of the impairment (to the rights of other States), benefit (to the coastal State) and availability of alternatives, and, notably, consultation.

The concept of due regard is closely related to—and has been equated to—that of reasonableness, which is often invoked by courts and tribunals to assess the extent of the rights that may legitimately be asserted by a coastal State where the freedoms of another State are affected. In this regard, the concept of reasonableness operates as 'an instrument for courts to control the exercising of the discretionary power of the State'.[143] In its application to coastal State jurisdiction over living resources, the rule of reasonableness 'requires State behavior to be proportional to the aim legally pursued, with due regard to the rights and freedoms granted to another State'.[144] Accordingly, the coastal State may not exercise its regulatory authority in such a way as to subject the rights of other States to requirements that in effect make their exercise impossible.[145] And in the context of enforcement, reasonableness has been found to encompass the principles of necessity and proportionality.[146]

The importance of 'reasonableness' and 'due regard' to maintaining an effective balance between the rights of coastal States and other States is reflected in the structure of the LOSC's dispute settlement provisions. While disputes concerning the coastal State's exercise of sovereign rights over living resources are *excluded* from compulsory jurisdiction under Article 297(3)(a),[147] allegations of coastal State contraventions of the freedoms of Article 58 are *included* under Article 297(1)(a).

[141] Ibid [519] (emphasis added).

[142] This aspect of the *Chagos Arbitration* decision was referenced directly in the *South China Sea Arbitration*, which involved the 'reversed situation' of the due regard owed by a flag State to the rights and duties of the coastal State in its EEZ under art 58(3): *South China Sea Arbitration* [742]. This reflects the fact that the rule of due regard is reciprocal and applies in identical terms to the activities of other States in the EEZ under art 58(3): see n 10 and associated text.

[143] *'Volga' (Russian Federation v Australia)* (Prompt Release, Judgment) (2002) ITLOS Rep 10 [18] (*Volga*).

[144] *Dispute Concerning Filleting within the Gulf of St Lawrence (Canada v France)* (1990) 82 ILR 591 [54] (*Filleting in the Gulf of St Lawrence*). See also *Volga* (Sep Op Cot) [21].

[145] *Filleting in the Gulf of St Lawrence* [54].

[146] *Arctic Sunrise Arbitration (Netherlands v Russia)* [2015] PCA Case 2014-02 [222] (*Arctic Sunrise Arbitration*); *Duzgit Integrity Arbitration (Malta v Sao Tome and Principe)* [2016] PCA Case 2014-07 [209] and [254] (*Duzgit Integrity Arbitration*).

[147] On compulsory dispute settlement, see Section 2.1.2.

The practical effect of this 'exception to the exception' is to ensure that no preference is given to the rights of either the coastal or other States in the EEZ, since disputes concerning the coastal State's obligation to have 'due regard' for the freedoms of other States may be subjected to compulsory dispute settlement.[148] It is thus particularly important for the coastal State to ensure that, in interpreting and implementing its sovereign rights under Article 56, it acts reasonably and gives due regard to the freedoms of other States under Article 58.

There is an important distinction between rights that are specifically attributed to coastal States or other States under the LOSC (but whose exercise is limited by the obligation of due regard), and rights that are *not* attributed under the LOSC (and whose right of exercise thus fall to be determined by reference to the rule on residual rights in Article 59). The underlying objective of Article 59 is to preserve the *sui generis* nature of the EEZ by ensuring that, in the case of unattributed rights or jurisdiction, there is no presumption in favour of either coastal States or third States; in short, that the EEZ is not assimilated to either the regime of high seas freedoms or to the coastal State regime of the territorial sea.[149] To achieve this objective, Article 59 provides a formula for resolving conflicts over unattributed rights, which involves equity, the assessment of relevant circumstances, and the importance of the interests involved not only to the parties, but to the international community as a whole. In practice, however, this formula simply gives rise to an obligation to seek a solution, whether through negotiation or dispute settlement.[150] Accordingly, the effect of Article 59 ultimately falls to be determined through the practice of States and the decisions of international courts and tribunals on a case-by-case basis as questions of 'residual rights' arise.

While this issue was of significant concern during the negotiation of the LOSC, in practice there has been very limited application of Article 59—at least in dispute settlement. For example, in the *Saiga (No 2)*[151] and *Virginia G* cases, the question of jurisdiction over bunkering of fishing vessels in the EEZ was addressed (by both the Parties and the Tribunal) on the basis that it either fell within the freedom of navigation of the flag State or the economic rights of the coastal State.[152] Accordingly, there was no consideration of the Article 59 formula for unattributed

[148] Tullio Treves, 'Coastal States' Rights in the Maritime Areas under UNCLOS' (2015) 12(1) BrazilJIntlLaw 39, 42; Alexander Proelss, 'The Law on the Exclusive Economic Zone in Perspective: Legal Status and Resolution of User Conflicts Revisited' (2012) 26 OceanYB 87, 92.

[149] Jorge Castaneda, 'Negotiations on the Exclusive Economic Zone at the Third United Nations Conference on the Law of the Sea' in Jerzy Makarczyk (ed), *Essays in International Law in Honor of Judge Manfred Lachs* (Brill 1984) 615–6.

[150] Orrego Vicuna, *The EEZ* (n 6) 36.

[151] *MV 'Saiga' (No 2) (Saint Vincent and the Grenadines v Guinea)* (Judgment) (1999) ITLOS Rep 10 (*Saiga (No 2)*).

[152] Similarly, neither of the Parties in the *MT San Padre Pio* case has sought to apply art 59 in relation to a dispute relating to jurisdiction over the ship-to-ship transfer of gasoil in the EEZ (although at the time of writing the case had yet to be argued on the merits): *MT 'San Padre Pio' (Switzerland v Nigeria)* (Provisional Measures, Order of 29 May 2019) (2018–2019) ITLOS Rep 369 (*San Padre Pio*).

'residual rights', only the proper extent of *existing* rights, taking into account the obligation of 'due regard' under Articles 56 and 58.[153]

In the case of a conflict between the actual or potential rights of a coastal State and other States in the EEZ, the threshold question is thus whether the LOSC has already attributed the right (explicitly or implicitly) to the coastal State or other States.[154] If the right *has* been attributed in one of these ways, it is necessary to determine the legitimate content and extent of the right, taking into account the rule of due regard; if the right has *not* been attributed, Article 59 must be applied.[155] In the latter instance, while there has been no indication from international courts and tribunals on this issue, the leading commentaries suggest that, given the functional nature of the EEZ, Article 59 would operate in favour of the coastal State where economic interests are concerned, and in favour of the international community as a whole where conflicts arise on issues not related to the exploration or exploitation of resources.[156]

2.3.2.2 The Rule of Due Diligence

The second rule that coastal States must observe is that of due diligence, which has an important application in relation to shared stocks and is reflected in some of the primary norms in the LOSC. The concept of due diligence arises from the well-established principle that States must ensure that the exercise of their sovereignty and sovereign rights does not unduly infringe the sovereignty and sovereign rights of other States—it is the duty of care that States owe to each other as a corollary of their sovereignty,[157] identified in a string of general international law cases from the 1872 *Alabama Claims* arbitration[158] to the 2010 *Pulp Mills* case.[159] Due diligence is part of the framework for accountability in international law; it plays an important role in establishing standards of conduct, while preserving flexibility and autonomy for sovereign States in the implementation of their international obligations.[160]

[153] Art 59 was raised in two dissenting opinions in *Saiga (No 2)*, which noted that the LOSC regime does not exhaustively allocate all possible rights and jurisdiction (whether in relation to economic activity, freedom of navigation, or other internationally lawful uses of the sea), but did not attempt to apply the art 59 formula to the case at hand: *Saiga (No 2)* (Sep Op Vukas) [21], (Sep Op Laing) [55]–[56]. It was also noted (but once again not applied) by one judge in the provisional measures phase of *San Padre Pio* (Dec Kittichaisaree) [2]–[3].

[154] Philip Allott, 'Power Sharing in the Law of the Sea' (1983) 77 AJIL 1, 37.

[155] Orrego Vicuna, *The EEZ* (n 6) 39.

[156] See Nandan and Rosenne, *UNCLOS Commentary, Vol II* (n 7) 569; Alexander Proelss, 'Article 59' in Alexander Proelss (ed), *United Nations Convention on the Law of the Sea: A Commentary* (CH Beck 2017) 463.

[157] Ellen Hey, *The Regime for the Exploitation of Transboundary Marine Fisheries Resources: The United Nations Convention on the Law of the Sea Cooperation Between States* (Kluwer 1989) 26–7.

[158] *Alabama Claims Arbitration (United States/Great Britain)* (1872) 29 RIAA 125.

[159] *Pulp Mills on the River Uruguay (Argentina v Uruguay)* (Judgment) (2010) ICJ Rep 14 [197] (*Pulp Mills*).

[160] International Law Association Study Group on Due Diligence in International Law, *Second Report* (2016) 2, available at <http://www.ila-hq.org/en/study-groups/index.cfm/cid/1045> > accessed 29 June 2021.

The core content of the principle—articulated in the *Corfu Channel* case—is 'every State's obligation not to allow knowingly its territory to be used for acts contrary to the rights of other States'.[161] While the exact scope and content of due diligence are context-dependent, in general it 'may be read as establishing positive obligations of conduct that are to be assessed in light of a general regulatory position that extends beyond immediate treaty obligations'.[162] In this regard, there are three key aspects of due diligence that have important ramifications for coastal States (and other States) in the EEZ.

First, as the International Court of Justice (ICJ) identified in the *Pulp Mills* case, due diligence is an obligation of conduct, and not result, which requires that States adopt the rules and measures necessary to give effect to the primary obligation.[163] Second, due diligence gives rise to the 'no harm' principle, which originated in the *Alabama Claims* arbitration and has developed into a customary obligation for States to ensure that activities within their jurisdiction and control respect the environment of other States or of areas beyond national control.[164] Third, in relation to shared natural resources, the jurisprudence clearly indicates that where the interests of other States cannot be sufficiently taken into account through unilateral conduct, cooperation and negotiation may be the only way to fulfil the duty of due diligence.[165] These three aspects of due diligence are reflected in primary obligations for all States in the LOSC, including the rule of due regard, the duty to cooperate, and the requirement to prevent harm to the marine environment. In addition, recent decisions of international courts and tribunals have invoked and applied the rule of due diligence as a standard of conduct in assessing the content and implementation of a range of rights and obligations under the LOSC. These decisions help to clarify the way in which the rule of due diligence applies in the law of the sea, and specifically in the EEZ.

In the *SRFC Advisory Opinion,* the concept of due diligence was specifically stated to apply in relation to the duty to cooperate in the conservation and management of shared stocks under the LOSC[166] and the responsibility of flag States to ensure their vessels comply with coastal State laws and regulations in the EEZ.[167] Curiously, the Tribunal made no reference to a due diligence standard in its discussion of the coastal State's responsibility to 'ensure that the maintenance of the living resources in the EEZ is not endangered by over-exploitation' under Article 61(2) of the LOSC.[168] Nonetheless, since the fulfilment of this obligation involves

161 *Corfu Channel Case (UK v Albania)* (Judgment) (1949) ICJ Rep 4 [4].

162 Richard A Barnes, 'The Continuing Vitality of UNCLOS' in J Barrett and R Barnes (eds), *Law of the Sea: UNCLOS as a Living Treaty* (BIICL 2016) 480.

163 *Pulp Mills* [197].

164 *Nuclear Weapons Advisory Opinion* [29]. This obligation is codified in arts 192 and 194 of the LOSC.

165 See the discussion in Hey, *Regime for Exploitation of Transboundary Resources* (n 157) 32–5.

166 SRFC *Advisory Opinion* [210].

167 Ibid [125]–[140].

168 Ibid [104]–[107].

not only the adoption and enforcement of regulatory or administrative measures, but the actions of a wide range of private persons and entities (including vessels flagged to other States),[169] it must logically be an obligation of conduct and not result. Similarly, while the statements in the *South China Sea Arbitration* with respect to the protection and preservation of the marine environment concerned the due diligence obligation of the flag State,[170] this obligation must also apply to coastal States, since the obligation to protect and preserve the marine environment in Article 192 applies to all States in all maritime zones. Accordingly, the requirement of due diligence can be said to apply to the obligations of coastal States under the LOSC to: ensure the maintenance of the living resources of the EEZ (Article 61); cooperate with other States to conserve and develop shared stocks (Articles 63 and 64); and protect and preserve the marine environment (Articles 192 and 194).[171]

Of course, the substantive content of this requirement is a separate issue. In general terms, it is clear that due diligence is an obligation 'to deploy adequate means, to exercise best possible efforts, to do the utmost'[172] in pursuit of the relevant outcome. Fulfilment of this obligation requires, first, the adoption of appropriate rules and measures, and second, 'a certain level of vigilance' in their enforcement and in the administrative control of relevant actors.[173] In practice, however, the content of due diligence varies according to the specific nature and context of the obligation in question. As applied to the duty to cooperate under the LOSC, due diligence has been found to require engagement in meaningful, good faith consultations involving substantive effort from all States concerned, 'with a view to adopting effective measures necessary to coordinate and ensure the conservation and development of shared stocks'.[174] In relation to the protection and preservation of the marine environment, it requires States to adopt and enforce the measures necessary to prevent harm to depleted, threatened, or endangered species, whether the harm is caused directly or through the destruction of their habitat.[175] Importantly, while the content of due diligence is often understood to vary in light of the capacity or development status of the State concerned, ITLOS has indicated that this

[169] As the ITLOS Seabed Disputes Chamber has made clear, the responsibility 'to ensure' entails an obligation for States to exercise power over persons and entities of their nationality or within their control: *Responsibilities and obligations of States sponsoring persons and entities with respect to activities in the Area* (Advisory Opinion) (2011) ITLOS Rep 10 [107]–[116] (*Seabed Advisory Opinion*).

[170] *South China Sea Arbitration* [956]–[959] and [974].

[171] For a broader examination of the duties in the LOSC to which due diligence applies, see Irina Papanicolopulu, 'Due Diligence in the Law of the Sea' in Heike Krieger et al (eds), *Due Diligence in the International Legal Order* (OUP 2020) 150–2.

[172] *SRFC Advisory Opinion* [129], quoting *Seabed Advisory Opinion* [110].

[173] *South China Sea Arbitration* [944], quoting *SRFC Advisory Opinion* [131] and *Pulp Mills* [197].

[174] *SRFC Advisory Opinion* [210]. Judge Paik notes that (unlike disputes arising from the coastal State's exercise of sovereign rights with respect to the living resources in its EEZ) any dispute arising from a failure to consult or negotiate in relation to art 63(1) may be submitted to compulsory dispute resolution under Part XV Section 2 of the LOSC: *SRFC Advisory Opinion* (Sep Op Paik) [37]. Presumably, this would also apply with respect to arts 63(2) and 64(1).

[175] *South China Sea Arbitration* [959].

is not the case in the law of the sea, since equality of treatment between developed and developing States is needed to ensure that companies do not seek to acquire the nationality or sponsorship of developing States 'in the hope of being subjected to less burdensome regulations and controls'.[176]

At present, there is no jurisprudence on the specific content of any due diligence requirement for the coastal State to ensure the maintenance of living resources in the EEZ, although it could be expected to involve a requirement to adopt and enforce the necessary legislative and administrative measures to ensure this result, including through the effective exercise of jurisdiction and control over its own flagged vessels, effective sanctions to ensure compliance, and the necessary measures to prevent, deter and eliminate illegal fishing by foreign flagged vessels.[177] In any case, the content of these due diligence requirements is not fixed; due diligence is a variable concept that may change over time as a consequence of new scientific knowledge, technical advances, or changes in the nature of the risks involved.[178] Moreover, since due diligence commonly applies in situations marked by an absence of specific rules, international courts and tribunals retain significant flexibility in determining the content and application of the rule in the circumstances of each case.[179] Accordingly, coastal States should be vigilant in their diligence.

2.3.2.3 Other Applicable Rules of International Law

Finally, in exercising its rights with respect to living resources in the EEZ, the coastal State must take into account other applicable rules of international law. This arose in *Saiga (No 2)*, in which ITLOS considered the lawfulness of the force used by the coastal State in arresting the *Saiga*.[180] The majority approached the question by noting that: '[a]lthough the [LOSC] does not contain express provisions on the use of force in the arrest of ships, international law, which is applicable by virtue of article 293 of the [LOSC], requires that the use of force must be avoided as far as possible and, where force is unavoidable, it must not go beyond what is reasonable and necessary in the circumstances. Considerations of humanity must apply in the law of the sea, as they do in other areas of international law.'[181]

The Tribunal thus found that it had to consider the circumstances in which the *Saiga* was arrested in the context of the applicable rules of international law on the

[176] *Seabed Advisory Opinion* [159].

[177] These requirements are adapted from the criteria set out in the *SRFC Advisory Opinion* with respect to the due diligence obligation of flag States, and the Tribunal's statement that the coastal State bears the primary responsibility for preventing, deterring, and eliminating IUU fishing: *SRFC Advisory Opinion* [105] and [133]–[140].

[178] *Seabed Advisory Opinion* [117].

[179] Valentin Schatz, 'Fishing for Interpretation: The ITLOS Advisory Opinion on Flag State Responsibility for Illegal Fishing in the EEZ' (2016) 47(4) ODIL 327, 337.

[180] In this context, the term 'use of force' equates broadly to the use of coercive (or 'police') measures as part of maritime law enforcement, rather than to the use of armed force in the sense in which the term is employed in art 2(4) of the Charter of the United Nations.

[181] *Saiga (No 2)* [155].

use of force.[182] This also applies with respect to international human rights standards, which may be used to assist in the interpretation and application of the provisions of the LOSC relating to the arrest or detention of a vessel or persons,[183] or the confiscation of a vessel.[184]

As the *Arctic Sunrise Arbitration* Tribunal made clear, however, this is not the same as directly applying the relevant international law standards or determining whether a breach of other international law rules has occurred.[185] Rather, it is limited to a requirement to have reference to standards from other areas of international law (such as freedom from arbitrary detention, freedom of expression, and right to a fair hearing) in order to characterize or inform the interpretation of rights and obligations under the LOSC.[186] Accordingly, coastal States should have regard to the applicable rules of international law relating to the use of force and the protection of human rights when considering how to strike the balance in exercising their enforcement powers in the EEZ.

2.3.3 The Rights of Coastal States: Things They May Do

There is a growing body of jurisprudence regarding things that coastal States *may* do in the exercise of their jurisdiction in the EEZ. This includes judicial consideration of the 'margin of appreciation' afforded each State in its implementation of the LOSC, as well as formal recognition that coastal States may legitimately take reasonable steps to 'protect or prevent interference with' their sovereign rights and make use of modern technology in maritime enforcement.

2.3.3.1 The Margin of Appreciation

As the Permanent Court of International Justice (PCIJ) famously stated in the *Lotus* case, international law leaves States 'a wide measure of discretion'.[187] This is reflected in the flexibility afforded to States by the so-called 'margin of appreciation', a concept that is related to other notions of flexibility such as reasonableness and discretion.[188] The margin of appreciation is best known for its extensive application by the European Court of Human Rights as a methodology for scrutiny of

[182] Cited with approval in *Guyana v Suriname* (2007) 139 ILR 566 [405]–[406].

[183] *Arctic Sunrise Arbitration* [197]–[198]; cited with approval in *Duzgit Integrity Arbitration* [207].

[184] *'Juno Trader' (Saint Vincent and the Grenadines v Guinea-Bissau)* (Prompt Release, Judgment) (2004) ITLOS Rep 17 [77] (*Juno Trader*).

[185] *Arctic Sunrise Arbitration* [197].

[186] Douglas Guilfoyle and Cameron A Miles, 'Provisional Measures and the MV Arctic Sunrise' (2014) 108 AJIL 271, 285. See also *Duzgit Integrity Arbitration* [208].

[187] *Lotus* 18–19.

[188] Jean-Pierre Cot, 'The Law of the Sea and the Margin of Appreciation' in Tafsir Malick Ndiaye and Rüdiger Wolfrum (eds), *Law of the Sea, Environmental Law and Settlement of Disputes: Liber Amicorum Judge Thomas A Mensah* (Martinus Nijhoff 2007) 389, 390.

the decisions of national authorities,[189] but it has also been applied in other areas of international law and by other courts and tribunals, either through explicit invocation or implicit adoption as a methodological choice.[190] It is characterized by two principles: 'judicial deference', involving a certain degree of deference or respect by international courts for the discretion of national authorities; and 'normative flexibility', reflecting its application to international norms that are open-ended or unsettled and preserve a significant margin within which states can exercise their discretion.[191] The margin of appreciation does not provide an unlimited discretion or preclude judicial review of State actions,[192] nor is it a 'doctrine' or set of principles; rather, it is 'a methodological approach, a standard of review'.[193]

While the margin of appreciation has received almost no treatment in the academic literature on the law of the sea,[194] it features in the jurisprudence of ITLOS and other tribunals. As Judge Wolfrum has explained, under the LOSC: 'coastal States enjoy considerable discretion in laying down the content of laws concerning the conservation and management of marine living resources in their [EEZ] and of the corresponding laws on enforcement.'[195] The margin of appreciation afforded coastal States under the LOSC thus includes both 'discretionary' powers to set laws for the regulation of living resources (such as the power to determine the allowable catch, allocate surplus resources to third States, and set conditions under which living resources may be accessed), as well as powers to take enforcement measures in respect of those laws subject to the requirement of 'reasonableness' (which restricts the coastal State to the exercise of such enforcement powers 'as may be necessary', and requires that a 'reasonable' bond be set to secure the prompt release of a vessel).

However, the nature and extent of the review of coastal State actions that can or should be undertaken by ITLOS (and other courts and tribunals) remains controversial. While the majority in the *Monte Confurco* case clearly stated that ITLOS 'is not an appellate forum against a decision of a national court', it also noted that the Tribunal is 'not precluded from examining the facts and circumstances of the case to the extent necessary for a proper appreciation of the reasonableness of the bond'.[196] This distinction is exemplified in the decision of the *Duzgit Integrity*

[189] Yuval Shany, 'Toward a General Margin of Appreciation Doctrine in International Law?' (2005) 16 EJIL 907, 909 and 927–8.
[190] In particular, it has been invoked or applied in cases relating to trade, the use of force, and consular assistance: see generally ibid 926–31; Cot, 'The LOS and the Margin of Appreciation' (n 188) 392–395; *Volga* (Sep Op Cot) [14]–[20].
[191] Shany, 'Toward a General Margin of Appreciation Doctrine' (n 189) 909–10.
[192] Ibid 910.
[193] Cot, 'The LOS and the Margin of Appreciation' (n 188) 390.
[194] Ibid 389.
[195] *'Camouco' (Panama v France)* (Prompt Release, Judgment) (2000) ITLOS Rep 10 (Diss Op Wolfrum) [11] (*Camouco*).
[196] *'Monte Confurco' (Seychelles v France)* (Prompt Release, Judgment) (2000) ITLOS Rep 86 [72]–[74] (*Monte Confurco*).

Tribunal, which carefully distinguished between measures that fell within the discretion of the coastal State, to which deference was given by the Tribunal, and measures that were so unreasonable and disproportionate that they exceeded the rights of the coastal State and were subject to review by that Tribunal.[197]

Although ITLOS has been conscious of the need to accord a margin of appreciation to the coastal State (particularly in relation to the exercise of enforcement jurisdiction under Article 73 of the LOSC), there have been significant differences of opinion between members of the Tribunal concerning the appropriate standard to be applied in order to maintain a proper balance between the interests of coastal and flag States.[198] The division of approach on this issue was particularly clear in the *Virginia G* case, in which the majority concluded that the coastal State's confiscation of a vessel that had engaged in unauthorized bunkering activities in the EEZ went beyond what was 'necessary' to ensure compliance with its laws and regulations and was thus inconsistent with Article 73(1) of the LOSC. There was strong disagreement from a significant minority who thought that the confiscation was reasonable, and that the Tribunal's approach threatened to undermine the ability of coastal States to take appropriate measures to combat illegal fishing in their EEZs.[199] The minority considered that the Tribunal had overstepped its role in judicial review of the coastal State's exercise of enforcement jurisdiction, and functioned akin to an appellate court by substituting its own view for that of the local authorities.[200] While the exercise of sovereign rights by the coastal State in its EEZ should, in theory, attract a 'degree of deference' from international courts and tribunals,[201] in practice the approach adopted by ITLOS has provided little clarity regarding the standard to be applied in the review of coastal State jurisdiction, or the way in which the balance should be struck.[202]

2.3.3.2 The Protection of, or Prevention of Interference with, Sovereign Rights

Beyond the regulation of activities 'directly connected with' sovereign rights, recent jurisprudence has also confirmed that a coastal State may take steps to protect or prevent interference with its sovereign rights, provided that such measures are reasonable, necessary, and proportionate. This issue was considered by the *Arctic*

[197] *Duzgit Integrity Arbitration* [255]–[262] and [277].

[198] See, eg, *Camouco* (Diss Op Wolfrum) [11]–[12], (Diss Op Anderson) [50]; *Volga* (Diss Op Anderson) [18]–[23], (Diss Op Shearer) [19].

[199] Robin Churchill, 'Dispute Settlement in the Law of the Sea: Survey for 2014' (2015) 30 IJMCL 585, 595 fn 47.

[200] *Virginia G* (Joint Diss Op Hoffmann, Marotta Rangel, Chandrasekhara Rao, Kateka, Gao, and Bouguetaia) [50]–[56], (Diss Op Jesus) [9]–[22], (Diss Op Ndiaye) [163], (Diss Op Servulo Correia) [16]–[27].

[201] Ibid (Joint Diss Op Hoffmann, Marotta Rangel, Chandrasekhara Rao, Kateka, Gao, and Bouguetaia) [49]. See also Cot, 'The LOS and the Margin of Appreciation' (n 188) 396.

[202] Harrison, 'Safeguards Against Excessive Enforcement Measures' (n 2) 220. On the standards applied by ITLOS in reviewing coastal State enforcement actions, see generally Chapter 6.

Sunrise Arbitration Tribunal, which considered the types of protest actions that could reasonably be considered to constitute an interference with the exercise of the coastal State's sovereign rights, and concluded that:

> it would be reasonable for a coastal State to act to prevent: (i) violations of its laws adopted in conformity with the [LOSC]; (ii) dangerous situations that can result in injuries to persons and damage to equipment and installations; (iii) negative environmental consequences . . . ; and (iv) delay or interruption in essential operations. All of these are legitimate interests of coastal States.
>
> At the same time, the coastal State should tolerate some level of nuisance through civilian protest as long as it does not amount to an 'interference with the exercise of its sovereign rights.' Due regard must be given to rights of other States, including the right to allow vessels flying their flag to protest.[203]

The *Arctic Sunrise Arbitration* related to the exercise of sovereign rights over the *non*-living resources of the EEZ, but logically this aspect of the Tribunal's judgment would apply equally to sovereign rights over living resources, since they arise under the same provision of the LOSC. Although Article 73(1) specifically provides that the coastal State's jurisdiction over living resources extends to such measures 'as may be necessary' to ensure compliance with its laws and regulations, the extent of this jurisdiction—and whether or not it includes a right to protect and prevent interference with its sovereign rights—has not been tested. Given the incidence and potential impact of direct action protests at sea in relation to the exploitation of living resources,[204] coastal States are likely to welcome the Tribunal's affirmation that 'the protection of a coastal State's sovereign rights is a legitimate aim that allows it to take appropriate measures for that purpose', provided such measures fulfil the tests of reasonableness, necessity, and proportionality.[205]

2.3.3.3 The Use of Modern Technology

The *Arctic Sunrise Arbitration* also made clear that the LOSC should be interpreted so as to permit the use of modern technology in maritime law enforcement. Noting the 'large areas that must now be policed by coastal States and the availability of more reliable advanced technology (sea-bed sensors, satellite surveillance, over-the-horizon radar, unmanned aerial vehicles)', the Tribunal concluded

[203] *Arctic Sunrise Arbitration* [327]–[328].

[204] See the discussion of such protest action in G Plant, 'International Law and Direct Action Protests at Sea: Twenty Years On' (2002) 33 NYIL 75; Richard Caddell, 'Platforms, Protestors and Provisional Measures: The Arctic Sunrise Dispute and Environmental Activism at Sea' (2014) 45 NYIL 359; Maria Chiara Noto, 'The Arctic Sunrise Arbitration and Acts of Protest at Sea' (2016) 2 MarSafety&SecLJ 36.

[205] *Arctic Sunrise Arbitration* [326]. On the application of 'protective' measures to foreign fishing vessels in the EEZ, see further Chapter 5 nn 63–71 and associated text.

that it 'would not make sense to limit valid orders to stop to those given by an enforcement craft within the proximity required for an audio or visual signal that makes no use of radio communications'.[206] The Tribunal thus rejected a narrow, textual interpretation of Article 111, and stated that the hot pursuit provisions of the LOSC must be interpreted 'in the light of their object and purpose, having regard to the modern use of technology'.[207] The importance of interpreting the LOSC in light of the developments of modern technology has been emphasized in separate and dissenting opinions in a number of earlier cases[208] and in some domestic court decisions.[209] However, the *Arctic Sunrise Arbitration* is the first occasion on which an evolutionary approach to the interpretation of the LOSC's enforcement provisions has been clearly endorsed by the judgment of an international court or tribunal.[210]

While there is no standard definition of the term 'evolutionary interpretation', the effect of this approach is that the meaning of treaty terms can change over time, without requiring the specific intervention of the Parties to amend or modify them.[211] In this respect, as the ICJ has confirmed, evolutionary interpretation looks to the original intention of the Parties in order to ascertain whether they intended that the terms used would have 'a meaning or content capable of evolving, not one fixed once and for all, so as to make allowance for, among other things, developments in international law'.[212] Accordingly, while evolutionary interpretation can serve the same purpose as the process of subsequent practice under Article 31(3)(b) of the VCLT in ensuring that the instrument can survive and adapt to contemporary priorities and realities, and both principles rely on the intention of the Parties, they operate by different mechanisms: the former looks to the *original* intention of the Parties, and the latter to their *subsequent* intention.[213] However, as in the *Navigational Rights* case, these two approaches may lead to the same conclusion.[214]

[206] *Arctic Sunrise Arbitration* [259].

[207] Ibid [260].

[208] See *Volga* (Diss Op Shearer) [17]; *Juno Trader* (Sep Op Lucky) [41]; *SRFC Advisory Opinion* (Sep Op Lucky) [18]–[19].

[209] See William C Gilmore, 'Hot Pursuit: The Case of R v Mills and Others' (1995) 44 ICLQ 927, 956–7; *Regina v Sunila and Solayman* (1986) 28 (4th) Dom Law Rep 450.

[210] James Harrison, 'The Arctic Sunrise Arbitration (Netherlands v. Russia)' (2016) 31 IJMCL 145, 151.

[211] Eirik Bjorge, 'Introducing "The Evolutionary Interpretation of Treaties"' *EJIL: Talk!* 5 December 2014, available at <http://ejiltalk.org/introducing-the-evolutionary-interpretation-of-treaties/> accessed 6 February 2021.

[212] *Dispute Regarding Navigational and Related Rights (Costa Rica v Nicaragua)* (Judgment) (2009) ICJ Rep 213 [64].

[213] Irina Buga, *Modification of Treaties by Subsequent Practice* (OUP 2018) 93.

[214] Eirik Bjorge, *The Evolutionary Interpretation of Treaties* (OUP 2014) 76–7.

2.3.4 The Prohibitions on Coastal States: Things They May Not Do

Finally, there is a small but important category of material on the things that coastal States may *not* do in exercising jurisdiction over living resources in the EEZ. This includes recognition of some issues that have been determined not to come within the scope of the coastal State's sovereign rights in the EEZ, and some specific restrictions on the interpretation of enforcement powers under Article 73 of the LOSC.

2.3.4.1 The Assertion of 'Customs' or 'Public Interest' Jurisdiction

In contrast to the decision in *Virginia G* concerning activities that coastal States *may* regulate in the EEZ, *Saiga (No 2)* provides some clear guidance regarding things that coastal States may *not* regulate. Although both cases concerned the bunkering of fishing vessels, *Saiga (No 2)* was not based on the coastal State's sovereign rights over living resources, but on an assertion of customs jurisdiction exercised in the 'public interest' or in an exercise of 'self-protection'. In essence, Guinea asserted that the sovereign rights of the coastal State must include an inherent right to protect itself against unauthorized economic activities in the EEZ, particularly where those activities entail 'considerable fiscal losses' for the coastal State.[215] This assertion was flatly rejected by ITLOS, on the basis that it would 'entitle a coastal State to prohibit any activities in the EEZ which it decides to characterize as activities which affect its economic "public interest" or entail "fiscal losses" for it', which would curtail the rights of other States in the EEZ.[216]

ITLOS also confirmed that coastal States may not extend their customs laws to the EEZ.[217] Guinea's insistence that its regulation of bunkering was based on customs jurisdiction—even after ITLOS justified the admissibility of the earlier prompt release case on the basis of fisheries jurisdiction[218]—is one of the most notable aspects of this case. While the *Saiga* saga does not directly concern living resources in the EEZ, it confirms the 'functionally limited' nature of the sovereign rights afforded the coastal State in the EEZ,[219] and provides some useful guidance regarding the types of innovative interpretations of the LOSC on which coastal States may *not* rely. Further clarification on the functional limits of the coastal State's sovereign rights may be provided in the merits phase of the *San Padre Pio* case currently pending before ITLOS, which concerns Nigeria's arrest of a Swiss-flagged tanker that was conducting ship-to-ship transfers of gasoil to vessels

[215] *Saiga No 2* [129]–[130].
[216] Ibid [131].
[217] Ibid [136].
[218] *MV 'Saiga' (Saint Vincent and the Grenadines v Guinea)* (Prompt Release, Judgment) (1997) ITLOS Rep 16 [56]–[57] (*Saiga*).
[219] Proelss, 'The Law on the EEZ in Perspective' (n 148) 94.

supporting the operation of an oilfield in Nigeria's EEZ, in contravention of relevant Nigerian laws and regulations.[220]

2.3.4.2 The Exercise of Enforcement Measures that are Not 'Necessary'

Finally, there are a number of important restrictions on the way in which coastal States may exercise their enforcement powers in the EEZ. As Harrison points out, since the conditions attached to the enforcement jurisdiction of coastal States under the LOSC were intended to ensure the maintenance of an effective balance between the rights of coastal States and other States in the EEZ, the way in which courts and tribunals interpret these provisions is crucial.[221] Since coastal State jurisdiction under these provisions is specifically tied to what is 'necessary' and 'reasonable', their interpretation necessarily involves balancing the rights of coastal States and other States.[222] While 'necessary' can be interpreted to mean anything from 'indispensable' to 'making a contribution to',[223] the jurisprudence evidences an observable trend toward a narrow, textual interpretation of the coastal State's enforcement powers, particularly with respect to the penalties that may be imposed for breaches of the coastal State's laws and regulations in the EEZ under Article 73(1), and the amount and form of the bond that may be set for the prompt release of a vessel under Article 73(2).[224]

For example, while ITLOS has confirmed that confiscation of a vessel is (in theory) within the powers of the coastal State to take such enforcement measures as are 'necessary' under Article 73(1),[225] in practice it has interpreted the criterion of 'necessity' very strictly. Accordingly, in the *Virginia G* case, notwithstanding the serious nature of the infraction committed by the vessel, its confiscation by the coastal State was considered to contravene Article 73(1) on the basis that confiscation was not 'necessary'.[226] The Tribunal also stated that the principle of reasonableness 'applies generally to enforcement measures under Article 73 of the Convention' and found that the confiscation of the vessel was not 'reasonable' in light of the circumstances of the case.[227] Similarly, despite having enumerated a long list of issues that must be considered in determining the 'reasonableness' of a bond under Article 73(2),[228] in several cases ITLOS has simply substituted the bond set by the coastal State with a lower amount, without providing any clear

[220] See further Chapter 3 nn 122–5 and associated text.
[221] Harrison, 'Safeguards Against Excessive Enforcement Measures' (n 2) 217–18.
[222] Harrison, 'Article 73' (n 56) 558.
[223] Ibid.
[224] On the approach of ITLOS to penalties and bonds for fisheries offences, see generally Chapter 6.
[225] *'Tomimaru' (Japan v Russian Federation)* (Prompt Release, Judgment) (2005–2007) ITLOS Rep 74 (*Tomimaru*); *Virginia G* [255]–[257].
[226] Ibid [269].
[227] Ibid [270].
[228] These include: the gravity of the alleged offences, the penalties imposed or imposable under the laws of the detaining State, the value of the detained vessel and of the cargo seized, the amount of the bond imposed by the detaining State and its form, and all the circumstances of the particular case.

reasoning on why this amount was more 'reasonable' than that set by the coastal State.[229] Accordingly, even after nine prompt release cases, the Tribunal's approach to determining 'reasonableness' is still not clear enough to be relied on predictably by coastal States in setting their own bonds under Article 73(2).[230]

2.4 Conclusion

The framework that governs the continuum of jurisdiction over the living resources of the EEZ is based on two sets of competing interests.[231] First, the interests of the coastal State, represented by the coastal State's sovereign rights over living resources, and safeguarded by its exclusive right to take decisions with respect to the exploitation, exploration, conservation, and management of those resources. Second, the interests of the international community as a whole, expressed in the twin objectives of conservation (to ensure that the resources are not endangered by over-exploitation) and optimum utilization (to ensure they are not wasted by under-exploitation),[232] and safeguarded by the requirement for the coastal State to adopt proper conservation and management measures, and grant other States access to any surplus. However, since both sets of interests are implemented and effected through the actions and decisions of the coastal State, the overriding characteristic of this regime is the substantial discretion enjoyed by the coastal State with respect to the exercise of its sovereign rights to explore, exploit, conserve, and manage the living resources of the EEZ.[233]

Of course, this discretion is not unlimited; in order to preserve the balance that lies at the heart of the EEZ regime the coastal State's sovereign rights are subject to a number of additional constraints—in particular, the requirement of due regard, the duty to cooperate, the requirement that enforcement measures be 'necessary', and the obligation to protect and preserve the marine environment. Over time, the 'non-specific' standards of the LOSC have been strengthened by the recognition of additional conservation and management concepts developed in other instruments. These include: the precautionary approach and the ecosystem approach, which must be applied widely in the conservation, management, and exploitation of living resources; the principle of compatibility, which gives additional substance to the duty to cooperate; and the concept of IUU fishing, which informs the

[229] For a useful discussion of this issue, see Alan Vaughan Lowe, 'The International Tribunal for the Law of the Sea: Survey for 2000' (2001) 16 IJMCL 549, 560–5.

[230] Taisaku Ikeshima, 'The "Reasonableness" of Unreasonable Arguments in Prompt Release Cases in the ITLOS' (2009) 6 Waseda GlobalFor 107, 107–8. See also *Volga* (Dec Marsit) [4].

[231] Hey, *Regime for Exploitation of Transboundary Resources* (n 157) 47.

[232] Mohamed Dahmani, *The Fisheries Regime of the Exclusive Economic Zone* (Martinus Nijhoff 1987) 43.

[233] Ibid 156; Kwiatkowska, *The 200 Mile EEZ* (n 16) 91.

measures that should be taken by all States—separately and collectively—to ensure the proper conservation and management of global fish stocks.

Notwithstanding these developments, the ambiguous, open-ended and highly qualified nature of the basic rights and obligations established in the LOSC, as well as the varied and constantly developing nature of activities at sea, make it difficult to determine the actual extent of the coastal State's jurisdiction over living resources in the EEZ. While unilateral assertions of jurisdiction have played a decisive role in changing and developing the law of the sea,[234] the establishment of new or innovative precedents within the laboriously negotiated and widely ratified LOSC framework is likely to present significant challenges, and 'unsuccessful unilateralism is far more likely today to result not merely in protest, but in litigation, and probable defeat.'[235] Accordingly, coastal States need a clear understanding of the obligations and prohibitions that apply under the LOSC, in order to find effective and workable solutions to the contemporary challenges of fisheries governance and maximize the effectiveness of their jurisdiction within the limits of existing law. In this context, the first question to determine is: what is 'fishing'? In other words, what activities and which vessels may be regulated by the coastal State on the basis of its sovereign rights over living resources? This will be the subject of Chapter 3.

[234] DP O'Connell, *The International Law of the Sea, Vol I* (OUP 1982) 31.
[235] Alan E Boyle, 'EU Unilateralism and the Law of the Sea' (2006) 21 IJMCL 15, 20.

3

The Regulation of 'Fishing' and Related Activities

Vessels ply the oceans for many purposes, transporting all manner of cargo and passengers, laying submarine cables, undertaking scientific research, exploiting resources, and providing at-sea support and supplies.[1] Some of these vessels are simply engaged in the free exercise of navigation through the exclusive economic zone (EEZ) under the jurisdiction of their flag State pursuant to Article 58(1)(a) of the United Nations Convention on the Law of the Sea (LOSC). Others are directly involved in 'fishing' in a traditional sense, and clearly attract the coastal State's rights and jurisdiction over living resources under Articles 56(1)(a) and 62(4) of the LOSC. In between these two categories, however, there are other, less traditional, types of vessels, which are engaged in—or are *equipped* to engage in—a range of other, less traditional, 'fishing related' activities.

In the late nineteenth century, the fishing industry was revolutionized by the development of steam-powered ships, capable of staying at sea for weeks at a time and fishing with much greater efficiency than their sail-powered predecessors. Similarly, over the last four decades, the development of technology and infrastructure facilitating transhipment and resupply at sea has changed the nature of commercial fishing. Large industrial fishing vessels can now stay at sea for months at a time, assisted by a wide range of 'fishing support' vessels in the conduct of various 'fishing related' activities—from the on-board processing, packaging, and freezing of fish by factory vessels and the transhipment of catch to refrigerated fish carrier or reefer vessels for transport to port,[2] to refuelling (commonly described as 'bunkering')[3] and the supply of food, water, bait, fishing gear, and other items, the rotation of personnel and the conduct of repairs. These fishing related activities fall broadly within two functional categories: the first consisting of 'fish-handling' activities, such as processing, packaging, transhipping, and transporting catch, and

[1] Rainer Lagoni, 'Offshore Bunkering in the Exclusive Economic Zone' in Tafsir Malick Ndiaye and Rüdiger Wolfrum (eds), *Law of the Sea, Environmental Law and Settlement of Disputes: Liber Amicorum Judge Thomas A Mensah* (Martinus Nijhoff 2007) 613.

[2] Transhipment is the transfer of fish that have not previously been landed from one vessel directly to another, either at sea or in port: United Nations (UN) Food and Agriculture Organization (FAO) Term Portal, available at <http://fao.org/faoterm/en/> accessed 24 November 2020.

[3] The activity of refuelling ships is commonly described as 'bunkering', because it involves filling the fuel bunkers of the ship. The vessels that deliver the fuel are known as 'bunkers'.

Coastal State Jurisdiction over Living Resources in the Exclusive Economic Zone. Camille Goodman, Oxford University Press.
 DOI: 10.1093/oso/9780192896841.003.0003

the second involving other activities to support the operation of fishing vessels, such as bunkering and the supply of provisions and personnel.[4]

While it has long been accepted that the coastal State's sovereign rights encompass all rights 'necessary for and connected with' the exploration, exploitation, conservation, and management of natural resources in the EEZ, including the right to take the necessary enforcement measures,[5] the scope of actors and activities that the coastal State may regulate on the basis of these rights has never been fully explored. Part V of the LOSC includes detailed and extensive provisions regarding the coastal State's jurisdiction over 'living resources' and refers in several places to 'fishing' and 'fishing vessels', but does not provide any definitions for these traditional terms, let alone refer to the various fishing related activities which are an integral part of modern industrial fishing, or the fishing support vessels that perform them.[6]

This gives rise to two important questions. First, do such fishing related activities fall to be regulated by the coastal State on the basis of its sovereign rights under Article 56(1) or do they constitute an exercise of the freedom of navigation under Article 58(1) or even a residual right requiring the application of Article 59? And second, if the regulation of such activities does come within the jurisdiction of the coastal State, what is the scope and substance of this jurisdiction? Does it only enable the coastal State to regulate fishing related activities involving vessels that are *actively engaged in fishing* in its own EEZ under Article 62(4), or does it extend to the regulation of fishing vessels that are merely transiting to or from fishing grounds elsewhere? And does it allow the regulation of vessels that are *equipped to engage* in fishing related activities, or only the regulation of the activities themselves? These

[4] Valentin Schatz, 'Combating Illegal Fishing in the Exclusive Economic Zone—Flag State Obligations in the Context of the Primary Responsibility of the Coastal State' (2016) 7(2) GoettingenJIntlLaw 383, 389.

[5] This language was used by the International Law Commission (ILC) in its 1956 commentary on the Articles on the Law of the Sea to explain the expression 'sovereign rights' in relation to the continental shelf, and has been endorsed as applying equally to the coastal State's sovereign rights over resources in the EEZ: ILC, 'Articles Concerning the Law of the Sea with Commentaries' *Yearbook of the International Law Commission (1956) Volume II*, UN Doc A/CN.4/SER.A/1956/Add.l 265, 297; Satya Nandan and Shabtai Rosenne (eds), *United Nations Convention on the Law of the Sea 1982: A Commentary, Vol II* (Martinus Nijhoff 1993) 541–2; *Virginia G* [211].

[6] The official records of the Third United Nations Conference on the Law of the Sea (UNCLOS III) do not contain any reference to 'related activities' in the context of fishing, nor to related concepts such as 'transhipment', 'refuelling', or 'support vessels.' The concepts of 'ancillary rights' and 'factory ships' were raised at UNCLOS III but were not discussed in any detail. See Ogundere (Nigeria), 22nd meeting of the Second Committee, 31 July 1974 and 31st meeting of the Second Committee, 7 August 1974, and Warioba (Tanzania), 23rd meeting of the Second Committee, 1 August 1974, extracted in UN, *Official Records of the Third United Nations Conference on the Law of the Sea, Volume II, (Summary Records of Meetings of the First, Second and Third Committees, Second Session (Caracas, 20 June to 29 August 1974)* 172, 182, and 232. The concept of 'bunkering' was raised in the context of sea-bed mining in the Area, but not in relation to fisheries: 'Economic implications of sea-bed mineral development in the international area: report of the Secretary-General', Document A/CONF.62/25, extracted in UN, *Official Records of the Third United Nations Conference on the Law of the Sea, Volume III, (Documents of the Conference, First (New York, 3–15 December 1973) and Second (Caracas, 20 June to 29 August 1974) Sessions)* 36.

questions have been raised in several high-profile disputes before international tribunals over the last thirty years, but have received conflicting and incomplete treatment in judicial decisions, and surprisingly little attention in the literature.[7]

This Chapter examines the coastal State's jurisdiction over foreign vessels in the EEZ on the basis of its sovereign rights over living resources, in order to clarify *what activities* and *which vessels* come within this regulatory power. It considers the legal regime that is the source of this jurisdiction (Section 3.1) and analyses the approaches taken by international courts and tribunals to determining its scope (Section 3.2). It also looks beyond the caselaw and literature and examines the extensive national and international practice of States (Section 3.3) in order to comprehensively illustrate the contemporary substance of coastal State jurisdiction with respect to fishing related activities and fishing support vessels in the EEZ.

3.1 The Source of Jurisdiction over Fishing in the EEZ: Part V of the LOSC

Historically, the regime governing offshore maritime jurisdiction was based on a binary distinction between sovereignty and freedom.[8] Landward of the territorial sea boundary, the governing principle was sovereignty; in the internal waters and territorial sea, the dominant legal presumption was the sovereignty of the coastal State and any rights attributed to other States (such as innocent passage) constituted exceptions to be interpreted restrictively. Seaward of the territorial sea boundary, this presumption was reversed; although certain specific rights were attributed to coastal States in the contiguous zone, in the context of the continental shelf and the exclusive fishery zone they operated as exceptions to the dominant

[7] Three authors have examined this question in some detail, all of whom were involved in the *Saiga* cases heard by the International Tribunal for the Law of the Sea (ITLOS) in the 1990s (*Saiga* and *Saiga (No 2)*). Anderson's academic contributions (combined with his opinions as a judge in the *Saiga* cases) show the evolution of his approach over time: David Anderson, 'The Regulation of Fishing and Related Activities in Exclusive Economic Zones' in Erik Franckx and Philippe Gauthier (eds), *The Exclusive Economic Zone and the United Nations Convention on the Law of the Sea, 1982–2000: A Preliminary Assessment of State Practice* (Bruylant 2003); David Anderson, *Modern Law of the Sea: Selected Essays* (Martinus Nijhoff 2008); David Anderson, 'Coastal State Jurisdiction and High Seas Freedoms in the EEZ in the Light of the Saiga Case' in Clive R Symmons (ed), *Selected Contemporary Issues in the Law of the Sea* (Brill Nijhoff 2011). Ndiaye (who was also a judge in the *Saiga* cases) considers these issues in the West African context: Tafsir Malick Ndiaye, 'Illegal, Unreported and Unregulated Fishing: Responses in General and in West Africa' (2011) 10 ChineseJIntlL 373. Lagoni (who was counsel for Guinea in the *Saiga* cases) thoroughly examines the applicable legal regime in the LOSC but does not consider the extent of State practice: Lagoni, 'Offshore Bunkering' (n 1). In addition, Molenaar and Tsamenyi have explored this question in the context of satellite-based monitoring of fishing support vessels: Erik Jaap Molenaar and Martin Tsamenyi, 'Satellite-Based Vessel Monitoring Systems for Fisheries Management: International Legal Aspects' (2000) 15 IJMCL 65, 87–93. However, these contributions all pre-date the key decision of ITLOS on this issue in *Virginia G*.

[8] Julio Cesar Lupinacci, 'The Legal Status of the Exclusive Economic Zone in the 1982 Convention on the Law of the Sea' in Francisco Orrego Vicuna (ed), *The Exclusive Economic Zone: A Latin American Perspective* (Westview Press 1984) 101.

principle of freedom of the high seas, and any conflicts were resolved by reference to the presumption of freedom and the interests of the international community as a whole.[9]

In the context of fishing, this dualist approach resulted in two distinct regimes, namely, the unquestioned right of regulation by the coastal State within the territorial sea, and the presumption of exploitation free from coastal State interference in the high seas beyond.[10] In case of doubt, or where legal texts were mute, conflicts between the fishing rights of the coastal State and the navigational rights of other States would be resolved by reference to these legal presumptions, in relation to which exceptions were interpreted strictly. With the adoption of the LOSC, however, the long-standing dualism of the traditional approach was overtaken by the 'precarious compromise notion between sovereignty and freedom' embodied in the concept of the EEZ.[11]

Under the *sui generis* legal regime established for the EEZ in the LOSC, the activities of a foreign vessel may either be subject to the regulation of the coastal State under Article 56(1) or come within the rights and freedoms of the flag State under Article 58(1)—and as Articles 55 and 59 make clear, if the activity of the vessel is one in relation to which rights and jurisdiction have not been attributed by the LOSC, there is no legal presumption in favour of either regime. While the carefully constructed ambiguity of this framework has left scholars, judges, and practitioners alike at a loss to identify the exact powers of States in the EEZ,[12] it is nonetheless necessary to commence at the source and examine its terms in detail.

3.1.1. The 'Functional Sovereignty' of the Coastal State

Sovereignty 'signifies independence'; it is the 'principle of the exclusive competence of the State in regard to its own territory', and 'in regard to a portion of the globe is the right to exercise therein, to the exclusion of any other State, the functions of a State.'[13] Pursuant to Article 56(1)(a) of the LOSC, the coastal State has 'sovereign rights' to explore and exploit, conserve and manage the living resources of the EEZ. The notion of sovereign rights is 'an extract of the comprehensive concept of sovereignty' which has been extended to the EEZ for the limited purposes

[9] Edward Duncan Brown, *The International Law of the Sea: Vol 1* (Dartmouth Publishing 1994) 218–19.

[10] Shigeru Oda, 'Fisheries under the United Nations Convention on the Law of the Sea' (1983) 77 AJIL 739, 739.

[11] Rene-Jean Dupuy, 'The Sea Under National Competence' in Rene-Jean Dupuy and Daniel Vignes (eds), *A Handbook on the New Law of the Sea, Vol 1* (Martinus Nijhoff 1991) 276.

[12] Maria Gavouneli, *Functional Jurisdiction in the Law of the Sea* (Martinus Nijhoff 2007) 66.

[13] *The Island of Palmas (United States of America v The Netherlands)* (1928) 2 RIAA 831, 838 (*Island of Palmas*).

specified in Article 56(1)(a).[14] The coastal State's sovereign rights thus constitute a 'functionally limited variation' of the broad concept of sovereignty,[15] meaning that with respect to the exploration and exploitation, conservation and management of the living resources of the EEZ, the coastal State's competence is equivalent to that it enjoys in the territorial sea.[16] Within their functional limits, the coastal State's sovereign rights are plenary and exclusive, and allow the coastal State to conduct or regulate relevant activities to the exclusion of all others.[17]

The functional limits of the coastal State's sovereign rights are clearly expressed in the two linked purposes for which they are conferred: they may be exercised for 'exploring and exploiting' and 'conserving and managing' the living resources of the EEZ.[18] If the ordinary meaning of these terms is considered in their context,[19] it is clear that the coastal State is thus entitled to:

- assess, examine, evaluate, and investigate the living resources of the EEZ ('explore');
- harvest, extract, make use of or derive benefit from them ('exploit');
- preserve, retain or husband them, and prevent their being used in a wasteful or destructive manner ('conserve'); and
- maintain or conserve them and control their use and exploitation ('manage').[20]

As Burke has observed: 'These terms are sufficiently wide to embrace all normal enterprisory and governmental functions that pertain to living resources. "Exploring and exploiting" would normally be considered to cover all the activities involved in commercial or recreational fishing.... Similarly, "conserving and managing" are broad concepts that incorporate all the activities that bear on deciding about the wise use and disposition of living resources.'[21]

[14] Alexander Proelss, 'The Law on the Exclusive Economic Zone in Perspective: Legal Status and Resolution of User Conflicts Revisited' (2012) 26 OceanYB 87, 93.

[15] See Edward Duncan Brown, 'The Exclusive Economic Zone: Criteria and Machinery for the Resolution of International Conflicts between Different Users of the EEZ' (1977) MarPolManagement 325, 333; Proelss, 'The Law on the EEZ in Perspective' (n 14) 101.

[16] *Tunisia v Libya* (Diss Op Oda) [124]. The historical development of the term makes clear that 'sovereign rights' are not equivalent to 'sovereignty', but that they are 'more than exclusive rights, in the sense that their scope must be extensively interpreted to include whatever powers are needed to ensure that the coastal State is enabled to enjoy its rights in full': Brown, *The International Law of the Sea, Vol I* (n 9) 220.

[17] *Island of Palmas* 838. See Giuseppe Cataldi, 'La Pêche dans les Eaux Soumises à la Souveraineté ou la Juridiction des États Côtiers' in Daniel Vignes, Rafael Casado Raigon, and Giuseppe Cataldi (eds), *Le Droit International de la Pêche Maritime* (Editions Bruylant 2000) 46, 83; Donald R Rothwell and Tim Stephens, *The International Law of the Sea* (2nd ed, Hart 2016) 92; Alexander Proelss, 'Article 56' in Alexander Proelss (ed), *United Nations Convention on the Law of the Sea: A Commentary* (CH Beck 2017) 424.

[18] Nandan and Rosenne, *UNCLOS Commentary, Vol II* (n 5) 542.

[19] Vienna Convention on the Law of Treaties (VCLT) art 31(1).

[20] See *Oxford English Dictionary Online* (OUP September 2020) <http://www.oed.com> accessed 24 November 2020.

[21] William T Burke, *The New International Law of Fisheries* (Clarendon Press 1994) 40.

This broad remit is reinforced by the rights and discretions established in Articles 61 and 62, and particularly by Article 62(4), which sets out an extensive and non-exhaustive list of the types of terms and conditions that may be imposed and enforced by the coastal State in relation to foreign fishing in the EEZ. In addition, the coastal State has to fulfil a range of conservation and management obligations, and has the 'primary responsibility' for taking the measures necessary to prevent, deter, and eliminate illegal, unreported, and unregulated (IUU) fishing.[22]

Given the extensive nature of these rights and obligations, it seems reasonable to conclude that the coastal State's regulatory powers extend not only to the catching of fish, but to all fishing related activities, including fish-handling activities (such as processing, packaging, transhipment, and transport), and activities to support the operation of fishing vessels (such as bunkering and resupply). This approach was endorsed very early on by Burke, who concluded that: '[t]he coastal state is clearly not prohibited from regulating any phase of the fishing industry that occurs within its EEZ. If such regulation were impermissible, the coastal state would not have "sovereign rights for the purpose of exploring, exploiting, conserving and managing" as provided in Article 56, nor the discretion to select applicable "terms and conditions".'[23]

However, this interpretation has not been universally shared.[24] Since there is no express mention of these broader fishing related activities in the LOSC—and many of them were not common practice at the time the LOSC was negotiated—they have also been interpreted to fall within the freedoms that may be exercised by other States in the EEZ under Article 58(1).

3.1.2 The Right of 'Non-Interference'

Article 58(1) of the LOSC safeguards the rights of other States in the EEZ by providing that all States enjoy 'the freedoms referred to in Article 87 of navigation and overflight and of the laying of submarine cables and pipelines, and other internationally lawful uses of the sea related to these freedoms'. Two key observations must be made about the effect of this provision. First, it does not preserve *all*

[22] *SRFC Advisory Opinion* [106].

[23] William T Burke, 'Coastal State Fishery Regulation Under International Law: A Comment on the La Bretagne Award of July 17, 1986 (The Arbitration Between Canada and France)' (1988) 25 SanDiegoLRev 495, 523.

[24] For a long time, there was very little support for this position aside from the authors of the FAO series of studies on coastal State requirements for foreign fishing, who noted as early as 1983 that the general trend among coastal States was toward the regulation of a broad range of 'fishery support' vessels, such as mother ships, transport ships, and refuelling ships, as well as vessels actually engaged in fishing operations: Gerald Moore, *Coastal State Requirements for Foreign Fishing* (Rev 1, FAO 1983) 13. See also: Gerald Moore, *Coastal State Requirements for Foreign Fishing* (Rev 2, FAO 1985) 14; Gerald Moore, *Coastal State Requirements for Foreign Fishing* (Rev 3, FAO 1988) 9; FAO Legal Office, *Coastal State Requirements for Foreign Fishing* (Rev 4, FAO 1993) 4.

the high seas freedoms mentioned in Article 87, since three important freedoms (fishing, marine scientific research, and the construction of artificial islands and installations) have already been subjected to coastal State jurisdiction under Article 56(1). Second, despite being defined by reference to Article 87, the remaining freedoms do not encompass the same spectrum as they do on the high seas but are subject to the measures relating to the rights of coastal States in the EEZ and to the duty of due regard pursuant to Article 58(2). Subject to these inherent limitations, the freedoms of other States in the EEZ operate—like the high seas freedoms—as rights of non-interference. Accordingly, a ship exercising the freedom of navigation through the EEZ is subject to the jurisdiction of its flag State, and protected from interference by the coastal State, except as otherwise provided in the LOSC.[25] Thus while the coastal State has sovereign rights to regulate fishing in the EEZ, this does not, of itself, deprive a fishing vessel of its freedom to navigate in the EEZ.[26] The question is: does the freedom of navigation include the freedom to engage in activities that are not 'fishing', but are only 'fishing related'?

As Rothwell and Stephens observe, the 'freedom of navigation' has significant historical importance in the law of the sea, and—as confirmed by the absence of any further definition or elaboration of this term in the text of the LOSC—reflects considerable State practice and customary international law.[27] Nonetheless, the constantly changing nature of the activities taking place at sea make it necessary to examine the contemporary meaning and application of this iconic concept. The term 'navigation' is ordinarily understood to mean the action or practice of travelling on water in a ship or other vessel,[28] or—as it is employed in Article 90 of the LOSC to describe the right of navigation—'sailing ships' on the sea. Accordingly, the 'freedom of navigation' can be interpreted to mean the free or unimpeded movement or passage of a ship,[29] as distinct from the conduct of any other activities at sea.[30] When considered in context in the LOSC, this interpretation is reinforced by the distinction between the freedom of navigation in the EEZ under Article 58(1), and the all-encompassing 'freedom of the high seas' in Article 87, which comprises a non-exhaustive list of elements, of which the freedom of navigation is

[25] In particular, art 58(2) provides that arts 88 to 115 and other pertinent rules of international law apply to the EEZ in so far as they are not incompatible with Part V. Accordingly, the freedom of navigation in the EEZ remains subject not only to the laws and regulations of the coastal State under art 58(3), but to the right of visit and the prohibition of acts such as piracy, the transport of slaves, and illicit traffic in narcotic drugs.

[26] Nandan and Rosenne, *UNCLOS Commentary, Vol II* (n 5) 565; David Joseph Attard, *The Exclusive Economic Zone in International Law* (Clarendon Press 1987) 80.

[27] Rothwell and Stephens, *The International Law of the Sea* (n 17) 164.

[28] *Oxford English Dictionary Online* (n 20).

[29] Satya Nandan and Shabtai Rosenne, *United Nations Commentary on the Law of the Sea: A Commentary, Vol III* (Martinus Nijhoff 1995) 81.

[30] Lagoni, 'Offshore Bunkering' (n 1) 621. In a similar vein, the regime of innocent passage that applies in the territorial sea also distinguishes between the passage or movement of the ship (art 18) and activities undertaken during that passage (art 19).

but one.[31] On this basis, it can be concluded that fishing related activities (in particular, bunkering) do *not* fall within the freedom of navigation in the EEZ.[32]

However, in the specific context of the offshore bunkering of fishing vessels, a number of alternative interpretations have also been offered. The most straightforward relies on the absence of any specific reference to bunkering in Part V, and the nature of activities listed in Article 62(4), to conclude that the relevant legal regime for bunkering is that of navigation.[33] It has also been suggested that bunkering of fishing vessels cannot be conceived as economic exploration or exploitation *of* the zone (which would fall within the coastal State's sovereign rights under Article 56(1)(a)), but is merely an activity conducted *in* the zone, which therefore falls outside the coastal State's sovereign rights over living resources.[34] However, both these interpretations use negative reasoning to reach this result—they rely on the conclusion that since bunkering does not come within Article 56(1), it must come within Article 58(1)—which is inconsistent with the *sui generis* legal nature of the EEZ. Neither of them provides any substantive basis to support the argument that fishing related activities form part of the freedom of navigation, which, in the EEZ, operates as a functional right, the extent of which must be determined according to its purpose.[35]

In a slightly different vein, it could be argued that bunkering does not fall within the freedom of navigation itself, but is one of the 'internationally lawful uses of the sea related to the freedom of navigation' protected by Article 58(1).[36] However, since the term 'related' is not defined in the LOSC, this argument is inconclusive: this provision can be interpreted broadly, so as to classify a wide range of internationally lawful uses of the sea as related to the freedom of navigation, or interpreted narrowly, by arguing that any activities that are not directly linked to the specific operation of the ship are unrelated to its navigation.[37] In addition, since container ships normally have large bunker tanks and carry cargo from one port to another, it is rarely necessary for them to refuel at sea—added to which, the safety

[31] Ibid. As Rothwell and Stephens explain, the non-exhaustive nature of the list in art 87(1) has significance with respect to the capacity of States to engage in other activities that are not listed in art 87(1) but are nonetheless consistent with the freedom of the high seas (such as military exercises and weapons testing): Rothwell and Stephens, *The International Law of the Sea* (n 17) 164.

[32] Lagoni, 'Offshore Bunkering' (n 1) 621; *Saiga (No 2)* (Sep Op Zhao) [3].

[33] *Saiga* (Diss Op Wolfrum and Yamamoto) [22]. See also Barbara Kwiatkowska, 'The Saint Vincent and the Grenadines v Guinea M/V Saiga Cases before the International Tribunal for the Law of the Sea' in Donald R Rothwell and Sam Bateman (eds), *Navigational Rights and Freedoms of the New Law of the Sea* (Kluwer Law International 2000) 286; Clayton Vignocchi, 'ITLOST? The International Tribunal for the Law of the Sea Sounds the Charge to Expand Coastal State Jurisdiction' (2014) 39 TulMarLJ 791, 800–3.

[34] *Saiga (No 2)* (Sep Op Laing) [38] and [55]–[56]. See also Lagoni, 'Offshore Bunkering' (n 1) 619.

[35] Gavouneli, *Functional Jurisdiction* (n 12) 68–9.

[36] *Saiga (No 2)* (Sep Op Anderson) [14], (Sep Op Vukas) [17]. See also Lagoni, 'Offshore Bunkering' (n 1) 621–2.

[37] Ibid; Alexander Proelss, 'Article 58' in Alexander Proelss (ed), *United Nations Convention on the Law of the Sea: A Commentary* (CH Beck 2017) 452.

and environmental risks involved in bunkering provide a strong incentive for such vessels to refuel in port.[38] In any event, there seems to be no reason why a licensing or authorization regime could not be appropriately designed to regulate the fishing related activities of fishing support vessels—whether bunkering or other forms of resupply—without unnecessarily restricting their ability to engage in non-fishing related activities in support of other vessels.

3.1.3 A Question of Residual Rights?

It has also been suggested that the question of jurisdiction over fishing related activities could be resolved (whether directly or by analogy) by reference to the formula in Article 59,[39] which provides that any conflict involving unattributed rights should be resolved 'on the basis of equity and in the light of all the relevant circumstances, taking into account the respective importance of the interests involved to the parties as well as to the international community as a whole'.[40] However, this formula only applies if rights or jurisdiction over the issue in question have not already been attributed to the coastal State or to other States within the EEZ; it is only a 'backup clause',[41] which applies if there is a gap in the LOSC and the activity in question is completely new and unrelated to any type of activity already regulated.[42] Once again, it must be interpreted in light of the functional nature of the rights allocated to States in the EEZ.[43]

While many of the fishing related activities that form part of modern industrial fishing have evolved since the adoption of the LOSC and might thus be considered 'new', they are all directly related to fishing—an activity that is already regulated by the LOSC. In contrast, the types of activities that are commonly suggested to fall within the category of unattributed rights suitable for resolution under Article 59 include the conduct of military manoeuvres and the construction of military installations and structures in the EEZ, the protection and preservation of underwater cultural heritage in areas beyond the contiguous zone, and the use of acoustic emplacements and other ocean data acquisition systems.[44] While some coastal States

[38] Lagoni, 'Offshore Bunkering' (n 1) 615. This book only examines the regulation of bunkering as a fishing related activity under art 56(1)(a) of the LOSC. However, there is a separate body of literature—and, potentially, practice—on the coastal State's right to regulate bunkering as an aspect of marine environmental protection pursuant to arts 56(1)(b)(iii), 211, or 220 of the LOSC, a concept which has been endorsed by Judges Kelly and Attard: *Virginia G* (Joint Dec Kelly and Attard) 142.

[39] *Saiga (No 2)* (Sep Op Laing) [55]–[56]; *Virginia G* (Dec Treves) [8]. See also Molenaar and Tsamenyi, *Satellite-Based Vessel Monitoring Systems* (n 7) 109; Lagoni, 'Offshore Bunkering' (n 1) 623.

[40] On the issue of art 59 and residual rights, see also Section 2.3.2.1.

[41] Alexander Proelss, 'Article 59' in Alexander Proelss (ed), *United Nations Convention on the Law of the Sea: A Commentary* (CH Beck 2017) 460.

[42] Lagoni, 'Offshore Bunkering' (n 1) 623.

[43] Nandan and Rosenne, *UNCLOS Commentary, Vol II* (n 5) 569.

[44] See, eg, Brown, *The International Law of the Sea, Vol I* (n 9) 239–44; Petros Liacouras, 'Intelligence Gathering on the High Seas' in Anastasia Strati, Maria Gavouneli and Nikolaos Skourtos (eds),

assert the right to regulate these activities in the EEZ, they are not directly related to any of the rights attributed to coastal States under Article 56(1) and highlight, by apposition, the functional nature of the relationship between fishing related activities and the coastal State's sovereign rights over living resources in the EEZ.

Even if Article 59 were to be applied to determine whether jurisdiction over fishing related activities should be attributed to the coastal State or to other States, given the 'functional' nature of the EEZ it seems likely that the interests of the coastal State would prevail.[45] While the criteria by which the matter is to be decided are 'imprecise' and 'elusive',[46] the requirement that the conflict be resolved on the basis of equity and consideration of all relevant circumstances implies a standard of reasonableness and a case-by-case approach.[47] In this regard, issues such as the organized nature and economic impact of fishing related activities, their essential role in the infrastructure that supports both the legitimate and illegal operation of fishing vessels, and the coastal State's responsibility for the prevention of illegal fishing in the EEZ are persuasive factors in favour of the coastal State.

However, Article 59 only applies if a 'conflict arises', and since neither the parties nor the international courts and tribunals involved in the various disputes about fishing related activities have invoked this provision, it seems safe to conclude that they are *not* unattributed or residual rights to be resolved on the basis of Article 59.

3.2 The Scope of Jurisdiction over Fishing: The Jurisprudence

Article 59 aside, the journey to judicial clarity regarding jurisdiction over fishing related activities has been lengthy and circuitous, including detours through the 1986 *Dispute Concerning Filleting within the Gulf of St Lawrence*, in which coastal State jurisdiction was found *not* to extend to the filleting of fish caught in the EEZ,[48] and the *Saiga* cases of the late 1990s, which involved a lot of equivocation on the point. While the judgment in the 2014 *Virginia G* case concluded that 'bunkering of foreign vessels fishing in its EEZ is among those measures which the coastal State may take in its EEZ to conserve and manage its living resources',[49] the qualifications that accompanied this statement still leave a good deal of uncertainty about the extent of the coastal State's regulatory powers. The different approaches

Unresolved Issues and New Challenges to the Law of the Sea: Time Before and Time After (Martinus Nijhoff 2006) 142–6; Tullio Treves, 'Coastal States' Rights in the Maritime Areas under UNCLOS' (2015) 12(1) BrazilJIntlLaw 39, 43; Proelss, 'Article 59' (n 41) 460–1.

[45] Nandan and Rosenne, *UNCLOS Commentary, Vol II* (n 5) 569; Rothwell and Stephens, *The International Law of the Sea* (n 17); Proelss, 'Article 59' (n 41) 461.
[46] Anderson, 'Coastal State Jurisdiction' (n 7) 108.
[47] Proelss, 'Article 59' (n 41) 461.
[48] *Filleting in the Gulf of St Lawrence* [52].
[49] *Virginia G* [217].

taken in these judgments—and the significant differences of view expressed in the separate and dissenting opinions which accompanied them—make them a useful vehicle for exploring the questions raised in this Chapter, if not necessarily a complete basis for answering them.

3.2.1 The *Filleting in the Gulf of St Lawrence* Arbitration: Processing of Fish at Sea

In *Filleting in the Gulf of St Lawrence,* the Arbitral Tribunal took a very narrow approach to the interpretation of coastal State authority over living resources in the EEZ. The dispute concerned an application by a French vessel, registered in St Pierre and Miquelon, for a licence to fish in Canadian waters under a 1972 Agreement between France and Canada.[50] The vessel in question, *La Bretagne,* was a 'freezer-trawler', equipped not only to catch fish but to process and store it aboard, giving it much greater capacity than a normal fishing trawler. The Canadian authorities granted the vessel's application to fish in the Gulf of St Lawrence, but limited the extent of processing that could be carried out on board to heading and gutting (and not filleting), in line with the regulations that applied to Canadian trawlers in the area.[51] The French Government objected on the basis that this limitation contravened the 1972 Agreement, and the Parties established an Arbitral Tribunal to settle the dispute pursuant to the compulsory dispute resolution procedure in the Agreement. The question before the Arbitral Tribunal was whether or not Canada could prohibit the French vessels licensed under the 1972 Agreement from engaging in fish filleting in the Gulf of St Lawrence. While the 1972 Agreement pre-dated the adoption of the LOSC—indeed the LOSC had not entered into force at the time of the proceedings— the decision nonetheless involved some consideration of the relationship between the rights arising under both instruments, and under customary international law.

In a split decision focused heavily on treaty interpretation and application, the Arbitral Tribunal found that neither the 1972 Agreement nor international law gave Canada the authority to prohibit filleting by the French trawlers. In reaching this decision, the majority found that Canada's authority to regulate the French trawlers stemmed solely from the 1972 Agreement, and effectively excluded the broader effect of Canada's sovereign rights as a coastal State pursuant to the LOSC

[50] *Agreement between Canada and France on their Mutual Fishing Relations* (1972 Agreement) (signed and entered into force 27 March 1972) UNTS 12353. The 1972 Agreement sought to phase out French metropolitan fishing in the newly extended area of exclusive Canadian fisheries jurisdiction in the Gulf of St Lawrence, while allowing locally based fisheries from St Pierre and Miquelon to continue as 'an arrangement between neighbours'.

[51] *Filleting in the Gulf of St Lawrence* [14].

and customary international law.[52] This narrow approach to the *source* of Canada's jurisdiction directly affected the *scope* of that jurisdiction; since the source of Canada's regulatory power was the 1972 Agreement, Article 6 of that Agreement—which provided for Canadian fishery regulations to be applied 'without discrimination in form or in fact' to French vessels licensed under the Agreement—also governed the scope of regulations that could be issued by Canada.[53] In this regard, the majority found that in its 'natural and ordinary sense', the term 'fishery regulations' was limited to laws and regulations that 'fix the conditions to which all fish-catching activities are subject and are generally designed to maintain order on fishing grounds as well as to protect and preserve resources.'[54] The effect of this narrow approach was to confine the coastal State's regulatory authority to the regulation of the harvesting (or 'fish-catching') phase of fishing activities.

Although the decision focused primarily on the interpretation and application of the 1972 Agreement, the majority recognized that it had to consider other relevant rules of international law applicable between the Parties—in particular the LOSC, which both Parties had raised in support of their arguments.[55] In this regard, too, the decision reflects a narrow, technical approach to the interpretation of coastal State rights. While accepting that the coastal State has sovereign rights for the exploitation and management of living resources under Article 56 of the LOSC, the majority found that these rights are limited to 'conservation' purposes,[56] and that the coastal State's regulatory power does not include the authority to regulate subjects of a 'different nature' than those described in the—admittedly non-exhaustive—list set out in Article 62(4). On this basis, the majority concluded, 'the regulation of filleting at sea cannot *a priori* be justified by coastal State powers under the new law of the sea rules'.[57] Thus, the coastal State's management powers

[52] Ibid [31] and [55]. The majority decision was issued by the Chairperson (de Visscher) and the French appointee (Queneudec). The Canadian appointee (Pharand) issued a dissenting opinion that (in contrast to the majority decision) placed great weight on the modern developments in international fisheries law—particularly the fisheries provisions of the LOSC, which he viewed as customary international law—and concluded that '[t]here is no doubt that, in the absence of an agreement or arrangement to the contrary, the coastal State may regulate processing, including filleting', and that the 1972 Agreement did not provide any indication to the contrary: ibid (Diss Op Pharand) [11]–[17] and [31].

[53] *Filleting in the Gulf of St Lawrence* [36]–[38].

[54] Ibid [38]. In contrast, Pharand concluded (at [31] of his dissenting opinion) that 'fishery regulations' covered more than just 'the simple act of fishing' and included processing and filleting.

[55] *Filleting in the Gulf of St Lawrence* [49].

[56] Ibid [50].

[57] Ibid [52]. This is difficult to reconcile with the next paragraph of the decision, which recognizes that the regulations of some coastal States requiring catch to be landed in port—which have the effect of regulating the processing of catch by foreign vessels at sea—can be based on art 62(4)(h) of the LOSC ('the landing of all or any part of the catch by such vessels in the ports of the coastal State') provided the coastal State is 'acting within its sovereign rights, is not bound by any treaty or if a provision to this effect is included in a specific treaty concluded by the coastal State': ibid [53]. While it is possible to draw a distinction between regulations that prohibit processing at sea and regulations that require the landing of catch in port, since both involve the regulation of post-harvesting (or post 'fish-catching') activities, it is not tenable to argue that one activity may be regulated on the basis of the coastal State's sovereign rights and the other may not.

would be confined to the 'conservation' of living resources, to the exclusion of environmental, social, political, and other matters.[58]

This decision has been subject to widespread criticism, including with respect to the approach taken to treaty interpretation, the views expressed on the substantive international law governing fisheries, and the lack of attention to relevant State practice.[59] At the heart of all these criticisms lies the major flaw in this decision: contrary to the 'unjustifiably narrow' approach taken by the majority,[60] fishery regulations are concerned with considerably more than 'conservation' of a resource. Coastal State fishery jurisdiction is commonly used to address a wide range of social, political, and economic aims, through the regulation of a variety of actors and activities involved in or related to the exploitation of living marine resources.[61] In addition, the majority's assertion that in the common usage of States 'fishery regulations' do not extend beyond the harvesting phase of fishing[62] failed to take account of the practice of a significant number of coastal States—including not only France and the then European Economic Community, who were involved in the case, but Asian and African States, whose regulations at the time of the decision extended beyond 'fish-catching' to govern 'fish-handling' activities such as the processing and landing of catch.[63] In short, the Arbitral Tribunal's 'slavish reliance on technical legal status seems at odds with the reality of modern international fisheries law',[64] and certainly were such a case brought today, a court or tribunal would adopt a 'less restrictive' approach, given the practices of coastal States observed in the last thirty years.[65]

3.2.2 The *Saiga* Saga: Bunkering of Vessels at Sea

A decade after *Filleting in the Gulf of St Lawrence*, ITLOS was called upon to consider similar issues in its inaugural jurisprudence in the *Saiga* cases. While the *Saiga* cases involved the bunkering of fishing vessels—rather than the processing of fish—in the EEZ, they raised the same underlying question: what types of activity can be assimilated to the exercise by the coastal State of its sovereign rights to

58 Anderson, 'The Regulation of Fishing and Related Activities' (n 7) 37.
59 See Burke, 'Coastal State Fishery Regulation' (n 23) 501; Ted L McDorman, 'French Fishing Rights in Canadian Waters' (1989) 4(1) IJMCL 52, 57; Barbara Kwiatkowska, *The 200 Mile Exclusive Economic Zone in the New Law of the Sea* (Martinus Nijhoff 1989) 67; Ndiaye, 'IUU Fishing' (n 7) 388.
60 RR Churchill and AV Lowe, *The Law of the Sea* (3rd ed, MUP 1999) 291–2.
61 Burke, 'Coastal State Fishery Regulation' (n 23) 512.
62 *Filleting in the Gulf of St Lawrence* [37].
63 Burke, 'Coastal State Fishery Regulation' (n 23) 514–15. See also the comprehensive summary of coastal State requirements applicable to foreign fishing at the time: Moore, *Coastal State Requirements for Foreign Fishing, Rev 2* (n 24).
64 McDorman, 'French Fishing Rights' (n 59) 57.
65 Ndiaye, 'IUU Fishing' (n 7) 388. On the treatment of this decision by ITLOS in *Virginia G*, see Section 3.2.4.

explore, exploit, conserve, and manage living resources in the EEZ?[66] Interestingly, despite the underlying similarity of the issues (and despite it being raised by both Parties in the merits phase),[67] not one of the nineteen judgments, declarations, and separate and dissenting opinions issued in the course of the *Saiga* proceedings considered or referred to the jurisprudence of the Arbitral Tribunal in *Filleting in the Gulf of St Lawrence*.[68] And although the Tribunal did not come to a clear conclusion about the type of activities that come within the coastal State's fisheries jurisdiction, the judgments issued by the Tribunal—in particular, the wide variety of separate and dissenting opinions—examine various arguments to support different answers to this question.

The *Saiga* was an oil tanker registered in Saint Vincent and the Grenadines, and bunkering fishing vessels operating off the coast of Guinea. On 27 October 1997, the *Saiga* supplied gasoil to three fishing vessels in the Guinean EEZ (all of which were authorized by Guinea to fish in that zone),[69] before sailing on towards the southern boundary of the EEZ. The following day, the *Saiga* was boarded and arrested by Guinean patrol boats at a point outside Guinea's EEZ, and taken to the port of Conakry, where the Master and crew were detained. Although two injured crew members were subsequently allowed to leave, no bond or other financial security for the release of the vessel and remaining crew was requested by Guinea (or offered by Saint Vincent and the Grenadines). On 13 November 1997, Saint Vincent and the Grenadines submitted a request to ITLOS for prompt release under Article 292 of the LOSC, which was granted in a decision issued on 4 December 1997.[70] On 22 December 1997, Saint Vincent and the Grenadines instituted arbitral proceedings pursuant to Annex VII of the LOSC, which were subsequently transferred to ITLOS and resulted in a decision on the merits issued on 1 July 1999.[71]

Notwithstanding Guinea's insistence throughout the proceedings that its regulation of bunkering rested on customs jurisdiction, in considering the application for prompt release, the majority characterized Guinea's actions as being based on Article 73 of the LOSC.[72] This approach necessitated consideration of whether

[66] *Saiga* [57].

[67] *ITLOS Pleadings, Minutes of Public Sittings and Documents, Vol 3* (1999) *'MV Saiga' (No 2) (Saint Vincent and the Grenadines v Guinea)* Memorial of Saint Vincent and the Grenadines [133] and Counter-Memorial of Guinea [107].

[68] In the prompt release phase, the majority decision was accompanied by four dissenting opinions. In the merits phase, the majority decision was accompanied by one joint declaration, eight separate opinions, and two dissenting opinions. The only one of these to refer in any way to *Filleting in the Gulf of St Lawrence* was Judge Ndiaye's dissenting opinion in the merits phase, quoting a passage relating to the right of a flag State to decide on the conditions for the registration of ships: *Saiga (No 2)* (Diss Op Ndiaye) [36].

[69] The *Giuseppe Primo* and the *Kriti*, both flying the flag of Senegal, and the *Eleni S*, flying the flag of Greece.

[70] *Saiga*.

[71] *Saiga (No 2)*.

[72] The majority noted that classifying bunkering as a 'customs' offence made it very arguable that the Guinean authorities acted from the beginning in violation of international law, while classifying it under art 73 permitted the assumption that Guinea was convinced that in arresting the *Saiga* it was

or not bunkering is an activity that falls within the coastal State's sovereign rights to explore, exploit, conserve, and manage the living resources of the EEZ (and thus within the auspices of the Tribunal's power to order prompt release under Articles 73(2) and 292). The Tribunal was almost evenly divided on this question. The majority judgment (adopted by twelve judges) found it arguable that 'refuelling is by nature an activity ancillary to that of the refuelled ship', citing the definition of 'fishing activities' in the *Convention for the Prohibition of Fishing with Long Driftnets in the South Pacific* (Driftnet Convention)[73] and the domestic laws of Guinea-Bissau, Sierra-Leone, and Morocco.[74] However, the majority also noted that bunkering at sea could be classified as an independent activity governed by the freedom of navigation—or perhaps even the 'residual rights' regime of Article 59.[75]

The nine dissenting judges cast significantly more doubt on the question: Judge Anderson stated that bunkering 'is an internationally lawful use of the sea related to navigation',[76] and Vice President Wolfrum and Judge Yamamoto (with whom President Mensah agreed), expressed doubt as to whether services rendered to fishing vessels fall under the 'laws and regulations' referred to in Article 73(1), since Article 62(4) 'gives no indication that the competence of the coastal State concerning fishing might encompass activities of merchant ships, associated with the freedom of navigation, for the sole reason that they service fishing vessels.'[77] In the event, none of these views were conclusive; the majority found that, for the purpose of determining the admissibility of a prompt release application, it was not necessary to come to a view about which approach was better founded in law, but simply noted that alleged non-compliance with Article 73(2) was arguable, or at least 'sufficiently plausible'[78] and, on this basis, ordered the prompt release of the *Saiga* and its crew from detention on the payment of a reasonable bond or security.[79]

acting within its rights under the LOSC. On this basis, the majority concluded that 'given the choice between a legal classification that implies a violation of international law and one that avoids such implication it must opt for the latter': *Saiga* [72].

[73] (Opened for signature 24 November 1989, entered into force 17 May 1991) 1899 UNTS 3.

[74] *Saiga* [57]. These laws were cited by Saint Vincent and the Grenadines in support of its argument that bunkering is an activity that comes within arts 73 and 292 of the LOSC (although by reference to the laws of *Mauritania*, rather than Morocco): *ITLOS Pleadings, Minutes of Public Sittings and Documents, Vol 1* (1997) *'MV Saiga' (Saint Vincent and the Grenadines v Guinea)* Verbatim Record of the Public Hearing held on 27 November 1997 at 3pm, 33–4.

[75] *Saiga* [58].

[76] Ibid (Diss Op Anderson) [14].

[77] Ibid (Joint Diss Op Wolfrum and Yamamoto) [22]–[25] and (Diss Op Mensah) [6]. In a further joint dissenting opinion, five judges declined to discuss the question, on the basis that the Applicant (Saint Vincent and the Grenadines) had not proved, and the Respondent (Guinea) had denied, that the measures taken with respect to the *Saiga* related to fisheries or were exercised pursuant to art 73: ibid (Joint Diss Op Park, Nelson, Chandrasekhara Rao, Vukas and Ndiaye) [10]–[17].

[78] *Saiga* [59].

[79] Ibid [86]. The four dissenting opinions (two individual and two joint) strenuously agreed with each other that the 'sufficiently plausible' test adopted by the majority was an insufficient standard to apply for prompt release proceedings under art 292 of the LOSC, which are not merely preliminary but

The second phase of the proceedings was no more conclusive; although both parties requested the Tribunal to make declarations regarding the rights of coastal States and of other States in connection with offshore bunkering,[80] having decided that the LOSC does not empower a coastal State to apply its customs laws in the EEZ in the way asserted by Guinea,[81] the majority once again found that it was not necessary to decide the broader question with regard to bunkering, and did not make any findings on the issue.[82] Although almost all the judges who had dissented in the earlier proceedings joined the majority decision (indicating, perhaps, that their previous dissent had centred on the view that Saint Vincent and the Grenadines should have challenged the legality of Guinea's actions on their merits rather than through the prompt release mechanism),[83] several of the separate and dissenting opinions nonetheless demonstrated the continued disparity of views on the extent of the coastal State's jurisdiction over 'fishing'.

At one end of the spectrum, Judge Vukas (who joined in the majority decision) took the position previously adopted by Judge Anderson, stating that bunkering should be considered an internationally lawful use of the sea under Article 58(1) of the LOSC, related to the freedom of navigation and associated with the operation of ships. His separate opinion noted that '[s]upply of bunkers is the purpose of the navigation of a tanker, and refuelling is essential for further navigation of the ship to which gas oil has been supplied.'[84] At the other end of the spectrum, Judge Zhao (also a member of the majority) took the opposite view, concluding not only that

dispositive of the merits of the question. Instead, the minority considered that the Applicant's allegation needed to be 'well founded', a burden which could only be successfully discharged by establishing that there is a 'direct connection' between the arrest of the vessel and laws and regulations referable to art 73 of the LOSC: ibid (Diss Op Mensah) [5], (Diss Op Anderson) [4], (Joint Diss Op Park, Nelson, Chandrasekhara Rao, Vukas and Ndiaye) [8]–[9], (Joint Diss Op Wolfrum and Yamamoto) [4].

80 Saint Vincent and the Grenadines argued that bunkering in the EEZ constitutes an exercise of the freedom of navigation and other internationally lawful uses of the sea related to the freedom of navigation, as provided for in arts 56 and 58 of the LOSC. In contrast, Guinea maintained that bunkering is not an exercise of the freedom of navigation or any of the internationally lawful uses of the sea related to freedom of navigation, but a commercial activity. Guinea also noted that bunkering in the EEZ may not have the same status in all cases, and that different considerations might apply to bunkering of ships operating in the zone, as opposed to the supply of oil to ships that are in transit: *Saiga (No 2)* [138].

81 Ibid [127].

82 Ibid [138]. The approach taken by the Tribunal is not criticized; it is common practice for courts and tribunals to decide a case solely on the basis of the issues that actually arise for decision, leaving hypothetical questions to be decided in cases where they arise directly on the facts. The restraint shown by the Tribunal in this case stands in contrast to the *obiter* statements made in the prompt release proceedings (which were the subject of regret by some members of the minority: *Saiga* (Joint Diss Op Wolfrum and Yamamoto) [20]).

83 Bernard H Oxman and Vincent Bantz, 'The M/V "Saiga" (No 2) (Saint Vincent and the Grenadines v Guinea), Judgment (ITLOS Case No 2)' (2000) 94(1) AJIL 140, 149.

84 *Saiga (No 2)* (Sep Op Vukas) [17]. However, Judge Vukas noted that he did not 'rule out' the possibility that the constant practice of States might lead to the development of additional international rules concerning the rights and duties of coastal and/or other States in the EEZ beyond those in the LOSC (at [21]). Judge Nelson expressed concern that Guinea's position seemed to 'contain within it the seeds of destruction' of the LOSC, but concluded by commenting '[t]hat is far from saying that the tribunal should disregard the development of customary international law': ibid (Sep Op Nelson) [125].

the freedom of navigation does *not* include bunkering and ancillary activities, but that the coastal State's agreement is required for bunkering in the EEZ, and that fishing vessels should obtain licences or approval for bunkering from the coastal State.[85] The rights of the coastal State were also emphasized by Judge Warioba (the only member of the Tribunal to dissent on the question of customs jurisdiction), who found that the coastal State's right to regulate fishing in the EEZ extends to the regulation of customs matters, and particularly to the establishment of the laws and regulations necessary to deal with smuggling by fishing vessels.[86]

In a separate opinion that sat between these two extremes, Judge Anderson endorsed the Tribunal's decision not to make any general findings about bunkering, on the basis that these questions are far from being straightforward since 'bunkering is conducted under all manner of different circumstances and may involve distinct types of recipient vessels, including passenger vessels, warships, cargo ships and fishing vessels.'[87] As explained in more detail in his extra-judicial and post-judicial writing, Judge Anderson's position is that bunkering is a service: when it serves navigation, the rules on navigation apply, whereas when it serves fishing in the EEZ, the regime for fishing applies.[88] On this view the coastal State may regulate bunkering as part of the conditions attached to a licence to fish in the EEZ under Article 62(4).[89]

This position is similar to that put by Saint Vincent and the Grenadines itself, whose argument was not that the coastal State's sovereign rights over *living resources* do not extend to the regulation of bunkering of fishing vessels in the EEZ, but that the coastal State's *customs jurisdiction* does not extend to the regulation of bunkering in the EEZ.[90] This argument was also put another way, on the basis that the application of *customs duties* does not fall within the coastal State's sovereign rights to explore, exploit, conserve, and manage the living resources of the EEZ.[91] This approach is explained by the domestic fisheries legislation of Saint Vincent and the Grenadines which, as in force both at the time and at present, provides that 'no foreign fishing vessel shall be used for fishing *or related activities* in the fishery waters without a valid foreign fishing licence', and defines 'related activities' to mean: '(a) transhipping fish to or from any vessel; (b) storing, processing or transporting fish taken from the fishery waters up to the time it is first landed; (c) *refuelling or supplying fishing vessels* or performing other activities in support of fishing operations; (d) attempting or preparing to do any of the above.'[92]

85 *Saiga (No 2)* (Sep Op Judge Zhao) [3]–[4].
86 Ibid (Diss Op Warioba) [75]–[76].
87 Ibid (Sep Op Anderson) 137.
88 Anderson, 'The Regulation of Fishing and Related Activities' (n 7) 49; Anderson, *Modern Law of the Sea* (n 7) 227; Anderson, 'Coastal State Jurisdiction' (n 7) 114.
89 Ibid 112–13.
90 *ITLOS Pleadings, Saiga No 2* (n 67) Memorial of Saint Vincent and the Grenadines [5].
91 Ibid [114]–[137] and Reply Submitted by Saint Vincent and the Grenadines [121]–[140].
92 Saint Vincent and the Grenadines, *Act 1986* ss 2 and 8(1) (emphasis added).

Moreover, during oral argument in the prompt release proceedings, Saint Vincent and the Grenadines cited examples from other States in the region to demonstrate that the bunkering of fishing vessels in the EEZ is regulated through domestic fisheries legislation.[93] In this regard, reference to the relevant State practice of the time would have revealed the general trend toward coastal State regulation of a broad range of fishing support vessels, including mother ships, transport ships, and refuelling ships, as well as vessels actually engaged in fishing operations.[94]

3.2.3 The *Juno Trader* Case: Transhipment of Fish at Sea

The next prompt release application made to the Tribunal by Saint Vincent and the Grenadines also involved a fishing support vessel—this time the *Juno Trader*, a refrigerated cargo vessel, which had received a transhipment of frozen fish in Mauritania's EEZ (from a vessel licensed to fish in that zone) and was passing through Guinea-Bissau's EEZ en route for Ghana when it was boarded and arrested by Guinea-Bissau's navy, and escorted to the port of Bissau. Having inspected the catch on board and found that it consisted predominantly of species found in Guinea-Bissau's EEZ, the local authorities found that the *Juno Trader* had 'violated the provisions of the fishing legislation of Guinea-Bissau, regarding operations related to fishing'. Fines were imposed on the vessel and captain, and all the products on board the vessel were confiscated on suspicion of having been transhipped in the waters of Guinea-Bissau without authorization.[95]

Similarly to Saint Vincent and the Grenadines, the domestic legislation of Guinea-Bissau provided that coastal State authorization was required for all 'fishing related operations', defined to mean: '(a) the transhipment of fish or fishery products in the maritime waters of Guinea-Bissau; (b) the transport of fish or any other aquatic organisms which have been caught in the maritime waters of Guinea-Bissau until the first landing; (c) activities of logistic support to fishing vessels at sea; (d) the collection of fish from fishermen.'[96]

As in the *Saiga* proceedings, the written and oral arguments of Saint Vincent and the Grenadines did not dispute the formal extent of the coastal State's regulatory authority, or the validity of Guinea-Bissau's fisheries regulations; rather, the dispute concerned whether or not the activities of the *Juno Trader* had in fact infringed these regulations, since the fish had (on the account of Saint Vincent and

[93] *ITLOS Pleadings, Saiga* (n 74) Verbatim Record of the Public Hearing held on 27 November 1997 at 3pm, 33–4.

[94] FAO Legal Office, *Coastal State Requirements for Foreign Fishing, Rev 4* (n 24) 4.

[95] *Juno Trader* [33]–[43].

[96] Guinea-Bissau, *Decree-Law 6A-2000*, arts 3(3) and 23. This legislation was repealed and replaced in 2011, but the definition of 'fishing related operations' and the requirement for coastal State authorization are unchanged: *Dec Law 10/2011*, arts 6(3) and 35.

the Grenadines) been both caught and transhipped in the EEZ of Mauritania, rather than Guinea-Bissau.[97]

As Churchill has observed,[98] since the *Saiga* proceedings, the Tribunal has ruled that in a prompt release case it will not inquire into the circumstances in which the detained vessel was arrested,[99] and will not consider whether the coastal State's laws relating to fishing in the EEZ are compatible with the LOSC.[100] Nonetheless, although the Tribunal did not expressly consider the extent of the coastal State's competence to regulate the activities of transhipment vessels in the EEZ, '[t]he fact that the *Juno Trader* was used for carrying frozen fish probably after transhipment from the vessel having fished them was not even envisaged as an argument for holding that Article 73 was not applicable.'[101] Moreover, the Tribunal took into account Guinea-Bissau's transhipment legislation for the purposes of calculating the reasonableness of the bond pursuant to Article 73(2), which can be read as an implicit acknowledgment of its conformity with the LOSC.[102] And unlike the disputed and disparate approaches taken in the *Saiga* proceedings, not only was the *Juno Trader* judgment adopted unanimously, but none of the accompanying declarations or separate opinions questioned the competence of the coastal State to regulate transhipment in its EEZ.

3.2.4 The *Virginia G* Case: Activities 'Directly Connected' to Fishing

After nearly thirty years of uncertainty on this question, in the 2014 *Virginia G* case ITLOS was directly called upon to decide whether the bunkering of foreign fishing vessels falls within the sovereign rights of the coastal State under Article 56, or the flag State's freedom of navigation under Article 58. The *Virginia G* was a Panamanian-flagged oil tanker providing bunkering services to fishing vessels operating off the coast of West Africa. On 21 August 2009, the *Virginia G* provided

[97] Saint Vincent and the Grenadines implicitly recognized the right of the coastal State to regulate transhipment, by specifically noting that the transhipment had been 'explicitly authorized' by the Mauritanian authorities. See *ITLOS Pleadings, Minutes of Public Sittings and Documents, Vol 12* (2004) *'Juno Trader' (Saint Vincent and the Grenadines v Guinea-Bissau)* Verbatim Record of the Public Sitting held on 6 December 2004 at 10am, 7.

[98] Robin Rolf Churchill, 'The Jurisprudence of the International Tribunal for the Law of the Sea Relating to Fisheries: Is There Much in the Net?' (2007) 22 IJMCL 383, 404.

[99] *Volga* [83].

[100] *Camouco* [60].

[101] Tullio Treves, 'Some International Law Aspects of the Use of Vessel Monitoring Systems for Preventing Illegal Unreported and Unregulated Fishing' in Tafsir Malick Ndiaye and Rüdiger Wolfrum (eds), *Law of the Sea, Environmental Law and Settlement of Disputes: Liber Amicorum Judge Thomas A Mensah* (Martinus Nijhoff 2007) 816. Judge Treves was a member of the majority in *Juno Trader* and voted in favour of all operative parts of the judgment (although he also issued a separate opinion addressing due process issues associated with art 73(2)).

[102] Schatz, 'Combating Illegal Fishing in the EEZ' (n 4) 390.

gasoil to two Mauritanian vessels fishing under licence in the EEZ of Guinea-Bissau. Although the fishing vessels had sought and obtained authorization to receive bunkering from the *Virginia G* at the relevant place and time, Guinea-Bissau alleged that the *Virginia G* had not received the authorization—or made the payment—required in order to provide bunkering services in the EEZ of Guinea-Bissau.[103] Accordingly, all three vessels were arrested and escorted to the port of Bissau, where the *Virginia G* (together with the gasoil on board) was confiscated in September 2009 for conducting unauthorized bunkering activities in the EEZ, and not released until a year later.[104]

In contrast to Saint Vincent and the Grenadines' approach in the *Saiga* and *Juno Trader* cases, Panama did not seek prompt release of the *Virginia G* under Article 73(2) of the LOSC (which might have implied some acceptance that the actions in question were taken pursuant to the coastal State's regulatory powers over living resources), but instituted proceedings against Guinea-Bissau on the grounds that the requirement of authorization and imposition of fees for bunkering violated Articles 56 and 58 of the LOSC, and that the arrest and confiscation of the vessel thus contravened Article 73(1). Accordingly, from the outset, the dispute was clearly framed around the question of whether or not Guinea-Bissau, as a coastal State, had jurisdiction to regulate the bunkering of foreign vessels fishing in its EEZ, and the arguments put forward by the parties reflected this.

Panama (which, unlike Saint Vincent and the Grenadines did not, at the time, have legislation regulating bunkering of foreign fishing vessels in the EEZ)[105] argued that the provision of bunkering services is encompassed by the freedom of navigation and other internationally lawful uses of the sea related to that freedom pursuant to Article 58(1) of the LOSC, and is not reserved or recognized to the coastal State. While noting the potential distinction between the coastal State's regulation of bunkering by *fishing vessels* on the basis of their fishing activities in the EEZ, and the regulation of *bunkering vessels* such as the *Virginia G*,[106] Panama nonetheless rejected the idea that bunkering in the EEZ could be qualified as a

[103] *Virginia G* [59]–[60].

[104] Following various legal proceedings brought by the *Virginia G's* owner in the courts of Guinea-Bissau, the confiscation order was rescinded and the vessel released in August 2010. While the fishing vessels were also arrested for bunkering violations relating to the *Virginia G's* lack of authorization, since they had valid fishing licences and had sought authorization to receive bunkering from the *Virginia G* at the relevant place and time, Guinea-Bissau considered their violations to be much less serious than those of the *Virginia G*: *ITLOS Pleadings, Minutes of Public Sittings and Documents, Vol 21* (2004) *'Virginia G' (Panama v Guinea-Bissau)* Counter-Memorial of the Republic of Guinea-Bissau [122].

[105] Panama's fisheries legislation has recently been updated with the passage of *Law 204 of 2021 Regulating Fishing, Aquaculture and Related Activities* which is expressed to apply in the same way to all vessels engaged in fishing and fishing related activities in the EEZ, and defines 'fishing related activities' to include 'any operation in support of or preparation for fishing, including landing, packaging, processing, transhipment or transport of fishery products that have not been previously landed in port, as well as the provision of personnel, fuel, fishing gear and other supplies necessary for fishing': *Law 204 of 2021* arts 1 and 11.

[106] *ITLOS Pleadings, Virginia G* (n 104) Memorial of the Republic of Panama [284].

fishing related activity subject to national regulation and control.[107] In contrast, Guinea-Bissau argued that 'the interests of the coastal state in the preservation of maritime resources and the regulation of fisheries prevail over the economic interests of bunkering activities carried out by tankers.'[108] Guinea-Bissau stressed that bunkering is instrumental to fishing operations, has a much stronger connection to the conduct of fishing than the freedom of navigation, and is considered throughout the West African region to be a 'fishing related operation' subject to the prior authorization of the coastal State.[109]

The Tribunal agreed with Guinea-Bissau's argument, finding unanimously that:

> the regulation by a coastal State of bunkering of foreign vessels fishing in its [EEZ] is among those measures which the coastal State may take in its [EEZ] to conserve and manage its living resources under Article 56 of the [LOSC] read together with Article 62, paragraph 4, of the [LOSC]. This view is also confirmed by State practice which has developed after the adoption of the [LOSC].
>
> The Tribunal acknowledges that the national legislation of several States, not only in the West African region, but also in some other regions of the world, regulates bunkering of foreign vessels fishing in their [EEZ]s in a way comparable to that of Guinea-Bissau. The Tribunal further notes that there is no manifest objection to such legislation and that it is, in general, complied with.[110]

In reaching this decision, the Tribunal noted that the terms 'conserving' and 'managing' in Article 56(1) indicate that the rights of the coastal State 'go beyond conservation in its strict sense',[111] and that the laws and regulations that may be adopted by the coastal State pursuant to the non-exhaustive list in Article 62(4) include measures that may be considered as 'management'.[112] Despite being 'aware' of the decision in *Filleting in the Gulf of St Lawrence* that the coastal State does not have authority to regulate subjects of a 'different nature' than those described in Article 62(4),[113] the Tribunal applied a different test—that of 'direct connection'. The Tribunal noted that: 'it is apparent from the list in article 62, paragraph 4, of the [LOSC] that for all activities that may be regulated by a coastal State there must be a *direct connection* to fishing. The Tribunal observes that such connection to fishing exists for the bunkering of foreign vessels fishing in the [EEZ] since this enables them to continue their activities without interruption at sea.'[114]

[107] Ibid Memorial of the Republic of Panama [291].
[108] Ibid Counter-Memorial of the Republic of Guinea-Bissau [218].
[109] Ibid Counter-Memorial of the Republic of Guinea-Bissau [76]–[99] and Rejoinder of the Republic of Guinea-Bissau [50].
[110] *Virginia G* [217]–[218].
[111] Ibid [211]–[212].
[112] Ibid [213].
[113] *Filleting in the Gulf of St Lawrence* [52].
[114] *Virginia G* [215] (emphasis added).

In reaching this conclusion, the Tribunal was guided by the definitions of 'fishing', 'fishing vessels', and 'fishing related activities' in a range of international agreements which 'all establish the close connection between fishing and the various support activities, including bunkering'.[115] For example, the Tribunal referred particularly to the Port State Measures Agreement, in which the term 'fishing related activities' is defined broadly in Article 1(f) to include: 'any operation in support of, or in preparation for, fishing, including the landing, packaging, processing, transhipping or transporting of fish that have not been previously landed at a port, as well as the provisioning of personnel, fuel, gear and other supplies at sea'.

On its face, this suggests that ITLOS considers not only bunkering but other 'fishing related activities', including landing, packaging, processing, transhipping, and transporting of fish not previously landed in port, as well as the provision of personnel and supplies at sea to be 'directly connected' to fishing, and thus within the jurisdiction of the coastal State. However, as Judge *ad hoc* Treves pointed out with regret in his declaration, the Tribunal's approach to resolving the dispute ultimately produced a much narrower finding.[116]

The Tribunal did not base its decision on the functional relationship between fishing related activities and the conduct of fishing itself, nor consider the possibility of making a characterization based on the activity of the fishing vessel receiving the bunker—which approaches might have allowed for the logic of the opinion to be applied more broadly (such as in relation to fishing related activities generally, or with respect to the bunkering of vessels engaged in activities other than fishing).[117] Instead, the Tribunal relied on a combined interpretation of Articles 56(1) and 62(4) to find that the sovereign right to 'manage' living resources includes the right to regulate the bunkering of foreign vessels engaged in fishing in the EEZ, but qualified this by stating that the coastal State 'does not have such competence with regard to other bunkering activities, unless otherwise determined in accordance with the [LOSC]'.[118] Moreover, the Tribunal did not establish a positive right for coastal States to regulate *any* activity having a 'direct connection' to fishing, but constructed a negative rule pursuant to which 'for all activities that may be regulated by a coastal State there must be a direct connection to fishing'.[119] Notwithstanding the broad range of fishing related activities regulated in the international conventions by which the Tribunal was 'guided', these qualifications make

[115] Ibid [216].

[116] *Virginia G* (Dec Treves) [8]. See also Treves, 'Coastal States' Rights' (n 44) 44. Several other members of the Tribunal also expressed support for a more expansive approach to the question. Kelly and Attard stated that bunkering generally comes within the coastal State's jurisdiction under art 56(1)(b)(iii); Nelson regretted that more attention was not paid to the formula in art 59 for determining residual rights; and Ndiaye noted that there is widespread coastal State regulation of fishing related activities in the EEZ, which has not suffered any challenge whatsoever, and lies well within the sovereign rights conferred on the coastal State under the LOSC.

[117] *Virginia G* (Dec Treves) [8]–[9].

[118] *Virginia G* [223].

[119] Ibid [215]. This was reiterated in the *SRFC Advisory Opinion* [100].

it difficult to determine precisely which activities the Tribunal considers may be regulated by the coastal State in the EEZ.

Furthermore, the judgment does not clearly establish which vessels may be regulated by the coastal State. For example, the Tribunal stated that the coastal State's regulatory authority, which arises under Article 56 'read together with' Article 62(4), extends to fishing related activities when they are undertaken in support of foreign vessels *engaged in fishing* in the EEZ—not in support of foreign fishing vessels in the EEZ.[120] This distinction is important, because it implies that the coastal State's regulatory power is limited to foreign-flagged vessels that are fishing in the EEZ pursuant to a licence issued by the coastal State under Article 62(4), and does not extend to the broader regulation of foreign fishing vessels that are—or purport to be—merely in transit through the zone under Article 56(1). This has important consequences for the coastal State's ability to prevent, deter, and eliminate illegal fishing in the EEZ. In addition, the judgment does not clarify the extent of the coastal State's jurisdiction over fishing support vessels (such as bunkers and carrier vessels) operating in the EEZ; in particular, whether the coastal State may only regulate such vessels during the conduct of fishing related activities, or may also regulate other aspects of their navigation in the EEZ. Once again, this question has significant practical consequences for the coastal State.

The decision in *Virginia G* has subsequently been applied, to different effects, in other disputes relating to bunkering operations. In the *Norstar* case, which involved the bunkering of leisure boats on the high seas, the Tribunal explicitly recalled its decision in *Virginia G* that 'the bunkering of foreign vessels engaged in fishing in the [EEZ] is an activity which may be regulated by the coastal State concerned', and distinguished this from bunkering on the high seas, which it found is part of the freedom of navigation.[121] In the provisional measures phase of the *San Padre Pio* dispute, which relates to a ship-to-ship transfer of gasoil between transport vessels in the Nigerian EEZ, Nigeria sought to apply and extend the Tribunal's finding in *Virginia G* that the coastal State's competence to regulate bunkering of foreign vessels engaged in fishing in the EEZ derives from its sovereign rights over living resources in order to support a similar competence in relation to *non*-living resources.[122] This may provide an opportunity for the Tribunal to clarify some of the questions from *Virginia G* raised above—including how 'direct' the connection between the bunkering and the activity needs to be, and whether the coastal State

[120] *Virginia G* [217], and see generally the discussion at [212]–[215].

[121] *Norstar* [219]. The lawfulness of bunkering on the high seas *per se* was not disputed by either Party—the unlawfulness arose (from Italy's perspective) in relation to a broader 'criminal plan concerning the commission of the crimes of tax evasion and smuggling in Italian territory': ibid [250].

[122] *MT 'San Padre Pio' (Switzerland v Nigeria)* (Provisional Measures) (2019) ITLOS Case No 27, Statement in Response of the Federal Republic of Nigeria of 17 June 2019 [3.13]–[3.14]. In contrast, Switzerland sought support from the *Norstar* decision in arguing that the freedom of navigation in the EEZ includes non-interference with bunkering activities, provided they are not connected with fishing: ibid Request for the Prescription of Provisional Measures of the Swiss Confederation [29].

has a broad regulatory power supported by Article 56(1), or a narrower jurisdiction reliant on the support of Article 62(4).[123] At the time of writing, the merits of the *San Padre Pio* dispute are yet to be considered; the Tribunal has 'noted' the claims of both Parties regarding their asserted rights and obligations, and on the basis of a finding that the rights to freedom of navigation claimed by Switzerland under Article 58 are at least 'plausible',[124] has ordered the release of the vessel on posting of a bond or other financial security of $14 million USD.[125]

As Judge Gao has observed, although the *Virginia G* decision only takes one small step beyond the Tribunal's position in the *Saiga* cases, 'this step is an important one in the right direction'.[126] Regrettably, however, it still does not provide a comprehensive answer to the key question raised in this Chapter—*what activities* and *which vessels* may be regulated by the coastal State on the basis of its sovereign rights over the living resources of the EEZ? Fortunately, there is a significant amount of 'robust international practice' at the global, regional, and national level that clearly demonstrates the scope and substance of the coastal State's sovereign rights and jurisdiction over living resources in the EEZ.[127]

3.3 The Substance of Jurisdiction over Fishing: The State of Practice

Although the concept of 'fishing related activities' was not raised at UNCLOS III,[128] the regulation of activities and vessels that support the conduct of fishing operations is evident in international practice as early as 1967, when the term 'vessel' was defined in the *Convention on Conduct of Fishing Operations in the North Atlantic* to mean 'any fishing vessel and any vessel engaged in the business of processing fish or providing supplies or services to fishing vessels'.[129] Similar approaches have been adopted in multilateral treaties in the Pacific region since the 1980s, starting with the 1987 *Treaty on Fisheries between the Governments of Certain Pacific Island States and the Government of the United States of America* (US Tuna Treaty) in which 'fishing' was defined to include 'any operations at sea directly

[123] There is also likely to be a question about whether ship-to-ship transfers should be treated in the same way as bunkering, since they essentially involve the transfer of cargo from one vessel to another, rather than refuelling vessels to facilitate their uninterrupted navigation at sea. See further David Testa, 'Coastal State Regulation of Bunkering and Ship-to-Ship (STS) Oil Transfer Operations in the EEZ: An Analysis of State Practice and of Coastal State Jurisdiction Under the LOSC' (2019) 50(4) ODIL 363.
[124] *San Padre Pio* [107]–[108].
[125] Ibid [146].
[126] *Virginia G* (Dec Gao) [12].
[127] Ibid (Diss Op Ndiaye) [182].
[128] See n 6.
[129] (Opened for signature 1 June 1967, entered into force 29 September 1976) 1051 UNTS 102, art 2(1).

in support of, or in preparation for any activity described in this paragraph.'[130] This approach was further developed by the 1994 *Federated States of Micronesia Arrangement for Regional Fisheries Access* (FSM Arrangement),[131] in which 'related activities' was defined to mean: '(i) refuelling or supplying fishing boats, selling or supplying fishing equipment or performing other activities in support of fishing; (ii) on-shore storing, buying or processing of fish or fish products from the time they are first landed; or (iii) storing, buying, transhipping, processing or transporting fish or fish products taken from the Arrangement Area up to the time such fish or fish products are first landed.'

Most recently, global fisheries instruments such as the Port State Measures Agreement have included the term 'fishing related activities', which are defined to mean 'any operation in support of, or in preparation for, fishing, including the landing, packaging, processing, transhipping or transporting of fish that have not been previously landed at a port, as well as the provisioning of personnel, fuel, gear and other supplies at sea.'[132]

Beyond the inclusion of defined terms referring to them, the important role that fishing related activities and fishing support vessels play in modern industrial fishing is also reflected in the scope and substance of key global and regional fisheries instruments. It is evident in the range of rights and responsibilities assigned to coastal, flag, and port States in the Compliance Agreement,[133] the UNFSA,[134] and the IPOA-IUU.[135] It is also demonstrated by the development of the Global Record of Fishing Vessels, Refrigerated Transport Vessels, and Supply Vessels,[136]

[130] (Opened for signature 2 April 1987, entered into force 15 June 1988) [1988] ATS 42, art 1.1(c)(v). This approach was subsequently adopted in other agreements adopted in the Pacific during the 1990s, including art 1(c)(vi) of the Driftnet Convention and art 1(a)(v) of the *Niue Treaty on Fisheries Surveillance and Law Enforcement Cooperation in the South Pacific Region* (Niue Treaty) (opened for signature 21 December 1992, entered into force 20 May 1993) [1993] ATS 31.

[131] (Opened for signature 30 November 1994, entered into force 23 September 1995) LEX-FAOC067613.

[132] Art 1(d). See also FAO Voluntary Guidelines for Flag State Performance [4].

[133] Since the Compliance Agreement defines 'fishing vessel' to include 'any vessel used or intended for use for the purposes of the commercial exploitation of living marine resources, *including mother ships and any other vessels directly engaged in such fishing operations*' (emphasis added), the flag State obligations apply to support vessels engaged in related activities. Interestingly, Edeson notes that this definition was actually included as a restriction, in order to exclude support vessels not directly engaged in fishing operations and was a point of contention in the negotiations: William Edeson, 'Closing the Gap: The Role of "Soft" International Instruments to Control Fishing' (1999) 20 AustYBIL 83, 88.

[134] Art 18(3)(g) and (h) refer to flag State obligations relating to vessels engaged in fishing related activities and the control of transhipment on the high seas.

[135] While the IPOA-IUU does not include definitions of any relevant terms, a number of its provisions involve the regulation of related activities and support vessels, including: flag State duties with respect to transport vessels and supply vessels (at [48]–[49]); coastal State duties with respect to the authorization and oversight of at-sea transhipment and processing of fish and fish products (at [51]); and port State duties regarding the port access of vessels engaged in fishing related activities (at [55]–[59]).

[136] The Global Record of Fishing Vessels, Refrigerated Transport Vessels and Supply Vessels is a comprehensive and updated online repository which provides a single point for information on vessels used for fishing and fishing-related activities, which has the primary objective of combating IUU fishing: available at <http://www.fao.org/global-record/information-system/en/> accessed 26 November 2020.

the endorsement of the obligations and initiatives referred to in the United Nations General Assembly (UNGA) Resolutions on Sustainable Fisheries,[137] and the scope and substance of constituent instruments or conservation and management measures of regional fisheries management organizations (RFMOs) or arrangements in every ocean.[138]

The international developments are matched by extensive regulation at the national level, where the concept of 'related activities' appears in fisheries legislation as early as 1979.[139] Since national legislation is drawn up to address the conditions, issues, and objectives faced by each coastal State in its own EEZ, different approaches are taken to the regulation of foreign vessels by different countries. However, a comprehensive review of coastal State legislation reveals two related and observable trends: (i) the widespread regulation of a broad range of fishing related activities; and (ii) the application of such regulations to both fishing vessels and fishing support vessels in the EEZ, including those engaged in fishing under licence from the coastal State, and those navigating through the EEZ. These trends are reflected in the practice of States with both coastal and distant water fishing interests, in developed and developing States, and in States located in all regions of the world and from all legal traditions. They are reinforced by the collective practice of States in global, regional, and sub-regional agreements and arrangements, each of which involve different maritime areas, marine species, and member States, but all of which recognize the importance of regulating all the actors and activities that make up the global fishing industry.

More specifically, the practice shows that most coastal States adopt one of two general approaches to fishing related activities in the EEZ, distinguished by the scope of vessels and activities to be regulated. The first approach involves regulating the full range of fishing related activities in the EEZ, including both: (i)

[137] See UNGA Res 75/89 (8 December 2020) UN Doc A/75/89 Preamble [42] and [84], [92], [102] and [121].

[138] In the case of the newer RFMOs, the regulation of fishing related activities and support vessels is provided for in their constituent instruments. See, eg, *Convention on the Conservation and Management of Highly Migratory Fish Stocks in the Western and Central Pacific Ocean* (WCPFC Convention) (opened for signature 5 September 2000, entered into force 19 June 2004) [2004] ATS 15, arts 1(d) and 1(e); *Southern Indian Ocean Fisheries Agreement* (SIOFA Agreement) (opened for signature 29 December 2006, entered into force 13 September 2011) [2012] ATS 21, arts 1(g)(iv) and 1(i); *Convention on the Conservation and Management of Fishery Resources in the South East Atlantic Ocean* (opened for signature 20 April 2001, entered into force 13 April 2003) 2221 UNTS 189, arts 1(h)(iv) and 1(j). While the constituent instruments of older organizations do not refer to such activities and vessels, they are nonetheless commonly regulated in conservation and management measures. See, eg, Indian Ocean Tuna Commission (IOTC), *Resolution 15/04 Concerning the IOTC Record of Vessels Authorized to Operate in the IOTC Area of Competence* [1], available at <http://iotc.org/sites/default/files/documents/compliance/cmm/iotc_cmm_15-04_en.pdf> accessed 27 November 2020; North East Atlantic Fisheries Commission (NEAFC), *NEAFC Scheme of Control and Enforcement, 9 February 2017*, art 1(e) and (f), available at <http://www.neafc.org/scheme/Chapter1/article1> accessed 26 November 2020.

[139] See Sri Lanka, *Act 1979* s 28: 'related activities' in relation to fishing means: '(a) transhipping fish to or from any boat or vessel; (b) storing, processing or transporting fish or aquatic plants obtained from fishing operations; (c) refuelling or resupplying fishing boats or performing other activities in support of, or ancillary to, fishing operations; (d) attempting or preparing to do any of the above.'

'fish-handling' activities, such as processing, packaging, storing, transhipping, and transporting fish up until the first time it is landed; and (ii) activities in support of fishing operations, such as bunkering, resupplying, and providing other logistical services to vessels at sea.[140] This approach is reflected in the domestic practice of roughly half the coastal States, and is the dominant approach in Africa, the Asia-Pacific, and parts of the Caribbean—particularly in areas where collective minimum standards have been established for the regulation of foreign fishing in the EEZ through regional and sub-regional fisheries bodies. While this approach is given effect through national legislation in a variety of ways, in most cases the legislation defines an activity or a vessel in a way that includes all relevant forms of conduct, and then prohibits the conduct of the activity or the use of the vessel without an appropriate authorization or licence.[141]

The second approach involves regulating a sub-set of 'fish-handling' activities only (and not other activities in support of fishing operations). Once again, this approach is reflected in the domestic practice of about half the coastal States, and particularly in the practice of the European Union (EU) member States (who dominate both the Eastern and Western Europe regional groups) and in the Latin American focus on regulating the extraction, processing, and commercialization of the living resources of the EEZ. Leaving aside the collective practice of the EU—and noting the difficulties of obtaining and translating the legislation of foreign countries, and the consequent potential for interpretive errors—there appears to be less uniformity in the way that this approach is given effect in domestic legislation. However, it commonly includes regulation of the on-board processing, packaging, and freezing of fish by factory vessels, the transhipment of catch to refrigerated fish carrier or reefer vessels for transport to port, and the landing of catch, or a sub-set of these activities.[142]

It is worth noting that while activities in support of fishing operations are widely regulated, 'fish-handling' activities are almost *universally* regulated. This reflects the importance of these activities in the modern fishing industry, as well as their significant potential to facilitate illegal fishing by obscuring the real source of the catch and providing a legitimate pathway for its entry to port. In particular,

[140] On the distinction between these two 'functional' categories of fishing related activities, see Schatz, 'Combating Illegal Fishing in the EEZ' (n 4) 389.

[141] See, eg, Mauritius, *Act 2007* s 2: 'related activity' in relation to fishing means 'the operation of a boat, vessel or mother vessel in conjunction with fishing operations and includes—(a) storing, transhipping, processing or transporting of fish or any fish product taken in the maritime zones, or in the course of high seas fishing up to the time it is first landed; (b) refuelling or supplying fishing boats or fishing vessels; or (c) performing any other activity in support of fishing operations.' S 34(1) provides that 'No person shall use a foreign fishing boat or foreign fishing vessel for fishing or any related activity within the maritime zones unless he is the holder of a foreign fishing boat or foreign fishing vessel licence.'

[142] For example, the legislation of some coastal States focuses only on either the processing and 'commercialization' of resources, the conduct of transhipment, or the landing of catch in port, while others regulate all of these activities.

by transhipping at sea, vessels can avoid the scrutiny and enforcement associated with port calls. Accordingly, not only is at-sea transhipment commonly associated with higher incidences of illegal fishing, but it also facilitates other forms of transnational crime including human trafficking, forced labour, and other human rights abuses, as well as drug trafficking.[143] At the international level, this is reflected in the measures adopted by RFMOs and other regional fisheries bodies to regulate the conduct of transhipment,[144] and supported by the programmes established by non-government and civil society organizations to monitor and identify unregulated transhipment.[145] It is also reflected in the national practice of coastal States, which commonly apply additional conditions to transhipment activities—ranging from requirements for case-by-case authorization, the payment of fees, and supervision by authorized observers, to a complete prohibition on at-sea transhipment.

As demonstrated by the practice listed in Table 3.1 and discussed in this Section, these approaches and trends are clearly identifiable in national legislation, particularly in areas where regional fisheries bodies have established collective standards regulating fishing related activities in the EEZ.

3.3.1 Africa

The scale of illegal fishing off the coast of Africa—in particular its impact on the sustainability of marine resources and the economic, political, and social security of the coastal communities that depend upon them—has been well documented,[146] and a wide range of regulatory measures adopted in response, particularly with respect to the fishing related activities that 'enable' illegal fishing,

[143] See Matt Gianni and Walt Simpson, 'Flags of Convenience, Transhipment, Re-Supply and At-Sea Infrastructure in Relation to IUU Fishing' in *Fish Piracy: Combating Illegal, Unreported and Unregulated Fishing* (OECD 2009) 158; Eve de Coning and Alexia Taveau, *Transnational Organized Crime in the Fishing Industry* (UNODC 2011); International Labour Office, *Caught at Sea: Forced Labour and Trafficking* (ILO 2013); Anastasia Telesetsky, 'Laundering Fish in the Global Undercurrents: Illegal, Unreported, and Unregulated Fishing and Transnational Organized Crime' (2014) 41(4) ELQ 939.

[144] Six RFMOs have implemented a ban on transhipment at sea by all or a certain category of vessels. For an excellent overview of this issue, see Christopher Ewell et al, 'Potential Ecological and Social Benefits of a Moratorium on Transhipment on the High Seas' (2017) 81 MarPol 293.

[145] See DA Kroodsma, NA Miller, and A Roan, *The Global View of Transhipment: Preliminary Findings* (Global Fishing Watch and SkyTruth 2017); Lacey Malarky and Beth Lowell, *No More Hiding at Sea: Transhipping Exposed* (Oceana 2017), available at <https://usa.oceana.org/TranshippingExposed> accessed 29 November 2020.

[146] See David J Agnew et al, 'Estimating the Worldwide Extent of Illegal Fishing' (2009) 4(2) PLOS ONE, available at <https://journals.plos.org/plosone/article?id=10.1371/journal.pone.0004570> accessed 29 November 2020; Interpol Environmental Security Sub-Directorate, Study on Fisheries Crime in the West African Coastal Region (2014), available at <https://www.interpol.int/en/content/download/5144/file/INTERPOL%20Study%20on%20Fisheries%20Crime%20in%20the%20West%20African%20Coastal%20Region%20EN.pdf> > accessed 1 August 2021; Environmental Justice Foundation, 'Transhipment at Sea: The Need for a Ban in West Africa' (2013), available at <http://ejfoundation.org/reports/transhipment-at-sea-briefing> accessed 29 November 2020.

Table 3.1 Coastal State approaches to regulating fishing related activities by foreign vessels in the EEZ

	Authorization required for all fishing related activities, including fish-handling activities and activities in support of fishing operations (bunkering and resupply)	Authorization required for fish-handling activities (processing, packaging, transhipping, transporting catch)	Specific regulation/prohibition of transhipment at sea	Relevant legislation and regulations
African Group				
Algeria		X	X	*Law 01-11 of 2001* arts 57, 58
Angola	X		X	*Law 6-A/04 of 2004* arts 5(5),108(d); *Dec 41/05* arts 109–10; *Dec 14/05* arts 47–55
Benin	X			*Dec 2018-335* arts 1(b), 3, 10, 32, 34
Cameroon		X		*Law 94/01* arts 139, 140(1); *Dec 95/413* art 5(2)
Cape Verde	X		X	*Leg Dec 2/2020* arts 3(ii), 8(3), 43
Comoros	X			*Law 82-015* arts 1, 3, 5(f), 21(l)
Congo		X		*Law 2-2000* arts 2, 93
Cote d'Ivoire	X		X	*Law 2016-554* arts 1, 27–8, 41
Equatorial Guinea		X	X	*Law 11/2017* arts 1, 21(1), 30(2), 92, 125
Eritrea	X		X	*Proc 176/2014* arts 3(y), 16(1); *Regs 1998* arts 6(k), 9
Gabon	X		X	*Law 15/2005* arts 5, 18; *Dec 579/PR/MPE* art 47
Gambia	X		X	*Act 2007* ss 2, 23(1); *Regs 2008* s 26(e)
Ghana	X		X	*Act 2002* ss 63(3), 132–3, 140; *Regs 2010* s 33
Guinea	X		X	*Code 2015* arts 7, 66, 83, 122–4
Guinea-Bissau	X			*Dec Law 10/2011* arts 6(3), 35
Kenya	X		X	*Act 2016* ss 2, 84(1)(a), 107
Liberia	X		X	*Law 2019* ss 1.3, 10.1(1)(a), 10.25
Libya			X	*Law 14 of 1989* art 13(i); *Res 71 of 1990* art 11
Madagascar	X		X	*Code 2015* arts 1, 3(a), 40, 60

Continued

Table 3.1 *Continued*

	Authorization required for all fishing related activities, including fish-handling activities and activities in support of fishing operations (bunkering and resupply)	Authorization required for fish-handling activities (processing, packaging, transhipping, transporting catch)	Specific regulation/prohibition of transhipment at sea	Relevant legislation and regulations
Mauritania	X			*Law 2015-017* arts 4, 34
Mauritius	X		X	*Act 2007* ss 2, 34(1), 39
Morocco			X	*Law 15-12* art 4
Mozambique	X			*Law 22/2013* Glossary, art 39(1)
Namibia		X	X	*Act 2000* ss 50, 52(3)(3); *Regs 2001* ss 36(2) and (3)
Nigeria				*Act 1992* s 1; *Act 1969* s 4(1) (licence required for fishing, discharging fish, and bunkering in the EEZ)
Sao Tome & Principe	X			*Law 9/2001* arts 4, 30; *Dec 28/2012* art 30
Senegal	X		X	*Code 2015* arts 8, 55–6
Seychelles	X		X	*Act 2014* ss 3(2), 11(1); *Regs 1987* s 5
Sierra Leone	X		X	*Act 2018* ss 1, 14(1)(a); *Regs 2019* s 31
Somalia	X			*Law 2016* arts 2, 15
South Africa	X		X	*Act 1998* ss 1, 39(1); *Regs 1998* s 85
Tanzania	X		X	*Act 2020* ss 3, 39, 46(1)
Togo	X		X	*Law 2016-026* arts 2(a) and (b), 30, 44, 86–90
Tunisia			X	*Law 94-13* arts 15–16
Asia-Pacific Group				
Bangladesh	X		X	*Act 2020* s 24; *Rules 1983* s 8(e)
Brunei	X			*Order 2009* ss 2, 17(1), 35
Cambodia			X	*Law 2006* arts 47, 64
China	X			*Prov Regs 1999* arts 8, 9
Chinese Taipei	X			*Act 2016* arts 4,11, 12 (as a flag State)

Table 3.1 *Continued*

	Authorization required for all fishing related activities, including fish-handling activities and activities in support of fishing operations (bunkering and resupply)	Authorization required for fish-handling activities (processing, packaging, transhipping, transporting catch)	Specific regulation/prohibition of transhipment at sea	Relevant legislation and regulations
Cook Islands	X		X	*Act 2005* ss 2, 20(1), 37; *Regs 2012* ss 31–6
Fiji	X		X	*Dec 2012* arts 2(1), 33(2); *Regs 2014* ss 34–6
India	X			*Act 1981* ss 2(c), 3; *Rules 1982* s 3(4)
Indonesia		X	X	*Law 2004* arts 1(1), (5) and (9), 26(1), 27(2), 28(2); *Reg 57/2014*
Iran	X			*Law 1995* arts 3(1) and (3), 7
Japan	X		X	*Act 1996* arts 2(2), 9; *Act 2001* art 6
Kiribati	X			*Act 2010* ss 3, 12
Korea	X		X	*Fishing Act 1996* arts 2(4), 5(1), 11
Malaysia	X		X	*Act 1985* ss 2, 15(2)
Maldives	X		X	*Act 2019* ss 73(a), 88(a)
Marshall Islands	X		X	51 *MIRC* §§102(56), 409; *Regs 1998* s 4(1)(a)
Micronesia	X		X	24 *FSM Code* §§102(56), 103, 407
Myanmar		X		*Law 1989* ss 2(p) and (q), Chapter III, 32(a)
Nauru	X		X	*Act 1997* ss 2, 24(1); *Regs 1997* s 30(3)
Niue	X			*Act 1996* ss 2(1), 18(2)
Oman		X	X	*Law 2019* arts 9, 44, 37
Pakistan		X	X	*Act 1975* arts 2(d), 3; *Deep Sea Policy 2018* 6(2)(h)
Palau	X			27 *PNC* §§102(j), 203
Papua New Guinea	X		X	*Act 1998* ss 2(1), 39, 46(1); *Reg 2000* s 25
Philippines	X		X	*Code 1998* ss 41, 42, 86

Continued

Table 3.1 *Continued*

	Authorization required for all fishing related activities, including fish-handling activities and activities in support of fishing operations (bunkering and resupply)	Authorization required for fish-handling activities (processing, packaging, transhipping, transporting catch)	Specific regulation/prohibition of transhipment at sea	Relevant legislation and regulations
Qatar		X		*Law 4 of 1983* arts 1, 10; *Exec Reg 2 of 1985* arts 30, 31*bis*, 31*bis*(2)
Samoa	X		X	*Act 2016* ss 2(1), 26(1), 44
Solomon Islands	X		X	*Act 2015* ss 2(1), 43(1)(a) and (g), 60–2
Sri Lanka	X		X	*Act 1979* ss 4, 28; *Regs 1981* s 8
Thailand		X	X	*Ordinance BE 2558, 2015* ss 5, 36, 86–8
Timor-Leste	X		X	*Dec Law 2004* arts 1(aa), 22(2), 103; *Dec 5/2004* art 151
Tonga	X		X	*Act 2002* ss 2(1), 38(1); *Regs 1992* s 26
Tuvalu	X		X	*Act 2006* ss 2, 13(1), 33
United Arab Emirates		X		*Law 23 of 1999* arts 44, 49
Vanuatu	X		X	*Act 2014* ss 1, 59(1), 104–5
Vietnam				*Law 2017* arts 3(18) and (19), 60(1) (licence required for fishing and 'fishing logistics', which includes transport of fish)
Yemen	X			*Law 2 of 2006* arts 2, 4(a), 9(3)
Eastern Europe Group				
Albania		X	X	*Law 64/2012* arts 4(1), 68(1), 85
European Union		X	X	*Reg 1380/2013* art 4(1)(28); *Reg 1005/2008* arts 2(1) and (2); *Reg 1224/2009* art 20(1)
Montenegro		X	X	*Law 2009* arts 4 (26) and (28), 111
Russia	X		X	*Act 1998* arts 4(1), 10(1), 12(4), 40

Table 3.1 *Continued*

	Authorization required for all fishing related activities, including fish-handling activities and activities in support of fishing operations (bunkering and resupply)	Authorization required for fish-handling activities (processing, packaging, transhipping, transporting catch)	Specific regulation/prohibition of transhipment at sea	Relevant legislation and regulations
Latin America and the Caribbean Group				
Antigua & Barbuda	X			*Act 2006* ss 2, 27(1)
Argentina		X		*Law 24.922 of 1998* arts 2, 25, 46
Bahamas		X		*Info Bulletin 155* paras 2.1, 5.5 (as a flag State)
Barbados	X			*Act 1993* ss 2, 8(1)
Belize	X		X	*Act 2020* ss 2, 28, 39
Brazil		X	X	*Law 11.959 of 2009* arts 4, 10, 12, 24
Chile		X		*Law 1991* arts 1, 2(1), (2) and (30), 14
Colombia		X	X	*Statute 13 of 1990* arts 3, 30, 54(1), (8), and (9)
Costa Rica		X	X	*Law 8436 of 2005* arts 2(2), 7, 41, 149
Dominica	X		X	*Act 1987* ss 2, 8(1)
Dominican Republic		X	X	*Law 307-04* arts 2(II), 14–15, 39(1)
Ecuador	X		X	*Law 2020* arts 7(3) and (4), 65, 95
El Salvador		X	X	*Law 2001* arts 6(19) and (30), 23–4, 34; *Reg 38 of 2007* art 63
Grenada	X		X	*Act 1986* ss 2, 8(1); *Regs 1987* s 6
Guyana	X		X	*Act 2012* ss 2(2)(g), 18(1)
Honduras		X	X	*Dec 106-2015* arts 5, 68
Jamaica	X			*Act 2018* ss 2, 25(1)(a)
Mexico		X		*Law 2007* arts 76–7
Nicaragua		X		*Law 2004* arts 7, 12, 38

Continued

Table 3.1 *Continued*

	Authorization required for all fishing related activities, including fish-handling activities and activities in support of fishing operations (bunkering and resupply)	Authorization required for fish-handling activities (processing, packaging, transhipping, transporting catch)	Specific regulation/prohibition of transhipment at sea	Relevant legislation and regulations
Panama	X		X	*Law 204 of 2021* arts 1, 11, 32, 62
Peru		X	X	*Law 25977 of 1992* arts 19, 27, 76(1)–(2) and (8); *Dec 012/2001/PE* art 71
Saint Kitts and Nevis	X		X	*Act 2016* ss 2(1), 63(1)(a), 78–9
Saint Lucia	X		X	*Act 1984* ss 2, 8(1); *Regs 1994* s 13(c)
Saint Vincent & Grenadines	X		X	*Act 1986* ss 2, 8(1); *Regs 1987* s 6(1)(c)
Trinidad & Tobago	X			*Act 1986* ss 2, 26(1)
Uruguay		X	X	*Law 19.175 of 2013* arts 4, 9, 20; *Dec 115/018* art 4
Venezuela	X			*Dec Law 1,408 of 2014* arts 15(1), (9) and (25), 25
Western Europe and Others Group				
Australia	X		X	*Act 1991* ss 4(1), 100, 103
Canada	X			*Act 1985* ss 2(1), 4(1); *Regs 2014* s 5(1)(a)
France (Mayotte)	X		X	*Dec 2010-727* art 1; *Code* art L945-2
France (New Caledonia)	X		X	*Deliberation 50/CP 2011* arts 2, 5, 9
France (SAAT)		X		*Code* arts L958-5, L-958-8
Iceland		X		*Act 1998* arts 1–3
New Zealand	X		X	*Act 1996* ss 2(1), 83(1) and (4)(f); *Regs 2001* s 27
NZ (Tokelau)	X		X	*Act 1977* s 2; *Regs 2012* regs 6, 33
Norway		X	X	*Dec 2 of 1977* s 1; *Regs 2010* s 7

Table 3.1 *Continued*

	Authorization required for all fishing related activities, including fish-handling activities and activities in support of fishing operations (bunkering and resupply)			
		Authorization required for fish-handling activities (processing, packaging, transhipping, transporting catch)		
			Specific regulation/prohibition of transhipment at sea	
				Relevant legislation and regulations
United Kingdom		X	X	*Act 2020* s 52; *Act 1967* s 4A
UK (Falklands)	X		X	*Ordinance 2005* ss 2(1), 8(3), 46; *Regs 1987* Part IV
UK (Montserrat)	X			*Act 2000* ss 2, 14(1)
UK (Pitcairn)	X			*Ordinance 2016* ss 3, 8, 24(1)(a)
UK (SGSSI)		X	X	*Ordinance 2000* ss 2, 6(2); *Regs 1990* s 3
UK (Turks & Caicos)			X	*Regs 1998* s 33
United States	X		X	16 *USC* 38 §1824(a) and (d); 50 *CFR* §§600.10, 600.501

Notes

a. The practice of EU member States is examined by reference to EU regulations.

such as transhipment and bunkering at sea.[147] In addition, the practice of coastal States in the western and eastern parts of Africa is clearly influenced by the collective minimum standards for the regulation of foreign fishing in the EEZ established through regional and sub-regional fisheries bodies.

On the west coast of Africa, the seven members of the Sub-Regional Fisheries Commission (SRFC) have collectively agreed the *Convention on the Determination of the Minimal Conditions for Access and Exploitation of Marine Resources within the Maritime Areas under the Jurisdiction of the Member States of the Sub-Regional Fisheries Commission (SRFC)* (SRFC MCA Convention),[148] pursuant to which the activities of all factory vessels, support vessels, and reefer vessels operating in the

[147] See, eg, *ITLOS Pleadings, Minutes and Documents, Vol 22* (2015) *SRFC Advisory Opinion,* Written pleadings of the SRFC; Ndiaye, *IUU Fishing* (n 7).

[148] (Opened for signature 8 June 2012, entered into force 16 September 2012). The members of the SRFC are Cape Verde, Gambia, Guinea, Guinea-Bissau, Mauritania, Senegal, and Sierra Leone.

EEZ must be regulated, and foreign vessels may only tranship in designated ports unless a specific exemption is granted.[149] This approach is reflected in Section 14 of Sierra Leone's *Fisheries and Aquaculture Act 2018,* which provides that a valid licence or authorization is required for the conduct of fishing or 'related activities', defined in Section 1 to include: '(a) refuelling or supplying fishing vessels or performing other activities in support of fishing operations; (b) transhipping, storing, processing or transporting fish or fish products up to the time they are first landed; (c) on-shore storing, or processing fish or fish products from the time they first landed; and (d) attempting or preparing to do any of the above activities.'

The legislation of the other SRFC members has a similar approach and effect.[150] The area covered by the EEZs of member States of the SRFC and other regional and sub-regional fisheries bodies in Africa is depicted in Figure 3.1.

Immediately to the south of the SRFC, the six members of the Fisheries Committee for the West Central Gulf of Guinea (FCWC) have taken a similar approach, establishing the *Convention on Minimum Requirements for Access to the Fishery Resources of the Area of the Fisheries Committee for the West Central Gulf of Guinea* (FCWC MRA Convention),[151] which provides that foreign fishing vessels—defined to include all support ships and carrier vessels—may not fish or carry out transhipment or support operations in the EEZ of a member State unless they are listed on the sub-regional register of authorized vessels, and that transhipment at sea is prohibited except in emergency situations.[152] This approach is reflected in Section 10(1)(a) of Liberia's *Fisheries and Aquaculture Management and Development Law 2019*, which provides that a valid and applicable authorization is required to use a fishing vessel or reefer for industrial fishing or 'related activities', defined in Section 1.3 to include: '(a) storing, transhipping, processing or transporting fish or fish products up to the time they are first landed; (b) onshore storing, buying, or processing fish or fish products from the time they are first landed; (c) refuelling or supplying fishing vessels, selling or supplying fishing equipment or performing other activities in support of fishing operations; (d) exporting fish or fish products from the country, and (e) attempting or preparing to do any of the above.'

The regulations of the other FCWC members have a similar scope and effect.[153]

On the eastern coast of Africa, the twelve members of the South West Indian Ocean Fisheries Commission (SWIOFC) have established the *Guidelines for Minimum Terms and Conditions (MTC) for Foreign Fisheries Access in the South*

[149] SRFC MCA Convention arts 4, 7, and 26.
[150] See Table 3.1.
[151] (Signed 13 December 2013). The members of the FCWC are Benin, Côte d'Ivoire, Ghana, Liberia, Nigeria, and Togo.
[152] FCWC MRA Convention arts 1, 7, and 16.
[153] See Table 3.1. The exception is Nigeria, which only regulates 'fish-handling' activities (*Act 1992* s 1), but bunkering activities nonetheless require a licence under s 4(1) of the *Petroleum Act 1969.*

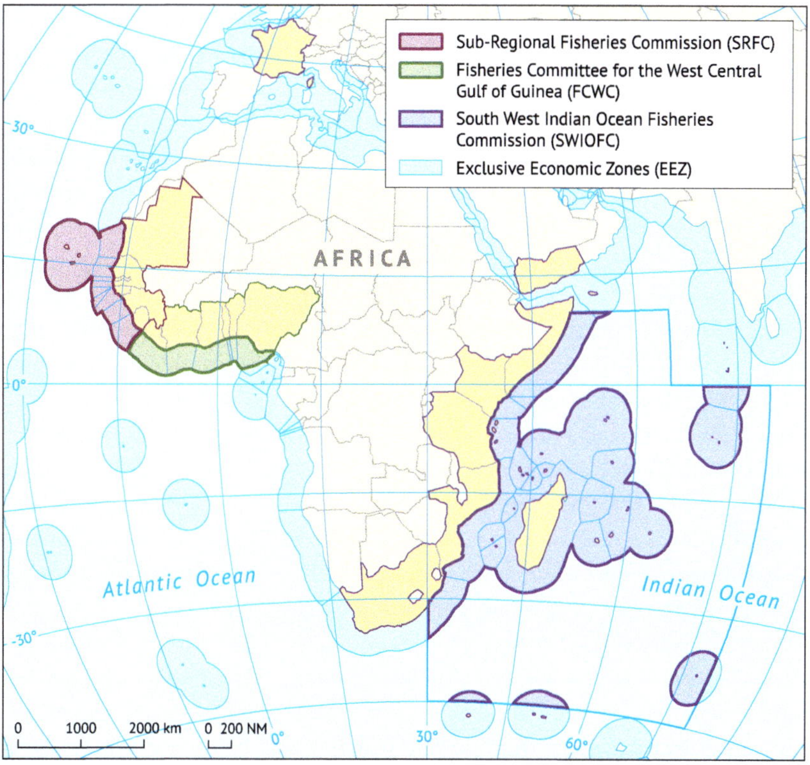

Figure 3.1 EEZs of the members of regional and sub-regional fisheries bodies in Africa

Notes

Created using Natural Earth raster and vector map data available at <http://naturalearthdata.com> and the Flanders Marine Institute Maritime Boundaries Geodatabase, *Maritime Boundaries and Exclusive Economic Zones* (200NM) (Version 11, 2019) available at <http://www.marineregions.org/>.

West Indian Ocean Fisheries Commission (SWIOFC) Region (SWIOFC MTCs),[154] which provide that all foreign fishing vessels, including supply and transport vessels, operating in the EEZs of a member State in regards to tuna and tuna-like species should possess a valid licence issued by the participating State, and that transhipment should only take place in ports.[155] These requirements are consistent

[154] (Finalized by the SWIOFC bureau and circulated to all Parties by the Secretariat on 18 February 2019). The members of SWIOFC are Comoros, France (Mayotte), Kenya, Madagascar, Maldives, Mauritius, Mozambique, Seychelles, Somalia, South Africa, Tanzania, and Yemen. The SWIOFC includes three members who are from outside the African region pursuant to formal UN geographic groupings, but whose practice is consistent with that of the African region members: France (on behalf of Mayotte) is in the Western Europe and Others Group, and Maldives and Yemen are in the Asia-Pacific Group. As SWIOFC was established under art VI of the FAO Constitution, it only has an advisory function and cannot adopt binding instruments.

[155] SWIOFC MTCs arts 5 and 20.

with Section 84(1) of Kenya's *Fisheries Management and Development Act 2016* which provides that a valid licence is required for the conduct of any 'fishing related activities' in the EEZ, defined in Section 2 to mean any activity in support of, or in preparation for, fishing including: '(a) transhipping of fish to or from any vessel; (b) landing, packaging, processing, handling or transporting of fish that have not been previously landed at port; (c) provision of personnel, fuel, gear and other supplies at sea or performing other activities in support of fishing operations; (d) exporting fish or fish products from the country; and (e) attempting or preparing to do any of the above.'

The legislation of all other SWIOFC members contains provisions with a similar substance and effect,[156] as does the legislation of a number of other coastal States who are not members of any of these regional fisheries bodies, namely Angola, Eritrea, Gabon, and Sao Tome and Principe.[157] In addition, the majority of all the African countries so far examined have also enacted further specific provisions relating to the conduct of transhipment—such as requiring advance notification and authorization to be sought on a case-by-case basis, requiring that transhipment take place in port or under the supervision of an authorized observer, and imposing fees and reporting requirements.[158]

There are also a small number of African coastal States—principally in northern and central Africa—whose legislation only extends to the regulation of 'fish-handling' activities. The legislation of most of these States is focused principally on regulating the conduct of landing and transhipment of catch, whether by placing a complete prohibition on at-sea transhipment or regulating it through licensing or authorization requirements. In Morocco, for example: '[e]xcept in the case of *force majeure* or distress, transhipment operations at sea of fishery products between foreign fishing vessels or between a Moroccan fishing vessel and a foreign fishing vessel are prohibited in the [EEZ] and must take place exclusively in a Moroccan port . . . '.[159] The legislation of Algeria, the Republic of Congo, Equatorial Guinea, Libya, and Tunisia contains similar prohibitions, Cameroon's legislation regulates the landing of catch (but does not refer to transhipment), and Namibia prohibits the conduct of transhipment outside a port except in accordance with the conditions of a valid licence or authorization, and subject to the payment of relevant fees and charges.[160]

156 See Table 3.1.
157 Ibid.
158 Ibid.
159 Morocco, *Law 15-12* art 4.
160 Ibid.

3.3.2 Asia-Pacific

Regulation of the full spectrum of fishing related activities and fishing support vessels is also the dominant approach in the Asia-Pacific region, where the influence of collective standards is similarly evident in the practice of the seventeen members of the Pacific Islands Forum Fisheries Agency (FFA)[161] whose EEZs cover the vast area depicted in Figure 3.2.

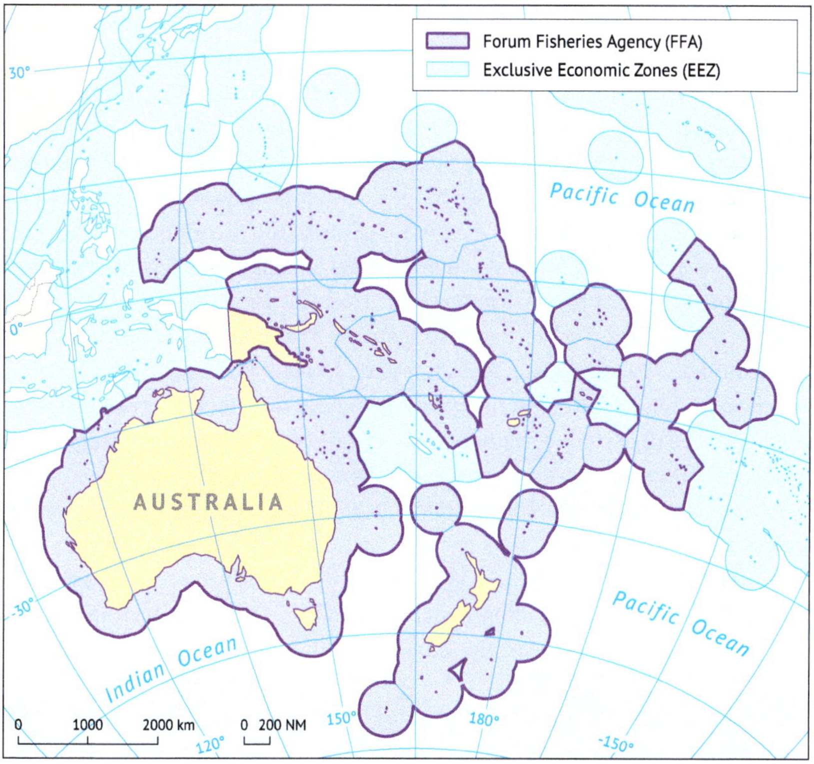

Figure 3.2 EEZs of the members of the Pacific Islands Forum Fisheries Agency

Notes

Created using Natural Earth raster and vector map data available at <http://naturalearthdata.com> and the Flanders Marine Institute Maritime Boundaries Geodatabase, *Maritime Boundaries and Exclusive Economic Zones* (200NM) (Version 11, 2019) available at <http://www.marineregions.org/>.

[161] Australia, Cook Islands, Micronesia, Fiji, Kiribati, Nauru, New Zealand, Niue, Palau, Papua New Guinea, Marshall Islands, Samoa, the Solomon Islands, Tokelau, Tonga, Tuvalu, and Vanuatu. Pursuant to the UN geographic groupings used in Table 3.1, FFA members Australia and New Zealand (both on its own behalf and on behalf of Tokelau) are from the Western Europe and Others Group.

The FFA members have adopted *Harmonized Minimum Terms and Conditions for Access by Fishing Vessels* (FFA Harmonized MTCs), which provide that foreign fishing vessels and support vessels may not be granted a licence to operate in the EEZ of a member State unless they are in 'good standing' on the Regional Register of Foreign Fishing Vessels, and include particular conditions for the monitoring and control of transhipment.[162] This is given effect in the national legislation of most FFA members through authorization or licensing requirements. A typical example is Samoa's *Fisheries Management Act 2016*, which provides that a foreign fishing vessel must not be used for fishing or related activities except under a licence or fisheries treaty, and defines 'related activities' to include: '(a) transhipment of fish or fish products to or from any vessel; (b) storing, processing, or transporting from fishery waters up to the time the fish or fish products are first landed; (c) refuelling or supplying fishing vessels or performing other activities in support of fishing operations.'

Provisions with similar effect are found in the legislation of the other FFA members in the Asia-Pacific region.[163] In the legislation of those FFA members that are also party to the sub-regional FSM Arrangement, the definition of 'fishing related activities' is extended beyond activities at sea to include the 'on-shore storing, buying or processing of fish or fish products from the time they are first landed', consistent with Article 1(1) of that arrangement.[164] Pursuant to Article 6 of the FFA Harmonized MTCs, at-sea transhipment is prohibited in the EEZs of FFA members except in certain prescribed circumstances, and vessels wishing to tranship are required to provide seventy-two hours' notice, pay all fees, tranship only at the designated time and port, and submit relevant reports upon completion. This is also reflected in further, specific requirements in the legislation of most of the FFA members.[165]

In contrast to the Pacific Island countries' firmly established regional approach to the regulation of foreign fishing vessels in the EEZ, there is little in the way of collective or regional practice in the broader Asian and Middle-Eastern parts of the Asia-Pacific region.[166] The practice of coastal States in this region may be influenced by their participation in the *Regional Plan of Action to Promote Responsible Fishing Practices including Combating Illegal, Unreported and Unregulated Fishing in the Region* (RPOA-IUU)[167] or membership of the Western and Central Pacific

[162] (Adopted in April 1990, as amended May 2019) annex 4 [3.1] and art 7. The FFA Harmonized MTCs are regularly revised and updated.

[163] See Table 3.1.

[164] See the legislation of the FSM Arrangement members (Micronesia, Kiribati, Nauru, Papua New Guinea, Marshall Islands, the Solomon Islands, and Tuvalu) in Table 3.1.

[165] See Table 3.1.

[166] In this context, the terms 'Pacific', 'Asian', and 'Middle Eastern' are used to distinguish between the three broad geographic areas that together make up the 'Asia-Pacific' Regional Group in the UN system.

[167] The RPOA-IUU is a voluntary instrument adopted by eleven countries (Australia, Brunei, Cambodia, Indonesia, Malaysia, Papua New Guinea, Philippines, Singapore, Thailand, Timor-Leste, and Vietnam) in order to enhance and strengthen fisheries management in the region, and to prevent, deter, and eliminate IUU fishing in the Southern and Eastern South China Sea and Sulu-Sulawesi Seas,

Fisheries Commission (WCPFC).[168] However, there are no regionally agreed standards or measures regarding the regulation of foreign fishing in the EEZs of the Asian countries. Nonetheless, the fisheries legislation of coastal States in this region demonstrates a long and widespread practice of regulating all fishing related activities and fishing support vessels in the EEZ.

Some Asia-Pacific coastal States have adopted a broad definition of 'fishing' that includes all related activities, for which a licence is required. This is reflected in the Republic of Korea's *Act on the Exercise of Sovereign Rights on Foreigners' Fishing Etc within the Exclusive Economic Zone 1996*, in which 'fishery activities' are defined in Article 2(4) to include 'fisheries or a search and gathering activity related to fisheries; keeping, storage, and processing of fishery products; transportation of the catch and its products; supply of materials necessary for vessels; and other acts related to fisheries', and a licence is required for each foreign vessel engaged in fishery activities in the EEZ, pursuant to Article 5. A similar approach is taken by Iran and (as a flag State regulating the activities of its own vessels in the EEZs of other States) the fishing entity of Chinese Taipei.[169]

Other countries use the term 'fishing vessel' to regulate a similarly broad category of activities—such as Brunei's *Fisheries Order 2009*, which provides in Section 17 that no foreign fishing vessel shall be used for fishing without a licence, and defines 'fishing vessel' in Section 2 to mean 'any vessel which is used for, equipped to be used for, or of a type used for (a) fishing; or (b) aiding or assisting any vessel in the performance of any activity related to fishing, including any of the activities of preparation, processing, refrigeration, storage, supply or transportation of fish'. The legislation of Malaysia, Palau, and the Philippines is similarly crafted.[170]

Some States require that a permit or authorization be obtained in order to engage in a defined category of 'related activities' (or other similar terms). For example, pursuant to Section 4 of Sri Lanka's *Foreign Fishing Boat Act 1979*, 'no foreign fishing boat shall be used for fishing or related activities in Sri Lankan waters except under the authority of a permit'; Article 9 of Japan's *Act on the Exercise of Sovereign Rights concerning Fisheries in the Exclusive Economic Zone 1996*

the Gulf of Thailand, and the Arafura-Timor Seas. In 2010, a study for the RPOA-IUU produced a Framework for Model Fisheries Legislation in South East Asia, which proposed that foreign fishing vessels be prohibited from engaging in fishing or related activities (defined to include all ancillary activities) in the EEZ without a valid licence: available at <http://rpoaiuu.org/model-fisheries-legislation/> accessed 29 November 2020.

168 WCPFC members in the Asia-Pacific include all FFA members as well as China, Chinese Taipei, Japan, Korea, Philippines, and Indonesia. Thailand and Vietnam are cooperating non-members. Pursuant to art 1(e) of the WCPFC Convention, 'fishing vessel' means 'any vessel used or intended for use for the purpose of fishing, *including support ships, carrier vessels and any other vessel directly involved in such fishing operations*' (emphasis added). Since coastal State members of the WCPFC are required to apply conservation and management measures to waters within national jurisdiction, this could potentially influence national legislation regulating fishing related activities in the EEZ.

169 See Table 3.1.

170 Ibid.

provides that foreign nationals intending to engage in 'fishery incidental acts' in the EEZ must obtain authorization for each vessel engaging in such acts; and Article 22(2) of Timor-Leste's *Decree-Law on the General Bases of the Legal Regime for the Management and Regulation of Fisheries and Aquaculture 2004* states that 'fishing vessels engaged in fishing related operations shall be equally subject to a fishing related operations permit in accordance with the provisions of applicable regulations.'[171]

Another approach, the implementation of which is more varied, is to specify the particular related activities or support vessels to which regulations apply. For example, pursuant to Section 24 of the Bangladesh *Marine Fisheries Act 2020* it is an offence for a foreign fishing vessel to load, unload, transfer, or tranship fish, or load or unload fuel or supplies without a licence. Another example is found in China's *Provisional Regulations on Foreigners and Foreign Fishing Vessels in the Jurisdictional Waters of the People's Republic of China 1999*, which provide that:

> Article 8. Aliens and foreign ships within the waters under the jurisdiction of the People's Republic of China shall not, without the approval of the fishery and fishing harbor supervision and administration bureau of the People's Republic of China, distribute the catch and their products or supplies within the ship.
>
> Article 9. The foreign fish cargo ship and the supply ship that have been approved for reproduction shall, according to regulations, declare to the relevant fishery and fishing port supervision and administration authorities of the People's Republic of China the time and place of the inspection of the fish stock or supply in the waters under the jurisdiction of the People's Republic of China including the name of the ship, the amount of the fish, the quantity of the ship, or the major supply items and quantities. At the end of the transhipment or refueling, the exact number of rebates should be declared.

Notwithstanding the variety of terms and approaches adopted in this region, the legislation demonstrates the clear intent of the majority of coastal States to regulate all types of fishing related activities, including both fish-handling activities and activities that support the operation of fishing vessels. In addition, there is once again a widespread practice of imposing additional regulation on the conduct of transhipment in the EEZ (or prohibiting its conduct at sea).[172]

[171] The term 'fishing related operations' is defined in art 1(aa) to include: 'the transhipment of catches or of fish products from one vessel to another and the storing or the processing of such products aboard, as well as the maritime transportation of any marine species caught in national maritime waters until the first port of disembarkation, the maritime transport from/to fishing sites or the supply of provisions, fuel and other products to fishing vessels or any other logistical activity of support to such vessels when they take place at sea.'

[172] See Table 3.1.

As in the African region, there is also a small but significant group of States whose legislation regulates only on fish-handling activities. While the legislation of Cambodia and Pakistan is focused on transport and transhipment (including a ban on transhipment at sea),[173] other States in this group use a licensing or authorization requirement to regulate a broader range of fish-handling activities including the processing, storing, receiving, transferring, and transporting of fish in the EEZ. For example, pursuant to Section 44 of Oman's *Law on Living Aquatic Resources 2019*, activities relating to living aquatic resources (which require a permit under Section 9) include the preparation, manufacturing, drying, smoking, transporting, marketing, cooling, freezing, storage, export, and import of living aquatic resources. Provisions of similar effect are found in the legislation of Indonesia, Myanmar, Qatar, Thailand, and Vietnam, including (in the case of Indonesia and Thailand) additional conditions regarding the conduct of transhipment at sea.[174]

3.3.3 Eastern Europe

There are two very distinct approaches to the regulation of fishing related activities in the Eastern Europe group: that of the EU, and that of the Russian Federation.

Since almost all the coastal States in Eastern Europe are members of—or candidates for membership of—the EU,[175] their practice generally follows the relevant EU regulations, which only address fish-handling activities (and not other activities in support of fishing vessels) in the EEZ. Article 4 of *Regulation (EU) No 1380/2013 of the European Parliament and of the Council of 11 December 2013 on the Common Fisheries Policy* defines 'fishing activity' to mean 'searching for fish, shooting, setting, towing, hauling of a fishing gear, taking catch on board, transhipping, retaining on board, processing on board, transferring, caging, fattening and landing of fish and fishery products'. Pursuant to Article 2(1)(a) of *Council Regulation (EC) No 1005/2008 of 29 September 2008 Establishing a Community System to Prevent, Deter and Eliminate Illegal, Unreported and Unregulated Fishing* (Regulation 1005/2008), fishing activities that are conducted in waters under the jurisdiction of a State without its permission or in contravention of its regulations constitute 'illegal fishing'—and therefore IUU fishing, attracting serious consequences. Waters under the jurisdiction of EU member States are shown in Figure 3.3, which depicts the EEZs appurtenant to the metropolitan territory and

173 Ibid.

174 Ibid.

175 EU member States in the Eastern Europe group are Bulgaria, Croatia, Estonia, Latvia, Lithuania, Poland, Romania, and Slovenia. The EU regulations also represent the practice of EU members in other regional groups: Cyprus in the Asia-Pacific group; and Belgium, Denmark, Finland, France, Germany, Greece, Ireland, Italy, Malta, Netherlands, Portugal, Spain, and Sweden in the Western Europe and Others group.

Figure 3.3 EEZs of the members of the European Union

Notes

Created using Natural Earth raster and vector map data available at <http://naturalearthdata.com> and the Flanders Marine Institute Maritime Boundaries Geodatabase, *Maritime Boundaries and Exclusive Economic Zones* (200NM) (Version 11, 2019) available at <http://www.marineregions.org/>.

outermost territories of EU member States (collectively, 'Union waters') as well as their overseas territories.[176]

While EU fisheries regulations do not generally apply to the activities of other foreign-flagged fishing support vessels (such as bunkering and resupply vessels) in the EEZ, the importance of regulating a broad range of fishing related activities is implicitly acknowledged in Regulation 1005/2008, in which a 'fishing vessel' is defined to include 'any vessel of any size used or intended for use for the purposes of commercial exploitation of fishery resources, including support ships, fish processing vessels, vessels engaged in transhipment and carrier vessels equipped for the transportation of fishery products, except container vessels', and a fishing vessel is presumed to have engaged in IUU fishing if it has 'supported or resupplied other fishing vessels identified as having engaged in IUU fishing'.[177] The EU's

[176] As defined in art 4.1(1) of *Reg 1380/2013*, 'Union waters' means waters under the sovereignty or jurisdiction of the EU member States, with the exception of the waters adjacent to the territories listed in Annex II to the *Treaty on the Functioning of the European Union* (signed 13 December 2007, entered into force 1 December 2009) OJ C 326/47.

[177] Arts 2(5) and 3(1)(j). The role of support vessels is also acknowledged in the preamble to *Reg 1380/2013* (at [16]), which states: 'Support vessels may have a substantial impact on the way fishing vessels are able to carry out their operations and on the quantity of fish they can retrieve. It is therefore necessary to take them into account in the authorization and reporting processes set out in this Regulation.'

strong focus on combating IUU fishing is also reflected in its strict controls on transhipment. Article 20 of *Council Regulation (EC) No 1224/2009 Establishing a Community Control System for Ensuring Compliance with the Rules of the Common Fisheries Policy* prohibits transhipment at sea in 'Union waters' unless conducted in designated ports or places close to the shore of member States, pursuant to an authorization and subject to strict conditions.

The fisheries legislation of Albania and Montenegro—both candidates for EU membership—is similarly directed toward the regulation of fish-handling activities and also includes strict requirements for the conduct of transhipment (which in the case of Montenegro, is prohibited at sea, and in the case of Albania, requires authorization and is subject to conditions).[178] In contrast, a broader approach is adopted in the laws of the Russian Federation, which regulate all fishing related activities (including both fish-handling activities and other activities in support of fishing operations). Pursuant to Article 10(1) of the *Federal Act on the Exclusive Economic Zone of the Russian Federation 1998*, both Russians and foreign nationals must obtain licences from the relevant federal executive body in order to engage in the 'commercial exploitation of living resources', defined in Article 4(1) as: 'a comprehensive process including searching for and fishing (harvesting) aquatic biological resources, accepting, processing, transporting, storing and reloading products and supplying commercial vessels and facilities with fuel, water, food, packing material and other materials.' In addition, specific regulation of transhipment is provided under Article 12(4), pursuant to which both Russian and foreign vessels may not load, unload, or transfer living resources of any species caught in the EEZ except as provided for in their licences, and any such loading, unloading, or transfer must be supervised by an authorized official.

3.3.4 Latin America and the Caribbean

The regulation of fishing related activities in Latin America and the Caribbean is characterized by a clear distinction between the practice of the Latin American States—who regulate fish-handling activities only—and that of the Caribbean States, who were amongst the earliest coastal States to develop a collective approach to regulating the conduct of a defined set of fishing related activities.

In the 1980s, the ten members of the Organization of Eastern Caribbean States (OECS)[179] developed harmonized fisheries legislation that included almost

[178] See Table 3.1.

[179] The OECS is a ten member group of islands in the Eastern Caribbean region. The members are Anguilla, Antigua and Barbuda, the British Virgin Islands, Dominica, Saint Kitts and Nevis, Grenada, Montserrat, Saint Lucia, Saint Vincent and the Grenadines, and Martinique. Since Anguilla, the British Virgin Islands, and Montserrat are British overseas territories, and Martinique is an overseas department of France, their practice falls formally within the Western Europe and Others Group.

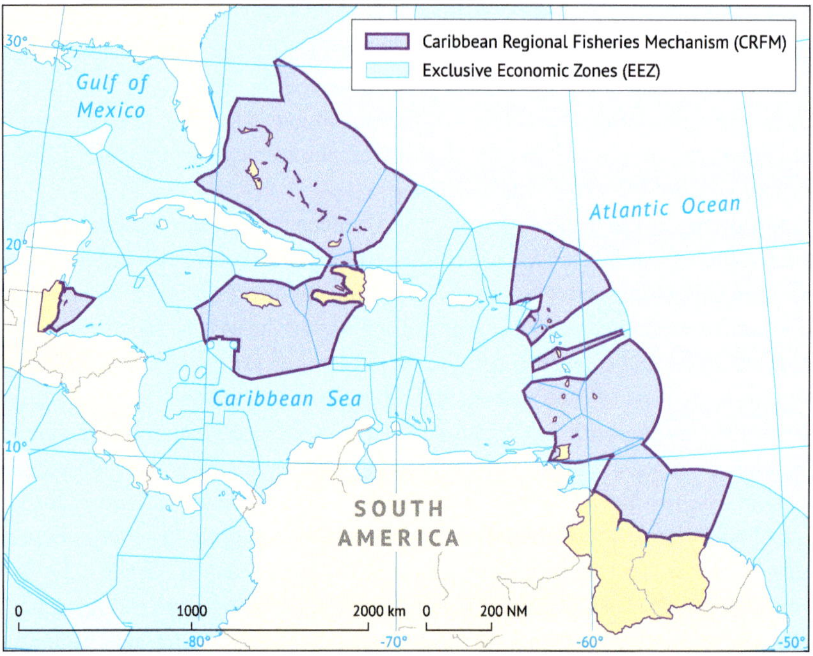

Figure 3.4 EEZs of the members of the Caribbean Regional Fisheries Mechanism

Notes

Created using Natural Earth raster and vector map data available at <http://naturalearthdata.com> and the Flanders Marine Institute Maritime Boundaries Geodatabase, *Maritime Boundaries and Exclusive Economic Zones* (200NM) (Version 11, 2019) available at <http://www.marineregions.org/>.

identical provisions prohibiting any foreign fishing vessel from engaging in fishing or 'related activities' without a foreign fishing licence. These provisions are still evident in the laws of the OECS members, as well as amongst the broader membership of the Caribbean Regional Fisheries Mechanism (CRFM), whose EEZs are depicted in Figure 3.4.[180]

For example, Section 8 of Grenada's *Fisheries Act 1986* provides that 'no foreign vessel shall be used for fishing or related activities in the fishery waters without a valid foreign fishing licence', and Section 2 defines 'related activities' to mean: '(a) transhipping fish to or from any vessel; (b) storing, processing or transporting

[180] The CRFM comprises seventeen developing and small island States in the Caribbean: Anguilla, Antigua and Barbuda, Bahamas, Barbados, Belize, Dominica, Grenada, Guyana, Haiti, Jamaica, Montserrat, Saint Kitts and Nevis, Saint Lucia, Saint Vincent and the Grenadines, Suriname, Trinidad and Tobago, and Turks and Caicos Islands. The CRFM operates as a specialized forum within the Caribbean Community (CARICOM) and aims to promote the sustainable use of fisheries and aquatic resources amongst its members. In addition to those identified in the OECS, the Turks and Caicos Islands is an overseas territory of the United Kingdom, formally in the Western Europe and Others Group.

fish taken from the fishery waters up to the time it is first landed; (c) refuelling or supplying fishing vessels or performing other activities in support of fishing operations; (d) attempting or preparing to do any of the foregoing.'

Similar provisions (with updates and modernization in some cases) are found in the legislation of Antigua and Barbuda, Barbados, Belize, Dominica, Guyana, Jamaica, Montserrat, Saint Kitts and Nevis, Saint Lucia, Saint Vincent and the Grenadines, and Trinidad and Tobago.[181] This approach is also adopted in recently updated legislation from coastal States beyond the Caribbean sub-region—specifically, that of Ecuador and Panama.[182] Since this legislation requires that a vessel obtain a 'licence' to engage in fishing related activities, the full suite of fisheries licensing provisions apply to the conduct of such activities in the EEZ. Nonetheless, as in other regions, some coastal States in the Caribbean also require that further authorization be sought prior to the conduct of transhipment in the EEZ (although, with the exception of Ecuador and Panama, they do not generally prohibit transhipment taking place at sea).[183] Unlike other Caribbean coastal States, the Bahamas does not appear to regulate fishing related activities as a coastal State, but clearly accepts their regulation by other coastal States—as indicated by its requirement (as a flag State) that its carrier vessels obtain all requisite permissions and licences from the coastal State when participating in transhipment operations in foreign EEZs.[184]

Despite their collective success in influencing the development of the EEZ, the subsequent practice of the Latin American coastal States has not been marked by regional cooperation in the same way as much of Europe, Africa, the Pacific, and the Caribbean. Although some coastal States are members of regional fisheries bodies such as the Central American Fisheries and Aquaculture Organization (OSPESCA),[185] the Latin American Organization for Fisheries Development (OLDEPESCA)[186] and the Permanent Commission of the South Pacific (CPPS),[187]

[181] See Table 3.1.
[182] Ibid.
[183] Ibid.
[184] Ibid.
[185] OSPESCA is a sub-regional organization comprising eight Central American countries (Belize, Costa Rica, the Dominican Republic, El Salvador, Guatemala, Honduras, Nicaragua, and Panama), which aims to encourage the development and coordinated management of regional fisheries and aquaculture activities. Although a number of regional measures have been adopted, including a second ten-year Fisheries and Aquaculture Integration Policy (2015–2025), and Regulations regarding IUU fishing and the establishment of a vessel monitoring system, they do not include standardized conditions for the regulation of fishing related activities by foreign fishing vessels.
[186] OLDEPESCA comprises twelve Latin American countries (Belize, Bolivia, Costa Rica, Cuba, Ecuador, El Salvador, Guyana, Honduras, Mexico, Nicaragua, Peru, and Venezuela) and is focused on making use of fishery resources to meet Latin American food requirements through the promotion of fisheries development and the strengthening of regional cooperation. While OLDEPESCA serves as a forum for coordination and information exchange regarding IUU fishing, it does not appear that any collective standards or approaches to the regulation of foreign fishing have been adopted by OLDEPESCA.
[187] The CPPS provides a mechanism for four Latin American countries (Chile, Colombia, Ecuador, and Peru) to coordinate their maritime policies at a regional level. The area of competence of the CPPS

there are no collective minimum standards for the regulation of foreign fishing in the EEZs of the Latin American countries—perhaps due to the long-standing approach in this region to issues of sovereignty and sovereign rights in the 'patrimonial sea'. Indeed, the national legislation in this region reflects a strong emphasis on national patrimony over marine resources and a tendency to restrict foreign fishing in the EEZ in favour of expansion of the domestic fishing industry, including through joint ventures, partnership agreements, and charter arrangements.[188] Similarly, the regulation of fishing related activities is primarily focused on 'fish-handling' activities involving fishery resources taken from the waters of the EEZ and—unlike the practice in other regions—does not generally extend to activities involving the processing or transhipment of fish caught elsewhere.

While the structure of the legislation varies significantly between States in this region,[189] 'fishing activity' is commonly expressed to include extraction, processing, and commercialization of fishery resources, and in order to engage in any of these 'phases' of fishing activity in the EEZ, a person must be registered with the relevant authority or obtain a licence, permit, or authorization. For example, El Salvador's *General Law on the Management and Promotion of Fisheries and Aquaculture 2001* provides:

> Article 23. For the purposes of this Law, fishing, extraction, processing and marketing are considered as phases of fishing. For aquaculture, in addition to the fishing phases, reproduction and cultivation are also considered as such.
>
> Article 24. Any natural or legal person interested in engaging in any of the different phases of fishing and aquaculture shall be authorized by CENDEPESCA [the Centre for the Development of Fisheries and Aquaculture].

Similarly, pursuant to Article 4 of Brazil's *Law No 11.959 providing for the National Policy on Sustainable Development of Fishery and Aquaculture 2009*, fishing activity comprises 'all the processes of fishing, exploitation and exploration, cultivation,

includes the territorial sea and EEZs of its member States, and its activities include promoting the implementation of the IPOA-IUU and combatting IUU fishing. However, like OLDEPESCA, it does not appear that the CPPS has adopted any collective standards or approaches to the regulation of foreign fishing.

[188] See, eg, El Salvador, *Law 2001* art 2: 'The hydrobiological resources found in jurisdictional waters of both the sea and inland, continental and insular marine bodies of water, as well as national lands and waters suitable for aquaculture, are part of the national heritage'; Peru, *Law 25977 of 1992* art 2: 'The hydrobiological resources contained in the jurisdictional waters of Peru are the national patrimony. Consequently, it corresponds to the State to regulate the integral management and the rational exploitation of said resources, considering that the fishing activity is of national interest.'

[189] The majority of national and regional practice examined in this book defines the scope of the relevant activities or vessels, and then employs those definitions in substantive provisions involving an obligation or prohibition on relevant conduct. These two elements are not always so clearly identifiable in the legislation of the Latin American countries, which is commonly structured around the 'phases' of fishing activity.

conservation, processing, transport, commercialization and research', and Article 24 provides that 'any person, whether physical or juridical, who is engaged in fishing activities, as well as the fishing vessel, must be previously registered in the General Register of Fishing Activity.' Provisions with similar effect can be found in the legislation of Argentina, Chile, Colombia, Costa Rica, the Dominican Republic, Nicaragua, Peru, Uruguay, and Venezuela, while the legislation of Honduras and Mexico is focused more narrowly on transhipment.[190] The conduct of transhipment is generally subject to specific authorization, including, in the cases of Argentina, Brazil, Colombia, the Dominican Republic, Honduras, Peru, and Uruguay, a requirement that all fish caught in the EEZ be landed or transhipped in a national port.[191]

3.3.5 Western Europe and Others

The practice in the Western Europe and Others Group is more diverse than in other groups, which is not surprising since it does not comprise a distinct or co-located geographic 'region' but a dispersed group of States with widely varying circumstances. While a range of different approaches are taken in the legislation of these States, they all have the general effect of regulating foreign vessels engaged in a broad range of fishing related activities in the EEZ—and where they are ambiguous, they can generally be interpreted in light of the relevant State's commitments under regional agreements and arrangements.

More than half of the Western Europe and Others Group are members of the EU, and are thus bound by the approach set out in the EU Regulations, involving the regulation of 'fish-handling' activities, and in particular the conduct of transhipment.[192] While the United Kingdom is no longer an EU member, the approach adopted in its *Fisheries Act 2020* has a similar scope: 'fish activities' are defined in Section 49 to include: '(a) catching fish; (b) operating vessels for catching or processing fish; (c) transporting fish or fish products; (d) loading and unloading fish or fish products; (e) processing fish' (and there is no reference to any broader activities in support of fishing operations). In addition, Section 4A of the *Sea Fish (Conservation) Act 1967* prohibits the unauthorized transhipment of fish between any vessels in British fishery waters.

Elsewhere in Western Europe, the scope of activities subject to coastal State regulation in Iceland and Norway can be established by reference to the vessels to which the regulations apply. While there is no definition or specific regulation of fishing related activities in the *Act on Fishing and Processing by Foreign Vessels in Iceland's*

[190] See Table 3.1.
[191] See Table 3.1.
[192] See Section 3.3.3.

Exclusive Fishing Zone 1998, Article 2 provides that foreign fishing and processing vessels must sail 'without interruption' through the exclusive fishing zone, which precludes the conduct of fishing related activities such as bunkering and transhipping, which require the vessel to stop. In Norway, foreign fishing is regulated by *Decree No 2 of 1977 Relative to Fishing and Hunting Operations by Foreign Nationals in the Economic Zone of Norway and Landing of Fish in Norwegian Ports,* which is expressed by Section 1 to apply to foreign vessels of any type that are fishing and hunting for commercial purposes, including transhipment. It also applies to vessels assisting the fishing fleet, including transport vessels to which catches are transhipped, and regardless of which area the catch was taken in.

In North America, the relevant legislation of Canada and the United States individually lists the various types of related activities for which licences are required. Under Section 5(1)(a) of Canada's *Coastal Fisheries Protection Regulations 2014,* the Minister may issue a licence authorizing a foreign fishing vessel and its crew to enter Canadian fisheries waters for any of the following purposes: '(i) to engage in commercial fishing, (ii) to tranship or take on board any fish, outfit or supplies while at sea, (iii) to process fish at sea, (iv) to transport fish from fishing grounds, (v) to provision, service, repair or maintain any other foreign fishing vessel while at sea [. . .].' Pursuant to Section 1824 of Title 16 of the *United States Code*, no foreign fishing vessel shall engage in fishing within the EEZ without a valid permit. The definition of 'fishing' in Section 600.10 of Title 50 of the *Code of Federal Regulations* includes 'any operations at sea in support of, or in preparation for' the catching of fish, and 'support' is defined to include 'any operation by a vessel assisting fishing by foreign or US vessels, including supplying water, fuel, provisions, fish processing equipment, or other supplies to a fishing vessel'. In addition, Section 600.501 establishes different permits for different types of fishing activities by foreign vessel—including transhipping with, scouting for, and supporting both US and foreign vessels—which apply in relation to fish caught both within and beyond the United States' EEZ.[193]

Reflecting the regional agreements and arrangements in the Pacific to which they are party,[194] the legislation of both Australia and New Zealand defines the term 'fishing' to include 'any operations at sea directly in support of, or in preparation for any activity described in this definition'.[195] Pursuant to Section 100 of the *Fisheries Management Act 1991* (Cth), it is an offence to use a foreign boat

[193] In the United States, 50 *CFR* Chapter VI governs all foreign fishing under the *Magnuson-Stevens Fisheries Conservation Act* (16 *USC* 38). The Act applies throughout the EEZ, which encompasses waters adjacent to the United States including Puerto Rico, the Northern Mariana Islands, and United States overseas territories and possessions: *Proclamation 5030* 'Exclusive Economic Zone of the United States America', 10 March 1983, 48 FR 10605.

[194] Relevant agreements and arrangements to which Australia and New Zealand are party include the FFA Harmonized MTCs, the US Tuna Treaty, the Niue Treaty, and the WCPFC Convention (on which, see the discussion in n 168).

[195] See Table 3.1.

for commercial fishing in the Australian Fishing Zone (AFZ) without a valid licence,[196] and Section 103 establishes a specific offence of transhipping fish between vessels in the EEZ without a licence or approval. Similarly, under Section 83 of the New Zealand *Fisheries Act 1996*, the operator of any foreign fishing vessel who proposes to use that vessel for fishing within the EEZ may apply for a licence for that purpose, while Section 27 of the *Fisheries (Foreign Fishing Vessel) Regulations 2001* prohibits the unauthorized transhipment of fish from a foreign vessel in the New Zealand EEZ.

While the regulation of fishing related activities in the fishery waters of the metropolitan territory of the United Kingdom follows the EU approach, the regulations that apply in the EEZs appurtenant to its overseas territories are more varied. The regulations that apply in the Falkland Islands and the Pitcairn Islands follow a similar approach to Australia and New Zealand, requiring a licence for the conduct of 'fishing', defined to include not only fish-handling activities such as processing and transhipping, but 'any operation in support of or preparation for' fishing. In the Caribbean, while Montserrat regulates a specific set of 'related activities' in a similar way to other CRFM members, the regulations that apply in the Turks and Caicos Islands are focused solely on the regulation of transhipment, and require authorization for the transhipment of any fish caught in the EEZ. The regulations in South Georgia and the South Sandwich Islands are similarly focused on transhipment and extend to the transhipment of 'any fish within South Georgia and South Sandwich Islands waters ... whether that fish was caught within those waters or not'.[197]

The regulations of the French overseas territories are also quite varied. For example, New Caledonia's legislation takes a similar approach to that of Australia and New Zealand (possibly reflecting its membership of the WCPFC) and prohibits transhipment at sea except in case of *force majeure*. Mayotte (which is a member of SWIOFC) requires 'foreign assistance vessels' operating in its EEZ to have a licence, but otherwise generally applies the provisions of the French *Rural and Marine Fisheries Code*, pursuant to which foreign vessels are prohibited from transhipping without or contrary to a licence. In the remote Southern Ocean EEZ of the French Southern and Antarctic Territories, it is specifically prohibited for any fishing or fish transport vessel to enter or exit without reporting to the authorities, and significant fines apply for the unauthorized exploitation of fish products on board a ship.[198]

[196] The AFZ encompasses the area extending from three nautical miles seaward of the territorial sea baseline to the outer limits of the EEZ: Australia, *Act 1991* s 4(1).

[197] See generally Table 3.1.

[198] Ibid.

3.4 Conclusion

In the modern industrial fishing complex, 'fishing' is not simply a process that involves fishing vessels catching fish. Given the intricate off-shore infrastructure providing bunkering, supply, and transhipment services that allow fishing vessels to stay at sea for prolonged periods of time, and the logistical networks for processing, packaging, and distribution, 'fishing' is merely part of a chain of events more properly understood as a 'fishing operation' involving multiple actors and activities.[199] Accordingly, it is important to clearly establish the parameters of coastal State jurisdiction over foreign fishing vessels and fishing support vessels in the EEZ, in order to ensure a predictable and stable framework for the prescription and enforcement of coastal State fisheries jurisdiction, and for the conduct of fishing operations.

While reference is often had to the decisions of international courts and tribunals in order to determine authoritative interpretations of international law, such third party decisions are not the only—or necessarily the best—way to ascertain the meaning and application of treaty provisions.[200] In particular, the focus on the specific facts and circumstances required to decide a particular case can result in partial or incomplete interpretations of relevant issues, or remarks made in *obiter*, which can become unduly influential if not considered in a wider context. Accordingly, it is important to look at State practice in order not only to arrive at an authentic interpretation of international law, but to discern specific regulatory trends and alternatives, and establish the bounds of 'permissible regulatory competence'.[201]

In the *Virginia G* case, the Tribunal did make reference to State practice, observing that fishing related activities such as bunkering are regulated in the national legislation of 'several' States, not only in the West African region, but also in 'some other regions of the world'.[202] However, as this Chapter has shown, this statement fails to adequately convey the 'common, concordant and consistent' nature of State practice on this issue,[203] which constitutes objective evidence of the understanding of the parties regarding the meaning of relevant provisions of the LOSC, to which recourse can be had as an authentic means of interpretation under Article 31(3)(b) of the Vienna Convention on the Law of Treaties (VCLT).[204] Given the comprehensive national, regional, and global practice examined in this Chapter, some firm conclusions can be drawn about the contemporary extent of coastal State jurisdiction over 'fishing' under the LOSC.

199 de Coning and Taveau, 'Transnational Organized Crime in the Fishing Industry' (n 143) 20.
200 Michael Reisman, 'International Incidents: Introduction to a New Genre in the Study of International Law' (1984) 10 YJIL 1, 10.
201 Burke, 'Coastal State Fishery Regulation' (n 23) 500.
202 *Virginia G* [218].
203 *Japan: Alcoholic Beverages II* 12–13.
204 On the effect of subsequent practice under the VCLT, see Section 1.2.2.

First, on the basis of their sovereign rights over living resources in the EEZ under Article 56(1)(a) of the LOSC, coastal States can regulate a wide range of fishing and fishing related activities, including all the ancillary operations that form part of modern industrial fishing: processing, packaging, storing, transporting, and transhipping fish and fish products; bunkering fishing vessels at sea; supplying water, food, fuel, and fishing gear; and assisting with the rotation of personnel and conduct of repairs at sea. In the future, this jurisdiction could extend to other activities for which technology or infrastructure does not yet exist, provided they are 'directly connected' to fishing.[205]

Second, the coastal State's jurisdiction extends to the regulation of all fishing and fishing support vessels that are engaged in fishing related activities in the EEZ, including:

- foreign fishing vessels harvesting fish in the EEZ pursuant to a licence;
- foreign fishing vessels engaged in fishing related activities during transit through the EEZ; and
- fishing support vessels that engage in fishing related activities in support of any fishing vessel (licensed or transiting) in the EEZ.

Depending on the activities in question, these vessels may be regulated through terms and conditions applied via a licensing regime under Article 62(4) or simply through case-by-case authorization as an exercise of the coastal State's sovereign rights and jurisdiction under Article 56(1)(a). They may be subject to a range of additional conditions including advance notification, the presence of observers, the payment of relevant fees, and compliance with reporting requirements.

Third, the coastal State's jurisdiction with respect to transhipment includes the transfer of any fish or other living marine resources between any two vessels in the EEZ, regardless of whether or not they were harvested within that zone.[206] In addition, the coastal State may—and in the case of members of some RFMOs and regional fisheries bodies, *must*—prohibit at-sea transhipment in the EEZ.

Fourth, notwithstanding the breadth of this jurisdiction, the coastal State is not free to simply regulate fishing related activities in any way that it chooses; the coastal State's sovereign rights over living resources under Article 56(1) are functionally limited, and can only be exercised for the purpose for which they were conferred. Accordingly, the regulation of fishing support vessels must be firmly based on and directed toward their involvement in fishing related activities (rather than an exercise of customs, economic or 'public interest' jurisdiction).

As the International Law Commission (ILC) observed in its 'Commentary to the 1956 Articles on the Law of the Sea', not only does the inadequate protection

[205] *Virginia G* [215]. See also *SRFC Advisory Opinion* [100].
[206] For an opposing view on this issue, see Anderson, 'Coastal State Jurisdiction' (n 7) 115.

of marine living resources threaten the world's food supply, but 'in so far as it renders the coastal State or the States directly interested helpless against wasteful and predatory exploitation of fisheries by foreign nationals, it constitutes an inducement to the State or States in question to resort to unilateral measures of self-protection, which are sometimes at variance with the law.'[207]

Similarly, in a contemporary context, overly narrow or rigid interpretations of the fishery provisions of the LOSC could seriously impact the effectiveness of the framework established in Part V of the LOSC, and lead to 'confusion and misunderstanding about the economic, social, and political goals of fisheries management, and about the authority of the coastal State to adopt appropriate regulations.'[208] Fortunately, there is no longer any need for confusion regarding the coastal State's right to regulate a broad range of fishing and fishing related activities, and a wide variety of fishing and fishing support vessels in the EEZ. Instead, the question becomes: what is the extent of the coastal State's regulatory authority with respect to such vessels and how can coastal States use that jurisdiction most effectively? More specifically: what is the extent of the coastal State's prescriptive jurisdiction with respect to the access and activities of foreign fishing vessels in the EEZ; how far does coastal State jurisdiction extend in relation to unlicensed foreign fishing vessels exercising the freedom of navigation to transit through the EEZ; and what jurisdiction does the coastal State have to enforce all of these regulations, within and beyond the EEZ? These questions will be the focus of Chapters 4, 5, 6, and 7.

[207] ILC, *Yearbook 1956, Vol II* (n 5) 286.
[208] Burke, 'Coastal State Fishery Regulation' (n 23) 503.

4

Prescriptive Jurisdiction over Foreign Fishing in the EEZ

Under the traditional law of the sea as it existed prior to the development of the United Nations Convention on the Law of the Sea (LOSC), the exploitation of living resources was underpinned by two disparate regimes—coastal State sovereignty in the territorial sea, and the freedom of fishing for all on the high seas.[1] These regimes were inherently linked: since the territorial sea coincided with the coastal State's individual monopoly on fishing, and the high seas represented the community right to fishing, any increase in the extent of the territorial sea would automatically encroach upon the high seas freedom of fishing.[2] It was clear by the 1930s that this arrangement was inadequate for the conservation and management of fishery resources, but there was widespread reluctance to entrust greater jurisdiction to coastal States, amid fears that if they were allowed to establish rules on fisheries beyond the territorial sea, 'extremist' and 'arbitrary' measures would result.[3] Nonetheless, in a 'triumph of individualism over collectivism',[4] the exclusive economic zone (EEZ) established in Part V of the LOSC expanded the coastal State's resource monopoly to 200 nautical miles, enclosing more than one third of the world's ocean space and 90 per cent of its fishery resources within national jurisdiction.

By replacing the freedom to fish with the coastal State's exclusive title to living resources, the establishment of the EEZ 'radically changed the pattern of world fisheries, especially the distribution of access to the living resources and to the benefits derived from their exploitation'.[5] In order to balance the exclusive fishery jurisdiction of coastal States with the interests and concerns of the international community, a range of carefully negotiated compromises were embedded in Articles 61 and 62 of the LOSC, including in particular:

[1] See Ram Prakash Anand, *Origin and Development of the Law of the Sea* (Dordrecht 1982) 225–41; Arvid Pardo, 'The New Law of the Sea and Some of Its Implications' (1987) 87(3) Law&Env 1, 3.

[2] Shigeru Oda, 'Fisheries under the United Nations Convention on the Law of the Sea' (1983) 77 AJIL 739, 739.

[3] Tullio Treves, 'Historical Development of the Law of the Sea' in Donald R Rothwell et al (eds), *The Oxford Handbook of the Law of the Sea* (OUP 2015) 10, quoting Gilbert Gidel, *Le Droit International Public de la Mer, Vol III* (Mellottée Chateauroux 1932) 468.

[4] DP O'Connell, *The International Law of the Sea, Vol I* (OUP 1982) 552.

[5] Barbara Kwiatkowska, *The 200 Mile Exclusive Economic Zone in the New Law of the Sea* (Martinus Nijhoff 1989) 45.

Coastal State Jurisdiction over Living Resources in the Exclusive Economic Zone. Camille Goodman, Oxford University Press.
 DOI: 10.1093/oso/9780192896841.003.0004

(i) the coastal State's obligation to promote optimum utilization of marine resources by determining a total allowable catch and ascertaining the availability of a surplus;
(ii) the detailed description of the way in which—and the States to which—access to such a surplus should be given; and
(iii) the terms and conditions that might be applied to foreign nationals granted access to the surplus.

While the coastal State's sovereign rights are thus clearly conditioned with an obligation to provide other States with access to the living resources of the EEZ in certain circumstances, the impact of these compromises is less clear—in particular, how 'real and enforceable' are these obligations to share?[6]

In practice, given the open-ended and discretionary nature of these provisions, and their general exclusion from compulsory dispute settlement,[7] coastal States can be seen to have secured almost unlimited powers over their living resources.[8] The LOSC regime for fisheries 'leaves the coastal state in the preeminent position in determining what gets fished, how much gets fished, how it gets fished, and who fishes' in its EEZ.[9] Accordingly, the regulation of foreign fishing in the EEZ is not an issue whose scope can be determined simply by reference to the text of the LOSC, nor the decisions of international courts and tribunals, but only by examining the way in which coastal States have exercised this jurisdiction since the adoption of the LOSC and the establishment of the EEZ. In this respect, the highest conclusion that could be reached in the leading commentary at the time the LOSC entered into force in 1994 was that 'accepted practice for the implementation of Article 62 is still in the process of development.'[10] After the passage of more than twenty-five years, it is timely to assess the outcome of that process and consider how the regime for foreign fishing in the EEZ has developed.

In particular: what *is* the accepted practice of States in exercising their prescriptive jurisdiction to regulate foreign fishing in the EEZ? How does this practice implement, develop, or vary the framework established in the LOSC or affect the carefully negotiated 'balance' between the rights and interests of coastal States and other States in the EEZ? And to what extent does the regime for foreign fishing actually qualify or limit the coastal State's sovereign rights over living resources in

[6] Edward Duncan Brown, *The International Law of the Sea, Vol 1* (Dartmouth 1994) 222.

[7] See Section 2.1.2.

[8] Guifang Xue, *China and International Fisheries Law and Policy* (Martinus Nijhoff 2005) 16. Similarly, Brown concludes that the regime in the LOSC 'imposes few restraints upon coastal States which may wish to transform their limited sovereign rights into practically unlimited sovereignty over the living resources of the zone': Brown, *The International Law of the Sea, Vol I* (n 6) 224.

[9] Lawrence Juda, 'The Exclusive Economic Zone: Compatibility of National Claims and the UN Convention on the Law of the Sea' (1986) 16 ODIL 1, 22.

[10] Satya Nandan and Shabtai Rosenne (eds), *United Nations Convention on the Law of the Sea 1982: A Commentary, Vol II* (Martinus Nijhoff 1993) 638.

the EEZ? This Chapter will address these questions by exploring the approaches adopted by coastal States to regulating foreign access to the surplus living resources of the EEZ under Article 62(2) of the LOSC (Section 4.1), examining the criteria used to allocate and apportion any surplus resources to foreign States pursuant to Article 62(3) (Section 4.2), and analysing the terms and conditions applied to foreign fishing vessels operating under licence in the EEZ as envisaged in Article 62(4) (Section 4.3).

4.1 Approaches to Regulating Foreign Fishing in the EEZ: Article 62(2)

Despite—or perhaps due to—its vast transfer of resources from the traditional regime of common access to the EEZ jurisdiction of coastal States, the LOSC demonstrates a clear concern to ensure the 'equitable and efficient utilization' of these resources, and to realize a 'just and equitable international economic order which takes into account the needs and interests of mankind as a whole'.[11] In this regard, the interests of three key groups of States are sought to be balanced through the objective of 'optimum utilization' established in Article 62(1) of the LOSC: the exclusive or preferential rights of coastal States, the historic interests of distant water fishing States, and the equitable interests of land-locked and geographically disadvantaged States.[12] In theory, the function of Article 62 is to allow other States to access the living resources of the EEZ if the coastal State itself cannot harvest them all, thereby ensuring that these resources are not under-utilized by coastal States at the expense of the international community.[13] Accordingly, pursuant to Article 62(2) of the LOSC, where the coastal State does not have the capacity to harvest the entire allowable catch of the living resources in its EEZ, it shall give other States to access the surplus 'through agreements or other arrangements'.

The LOSC does not elaborate on the type of 'agreements or other arrangements' that are envisaged to give effect to this requirement, and the approaches of coastal States to the implementation of this obligation, by granting—or, as the case may be, limiting—foreign fishing access vary widely. Three broad approaches are commonly discernible in the practice of coastal States, each of which has different benefits and limitations and allows coastal States to pursue different objectives with respect to foreign fishing in the EEZ:[14]

[11] LOSC Preamble [4] and [5].

[12] David Joseph Attard, *The Exclusive Economic Zone in International Law* (Clarendon Press 1987) 157.

[13] Ibid.

[14] Coastal State regulation of 'foreign fishing' can be directed at a variety of subjects, including foreign States, legal or natural persons who are nationals of foreign States, and foreign-flagged or foreign-owned vessels. In this regard, art 62(2) and (3) refer to giving 'other States' access to the surplus catch in the EEZ, and art 62(4) sets terms and conditions applicable to 'nationals of other States' fishing in the EEZ. However, since the majority of regulation is directed at the level of vessels—which are the primary

- the regulation of foreign fishing through access agreements with States or fishing industry associations, or by direct licensing arrangements with individual vessels;
- the restriction of foreign fishing to operations carried out in association with national partners or by some form of assimilation with a national vessel; and
- the exclusion of foreign fishing in the EEZ by explicit or implicit prohibition.

While each of these regulatory approaches might properly be described as the dominant policy of a coastal State toward foreign participation in fisheries, they do not operate as 'uniquely defined choices', but as broad categories that may be adopted individually or in combination.[15] Given the complex multi-national interests and structures involved in the global fishing industry, none of them is truly exclusive,[16] and coastal States may adopt one or a combination of these techniques in order to reflect their own fisheries management framework, support a wide range of policy objectives, assert jurisdiction over a variety of fisheries issues (including research, data collection, stock identification, fisheries development, conservation, management, surveillance, and enforcement), or pursue political, social, economic, security, or other interests. Table 4.1 summarizes the principal approach—or combination of approaches—taken by each coastal State with respect to allowing foreign fishing access in the EEZ, each of which is examined in more detail in this Section.

4.1.1 Regulating Foreign Participation through Access Agreements and Direct Licensing

The approach most commonly taken by coastal States is to regulate the extent to which, and the way in which, foreign vessels can access and exploit the surplus living resources of the EEZ by means of an access agreement or direct licensing arrangement. These legal instruments can take different forms, involve different parties, and provide useful levers for coastal States to pursue a broad range of policy objectives in the exercise of their sovereign rights over the living resources of the EEZ.

unit of regulation in the law of the sea—rather than persons or companies, references in this book to the regulation of 'foreign fishing' generally refer to the activities of foreign-flagged fishing vessels, unless otherwise specified.

[15] LC Christy and Gerald Moore, 'Forms of Foreign Participation in Fisheries: Coastal State Practice' in *Report of the Expert Consultation on the Conditions of Access to the Fish Resources of the Exclusive Economic Zones* (FAO 1983) 95.

[16] Ibid. As Christy and Moore point out, even a policy to exclude foreign participation will have exceptions dictated by the need for foreign inputs and markets, the presence of immigrant foreigners, and the difficulty of defining and controlling the ownership, structure, and activities of corporations.

Table 4.1 Coastal State approaches to regulating foreign fishing access in the EEZ

African Group	
Algeria	*Law 01-11 of 2001* arts 23, 24: by direct licensing.
Angola	*Law 6-A/04* arts 32(4), 50: foreign fishing may be permitted if resources are available once the priority of granting fishing rights to Angolan people has been met, in association with residents/nationals or under State-to-State access agreement.
Benin	*Law 2014-19* art 20: under State-to-State access agreement.
Cameroon	*Law 94/01* art 118: only natural persons resident, or legal persons headquartered, in Cameroon whose capital composition is known to the fisheries administration.
Cape Verde	*Leg Dec 2/2020* arts 21(2), 66: only under State-to-State or Govt-to-industry access agreement, for tuna and tuna-like species.
Comoros	*Law 82-005* art 9: where Comoros does not have the capacity to harvest all of the allowable catch, it shall give other States access through agreements; *Law 82-015* art 5: foreign fishing may be authorized by direct licensing.
Congo	*Law 2-2000* arts 44 (b) and (c), 52: by direct licensing or State-to-State access agreement within the limits of the surplus of exploitable stocks.
Cote d'Ivoire	*Law 2016-554* art 19: under chartering arrangement with nationals or State-to-State access agreement.
Djibouti	*Law 187 of 2002* art 7: no foreign fishing (Djibouti nationals and vessels only).
Egypt	*Act 124 of 1983* art 25: no foreign fishing (foreign vessels may not be licensed to fish in the EEZ).
Equatorial Guinea	*Law 11/2017* art 30: by direct licensing or under a treaty or access agreement.
Eritrea	*Proc 176/2014* art 16(3): only under State-to-State or Govt-to-industry access agreement, or if the Minister determines an agreement is not feasible and the applicant provides sufficient financial or other guarantees.
Gabon	*Law 15/2005* art 30: under chartering arrangement with nationals or an access agreement.
Gambia	*Act 2007* s 39(1)(d): only pursuant to a State-to-State or Govt-to-industry access agreement (bilateral or multilateral) or a related agreement or arrangement.
Ghana	*Act 2002* s 63: under an access agreement or if determined by the Minister on the recommendation of the Commission.

Continued

Table 4.1 *Continued*

Guinea	*Code 2015* arts 56, 58: access to surplus resources shall be accorded to foreign vessels taking into account management plans, the level of effort, the fishing capacity of the Guinean fleet and the interests of fishermen and local communities; access only under an agreement with State or competent entity.
Guinea-Bissau	*Dec Law 10/2011* art 8(4): only pursuant to a State-to-State or Govt-to-industry access agreement, or under charter contracts.
Kenya	*Act 2016* s 128(2)(a) and (b): by direct grant of an access right or licence, or pursuant to a State-to-State or Govt-to-industry access agreement or arrangement.
Liberia	*Law 2019* s 5.1: by direct grant of an access right or licence or pursuant to a State-to-State or Govt-to-industry access agreement or arrangement.
Libya	*Res 71 of 1990* arts 38–40: only pursuant to a partnership contract with a Libyan organization, whose flag State is party to an access agreement.
Madagascar	*Code 2015* arts 28, 35: only pursuant to a State-to-State or Govt-to-industry access agreement or under charter to Malagasy nationals.
Mauritania	*Law 2015-017* art 33: pursuant to State-to-State or Govt-to-industry access agreements or by direct licensing in special circumstances.
Mauritius	*Act 2007* art 35: only under a State-to-State or Govt-to-industry access agreement, or if otherwise determined by the Minister with a sufficient financial guarantee.
Morocco	*Act 1-81 of 1980* art 3: no foreign fishing (only Moroccan flagged or chartered vessels operated by Moroccan natural or legal persons with prior approval of the Minister).
Mozambique	*Law 22/2013* arts 37, 42: only under a State-to-State or Govt-to-industry access agreement (bilateral or multilateral).
Namibia	*Act 2000* ss 33, 40: a right of access can be granted under a State-to-State access agreement or directly by the Minister.
Nigeria	*Regs 1992* s 3: no foreign fishing (fishing only by Nigerian-flagged vessels).
Sao Tome & Principe	*Law 9/2001* arts 27–8: only under a State-to-State or Govt-to-industry access agreement, or if locally-based, or if authorized in exceptional cases which may be conditional on deposit of a bond.
Senegal	*Code 2015* art 27: only under a State-to-State or Govt-to-industry access agreement, or chartering arrangement with Senegalese nationals.

Table 4.1 *Continued*

Seychelles	*Act 2014* s 12: only under a State-to-State or Gov-to-industry access agreement, or if the Minister determines an agreement is not feasible and the applicant provides sufficient financial or other guarantees.
Sierra Leone	*Act 2018* s 14: by direct licensing.
Somalia	*Law 2016* art 16: foreign fishing may be permitted by direct licensing if the resources are surplus to the needs and employment capacity of the Somali fishing community.
South Africa	*Act 1998* s 39: only under State-to-State or Govt-to-industry access agreement or if licence issued by the Minister with sufficient guarantees and conditions relating to insurance and pollution.
Tanzania	*Act 2020* ss 47, 49: under an access agreement or arrangement or through a joint venture or charter agreement approved by the Minister.
Togo	*Law 2016-026* arts 21–3: under a State-to-State access agreement, by direct licensing with a sufficient bond to ensure compliance, or under charter by Togolese natural or legal persons.
Tunisia	*Law 94-13* art 3: no foreign fishing (no fishing by foreign vessels except for research or training).
Asia-Pacific Group	
Bahrain	*Leg Dec 20 of 2002* art 3: no foreign fishing (fishing by non-Bahraini citizens prohibited).
Bangladesh	*Act 2020* s 7: by direct licensing.
Brunei	*Order 2009* s17: only under a State-to-State or Govt-to-industry access agreement.
Cambodia	*Law 2006* art 38: direct license from the Ministry after obtaining approval from the Government.
China	*Law 2004* art 8: direct licensing by approval of the Fisheries Administration, including within the framework of access agreements.
Chinese Taipei	*Act 1929* arts 4–6: only in cooperation with nationals.
Cook Islands	*Act 2005* s 35: only under a State-to-State access agreement (bilateral or multilateral) or regional agreement.
Fiji	*Dec 2012* s 33: by direct licensing or under a State-to-State or Govt-to-industry access agreement (bilateral or multilateral), or regional agreement.
India	*Act 1981* ss 4–5: by direct licensing or chartering by nationals.

Continued

Table 4.1 *Continued*

Indonesia	*Dec 15 of 1984* art 3: foreign fishing shall be permitted if Indonesian nationals or bodies corporate are unable to make complete use of the allowable catch; *Law 2004* art 30: only under a State-to-State access agreement; *Pres Reg 44/2016* App III, Table C, No 124: fishing may only be funded with Indonesian capital.
Iran	*Law 1995* art 7: only under a State-to-State or Govt-to-industry access agreement.
Japan	*Act 1996* art 6: only under a State-to-State access agreement.
Kiribati	*Act 2010* ss 12, 17: by direct licensing or under an access agreement.
Korea	*Fishing Act 1996* art 5: by direct licensing.
Kuwait	*Law 1980* art 2: only under an access agreement.
Malaysia	*Act 1985* s 15: only under a State-to-State access agreement.
Maldives	*Act 2019* s 36: no foreign fishing (licences not issued to foreign vessels).
Marshall Islands	51 *MIRC* §403: only under an access agreement or arrangement.
Micronesia	24 *FSM Code* §105: only under an access agreement or arrangement.
Myanmar	*Law 1989* Chapter III: by direct licensing.
Nauru	*Regs 1997* s 27: only under a State-to-State or Govt-to-industry access agreement.
Niue	*Act 1996* s 28: by direct licensing or under a State-to-State access agreement (bilateral or multilateral).
Oman	*Law 2019* art 31: no foreign fishing (licences granted only to Omani corporations; use of foreign vessels for fishing may be authorized if insufficient Omani vessels).
Pakistan	*Deep Sea Policy 2018* para 2.3: no foreign fishing (licences issued only to local individuals, companies or partnerships, or joint ventures with foreign companies).
Palau	27 *PNC* §166: by direct licensing or under an access agreement (but only in Domestic Fishing Zone, with limited possibilities for export).
Papua New Guinea	*Act 1998* s 33: only under a State-to-State access agreement.
Philippines	*Code 1998* s 5: no foreign fishing (use and exploitation of living resources reserved exclusively to Philippines nationals).

Table 4.1 *Continued*

Qatar	*Law 4 of 1983* arts 7, 38: no foreign fishing (only vessels that are wholly owned by Qatari nationals may be licensed to fish in the EEZ).
Samoa	*Act 2016* s 28: only under a multilateral access agreement.
Solomon Islands	*Act 2015* s 38(6): under a written agreement with the Minister.
Sri Lanka	*Act 1979* s 6: by direct licensing.
Thailand	*Ordinance BE 2558, 2015* ss 5, 7: no foreign fishing (fishing rights only granted to Thai persons/companies; foreign vessels only used by State-to-State agreement).
Timor-Leste	*Dec Law 2004* arts 10, 32: under a State-to-State or Govt-to-industry access agreement or individual contracts.
Tonga	*Act 2002* s 38: only under a State-to-State or Govt-to-industry access agreement.
Turkey	*Law 1380* art 21: no foreign fishing (foreign nationals may not enter the fishery waters or practice fishing, except for recreational purposes or authorized research).
Tuvalu	*Act 2006* s 28: only under an access agreement.
United Arab Emirates	*Law 23 of 1999* art 40: no foreign fishing (foreign vessels may not fish in the EEZ).
Vanuatu	*Act 2014* ss 53, 57: by direct licensing or under a State-to-State access agreement.
Vietnam	*Law 2017* art 55: only under a State-to-State access agreement and with issue of investment registration certificates or approval of cooperation projects.
Yemen	*Law 2 of 2006* art 6(a): only under an access agreement.
Eastern Europe Group	
Albania	*Law 64/2012* art 30: no foreign fishing (fishing licences not granted to foreign vessels, and Albanian-flagged vessels may not be majority foreign-owned).
European Union	*Reg 2371/2002* art 17: all EU-flagged vessels have equal access to waters and resources of EU Members; *Reg 2017/2403* art 33(1): third country (non-EU) vessels may only fish under an access agreement.
Montenegro	*Law 2009* art 95: only under a State-to-State access agreement.

Continued

Table 4.1 *Continued*

Russia	*Act 1998* art 9: foreign fishing may be allowed if there is an access agreement and Russian applicants do not have the capacity to harvest the allowable catch of relevant resources in the specific fishing area; *Law N57-FZ of 2008* art 6(40): acquisition of fishing rights by a non-Russian company requires government approval.
Latin America and the Caribbean Group	
Antigua & Barbuda	*Act 2006* s 27: only under a State-to-State or Govt-to-industry access agreement.
Argentina	*Law 24.922 of 1998* arts 37, 38: only in association with nationals and under a State-to-State access agreement.
Bahamas	*Act 1977* s 7: only under a State-to-State access agreement.
Barbados	*Act 1993* s 8: only under a State-to-State or Govt-to-industry access agreement, or if otherwise determined by the Minister in the national interest.
Belize	*Act 2020* ss 27, 28: under a State-to-State or Govt-to-industry access agreement or if otherwise determined by the Minister with sufficient guarantees.
Brazil	*Law 11.959 of 2009* art 9 and *Dec 4.810 of 2003* art 4: only under a chartering arrangement with nationals or a State-to-State access agreement.
Chile	*Law 1991* arts 17, 115: no foreign fishing (licences not granted to foreign fishing vessels; fishing rights only for Chilean legal or natural persons).
Colombia	*Statute 13 of 1990* art 31: foreign fishing vessels may only be used under a contract with a Colombian company delivering part of the catch to the domestic market.
Costa Rica	*Law 8436 of 2005* arts 7, 57: no foreign fishing except for tuna seining, pursuant to direct licensing or charter arrangements with nationals.
Cuba	*Leg Dec 2 of 1977* art 4: other States shall be given access to the surplus of the allowable catch through the conclusion of appropriate agreements; *Law 129/2019* art 11(3): by direct licensing, authorized by the Council of Ministers.
Dominica	*Act 1987* s 7(1): under a State-to-State or Govt-to-industry access agreement.
Dominican Republic	*Law 307-04* arts 15(1), 19: under a State-to-State access agreement or by direct licence, or foreign vessels with locally domiciled operators.

Table 4.1 *Continued*

Ecuador	*Law 2020* arts 7(24), 156–8: foreign fishing vessels may operate under a lease or charter with nationals, or a contract to supply fish exclusively to a national processor.
El Salvador	*Law 2001* art 24: by direct licensing.
Grenada	*Act 1986* s 8: only under a State-to-State or Govt-to-industry access agreement.
Guatemala	*Dec 80-02* art 75: by direct licensing.
Guyana	*Act 2012* s 18(5): only under a State-to-State or Govt-to-industry access agreement.
Honduras	*Dec 172-99* art 8(1): under an access agreement with States who have customarily exercised fishing rights; *Dec 106-2015* art 50: or by temporary direct licensing in association with a national processor to land fish domestically.
Jamaica	*Act 2018* ss 25, 49: only under a State-to-State or Govt-to-industry access agreement.
Mexico	*Act 1986* art 56: the Federal Executive shall give foreign ships access to the surplus of the allowable catch, having regard to the national interest; *Law 2007* art 62: by exception, under a State-to-State access agreement.
Nicaragua	*Law 2004* art 55: no foreign fishing for limited access fisheries; direct licensing for open access resources depending on capacity of national fleet.
Panama	*Law 204 of 2021* art 60: no foreign fishing (fishing in Panama's waters by foreign-flagged vessels is prohibited).
Peru	*Law 25977 of 1992* art 48: by direct licensing, or under contract with a Peruvian company or State-to-State or Govt-to-industry access agreement.
Saint Kitts & Nevis	*Act 2016* s 40(1): only under an access agreement.
Saint Lucia	*Act 1984* s 8(4): only under a State-to-State or Govt-to-industry access agreement.
Saint Vincent & Grenadines	*Act 1986* s 8(4): only under a State-to-State or Govt-to-industry access agreement.
Trinidad & Tobago	*Act 1986* ss 25–7: under a State-to-State access agreement or by direct licensing.
Uruguay	*Dec 115/018* art 33: by direct licensing, requiring approval from the Ministries of Foreign Affairs and National Defence.

Continued

Table 4.1 *Continued*

Venezuela	*Dec Law 1,408 of 2014* art 41: if there is a surplus the domestic fleet cannot harvest, foreign fishing vessels may be allowed to participate pursuant to a State-to-State access agreement, taking into account the social and economic benefits to Venezuela.
Western Europe and Others Group	
Australia	*Act 1991* ss 4(2), 34–7: by direct licensing or under an access agreement (policy that foreign fishing licences are not currently issued outside the framework of existing access agreements), or by 'declaring' a foreign boat to be an Australian boat.
Canada	*Regs 2014* s 5(1): by direct licensing (if Canada has 'favourable fisheries relations' with the flag State) or bilateral agreement.
France (Mayotte)	*Code* arts L921-2, 951-5 and *Dec 2010-727* arts 3–4: by direct licensing, on decision of the Prefect after consulting the Ministers responsible for foreign affairs, maritime fishing and overseas.
France (New Caledonia)	*Code* art L957-2 and *Deliberation 50/CP 2011* arts 5, 7: by direct licensing, subject to an order of the Government of New Caledonia setting the conditions.
France (SAAT)	*Code* art L958-5 and *Order 2017-48* art 1: by direct licensing, on decision by the senior administrator.
Iceland	*Act 1998* art 3: only under State-to-State access agreements.
New Zealand	*Act 1996* ss 82(1), 103(1): The Minister may from time to time apportion the foreign allowable catch among other countries in respect of any stock (other than any highly migratory species); vessels must not be used for fishing unless flagged to New Zealand, except if an exemption is granted by the Chief Executive.
NZ (Tokelau)	*Regs 2012* ss 8, 27: by direct licensing or under a multilateral access agreement.
Norway	*Dec 2 of 1977* s 4: only under a State-to-State access agreement.
United Kingdom	*Act 2020* ss 16–17: by direct licensing.
UK (BIOT)	*Proc 1 of 2010*: no foreign fishing (marine protected area in which all commercial fishing is prohibited).
UK (Falklands)	*Ordinance 2005* s 41: by direct licensing.
UK (Montserrat)	*Act 2000* s 18: only under a State-to-State or Govt-to-industry access agreement.
UK (Pitcairn)	*Ordinance 2016* ss 4, 8: no foreign fishing (marine protected area in which foreign fishing is prohibited).

Table 4.1 *Continued*

UK (SGSSI)	*Ordinance 2000* s 5: by direct licensing.
UK (Turks & Caicos)	*Regs 1998* s 6: only under a State-to-State or Govt-to-industry access agreement.
United States	16 *USC* §§1821(c) and (e)(1)(A): the Secretary of State may make allocations to foreign nations from the total allowable level of foreign fishing that is permitted with respect to each fishery; foreign fishing may only be authorized under a State-to-State access agreement.

Notes

a. The practice of EU member States is examined by reference to EU regulations.

4.1.1.1 State-to-State Access Agreements

The dominant type of 'agreements or other arrangements' employed to facilitate foreign fishing in the EEZ are fisheries access agreements, which were already common practice at the time the LOSC was negotiated.[17] While fisheries access agreements may take a number of different forms, the most common is a bilateral agreement between States, which establishes a right of access, subject to agreed terms and conditions, for fishing vessels of a flag State to exploit the living resources in the EEZ of the coastal State. Such bilateral access agreements (which will be referred to as 'State-to-State' access agreements) constitute 'treaties' for the purposes of the Vienna Convention on the Law of Treaties (VCLT): they are written agreements entered into between States with an intention to create legal relations, governed by international law.[18] Unfortunately, although the legal framework for such agreements is generally established in national legislation, and there is a significant body of literature seeking to analyse their typology, structure, economic benefits, and development impact,[19] it is often difficult to evaluate their terms and effect because (despite being treaties)[20] many of them are not in the public

[17] See, eg, the list of bilateral fishery agreements in Jean Carroz and Michel Savini, 'The Practice of Coastal States Regarding Foreign Access to Fishery Resources (An Analysis of Bilateral Agreements)' in *Report of the Expert Consultation on the Conditions of Access to the Fish Resources of the Exclusive Economic Zones* (FAO 1983) 59–72.

[18] VCLT art 2(1)(a).

[19] See Elizabeth Havice, 'The Structure of Tuna Access Agreements in the Western and Central Pacific Ocean: Lessons for Vessel Day Scheme Planning' (2010) 34(5) MarPol 979; Antonius Gagern and Jeroen van den Bergh, 'A Critical Review of Fishing Agreements with Tropical Developing Countries' (2013) 38 MarPol 375; World Bank, *Trade in Fishing Services: Emerging Perspectives on Foreign Fishing Arrangements* (World Bank 2014), available at <http://documents1.worldbank.org/curated/en/504571468164949623/pdf/92622-REVISED-PUBLIC-Trade-in-Fishing-Services-WEB-withaddendum.pdf> accessed 7 December 2020; Rachel Nichols et al, 'Fishing Access Agreements and Harvesting Decisions of Host and Distant Water Fishing Nations' (2015) 54 MarPol 77.

[20] Pursuant to art 102 of the Charter of the United Nations, treaties that are not registered with the Secretariat may not be invoked before any organ of the United Nations (UN). Given the limitations on compulsory dispute settlement in relation to the EEZ, this may have limited importance for fisheries

domain—particularly those with key distant water fishing nations such as China, Japan, Korea, Russia, and Chinese Taipei.[21]

Historically, access agreements provided an important way to concretize the concept of extended fisheries jurisdiction, by allowing coastal States to secure the agreement of flag States to key aspects of the LOSC and ensure recognition of their sovereign rights over living resources in the EEZ.[22] Although no longer required for this particular purpose, they still offer some significant advantages. In particular, as binding agreements, they provide a firm basis for coastal States to negotiate with flag States in order to secure a range of benefits that are not achievable through a vessel-by-vessel approach to licensing—such as trade and economic incentives, technology transfer and training, undertakings regarding flag State responsibility for compliance, and even support for strategic and geo-political objectives. They may be structured in a variety of ways, including as a framework agreement for cooperation (to be supplemented on a regular basis by the adoption of protocols for implementation) or as a self-contained agreement providing directly for the conduct of foreign fishing in the EEZ.

Of course, bilateral agreements need not be restricted to a one-directional grant of access from a coastal State to a flag State; reciprocal access agreements between two coastal States also provide an important mechanism for managing foreign fishing, particularly where the fishermen of neighbouring countries have historically fished for a shared or straddling stock—such as in the North Atlantic and various parts of Africa—or in areas where two or more States border an enclosed or semi-enclosed sea in which fishery resources are shared and the seas are not wide enough for coastal States to establish a full 200 nautical mile EEZ—such as the Yellow Sea and East China Sea.[23] For example, while the member States of the EU are more than capable of taking the entire allowable catch in EU waters, the EU has maintained a practice of granting some access to vessels of other coastal States, in return for EU vessels being granted access to their waters, in order to maintain

access agreements. However, it might be a relevant consideration for coastal States wanting to invoke issues of flag State responsibility before an organ of the UN system.

[21] Daniel Pauly et al, 'China's Distant-Water Fisheries in the 21st Century' (2014) 15(3) Fish&Fisheries 474, 475; Jane Mbendo, *Developing Regional Minimum Terms and Conditions for Granting Tuna Fishing Access in the Western Indian Ocean* (WWF Coastal East Africa Initiative 2012) available at <http://d2ouvy59p0dg6k.cloudfront.net/downloads/mtc__consultancy_new_.pdf> accessed 7 December 2020. A notable exception is the European Union (EU) which provides the text of its Fisheries Partnership Agreements in a publicly available online database, available at <http://ec.europa.eu/fisheries/cfp/international/agreements_en> accessed 7 December 2020. Some coastal States specifically require the publication of access agreements. See, eg, Mozambique, *Dec 74/2017* art 28; Namibia, *Act 2000* §36.

[22] Les Clark, 'Case Study on Foreign Fishing Agreements in the Western Pacific' in *Trade in Fishing Services: Emerging Perspectives on Foreign Fishing Arrangements* (World Bank 2014) 61.

[23] Art 123 of the LOSC requires States bordering an enclosed or semi-enclosed sea to cooperate in the exercise of their rights and performance of their duties under the LOSC, and to co-ordinate the management, conservation, exploration, and exploitation of the living resources of the sea.

existing patterns of historic fishing and reduce dislocation.[24] As such, reciprocal access agreements are commonly based not on the existence of a surplus (or the payment of a fee), but on the principle of a 'balanced exchange of access to stocks'.[25]

State-to-State access agreements can also be regional or multilateral, allowing the vessels of one flag State to fish in the waters of two or more coastal States, or providing reciprocal access for the vessels of all Parties to their combined waters. For example, since 1988 the US Tuna Treaty has enabled purse seine vessels from the United States to fish for tuna in the combined EEZs of the members of the Pacific Islands Forum Fisheries Agency (FFA), in return for an annual payment and commitments regarding broader cooperation in fishing and fisheries development, training, technical assistance, and capacity building.[26] Such multilateral access agreements are particularly important for the effective management of straddling and highly migratory species, as they allow coastal States to take regional approaches to regulating foreign fishing for these shared stocks. In addition, the multilateral approach to access negotiations with flag States can have a wide range of benefits for coastal States—particularly developing or small island developing coastal States—with respect to securing the resources, expertise, information, and political leverage necessary to negotiate equitable access arrangements with distant water fishing nations.[27] Reciprocal multilateral access agreements can help to promote other objectives—as in the case of the FSM Arrangement, which provides preferential reciprocal access to the EEZs of all Parties for the domestic vessels of those Parties, as a method of promoting participation in fishing and developing national fisheries industries. Multilateral access agreements can also be used to address unregulated fishing in high seas pockets. For example, the Barents Sea Loophole Agreement—adopted by Norway, Russia, and Iceland in 1999—provides for Icelandic vessels to fish in the EEZs of Norway and Russia, in return for ceasing to fish in the area of high seas known as the Barents Sea 'Loophole' which they enclose.[28]

[24] Robin Churchill and Daniel Owen, *The EC Common Fisheries Policy* (OUP 2010) 330.

[25] Graeme Parkes, 'The Payment of Fees for Access to Fisheries in Exclusive Economic Zones' in *Report of a Regional Workshop on Fisheries Monitoring, Control and Surveillance, Kuala Lumpur and Kuala Terengganu, Malaysia, 29 June–3 July 1998 (Supplement 2, Technical Papers) FAO/Norway Government, Cooperative Programme, GCP/INT/648/NOR–Field Report C-1)* (FAO 1999) 138.

[26] The US Tuna Treaty has been renewed and amended several times. The most recent (2016) amendments are available at <https://www.congress.gov/115/cdoc/tdoc3/CDOC-115tdoc3.pdf> accessed 1 August 2021. The EEZs of the FFA members are depicted in Figure 3.2.

[27] On the challenges faced by developing coastal States in negotiating access agreements, see further: Oda, 'Fisheries under the LOSC' (n 2); Camille Goodman, 'The Cooperative Use of Coastal State Jurisdiction with Respect to Highly Migratory Stocks: Insights from the Western and Central Pacific Region' in Larry Martin, Christina Houreas, and Constantinos Salonidis (eds), *Natural Resources and the Law of the Sea: Exploration, Allocation, Exploitation of Natural Resources in Areas under National Jurisdiction and Beyond* (Juris 2017) 221–2.

[28] *Agreement between Iceland, Norway and Russia Concerning Certain Aspects of Cooperation in the Area of Fisheries* (signed 15 May 1999, entered into force 15 June 1999) (1999) 14 IJMCL 484. See further: Robin Rolf Churchill, 'The Barents Sea Loophole Agreement: A "Coastal State" Solution to a Straddling Stock Problem' (1999) 14 IJMCL 467.

The national legislation of some coastal States provides that foreign fishing in the EEZ may only be permitted pursuant to, or within the framework of, a State-to-State access agreement. For example, Article 15 of Malaysia's *Fisheries Act 1985* provides that no foreign fishing vessel shall engage in fishing in Malaysian fishery waters 'unless authorized so to do under an international fishery agreement in force between the Government of Malaysia and the government of the country, or between the Government of Malaysia and the international organization, to which such vessel belongs or in which such vessel is registered.'

Similar provisions (or provisions with similar effect) are found in the legislation of coastal States in all regions of the world, including a number of Asia-Pacific countries—Cook Islands, Fiji, Indonesia, Japan, the Marshall Islands, Micronesia, Papua New Guinea, Samoa, and Tuvalu—as well as Benin, the EU, Montenegro and Russia, Argentina, Bahamas, Mexico and Venezuela, and Iceland, Norway, and the United States.[29] In addition, the legislation of a large number of other coastal states provides that State-to-State access agreements are one way in which foreign fishing may be authorized (along with various combinations of other approaches).[30]

4.1.1.2 Government-to-Industry Access Agreements

While significant advantages can be obtained by ensuring that foreign fishing is conducted on the basis of a State-to-State agreement—particularly by negotiating benefits that can only be provided by a State—there may also be circumstances in which it is preferable for the coastal State to conclude an access agreement with a corporation or private sector association rather than a flag State, whether for political or diplomatic reasons, to avoid formal or lengthy treaty ratification processes, or for simple expediency.[31] Such agreements—which do not constitute treaties—may be negotiated directly with an individual fishing company, but are most commonly entered into between a coastal State and an association representing the fishing industry of the flag State,[32] such as the National Ocean Tuna Fishery Association of Japan or the China Overseas Fisheries Association.[33] These associations are composed of fishing companies, local fishing cooperative associations, and fishing boat owners engaged in deep sea or distant water fishing. Their principal objectives generally include securing fishing access through negotiation and cooperation with coastal States, strengthening cooperation with regional or international fisheries organizations and contributing to the development of the

[29] See Table 4.1.

[30] Ibid. The use of State-to-State access agreements as a means to regulate foreign fishing is contemplated in the legislation of at least half the coastal States examined in this book.

[31] Carroz and Savini, 'The Practice of Coastal States Regarding Foreign Access' (n 17) 45.

[32] These agreements are mainly concluded with industry associations from Japan, Taiwan, Korea, and China: Elizabeth Havice, 'The Structure of Tuna Access Agreements' (n 19) 981.

[33] See the details of the national tuna fisheries associations provided by the Organization for the Promotion of Responsible Tuna Fisheries, available at <http://oprt.or.jp/eng/members/> accessed 7 December 2020.

fishing industry. Such 'Government-to-industry' access agreements do not explicitly involve financial contributions from the flag State, although officials from the flag State may be involved in the negotiations (and may seek to link the negotiation of such agreements to the provision of other benefits or development assistance to the coastal State).[34]

The national legislation of many coastal States provides for the granting of foreign fishing access pursuant to Government-to-industry agreements—generally as an alternative to a State-to-State access agreement. For example, pursuant to Article 37 of Mozambique's *Fisheries Law No 22/2013*, the Government may conclude: '(a) multilateral or bilateral agreements with third States interested in obtaining fishing rights, or for the purpose of research, experimentation and fisheries inspection, in the jurisdictional waters of Mozambique; or (b) contracts with international organizations or foreign fishing associations, granting fishing rights, with priority to those whose countries have signed agreements with Mozambique.'

The adoption of such agreements as an alternative to State-to-State access agreements is also envisaged in the legislation of a large number of other coastal States, in particular developing countries in Africa, the Asia-Pacific, and the Caribbean.[35] And the legislation of some coastal States provides for foreign fishing to be authorized pursuant to 'access agreements' generally, which, unless the context indicates otherwise, could be interpreted to mean either a State-to-State or Government-to-industry agreement.[36]

4.1.1.3 Direct Licensing

Not all States require an access agreement to provide a framework for regulating foreign fishing; another option is direct licensing. Exercising jurisdiction in this way allows foreign fishing licences to be issued quickly and for short periods, giving the coastal State flexibility to adjust the fishing levels as dictated by biological, social, and economic drivers, and providing a direct resource rent to the government.[37] Of course, it also has some limitations. While a broad range of terms and conditions can be imposed under a vessel licence—including with respect to important fisheries management issues like catch reporting, and fisheries development issues such as technology transfer, employment of local crew, and domestic landing of catch—in the long term the 'unsubstantiality of the arrangement counsels against great expectations' in this regard.[38] In particular, without the participation of a flag State or national fisheries association, it will be more difficult for the coastal State to secure the broader, long-term, enforceable forms of cooperation that might be

[34] Havice, 'The Structure of Tuna Access Agreements' (n 19) 981. On linking development assistance to fisheries access, see nn 97–101 and associated text.
[35] See Table 4.1.
[36] Ibid.
[37] Christy and Moore, 'Forms of Foreign Participation in Fisheries' (n 15) 96–7.
[38] Ibid 97.

achieved through an access agreement. In addition, the direct issuance of commercial licences to foreign fishing vessels is also potentially a less transparent method by which to grant access to the natural resources of the coastal State.[39] Nonetheless, direct licensing of foreign fishing vessels is provided for in the national legislation of a significant number of coastal States, either on its own or as an alternative or exception to the adoption of an access agreement.[40]

4.1.2 Harnessing Foreign Participation through Association or Assimilation with Domestic Interests

While Article 62(2) establishes an obligation to provide other States with access to the surplus in situations where the coastal State 'does not have the capacity to harvest' the entire allowable catch, the concept of 'harvesting capacity' is not defined in the LOSC, nor are there any restrictions on the coastal State artificially enhancing its capacity by contracting foreign vessels, crews, capital, tools, technology, or know-how in order to harvest the catch itself.[41] As Oda has observed, it is thus possible that even the least-developed coastal States may be considered to always have the capacity to harvest the entire catch.[42] In this regard, a wide variety of arrangements have been adopted that require foreign fishing interests to be associated with, or assimilated to, the domestic interests of the coastal State. These may take the form of residency, headquarter, or capital requirements; special arrangements for 'locally-based' foreign fishing vessels; joint ventures involving foreign partners; chartering arrangements; or other types of contractual arrangements.[43] Such arrangements are specifically envisaged in Article 62(4)(i) of the LOSC, which provides that the terms and conditions for foreign fishing that may be established in the laws and regulations of the coastal State might include 'terms and conditions relating to joint ventures or other cooperative arrangements'.

[39] However, access agreements also pose significant challenges to transparency, since they are commonly negotiated in private and not made publicly available.

[40] See Table 4.1. Perhaps reflecting these limitations, a number of coastal States provide that direct licensing may only be used in exceptional circumstances (in particular, if the negotiation of an access agreement is not practicable) and/or require high level approval or the provision of a bond or other financial security. See, eg, Eritrea, Mauritius, Sao Tome and Principe, Seychelles, Togo, South Africa, and Belize.

[41] James Harrison and Elisa Morgera, 'Article 62' in Alexander Proelss (ed), *United Nations Convention on the Law of the Sea: A Commentary* (CH Beck 2017) 497–8.

[42] Oda, 'Fisheries under the LOSC' (n 2) 744.

[43] See Christy and Moore, 'Forms of Foreign Participation in Fisheries' (n 15) 97–9; World Bank, *Trade in Fishing Services* (n 19) 18–20; Pierre Failler, *Review of Previous and Current Fisheries Agreements Concluded by Some African Union Member States in West and Central Africa* (AU-IBAR 2015) 12–14, available at <https://www.researchgate.net/publication/299513786_Review_of_previous_and_current_fisheries_agreements_concluded_by_some_African_Union_Member_States> accessed 1 August 2021.

In Angola, for example, fishing rights may be granted to foreign natural or legal persons conducting their activities 'in association with' Angolan nationals, while Cameroon's legislation provides that fishing licences may only be granted to natural or legal persons resident or headquartered in Cameroon whose capital composition is known to the administration responsible for fisheries.[44] Similarly, Argentina's legislation provides for foreign fishing vessels to be authorized to access surplus stocks in the EEZ through joint ventures with Argentinian companies, the chartering of foreign fishing vessels by Brazilian companies is considered 'an instrument of national oceanic fisheries development policy', and Colombia's legislation states that foreign fishing vessels may only be used in the Colombian EEZ pursuant to a contract with a Colombian company that has agreed to deliver part of the catch to supply the domestic market.[45] A number of other coastal States, particularly in Africa and Latin America, also provide for foreign vessels to access the living resources of the EEZ through residency or domicile requirements, or by chartering, joint venture, or other forms of association with nationals.[46]

Such arrangements can have significant benefits for coastal States. Rather than simply allowing foreign vessels to harvest the fishery resources of the EEZ in return for a one-off access fee, approaches involving association with national interests can provide a mechanism for coastal States to obtain the capital, infrastructure, or expertise required to develop their domestic fishing industry, or stimulate on-shore investment in port services, processing, or marketing. They can also enable two States to combine their skills and resources (such as labour, capital, infrastructure, markets, technology, and fishery resources) to best advantage.[47] However, these arrangements can also have drawbacks, such as the possibility for foreign interests to dominate the most profitable aspects of the fishing operation or use complex business structures to evade measures designed to regulate foreign fishing,[48] and the limits on the extent of the coastal State's jurisdiction over certain aspects of the operation of foreign fishing vessels—particularly 'internal' matters such as labour standards and rights protections—in its EEZ.

Should such forms of 'association' not prove sufficient to give effect to the coastal State's objectives, another option is to assimilate foreign-flagged vessels to national vessels, such as by requiring them to re-flag or be 'declared' to be national boats in order to access fishery resources in the EEZ. For example, while Section 82 of the New Zealand *Fisheries Act 1996* contemplates the allocation of surplus resources to other States, Section 103(1) requires that all fishing vessels operating in the New Zealand EEZ be flagged to New Zealand. Following serious allegations

[44] See Table 4.1.
[45] Ibid.
[46] Ibid.
[47] On the benefits and drawbacks of joint ventures, see World Bank, *Trade in Fishing Services* (n 19) 17–18.
[48] Christy and Moore, 'Forms of Foreign Participation in Fisheries' (n 15) 97–8.

of mistreatment and underpayment of foreign crews working on some foreign charter vessels,[49] this requirement was introduced in 2014 in order to protect the human rights of crews and ensure the maintenance of New Zealand's reputation as a responsible and sustainable fishing nation.[50] As a result, foreign-owned fishing vessels and crews operating in New Zealand's EEZ are subject to the same regulations as New Zealand domestic vessels—not only with respect to the fisheries law, but in relation to minimum wages and other employment conditions.[51]

In Australia, although Sections 34 to 37 of the *Fisheries Management Act 1991* (Cth) provide a basis to allow foreign fishing in the EEZ, the current policy is that foreign fishing licences are not issued outside the framework of existing State-to-State access agreements (which provide for traditional fishing by nationals of Indonesia and Papua New Guinea in specific areas).[52] However, under Section 4(2) of the Act, a foreign vessel may be 'declared' to be an 'Australian boat' under the Act, allowing it to operate in Australian waters provided that the vessel is only to be used in Australia for a limited period of time, and the authorities are satisfied that there will be sufficient Australian control of the operations of the vessel during that period. Once declared to be an 'Australian boat', the vessel will be subject to the operation of the fisheries management and enforcement regime (and other relevant legislation) in the same way as Australian-flagged and Australian-owned vessels in the EEZ.[53] As these examples demonstrate, by assimilating foreign vessels with national vessels, coastal States may seek to apply the same fisheries management and enforcement regime with respect to both domestic and foreign-flagged or foreign-owned vessels in their EEZs, or leverage their fisheries jurisdiction to have a broader regulatory effect with respect to issues such as human rights and labour standards.

[49] Christina Stringer et al 'Not in New Zealand's Waters, Surely? Labour and Human Rights Abuses Aboard Foreign Fishing Vessels' [2011] *New Zealand Asia Institute Working Paper Series No 11:01*, available at <http://docs.business.auckland.ac.nz/Doc/11-01-Not-in-New-Zealand-waters-surely-NZAI-Working-Paper-Sept-2011.pdf> accessed 8 December 2020.

[50] Joanna Mossop, 'New Zealand Requires Foreign Charter Vessels to Reflag' (2016) 1 APacJOceanL&Pol 106, 106–7.

[51] An exemption may be granted for the purposes of fisheries-related research where no New Zealand ship is available, in which case the vessel must also comply with New Zealand employment law including the payment of minimum wages: New Zealand, *Act 1996* s103A.

[52] See Australia, *Second National Plan of Action to Prevent, Deter and Eliminate Illegal, Unreported and Unregulated Fishing* [46], available at <http://fao.org/3/a-ax408e.pdf> accessed 8 December 2020; David Borthwick, *Review of Commonwealth Fisheries: Legislation, Policy and Management* (2012) 89–90, available at <https://www.agriculture.gov.au/fisheries/fisheries-management-review> accessed 1 August 2021.

[53] In contrast to the New Zealand approach, this declaration does not affect the vessel's flag status. A foreign-flagged boat that has been 'declared' to be an Australian boat remains foreign-flagged and will only be authorized to fish in the Australian EEZ; any high seas fishing must be authorized by the flag State: Australian Fisheries Management Authority, *Declaring a Foreign Boat to Be an Australian Boat* (2003) 4, available at <http://afma.gov.au/sites/default/files/uploads/2014/12/boatdeclaration.pdf> accessed 8 December 2020.

4.1.3 Excluding Foreign Participation by Directly or Indirectly Prohibiting Foreign Fishing

Although Article 62(2) appears to establish an obligation for coastal States to allow other States to access any surplus fisheries resources in the EEZ, this requirement is more ostensible than real. Since the coastal State has complete discretion to determine whether there is a surplus or whether the nationals of the coastal State can harvest the entirety of the allowable catch, it is generally considered to be within the power of the coastal State to effectively prohibit foreign fishing through the exercise of this discretion.[54] In this respect, some coastal States have used their discretion very broadly to directly prohibit all foreign fishing in the EEZ, whether by reference to foreign nationals, or foreign vessels.

For example, pursuant to Section 5 of the Philippines *Fisheries Code 1998*, 'the use and exploitation of the fishery and aquatic resources in Philippine waters shall be reserved exclusively to Filipinos' (although research and survey activities may be allowed, under strict regulations, for purely research, scientific, technological, and educational purposes that would also benefit Filipino citizens). Egypt's legislation simply provides that 'fishing licences shall not be issued to foreign vessels.'[55] Provisions prohibiting the grant of fisheries access to foreign nationals or foreign vessels also appear in the legislation of Bahrain, Djibouti, Indonesia, Morocco, Qatar, Thailand, Tunisia, Turkey, the United Arab Emirates, Albania, Chile, and Panama.[56]

There are also instances in which coastal States have indirectly prohibited foreign fishing by declaring a marine protected area (MPA) over the EEZ, with the effect that no surplus will be declared, and no foreign fishing allowed. While the establishment of MPAs is clearly within the sovereign rights of the coastal State under Article 56 of the LOSC, recently there has been a noticeable trend toward the protection of vast areas of the EEZ within which commercial fishing is completely prohibited—predominantly in remote locations where surveillance and enforcement is difficult and expensive. For example, in 2016 an MPA was declared over the 834,000 square kilometres EEZ of the Pitcairn Islands, within which all commercial fishing is prohibited.[57] This followed the United Kingdom's 2010 proclamation of an MPA over the entirety of the 200 nautical mile Environment (Protection and

[54] See, eg, William T Burke, '1982 Convention on the Law of the Sea Provisions on Conditions of Access to Fisheries Subject to National Jurisdiction' (1984) 63 OrLR 73, 89–90; Mohamed Dahmani, *The Fisheries Regime of the Exclusive Economic Zone* (Martinus Nijhoff 1987) 55; Gordon Munro, 'The Legal and Economic Principles Underlying Foreign Fishing Arrangements' in *Trade in Fishing Services: Emerging Perspectives on Foreign Fishing Arrangements* (World Bank 2014) 45. See also the discussion in Section 2.1.2 regarding the effect of the obligation to set a total allowable catch under art 61(1).

[55] Egypt, *Act 124 of 1983* art 125.

[56] See Table 4.1.

[57] United Kingdom (Pitcairn Islands), *Ordinance 2016* ss 4 and 8. Since the Pitcairn Islands is an overseas territory of the United Kingdom, this marine park forms part of the United Kingdom's EEZ.

Preservation) Zone established for the British Indian Ocean Territory (BIOT), within which all commercial fishing and extractive activities are prohibited.[58] Similarly, in 2015 Palau established a national marine sanctuary covering 80 per cent of its EEZ, within which all commercial fishing is prohibited.[59] Fishing has also been completely prohibited in large MPAs established by Kiribati, Chile, New Zealand, and the United States.[60] It is thus important to consider whether the legislative exclusion of any possibility of foreign access to the surplus resources in large parts of the EEZ—with no temporal limit that might allow for a periodic reassessment of the situation—has the potential to undermine the objective of 'optimum utilization', which was an important *quid pro quo* in the 'package deal' under which coastal States gained the right to extend their jurisdiction over living resources to 200 nautical miles.

While it has been argued that 'all-encompassing nature protection areas purporting to occupy the full extent of the EEZ and exercising degrees of exclusive control' require some form of multilateral mandate for legitimacy,[61] the better view is that they are consistent with the LOSC, provided the coastal State has 'due regard' to the rights and duties of other States in their establishment and operation.[62] A wide range of considerations may legitimately underpin a coastal State's decision to proclaim a permanent MPA and prohibit foreign fishing—including an ongoing absence of any surplus resources, the needs of coastal fishing communities or the overwhelming dependence of the coastal State on the exploitation of

[58] United Kingdom (BIOT), *Proclamation 1 of 2010*. Since the United Kingdom has continued to administer the Chagos Archipelago and the surrounding EEZ as the BIOT since the independence of Mauritius, this marine park currently forms part of the United Kingdom EEZ. However, sovereignty over the Chagos Archipelago is disputed by Mauritius. In 2015, the *Chagos Arbitration* Tribunal recognized, without prejudice to the question of sovereignty, that Mauritius has certain rights in respect of the Chagos Archipelago, including fishing rights, and found that the United Kingdom's establishment of the MPA breached arts 2(3) and 56 of the LOSC, on the basis that Mauritius' rights had been significantly affected by its establishment, and the United Kingdom had failed to properly consult with Mauritius or balance its rights and interests: *Chagos Arbitration* [449]–[455] and [520]–[536]. In addition, the International Tribunal for the Law of the Sea (ITLOS) has found that while the process of decolonization has yet to be completed, Mauritius' sovereignty can be inferred from the determinations of the International Court of Justice (ICJ) in *Legal Consequences of the Separation of the Chagos Archipelago from Mauritius in 1965* (Advisory Opinion) (2019) ICJ Rep 95: see *Dispute Concerning Delimitation of the Maritime Boundary Between Mauritius and Maldives in the Indian Ocean (Mauritius/Maldives)* (Preliminary Objections, Judgment) [2021] ITLOS Case No 28 [246].

[59] Palau, 27 *PNC* §161. The remaining 20 per cent of the EEZ has been declared a 'Domestic Fishing Zone' within which commercial fishing is limited to tuna and billfish caught through free-school purse-seining and long-lining and fish must be landed in Palau prior to export unless otherwise authorized by the Minister.

[60] For details of the extended MPAs established within EEZs by coastal States see: <http://mpatlas.org/> accessed 8 December 2020.

[61] Richard P Dunne et al, 'The Creation of the Chagos Marine Protected Area. A Fisheries Perspective' (2014) 69 Advances in MarBiol 79, 114.

[62] Nicola R Wheen, 'Marine Protected Areas in the Exclusive Economic Zone: UNCLOS or the TPPA's Looming Presence?' (2016) 14(2) OtLR 351, 355–6. See also New Zealand Government Cabinet Paper, 'Establishment of a Kermadec Ocean Sanctuary' 10 September 2015 [36]–[41], available at <http://beehive.govt.nz/sites/default/files/3_%20Cabinet_paper-Establishment_of_a_Kermadec_Ocean_Sanctuary.pdf> accessed 11 November 2020.

the living resources of the EEZ,[63] a lack of economic viability,[64] and difficulties in preventing illegal fishing. In addition, since the current marine reserves only relate to a portion of the EEZs of the coastal States in question, it remains possible for the coastal State to establish a total allowable catch, calculate a surplus, and allow foreign fishing in the remaining parts of the EEZ. Nonetheless, the increasing practice of establishing extended MPAs—and the consequent exclusion of all foreign fishing—represents a potentially noteworthy development in the interpretation and implementation of Article 62.

4.2 Allocating a Surplus to Foreign States: Article 62(3)

Notwithstanding the developments highlighted in Section 4.1, it is clear that most coastal States do provide for the possibility of foreign access to the surplus living resources of the EEZ as envisaged in Article 62(2), using one or more of the approaches discussed. However, very few States follow the mechanism established in Article 62(3) of the LOSC, which sets out a number of criteria for allocating a surplus among foreign States. It is difficult to comprehensively evaluate State practice in this regard, including because: the question of whether or not to allocate foreign access to a particular State is commonly an executive or administrative decision; most coastal States do not expressly reflect obligations of this type in their national legislation; and the substantive content of fisheries access agreements is not widely available. However, by analysing the national legislation of States against the regime described in Article 62(3), it is possible to draw some conclusions about the way in which coastal States have interpreted, implemented, and developed this provision, which highlight:

- the very limited number of references to any requirement to allocate a surplus;
- the limited extent to which coastal States apply the criteria for allocation developed in Articles 62(3), 69, and 70; and
- the development of a range of additional criteria to guide the coastal State's decision-making regarding the allocation of surplus resources among other States.

63 LOSC arts 61(3) and 71.

64 For example, the United Kingdom asserted the BIOT fishery to be 'a loss-making venture and heavily subsidized': UK Foreign and Commonwealth Office, Overseas Territories Directorate, 'UK/Mauritius Talks on the British Indian Ocean Territory', 24 July 2009, cited in *Chagos Arbitration* [128] and fn 167. Similarly, an assessment of the Pitcairn Islands' EEZ in May 2013 concluded that large-scale commercial fishing is not commercially viable, particularly taking into account the cost of monitoring and enforcement required to ensure the sustainability of stocks: Pew Charitable Trusts, *Is Offshore Commercial Fishing a Prospect in the Pitcairn Islands?* (May 2013), available at <http://pewtrusts.org/-/media/legacy/uploadedfiles/peg/publications/report/ioffshorecommercialfishinginthepitcairnislands pdf.pdf> accessed 8 December 2020.

4.2.1 Incorporation of the Obligation to Allocate a Surplus

While some of the early reviews of State practice do identify a number of coastal States whose national legislation refers to allowing other States access to a surplus in similar terms to the LOSC,[65] from the 1990s onwards the literature observes that the majority of coastal States do not make any specific reference in their national legislation to the requirement to allocate a surplus to foreign States.[66] This is borne out in contemporary practice, in which the national legislation of only five of the coastal States examined in this book—Comoros, Cuba, Guinea, Indonesia, and Mexico—clearly establishes a positive requirement that the coastal State *shall* determine and allocate any surplus resources among foreign States.[67] Another small group of coastal States—Angola, New Zealand, Russia, Somalia, the United States and Venezuela—approach the determination and allocation of a surplus on a permissive basis, by specifically noting that surplus resources *may* be allocated to foreign nationals.[68]

Rather than providing either a positive obligation or a permissive right regarding surplus resources, a number of coastal States address the potential for foreign access in the negative, by providing that fishing rights allocated to foreign vessels 'must not exceed the total amount allocated' under the relevant fisheries management plan. This approach—which implies compliance with the coastal State's obligations regarding conservation and optimum utilization as well as the establishment of a surplus, while retaining significant flexibility regarding the extent of its allocation—features in the legislation of several Caribbean countries, as well as some African and Asia-Pacific States.[69] Beyond this, even where no particular reference is made regarding the allocation of resources to other States, it is clear

[65] See Gerald Moore, *Coastal State Requirements for Foreign Fishing* (Rev 1, FAO 1983) 6–8; Barbara Kwiatkowska, 'Conservation and Optimum Utilization of Living Resources' in Thomas A Clingan (ed), *The Law of the Sea: What Lies Ahead? Proceedings of the 20th Annual Conference of the Law of the Sea Institute, July 21–24, 1986* (Law of the Sea Institute 1988) 249.

[66] Dahmani, *The Fisheries Regime* (n 54) 75; Attard, *The EEZ* (n 12) 161; William T Burke, *The New International Law of Fisheries* (Clarendon Press 1994) 64. Some of the key reasons for, and implications of, this approach are helpfully summarized in Moore, *Coastal State Requirements for Foreign Fishing, Rev 1* (n 65) 6 fn 4: 'National legislation tends by its very nature to be concerned more with relations between the State and individuals, whether national or foreign, and with relations among individuals rather than with inter-state relations. Legislative drafters are also traditionally cautious in using language that unnecessarily acknowledges obligations of the State under international law. The absence of any reference in national legislation to responsibilities of the coastal State under international law does not, of course, mean that such responsibilities do not exist or are not accepted by the State.'

[67] See Table 4.1. In Indonesia, the practical effect of this requirement has been neutralized through subsequent regulations prohibiting foreigners, foreign vessels, and foreign entities from fishing, working, and investing in the fisheries sector.

[68] See Table 4.1.

[69] See Antigua and Barbuda, *Act 2006* s 26(2); Dominica, *Act 1987* s 7(2); Eritrea, *Proc 176/2014* art 15(1); Gambia, *Act 2007* s 38(1); Guyana, *Act 2012* §17(2); Japan, *Act 1996* art 6(1); Korea, *Fishing Act 1996* art 6(1); Saint Lucia, *Act 1984* s 7(2); Saint Vincent and the Grenadines, *Act 1986* s 7(2); Equatorial Guinea, *Law 11/2017* arts 142 and 143(1)(d); South Africa, *Act 1998* s 38(1); Tonga, *Act 2002* s 36(2); United Kingdom (Montserrat), *Act 2000* s 23(3), (Turks and Caicos Islands), *Regs 1998* reg 8(3).

that the national legislation of most coastal States does envisage the possibility of foreign fishing access in the EEZ, pursuant to the various approaches described in Section 4.1 and Table 4.1. However, this raises a more difficult question—how are surplus resources to be allocated among foreign States?

4.2.2 Application of the LOSC Criteria for Allocating the Surplus

The question of how the surplus resources of the EEZ would be allocated was the subject of 'difficult and arduous negotiations' during the development of the LOSC,[70] as countries with different interests all sought to ensure some form of priority access.[71] Distant water fishing nations proposed the inclusion of criteria such as patterns of traditional fishing in the area, and contribution to the cost and conduct of fisheries research, exploration, and development; land-locked and geographically disadvantaged States made a wide range of proposals regarding the way in which they might be given preferential rights or otherwise assured a fair and equitable share of the resources; developing States argued for particular recognition of their need to access the surplus catch; and coastal States sought to maximize their discretion and avoid any priority or preference being applied to the allocation criteria.[72]

The hard-fought compromise that was ultimately reached between these positions is reflected in Article 62(3) of the LOSC, which requires that in giving other States access to its EEZ, the coastal State: 'shall take into account all relevant factors, including, *inter alia*, the significance of the living resources of the area to the economy of the coastal State concerned and its other national interests, the provisions of articles 69 and 70, the requirements of developing States in the subregion or region in harvesting part of the surplus and the need to minimize economic dislocation in States whose nationals have habitually fished in the zone or which have made substantial efforts in research and identification of stocks.'

While this provision clearly attempts to balance the rights of the coastal State with the legitimate interests of other States, the breadth of criteria that can be considered by the coastal State—combined with the lack of any formula requiring prioritization or preference—has effectively allowed the coastal State the 'broadest discretion to decide to whom and under what conditions access will be granted, which constitutes a new expression of compatibility with its sovereign

[70] Jorge Castaneda, 'Negotiations on the Exclusive Economic Zone at the Third United Nations Conference on the Law of the Sea' in Jerzy Makarczyk (ed), *Essays in International Law in Honor of Judge Manfred Lachs* (Brill 1984) 618.

[71] Francisco Orrego Vicuna, *The Exclusive Economic Zone* (CUP 1989) 54.

[72] For further detail on the proposals put forward by these groups of States during the negotiations, see Nandan and Rosenne, *UNCLOS Commentary, Vol II* (n 10) 613–34; Burke, *The New International Law of Fisheries* (n 66) 69–80.

rights regarding these resources'.[73] Nonetheless, given the difficulty experienced in negotiating this provision, and its importance to achieving consensus on the overall EEZ regime, fishing States might reasonably have expected that in negotiations regarding access, coastal States would exercise their discretion by reference to the criteria in Article 62(3).[74] If that were indeed their expectation, it is likely that they have been disappointed.

Notwithstanding the critical role attributed to the rights of land-locked and geographically disadvantaged States during the negotiation of the LOSC—reflected in their inclusion in Article 62(2) and (3), as well as in the detailed provisions of Articles 69 and 70 regarding the 'right' of such States to participate in the exploitation of any surplus—the practical effect of these rights is very tenuous, since nothing in any of the relevant provisions constrains the coastal State's discretion to grant (or refuse) access to foreign States on the basis of any particular criteria. And while the rights of land-locked and geographically disadvantaged States have been the focus of extensive analysis in the literature over the last thirty years,[75] this has not been matched by any extensive attention in the practice of coastal States. Indeed, only two coastal States actually refer to this issue in their fisheries legislation: Angola, which states that in the case of a surplus, preference is to be given to 'inland and/or geographically disadvantaged and South African Development Community (SADC) States';[76] and Morocco, which 'adheres to the principle of privileged cooperation, concerning the living resources, with neighbouring land-locked countries'.[77] Of course, coastal States may choose to grant fishing access to land-locked or geographically disadvantaged States notwithstanding the lack of a reference to this criterion in their national legislation, but while there are some reports of access being granted to developing landlocked States, doubts have been raised about their practical effect.[78] In addition, the UN Food and Agriculture Organization's (FAO) fishery statistics do not report any marine capture landings from vessels flagged to any land-locked country between 2009 and 2018—which suggests that such countries are either not seeking (or not being granted) access to fishing in the EEZ, or are being required to attribute their catches to the relevant coastal State.[79]

73 Orrego Vicuna, *The EEZ* (n 71) 54.

74 William Edeson and JF Pulvenis, *The Legal Regime of Fisheries in the Caribbean Region* (Springer-Verlag 1983) 28.

75 See Burke, '1982 Convention on the Law of the Sea' (n 54) 95–100; Dahmani, *The Fisheries Regime* (n 54) 67–74; Kwiatkowska, *The 200 Mile EEZ* (n 5) 70–4; Orrego Vicuna, *The EEZ* (n 71) 55–9; Burke, *The New International Law of Fisheries* (n 66) 69–77; Marion Markowski, *The International Law of EEZ Fisheries* (Europa Law 2010) 70–4.

76 Angola, *Law 6-A/04 of 2004* art 59(2).

77 Morocco, *Act 1-81 of 1980* art 13.

78 Helmut Tuerk, 'Landlocked and Geographically Disadvantaged States' in Donald R Rothwell et al (eds), *The Oxford Handbook of the Law of the Sea* (OUP 2017) 343.

79 FAO, *Yearbook of Fishery and Aquaculture Statistics 2018* (FAO 2020).

Evidence of national legislation addressing 'the requirements of developing States in the subregion or region' is similarly lacking. Besides the reference to 'SADC States' in the Angolan legislation, only two other coastal States have legislation that addresses this issue: Namibia, where Section 35(1) of the *Marine Resources Act 2000* specifies that a fisheries agreement may be entered into with a member country of the SADC; and Niue, which specifies in Section 22 of the *Territorial Sea and Exclusive Economic Zone Act 1996* that preferential access may be granted to vessels owned or controlled by member countries of the FFA.

Similarly, while the 'need to minimize economic dislocation in States whose nationals have habitually fished' in the EEZ was clearly seen as important during the negotiation of the LOSC, very few coastal States recognize it as a criterion for the allocation of surplus fishery resources.[80] One example is the Bahamas' *Fisheries Resources (Jurisdiction and Conservation) Act 1977*, which provides in Section 10(4)(a) that the proportion of the total allowable level of foreign fishing to be allocated to a foreign State will be calculated 'taking into account the extent to which fishermen of that foreign State have traditionally engaged in fishing activity in the fishery concerned'. Similar provisions are included in the legislation of Honduras, Nauru, New Zealand, and the United States.[81]

The criterion of having made 'substantial efforts in research and identification of stocks' in the EEZ is taken into consideration by a slightly larger number of States. For example, pursuant to Section 5(a) of Nauru's *Fisheries Act 1997*, in exercising powers in respect of foreign fishing in the EEZ, the Minister or relevant official shall have regard to whether the relevant State 'has cooperated with the Republic in, and made substantial contributions to, the development of Nauru's fishing industry, fishery research and the identification and management of fishing resources'. Similar criteria are found in the legislation of Equatorial Guinea, Brunei, Malaysia, the Marshall Islands, Micronesia, New Zealand, and the United States.[82] In addition, some coastal States include ongoing or *future* cooperation in fishery research as a criterion for foreign fishing access, by means of both access agreements[83] and licensing conditions.[84]

[80] Historical or habitual fishing may also be protected through ongoing access agreements or arrangements, rather than by the allocation of a surplus. For example, pursuant to a bilateral memorandum of understanding (MOU), some Indonesian fishermen are permitted to engage in fishing in a certain area of the Australian EEZ using traditional methods, in recognition of the long history of traditional Indonesian fishing in that area: *Australia-Indonesia Memorandum of Understanding regarding the Operations of Indonesian Traditional Fishermen in Areas of the Australian Fishing Zone and Continental Shelf* (signed 7 November 1974) LEX-FAOC001631.

[81] Honduras, *Dec 172-99* art 8(1); Nauru, *Act 1997* s 5(d); New Zealand, *Act 1996* s 82(2)(a); United States, 16 *USC* §1821(e)(1)(E)(vi).

[82] Equatorial Guinea, *Law 11/2017* art 143(1)(c); Brunei, *Order 2009* s 22(b); Malaysia, *Act 1985* s 18(1)(b); Marshall Islands, 51 *MIRC* §206(2)(b); Micronesia, 24 *FSM Code* §504(2)(b); New Zealand, *Act 1996* s 82(2)(b); United States, 16 *USC* §1821(e)(1)(E)(vi).

[83] Mozambique, *Law 22/2013* art 37(3)(d); Timor-Leste, *Dec Law 2004* art 32(2).

[84] Art 62(4)(f) of the LOSC specifically identifies fisheries research as a licence condition that may be imposed by the coastal State, which may require 'the conduct of specified fisheries research programmes … including the sampling of catches, disposition of samples and reporting of associated scientific data'.

Of course, in addition to these four criteria relating to the interests of other States, Article 62(3) also expressly entitles the coastal State to take into account the significance of the living resources of the area to its own economy and national interests in allocating or apportioning any surplus resources. Indeed, it has been suggested that the importance attached by coastal States to the right to choose the participants in the surplus stock was 'mainly due to the fact that many States envisaged trading the right of access against non-marine concessions'.[85] As various commentators have observed, such 'national interests' need not relate to fisheries; they may be political, strategic, educational, cultural, environmental, religious, or ideological.[86] As a result, despite it having been expected that negotiations regarding foreign State access would refer to the criteria in Article 62(3),[87] it quickly became clear that the chief criterion that would guide the granting of access was the coastal State's own national interest.[88] This is reflected in the range of additional criteria for foreign fishing access that have developed in State practice.

4.2.3 Additional Criteria Governing Access to or Allocation of Surplus Resources

As may be obvious from the preceding discussion, very few coastal States have incorporated a set of allocation or apportionment criteria into their national legislation in a way that clearly reflects Article 62(3) of the LOSC.[89] The approach more commonly taken by coastal States is to prescribe conditions to be included in access agreements, or taken into consideration in granting licenses, which then operate in practice as criteria—or pre-requisites—for allocation or apportionment of the surplus to a particular foreign State.[90] In this regard, a number of common themes or interests can be distilled from the wide variety of criteria for access set out in the national legislation of coastal States, including:

- the payment of access fees or other forms of compensation;
- the exercise of flag State responsibility or cooperation in enforcement of fisheries laws;

[85] Attard, *The EEZ* (n 12) 168.
[86] Burke, '1982 Convention on the Law of the Sea' (n 54) 93; Kwiatkowska, *The 200 Mile EEZ* (n 5) 65.
[87] Edeson and Pulvenis, *The Legal Regime of Fisheries in the Caribbean* (n 74) 28.
[88] Orrego Vicuna, *The EEZ* (n 71) 54–5.
[89] Of the coastal States examined in this book, only eight set out a legislated list of criteria to be considered in allocating fishing opportunities to foreign States: Brunei, *Order 2009* s 22; Malaysia, *Act 1985* s 18; Marshall Islands, 51 *MIRC* §206; Micronesia, 24 *FSM Code* §504; Nauru, *Act 1997* s 5; Papua New Guinea, *Act 1998* s 34; New Zealand, *Act 1996* s 82(2); United States, 16 *USC* §1821(e) and (f).
[90] These criteria, or pre-requisites, for the granting of access under art 62(3) are separate to the 'terms and conditions' in the laws and regulations of the coastal State envisaged under art 62(4), which apply to the activities of foreign nationals or the operation of foreign fishing vessels during the period of the licence, discussed in Section 4.3.

- the reciprocity of access for the coastal State to the resources or markets of the flag State; and
- the development and application by individual coastal States of specific criteria that give effect to particular national interests.

4.2.3.1 Access Fees and Other Forms of Compensation

In essence, foreign fishing access is a form of trade. It has been described as form of *export,* involving the sale of a fishing right (defined by species, catch, vessels, time, or area) by a coastal State in return for compensation from the flag State (through an access payment, or some other form of remuneration).[91] It can also be understood as a trade in services, involving the *import* by the coastal State of fishing services from the flag State (such as harvesting, processing, packaging, and distributing) in order to maximize the returns from (or optimize the utilization of) the living resources in its EEZ.[92] While the latter approach appears to involve the exporter (the flag State or vessel) paying the importer (the coastal State) for the right to provide the service, the coastal State's payment for the services is implicitly contained within the gains made by the flag State or vessel from the exploitation of the resources. On either view, it is clear that coastal States need to understand where their 'comparative advantage' lies in relation to the conduct of fishing operations in the EEZ,[93] and what form of and level of compensation for access will allow them to maximize the returns on their resources.

While Article 62(4)(a) lists the 'payment of fees and other forms of remuneration' as one of the terms and conditions that may be established in the laws and regulations of the coastal State, in practice the financial or other forms of 'resource rent' actually constitute a fundamental consideration for coastal States in allocating access to other States.[94] However, there are no rules of international law regarding

[91] Stephen Mbithi Mwikya, *Fisheries Access Agreements: Trade and Development Issues* (International Centre for Trade and Sustainable Development 2006) IX–X; Marcos Orellana, *Towards Sustainable Fisheries Access Agreements* (United Nations Environment Programme 2008) ix.

[92] World Bank, *Trade in Fishing Services* (n 19) 16; Munro, 'The Legal and Economic Principles Underlying Foreign Fishing Arrangements' (n 54) 49–53.

[93] On the various factors that need to be considered in establishing comparative advantage, see generally: World Bank, *Trade in Fishing Services* (n 19); Munro, 'Legal and Economic Principles Underlying Foreign Fishing Arrangements' (n 54).

[94] Such compensation can take two forms: first, compensation from the flag State to the coastal State (State-to-State compensation); and second, a payment made by the fishing industry to the coastal State, whether through a fishing association or by an individual company or vessel (industry-to-State compensation): Will Martin et al, *A Handbook for Negotiating Fishing Access Agreements* (World Wildlife Fund 2001) 12. The concept of State-to-State compensation for foreign fishing has generated a range of complex questions regarding whether such payments constitute subsidies that should be subject to disciplines under international trade law. See further Mbithi Mwikya, *Fisheries Access Agreements* (n 91); Orellana, *Towards Sustainable Fisheries Access Agreements* (n 91); Margaret A Young, 'Fragmentation or Interaction: The WTO, Fisheries Subsidies, and International Law' (2009) 8 WTrRev 477.

the amount of compensation that should be paid in return for foreign fishing access, and it ultimately falls to each coastal State to negotiate a package that most fully realizes the benefits it seeks to achieve from the living resources of its EEZ. As Burke has observed: 'The [LOSC] contains no specific limitation or restriction on fee level, and although good faith is required the treaty gives ample leeway to coastal States to secure monetary benefits from EEZ fisheries. Charging fees that reflect the actual value of the right to the foreign nation involved would certainly fall well within coastal State authority.'[95]

While the payment of fees or compensation in return for access to the surplus—whether under an access agreement or by direct licensing—is required under the national legislation of most coastal States, the rate and value of such payment is highly unclear due to the lack of data and transparency from a wide range of actors, including foreign fleets, processing companies, fishing associations, and governments. However, the general consensus in the literature is that most arrangements provide coastal States with a very low 'rate of return' on their fishery resources.[96]

Fishing access commonly forms part of the broader diplomatic engagement between developed and developing States, and access agreements may be used as a mechanism for providing development assistance—or development assistance may be used as a form of leverage for influencing negotiations in favour of a foreign fleet.[97] However, as Petersen notes, greater benefits could accrue to coastal States, including a reduction in aid dependency, if access fees for foreign States were set at appropriate levels in the first place.[98] In this regard, some developing coastal States have specifically sought to de-link the fees paid for access to fishery resources from the provision of development assistance. For example, in relation to determining the access fee and other benefits provided in return for foreign access, Section 128(4)(b) of Kenya's *Fisheries Management and Development Act 2016* provides that 'such fee or benefits shall not include development assistance or benefits that are unrelated to the value of the fisheries access.' Similar provisions are included in the legislation of Gambia, Liberia, Papua New Guinea, the Solomon Islands, Tonga, and Jamaica.[99]

[95] Burke, *The New International Law of Fisheries* (n 66) 66.

[96] See Elizabeth Petersen, 'The Catch in Trading Fishing Access for Foreign Aid' (2003) 27(3) MarPol 219; Havice, 'The Structure of Tuna Access Agreements' (n 19); Nichols et al, 'Fishing Access Agreements' (n 19); Frédéric Le Manach et al, 'Who Gets What? Developing a More Equitable Framework for EU Fishing Agreements' (2013) 38 MarPol 257.

[97] Havice, 'The Structure of Tuna Access Agreements' (n 19) 985.

[98] Benefits of increasing access fees from distant water fishing nations would include the elimination of incentives for underreporting catch, a reduction in the present level of aid dependency, more transparency in fishing treaties, increased flexibility in government spending, and increased capital and opportunity for the coastal State's own efforts in fisheries development and broader economic development: Petersen, 'The Catch in Trading Fishing Access' (n 96) 227.

[99] Gambia, *Act 2007* s 38(5); Liberia, *Law 2019* s 5.1(a); Papua New Guinea, *Act 1998* s 35(4); Solomon Islands, *Act 2015* s 38(4); Tonga, *Act 2002* s 37(3); Jamaica, *Act 2018* s 49.

For other coastal States, the compensation available through access agreements may provide a means to gradually phase out foreign fishing altogether by developing the domestic fishing industry, including through the establishment of downstream and value-added operations that can increase the return from the living resources of the EEZ. For these countries, agreement to provide assistance with the construction of on-shore infrastructure, technical training and the transfer of technology constitute important criteria for providing access to foreign States.[100] This approach is envisaged in Article 62(4)(a), which notes that the compensation provided in return for fishing access 'may consist of adequate compensation in the field of financing, equipment and technology relating to the fishing industry', and Article 62(4)(j), which envisages terms and conditions for foreign fishing that relate to 'requirements for the training of personnel and the transfer of fisheries technology, including enhancement of the coastal State's capability of undertaking fisheries research'. Other coastal States apply this criterion retrospectively, by considering whether the foreign State has a proven history of providing assistance or cooperation in these areas.[101]

4.2.3.2 Flag State Responsibility, Compliance, and Cooperation

The concept of flag State cooperation with respect to the enforcement of fisheries laws—in effect, flag State responsibility—is another important pre-requisite for coastal States in considering whether or not to exercise their jurisdiction to grant foreign fishing access. Although the practice of including flag State 'compliance clauses' in access agreements actually pre-dates the LOSC,[102] the issue of flag State responsibility for illegal fishing in the EEZ of a coastal State is not directly addressed anywhere in the LOSC—let alone as part of the regime for foreign fishing access established in Article 62.[103] However, as ITLOS confirmed in the *SRFC Advisory Opinion,* while the 'primary responsibility' to prevent, deter, and eliminate illegal, unreported, and unregulated (IUU) fishing rests with the coastal State, flag States also have a responsibility to ensure that vessels flying their flag do not conduct IUU fishing activities within the EEZs of coastal States.[104] This is acknowledged in the

[100] Iran, *Law 1995* art 8; Marshall Islands, 51 *MIRC* §206; Micronesia, 24 *FSM Code* §504; Brazil, *Dec 4810 of 2003* art 4.

[101] Brunei, *Order 2009* s 22(b); Malaysia, *Act 1985* s 18; United States, 16 *USC* §1821(e)(E)(v).

[102] Valentin Schatz, 'The Contribution of Fisheries Access Agreements to Flag State Responsibility' (2017) 84 MarPol 313, 314.

[103] This omission may be due to the 'spatial' way in which rights and duties are allocated under the LOSC, which leads to a clear division of responsibilities between coastal and flag States with regard to different issues in different maritime zones. With respect to fisheries, for example, arts 56, 61, 62, and 73 clearly establish the prescriptive and enforcement jurisdiction of the coastal State as the dominant regime in the EEZ: Valentin Schatz, 'Fishing for Interpretation: The ITLOS Advisory Opinion on Flag State Responsibility for Illegal Fishing in the EEZ' (2016) 47(4) ODIL 327, 328–9.

[104] *SRFC Advisory Opinion* [124]. In considering the substantive content of flag State responsibility for fishing vessels in the EEZ, ITLOS placed significant weight on both the 'specific obligations' relating to fisheries and the EEZ in arts 58(3) and 62(4), and the 'general obligations' of arts 94(2) and (6) and 192, which are not limited spatially but apply to all areas, including maritime zones under the jurisdiction of a coastal State.

FAO Voluntary Guidelines on Flag State Responsibility, which provide that the flag State should 'take measures to ensure that persons subject to its jurisdiction, including owners and operators of vessels flying its flags, do not support or engage in IUU fishing and fishing related activities in support of such fishing', and specifically encourage coastal and flag States entering into an access agreement 'to agree on how to implement their respective roles and responsibilities under that agreement in advance of any fishing activities by flag State vessels while in the national jurisdiction of the coastal State'.[105]

The criterion of flag State responsibility and cooperation in enforcement has been taken up by coastal States in a number of different ways. The most common approach, adopted by the majority of coastal States in Africa, the Caribbean, and the Asia-Pacific, is to require that an access agreement include a provision that establishes the responsibility of the foreign party to ensure compliance by its vessels with both the agreement itself, and with the fisheries legislation (and in some instances environmental, customs, quarantine, or other legislation) of the coastal State. For example, Article 37(3) of Mozambique's *Fisheries Law 22/2013* provides that: 'The agreements and contracts referred to in this Article shall include the obligation on the part of the Contracting State, international organization or association to take all necessary measures to ensure that their vessels comply with: (a) the terms and conditions of the agreement, the contract and the fishing licence; (b) the relevant legislation in force in Mozambique; (c) customs and health procedures on the export of fishery products.'[106]

Flag State responsibility is also addressed in Section 37(1) of Tonga's *Fisheries Management Act 2002*, which states that any access agreement: 'shall include a provision, in relation to a State, that such State shall assume flag state responsibility, and otherwise establish the responsibility of the foreign party or parties to ensure compliance by its vessels with the terms and conditions of the agreement, international conservation and management measures, international law and with the laws relating to fishing in the fisheries waters.'[107]

To similar effect, pursuant to Section 7(3) of Dominica's *Fisheries Act 1987*, any access agreement entered into by Dominica 'shall include a provision establishing the responsibility of the foreign State or association to take necessary measures to

[105] [2(e)] and [39].

[106] See also in Africa: Angola, *Law 6-A/04 of 2004* art 50(3); Cape Verde, *Leg Dec 2/2020* art 22; Cote d'Ivoire, *Law 2016-554* art 20; Eritrea, *Proc 176/2014* art 15(3); Gabon, *Law 15/2005* art 31; Gambia, *Act 2007* s 38(4); Ghana, *Act 2002* s 64; Guinea, *Code 2015* art 61; Guinea-Bissau, *Dec Law 10/2011* art 14; Kenya, *Act 2016* s 129; Liberia, *Law 2019* s 10.16(2), Madagascar, *Code 2015* art 35; Mauritania, *Law 2015-017* art 37; Mozambique, *Law 22/2013* art 37(3); Sao Tome and Principe, *Law 9/2001* art 30; Senegal, *Code 2015* art 27; Seychelles, *Act 2014* s 9; Sierra Leone, *Regs 2019* reg 13; South Africa, *Act 1998* s 38; Togo, *Law 2016-026* art 22.

[107] See also in the Asia-Pacific: Brunei, *Order 2009* s 19; Cook Islands, *Act 2005* s 9(2)(c); Fiji, *Dec 2012* s 20(1)(c); Iran, *Law 1995* art 8; Kiribati, *Act 2010* s 12(2A); Malaysia, *Act 1985* s 17; Marshall Islands, 51 *MIRC* §406; Micronesia, 24 *FSM Code* §404; Nauru, *Act 1997* s 8; Papua New Guinea, *Act 1998* s 41A; Timor-Leste, *Dec Law 2004* art 32; Tuvalu, *Act 2006* s 31; Vanuatu, *Act 2014* s 57(4).

ensure compliance by its vessels with the terms and conditions of the agreement and with the laws relating to fishing in the fishery waters'.[108]

In addition to undertakings regarding *prospective* cooperation in securing compliance with the fisheries access agreement or licence or the enforcement of fisheries laws, a number of coastal States also specifically list the flag State's *historical* record of compliance or enforcement cooperation as a criterion to be taken into account when allocating fishing access to foreign States. For example, in the United States the criteria for apportionment of the surplus to foreign nations include 'whether, and to what extent, such nation and the fishing fleets of such nation have cooperated with the United States in the enforcement of United States fishing regulations'.[109] In Papua New Guinea, the exercise of any powers with respect to foreign fishing access must take into account whether the foreign State, its fishing associations and its fishing vessels have cooperated with Papua New Guinea in the enforcement of laws relating to: '(i) fishing and related activities; and (ii) the undertaking of flag State responsibility; and (iii) the conservation and management of fisheries resources; and (iv) the provision of information.'[110] Similar provisions—incorporating the criterion of demonstrated flag State cooperation in not only fisheries enforcement, but conservation and management, as well as the provision of fisheries information—are found in the legislation of Brunei, Malaysia, France (Mayotte), the Marshall Islands, Micronesia, Nauru, and New Zealand.[111]

4.2.3.3 Reciprocity

Another issue that features prominently in the national legislation of a number of coastal States despite not being included in the LOSC is the criterion of reciprocal fishing access for the vessels or nationals of the coastal State to the waters of the flag State or State of nationality.[112] In the United States, for example, Section 1821(f) of Title 16 of the *United States Code* provides unequivocally that: '[f]oreign fishing shall not be authorized for the fishing vessels of any foreign nation unless ... such nation extends substantially the same fishing privileges to fishing vessels of the United States.' The same effect is achieved in the negative by Section 5 of Korea's *Fisheries Act*, which provides that a ban or restriction on the acquisition of fishing

[108] See also in the Caribbean: Antigua and Barbuda, *Act 2006* s 26(3); Bahamas, *Act 1977* s 10(4); Barbados, *Act 1993* s 7; Belize, *Act 2020* s 27(3); Grenada, *Act 1986* s 7; Guyana, *Act 2012* s 17(3); Jamaica, *Act 2018* s 49; Saint Kitts and Nevis, *Act 2016* s 41; Saint Lucia, *Act 1984* s 7(3); Saint Vincent and the Grenadines, *Act 1986* s 7(3); United Kingdom (Montserrat), *Act 2000* s 23(3), (Turks and Caicos Islands), *Regs 1998* s 8(4).

[109] United States, 16 *USC* §1821(e)(E)(iii).

[110] Papua New Guinea, *Act 1998* s 34.

[111] Brunei, *Order 2009* s 22; Malaysia, *Act 1985* s 18; France (Mayotte), *Dec 2010-727* art 4(1) and (8); Marshall Islands, 51 *MIRC* §206(2); Micronesia, 24 *FSM Code* §504(2); Nauru, *Act 1997* s 5; New Zealand, *Act 1996* s 82(2).

[112] Imposing a criterion of reciprocity further marginalizes the idea of giving any preferential—or indeed any—access to the surplus by land-locked and geographically disadvantaged States as envisaged in arts 62(2) and (3), 69, and 70.

rights in Korean waters may be imposed with respect to nationals of countries that ban or restrict the acquisition of such rights in their waters by Korean nationals. In Argentina and the Bahamas, access agreements must include provision for reciprocal fishing access;[113] in Mexico, foreign fishing access will be subject to 'rigorous reciprocity';[114] and in Brunei, Malaysia, and Nauru, reciprocal access for local fishermen or fishing vessels to the waters of the flag State is listed as a criterion for the allocation of fishing access to the vessels of another State.[115]

Of course, the concept of reciprocity can take various forms, and in the national legislation of some coastal States the criterion of reciprocal access relates not only to fisheries, but markets. For example, pursuant to Article 37 of Argentina's *Law 24.922 on the Federal Fisheries Regime 1998*, an access agreement must make provision for tariff-free market access for Argentinian fishery products to an economic value equal to the fishing access granted, and under Article 10(4) of the Bahamas *Fisheries Resources (Jurisdiction and Conservation) Act 1977*, an access agreement must provide for market access for Bahamas fishery resources and products. Trade and market access issues also constitute a criterion for the allocation of foreign fishing access by the United States,[116] and previously formed an important plank in Canada's grant of fisheries access to vessels from the EU.[117] In this regard it is worth noting that while the FAO Code of Conduct provides that 'States should not condition access to markets on access to resources',[118] it does not specifically preclude coastal States from conditioning access to their *resources* on access to the markets of other States (although in practice this may be a very difficult distinction to draw).

4.2.3.4 Other Issues of 'National Interest'

While a myriad of other 'national interests' of coastal States are taken into account in the allocation of foreign access, many of these will never be public knowledge—whether because they form part of the internal decision-making process of the coastal State, fall within the undisclosed negotiating history between a coastal State and a flag State, or are contained in a confidential or 'closed' access agreement or licensing arrangement. However, a few examples of the sort of additional national interest criteria that are—or have been—part of the decision-making

[113] Argentina *Law 24.922 of 1998* art 37; Bahamas, *Act 1977* s 10(4).

[114] Mexico, *Law 2007* art 62.

[115] Brunei, *Order 2009* s 22; Malaysia, *Act 1985* s 18; Nauru, *Act 1997* s 5.

[116] United States, 16 *USC* §1821(e)(E)(i) and (ii).

[117] This was particularly important to Canada during the 1970s and 1980s, when the growing ability of Canada's industry to exploit the fishery resources that were newly available as a result of the displacement of foreign fleets from inside 200 miles increased the need for access to foreign markets for their domestic products: Donald Barry et al, *Fishing for a Solution: Canada's Fisheries Relations with the European Union, 1977–2013* (University of Calgary Press 2013) 14–16.

[118] Art 11.2.7.

framework applied by coastal States with respect to foreign fishing in the EEZ can be discovered.

In the national legislation of some coastal States, additional emphasis is placed on the protection of national fishery interests, such as artisanal fishing and the customary rights of indigenous fishers. For example: foreign fishing access in Papua New Guinea's EEZ must be based on 'recognition of and agreement to respect and comply with the customs, traditions and customary rights of the indigenous inhabitants',[119] and in Iran, it must include 'a commitment to observe the principles and measures taken by the government of Iran with respect to supporting the operations of traditional (artisanal) fishing'.[120] In Mexico, the emphasis is on developing the ship-building industry, with priority to be given to foreign-flagged vessels that prove their keel was manufactured in a Mexican shipyard.[121]

The national fishery interest is applied with a broader geographic scope in the legislation of Argentina, which requires that any agreement providing for foreign fishing must include measures regarding 'the conservation of resources in the area adjacent to the [EEZ]'.[122] This concept is taken further in Section 5(1.11) of Canada's *Coastal Fisheries Protection Regulations 2014*, pursuant to which a licence may not be granted to a foreign fishing vessel unless Canada has 'favourable fisheries relations' with the government of the vessel's flag State. The legislation itself does not expand on the criteria for measuring the 'favourability' of fisheries relations. However, a 1995 decision of the Canadian Federal Court involving a refusal to grant access to vessels from the United States on the basis that the United States was 'not cooperating with Canada's fisheries conservation objectives'[123] indicates that this criteria has been interpreted by reference to the adherence by a foreign country to both Canadian and international conservation practices and policies.[124] This conclusion is strengthened by Canada's application of the same criteria to deny port access to foreign fishing vessels on the basis of their flag State's failure to

119 Papua New Guinea, *Act 1998* s 35(1)(c).
120 Iran, *Law 1995* art 8(e).
121 Mexico, *Law 2007* art 62.
122 Argentina, *Law 24.922 of 1998* art 37(b).
123 *Antonsen v Canada (Attorney General)* [1995] 2 FCR 272 (17 February 1995) [9].
124 The Minister's decision reportedly involved the application of the 'Port Access Policy', which read in part: 'The relationship between Canada and the United States on fisheries conservation has become strained since 1990. The areas where the U.S. does not cooperate with Canada on fisheries conservation are as follows: (a) the continued overfishing by U.S. registered vessels on the nose and tail of the Grand Banks off Newfoundland of groundfish stocks straddling Canada's 200-mile zone; (b) rapidly increasing interceptions by U.S. fishermen of Canadian origin Pacific salmon, in contravention of the equity provisions contained in the Canada-United States Pacific Salmon Treaty; and (c) the continued promotion of overfishing of Pacific hake by the United States fishery management authorities in disregard of Canada's traditional share of this transboundary migratory species.' As cited in the judgment, the objectives of the Port Access Policy included: '(a) to reinforce Canadian sovereign rights to achieve our conservation objectives, (b) ensuring that Canada's competitive position in the fisheries market-place is not compromised through the facilitation of foreign fishing activity, and (c) optimizing benefits to the Canadian economy derived from the presence of the foreign fishing vessels within the Canadian zone.' See *Antonsen v Canada* (n 123) fn 6.

cooperate in the conservation of fishery resources under the management of the North Atlantic Fisheries Organization (NAFO).[125]

The consideration of these issues is also evident in the United Kingdom's approach to foreign fishing access in the EEZ surrounding South Georgia and the South Sandwich Islands (SGSSI). Section 10A of the SGSSI *Fisheries (Conservation and Management) Ordinance 2000* requires that before issuing or revoking a fishing licence, the SGSSI Director of Fisheries must consult the United Kingdom Secretary of State on 'whether there would be any implications for foreign policy'. Given the significant interest of some members of the Commission for the Conservation of Antarctic Marine Living Resources (CCAMLR) in the licences awarded for fishing in the waters of SGSSI, this provision enables consideration of the consequences and ramifications for the proper operation of CCAMLR and the achievement of the United Kingdom's objectives within CCAMLR if the award of licences is insensitive to those interests.[126] For example, in considering the issuance of four licences to foreign-flagged vessels for the 2006 fishing season, the United Kingdom advised that two should be given to Chilean vessels in recognition of the significant role that Chile had played in certain CCAMLR discussions, one to a Spanish vessel, and one to a South-African-flagged vessel (which also had Japanese interests, thus keeping two CCAMLR members onside). The advice noted that this would exclude a Uruguyan-flagged vessel (the *Isla Alegranza)* from the fishery but concluded that this was justified due to 'Uruguay's track record as a CCAMLR member on non-compliance and enforcement of CCAMLR conservation measures'.[127]

For other coastal States, the question of foreign fishing access can involve broader national security, foreign policy, or industrial relations considerations, or be used as a lever to encourage cooperation in issues of strategic, economic, or political importance. For example, Article 5 of the *Provisional Regulations on Foreigners and Foreign Fishing Vessels in the Jurisdictional Waters of the People's Republic of China, 1999* provides that a foreign vessel may only be licensed to fish in China's EEZ if it does not endanger China's national security. And while Australia's current policy settings do not allow foreign fishing in the EEZ, the *Guidelines for Application for the Use of Foreign Fishing Vessels in the Australian Fishing Zone, 1989* include both 'industrial relations' and 'foreign policy' considerations as factors to be taken into account in determining the nature and level of foreign involvement which will be authorized in a particular fishery.[128]

[125] During the 1980s and 1990s, access to Canadian ports was denied to the EU fishing fleet and to vessels from the Faroe Islands and Greenland on various occasions, on the basis that their flag States had failed to cooperate in the conservation and management of stocks under the purview of NAFO. See Barry et al, *Fishing for a Solution* (n 117).

[126] Cited in *R (on the application of Isla Alegranza SA) v The Director of Fisheries of the Government of South Georgia and the South Sandwich Islands* [2006] Falkland Islands Supreme Court SC/CIV/8/06 [23].

[127] Ibid [36].

[128] [6], available at <http://afma.gov.au/fisheries-services/guidelines-applications-use-foreign-fishing-vessels-australian-fishing-zone> accessed 21 January 2021.

Although it is difficult to find concrete instances of such criterion being applied in practice, there are some historic examples, such as the United States' denial of access to fishing vessels from the Union of Soviet Socialist Republics in response to the Soviet invasion of Afghanistan in 1979, and suspension of access to fishing by Polish vessels following the 1981 institution of martial law in Poland.[129] The denial of fishing access has also been employed by the United States to promote broader conservation issues, through Section 1821(e)(2) of Title 16 of the *United States Code*, which provides that if the Secretary of Commerce certifies that a foreign State is conducting fishing operations or engaging in trade which diminishes the effectiveness of the *International Convention for the Regulation of Whaling*,[130] the Secretary of State must diminish any fishing allocation to that nation by at least 50 per cent. The United States has previously used this provision to encourage compliance with measures of the International Whaling Commission by fishing nations including Korea, China, Norway, the USSR, Japan, and Iceland.[131] In addition, consideration of foreign fishing allocations may also be based on 'such other matters as the Secretary of State, in cooperation with the Secretary [of Commerce], deems appropriate',[132] thus providing a broad discretion for the application of a wide range of other issues of national interest.

4.3 Licence Terms and Conditions: Article 62(4)

Once it has been established that there is a surplus, and the relevant criteria have been applied to determine how that surplus will be allocated amongst foreign States, the coastal State must consider the regulations that will apply to the activities of the foreign vessels and crew that will be engaged in extracting it. In this regard, Article 62(4) makes clear that foreign nationals must comply with not only the conservation and management measures adopted under Article 61 of the LOSC, but such other 'terms and conditions' as may be established in the laws and regulations of the coastal State.[133] The coastal State has almost complete discretion in establishing such terms and conditions; not only is the list of potential terms and conditions set out in Article 62(4) specifically non-exhaustive, but Article 297(3)(a) protects any terms and conditions established by the coastal State from compulsory dispute settlement.

[129] David D Caron, 'International Sanctions, Ocean Management, and the Law of the Sea: A Study of Denial of Access to Fisheries' (1989) 16(2) ELQ 311, 315–16.

[130] (Concluded 2 December 1946, entered into force 10 November 1948) 161 UNTS 72.

[131] Caron, 'International Sanctions' (n 129) 317–26.

[132] United States, 16 *USC* §1821(e)(E)(vii).

[133] Many of these terms and conditions are commonly incorporated in the vessel licence, either by reference provisions in primary or secondary legislation, or through inclusion on the face of the licence itself—although they may also be included in an access agreement or other form of contract.

Nonetheless, without limiting this discretion, the terms and conditions specifically enumerated in Article 62(4) suggest that three broad areas of regulation were envisaged in the drafting of the LOSC. First, the establishment of criteria for licensing foreign fishers and foreign fishing vessels, including the type and amount of compensation required, the terms and conditions relating to joint ventures or cooperative agreements, and requirements for training of personnel and technology transfer.[134] As discussed in Section 4.2.3, despite being included in the list of 'terms and conditions' for foreign fishing under Article 62(4), in practice many of these criteria operate as pre-requisites for the allocation of foreign fishing access to other States under Article 62(3). Second, the adoption of fisheries conservation and management measures, including catch quotas, limits on the size, age, or species of fish to be caught, restrictions on fishing gear and locations, and limits on the type, size, and number of vessels to be employed in exploiting the resources.[135] And third, the development of compliance control and monitoring measures, including catch and effort reporting, vessel position reports, the carriage of observers, the landing of catch in national ports, and enforcement procedures.[136]

It is uniformly acknowledged that 'coastal States establish detailed terms and conditions for foreign fishing in the EEZ which are rarely challenged.'[137] Given the breadth of coastal State discretion evident in respect of every aspect of Article 62, this is not surprising—but the full extent of coastal State regulation over foreign fishing can only be established through a detailed, broad-based examination of the actual terms and conditions applied by coastal States. Accordingly, this Section will consider:

- the core group of standard terms and conditions applied by States to give effect to the basic criteria listed in Article 62(4) of the LOSC;
- the effect of collective application of these standard terms and conditions; and
- the ways in which coastal States have expanded the substantive, geographic, personal, and temporal reach of their jurisdiction through the application of innovative terms and conditions.

This examination of practice will provide a comprehensive foundation for establishing the contemporary extent of coastal State jurisdiction over living resources in the EEZ within—and potentially beyond—the framework in Part V of the LOSC.

[134] Art 62(4)(a), (i) and (j).
[135] Art 62(4)(b) to (d).
[136] Art 62(4)(e) to (h) and (k).
[137] Markowski, *The International Law of EEZ Fisheries* (n 75) 62. See also: Dahmani, *The Fisheries Regime* (n 54) 83; Attard, *The EEZ* (n 12) 172–8; Kwiatkowska, *The 200 Mile EEZ* (n 5) 67–9.

4.3.1 Standard Application of the LOSC Terms and Conditions

A list of the terms and conditions commonly used by coastal States to regulate foreign fishing vessels in the EEZ was developed and applied by the FAO in its series of studies on *Coastal State Requirements for Foreign Fishing*,[138] in order to assist coastal States in developing their national legislation, and to assist distant water fishing nations whose fleets are required to comply with such controls.[139] These terms and conditions reflect and give effect to many of the regulatory issues set out in Article 62(4), as well as some more specific standards elaborated in a number of the global fisheries instruments adopted after the LOSC,[140] and might now be described as generally accepted terms and conditions for the regulation of foreign fishing in the EEZ. They include:

- specified criteria for the marking of fishing vessels;[141]
- carriage of the fishing licence or authorization on board the vessel;[142]
- carriage of observers;[143]
- submission of a fishing plan;[144]
- putting in for port inspections on entering and leaving the EEZ;[145]
- carriage of position fixing equipment;[146]

[138] The first edition of *Legislation on Coastal State Requirements for Foreign Fishing* was published in 1981, and revised versions were published in 1983, 1985, 1988, 1993, and 1996, but the study has not been updated since. See Gerald Moore, *Coastal State Requirements for Foreign Fishing* (FAO and Bahamas Department of Marine Resources 1981); Moore, *Coastal State Requirements for Foreign Fishing, Rev 1* (n 65); Gerald Moore, *Coastal State Requirements for Foreign Fishing* (Rev 2, FAO 1985); Gerald Moore, *Coastal State Requirements for Foreign Fishing* (Rev 3, FAO 1988); FAO Legal Office, *Coastal State Requirements for Foreign Fishing* (Rev 4, FAO 1993); Danielle Mangatalle, *Legislation on Coastal State Requirements for Foreign Fishing* (6th ed, FAO 1996).

[139] Moore, *Coastal State Requirements for Foreign Fishing, Rev 1* (n 65) iii.

[140] These include: the *FAO Standard Specification and Guidelines for the Marking and Identification of Fishing Vessels* (FAO 1989); the FAO Code of Conduct; the IPOA-IUU; the Compliance Agreement; and the UNFSA.

[141] The marking of fishing vessels is listed in [47.8] of the IPOA-IUU as one of the conditions under which an authorization to fish may be issued, and is included (as a flag State responsibility) in art 8.3.3 of the FAO Code of Conduct, art 18(3)(d) of the UNFSA, and art III(6) of the Compliance Agreement.

[142] This requirement is also included in [46] of the IPOA-IUU and (as a flag State responsibility) in art 8.2.2 of the FAO Code of Conduct and art 18(3)(b)(iii) of the UNFSA.

[143] The carriage of observers is listed in [47.4] of the IPOA-IUU as one of the conditions under which an authorization to fish may be issued, included in arts 7.7.3 and 8.4.3 of the FAO Code of Conduct as an important aspect of ensuring compliance with fisheries conservation and management measures, and referred to in art 18(3)(g)(ii) of the UNFSA (in the context of flag State responsibility).

[144] Relatively few coastal States require foreign fishing vessels to submit a 'fishing plan'—or at least, they do not use this term in national legislation. It may be that 'fishing plan' is a term of art adopted in the FAO study and not commonly used by States, since it is not found in the LOSC or in any related instruments such as the IPOA-IUU or the FAO Code of Conduct. In practice, many coastal States require foreign fishing vessels to provide a detailed description of their proposed fishing operations addressing the issues described in art 62(4)(b) to (d) of the LOSC, but do not use the term 'fishing plan'.

[145] While this requirement would clearly fall within the concept of 'enforcement procedures' under art 62(4)(k), it is not commonly included in other post-LOSC instruments.

[146] While this requirement is not specifically envisaged in art 62(4), the original author of the FAO study referred to 'a possible requirement of installing transponders or other position-fixing equipment', which constituted new, expensive, and possibly unreliable technology at the time that the LOSC was

- appointing a local agent or representative;[147]
- posting a bond or guarantee prior to the commencement of fishing operations;[148]
- carrying an interpreter;[149]
- seeking authorization for transhipments;[150]
- stowing gear while in areas where the vessel is not authorized to fish;[151]
- landing or processing catch in the ports of the coastal State;[152]
- the protection of local fisheries and fishing gear;[153]
- employment or training of coastal State nationals in crew;[154]
- reporting on entry and exit to the EEZ, on commencement and cessation of fishing, and prior to entry into coastal State ports;[155]

adopted: Moore, *Coastal State Requirements for Foreign Fishing, Rev 1* (n 65) 21. The carriage and operation of such equipment (in particular, a vessel monitoring system (VMS)) is now a common requirement in coastal State legislation and is included in several of the post-LOSC fisheries instruments, as discussed in Section 4.3.3.

147 The original author of the FAO study suggested that this requirement was intended to ensure that foreign fishing operations were 'subject to coastal State jurisdiction in a real as well as a formal sense': Moore, *Coastal State Requirements for Foreign Fishing, Rev 1* (n 65) 21. While this may provide an important channel for communications (akin to a shipping agent), it is unlikely to solve the broader difficulties of effectively exercising coastal State jurisdiction over foreign fishing vessels.

148 While not specifically envisaged in the LOSC, this requirement comes within the ambit of enforcement procedures that may be applied under art 62(4)(k), discussed further in Chapter 6 nn 177–9 and associated text. It is particularly common in cases of direct licensing, where fishing is conducted outside the framework of an access agreement (see n 40 and associated text).

149 The potential benefits of this requirement are demonstrated by the facts of the *Duzgit Integrity Arbitration* in which, as a result of a conversation with a Coast Guard officer who only spoke limited English, the master of a Maltese vessel mistakenly believed he had been given permission to engage in a ship-to-ship transfer in the archipelagic waters of Sao Tome and Principe—which was not in fact the case, and led to the vessel being arrested by Sao Tome and Principe: *Duzgit Integrity Arbitration* [221]–[235].

150 Coastal State regulation of transhipment is discussed in detail in Chapter 3, and the potential for expanded interpretation and application of this requirement is considered further in Section 4.3.3.2.

151 Although not specifically listed in art 62(4) or addressed in the post-LOSC instruments, this requirement clearly relates to the conduct of foreign fishing in the EEZ and falls within the range of issues that may be regulated by coastal States. It is commonly applied not only to authorized vessels, but also to unlicensed vessels in transit through the EEZ, as discussed in Chapter 5.

152 As discussed in Chapter 3, coastal States commonly regulate the landing and processing of catch taken by foreign fishing vessels in the EEZ.

153 Coastal States commonly establish a wide range of conservation and management measures for the protection of local fisheries, including: prohibitions on the use of explosives and noxious substances; terms and conditions for the protection of fishing gear (which in most cases apply equally to domestic and foreign fishing vessels); and specific requirements for foreign fishing vessels relating to the protection of domestic fishing operations, particularly artisanal or small-scale fishing.

154 As discussed in Sections 4.1.2 and 4.2.3.1, the employment or training of nationals (together with other issues related to the development of the domestic fishing industry such as infrastructure, equipment, technology transfer, and technical training) may constitute allocation criteria or be relevant to compensation for access. However, a number of coastal States also include crewing requirements as a standard term of the foreign fishing licence. See, eg, Argentina, *Law 24.922 of 1998* art 38(l) (at least 50 per cent of the crew on a foreign fishing vessel must be Argentinian); Gambia, *Regs 2008* s 26(r) (at least 20 per cent of the crew must be Gambian nationals).

155 The author of the original FAO study noted that the critical points at which reporting is required tend to be entry into and departure from the EEZ: Moore, *Coastal State Requirements for Foreign Fishing,*

- timely reporting on vessel position;[156] and
- timely reporting on catch and effort, and the maintenance and submission of fishing logs.[157]

4.3.2 Collective Application of Minimum Terms and Conditions

In parts of the Asia-Pacific and Africa, a number of these requirements have been given greater effect through collective application, in the form of harmonized minimum terms and conditions for access to the EEZs of a regional or sub-regional group of coastal States. This approach has been adopted in the western and central Pacific through the FFA Harmonized Minimum Terms and Conditions (MTCs), in east Africa through the South West Indian Ocean Fisheries Commission (SWIOFC) MTCs, and in west Africa by the Sub-Regional Fisheries Commission (SRFC) MCA Convention and the Fisheries Committee of the West Central Gulf of Guinea (FCWC) MRA Convention. The members of the South African Development Community (SADC) have also committed to adopting harmonized minimum terms and conditions for access under the SADC *Protocol on Fisheries 2001* (SADC Protocol),[158] although to date they have not been developed. In addition, a number of the coastal States in Latin America and the Caribbean have established—or agreed to establish—harmonized national legislation for the regulation of foreign fishing, including through the Organization of Eastern Caribbean States (OECS)[159] and the Caribbean Regional Fisheries Mechanism (CRFM).[160]

Rev 1 (n 65) 15. As discussed in Chapter 5, many coastal States now require notice to be provided well in advance of entry to and departure from the EEZ, as well as at other points during the voyage.

[156] The requirement of timely reporting on position is clearly envisaged by the notion of 'vessel position reports' in art 62(4)(e). In contemporary practice, this is commonly given effect through the operation of VMS (as discussed in n 146), and expanded to incorporate reporting beyond the EEZ, as discussed in Section 4.3.3.

[157] The completion of catch and effort reports and fishing logbooks is a basic necessity for effective fisheries management and falls within the concept of 'catch and effort statistics' in art 62(4)(e).

[158] (Signed 14 August 2001, entered into force 8 August 2003) LEX-FAOC044398 art 10.

[159] The OECS members established harmonized national fisheries laws in the 1980s, which were revised in 1992: see generally Gerald Moore, H Walters, and D Robin, *Report on the Implementation of Harmonised Fisheries Legislation in the OECS Region* (FAO 1992), available at <http://fao.org/3/a-br465e.pdf> accessed 11 December 2020. Almost all the members of the OECS are now members of the broader CRFM group (see Chapter 3 nn 179–80).

[160] The *Agreement Establishing the Caribbean Community Common Fisheries Policy* (CCCFP) (adopted 2011, not yet in force) LEX-FAOC167228 provides in art 13.3 that participating Parties 'shall consider the development of harmonized procedures or common standards in relation to licensing systems'. The CCCFP has been approved by the competent Ministers of the Caribbean Community and is stated to 'reflect the CRFM Member States' current and intended practice in relation to responsible fishing within the territory and beyond of the CRFM members', although it has not yet entered into force: *ITLOS Pleadings, Minutes and Documents, Vol 22* (2015) *Request for an Advisory Opinion submitted by the Sub-Regional Fisheries Commission* Written Statement of the Caribbean Regional Fisheries Mechanism [28] and [140].

The membership and areas of competence of these organizations are discussed in Section 3.3 and depicted in Figures 3.1, 3.2, and 3.4.[161]

While there is some variation, the harmonized minimum terms and conditions adopted by these regional fisheries bodies commonly include:

- minimum fields of information to be provided in the licence application;
- carriage of a valid licence from the relevant coastal State on the vessel at all times;
- inclusion on the vessel register of relevant regional fisheries management organizations (RFMOs);
- the marking of fishing vessels and gear, and the conduct of pre-fishing inspections;
- reporting requirements relating to vessel position (on entry to and departure from the EEZ, when entering port and at other times during the course of fishing activities) and catch and effort (often through the use of standardized logbooks or forms);
- control and monitoring of transhipment and requirements for the landing of catch;
- carriage of an observer authorized by the coastal State or under a regional observer programme;
- employment of local crew; and
- installation and operation of an approved and functioning vessel monitoring system (VMS) that reports in accordance with regional specifications.

The harmonization of terms and conditions for foreign fishing has a range of advantages. For foreign fishing vessels wishing to operate in more than one EEZ in a particular region, there are significant benefits to consistency in regulation between those zones, particularly with respect to issues such as vessel marking, entry and exit reporting, and VMS requirements. From the point of view of coastal States, the collective application of harmonized minimum terms and conditions to all foreign vessels operating in the region not only demonstrates a consensus on the extent and application of their jurisdiction, but exponentially strengthens the position of each individual coastal State in setting stringent standards for access, since foreign vessels and distant water fishing nations cannot seek to manipulate or avoid the application of fisheries laws and regulations by simply transferring their operations—and their access fees—to the waters of another State in the region.

[161] The EU Common Fisheries Policy also has the effect of establishing harmonized minimum terms and conditions for foreign fishing, particularly through *Reg 2017/2403*. However, this is not its key focus—particularly given the limited surplus resources available for access by foreign vessels in Union waters. In respect of foreign fishing, the focus of EU regulations is more on the collective exercise of port and market State jurisdiction, which EU member States use to great effect, particularly through the measures established in *Reg 1005/2008*.

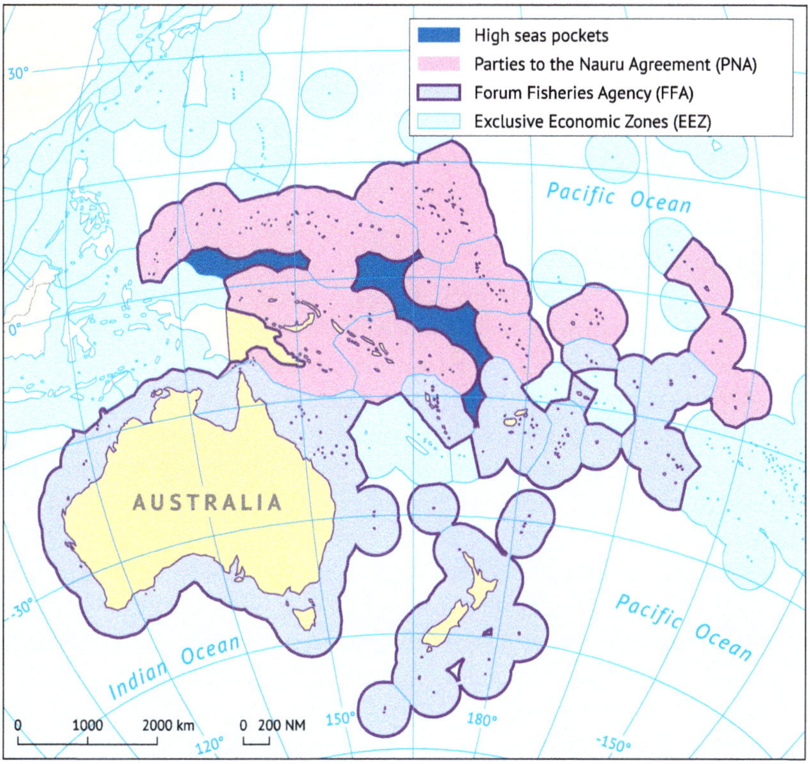

Figure 4.1 EEZs of the Parties to the Nauru Agreement

Notes

Created using Natural Earth raster and vector map data available at <http://naturalearthdata.com> and the Flanders Marine Institute Maritime Boundaries Geodatabase, *Maritime Boundaries and Exclusive Economic Zones* (200NM) (Version 11, 2019) available at <http://www.marineregions.org/>.

Some coastal States have extended the application of this collective approach to the compensation required for access to the EEZ. The most striking example is the Vessel Day Scheme (VDS) established by the Parties to the Nauru Agreement (PNA),[162] a sub-regional group comprising eight members of the FFA—Micronesia, Kiribati, Marshall Islands, Nauru, Palau, Papua New Guinea, Solomon Islands, and Tuvalu—with adjoining EEZs which contain the most productive tuna fishing grounds in the western and central Pacific region, depicted in Figure 4.1.

The VDS is a management scheme adopted by the PNA through the *Palau Arrangement for the Management of the Western Pacific Fishery* (Palau

[162] *Nauru Agreement Concerning Cooperation in the Management of Fisheries of Common Stocks* (Nauru Agreement) (adopted 11 February 1982, as amended April 2010).

Arrangement)[163] in order to encourage collaboration between Parties to enable them to maximize economic returns from the sustainable use of tuna resources. The VDS alters the structure of fisheries management to one of effort limits (rather than, for example, catch or vessel limits), calculated on the basis of 'fishing days'.[164] Under this system, PNA members establish a total allowable effort to apply within the entire area of their EEZs, which is allocated between individual members using a formula based on stock distribution and recent fishing history. Each PNA member can then grant foreign fishing vessels access to a certain number of 'fishing days' in its own EEZ. Through this collective, 'rights-based' approach to fisheries management, the PNA members have been able to maximize the effectiveness of their sovereign rights and extract a large number of additional benefits from the fishery—particularly in respect of the compensation paid for access to the EEZ.

For example, by establishing and applying a 'minimum benchmark price' to be paid by foreign fishing vessels in return for a 'fishing day', the PNA members have been able to exponentially increase the return from their resources. In 2004, the value of a day's fishing in PNA waters was approximately $1,350 USD. With the establishment of a minimum benchmark price, the cost of a day's fishing increased from $5,000 USD in 2012, to $6,000 USD in 2014, and $8,000 USD in 2015.[165] While the exact economic effect is difficult to ascertain (given the changing value of the catch and the changing costs of fishing), it is estimated that the PNA members have increased their returns from between 3 and 6 per cent of the total landed value of the tuna from their waters, to 14 per cent of that value.[166]

Of course, many of the factors that have contributed to the success of the PNA's harmonized approach to financial compensation are not easily replicable, including in particular the geography and stock distribution of the western and central Pacific region, and the high level of trust and integration that has developed through many years of close cooperation between the coastal States through the FFA and PNA, as well as other (non-fisheries) regional bodies. While it remains to be seen to what extent coastal States in other regions and sub-regions will follow the approach adopted by the PNA, there are some indications that they might seek

[163] (Opened for signature 28 October 1992, entered into force 1995, as amended June 2017). The VDS is implemented by two Management Schemes adopted pursuant to the Palau Arrangement: the Purse Seine VDS and the Long Line VDS, available at <https://pnatuna.com/index.php/key-documents> accessed 1 August 2021.

[164] A 'fishing day' includes any day (or part of a day) spent in the waters of a Party (but not in port) unless the vessel meets the requirements of a 'non-fishing day' (under the Purse Seine VDS) or the vessel is in transit (under the Long Line VDS). The calculation of a 'fishing day' includes an adjustment for different size vessels, to address changes in fishing technology and efficiency and prevent 'effort creep'.

[165] *Memorandum of Understanding between the Parties to the Palau Arrangement on a Minimum Benchmark Fee for a Fishing Day under the Vessel Day Scheme* (signed 13 June 2014).

[166] Elizabeth Havice, 'Rights-Based Management in the Western and Central Pacific Ocean Tuna Fishery: Economic and Environmental Change under the Vessel Day Scheme' (2013) 42 MarPol 259, 264; Agnes D Yeeting et al, 'Implications of New Economic Policy Instruments for Tuna Management in the Western and Central Pacific' (2016) 63 MarPol 45, 49.

to more extensively harness the collective strength of their jurisdiction over foreign fishing to increase the financial returns from the resources of their EEZs.

For example, in the south west Indian Ocean, the members of SWIOFC have sought to replicate the PNA's approach to benchmarking compensation for foreign fishing, by undertaking to: 'work together to standardize and harmonize financial compensation for access to resources of tuna and tuna-like species within waters under their national jurisdiction with at least a minimum of twelve (12%) percent of the average prevailing market value of the tuna and tuna-like species resources.'[167]

The coastal States of the Caribbean have sought to go even further by negotiating a Common Fisheries Policy, including a commitment to establish a common fisheries zone—although these efforts have yet to come to fruition.[168]

4.3.3 Application of Terms and Conditions with Expanded Effect

Of course, the list of potential terms and conditions set out in Article 62(4) is not exhaustive, and coastal States retain the right to establish such terms and conditions for foreign fishing as they see fit, provided they are 'consistent with' the LOSC. In this regard, the test for consistency seems to equate to a general standard of 'reasonableness'. Commentators generally agree that the coastal State may not prescribe criteria which are discriminatory, or which would make foreign access impossible—such as restricting access to fishing grounds or the use of fishing gear in such a way as to render fishing not physically possible or economically viable.[169]

Beyond this, it has also been suggested that the 'reasonableness' of the terms and conditions applied by the coastal State should be measured 'by their relationship to legitimate conservation and management goals and to other measures'.[170]

[167] SWIOFC MTCs art 7.2. See, eg, Mozambique, *Dec 74/2017* art 30(a), which stipulates that financial compensation under a fisheries access agreement must represent at least 12 per cent of the market value of expected catches. FCWC members are also seeking to develop a regionally harmonized approach to licence fees in order to maximize the resource rent: see FCWC, 'Consultancy Assignment: Minimum Terms and Conditions to Access Fisheries Including Fisheries License Regime' 9 February 2021, available at <https://fcwc-fish.org/our-news/consultancy-assignment-minimum-terms-and-conditions-to-access-to-fisheries-including-fisheries-license-regime-in-the-fcwc-region> accessed 25 February 2021.

[168] The attempt to establish a common fishing zone in the Caribbean has a long history—as early as 1991, the member States of the OECS decided to establish a common fishing zone for the OECS sub-region (although it was never fully implemented): Tricia Lovell, *Regionalism versus National Sovereignty: The Promise and Problems of a CARICOM Fisheries Agreement* (DOALOS 2008) 73–4, available at <http://un.org/Depts/los/nippon/unnff_programme_home/fellows_pages/fellows_papers/lovell_0708_antigua-barbuda.pdf> accessed 11 December 2020. Art 20(1)(e) of the CCCFP, which is not yet in force, provides that the Parties undertake to prepare a Protocol relating to the establishment of a common fisheries zone.

[169] See Dahmani, *The Fisheries Regime* (n 54) 55; Attard, *The EEZ* (n 12) 160; Kwiatkowska, *The 200 Mile EEZ* (n 5) 67; Burke, *The New International Law of Fisheries* (n 66) 66.

[170] Attard, *The EEZ* (n 12) 161; Harrison and Morgera, 'Article 62' (n 41) 504.

However, given the broad range of issues contemplated in Article 62(4)—which extend well beyond fisheries conservation and management—as well as the potential to effectively implement a wide range of 'terms and conditions' through the process of allocation and apportionment under Article 62(3), it is clear that coastal States retain and employ extremely broad discretionary powers over foreign fishing in the EEZ, which are not limited to the pursuit of 'conservation and management' objectives. Nonetheless, the coastal State's powers are not entirely open-ended; as ITLOS has clearly stated, 'it is apparent from the list in article 62, paragraph 4, of the Convention that for all activities that may be regulated by a coastal State there must be a direct connection to fishing.'[171]

The contemporary exercise of these powers is reflected in the wide variety of regulations adopted by coastal States with respect to foreign fishing vessels, which have expanded the spatial, temporal, personal, and substantive effect of their jurisdiction over living resources. This is most evident in the legislation of developing coastal States in Africa and the Asia-Pacific—which is not surprising, since they are the principal providers of access to fishing for foreign vessels from the large distant water fishing fleets—and particularly in areas where the harmonized minimum terms and conditions for foreign fishing adopted by regional and subregional fishery bodies have provided a basis for the collective development and application of innovative and ambitious licensing conditions.

4.3.3.1 Expanded Reporting Requirements for Fishing within the EEZ

In the contemporary practice of coastal States, the information required of foreign vessels fishing in the EEZ—and in particular the provision of 'vessel position reports'—have been given expanded spatial or temporal effect, including through reliance on modern technology that was not available or envisaged when the LOSC was negotiated. For example, foreign fishing vessels are commonly required to provide information about their plans significantly in advance of entering the coastal State's EEZ, including: the time and position of entry, the quantity of fish on board by species, and, in some cases, the port to which they will proceed immediately for inspection. The exact requirements of coastal States vary: while some seek only four hours advance notice of entry to and exit from the EEZ,[172] others require notice up to forty-eight hours in advance of entry and up to seventy-two hours prior to exit,[173] although the most common approach is to require vessels to provide this information twenty-four hours in advance.[174]

[171] *Virginia G* [215]; confirmed in *SRFC Advisory Opinion* [100]. See also the discussion regarding the requirement of a 'direct connection to fishing' in Section 3.2.4.

[172] Angola, *Dec 41/05* art 95.

[173] Fiji, *Regs 2014* s 39(3); Tonga, *Terms and Conditions 2002* s 7; Tuvalu, *Act 2006* s 21; Sri Lanka, *Regs 1981* art 8; India, *Rules 1982* s 5; Indonesia, *Dec 476/1985* art 2; Canada, *Regs 2014*, s 12(1)(a) and (c). See also SWIOFC MTCs art 11; SRFC MCA Convention art 14.

[174] Kenya, *Regs 1991* s 21; Liberia, *Law 2019* s 9.4; Mauritius, *Act 2007* art 53; Mozambique, *Terms and Conditions* [5]; Seychelles, *Act 2014* s 13; Bangladesh, *Rules 1983* s 8; Marshall Islands, 51 *MIRC* §420; Micronesia, 24 *FSM Code* §115. See also FCWC MRA Convention art 22.

In addition, the type and amount of information to be provided by fishing vessels has expanded through the development and application of satellite VMS. VMS can be used to determine the identity, location, speed, and direction of a vessel in near real-time, as well as to draw conclusions about its likely activities—such as a pattern of consecutive positions indicating possible fishing activity. Recent advances in technology have given rise to a range of additional functionalities, such as electronic catch reporting, integrated catch documentation schemes, and quota monitoring programmes, which mean that the information provided by VMS can be used to both enhance coastal State compliance capabilities, and to facilitate the development of broader, tailored fisheries management measures.[175] Accordingly, the requirement to install and operate a VMS falls squarely within not only the terms and conditions envisaged in Article 62(4), but the key concepts of gathering the data necessary to ensure that management measures are made on the basis of the 'best scientific evidence available' under Article 61(2), and taking the measures 'necessary to ensure compliance' with the laws and regulations of the coastal State pursuant to Article 73(1). This has been reinforced by obligations relating to the adoption of VMS in the key global fisheries instruments adopted subsequent to the LOSC, and by most RFMOs.[176] The installation and operation of a VMS on board foreign fishing vessels—and equally, in most cases, domestic fishing vessels—is now a ubiquitous requirement in the legislation of coastal States (and flag States) in every region of the world, and has substantively expanded the effect of the 'vessel position reports' envisaged in Article 62(4)(e).

4.3.3.2 Regulation of Fishing Activities beyond the EEZ

In the western and central Pacific region, the FFA members have further expanded the application and effectiveness of VMS by requiring foreign fishing vessels to consent to electronic monitoring at all times during the period of validity of the licence, both within *and beyond* the EEZ of the coastal State. This approach is underpinned by a common licensing provision in the FFA Harmonized MTCs,[177] and given effect in the legislation of FFA members. For example, under Section 31(3) of Fiji's *Offshore Fisheries Management Regulations 2014,* a fishing licence or authorization shall not be issued to a foreign fishing vessel unless a mobile transceiver unit has been installed on the vessel in accordance with relevant specifications, and

[175] Erik Jaap Molenaar and Martin Tsamenyi, 'Satellite-Based Vessel Monitoring Systems for Fisheries Management: International Legal Aspects' (2000) 15 IJMCL 65, 68–9.

[176] These include the IPOA-IUU, the FAO Code of Conduct and the UNFSA. Many RFMOs have also established VMS requirements. See Holly Koehler, 'RFMO Vessel Monitoring Systems: A Comparative Analysis to Identify Best Practices (Version 6)' *ISSF Technical Report 2021-08* (International Seafood Sustainability Foundation 2021), available at <https://stagerefresh.iss-foundation.org/research-advocacy-recommendations/our-scientific-program/best-practices-reports/> accessed 1 August 2021.

[177] [15(d)]: 'The operator shall ensure that the ALC/MTU is switched on and must be reporting normally, consistently and automatically to the FFA VMS at all times during the period of validity of the licence.'

'the master, owner, operator, or person chartering the fishing vessel, as the case may be, consents to the monitoring of such mobile transceiver unit at all times within and beyond Fiji fisheries waters during the period of validity of such licence or authorization.'[178] As a result, FFA members are able to continue monitoring the location and activity of a foreign fishing vessel throughout the period of its licence, even if the vessel should leave the licensing member's EEZ to fish or carry out other activities in the high seas or in the waters of another coastal State.[179] In addition, by entering into data sharing agreements, FFA members can also see the VMS data for the EEZs of other FFA members—allowing members to track the location and movements of all the foreign vessels licensed to fish in the region, rather than just those vessels that are licensed to fish in their own waters—which further multiplies the reach and effectiveness of the VMS.[180]

This technique has also been adopted sub-regionally by the PNA members, who have used a range of ambitious licensing conditions to assert control over the activities of foreign fishing vessels in areas of the high seas adjacent to their EEZs. Any foreign fishing vessel that is licensed to fish in the EEZ of a PNA member must not, during the period of validity of its licence:

- fish in prescribed areas of high seas;[181]
- tranship fish at sea, whether in an EEZ or on the high seas;[182] or
- conduct any bunkering or provisioning activities in prescribed areas of the high seas.[183]

[178] See also Kiribati, *Regs 2014* s 16; Marshall Islands, *Regs 2009* s 9; Nauru, *Regs 2009* s 10; Tuvalu, *Regs 2009* s 10; Vanuatu, *Act 2014* s 119.

[179] Similar requirements are also beginning to appear in the legislation of other coastal States. For example, in Eritrea, foreign vessels must install, maintain, and operate a satellite tracking device at all times while in Eritrean waters 'or such other areas as may be agreed or designated': *Proc 176/2014* art 13(4).

[180] On the use of this technology in the context of fisheries enforcement, see also the discussion in Chapter 6.

[181] *Third Arrangement Implementing the Nauru Agreement Setting Forth Additional Terms and Conditions of Access to the Fisheries Zones of the Parties* (PNA Third Implementing Arrangement) (signed 16 May 2008, as amended 1 May 2019) art 3. This prohibition applies in the two high seas pockets depicted in Figure 4.1: (a) the high seas pocket surrounded by the EEZs of Micronesia, Indonesia, Palau, and Papua New Guinea; and (b) the high seas area bounded by the EEZs of Micronesia, Fiji, Kiribati, Marshall Islands, Nauru, Papua New Guinea, Solomon Islands, and Tuvalu. See Kiribati, *Act 2010* s 12(2A); Marshall Islands, *Regs 2009* ss 7–8; Nauru, *Regs 2009* ss 7–9; Solomon Islands, *Regs 2012* ss 8–9; Tuvalu, *Regs 2009* ss 8–9. Some PNA members also require licensed vessels to stow their fishing gear while in the prescribed high seas areas, so that it is not readily available for fishing.

[182] *Second Arrangement Implementing the Nauru Agreement Setting Forth Additional Terms and Conditions of Access to the Fisheries Zones of the Parties* (PNA Second Implementing Arrangement) (adopted and entered into force 19 September 1990) LEX-FAOC005184 art 1.

[183] PNA Third Implementing Arrangement art 6. This prohibition applies to the transfer or receipt of fuel, oil, or any other supplies including food, cargo, crew, and spare parts in the high seas of the Western and Central Pacific Fisheries Commission (WCPFC) Convention Area east of 130° East. Similarly, the FFA Harmonized MTCs (at [18]) prohibit foreign fishing vessels from undertaking any fishing or related activity in the area of high seas bounded by the EEZs of the Cook Islands, French Polynesia, and Kiribati.

In addition, if a vessel licensed to fish in the EEZ of a PNA member is also used for high seas fishing during the course of a fishing trip, the vessel must provide the licensing State with catch and effort reports covering both the EEZ and the high seas for the whole trip.[184] These measures—which effectively operate as a condition for access to the resources of the EEZ—are an innovative way to expand the spatial application of the coastal State's jurisdiction over living resources.[185]

In considering these measures, it must be recalled that the extension of coastal State laws to the bunkering activities of foreign vessels on the high seas was recently considered by ITLOS in the *Norstar* case, in which the majority found that a foreign vessel's freedom of navigation under Article 87 may be breached if a coastal State extends its prescriptive jurisdiction to the activities of foreign ships on the high seas, unless 'justified by the [LOSC] or other international treaties'—even if the enforcement of those laws is carried out in internal waters.[186] This position (which was delivered with very little reasoning and departs from the widely accepted position that exclusive flag State jurisdiction is confined to enforcement activity on the high seas)[187] was opposed by the minority, who issued a strongly worded dissenting opinion arguing that there is nothing in the LOSC, its *travaux préparatoires*, other international treaties, customary international law, or State practice to suggest that Article 87 altogether excludes the right of non-flag States to exercise their prescriptive criminal jurisdiction with respect to activities on the high seas.[188] Notwithstanding this significant judicial difference of opinion, for the purpose of evaluating the PNA measures regulating the high seas activities of licensed foreign fishing vessels, it is sufficient to observe that they are justified by the LOSC, and thus meet the test set by ITLOS.

[184] Second PNA Implementing Arrangement art 2. Similarly, the FFA Harmonized MTCs state (at [7]) that foreign fishing vessels licensed by an FFA member must provide reports of all catch and bycatch 'taken in the fishery waters of the licensing member including the high seas'.

[185] A similar use of jurisdiction is evident in a series of bilateral State-to-State access agreements entered into by New Zealand with Korea, the Soviet Union, and Japan in the 1990s, in which the other parties agreed, as a condition of access to fishing opportunities in New Zealand's EEZ, to ensure that their vessels would not fish within the areas of high seas completely enclosed by the New Zealand EEZ: *Fisheries Agreement between the Government of New Zealand and the Government of the Republic of Korea* (signed 16 March 1978) 1167 UNTS 416; *Union of Soviet Socialist Republics and New Zealand Agreement on Fisheries (with Exchanges of Letters)* (signed 4 April 1978) 1151 UNTS 277; *New Zealand and Japan Agreement on Fisheries (with Memorandum of Understanding and Exchange of Letters)* (signed 1 September 1978) 1167 UNTS 441. See also the Barents Sea Loophole Agreement, the effect of which is that, in return for access to quotas in the Norwegian and Russian EEZs, Icelandic vessels will not fish in the high seas pocket known as the Barents Sea Loophole.

[186] *Norstar* [223]–[226]. This approach was subsequently applied by the Arbitral Tribunal in the *Enrica Lexie* arbitration in relation to the exclusivity of flag State jurisdiction under art 92 of the LOSC: *Enrica Lexie* [526]–[527].

[187] See Richard Collins 'Introductory Note to the M/V "Norstar" Case (Panama v Italy) (ITLOS)' (2019) 58 ILM 673, 674; Cameron Miles, 'The MV "Norstar" Case (Panama v Italy). ITLOS Case No 25. Preliminary Objections.' (2020) 114 AJIL 116, 121; Haomei Li, 'Letter to the Journal—Coastal State Jurisdiction in the "Norstar" Case at ITLOS' (2020) 19(1) ChineseJIntlL 177, 182.

[188] *Norstar* (Joint Diss Op Cot, Pawlak, Yanai, Hoffmann, Kolodkin, Lijnzaad, and Treves) [19]. On the *Norstar* decision, see further: Robin Churchill, 'Dispute Settlement in the Law of the Sea: Survey for 2019' (2020) 35 IJMCL 621, 623–32.

That is, in applying its laws to the high seas activities of a foreign fishing vessel as a condition of allowing that vessel access to the living resources of its EEZ, a coastal State is engaging in a legitimate exercise of its sovereign rights and jurisdiction under Articles 56 and 62 of the LOSC, to which the vessel's owners, operators, and flag State have consented, either explicitly or implicitly. This is because flag States have a responsibility to ensure that their vessels do not fish outside their national jurisdiction unless authorized to do so. Accordingly, if a flag State considers that the terms and conditions established in the laws and regulations of a coastal State are not consistent with the LOSC, it can refrain from authorizing its vessels to fish in those waters. Moreover, as specified in Article 62(4) and confirmed in the *SRFC Advisory Opinion*, the flag State is under an obligation to ensure compliance by vessels flying its flag with the conservation measures concerning living resources and other terms and conditions enacted by the coastal State for its EEZ.

Of course, given the freedoms enshrined in Article 87(1) of the LOSC, foreign fishing vessels may decide to continue engaging in fishing and related activities on the high seas in these areas—but if they do, they will not be able to access the lucrative fisheries in the EEZs of these coastal States.[189] In practice, fishing and fishing support vessels from a wide variety of distant water fishing nations—including the Bahamas, Belize, China, Ecuador, Japan, Liberia, New Zealand, Panama, Russia, South Korea, Spain, Chinese Taipei, and the United States—have continued to be authorized by their flag States to engage in fishing and related activities in the waters of the PNA members.[190] Moreover, in some instances the PNA have been able to extend the application of their regulations to the high seas through incorporation in the conservation and management measures of the Western and Central Pacific Fisheries Commission (WCPFC), reflecting the influence of coastal State rights in the management of highly migratory fisheries throughout their range.[191]

4.3.3.3 Compliance with Fisheries and Other Laws within and beyond the EEZ

In addition to regulations governing the operation of fishing vessels during the period of the licence, coastal States have developed a large—and ever-increasing—body of conditions relating to the history of compliance by foreign fishing vessels,

[189] Since the EEZs of the PNA members contain the most productive fishing grounds in the western and central Pacific region, the collective application of these conditions constitutes a 'powerful tool for managing fishing effort across the entire high seas/EEZ fishing area': Quentin Hanich et al, 'Sovereignty and Cooperation in Regional Pacific Tuna Fisheries Management: Politics, Economics, Conservation and the Vessel Day Scheme' (2010) 2(1) AustJMar&OceanAff 2, 10.

[190] See generally the flag States of the fishing vessels listed on the PNA Vessel Register, available at <https://pnatuna.com/index.php/registered-vessels> accessed 1 August 2021.

[191] Hanich et al, 'Sovereignty and Cooperation' (n 189) 10. See, eg, WCPFC, *CMM 2010-02 Conservation and Management Measures for the Eastern High Seas Pocket Special Management Area* (subsequently replaced by WCPFC, *CMM 2016-02 Conservation and Management Measures for the Eastern High Seas Pocket Special Management Area*), which prohibits transhipment in the high seas pocket bounded by the EEZs of the Cook Islands, French Polynesia, and Kiribati.

as well as their masters, owners, operators, and beneficial owners, with not only fisheries laws but a wide range of other legislation, both within and beyond the EEZ. Depending on the way in which they are crafted, these conditions have the potential to significantly expand the temporal, spatial, personal, and substantive effect of the influence that can be asserted by coastal States on the basis of their jurisdiction over living resources in the EEZ.

Some coastal States apply the fishing vessel's history of compliance with their own fishing regulations as a pre-condition for access to the living resources of their EEZ, or use inclusion on the IUU vessel list of an RFMO as a proxy for determining compliance.[192] Other States pursue similar objectives but with broader personal, spatial, and temporal effect, as in Section 128(2)(c) of Kenya's *Fisheries Management and Development Act 2016*, which provides that a foreign fishing licence may only be granted if the vessel, as well as its operator, master, and beneficial owner have not engaged in—or been reasonably suspected to have engaged in—IUU fishing in any place during the previous five years. Under Section 5(1.12) of the Canadian *Coastal Fisheries Protection Regulations*, a foreign fishing licence may not be granted if there are reasonable grounds to believe that the vessel is not in compliance with relevant conservation and management measures, or is providing supplies to *another* foreign fishing vessel that is not in compliance with relevant conservation and management measures. Provisions of similar object or effect can be found in the legislation of a range of other coastal States, particularly in Africa and the Asia-Pacific.[193]

In the legislation of some coastal States, such preconditions are substantively expanded to include a range of activities not related to fisheries—such as Section 7 of Gambia's *Fisheries Regulations 2008*, pursuant to which a licence may only be granted to a foreign fishing vessel provided that 'the vessel, or its owner, has not been convicted within the last five years of an offence under the laws of The Gambia governing navigation, customs, immigration, fiscal measures, health, narcotics or firearms'. Other coastal States have specifically sought to address aspects of labour exploitation, human rights standards, and transnational crimes including human trafficking and drug trafficking through the terms and conditions of foreign fishing licences. For example, pursuant to Sections 41A and B of Papua New Guinea's *Fisheries Management Act 1998*, a licence shall not be issued—or if already issued,

[192] See EU *Reg 2017/2403* art 33; Jamaica, *Act 2018* s 52. It is important to note that there are some limitations on the effectiveness of the IUU vessel lists as indicators of compliance, in particular a lack of transparency as to criteria and process. See Eva van der Marel, 'Problems and Progress in Combatting IUU Fishing' in Erik Jaap Molenaar and Richard Caddell (eds), *Strengthening International Fisheries Law in an Era of Changing Oceans* (Hart 2018) 302; European Commission *Community Action Plan for the Eradication of Illegal, Unreported and Unregulated Fishing* (2002) [3.3].

[193] See Cape Verde, *Leg Dec 2/2020* art 27; France (Mayotte), *Dec 2010-727* art 4(8); Guinea, *Code 2015* art 41; Liberia, *Law 2019* s 10.16(2); Madagascar, *Code 2015* art 40; Mauritius, *Act 2007* art 34(4); Seychelles, *Act 2014* s 12(6); Niue, *Act 1996* s 27; Papua New Guinea, *Act 1998* s 41A; Samoa, *Act 2016* s 29; Solomon Islands, *Act 2015* s 38(3); New Zealand, *Act 1996* s 83; Saint Kitts and Nevis, *Act 2016* s 42.

may be cancelled—'if there is reason to believe that the vessel has engaged in trafficking of people, drug trafficking, or has treated fish workers on board in a cruel or inhumane manner.'[194]

Issues of labour exploitation and human rights are the subject of specific regulation in Indonesia, where anyone operating a 'fishery business' (involving the capture, transportation, processing, or marketing of fish within the Indonesian EEZ) is required to obtain a fishery business licence, implement the Fishery Human Rights System and obtain a Fishery Human Rights Certificate.[195] In the Falkland Islands, Section 45(1) of the *Fisheries (Conservation and Management) Ordinance 2005* provides that an overseas master fishing licence (which is a pre-requisite for operating a foreign fishing vessel in the Falkland Islands EEZ) may be refused if during the last five years the person was convicted of any offence under the laws of the Falkland Islands or any other country or territory which involved violence towards, or maltreatment of, any member of the crew of a fishing vessel at which the person was at the time a master, mate, or officer.[196] The harmonized minimum terms and conditions agreed by the coastal States of the FFA and SWIOFC also include conditions relating to human rights violations and labour exploitation.[197]

Of course, ascertaining the facts necessary to apply some of these licensing conditions is likely to be difficult. In this regard, one possible approach can be found in Timor-Leste's legislation, which provides that on the expiration of a fishing permit, Timor-Leste will issue an 'acquittance' to the licence holder, indicating that there are no outstanding tariffs, fines, penalties, or tax charges towards the administration resulting from activities covered by the expired fishing permit.[198] While this is not a panacea for the difficulties involved in ascertaining the compliance history of foreign fishing vessels, some form of acquittal or certification issued to a foreign vessel by the coastal State upon the expiration of its fishing licence could be useful to other coastal States considering the grant of a licence to that vessel—perhaps functioning as a 'positive' indicator of compliance, in contrast to the records of 'negative' compliance, such as IUU vessel lists, which are commonly employed as licensing criteria.

[194] See also Sierra Leone, *Regs 2019* s 15; Tanzania, *Act 2020* ss 38 and 42; Tuvalu, *Act 2006* s 18.

[195] Indonesia, *Reg 35/2015*, art 4 and *Reg 2/2017*. This applies equally to Indonesian and foreign nationals operating a 'fishery business' but is focused particularly on the protection of foreigners working in the fishing industry. See Hadyu Ikrami, 'Indonesia's Reform of its Fisheries Law and Policy & Cooperation with ASEAN in Combating IUU Fishing' (2017) 2 APacJOceanL&Pol 318, 324–6.

[196] In addition, as noted in Section 4.1.2, following reports that serious human rights and employment abuses were occurring on board foreign fishing vessels operating under charter in its EEZ, the New Zealand government amended the *Fisheries Act 1996* to require all fishing vessels operating in New Zealand waters to be flagged to New Zealand, in order to ensure that all foreign vessels and their crews are covered by the full extent of New Zealand law, including employment relations and workplace health and safety law (nn 49–51 and associated text).

[197] SWIOFC MTCs arts 23 and 24; FFA Harmonized MTCs [22].

[198] Timor-Leste, *Dec Law 2004* art 6.

The reach and effectiveness of these terms and conditions can be strengthened through cooperation between coastal States, particularly by using a 'regional register' of foreign fishing vessels to collectively apply compliance conditions as part of the licensing process. For example, FFA members have agreed not to license any foreign fishing vessel or fishing support vessel to operate in their EEZs unless that vessel is first registered in 'good standing' on the FFA Vessel Register.[199] An application for good standing on the FFA Vessel Register will not be granted unless the vessel is not on an IUU vessel list, the application form with all relevant details has been received and the levy paid, and position reports are being received from the vessel by the FFA VMS.[200] Moreover, a vessel's 'good standing' can be suspended or withdrawn if the vessel or its owner, master, charterer, or operator contravenes the minimum terms and conditions of access or the fisheries laws and regulations of any FFA member, or is listed on an IUU vessel list.[201] The concept of 'good standing' on the FFA Vessel Register is also a crucial part of the arrangements in place between the PNA members for the regulation of vessels under the VDS: a vessel may not undertake any fishing in the EEZ of a PNA member unless registered on the relevant PNA VDS Register—which requires the vessel to first be in good standing on the FFA Vessel Register.[202]

The concept of 'good standing' not only strengthens the effectiveness of the FFA members' laws and regulations for foreign fishing, but also functions as a form of regional 'positive compliance' list, since a vessel cannot be licensed to fish in the EEZ of an FFA member unless it has good standing on the Vessel Register. While a number of other regional fishery bodies in Africa, central America, and the Caribbean have established—or have agreed to establish—regional or sub-regional vessel registers, these appear to be based on the compilation of national registers of foreign fishing vessels that have already been licensed by coastal States, rather than constituting a centralized, positive list of vessels to which licences *may be issued* by coastal States.[203] While useful for monitoring, control, and surveillance purposes, this approach does not have the same pre-emptive compliance effect as requiring vessels to maintain good standing on a single regional register in order to gain a licence to fish in the EEZ of any coastal State in the region. In this regard, the power of a regional register lies in the collective agreement of all member States to enforce particular legal consequences with respect to a vessel that is assigned as not

[199] FFA Harmonized MTCs Annex 4 'Procedures for the Operation of the FFA Vessel Register' [3.1].
[200] Ibid [4.1].
[201] Ibid [6] and [7].
[202] Palau Arrangement, Longline VDS art 7 and Purse Seine VDS art 8.
[203] SRFC MCA Convention art 19; SWIOFC MTCs art 8; *Convention on the Pooling and Sharing of Information and Data of the Area of the Fisheries Committee for the West Central Gulf of Guinea* (signed 12 December 2014) art 9(2); CCCFP art 13.2(d); OSPESCA, *Regulation OSP-01-09 of the Integrated System of Central American Fisheries and Aquaculture Registry (SIRPAC)* (in Spanish) (adopted 21 May 2009) arts 3 and 5, available at <http://extwprlegs1.fao.org/docs/pdf/sica180524.pdf> accessed 7 February 2021.

'responsible' or not of 'good standing'—in particular, refusing to register that vessel for fishing in the EEZ.[204]

4.3.3.4 Additional Benefits from the Regulation of Fishing Related Activities

As discussed in Chapter 3, coastal States regulate not only 'fishing' by foreign vessels in the EEZ, but a wide range of 'fishing related activities', including transhipment, bunkering, and the provision of water, food, fuel, and fishing gear. In many cases, detailed terms and conditions are established in national laws to regulate the conduct of these activities. For example, pursuant to Fiji's *Offshore Fisheries Management Decree 2012*, foreign fishing vessels may only engage in transhipment, bunkering, or provisioning: where authorized by the Director; with an authorized carrier or bunker vessel; on the provision of at least seventy-two hours' notice; at a place and time approved by the Director; subject to the provision of full reports in the approved form; under the supervision of an observer if directed; and subject to the payment of relevant fees, and any other condition imposed by the Director.[205] Similar approaches (involving, at a minimum, advance notice and authorization, supervision, reporting, and payment of fees) are found in the legislation of a number of other coastal States, particularly in Africa[206] and the Pacific.[207] Depending on the way in which such regulations are applied, they can have a range of advantages for the coastal State.

In addition to the ecological and social benefits to be gained through regulating the conduct of these activities,[208] coastal States can secure significant economic benefits by requiring that they take place in designated ports, including the payment of fees and service charges related to the conduct of transhipment or bunkering operations,[209] and private sector revenue from the provision of goods and services.[210] This revenue is additional to the fees that are paid for fishing access,

[204] Kieran Kelleher, 'Robbers, Reefers and Ramasseurs. A Review of Fisheries Monitoring, Control and Surveillance in Seven West African Countries' *Report for the Sub-Regional Fisheries Commission, Project FAO/GCP/INT/722/LUX (ARF/013)* (2002) 13, available at <http://researchgate.net/profile/Kieran_Kelleher/publication/278785493_Robbers_Reefers_and_Ramasseurs_A_review_of_fisheries_Monitoring_Control_and_Surveillance_in_seven_West_African_countries/links/5585e47008aeb0cdaddf7016/Robbers-Reefers-and-Ramasseu> accessed 14 December 2020.

[205] Fiji, *Dec 2012* ss 34–6. Similar provisions are established in the legislation of the Cook Islands, Tonga, and Vanuatu.

[206] Angola, *Dec 41/05* arts 109–110 and *Dec 14/05* arts 48–57; Guinea, *Code 2015*, arts 83 and 122–4; Kenya, *Act 2016* s 107; Liberia, *Law 2019* s 10.25; Mozambique, *Dec 43/2003* art 131; South Africa, *Regs 1998* s 85.

[207] Cook Islands, *Regs 2012* ss 31–6; Marshall Islands, 51 *MIRC* §409; Micronesia, 24 *FSM Code* §407; Solomon Islands, *Act 2015* ss 61–2; Tonga, *Regs 1992* s 26 and *Terms and Conditions 2002* s 8; Tuvalu, *Act 2006* s 33; Vanuatu, *Act 2014* ss 104–5.

[208] See Chapter 3 nn 143–6 and associated text.

[209] In addition to a transhipment or bunkering permit, these may include, for example, port entry fees, environmental levies, wharfage or anchorage fees, and customs or quarantine duties.

[210] Private sector goods and services likely to be used by vessels transhipping in port include shipping agency and pilot fees, garbage disposal, the purchase of fishing gear, salt and materials for constructing fish aggregating devices, water taxi or boat hire, and crew purchases.

and forms another component of the 'resource rent' that coastal States can extract from their fishery resources. In some instances, coastal States have sought to attract some of these additional economic benefits through the direct application of licensing conditions. For example, Section 5(c) of the Seychelles *Fisheries Regulations 1987* provides, as a condition of every fishing licence, that: 'All supplies and services required for the operation of the vessel shall be procured in Seychelles except if such supplies or services are not available locally.' A similar approach is taken in Kenya's legislation, which requires the holder of any licence issued for the purpose of fisheries access to give preference to materials and products made in Kenya, and service agencies located in Kenya and owned by Kenyan citizens, companies, or public corporations in the conduct of all relevant activities.[211] In practice, the implementation of such conditions is likely to be more effective if adopted collectively, through the framework of a cooperative management and enforcement regime, following the approach adopted by regional organizations such as the FFA and PNA.

4.4 Conclusion

Despite having been expressed in the language of obligation and recognized in the literature as the 'essence of the regime' for living resources in the EEZ,[212] the principles established in the LOSC for regulating access to the living resources of the EEZ bear little similarity to the contemporary regulation of foreign fishing by coastal States. While the LOSC formula was intended to afford a balance between the exclusive jurisdiction of coastal States over living resources in the EEZ and the interests of the international community, in practice it has proved poorly adapted to this task;[213] several of the key obligations are 'more apparent than real',[214] and although most coastal States do provide some opportunity for other States to have access to the EEZ, very few follow the specific mechanisms set out in Article 62.

In hindsight, this is not surprising; the scope and formulation of the principles necessary to transform traditional fishery conservation and utilization processes in the way required to implement the new and novel regime of the EEZ could not become evident or understood except through the experience gained by coastal states—and other States—over time in conserving and utilizing the resources of the zone.[215] Accordingly, while these provisions were critical to securing agreement to the adoption of the EEZ, and may have been 'the best compromise available at the

[211] Kenya, *Act 2016* §133.
[212] Orrego Vicuna, *The EEZ* (n 71) 50.
[213] Kwiatkowska, *The 200 Mile EEZ* (n 5) 45–6; Markowski, *The International Law of EEZ Fisheries* (n 75) 66–7.
[214] Burke, *The New International Law of Fisheries* (n 66) 44.
[215] Kwiatkowska, *The 200 Mile EEZ* (n 5) 46.

time they were negotiated',[216] their scope and effect has been significantly modified and developed—and additional considerations and priorities introduced—in the course of State practice. The practice examined in this Chapter clearly reveals the ways in which States have implemented, developed, and varied the framework established in the LOSC, and allows for conclusions to be drawn about the effect of these developments on the rights and interests of coastal and other States in the EEZ.

First, in practice, the grant or denial of foreign fishing access is not necessarily tied to the establishment of a surplus. At one end of the spectrum, some coastal States have effectively eliminated foreign fishing, including by placing a blanket prohibition on foreign fishing access, putting in place conservation and management measures which effectively preclude the establishment of a surplus, or adopting legislative measures that assimilate foreign fishing into the national system and allow the coastal State to exercise both coastal and flag State jurisdiction over foreign-owned or operated fishing vessels. At the other end of the spectrum, there are some coastal States for whom the act of providing access to surplus resources in accordance with the LOSC is seen as important—even if the exploitation of those resources is not economically viable, or they are not of any real interest to other States. In addition, some coastal States provide access for foreign fishing vessels even when there is no 'surplus', whether in order to ensure continued reciprocity of access to the resources of other States, or for economic or political reasons.

While some of these approaches appear to depart significantly from the central ideas of Article 62(2), it is important to recall both the broad discretion afforded coastal States in the implementation of their rights and obligations under Part V of the LOSC, as well as the complex mix of biological, economic, social, and political circumstances particular to each coastal State. Accordingly, a coastal State's approach to regulating foreign fishing access should not be measured against the exact formulas set out in the LOSC, but by the underlying—or overriding—objective of 'optimum utilization', pursuant to which a coastal State is competent to pursue a variety of management goals, policies, or tactics with respect to the living resources of the EEZ. In this regard, while most coastal States *do* envisage the possibility of foreign fishing, the objective of optimum utilization does not simply require coastal States to ensure the continued productivity of living marine resources for the common advantage of all by allowing access to other States in situations where there are surplus resources; it must also be observed as a principle of restraint, requiring the coastal State to ensure the conservation and sustainable management of those resources, which may require denial of access where there is *not* a surplus. Moreover, taking into account the range of management objectives that

[216] Ibid.

may inform the coastal State's decision-making in this regard, there may be sound reasons for determining that the 'optimum utilization' of living resources in the EEZ does not include access for foreign fishing vessels.[217]

Second, the exhaustively negotiated allocation criteria embedded in the LOSC have, for all practical purposes, become obsolete; notwithstanding the specific considerations listed in Article 62(3), coastal States allocate the resources of the EEZ solely on the basis of their own interests, without reference to the concerns of other States, or the 'rights' of land-locked or geographically disadvantaged States. In this respect, as the leader of the coastal State group at the Third United Nations Conference on the Law of the Sea (UNCLOS III) explained, provided the coastal State ensures optimum utilization, it has a right to 'marry the bride with the largest dowry.'[218]

The elements sought by coastal States in most contemporary 'dowries' do not include the interests of other States outlined in Article 62(3), but only issues relating to the coastal State's own economy and other national interests, including particularly:

- maximizing the financial or other forms of return or 'resource rent' provided in return for access to the living resources of the EEZ, including by moving from reliance on components provided as development assistance toward payments that contribute to coastal State fishery development;
- securing flag State commitments to cooperate in ensuring compliance with the terms of the access agreement and the fisheries laws and regulations of the coastal State, as well as agreement to broader cooperation in conservation and management of living resources in the EEZ and, in some cases, the high seas beyond;
- reciprocity in access, both with respect to fishing opportunities in the waters of the other party, and with respect to trade and investment opportunities in the markets of the other party; and
- a wide variety of 'national interest' objectives, relating not only to issues directly or indirectly connected with fishing—such as the protection of national fishery interests and the conservation and management of global fish stocks—but a range of broader environmental, national security, foreign policy, and even industrial relations considerations.

Importantly, while the coastal State's general duty to promote optimum utilization may oblige it to permit foreign access to the surplus, there is no particular 'right of

[217] Burke, '1982 Convention on the Law of the Sea' (n 54) 90.

[218] Jorge Castaneda, quoted in Bernard H Oxman, 'An Analysis of the Exclusive Economic Zone as Formulated in the Informal Composite Negotiating Text' in Thomas A Clingan (ed), *Law of the Sea Institute 13th Annual Conference 'Law of the Sea: State Practice in Zones of Special Jurisdiction'* (Law of the Sea Institute 1979) 72–3.

access' on the part of any other State or group of States,[219] and thus no limitations on the way in which the coastal State may exercise its discretion regarding the allocation of such access.

Third, while the terms and conditions for the conduct of foreign fishing envisaged in Article 62(4) of the LOSC have—in contrast to the other aspects of Article 62—generally been adopted and implemented consistent with their terms, coastal States have also developed additional or enhanced terms and conditions that have expanded the scope and effect of the jurisdiction that may be exercised on the basis of sovereign rights over living resources in the EEZ and broadened the substantive, geographic, personal, and temporal application of their influence. In many regions, these regulations have been strengthened and enhanced through the harmonization of conditions for foreign fisheries access, which has underpinned the collective development and application of a variety of innovative and ambitious licensing conditions, particularly by developing (and small island developing) coastal States. While all of these regulations can be described as being 'directly connected with' fishing—in so far as they constitute conditions relating to the conduct of fishing in the coastal State's waters—in practice, many of them have non-fisheries objectives (such as preventing transnational crime and human rights abuses, or enhancing coastal State control over industrial relations) or seek to secure or enhance cooperation within the framework of other legal regimes.

This trend is only likely to increase. As more and more coastal States become able to fully exploit their own resources, and the world's fish stocks continue to come under pressure from a growing population demanding protein, the competition for access to surplus resources will grow, enabling coastal States to further increase and expand the 'value' of the resource rent secured from their EEZs. In particular, it might be expected that coastal States will continue to develop criteria or conditions for access relating to non-fisheries issues or objectives, such as:

- heightened levels of control and higher standards in relation to labour and human rights issues throughout the supply chain, with respect to not only the actual harvesting of resources, but upstream and downstream processes;
- increasing demands for expanded opportunities in trade and market access, extending beyond fisheries products to other goods and services, or cooperation in eliminating harmful fisheries subsidies;
- the employment of increasingly 'rights-based' management approaches along the lines of those adopted in the western and central Pacific region, as a basis for expanding the spatial and substantive effect of the coastal State's sovereign rights; and

[219] In this regard, since there is no international 'right' of access to fishing in the waters of a coastal State, no right of a foreign State is breached if the coastal State denies access to its fisheries. As a result, there is no limitation on a coastal State applying denial of access to fishing as a form of sanction: Caron, 'International Sanctions' (n 129) 332–3.

- cooperation in relation to a wide variety of strategic and security issues, ranging from environmental protection and climate change to transnational crime and terrorism.

In light of the broad range of issues that are—or may be—regulated through the lens of foreign fishing access, the question becomes: what are the outer limits of coastal State jurisdiction, or do coastal States have a jurisdictional 'blank cheque' in this regard? Even prior to the adoption of the LOSC, Judge Oda predicted that: 'The principle of access of other nations to the surplus will eventually become meaningless, and the 200-mile [EEZ] will eventually be assimilated to the territorial sea, where the coastal State is free to grant any concession, to exploit the sea resources to any person or corporation by its own will, except that some land-locked States will continue to be allowed to participate in the exploitation of the living resources.'[220]

Of course, this vision has not proved completely accurate: no preference is granted to land-locked States, and the EEZ has not (or not yet) been assimilated to the territorial sea. However, the other aspects of Judge Oda's prediction are consistent with contemporary practice: it is clear that the principle of access to the surplus *has* become largely meaningless, and that the coastal State *is* free to grant access to any person or corporation on its own terms.

The 'jurisdictional continuum' governing the prescriptive exercise of coastal State power over foreign fishing in the EEZ can be defined—and the legitimacy of coastal State regulation can be assessed—by reference to the objective of 'optimum utilization', pursuant to which the coastal State has almost complete discretion to secure the 'optimum' value from the use of its resources, limited only by its obligations relating to conservation and management, the duty of cooperation with respect to shared stocks, and the general obligation to exercise its rights and fulfil its obligations under the LOSC in good faith. The value to be optimized is not limited to fisheries objectives: it may include a wide range of strategic, political, economic, environmental, social, or cultural objectives, and in practice is likely to require a balance to be achieved between a number of these things in order to maximize the overall 'value' to the coastal State.[221] While this does not amount to a 'blank cheque', it is certainly true that in exercising prescriptive jurisdiction with respect to foreign fishing access, the coastal State has extensive discretion, which is applied with minimal limitations. But to what extent does this discretion extend to the regulation of unlicensed vessels exercising the freedom of navigation through the EEZ, and to the enforcement of fisheries jurisdiction in the EEZ? These questions will be explored—and answers suggested—in Chapters 5 and 6.

[220] Shigeru Oda, *International Law of the Resources of the Sea* (Sijthoff & Noordhoff International 1979) 39–40.

[221] Matthew Hooper, 'Coherence through Co-Operation: The Challenge for Achievement of Policy Coherence for Fisheries Development in the Pacific' in *Fishing for Coherence: Proceedings of the Workshop on Policy Coherence for Development in Fisheries* (OECD 2006) 220–1.

5
Jurisdiction over Unlicensed Foreign Fishing Vessels in Transit through the EEZ

While the establishment of the exclusive economic zone (EEZ) in the United Nations Convention on the Law of the Sea (LOSC) extinguished the freedom of fishing in large areas of ocean, it did not extinguish the freedom of navigation, which continues to be exercisable by all vessels—not only container vessels, oil tankers, cruise ships, and warships, but fishing vessels and fishing support vessels travelling through the coastal State's EEZ without engaging in fishing or related activities within that zone. However, the passage of unlicensed foreign fishing vessels through a coastal State's EEZ, exercising (or claiming to exercise) the freedom of navigation, gives rise to a significant and legitimate interest on the part of a coastal State in ensuring that such vessels do not engage in fishing without authorization, in order to fulfil its 'special rights and responsibilities' in the EEZ,[1] protect its revenue stream, preserve the integrity and effectiveness of its management regime, and obtain reliable data on which to base future management decisions. In this regard, as the representative of Cambodia pointed out during the negotiation of the LOSC, the freedom of navigation in the EEZ ought not to be abused in any way which might affect the economic character of the zone, and 'foreign fishing vessels should not be permitted to use the pretext of the freedom of navigation to engage in clandestine fishing activities in the zone.'[2]

While all fishing activities 'conducted by national or foreign vessels in waters under the jurisdiction of a State, without the permission of that State, or in contravention of its laws and regulations' clearly fall within the broad category of 'illegal fishing',[3] the sub-set of 'unauthorized' fishing activities conducted by unlicensed foreign vessels, cloaked in the freedom of navigation, pose particular enforcement challenges for coastal States. This is not merely a theoretical concern, as demonstrated by the efforts of coastal States to combat unauthorized foreign fishing in their EEZs over the last twenty years—from the difficulties experienced by Australia and France in protecting remote areas of their EEZs in the Southern

[1] *SRFC Advisory Opinion* [106].

[2] Soth (Khmer Republic), 27th meeting of the Second Committee, 5 August 1974, extracted in *Official Records of the Third United Nations Conference on the Law of the Sea, Volume II (Summary Records of Meetings of the First, Second and Third Committees, Second Session (Caracas, 20 June to 29 August 1974))* 212.

[3] See IPOA-IUU [3.1.1].

Coastal State Jurisdiction over Living Resources in the Exclusive Economic Zone. Camille Goodman, Oxford University Press.
 DOI: 10.1093/oso/9780192896841.003.0005

Ocean in the early 2000s, reflected in the *Camouco*, *Monte Confurco*, and *Volga* cases, to the contemporary challenges faced by the developing coastal States of west Africa, where fishing by unlicensed industrial foreign fishing vessels accounts for a significant proportion of the estimated $1.3 billion USD annual loss to illegal, unreported, and unregulated (IUU) fishing.[4] At the same time, given the large expanse of ocean encompassed by the EEZs of coastal States, it is important that 'fishermen should be able to cross the economic zones of other countries with their catches, without the risk of being suspected of illegal fishing.'[5]

This clash of interests—between the flag State's desire to ensure free, efficient, and unimpeded movement of its vessels around the globe, and the coastal State's need to ensure that vessels do not use that freedom of movement to engage in illegal fishing and exploit the living resources of the EEZ—is not clearly resolved in the LOSC, or in any of the subsequent international instruments relating to fisheries.[6] The bulk of the early literature on this issue concluded that coastal State authority to apply regulatory measures to the navigation of foreign fishing vessels through the EEZ (such as requirements to stow gear, provide entry and exit notifications, or seek prior authorization) should only be accepted in narrowly defined 'exceptional circumstances'[7] or did not reach any conclusion about their legitimacy.[8] However, later authors have taken a more expansive view.[9] And in practice, regulations of this type have been widely adopted and enforced by coastal States, without any formal challenges from other States through litigation (even though Article 297(1)(a) of the LOSC preserves the possibility of compulsory dispute settlement where

[4] Africa Progress Panel, 'Grain, Fish, Money: Financing Africa's Green and Blue Revolutions' *Africa Progress Report 2014*, 89, available at <http://afdb.org/fileadmin/uploads/afdb/Documents/Project-and-Operations/Africa_Progress_Report_2014.PDF> accessed 17 December 2020.

[5] Van der Essen (Belgium), 35th meeting of the Second Committee, 9 August 1974, extracted in *Official Records of UNCLOS III* (n 2) 259.

[6] As discussed in Chapter 2, while a range of binding and non-binding instruments have been adopted to clarify and strengthen the LOSC framework for fisheries, these relate predominantly to the obligations of flag States, the governance of shared stocks, and the regulation of high seas fisheries. While the IPOA-IUU and the Port State Measures Agreement are focused on preventing, deterring, and eliminating IUU fishing, they do not address the issue of coastal State jurisdiction over unlicensed foreign fishing vessels in transit through the EEZ.

[7] William T Burke, 'Exclusive Fisheries Zones and Freedom of Navigation' (1983) 20 SanDiegoLRev 595, 623. See also: Horace B Robertson, 'Navigation in the Exclusive Economic Zone' (1984) 24 VaJIntlL 865, 890–5; Barbara Kwiatkowska, *The 200 Mile Exclusive Economic Zone in the New Law of the Sea* (Martinus Nijhoff 1989) 88 and fn 182.

[8] See Dean Robb, 'Access Conditions and Compliance Control' in *Report of the Expert Consultation on the Conditions of Access to the Fish Resources of the Exclusive Economic Zones* (FAO 1983) 159–60; David Joseph Attard, *The Exclusive Economic Zone in International Law* (Clarendon Press 1987) 180–2; Francisco Orrego Vicuna, *The Exclusive Economic Zone* (CUP 1989) 98–9.

[9] See Erik Jaap Molenaar and Martin Tsamenyi, 'Satellite-Based Vessel Monitoring Systems for Fisheries Management: International Legal Aspects' (2000) 15 IJMCL 65, 87; Jon M Van Dyke, 'The Disappearing Right to Navigational Freedom in the Exclusive Economic Zone' (2005) 29 MarPol 107, 108; Helmut Tuerk, *Reflections on the Contemporary Law of the Sea* (Martinus Nijhoff 2012) 175; Alexander Proelss, 'Article 58' in Alexander Proelss (ed), *United Nations Convention on the Law of the Sea: A Commentary* (CH Beck 2017) 444.

it is alleged that a coastal State has acted in contravention of the freedom of navigation in the EEZ).

In light of the obvious gaps between the text of the LOSC, the views in the literature and the state of the practice, it is important to examine the foundation and application of the legal regime governing this issue. First, given the lack of detail in the LOSC, what is the *nature* of the coastal State's jurisdiction over unlicensed foreign fishing vessels exercising the freedom of navigation through the EEZ: is it solely a question of enforcement jurisdiction, simultaneously enabled and limited by the terms of Article 73(1); or do coastal States also have prescriptive jurisdiction over such vessels? Second, what is the *extent* of such jurisdiction, and how can it be reconciled with, or balanced against, the freedom of navigation in the way envisaged by the rule of reciprocal due regard established in Articles 56(2) and 58(3)? And third, how does this translate to a practical, predictable framework for the regulation—and freedom—of navigation by foreign fishing vessels? This Chapter addresses these questions by analysing the broad framework established by the LOSC (Section 5.1) and examining the wide variety of regulatory measures that have been adopted in the law and practice of coastal States (Section 5.2), in order to establish the permissible scope and extent of coastal State jurisdiction over unlicensed foreign fishing vessels navigating through the EEZ (Section 5.3).

5.1 The LOSC Framework

By virtue of the general grant of 'sovereign rights to explore and exploit, conserve and manage' the living resources of the EEZ under Article 56(1)(a) of the LOSC, the coastal State has jurisdiction with respect to any foreign vessel or person—licensed or unlicensed—whose actions might impinge on those rights.[10] While Articles 61 and 62 clarify and confirm the scope and extent of this jurisdiction over *licensed* foreign fishing by establishing an extensive set of discretionary prescriptive powers, the LOSC does not provide similar guidance regarding the coastal State's jurisdiction over *unlicensed* fishing vessels in transit. In this regard, there is an important distinction to be drawn: the objective of coastal State jurisdiction over unlicensed foreign fishing vessels is not to regulate the details of their fishing activities, but simply to ensure that they do not engage in any such activities during their passage through the EEZ. Accordingly, the coastal State's authority over such vessels arises as a function of its enforcement jurisdiction, the scope of which must be initially determined by reference to the rule in Article 73(1) that the coastal State may 'take such measures, including boarding, inspection, arrest and judicial

[10] There are exceptions in respect of warships and ships used only on government non-commercial service, which have immunity from the jurisdiction of any State other than the flag State, as provided in arts 32 and 95.

proceedings, as may be necessary to ensure compliance with its laws and regulations', provided they are adopted in conformity with the LOSC.

5.1.1 Regulation by Enforcement Action or by Prescriptive Measures

There are two principal ways in which a coastal State can use this jurisdiction to try and ensure that unlicensed foreign vessels do not engage in fishing. The first is through traditional enforcement concepts, such as aerial surveillance and the boarding and inspection of foreign fishing vessels at sea.[11] While some commentators have taken a restrictive approach to the extent of this authority,[12] the majority of coastal States have interpreted the power of boarding and inspection under Article 73(1) broadly, applying it not only to vessels that are licensed to fish, or those currently engaged in fishing or related activities, or even those 'reasonably suspected' of having committed a violation of the coastal State's fisheries laws and regulations, but to *any* foreign fishing vessel in the EEZ.[13] However, while physical enforcement is possible as a matter of international *law*, it can be impractical—or even impossible—as a matter of *fact*, due to a shortage of physical and human resources, the high costs and practical challenges of conducting at-sea surveillance and enforcement operations, and the vast areas to be patrolled, which often pose an 'insuperable impediment' to effective physical monitoring and surveillance.[14]

Accordingly, the vast majority of coastal States supplement physical enforcement measures with some form of regulation, such as requirements that unlicensed foreign fishing vessels stow gear or give prior notification of their passage through the EEZ. Such requirements provide a cost-effective way to narrow the scope of the coastal State's surveillance effort, reduce the likelihood of unauthorized fishing, and help to ensure that clandestine fishing activities by unlicensed vessels are not legitimized by the defence that the vessel was merely exercising the freedom of navigation, and not fishing.[15] But while it is clear that coastal States can take physical enforcement measures to secure compliance with their fisheries laws pursuant to Article 73(1), the legitimate extent of these pre-emptive, *prescriptive* regulatory

[11] As discussed in Section 6.2.2, modern technology is increasingly being employed to reduce or replace physical at-sea enforcement, including with respect to detecting unauthorized foreign fishing in the EEZ.

[12] For example, Nandan and Rosenne state that a fishing vessel with its gear stowed would not be subject to the jurisdiction of the coastal State, but that the coastal State may be entitled 'to check by visual inspection' that the vessel is not engaged in any fishing activity: Satya Nandan and Shabtai Rosenne (eds), *United Nations Convention on the Law of the Sea 1982: A Commentary, Vol II* (Martinus Nijhoff 1993) 565.

[13] For more detail, see Section 6.2.1 and Table 6.1.

[14] Christopher J Carr and Harry N Scheiber, 'Dealing with a Resource Crisis: Regulatory Regimes for Managing the World's Marine Fisheries' (2002) 21 StanEnvLJ 45, 61.

[15] Robb, 'Access Conditions and Compliance Control' (n 8) 160.

requirements raises additional considerations, requiring the application of the reciprocal 'due regard' rule under Articles 56(2) and 58(3).[16]

5.1.2 Application of the Reciprocal Due Regard Rule

The reciprocal due regard rule is an express recognition of the need to accommodate the different uses (and users) of the EEZ,[17] and establishes a procedural obligation pursuant to which the State claiming the exercise of a right or freedom must consciously undertake a balancing exercise with the colliding rights or freedoms of other States.[18] As the *Chagos Arbitration* confirmed, this balancing exercise requires the coastal State to consider: all the circumstances of the case; the nature and importance of the different rights involved; the extent of impairment to the rights of flag States; and the availability of any alternatives; and may also involve consultation with affected States.[19] Since the outcome of this balancing exercise may be different in each individual situation, the rule of due regard does not impose 'a uniform obligation to avoid any impairment' of the rights of flag States, nor does it 'uniformly permit' the coastal State to proceed as it wishes, merely noting the rights of flag States.[20] While it is thus not possible to derive a 'universal rule of conduct' in this respect,[21] in seeking to establish how this framework applies to the regulation of unlicensed foreign fishing vessels in transit, it is useful to start by considering the general nature and importance to coastal and flag States of the rights involved.

For coastal States, the nature and importance of the rights in question is very clear; it arises not only from their sovereign rights over living resources under Article 56(1)(a) of the LOSC, but as a necessary means of giving effect to their responsibility to ensure the conservation and optimum utilization of those resources as required by Article 61, and as a particular function of the right and duty under Article 73(1) to ensure compliance with the laws and regulations adopted to achieve these ends. Illegal fishing can have severe economic impacts for coastal States (particularly developing coastal States) and undermine the effectiveness of fisheries management regimes and the collection of fisheries data. In addition, at-sea enforcement is notoriously difficult and costly.[22] Accordingly, coastal States have a legitimate interest in establishing appropriate regulatory measures to ensure that vessels passing through the EEZ do not conduct unauthorized fishing, and

[16] On the rule of due regard, see also Section 2.3.2.1.

[17] Myres S McDougal and William T Burke, *The Public Order of the Oceans: A Contemporary International Law of the Sea* (New Haven Press 1985) 777.

[18] Alexander Proelss, 'Article 56' in Alexander Proelss (ed), *United Nations Convention on the Law of the Sea: A Commentary* (CH Beck 2017) 432.

[19] *Chagos Arbitration* [519].

[20] Ibid.

[21] Ibid.

[22] See further Chapter 6 nn 8–13 and associated text.

that unauthorized fishing is not enabled by unauthorized fishing related activities (such as transhipment or bunkering) during passage through the EEZ. The importance of the coastal State's rights and responsibilities in this regard was underlined in the *SRFC Advisory Opinion,* in which ITLOS unequivocally stated that the primary responsibility for taking the necessary measures to prevent, deter, and eliminate illegal fishing—which includes unauthorized fishing in the EEZ—rests with the coastal State.[23]

At the same time, flag States have a legitimate right and interest in ensuring that their vessels can navigate freely and efficiently through EEZs without interference or impediment. In this regard, any regulations adopted by coastal States should not unduly burden the freedom of navigation of unlicensed fishing vessels or render their activities impractical or uneconomic—whether in terms of cost, time, convenience, planning or safety. This is clearly summarized by Burke: 'The freedom of navigation does not wholly insulate fishing vessels in transit from compliance with coastal State measures designed to enforce prohibition of illegal fishing, provided that such measures are essential to effective enforcement, do not significantly affect passage, and benefit the coastal State to a significant degree. Modest requirements that might occasion slightly longer voyages, or require specific measures aboard a fishing vessel, are consistent with the [LOSC].'[24]

In this context, Article 62(5) of the LOSC requires that coastal States give 'due notice' of their conservation and management laws and regulations. It is important to ensure that any applicable coastal State regulations are clear and publicly available, so that unlicensed foreign-flagged fishing vessels are not taken unawares. Nonetheless, it could still be difficult for such vessels to determine or comply with detailed requirements for transit—particularly if regulations are complex, there is a language barrier, or there is a change of plans during the voyage and a vessel needs to enter the EEZ of a coastal State to seek assistance or supplies, escape bad weather, or transit to another point beyond the zone. Since many coastal States regulate the conduct of not just fishing but *fishing related* activities in the EEZ, it is also important that vessels engaged in or equipped for such activities (such as transhipment or bunker vessels) are able to ascertain what regulations apply to them in the various EEZs through which they may pass.

In addition, flag States have a legitimate interest in ensuring that regulations or restraints which might be accepted in relation to fishing do not create difficulties for other types of vessels, develop into blanket rules that impede other types of navigation, or provide a stepping stone for the 'creeping' jurisdiction of coastal States to erode the freedoms and the balance preserved in the LOSC.[25]

23 *SRFC Advisory Opinion* [106].
24 Burke, 'Exclusive Fisheries Zones' (n 7) 605.
25 See Burke, 'Exclusive Fisheries Zones' (n 7) 600; Robertson, 'Navigation in the EEZ' (n 7) 894.

5.1.3 Prevention and Protection of Interference with Sovereign Rights

Of course, notwithstanding its vital importance and interest to all States, the freedom of navigation has never been absolute; over time, as maritime activities and technologies have changed and new exclusive interests have been recognized, limitations on the freedom of navigation have developed, and new ways have been found to balance the interests of coastal and flag States.[26] In this regard, one of the key lessons from the *Arctic Sunrise Arbitration* is that the coastal State has the right to take steps to prevent actions that would interfere with the exercise of its sovereign rights over the resources of the EEZ, including actions that would constitute violations of its laws adopted in conformity with the LOSC, and actions that would have 'negative environmental consequences.'[27] As Mossop has observed, this conclusion does not rely on any express provision in the LOSC, but flows automatically from the existence of the coastal State's sovereign rights over those resources.[28] However, the *Arctic Sunrise Arbitration* also made clear that the measures adopted by the coastal State must be reasonable, necessary, and proportionate. Accordingly, measures that are directed at limiting or preventing unauthorized interference with the living resources of the EEZ are likely to be a legitimate exercise of the coastal State's jurisdiction under Article 56(1), provided they are reasonable and proportionate to this aim, and thus respect the rule of due regard under Article 56(2).

Inevitably, the application of any coastal State regulation reduces the 'freedom' of navigation by foreign fishing vessels in transit—this is clearly envisaged in Article 58(1), which recognizes that the freedoms of other States in the EEZ are enjoyed 'subject to the relevant provisions' of the LOSC, which necessarily include the coastal State's sovereign rights over living resources. The pertinent question is whether any given regulation burdens the freedom of navigation in a way that is not 'necessary' or 'reasonable' in light of the coastal State's sovereign rights—and duties—to explore, exploit, conserve, and manage the living resources of the EEZ. In practice, this requires each jurisdictional assertion to be measured on its merits, with individual consideration given to the benefits, impairments, and alternatives available in relation to the wide variety of regulations that might be asserted by coastal States to prevent, deter, and eliminate unauthorized fishing in the EEZ. However, given the volume and consistency of contemporary State practice on this issue, it is also possible to draw some general conclusions about the types of

[26] RP Anand, '"Tyranny" of the Freedom-of-the-Seas Doctrine' (1973) 12(3) IntSt 416, 417.

[27] *Arctic Sunrise Arbitration* [327]. While the 'negative environmental consequences' in the *Arctic Sunrise Arbitration* related to marine pollution, this reasoning could be applied equally to negative environmental consequences relating to the living marine resources of the EEZ over which the coastal State has sovereign rights. See also Section 2.3.3.2.

[28] Joanna Mossop, 'Protests against Oil Exploration at Sea: Lessons from the Arctic Sunrise Arbitration' (2016) 31(1) IJMCL 60, 79–80.

regulations that are likely to meet these criteria, which help to give further content to the scope and extent of coastal State jurisdiction over unlicensed foreign fishing vessels in transit through the EEZ.[29]

5.2 The Contemporary Practice of Coastal States

Like the regulation of foreign fishing access discussed in Chapter 4, the approaches available to coastal States to regulate unlicensed foreign fishing vessels in transit through the EEZ are not uniquely defined choices, but regulatory options that may be employed singly or in combination depending on the needs and objectives of the coastal State. Since the last comprehensive examination of this issue was undertaken by Burke in the early 1980s,[30] the approach—or combination of approaches—now taken by each coastal State is summarized in Table 5.1, which shows that contemporary coastal State regulations generally include one or more of the following approaches:

- requirements relating to the stowage and carriage of fishing gear;
- routeing or passage requirements;
- entry to the EEZ restricted to purposes consistent with international law;
- requirements to notify details of passage to the coastal State, including vessel movements and catch on board;
- a prohibition on entering the EEZ without authorization;
- the use of presumptions; and
- maximizing the effect of other bases of jurisdiction.

While State practice has evolved significantly in the last forty years, these approaches still fall broadly within those suggested by Burke,[31] which provide a useful benchmark against which to understand and assess the contemporary practice of coastal States and consider the way in which the LOSC has been interpreted and implemented over time.

[29] This is a particularly important area in which to examine State practice because, in contrast to the regulation of issues associated with marine environmental protection and pollution, there are no externally established 'generally accepted standards', and the unilateral assertions of coastal State jurisdiction are not subject to consideration and adoption (or rejection) by the international community through another body (such as the International Maritime Organization (IMO)).

[30] William T Burke, 'Fisheries Regulations Under Extended Jurisdiction and International Law' *FAO Fisheries Technical Paper No 223* (FAO 1982). This study was revised in 1983: Burke, 'Exclusive Fisheries Zones' (n 7).

[31] Ibid 598.

Table 5.1 Coastal State approaches to regulating unlicensed foreign fishing vessels in the EEZ

African Group	
Algeria	*Law 01-11 of 2001* art 25: unlicensed foreign fishing vessels navigating in waters under national jurisdiction must clear the bridge or stow gear to prevent its use.
Angola	*Law 6-A/04 of 2004* art 103: unlicensed foreign vessels in Angolan waters must stow gear in sealed compartments so it cannot be used for fishing.
Benin	*Law 2014-19* arts 42, 43: unlicensed foreign fishing vessels in waters under Beninese jurisdiction must stow gear so that it cannot easily be used for fishing, and declare their movements and catches transported.
Cape Verde	*Leg Dec 2/2020* art 133(3): when any vessel reduces its speed below four knots for more than three hours there is a presumption that it is fishing.
Comoros	*Law 82-015* art 4: unlicensed foreign fishing vessels must stow fishing gear in the prescribed manner at all times while in the EEZ.
Cote d'Ivoire	*Law 2016-554* arts 22, 24: all foreign fishing vessels, including in transit, shall notify the position, date, and time of entry to and exit from waters under Ivorian jurisdiction and catches made; and stow gear when in an area where not authorized to operate.
Equatorial Guinea	*Law 11/2017*: arts 30(3), 31(1): unlicensed foreign fishing vessels in transit through the EEZ must stow gear so it is not easily usable for fishing or related activities and must submit a report including: the name of the vessel; date, time, and position; times of entry and exit to the zone; planned activities; and catch on board.
Eritrea	*Proc 176/2014* arts 17, 43 and *Regs 1998* art 15: unlicensed foreign fishing vessels must stow gear in the prescribed manner while in Eritrean waters. There is a presumption that all fish found on board any fishing vessel in Eritrean waters was caught in those waters.
Gabon	*Dec 579/PR/MPE* art 48: unlicensed foreign fishing vessels in transit through waters under Gabonese jurisdiction must stow gear so it cannot be used.
Gambia	*Act 2007* ss 41, 64 and *Regs 2008* s 27: unlicensed foreign fishing vessels must provide at least seventy-two hours' notice of intention to enter the fisheries waters. If the vessel has undermined international conservation and management measures, the Director may order the vessel not to enter the waters. The Secretary of State may direct any class of fishing vessel not to enter the waters where necessary to conserve and manage fisheries resources. These prohibitions do not apply to vessels involved in search and rescue, an emergency, or obtaining goods and services necessary to proceed safely and directly to a port elsewhere. Unlicensed foreign fishing vessels must stow gear in the prescribed manner so it is not available for fishing.

Table 5.1 *Continued*

Ghana	*Act 2002* ss 61–2: unlicensed foreign fishing vessels shall not enter the fishery waters except under 'circumstances recognized by international law'. Exception for a foreign fishing vessel entering for the sole purpose of 'innocent passage', by reason of force majeure or distress, for rendering assistance to persons, ships, or aircraft in danger or distress or for any other purpose recognized by international law. Vessels must stow gear in the prescribed manner and leave the waters as soon as the purpose for which they entered has been fulfilled or the reason has ceased to be valid.
Guinea	*Code 2015* art 112: unlicensed foreign fishing vessels must notify their entry to and exit from the EEZ, indicating the species and quantities of catches on board and stow gear so that it cannot easily be used for fishing.
Guinea-Bissau	*Dec 4/96* art 59: unlicensed fishing vessels shall stow gear in the prescribed manner for as long as they remain in the waters of Guinea-Bissau.
Kenya	*Act 2016* s 126 and *Regs 1991* s 19: unlicensed foreign fishing vessels must stow gear in the prescribed manner while in the Kenyan fishery waters.
Liberia	*Law 2019* ss 9.3–9.4: each foreign fishing vessel (licensed or unlicensed) must ensure that gear is stowed at all times so that it is not readily available for fishing, declare the type and quantity of fish on board at least twenty-four hours prior to entering or exiting the fisheries waters, and (if 15 metres or longer) shall be equipped with and ensure continuous operation of an AIS transceiver at all times while in the waters.
Madagascar	*Code 2015* art 61: unlicensed foreign fishing vessels wishing to transit the maritime waters must: inform the authorities of the place, date, and time of their entry to and exit from the waters; declare the species and quantities of the fishery resources held on board; and keep their fishing gear stowed during transit.
Mauritania	*Law 2015-017* art 47 and *Dec 2015-159* art 44: unlicensed foreign fishing vessels must stow gear as prescribed while in waters under Mauritanian jurisdiction.
Mauritius	*Act 2007* arts 52–3: each foreign fishing vessel shall provide twenty-four hours' notice of position at time of entry to or exit from the maritime zones and quantity of fish on board by species; unlicensed vessels must stow gear while in the maritime zones.
Morocco	*Act 1-81 of 1980* art 6(3): when exercising the freedom of navigation in the EEZ, foreign vessels must stow their fishing gear and equipment.
Namibia	*Act 2000* s 49: unlicensed vessels in Namibian waters must ensure that fishing gear is dismantled, stowed, or secured so as not to be readily available for fishing.
Nigeria	*Act 1992* s 2: unlicensed motor vessels within the EEZ shall stow their fishing gear wholly inboard as prescribed.

Continued

Table 5.1 *Continued*

Sao Tome & Principe	*Law 9/2001* art 39: unlicensed foreign fishing vessels must stow gear so it cannot be used for fishing while navigating through Sao Tome and Principe maritime space.
Seychelles	*Act 2014* s 6 and *Regs 1987* s 9: unlicensed foreign fishing vessels must keep their gear stowed in the prescribed manner and deactivate and not use any device for detecting fish at all times whilst in Seychelles waters.
Sierra Leone	*Regs 2019* s 7: unlicensed foreign fishing vessels must keep their gear stowed so that it is not available for fishing while in the fishery waters of Sierra Leone.
Somalia	*Law 2016* art 15: any fishing vessel that enters Somali waters without having a valid licence shall be presented to the Court and subjected to Somali fisheries law.
South Africa	*Act 1998* s 49 and *Regs 1998* ss 11, 81: foreign fishing vessels may not have any fishing gear on board in South African waters without a permit (accordingly, foreign fishing vessels must apply for a permit to enter the EEZ providing specified details and indicating their reason for entering the zone, and pay an application fee); foreign fishing vessels without a foreign fishing vessel licence must stow gear in the prescribed manner while in South African waters.
Tanzania	*Act 2020* s 37: unlicensed foreign fishing vessels in any place or at any time in the EEZ must stow gear so that it is not readily available for fishing.
Togo	*Law 2016-026* art 80: unlicensed foreign vessels navigating in waters under Togolese jurisdiction must stow gear so it cannot be easily used for fishing, and declare entry to and exit from the EEZ and the species and quantities of catches held on board.
Asia-Pacific Group	
Bangladesh	*Act 2020* ss 22: Unlicensed vessels may not enter Bangladesh fisheries waters except for: passage to a destination outside the waters; averting imminent danger or rendering assistance; obtaining emergency medical assistance; or 'any other purpose recognized by international law', which is subject to innocent passage. Vessels entering the fisheries waters for these purposes must notify their arrival and departure, observe prescribed rules, and return outside the waters as soon as the relevant purpose has been fulfilled.
Brunei	*Order 2009* ss 18, 55: a foreign fishing vessel may not enter Brunei waters except for the purpose of exercising 'innocent passage' in accordance with international law and must leave the waters as soon as that purpose is fulfilled. The vessel must notify its name, flag State, location, route and destination, types, and amount of fish on board and circumstances under which it is entering the waters. Any fish or gear on board will be presumed to have been caught, or to have been used for catching, fish in Brunei waters unless the requisite notification is provided on entry, fish are in a sealed hold, gear is stowed, and the vessel is travelling from one point outside the waters to another point outside the waters by the shortest practicable route.

Table 5.1 *Continued*

Cambodia	*Law 2006* art 50: unlicensed fishing vessels must stow their trawl gear so that it is not readily available for fishing while in the marine fishery domain.
China	*Prov Regs 1999* art 15: foreign fishing vessels navigating in the EEZ must stow their fishing gear in the prescribed manner.
Cook Islands	*Act 2005* s 19 and *Regs 1979* s 32: unlicensed foreign vessels that may be used for fishing or a related activity may not enter the fishery waters except for a purpose recognised under international law. Unlicensed foreign fishing vessels must stow gear so that it is not readily available for use for fishing.
Cyprus	*Fisheries Law* arts 3(6), 5A: the existence of fishing equipment on, inside, or towed by a vessel constitutes a presumption that the vessel is being used for fishing.
Fiji	*Dec 2012* s 33 and *Regs 2014* s 39(6): unlicensed foreign fishing vessels transiting Fiji fisheries waters must provide specified details (including name, flag, position, date and time, intended activity, and catch on board) at prescribed times and stow gear so it is not readily available for fishing or related activities. Otherwise, there is a presumption that fish on board was caught unlawfully in Fiji fisheries waters.
India	*Act 1981* s 22(2) and *Rules 1982* s 14: unlicensed foreign fishing vessels may enter the maritime zone of India for the purpose of passing through to a destination beyond, providing that all fishing gear is stowed and not readily available for fishing. If gear is not stowed, it shall be presumed, unless the contrary is proved, that the vessel was used for fishing within the maritime zone.
Indonesia	*Law 2004* art 38: foreign fishing vessels must keep their fishing gear stowed while in transit through areas of the Indonesian EEZ in which they are not licensed to fish.
Iran	*Law 1995* arts 30–31: unlicensed foreign fishing vessels in waters under the jurisdiction of Iran must stow gear so it cannot easily be used for fishing, and notify their arrival to and departure from those waters, as well as their geographical position periodically, during their stay within them.
Kiribati	*Act 2010* s 8: unlicensed foreign fishing vessels may only enter Kiribati waters for a purpose recognized under international law, must maintain a daily record of the date, time, and nature of every activity while in the waters, provide specified details to the authorities (name, flag, date and time, position, intended activity, and catch on board) at prescribed times, and leave the waters as soon as the purpose has been fulfilled. Gear must be stowed so it is not readily available for fishing. Otherwise, there is a presumption that fish on board was caught unlawfully in Kiribati waters.

Continued

Table 5.1 *Continued*

Malaysia	*Act 1985* ss 16, 56: unlicensed foreign fishing vessels may enter Malaysian fisheries waters for the purpose of transit to a destination beyond. Such vessels must notify their name, flag State, location, route and destination, types, and amount of fish on board and circumstances under which they are entering the waters; stow gear in the prescribed manner, and leave as soon as the purpose for which they entered has been fulfilled. Any fish on board will be presumed to have been caught in the fisheries waters unless the requisite notification is provided on entry, fish are in a sealed hold, gear is stowed, and the vessel is travelling from one point outside Malaysian fisheries waters to another point outside those waters by the shortest practicable route.
Maldives	*Act 2019* ss 25–6: foreign fishing vessels must obtain permission from the Ministry to enter the EEZ. The regulations for granting permission may include requirements for vessels to report entry and exit, provide information and stow gear. Unless the contrary is proven, any foreign fishing vessel entering the EEZ without obtaining permission shall be deemed to have entered for the purpose of engaging in fishing or related activity.
Marshall Islands	51 *MIRC* §§402, 522: vessels may not enter or remain within the fishery waters in violation of the fisheries law except for 'innocent passage' or force majeure in accordance with international law. Gear must be stowed so it is not readily available for use for fishing, or as may be prescribed.
Micronesia	24 *FSM Code* §§910–11: foreign vessels used for fishing or related activities shall report prescribed details upon entry and while within the fishery waters (including name, flag State, date and time, position, intended activity, and catch on board). Failure to comply gives rise to a refutable presumption that fish on board were caught unlawfully in the fishery waters (or, for a vessel used for fishing related activities, a presumption of unlawful engagement in such activities). Gear on board an unlicensed foreign fishing vessel must be stowed so it is not readily available for use in fishing.
Myanmar	*Law 1989* s 52: unlicensed foreign fishing vessels shall be deemed to be engaged in fishing if their fishing gear is not stowed during transit through the EEZ.
Nauru	*Act 1997* s 24: foreign boats may not enter or be in the fisheries waters except for 'a purpose recognised by international law' and must ensure that all fishing gear is stowed so it is not readily available for use in a place where not licensed to fish.
Niue	*Act 1996* s 18: a fishing craft shall not do anything in the EEZ that is not authorized or permitted by or under international law, and unless licensed for fishing in the relevant area, must not store fishing gear so it is readily available for fishing.
Palau	27 *PNC* §§191(c), 201(a), 203(c), 206(b): any vessel hovering in Palau's EEZ will be presumed to be violating the fisheries law. 'Hovering' means operating any unlicensed vessel within the EEZ which, taking into account its history, conduct, nature, navigation and character or location and other relevant data, is reasonable to believe is being or may be used to violate the fisheries law or any other law or regulation. There is a presumption that any fish on board a foreign vessel was caught and retained unlawfully.

Table 5.1 *Continued*

Papua New Guinea	*Act 1998* s 38: unlicensed foreign fishing vessels transiting the fisheries waters shall ensure that all gear on board is stowed so it is not readily available for fishing.
Philippines	*Code 1998* s 91 and *Order 200 of 2000* s 3: it is unlawful for any foreign person, corporation, or entity to operate any fishing vessel in Philippine waters. The entry of any foreign fishing vessel to Philippine waters shall constitute a prima facie presumption that the vessel is engaged in fishing. A foreign vessel is presumed to be fishing (or 'poaching') if: it enters the Philippines waters with its gear deployed or not stowed; it navigates with an irregular track or route, or in a manner that does not qualify as innocent passage, or is outside traditional routes or identified fishing grounds; or it is found in the Philippines waters lying-to or anchoring without any valid reason that may indicate force majeure, distress, or rendering assistance, or near known fishing grounds or marine protected areas:
Solomon Islands	*Act 2015* s 57: unlicensed foreign fishing vessels navigating in the fisheries waters must provide specified details (name, flag, date, time, position, intended activity, and catch on board) at prescribed times, and stow gear so it is not readily available for fishing or related activities. Otherwise, there is a presumption that fish on board was caught unlawfully in the fisheries waters.
Sri Lanka	*Act 1979* ss 5, 23(2) and *Regs 1981* art 2: unlicensed foreign fishing vessels shall stow gear in the prescribed manner while in Sri Lanka waters. If gear is not stowed in the prescribed manner or fish are found on board, it will be presumed that the boat has been used for fishing in contravention of the Act, unless the contrary is proved.
Timor-Leste	*Dec Law 2004* art 83: unlicensed foreign fishing vessels shall stow gear so as to render its use impossible while in transit through the EEZ.
Tonga	*Act 2002* ss 43, 68: foreign fishing and fish carrier vessels shall give seventy-two hours' notice of their intention to enter the fisheries waters. The Minister may direct any class of fishing or fish carrier vessel not to enter the waters where necessary for conservation and management. This shall not prevent a vessel from entering or remaining in the fisheries waters for a search and rescue operation or emergency, or for obtaining goods and services necessary to proceed safely and directly to a port outside Tonga. Foreign fishing vessels must stow gear so it is not readily available for use in fishing when in the fisheries waters.
Tuvalu	*Act 2006* s 27: a vessel may not be used to enter or remain in the fishery waters in contravention of the fisheries law, other laws, or an access agreement. An unlicensed foreign fishing vessel may enter the fishery waters for a purpose recognized by international law, including innocent passage and force majeure, but shall return outside as soon as that purpose has been fulfilled. Foreign fishing vessels transiting the fishery waters must provide specified details (name, flag, date, time, position, intended activity, and catch on board) in the manner prescribed, and stow gear so that it is not readily available for fishing or related activities.

Continued

Table 5.1 *Continued*

Vanuatu	*Act 2014* ss 53–4: unlicensed foreign fishing vessels navigating in Vanuatu waters must provide specified details (name, flag, date, time, position, intended activity, and catch on board) at prescribed times, and stow gear so that it is not readily available for fishing or related activities. If details are not notified as required, there is a presumption that fish on board was caught unlawfully in Vanuatu waters. Foreign fishing vessels must ensure that gear is stowed so it is not readily available for fishing.
Vietnam	*Dec 36/1999* art 9: it is an offence for a foreign fishing vessel not to stow fishing gear and devices in the EEZ.
Eastern Europe Group	
Albania	*Law 64/2012* arts 92, 106: unlicensed foreign fishing vessels must ensure that any fishing gear is stowed during transit through the fishery waters. In restricted fishing zones, unauthorized vessels must ensure that all gear is stow and must transit at a speed not less than six nautical miles per hour, except in the case of force majeure.
Bulgaria	*Act 2000* art 49(2): foreign fishing vessels must have their gear stowed while navigating through the EEZ.
European Union	*Reg 2017/2403* art 32(3), *Reg 1224/2009* arts 29, 47, 50: unlicensed foreign fishing vessels transiting Union waters must ensure that all gear on board is stowed during transit in the prescribed manner; during transit through a restricted fishing area, vessels must maintain a speed of not less than six knots, except in the case of force majeure or adverse conditions.
Russia	*Order 133 of 2005* art 9(5): unlicensed foreign fishing vessels must ensure that all fishing gear is stowed while in the EEZ.
Latin America and the Caribbean Group	
Antigua & Barbuda	*Act 2006* s 28 and *Regs 2013* s 27: unlicensed foreign vessels in Antigua and Barbuda waters must stow all fishing gear in the prescribed manner.
Argentina	*Law 24.922 of 1998* art 32 and *Dec 748/99* art 32: unlicensed foreign fishing vessels planning to enter maritime areas under Argentine jurisdiction must notify the authorities in advance, declare the catch and fishery products on board, and stow all gear. If a foreign fishing vessel is in the waters without express authorization, any fishery products found on board will be presumed to have been caught in those waters.
Bahamas	*Act 1977* s 20(2): any fish found on board a fishing vessel in the waters of the Bahamas shall be deemed to have been caught within those waters until the contrary is proved.
Barbados	*Act 1993* s 9: unlicensed foreign vessels must stow all fishing gear in the prescribed manner while in the waters of Barbados.
Belize	*Act 2020* s 38: unlicensed foreign fishing vessels in the EEZ of Belize shall keep fishing gear securely stowed so as not to be readily available for use.

Table 5.1 *Continued*

Dominica	*Act 1987* s 9: unlicensed foreign fishing vessels shall ensure that fishing gear is stowed in the prescribed manner during transit through the fishery waters.
Ecuador	*Dec 3,198 of 2002* arts 29–31: unlicensed foreign fishing vessels wishing to exercise 'innocent passage' through Ecuadorian waters shall provide: at least twelve hours notification; position before entering the waters; the date, time, and position of entry; the route, cruising speed and estimated day and time of exit from the waters; and whether or not the vessel has fish in its hold, by tonnage and species. Vessels must not engage in any activity other than simple passage and provide twenty-four hours' notice of their exit from the waters.
Grenada	*Act 1986* s 9 and *Regs 1987* s 7: unlicensed foreign fishing vessels shall ensure that all fishing gear is stowed in the prescribed manner while in the fishery waters.
Guyana	*Act 2012* s 31: unlicensed foreign fishing vessels shall ensure that all fishing gear is stowed in the prescribed manner while in the fisheries waters.
Honduras	*Dec 172-99* art 8(2): foreign fishing vessels exercising the freedom of navigation in the EEZ must comply with laws designed to prevent such vessels from engaging in fishing, including those relating to the stowage of fishing gear.
Jamaica	*Act 2018* s 55: unauthorized foreign fishing vessels must stow their gear in the prescribed manner while in the fisheries waters.
Nicaragua	*Dec 9/2005* art 209: unlicensed foreign fishing vessels must ensure that fishing gear is stowed in the prescribed manner during transit through the jurisdictional waters of Nicaragua.
Panama	*Exec Dec 161 of 2013* art 29: fishing vessels must stow their gear during transit through areas in which they are not authorized to fish and maintain a speed of not less than six knots except in case of force majeure or adverse conditions, in which case they must immediately notify the authorities (as a flag State).
Peru	*Dec 32/03* art 8: unlicensed foreign tuna fishing vessels navigating in transit through Peruvian waters shall keep their fishing gear properly stowed or stored.
Saint Kitts and Nevis	*Act 2016* ss 70, 75, 141 and *Regs 1995* s 10: unlicensed foreign fishing vessels navigating through the fisheries waters shall report details (including name, flag, date and time, position, intended activity, and catch on board) upon entry to and exit from the waters and at such other times as required. If a foreign vessel is navigating without reporting as required, it shall be presumed that any fish on board was caught illegally in the fisheries waters. Such vessels must ensure that ensure that gear is stowed or secured so that it is not readily available for fishing.
Saint Lucia	*Act 1984* s 9 and *Regs 1994* s 18: unlicensed foreign fishing vessels must stow gear in the prescribed manner while in the fishery waters.

Continued

Table 5.1 *Continued*

Saint Vincent & Grenadines	*Act 1986* s 9 and *Regs 1987* s 7: unlicensed foreign fishing vessels must stow gear in the prescribed manner while in the fishery waters.
Western Europe and Others Group	
Australia	*Act 1991* ss 95, 101: unlicensed foreign fishing vessels must not be within the Australian Fishing Zone (AFZ) unless gear is stowed in the prescribed manner and either: they have authorization or approval from the authorities; or they are travelling, by the shortest practicable route, from a point beyond the outer limits of the AFZ to another such point. It is an offence to possess fish on board a vessel in the AFZ if its taking was not authorized, but it is a defence if the court is satisfied that the fish was not taken in the AFZ.
Canada	*Act 1985* s 3 and *Regs 2014* ss 5(1)(b), 12.1, 14: unlicensed foreign fishing vessels may not enter Canadian fisheries waters unless authorized under the Act or the Regulations, any other law of Canada or a treaty. The Minister may issue a licence authorizing an unlicensed vessel to transit during a voyage to a destination outside the fisheries waters. A vessel may enter the fisheries waters without a licence to ensure the safety of the vessel and its crew, render assistance, or obtain emergency medical assistance. Unlicensed foreign fishing vessels entering the fisheries waters shall, as soon as is reasonably possible, notify the authorities of the name, flag state, location, route, and destination of the vessel and of the circumstances under which it entered Canadian fisheries waters. Such vessels shall ensure that all gear is stowed where it is not readily available for fishing; and, on request, proceed to a designated location for an inspection of the vessel.
France (New Caledonia)	*Deliberation 50/CP 2011* art 4: unlicensed fishing vessels must provide at least twenty-four hours' notice of entry to and exit from the New Caledonia maritime space, including at least the following details: date, time, position, name, flag, fishing authorizations, captain and owner details, call sign, satellite tracking system, gear on board, port visited and last port of call, quantity of each species on board.
France (SAAT)	*Code* art L958-7: any fishing vessel or vessel fitted out for the transport of fish entering the EEZ is required to report its entry and exit and to declare the tonnage of fish held on board.
Iceland	*Act 1998* art 4: unlicensed foreign fishing vessels must notify the Coast Guard of their transit six hours prior to entering and leaving Iceland's exclusive fishing zone, and send notification of their location, course, and speed at twelve-hour intervals during transit.
Ireland	*Act 2006* ss 8–9: it is unlawful for a foreign fishing vessel to enter the EEZ except for a purpose recognised by EU law, international law, a convention or arrangement in force between Ireland and the flag State, or another lawful purpose.
Malta	*Act 2001* ss 11, 14: foreign fishing vessels must notify the amounts, descriptions, and presentation of fish on board prior to entering the fisheries waters and before leaving an area of the fisheries waters in which the vessel is licensed to fish, and stow gear so it is not readily available for fishing.
Netherlands	*Regs 2011* art 10(5): fishing vessels must have their gear lashed and stowed in accordance with art 47 of EU *Regulation 1224/2009.*

Table 5.1 *Continued*

New Zealand	*Regs 2001* s 25 and *Act 1996* s 113: unlicensed foreign fishing vessels must stow all gear so that it is not readily available for fishing, and shall not possess any fish, aquatic life, or seaweed in New Zealand fisheries waters unless: it has previously been landed in another country; or approval has been given by the chief executive to possess that fish, aquatic life or seaweed; or it has been lawfully received by that vessel while in the fisheries waters. The burden of proving that an exception applies lies on the defendant.
United Kingdom	*Act 2020* s 12: an unlicensed foreign fishing boat must not enter the fishery limits except for a purpose recognized by international law or by any international agreement or arrangement to which the United Kingdom is a party. A vessel that enters the fishery limits for such a purpose must return outside as soon as the purpose has been fulfilled.
UK (Falklands)	*Ordinance 2005* s 169: it is an offence to have a fishing vessel equipped for fishing in the fishing waters unless the use or presence of the vessel is authorized by licence, or the gear is stowed in such a manner that it is not readily available for fishing. It is a defence for a person to show that they had no intention of fishing in the fishing waters.
UK (Montserrat)	*Act 2000* s 20: unlicensed foreign fishing vessels must ensure that all fishing gear is stowed during transit through the fishery waters.
UK (Pitcairn)	*Ordinance 2016* s 24(1): any fish on board an unlicensed foreign fishing vessel shall, unless the contrary is proved, be deemed to have been caught or taken in the marine protected area; any vessel found in the marine protected area in possession of fishing gear shall be deemed to have been fishing unless the gear is stowed so it is not readily accessible for fishing; and any vessel 'stationary, moored, drifting or sailing in a fishing pattern' in the marine protected area shall be deemed to be engaged in fishing. In each case the onus of proof to rebut the presumptions is on the person charged.
UK (SGSSI)	*Ordinance 2000* ss 8, 15, 18: twelve to twenty-four hours prior to entering a specified area (whether intending to fish or transit), every fishing vessel shall provide information including: name, registry, call sign, estimated time, date and location of entry into and departure from the specified area, and the quantity of fish, by species, on board. Unless otherwise proved, fish found on board that were not part of an entry or exit notification shall be presumed to have been caught in the fishery waters. Gear must be stowed in any area where the vessel is not authorized to fish.
UK (Turks & Caicos)	*Regs 1998* ss 32, 43(1): unlicensed foreign fishing vessels shall stow all gear so it is not readily available for fishing while in the fishery waters. Any marine products on board an unlicensed foreign fishing vessel in the fishery waters shall, unless the contrary is proved, be deemed to have been taken within those waters.
United States	16 *USC* §§1857(4), 1860(e): unlicensed foreign fishing vessels must ensure that all fishing gear on the vessel is stored below deck or in an area where it is not normally used, and not readily available, for fishing during transit through the EEZ.

Notes

a. The practice of EU member States is examined primarily by reference to EU regulations, but national legislation of individual member States is also included where relevant.

5.2.1 Stowage and Carriage of Gear

The most widely adopted approach—both at the time of Burke's study[32] and in contemporary practice—is a requirement for unlicensed foreign fishing vessels to stow gear while in transit through the EEZ. While the LOSC does not specifically reference coastal State restrictions on the stowage of fishing gear by vessels in transit through the EEZ, the relevance of stowage requirements to the prevention of unauthorized fishing is clearly recognized in the prescriptive powers provided to coastal States to regulate the passage of foreign vessels through straits and archipelagic waters under Articles 42(1)(c) and 54.[33] Not only does the requirement to stow fishing gear reduce the likelihood of a foreign vessel conducting illegal fishing during transit, it also reduces the complexities of proving the legality (or otherwise) of any catch on board—particularly when combined with the use of a presumption—thus alleviating the burden on both the coastal State and the vessel.

For example, pursuant to Section 22(2) of India's *Maritime Zones of India (Regulation of Fishing by Foreign Vessels) Act 1981*: 'Where any foreign vessel is found within any maritime zone and the fishing gear of such a vessel is not stowed in the prescribed manner or fish is found on board such vessel it shall be presumed, unless the contrary is proved, that the vessel was used for fishing within that zone.' As shown in Table 5.1, such measures are now employed by coastal States of every size and legal tradition, in every region. There is no evidence of any protest from flag States—indeed, a number of countries also apply these measures in their role as flag States, by actively requiring their flagged vessels to stow their gear while transiting through the EEZ of coastal States.[34] This is reflected in the literature, which notes that the requirement to stow gear is considered to be 'generally accepted', provided that it is not prescribed or enforced so rigidly as to have the effect of preventing entry to the EEZ.[35]

While the requirement to stow fishing gear is widely noted and accepted, very little has been written about the extent to which coastal States may regulate the *carriage* of certain types of gear by fishing vessels in transit through the EEZ. The limited literature on this issue—written in the 1990s—takes the view that prohibiting the 'mere possession of certain types of gear, properly stowed'[36] by a foreign

[32] Ibid 620.

[33] Pursuant to art 42(1)(c) of the LOSC, States bordering straits may adopt laws and regulations relating to transit passage including 'with respect to fishing vessels, the prevention of fishing, including the stowage of fishing gear'. Art 54 extends this to the regulation of archipelagic sea lanes passage.

[34] Kenya, *Act 2016* s 126(1)(b); Liberia, *Law 2019* s 9.3(1)(b); Sierra Leone, *Regs 2019* s 7(3)(a)(ii); Tanzania, *Act 2020* s 37(1)(b); China, *Regs 2020* art 32.

[35] See Burke, 'Exclusive Fisheries Zones' (n 7) 620; Gerald Moore, *Coastal State Requirements for Foreign Fishing* (Rev 1, FAO 1983) 22; Attard, *The EEZ* (n 8) 181. Since some fishing gear cannot easily be stowed (such as purse seine nets, which are too large to be stored below deck), it is important that the stowage requirements are applied reasonably with respect to different types of vessels.

[36] Ivan Shearer, 'High Seas: Drift Gillnets, Highly Migratory Species, and Marine Mammals' in Tadao Kuribayashi and Edward L Miles (eds), *The Law of the Sea in the 1990s: A Framework for Further*

fishing vessel in passage is not a valid exercise of coastal State jurisdiction.[37] However, there is a significant body of contemporary State practice demonstrating the adoption of regulations that prohibit the possession or carriage on board any fishing vessel in the EEZ of: (i) driftnets; and (ii) explosives, poisons, and other noxious substances, with an intention to use them for fishing. While neither of these categories of 'fishing gear' is specifically dealt with in the LOSC, the importance of regulating their use has subsequently been identified (to a greater or lesser extent) in various global fora—but to what extent does this provide a basis for coastal States to prohibit their carriage by fishing vessels merely transiting the EEZ?

Although it is well established that indiscriminate or 'destructive' fishing techniques such as driftnet fishing, dynamite fishing, and poisoning pose a significant threat of damage to living marine resources and the marine environment,[38] the international legal framework for the regulation of such activities is less clear. Since the marine environmental protection obligations established in Articles 192 and 194 of the LOSC apply to all States in all marine areas,[39] and the conservation of living resources is an element of these obligations,[40] coastal States (and flag States) have a due diligence obligation to ensure that activities within their jurisdiction or control do not harm the marine environment.[41] More specifically, the FAO Code of Conduct calls for States to adopt measures to minimize waste, discards, catch of non-target species, and negative impacts on associated or dependent species, including through the use of selective and environmentally safe gear, and to phase out gear which is not consistent with responsible fishing.[42] The FAO Code of Conduct also provides that States 'should prohibit dynamiting, poisoning and other comparable fishing practices'.[43] However, beyond these general (non-binding) statements, the activities of driftnet fishing, dynamiting, and poisoning are not mentioned in the principal global fisheries instruments adopted following the entry into force of the LOSC.

International Cooperation (Proceedings of the Law of the Sea Institute Twenty-Fourth Annual Conference, 24-27 July 1990, Tokyo, Japan) (The Law of the Sea Institute 1992) 253–4.

[37] William T Burke, 'Coastal State Authority over Driftnets on the High Seas' in *The Regulation of Driftnet Fishing on the High Seas: Legal Issues (FAO Legislative Study 47)* (FAO 1991) 30; Grant J Hewison, 'The Convention for the Prohibition of Fishing with Long Driftnets in the South Pacific' (1993) 25 CaseWResJIntlL 449, 505.

[38] See Grant J Hewison, 'High Seas Driftnet Fishing in the South Pacific and the Law of the Sea' (1993) 5 GeoIntlEnvtlLRev 313, 319–23; *Report of the FAO/UNEP Expert Meeting on Impacts of Destructive Fishing Practices, Unsustainable Fishing, and Illegal, Unreported and Unregulated (IUU) Fishing on Marine Biodiversity and Habitats, Rome, 23–25 September 2009* (FAO 2010), available at <http://fao.org/docrep/012/i1490e/i1490e00.pdf> accessed 22 December 2020;

[39] *SRFC Advisory Opinion* [120]; *South China Sea Arbitration* [940].

[40] *Southern Bluefin Tuna Cases* [40]; *SRFC Advisory Opinion* [216].

[41] *SRFC Advisory Opinion* [118]–[136]; *South China Sea Arbitration* [944].

[42] FAO Code of Conduct arts 7.2.2, 7.6.4, 7.6.9, 8.4.4, and 8.4.6.

[43] Ibid art 8.4.2.

With respect to driftnet fishing, a series of regional measures were adopted in the late 1980s,[44] which led to a 'global moratorium' on high seas fishing with large-scale pelagic driftnets, established by consensus through United Nations General Assembly (UNGA) Resolutions and given effect through a series of regulatory responses by coastal and flag States.[45] The most far-reaching of these measures is the Driftnet Convention adopted by the members of the Pacific Islands Forum Fisheries Agency (FFA) in 1989, which—in contrast to the UNGA Resolutions—focuses on prohibiting driftnet fishing activities not only on the high seas in the Convention Area, but within the fisheries jurisdiction of the Parties.[46] In addition to requiring the Parties to take measures such as prohibiting the use of driftnets and the transhipment of driftnet catches in areas within their jurisdiction, the Driftnet Convention provides that they may take measures 'consistent with international law' to 'prohibit the possession of driftnets on board any fishing vessel in an area under their jurisdiction'.[47]

A number of coastal States have enacted measures prohibiting the possession of driftnets on board any fishing vessel in the EEZ, including both Parties and non-Parties to the Driftnet Convention. The most comprehensive example is the New Zealand *Driftnet Prohibition Act 1991*, which states that '[n]o vessel in New Zealand fisheries waters shall have on board any driftnet', and authorizes an enforcement officer to stop, board, and inspect any vessel in the fisheries waters for the purpose of enforcing the Act, and to seize any vessel that the officer believes on reasonable grounds has been used in the commission of an offence against the Act.[48] A blanket prohibition on the possession of driftnets is also established in the legislation of a number of other Pacific Island States,[49] as well as Gambia, and Antigua and Barbuda.[50] Other coastal States have adopted slightly different approaches, such as prohibiting the conduct of driftnet fishing and then making it an offence to possess or control any fishing gear the use of which is prohibited,[51]

[44] These include the *Tarawa Declaration* adopted by the South Pacific Forum in July 1989; the *Langkawi Declaration on the Environment* adopted by the Commonwealth Heads of Government (CHOGM) meeting in October 1989; and the *Castries Declaration* adopted by the Organization of Eastern Caribbean States (OECS) in November 1989. See Linda Paul, 'High Seas Driftnetting: The Plunder of the Global Commons' (1994), available at <http://earthtrust.org/archive/dnpaper/contents.html> accessed 21 December 2020.

[45] UNGA Res 44/225 (22 December 1989) UN Doc A/44/225; UNGA Res 45/197 (21 December 1990) UN Doc A/45/197; UNGA Res 46/215 (20 December 1991) UN Doc A/46/215. On the measures taken to give effect to the moratorium, see the reports of the UN Secretary-General, *Large-Scale Pelagic Drift-Net Fishing and Its Impact on the Living Marine Resources of the World's Oceans and Seas*, UN Doc A/47/487 (6 October 1992); UN Doc A/48/451 (11 October 1993).

[46] Driftnet Convention arts 2 and 3(1).

[47] Ibid art 3(2)(e).

[48] See ss 6, 13, and 15.

[49] Cook Islands, *Act 2005* s 28; Fiji, *Dec 2012* s 25(1); Kiribati, *Act 2010* s 19; Nauru, *Act 1997* s 25; Niue, *Act 1996* s 19; Samoa, *Act 2016* s 43(1)(b); New Zealand (Tokelau) *Regs 2012* s 34; Tonga, *Act 2002* s 67; Tuvalu, *Act 2006* s 58; Vanuatu, *Act 2014* s 90.

[50] Gambia, *Act 2007* s 64; Antigua and Barbuda, *Act 2006* s 57.

[51] Ghana, *Act 2002* ss 87 and 135.

or providing that it is unlawful to have a driftnet on board a vessel for the purposes of fishing, on the basis that where a driftnet is found on board, such purpose shall be presumed.[52] These offences are commonly accompanied by significant financial and other penalties.

Despite constituting 'highly destructive fishing methods',[53] dynamite, poisons and other noxious substances are not subject to any globally agreed moratorium or regulation at the international level. Nonetheless, the national laws of a significant number of coastal States prohibit their carriage on board any fishing vessel in the EEZ. For example, pursuant to Article 73(c) of Benin's *Framework Law No 2014-19 on Fisheries and Aquaculture* it is prohibited to 'detain on board a fishing vessel or craft explosive substances or toxic substances or baits'. Similar provisions are included in the fisheries legislation of a number of other coastal States, predominantly in Africa.[54] Other coastal States prohibit the carriage of dynamite, poisons, and other noxious substances 'with the intention of using them for fishing', accompanied by the proviso that where such items are found on board a vessel, such intention will be presumed. This approach is most common in the Asia-Pacific region and in Latin America and the Caribbean but is also found in other regions.[55]

Given the global moratorium on the use of driftnets on the high seas, and the widespread ban on using both driftnets and other destructive fishing techniques in the EEZ, a prohibition on the carriage of driftnets, explosives, poisons, and other noxious substances is unlikely to impede the legitimate activity of foreign fishing vessels—and it could be argued that the balance of interests would still be adequately served if any vessel which does have a legitimate reason for carrying such gear through the EEZ of a coastal State were able to simply report that fact in advance of passage, to dispel any doubt.

[52] Mauritius, *Act 2007* art 13; United States, 16 *USC* §§1857(1)(M) and 1860(e).

[53] *South China Sea Arbitration* [970].

[54] Algeria, *Law 01-11 of 2001* arts 49 *bis* and *ter;* Angola, *Law 6-A/04 of 2004* art 104; Cameroon, *Law 94/01* art 127; Cape Verde, *Leg Dec 2/2020* art 89; Gabon, *Dec 579/PR/MPE* art 65; Guinea, *Code 2015* art 81; Guinea-Bissau, *Dec Law 10/2011* art 25; Mauritania, *Law 2015-017* art 38; Mozambique, *Dec 43/2003* art 50; Sao Tome and Principe, *Law 9/2001* art 40; Senegal, *Code 2015* art 65; Togo, *Law 2016-026* art 60; Tunisia, *Law 94-13* arts 10–11. See also: Iran, *Law 1995* art 24; Timor-Leste, *Dec Law 2004* art 92; Montenegro, *Law 2009* art 21; Argentina, *Law 24.922 of 1998* art 21; Jamaica, *Act 2018* s 89.

[55] Bangladesh, *Act 2020* s 27(2); Brunei, *Order 2009* s 31; Malaysia, *Act 1985* s 26; Marshall Islands, 51 *MIRC* §214; Nauru, *Act 1997* s 43; Papua New Guinea, *Reg 2000* s 32; Samoa, *Act 2016* ss 42–3; Tonga, *Act 2002* s 17; Tuvalu, *Act 2006* s 59; Vanuatu, *Act 2014* s 100; Antigua and Barbuda, *Act 2006* s 58; Barbados, *Act 1993* s 29; Belize, *Act 2020* s 37; Dominica, *Act 1987* s 24; Grenada, *Act 1986* s 25; Guyana, *Act 2012* s 29; Peru, *Dec 012/2001/PE* art 133; Saint Kitts and Nevis, *Act 2016* ss 22–5; Saint Lucia, *Act 1984* s 24; Saint Vincent and the Grenadines, *Act 1986* s 24. See also: Liberia, *Law 2019,* s 4.6(5); Mauritius, *Act 2007* art 13; Seychelles, *Act 2014* s 31; Sierra Leone, *Act 2018* s 40; Malta, *Act 2001* s 28; United Kingdom (Turks and Caicos Islands), *Regs 1998* ss 9(1) and 34(4).

5.2.2 Routeing or Passage Requirements

Another approach used by coastal States to regulate the transit of unlicensed foreign fishing vessels through the EEZ is to establish regulations governing their mode of passage, such as requirements relating to their route or speed. For example, Section 101 of the Australian *Fisheries Management Act 1991* (Cth) provides that unlicensed foreign fishing vessels must not be within the Australian fishing zone without authorization or approval from the Australian authorities, unless their fishing equipment is stowed in the prescribed manner and they are travelling 'by the shortest practicable route' from a point beyond the outer limits of the zone to another such point.[56] A requirement to transit by the 'shortest practicable route' is also found in the legislation of Brunei and Malaysia.[57] While this approach may have an 'impact' on the vessel's navigation, it would not necessarily impair it, provided it was left to the vessel to determine the actual course of its route, taking into account its departure point and destination, and other factors such as weather, navigational hazards, and the operational requirements of the vessel. Thus, this sort of measure can reasonably be said to effectively balance the relevant rights and interests and give appropriate respect to the navigational rights of the flag State.[58]

Since vessels that are legitimately transiting through the EEZ to a point outside it are likely to travel at a higher speed than vessels that are engaged in fishing operations, some coastal States require foreign fishing vessels to transit at a specified minimum speed. For example, under Article 133(3) of Cape Verde's *Legislative Decree 2/2020 approving the general regime regulating fishing activities in national maritime waters and the high seas*, a vessel is presumed to be fishing if it reduces its speed below four knots for more than three consecutive hours. Similarly, in Albania and the waters of European Union (EU) member States, unlicensed vessels transiting through 'restricted' fishing zones must maintain a speed of not less than six nautical miles per hour, except in case of *force majeure*.[59] This approach is also applied by Panama in its role as a flag State, to require that while transiting through the EEZs of coastal States in which they are not licensed to fish, Panamanian-flagged vessels must maintain a speed of not less than six knots, except in the case of *force majeure* or adverse conditions.[60]

Another variation on this approach is to prohibit activities that would *not* amount to continuous and expeditious navigation. For example, pursuant to

[56] As a flag State, Australia applies similar conditions to Australian-flagged vessels operating beyond the Australian EEZ. See *Conditions applying to High Seas Fishing Permits* [9], available at <http://afma.gov.au/sites/default/files/high_seas_general_conditions_2020_season.pdf> accessed 22 December 2020.

[57] See Table 5.1.

[58] For further discussion of the potential advantages and disadvantages of this approach, see Burke, 'Exclusive Fisheries Zones' (n 7) 611–17.

[59] See Table 5.1.

[60] Panama, *Exec Dec 161 of 2013* art 29.

Section 24(1) of the Pitcairn Islands' *Marine Protected Area Ordinance 2016*, any fishing vessel that is found or observed to be 'stationary, moored, drifting or sailing in a fishing pattern' in the marine protected area (which covers the entire EEZ) will be presumed to be engaged in fishing. Similarly, Palau prohibits unlicensed foreign fishing vessels from 'hovering' in the EEZ,[61] and a foreign vessel is presumed to be engaged in fishing in the Philippines EEZ if it 'navigates with an irregular track or route', or is found outside traditional routes, lying-to or anchoring without a valid reason.[62]

In the context of routeing or passage requirements, it is also useful to contemplate what possible applications there may be for the rule that the coastal State may take steps to prevent interference with the exercise of its sovereign rights, as confirmed in the *Arctic Sunrise Arbitration*.[63] To date, the principal application of 'preventive' or 'protective' coastal State regulation has been in situations involving protest activities at sea—predominantly non-violent direct action protests relating to controversial issues such as oil and gas exploration, whaling operations, and sealing. For example, following the 2011 protests at sea against the activities of the seismic survey vessel *Orient Explorer* in New Zealand's EEZ—during which a fishing vessel navigated into the path of the *Orient Explorer*, interrupting the conduct of the survey and requiring the dispatch of police and naval vessels at a cost of $1.7 million NZD ($1.225 million USD)[64]—New Zealand passed legislation providing for the creation of moving 'non-interference zones' of up to 500 metres around structures and vessels undertaking prospecting, mining, or exploration activity in the territorial sea and EEZ and above the continental shelf, which no person or vessel may enter 'without reasonable excuse'.[65] Similar provisions exist in the legislation of Canada and South Africa,[66] and analogous restrictions have reportedly also been used to address protest activities in respect of the exploitation of living resources, including Norway's establishment of moving 500 metre 'safety zones' around whaling vessels in its EEZ, and Canada's restrictions around the annual seal hunts on the ice floes of Newfoundland.[67]

These sort of 'zonal' restrictions around particular vessels—which appear to be modelled on the 500 metre safety zone that may be established around artificial islands, installations, and structures, pursuant to Article 60 of the LOSC—would probably have limited application to fisheries, other than in the context of direct

[61] See Table 5.1.
[62] Ibid.
[63] *Arctic Sunrise Arbitration* [327].
[64] For an excellent overview of this issue, see Mossop, 'Protests against Oil Exploration at Sea' (n 28) 77–8.
[65] New Zealand, *Crown Minerals Act 1991* s 101A–C.
[66] Canada, *Collision Regulations CRC c.1416* Rule 43; South Africa, *Marine Traffic Act 1981* ss 1 and 8B–C.
[67] G Plant, 'International Law and Direct Action Protests at Sea: Twenty Years on' (2002) 33 NYIL 75, 109.

action protests.[68] However, the concept of preventive or protective jurisdiction could underpin regulations requiring unlicensed fishing vessels to transit by the 'shortest practicable route' or at a certain minimum speed. Depending on the circumstances, it may also provide a basis for the adoption of broader preventive measures—probably not extending to the designation of mandatory sea-lanes for passage as contemplated by Burke,[69] but perhaps to the establishment of exclusion zones, which could be applied in a flexible, selective, temporal, and targeted way to address unusually difficult enforcement issues, or protect the coastal State's sovereign rights with respect to particularly important or vulnerable areas or stocks. For example, such measures may be appropriate in a remote area of a large EEZ where the risk of unlicensed fishing is so high (because of the potential value of the catch, or the distance from coastal State enforcement assets) and the potential impact so great (because it is a spawning ground for a key species or involves a vulnerable stock that requires stringent management) that the only reasonable way to protect the resources from unauthorized fishing is to establish an exclusion zone prohibiting passage through the area.

In this respect, the maritime zones legislation of a few coastal States includes the power to 'designate' areas of the EEZ for any purpose and apply provisions with respect to a wide range of issues, including entry into and passage through those zones.[70] Of course, any such measures would need to be carefully designed to address issues caused by fishing and fishing vessels—and not broader pollution or marine environmental protection issues, which are governed by the procedures in Part XII of the LOSC[71]—and any determination about their legitimacy would ultimately be based on the outcome of the 'balancing' process required to give effect to the obligation of due regard, including consideration of any alternatives that might reasonably be available.

[68] In Australia, for example, the 2012 arrival of the 142 metre factory trawler *FV Margiris* was met by protesters from Greenpeace who tried to board the vessel from rubber dinghies: 'Super Trawler Arrives amid Greenpeace Protest', *ABC News*, 31 August 2018, available at <http://abc.net.au/news/2012-08-30/greenpeace-tries-to-block-margiris-from-docking/4232548> accessed 21 December 2020.

[69] Burke, 'Exclusive Fisheries Zones' (n 7) 611. Under the conditions established in the LOSC, which include consistency with measures established by and requirements for adoption by the IMO, coastal States may establish sea-lanes and 'traffic separation schemes' in the territorial sea (art 22) and straits subject to the regime of transit passage (art 41).

[70] Barbados, *Marine Boundaries and Jurisdiction Act 1978* s 8; Guyana, *Maritime Zones Act 2010* s 30; India, *The Territorial Waters, Continental Shelf, Exclusive Economic Zone and Other Maritime Zones Act, 1976* ss 7(6)–(7); Jamaica, *Exclusive Economic Zone Act 1991* s 9; Pakistan, *Territorial Waters and Maritime Zones Act, 1976* ss 6(4)–(5). These provisions (together with other examples that have since been repealed) have been subject to protest by the United States: US Department of State, *Limits in the Seas No 112: United States Responses to Excessive National Maritime Claims* (1992) 45. See also Cyprus, *Fisheries Law* art 5A, which provides that the Minister may, by decree, prohibit fishing and/or the passage of vessels in any sea areas for reasons of national security or public safety or in the public interest.

[71] LOSC art 211(6)(a).

5.2.3 Entry to the EEZ Only for Purposes Consistent with International Law

A small but significant number of coastal States have enacted (and enforced) regulations pursuant to which unlicensed foreign fishing vessels are prohibited from entering the EEZ except for purposes consistent with international law. For example, Section 18 of Brunei's *Fisheries Order 2009* states that a foreign fishing vessel may not enter Brunei waters except for the purpose of 'exercising innocent passage in accordance with international law', and must return to a position outside Brunei waters as soon as the purpose for which it entered those waters has been fulfilled. Reference to 'innocent passage' can also be found in the legislation of Ghana, Bangladesh, the Marshall Islands, the Philippines, Tuvalu, and Ecuador.[72] Coastal States also use phrases such as 'circumstances recognized by international law' or 'a purpose recognized by international law'. For example, Section 12 of the United Kingdom's *Fisheries Act 2020* provides that a foreign fishing vessel must not enter the fishery limits except for a purpose 'recognized by international law' or under an international agreement or arrangement to which the United Kingdom is a party, and must return outside the fishery limits as soon as the purpose for which it entered has been fulfilled. This approach is also adopted in the legislation of Ghana, the Cook Islands, Kiribati, Nauru, Niue and Ireland.[73]

Unfortunately, none of these provisions indicate what is meant by 'innocent passage' or 'a purpose recognized by international law'. Clearly, any attempt to impose the requirements of innocent passage as defined in Part II, Section 3 of the LOSC and to substitute the territorial sea regime for the freedom of navigation would be inconsistent with both the LOSC and customary international law. In this respect, while the maritime zones legislation of a small number of coastal States still includes an assertion of 'sovereignty' over the EEZ,[74] or asserts that the powers of the territorial sea apply to fishing in the EEZ,[75] in practice they have not applied these asserted powers to regulate the conduct of foreign fishing in the EEZ, and their fisheries legislation distinguishes—either explicitly or by implicit differences in application—between the jurisdiction exercised in the territorial sea and the EEZ.[76] Given the combination of other requirements applied to the passage of

[72] See Table 5.1.

[73] See Table 5.1.

[74] Benin, *Decree No 76-92 Extending the Territorial Waters of the People's Republic of Benin to 200 Nautical Miles, 1976* art 1; Congo, *Ordinance No 049/77 of 20 December Amending Article 2 of Ordinance 26/71 of 18 October 1971* art 2; Ecuador, *Civil Code* art 628; El Salvador, *Constitution of 13 December 1983* art 84; Honduras, *Constitution of the Republic of Honduras 1982* art 12; Peru, *Political Constitution of Peru, Promulgated on 29 December 1993* art 54.

[75] Jamaica, *Exclusive Economic Zone Act 1991* s 8; Kuwait, *Decree No 317 of 2014 Concerning the Delimitation of the Marine Areas Pertaining to the State of Kuwait and Its Amendment* art 6.

[76] In the case of El Salvador, Honduras and Peru, the relevant provisions are incorporated in the Constitution, which could be difficult to amend. In addition, while Ecuador's reference to its 'sovereignty and jurisdiction' over the EEZ in a Declaration lodged upon accession to the LOSC in 2012 prompted objections from a number of States, several of them subsequently noted that Ecuador had

foreign fishing vessels by the coastal States in question (such as prior notification of entry to the EEZ), and the lack of any evidence that other elements of the territorial sea regime are being applied to these vessels (such as regulations relating to navigation, pollution, or security), it is more likely that the terms 'innocent passage' and 'a purpose consistent with international law' have been adopted—or *adapted*—by coastal States as terms of art, in order to protect their interests with respect to living resources. In that case, the relevant question is: what are these terms intended to mean, and is it consistent with the freedom of navigation under Article 58(1) of the LOSC?

In practice, any prosecution of an offence under these provisions would likely require the operator of the foreign fishing vessel to put in issue a purpose recognized by international law, and the coastal State to rebut it.[77] However, since the majority of these coastal States regulate the conduct of not only fishing but all 'fishing related activities' in the EEZ,[78] there is a very limited range of activities which an unlicensed foreign fishing vessel might realistically seek to undertake in their EEZs for a purpose 'consistent with international law'. Accordingly, while it is not clear how the concepts of 'innocent passage' or 'a purpose consistent with international law' are intended to differ from—or perhaps limit—the 'freedom of navigation' assured to all States in the EEZ, given the context in which they are used it seems likely that, in general, they contemplate:

- the exercise of passage through the EEZ to another point beyond it, without engaging in any fishing or fishing related activities; and
- that the passage should be continuous until its purpose has been fulfilled, unless there are exceptional circumstances (such as *force majeure,* or providing assistance to persons, ships, or aircraft in distress).

In essence, this would equate to a rule that unlicensed foreign fishing vessels must not 'hover'[79] in the EEZ without authorization from the coastal State.[80] While this

declared, in its discussions with their representatives, that it does not intend that the Declaration should exclude or modify the legal effect of the provisions of the LOSC. See United Nations (UN) Division for Ocean Affairs and the Law of the Sea (DOALOS), *Law of the Sea Bulletin No 80* (UN 2013) 14–15; DOALOS, *Law of the Sea Bulletin No 83* (UN 2014) 14–19.

[77] Unless the legislation includes a statutory presumption shifting the burden of proof to the defendant, as discussed in Section 6.2.4.1: P Flewwelling, *An Introduction to Monitoring, Control and Surveillance Systems for Capture Fisheries* (FAO 1994) 175.

[78] See the discussion in Chapter 3, and the practice summarized in Table 3.1.

[79] The concept of 'hovering' arises under the LOSC in the context of the territorial sea regime, where it constitutes a breach of innocent passage, which must be 'continuous and expeditious', and only includes stopping or anchoring in so far as these things are incidental to ordinary navigation, or are rendered necessary by *force majeure* or distress, or for the purpose of providing assistance to persons, ships, or aircraft in distress: LOSC art 18(2).

[80] As discussed in nn 61–2 and associated text, this rule is adopted more directly in the legislation of Palau, the Pitcairn Islands, and the Philippines.

is clearly a narrowing of the traditional 'freedom' of navigation, in practice it seems unlikely that it would impair the legitimate navigation of a foreign fishing vessel through the zone.

5.2.4 Notification and Reporting Requirements

A significant number of coastal States require unlicensed foreign fishing vessels in transit to provide advance notification of their entry to the EEZ, as well as other details such as their intended route of passage and exit point, and any fish on board. Such a requirement is in some ways more extensive than the territorial sea regime of innocent passage, which may be exercised without notification or reporting to the coastal State.[81] However, to the extent that it reduces the need for unlicensed vessels in transit to be subject to boarding and inspection, and reduces the complexities of proving the legality (or otherwise) of any catch on board, it offers useful possibilities for alleviating the burden on both the coastal State and the vessel.

While Burke was not able to discover any examples in 1983 of coastal State legislation positively requiring entry and exit notifications,[82] this approach has since been embraced by a wide range of coastal States and can now be found in national legislation in almost every region of the world. For example, under Section 53 of Mauritius' *Fisheries Act 2007*: 'The master of any foreign fishing boat or foreign fishing vessel or his agent shall provide, by letter, fax or email, to the Permanent Secretary at least 24 hours before the boat or vessel enters into, or exits from, the maritime zones, its position at the time of entry into, or exit from, the zones and the quantity of fish on board by species.'

A similar approach is taken in the legislation of other coastal States in Africa—including Benin, Cote d'Ivoire, Guinea, Liberia, Madagascar, and Togo—as well as Iran, Argentina, Canada, and France (in relation to its Southern and Antarctic Territories).[83]

A number of coastal States require more detailed notifications from unlicensed foreign fishing vessels. For example, the master of a foreign fishing vessel transiting the waters of Brunei or Malaysia must notify by radio the name, flag State, location, route, and destination of the vessel; the types and amount of fish it is carrying; and the circumstances under which it is entering the waters.[84] Unlicensed foreign fishing vessels transiting Fiji's EEZ are required to submit a report containing specified details (including the name of the vessel, International Radio Call Sign, flag registration, date and time, position to one minute of arc, crew complement,

[81] LOSC art 17.
[82] Burke, 'Exclusive Fisheries Zones' (n 7) 618–19.
[83] See Table 5.1.
[84] Ibid.

intended activity, and catch on board) at prescribed times, including: at least one hundred nautical miles prior to entry into Fiji fisheries waters; upon entry into Fiji fisheries waters; every two hours whilst within Fiji fisheries waters; and upon departure from Fiji fisheries waters.[85] This provision is included in almost identical terms in the legislation of other Pacific Island States—including Kiribati, Micronesia, the Solomon Islands, Tuvalu, and Vanuatu— and requirements of similar effect have been established by Equatorial Guinea, Ecuador, St Kitts and Nevis, Iceland, and the United Kingdom (in relation to South Georgia and the South Sandwich Islands).[86] This requirement is commonly applied by reference to a presumption, such that failure to comply with the notification requirement gives rise to a rebuttable presumption that all fish on board the vessel have been caught unlawfully within the coastal State's EEZ.

Less restrictive coastal State measures of this type are likely to be well adapted to the requirements of the due regard test: the requirement to report on entry, including with respect to the amount of fish on board, does not have any practical effect on navigation by foreign vessels and the potential benefit to the coastal State is significant, since it would provide a clearer surveillance picture from which to assess the potential risk of illegal fishing by the various vessels present in the EEZ at any given time. Compliance with such regulations can also have advantages for a vessel engaged in the legitimate freedom of navigation, since it reduces the need for boarding and inspection by the coastal State, and makes any inspection easier since it is only a question of ascertaining whether the fish on board exceeds that which was notified in advance.[87] Accordingly, as Burke observes, given the possible interference with the vessel's activities and the enforcement dilemmas that may otherwise result, such requirements 'may thus be seen as both assisting coastal State enforcement and removing a potential heavy burden from the fishing vessel'.[88]

Regulations requiring prior notification for the transit of unlicensed foreign fishing vessels have, in the past, been subject to protest by the United States[89] and Thailand.[90] Nonetheless, such requirements have been subject to implementation

[85] Ibid.

[86] Ibid.

[87] Tullio Treves, 'Jurisdiction over Vessels in the Areas of Pollution and Fisheries: General Report' in Erik Franckx and Philippe Gautier (eds), *The Exercise of Jurisdiction Over Vessels: New Developments in the Fields of Pollution, Fisheries, Crimes and Sea and Trafficking of Weapons of Mass Destruction* (Bruylant 2011) 12.

[88] Burke, 'Exclusive Fisheries Zones' (n 7) 619.

[89] In 1979 and 1992, the United States protested against provisions in the legislation of Costa Rica requiring prior notification of transit by unlicensed fishing vessels (which have since been repealed): J Ashley Roach, *Excessive Maritime Claims* (4th ed, Brill Nijhoff 2020) 464–6.

[90] In 1993, Thailand (which was not then a party to the LOSC) issued a circular stating that all vessels have the right to engage in navigation through the EEZ without having to give prior notification or obtain permission, approval, or consent from the coastal State: 'Statement of the Ministry of Foreign Affairs of Thailand', reproduced in DOALOS, *Law of the Sea Bulletin No 23* (UN 1993) 108. However, Thailand's declaration upon ratifying the LOSC in 2011 reflects a narrower position on the freedom of navigation and a broader approach to coastal State jurisdiction: Thailand, 'Declarations

and enforcement by coastal States. For example, in 2017 the St Kitts and Nevis' flagged *F/V Dzintars* was arrested by Liberia for failing to provide notification of the type and quantity of fish on board prior to entering the EEZ, as required under Section 12 of Liberia's *Regulations Relating to Fisheries, Fishing and Related Activities for the Marine Sector 2010.*[91] Similarly, in the 1999 case of *Republic v Jong Kim*, the master of the Korean-owned *Jasmine 9* was convicted for the offence of entering the fishery limits of Kiribati without a permit, for a purpose not recognized by international law, in violation of Section 5(1)(a) of the Kiribati *Fisheries Ordinance.*[92] This sort of requirement is even reflected in the legislation of flag States. For example, under Chinese law, before transiting waters under the jurisdiction of other countries, Chinese-flagged fishing vessels must store their catches, stow their gear, and notify the coastal State in advance in accordance with relevant regulations.[93] The legality of such requirements has not been challenged before an international court or tribunal—not even in the *Monte Confurco* and *Camouco* cases, in which such regulations formed part of the factual scenario underlying the requests for prompt release.[94] And apart from an oblique observation from Judge Kolodkin in the *Juno Trader* case about the existence of such requirements (without, however, making any specific comment regarding their legitimacy or otherwise)[95] there is no evidence in the jurisprudence of any concern about this form of coastal State regulation.

5.2.5 Authorization to Enter the EEZ

Burke observed in 1983 that 'a requirement for authorization of passage of fishing vessels is universally considered to exceed coastal State authority.'[96] Nonetheless, requirements of this sort appear in the national legislation of several coastal States. For example, under Canada's fisheries legislation, unlicensed foreign fishing

upon ratification of the Convention, 15 May 2011, under Articles 310 and 311 of the United Nations Convention on the Law of the Sea', reproduced in DOALOS, *Law of the Sea Bulletin No 76* (UN 2011) 14.

91 This offence is now contained in Liberia's *Law 2019* s 9.4.

92 *Republic v Jong Kim* [1999] KIHC 13. The *Fisheries Ordinance* was subsequently repealed and replaced—the relevant offence is now contained in Kiribati' *Act 2010* s 8.

93 China, *Regs 2020* art 32.

94 The legislation pursuant to which the vessels were seized provided, relevantly (as translated from French): 'any vessel entering the [EEZ] of the French Southern and Antarctic Territories shall be obliged to give notification of its presence and to declare the tonnage of fish held on board to the chief district administrator of the nearest archipelago': France, *Law No. 66-400 of 18 June 1966*, as amended by the *Law of 18 November 1997, on sea fishing and the exploitation of marine products in the French Southern and Antarctic Territories*, art 2). The legality of this requirement was not challenged by the Applicants or questioned by the Tribunal. This provision has since been repealed and replaced, but the requirement to give notice still applies: see Table 5.1.

95 *Juno Trader* (Dec Kolodkin) [4].

96 Burke, 'Exclusive Fisheries Zones' (n 7) 610.

vessels may not enter Canadian fisheries waters without authorization, except for the purpose of ensuring the safety of the vessel and its crew, rendering assistance to a vessel, or obtaining emergency medical assistance for a member of the crew at a Canadian port.[97] A similar approach is employed in Gambia, but in the form of a 'negative' authorization: pursuant to Section 41 of the *Fisheries Act 2007*, unlicensed foreign fishing vessels must provide at least seventy-two hours' notice of their intention to enter Gambia's fisheries waters, and may be ordered not to enter the waters (or, if they have already entered, to leave) if the Director is satisfied that the vessel in question has undermined conservation and management measures. This does not prevent a fishing vessel from entering or remaining in the fisheries waters for such period as is necessary when either the vessel is involved in a search and rescue operation or emergency, or for the purposes of obtaining food, fuel, and other goods and services necessary to enable the vessel to proceed safely and directly to a port outside Gambia. A similar 'negative' authorization requirement applies in the legislation of Tonga.[98]

Under the legislation of the Maldives, the entry of all foreign vessels (including unlicensed foreign fishing vessels) into the EEZ is prohibited except with prior authorization.[99] In South Africa, foreign fishing vessels may not have any fishing gear on board in the EEZ without a permit.[100] This provision operates in practice as a requirement for all foreign fishing vessels to apply for a permit to enter the EEZ, indicating their reason for entering the zone (such as bunkering, repair, discharge, transhipment, or emergency port call), accompanied by the requisite fee.[101] A similar effect is achieved by Somalia's *Fisheries Law 2016*, Article 15 of which provides that any fishing vessel entering Somali waters without a valid licence shall be presented to the court and subjected to Somalian fisheries law.

While foreign fishing vessels from a range of countries have been seized by coastal States in recent years on the basis of failure to obtain prior authorization for entry

[97] See Table 5.1 and the application form, available at <https://www.pac.dfo-mpo.gc.ca/fm-gp/licence-permis/forms/eez-zee-eng.html> accessed 1 August 2021.

[98] See Table 5.1.

[99] See Table 5.1 and the application form, available at <http://gov.mv/en/files/application-form-for-eez-entrance.pdf> accessed 22 December 2020. This prohibition has previously been subject to protest by the United States: United States Department of State, *Limits in the Seas No 126: Maldives Maritime Claims and Boundaries* (2005) 7.

[100] See Table 5.1 and the application form, available at <https://web.archive.org/web/20201222054425/http://dalrrd.gov.za/doaDev/sideMenu/fisheries/10_application_forms/docs/EEZ%20Appl.pdf> accessed 22 December 2020.

[101] At the time of writing, the application fee for a permit to enter the EEZ was 3,500 rand ($235 USD): South Africa, 'Fees Payable in Respect of Applications and the Issuing of Rights, Permits and Licences, 2010' para 1(f)(iii), available at <http://extwprlegs1.fao.org/docs/pdf/saf97454.pdf> accessed 22 December 2020. This is separate from the application fee required for a permit to engage in fishing or related activities under para 1(f)(i).

into, or passage through, the EEZ, there does not appear to have been any formal or informal protest about the legitimacy of these actions from their flag States or from other States.[102] For example: in 2005 the Portuguese-flagged vessel *Santa Mafalda* was seized and its master charged with offences of both unauthorized entry and unauthorized fishing in the Canadian EEZ;[103] a number of Chinese-flagged vessels have been fined for entering the South African EEZ without a permit, including six trawlers arrested in April 2020;[104] and the master of a vessel flagged by Chinese Taipei, which entered South Africa's EEZ on 7 September 2016 without having a permit, paid a fine of $6,700 USD as part of a plea and sentencing deal.[105] Given the sensitivity with which many flag States approach the issue of authorization for passage through the territorial sea and EEZ in other contexts—particularly with respect to the passage of warships, the carriage of nuclear and other hazardous materials, and the conduct of 'military activities'[106]—it is surprising that the relatively widespread enactment and enforcement of such a requirement in relation to the transit of fishing vessels has not generated more reaction in recent years. One possible explanation is that such requirements are set out in fisheries legislation, which is less likely to be deposited with the UN and circulated through formal channels, and thus less commonly reviewed by other States than maritime zones legislation. However, this does not explain the lack of reaction from countries whose vessels have been subject to seizure under these provisions—which supports the argument that they are accepted as a reasonable exercise of the coastal State's jurisdiction over unlicensed foreign fishing vessels.

Clearly, Burke's 1983 observation that a requirement of prior authorization for passage of fishing vessels 'lacks legal precedent' is no longer strictly true—there is

[102] While the United States has previously protested both the Maldives' requirement for prior authorization (see n 99) and Costa Rica's requirement for prior notification (now repealed) (see n 89), there are no further records of such complaints in the series of studies on *Limits in the Seas,* which is published by the United States Department of State to examine coastal States' maritime claims and assess their consistency with international law, nor does the fourth edition of Roach, *Excessive Maritime Claims* (n 89), published in 2020, detail any further instances of such protests.

[103] Government of Canada News Release, 'Fisheries and Oceans Canada Officers Seize Fishing Vessel Santa Mafalda', 30 May 2005, available at <http://canada.ca/en/news/archive/2005/05/fisheries-oceans-canada-officers-seize-fishing-vessel-santa-mafalda.html?=undefined&wbdisable=true> accessed 22 December 2020.

[104] South African Government, 'Environmental Affairs fines Chinese trawlers for being on South African waters' 26 April 2020, available at <https://www.gov.za/speeches/environmental-affairs-fines-chinese-fishing-trawlers-being-south-african-waters-26-apr-2020Environmental Affairs fines Chinese fishing trawlers for being on South African waters | South African Government (www.gov.za)> accessed 1 August 2021.

[105] Dave Chambers, 'Taiwanese Captain Pays R100,000 in Plea Deal on Fishing Charges' *Times Live,* 20 September 2016, available at <http://timeslive.co.za/news/south-africa/2016-09-20-taiwanese-captain-pays-r100000-in-plea-deal-on-fishing-charges/> accessed 22 December 2020.

[106] See generally Donald R Rothwell, 'Navigational Rights and Freedoms in the Asia Pacific Following Entry Into Force of the Law of the Sea Convention' (1995) 35 VaJIntlL 587; Stuart Kaye, 'Freedom of Navigation in a Post 9/11 World: Security and Creeping Jurisdiction' in David Freestone, Richard Barnes, and David Ong (eds), *The Law of the Sea: Progress and Prospects* (OUP 2006) 347; Van Dyke, *The Disappearing Right to Navigational Freedom* (n 9); Roach, *Excessive Maritime Claims* (n 89) 442–85.

a demonstrated practice of coastal States applying and enforcing such a requirement, and limited evidence of protest, even by the flag States affected. But what about the remainder of his conclusion—that such a requirement is inconsistent with the LOSC regime for freedom of navigation in the EEZ, and that the difficulties of enforcing fisheries regulations do not warrant such a drastic change to the navigation regime?[107]

The answer to this question is in two parts. The first part turns on whether a coastal State's requirement that an unlicensed vessel seek prior authorization burdens the vessel's freedom of navigation in a way that is not 'necessary' or 'reasonable' in light of the coastal State's sovereign rights, taking into account the particular circumstances of that coastal State, the relative benefits and impairments of the measure to both the coastal and flag State, and the alternatives that might be available.[108] For example, in the case of a developing coastal State with a large EEZ and a population that depends on fisheries for food and economic security, it could legitimately be argued that, given the significant area of the coastal State's responsibility and its limited capacity for at-sea enforcement, the requirement for an unlicensed foreign fishing vessel to seek prior authorization for entry to the EEZ is a reasonable and necessary means of using regulatory enforcement measures to achieve what cannot be accomplished through physical enforcement. In a similar vein, if, because of the geographic situation of a coastal State, it is unlikely that an unlicensed foreign fishing vessel would need to navigate through its EEZ (or a particular part of its EEZ) in order to access a point beyond that zone, the burden of a requirement for any such vessels to seek prior authorization might be considered reasonable in light of the benefit to the coastal State.

However, this conclusion is necessarily subject to the second part of the answer, which is that even if, in the particular circumstances of the case, it is reasonable for a coastal State to require a vessel to seek prior authorization to navigate through the EEZ, it would not be reasonable for a coastal State to refuse to *grant* such authorization—such a refusal would not simply 'impair' the vessel's freedom of navigation, but prevent it completely, and there is no basis in the LOSC (or customary international law) upon which a coastal State can exclude a foreign vessel from the EEZ.[109] Accordingly, the practical effect of such a requirement—if implemented consistently with international law—would be more akin to prior notification as discussed in Section 5.2.4, than prior authorization.

[107] Burke, 'Exclusive Fisheries Zones' (n 7) 611.
[108] *Chagos Arbitration* [519].
[109] This limitation only applies with respect to a request for authorization to navigate through the EEZ, and not for the conduct of any 'fishing related activities', which come within the coastal State's jurisdiction over living resources and may thus be denied, as discussed in Chapter 3.

5.2.6 Use of Presumptions

As the examples in this Chapter demonstrate, many coastal States use presumptions (in combination with other regulatory approaches) to regulate unlicensed foreign fishing vessels. For example, coastal State legislation relating to the transit of foreign fishing vessels through the EEZ includes presumptions:

- that all fish found on board a fishing vessel in the EEZ was caught in the EEZ;[110]
- that if gear is not stowed, the vessel was used for fishing in the EEZ;[111]
- that if a vessel transits below a certain speed, or does not take the shortest practicable route through the EEZ, it was engaged in fishing;[112] and
- that if a vessel has not provided prior notification of, or sought authorization for, its entry to the EEZ, any fish on board was taken unlawfully within the EEZ, or the vessel was engaged in unlawful fishing or related activities.[113]

Presumptions can be used in a variety of ways, with a variety of effects. Most of these presumptions have an *evidentiary* effect, shifting the burden of proof to the fishing vessel, and reducing the technical difficulties faced by the coastal State in proving an offence in a situation where evidence is exceptionally difficult to obtain.[114] However, presumptions can also be used to produce *practical* effects. For example, a presumption relating to compliance with a prior notification requirement can have the practical effect of narrowing the scope of enquiry; by encouraging unlicensed vessels to provide details about their transit, a presumption can reduce the number of unknown or potentially 'suspect' vessels in the EEZ, allowing the coastal State to focus its enforcement capacity on vessels that have not provided the relevant information. In addition, a presumption applied in relation to compliance with a requirement to carry or stow fishing gear can have a practical effect with respect to the conduct of an unlicensed vessel, by encouraging it to transit through the zone in a mode that reduces the risk of unauthorized fishing.

Finally, presumptions can have a *deterrent* effect in relation to a regulation that has limited jurisdictional support or may otherwise be difficult for the coastal State to apply or enforce. In this respect, presumptions allow the coastal State to make a minimal jurisdictional claim through a 'contingent' assertion of jurisdiction, which may deter a vessel that cannot successfully mount a rebuttal, but will not adversely

[110] See Table 5.1: Australia, Bahamas, Eritrea, New Zealand, Palau, United Kingdom (Pitcairn Islands and Turks and Caicos Islands).

[111] See Table 5.1: Brunei, India, Malaysia, United Kingdom (Falkland Islands).

[112] See Table 5.1: Cape Verde, Brunei, Malaysia.

[113] See Table 5.1: Argentina, Brunei, Fiji, Kiribati, Maldives, Malaysia, Micronesia, Philippines, Solomon Islands, Saint Kitts and Nevis, United Kingdom (SGSSI), Vanuatu.

[114] David Freestone, *The Burden of Proof in National Resources Legislation: Some Critical Issues for Fisheries Law* (FAO 1998) 8–9.

affect a vessel engaged in legitimate navigation, which can avoid potential delay or interference by the coastal State through compliance with the underlying regulation.[115] As Treves has observed, 'while a ship exercising the freedom of navigation may lawfully ignore the obligation set out in the national law, compliance with this obligation has some advantages, especially if the ship has nothing to hide.'[116]

5.2.7 Maximizing Other Bases of Jurisdiction

Coastal States can also harness existing forms of agreement, or bases of jurisdiction, to give effect to the type of regulatory measures outlined in this Chapter. The most straightforward approach is to maximize the application of the coastal State's prescriptive jurisdiction under Article 62(4). As demonstrated in Chapter 3, the coastal State can exercise its prescriptive jurisdiction under Article 62(4) to regulate not only vessels that are licensed to fish in the EEZ, but fishing support vessels engaged in 'fishing related activities', including: processing, packaging, storing, transporting and transhipping of fish and fish products; bunkering fishing vessels at sea; supplying water, food, fuel, and fishing gear; and assisting with the rotation of personnel and conduct of repairs at sea. Depending on the coastal State's particular legislative scheme and policy objectives, this prescriptive jurisdiction can be applied strategically to broaden the number of foreign vessels subject to the sort of regulations discussed in this Chapter, particularly through the targeted use of terms and conditions in access agreements, fishing licences, and authorizations for fishing related activities.

Alternatively—or in addition—coastal States can cooperate to establish collective conditions under Article 62(4), with the effect that a vessel which is licensed to conduct fishing or fishing related activities in the EEZ of any one coastal State in the group is required (as a condition of that licence) to comply with the requirements for transit through the zones of all the States involved. Such cooperative approaches can extend to the establishment of common conditions for transit, with significant benefits in terms of certainty and consistency for fishing vessels operating in—or transiting through—the EEZs of multiple coastal States. For example, pursuant to the FFA Harmonized MTCs, any unlicensed foreign fishing vessel that is transiting through the EEZ of an FFA member must keep all fishing gear stowed, and report its name, International Radio Call Sign, flag registration, date and time, position (to one minute of arc), compliment, intended activity, and catch on board to the designated authority at a prescribed distance or time prior to entry into the EEZ, upon entry, at prescribed intervals during transit, upon departure from the zone, and at any other times determined or directed by the coastal State.[117] Failure

115 Burke, 'Fisheries Regulations Under Extended Jurisdiction' (n 30) 15.
116 Treves, 'Jurisdiction over Vessels in the Areas of Pollution and Fisheries' (n 87) 12–13.
117 FFA Harmonized MTCs [12].

to comply with this requirement in the zone of a coastal State where the vessel is *not* licensed constitutes a breach of the licence conditions in the coastal State where the vessel *is* licensed. A number of other regional fisheries bodies have also established collective regulations for the transit of foreign fishing vessels.[118]

In the western and central Pacific Ocean, coastal States have been able to draw upon agreements reached within the framework of a regional fisheries management organization (RFMO) in order to gain additional information regarding the activities of unlicensed foreign fishing vessels in the region. Any coastal State member of the Western and Central Pacific Fisheries Commission (WCPFC) may request that the WCPFC vessel monitoring system (VMS) include waters under the member's national jurisdiction.[119] As a result, the coastal State will receive VMS data for the transit of any of the approximately 1,500 WCPFC-registered vessels through its EEZ. To date, fourteen coastal State members of the WCPFC have elected to receive this 'in-zone' VMS data.[120] In addition, coastal State members may receive continuous near real time WCPFC VMS data for the high seas in an area adjacent to and not more than one hundred nautical miles from their EEZs for the purpose of conducting monitoring, control, and surveillance activities on the high seas or in areas under their national jurisdiction.[121] It is clear that these measures, which appear to be unique to the WCPFC, significantly enhance the ability of coastal States to monitor, identify, and address the activities of unlicensed foreign vessels in the EEZ—particularly if used in combination with the other regulatory approaches discussed in this Chapter, and in the context of collaboration and collective action with other coastal States.

5.3 Conclusion

The primacy of the freedom of navigation has traditionally been the dominant narrative in the law of the sea, and was vigorously defended by maritime States in the negotiation of the regime for the EEZ in Part V of the LOSC, where it is 'safeguarded' by the rule of due regard in Articles 56 and 58, the residual rights clause in Article 59, and the right to resort to compulsory dispute settlement processes under Part XV.[122] Given this context, and the lack of specificity in Part V of the LOSC regarding the extent to which the exercise of this freedom may be affected

[118] SWIOFC MTCs [15]; SRFC MCA Convention art 15; FCWC MRA Convention art 23.

[119] WCPFC Convention art 24(8), implemented through WCPFC, *CMM 2014-02 Commission Vessel Monitoring System* [6(c)].

[120] See <http://wcpfc.int/vessel-monitoring-system> accessed 23 December 2020.

[121] WCPFC, *Rules and Procedures for the Protection, Access To, and Dissemination of High Seas Non-Public Domain Data and Information Compiled by the Commission for the Purpose of Monitoring, Control or Surveillance (MCS) Activities and the Access to and Dissemination of High Seas VMS Data for Scientific Purposes* [22].

[122] Robertson, 'Navigation in the Exclusive Economic Zone' (n 7) 882.

or impacted by the 'other provisions' of the Convention and 'the rights and duties of the coastal State' in the EEZ, it is not surprising that the common conclusion in the early literature was that 'in reconciling coastal fishery interests with navigation, only a very limited authority to affect navigation should be recognized, and then only in exceptional situations.'[123] However, as the LOSC has been implemented over time, this position has reversed: the importance of the coastal State's fishery interests is now accepted to provide a basis for coastal States to 'expect every foreign fishing vessel to identify itself and explain its intentions whenever it enters an EEZ, even if the fishing vessel is only transiting through the area on its way to distant fishing grounds.'[124]

While the extensive array of coastal State regulations now applied to the conduct of navigation by unlicensed foreign fishing vessels in the EEZ testifies to the general acceptance of this form of jurisdiction as a matter of *practice*, it remains important to clarify its basis within the LOSC as a matter of *law*, in order to enunciate a framework that can be understood and applied by all States—and all vessels—with certainty and predictability. From the review of national legislation undertaken in this Chapter, it is possible to draw some conclusions about the nature and extent of contemporary coastal State jurisdiction over unlicensed foreign fishing vessels—and the 'freedom of navigation' of such vessels—in the EEZ, and to identify some restraints and imperatives on the way this jurisdiction is exercised in practice.

First, this is an instance in which the coastal State's jurisdiction cannot be established simply by reference to an allocation of either prescriptive or enforcement jurisdiction in the LOSC. While the coastal State's authority over foreign fishing vessels in transit is enlivened by its enforcement powers under Article 73(1), which enable the coastal State to take the measures necessary to 'ensure compliance' with its laws and regulations, this authority is commonly exercised through prescriptive means, and in that sense is subject to the rule of reciprocal due regard established in Articles 56(2) and 58(3). In addition, any consideration of the legitimate extent of the laws and regulations that may be adopted (and enforced) by the coastal State 'in conformity with' the LOSC must take into account not only the coastal State's rights over living resources under Article 56(1), but its responsibilities to ensure the conservation and optimum utilization of those resources under Articles 61 and 62. Moreover, the coastal State's prescriptive and enforcement jurisdiction are both subject to a similar limitation—the extent to which the exercise of authority by the coastal State is 'reasonable' or 'necessary'—which in every case involves the complex process of striking an appropriate balance between the rights of coastal States and other States in the EEZ. Accordingly, the extent of the coastal State's jurisdiction over foreign fishing vessels in transit falls to be determined not on the basis of

[123] Burke, 'Exclusive Fisheries Zones' (n 7) 623.
[124] Van Dyke, 'The Disappearing Right to Navigational Freedom' (n 9) 108.

prescriptive or enforcement jurisdiction, but by reference to the functional jurisdiction assigned to each State by the LOSC.

Second, contrary to the previously accepted position that all vessels enjoy the freedom of navigation equally, and 'no distinction can be drawn according to the nature of a ship',[125] it is now clear that a distinction can, and in some cases *must*, be drawn in the application of coastal State regulations affecting navigation, depending on the nature and function of the ship in question. This distinction is important both to enabling the full extent of the coastal State's functional jurisdiction over living resources, and to restraining any improper assertion of coastal State jurisdiction with respect to other activities; in this respect 'States need to move carefully lest restraints become generalised and restrictions on vessel movement become both common and excessive.'[126] For example, while the coastal State's functional jurisdiction over living resources is widely used as the basis for applying prior notification or authorization requirements to foreign fishing vessels and fishing support vessels transiting through the EEZ, it would not justify the application of similar requirements to other (non-fishing) vessels.[127] In this regard, the developments in law and practice examined in this Chapter confirm Molenaar and Tsamenyi's conclusion that, 'in the context of fisheries, there may be considerations which allow for a balance of jurisdiction which is even more favourable to the coastal State.'[128]

Third, and consequently, it is now possible to articulate a more specific statement about the freedom of navigation that may be exercised by a foreign fishing vessel in the EEZ of a coastal State under the LOSC—or, stated in reverse, the extent to which the freedom of navigation exercisable by an unlicensed foreign fishing vessel may be limited by the jurisdiction of the coastal State. In this regard, the starting point must be the distinction between the freedom of navigation on the high seas under Article 87—which is subject only to the interests of other States in the exercise of their high seas freedoms—and the freedom of navigation in the EEZ under Article 58—which is subject to the 'relevant provisions' of the LOSC.[129] Since the relevant

[125] Tullio Scovazzi, 'Coastal State Practice in the Exclusive Economic Zone: The Right of Foreign States to Use This Zone' in Thomas A Clingan (ed) *The Law of the Sea What Lies Ahead? (Proceedings of the 20th Annual Conference of the Law of the Sea Institute, 21-24 July 1986, Miami, Florida)* (Law of the Sea Institute 1988) 315.

[126] Burke, 'Exclusive Fisheries Zones' (n 7) 623.

[127] Some coastal States have claimed a right of prior authorization or prior notification for the passage of nuclear-powered ships or vessels carrying nuclear waste or inherently dangerous or noxious cargoes through the EEZ, which have been subject to protest from several States (including, in particular, the United States): see generally Roach, *Excessive Maritime Claims* (n 89) 467–82. In practice, these assertions of jurisdiction have not led to major difficulties—perhaps because, as Churchill and Lowe observe, both the shipowner and the coastal State generally have a common interest in ensuring safe and expeditious passage for such vessels: RR Churchill and AV Lowe, *The Law of the Sea* (3rd ed, MUP 1999) 92.

[128] Molenaar and Tsamenyi, 'Satellite-Based Vessel Monitoring' (n 9) 87.

[129] As Van Dyke has observed, it is clear that 'it is no longer accurate to say that the freedom of navigation exists in the [EEZ] of other countries to the same extent that it exists on the high seas': Van Dyke, 'The Disappearing Right to Navigational Freedom' (n 9) 121.

provisions of the LOSC include the coastal State's sovereign rights and responsibilities with respect to living resources under Articles 56 and 61, the freedom of navigation of fishing vessels is necessarily a specific sub-set of the broader freedom of navigation that may be exercised by foreign vessels in the EEZ.

Since foreign fishing vessels only have the freedom to navigate—not the freedom to fish—in the EEZ, any activities that might constitute 'fishing' may not be conducted without the authorization of the coastal State. In this regard, the coastal State's power to regulate 'fishing' has been shown to include the full range of 'fishing related activities' that form part of modern industrial fishing, including: processing, packaging, storing, transporting, and transhipping fish and fish products; bunkering fishing vessels at sea; supplying water, food, fuel, and fishing gear; and assisting with the rotation of personnel and conduct of repairs at sea.[130] In light of the daily costs involved in operating a commercial fishing vessel, the only other activities in which a foreign fishing vessel is likely to be legitimately engaged are passage (moving from one fishing ground or port to another), or extraordinary activities relating to *force majeure* or seeking or rendering assistance in situations of distress. As such, the freedom of navigation that may be exercised by a foreign fishing vessel equates in practice to a right to undertake continuous and expeditious passage from one point beyond the EEZ to another point beyond the EEZ, except in circumstances involving *force majeure* or distress, or activities undertaken with the authorization of the coastal State. In this sense, it is perhaps similar to the 'freedom of communication' envisaged by the Tribunal in the *Croatia/Slovenia Arbitration* to ensure access to and from Slovenia through Croatia's territorial sea, which is 'not conditioned upon any criterion of innocence' and 'not suspendable under any circumstances'.[131] However, given the possibility that the coastal State may board and inspect foreign fishing vessels in transit through its EEZ, their freedom of navigation does not constitute an 'uninterrupted and uninterruptible' right of access in the sense described by the Tribunal.[132]

This understanding of the freedom of navigation for foreign fishing vessels transiting the EEZ provides a basis from which to establish the 'continuum' of jurisdiction that may be asserted by a coastal State over such vessels. At a minimum, the coastal State may adopt measures that effectively require unlicensed foreign fishing vessels to transit continuously and expeditiously, unless exceptional circumstances apply. Ascertaining the maximum extent of such jurisdiction still requires a balancing exercise, involving consideration of whether the coastal State's asserted regulation unduly burdens or affects the foreign fishing vessel's freedom of navigation, in light of the various issues identified in the *Chagos Arbitration*.[133]

[130] See Section 3.4.
[131] *Arbitration between the Government of the Republic of Croatia and the Government of the Republic of Slovenia* [2017] PCA Case 2012-04 [1127].
[132] Ibid [1123].
[133] *Chagos Arbitration* [519].

As the practice examined in this Chapter demonstrates, the regulatory approaches currently applied and enforced by coastal States to this end include measures relating to the purpose, route, or mode of navigation, the stowage or carriage of fishing gear, and the provision of information relating to passage through the zone, extending to prior notification or authorization of entry and exit. However, since there is no power to exclude a foreign fishing vessel from the EEZ, any measure that has the effect of precluding a foreign fishing vessel from exercising the freedom of navigation would be beyond the scope of the coastal State's jurisdiction.

Having explored the potential rights of coastal States with respect to the regulation of unlicensed foreign fishing vessels, it is important to note some correlative duties. In this respect, the starting point must be the duty in Article 62(5) of the LOSC for coastal States to 'give due notice of conservation and management laws and regulations'. This requirement is more complex than it first appears. While there is no indication of the form that such notice must take, presumably this involves the publication of laws and regulations—in the sense of making them publicly available[134]—but does not specifically require their deposit with a particular body or publication by any particular method.[135] Although it was originally suggested in respect of Article 62(5) that 'a systematic practice would develop for providing current information on the laws and regulations established by coastal States',[136] this has not so far eventuated.[137]

In the absence of any more specific rule, a coastal State might reasonably be expected to provide copies of relevant legislation and regulations to the FAO and ensure that they are available on the website of the relevant government agency. However, this is the minimum required to give effect to Article 62(5), which

[134] James Harrison and Elisa Morgera, 'Article 62' in Alexander Proelss (ed), *United Nations Convention on the Law of the Sea: A Commentary* (CH Beck 2017) 504.

[135] In contrast, for example, arts 16 and 84 of the LOSC require that in giving 'due publicity' to charts and lists of geographical coordinates, the coastal State deposit a copy with the Secretary-General of the UN and, in the case of those showing the outer limit lines of the continental shelf, with the Secretary-General of the International Seabed Authority. See also the requirement to give 'due notice' of the construction of artificial islands, installations, and structures pursuant to art 60(3), which has been substantiated by an IMO Regulation that refers to the publication of notices to mariners, radio warnings, and the depiction of such structures on all appropriate navigational charts: IMO Resolution A.672(16), *Guidelines and standards for the removal of offshore installations and structures on the continental shelf and in the exclusive economic zone*, adopted 19 October 1989.

[136] Nandan and Rosenne, *UNCLOS Commentary, Vol II* (n 12) 638.

[137] A wide range of national fisheries laws and regulations are available through the FAO website, including through the FAOLEX database (available at <http://fao.org/faolex/country-profiles/en/> accessed 23 December 2020) and the Fishlex database (available at <http://extwprlegs1.fao.org/fishery/index.htm> accessed 23 December 2020). However, since there is no legal requirement for coastal States to deposit their fisheries legislation with the Food and Agriculture Organization (FAO), this does not necessarily contain a comprehensive or current set of laws and regulations that could be relied upon by fishing vessel owners, operators, and masters to verify the requirements for transit through the EEZs of various coastal States. In addition, since these laws and regulations are likely to require interpretation—and, depending on the user, translation—the owner, operator, or master of an unlicensed foreign fishing vessel may find it difficult to ascertain exactly what requirements must be complied with during transit through the EEZ.

applies to all of the conservation and management laws and regulations adopted by the coastal State pursuant to Articles 61 and 62, the majority of which necessarily relate to the activities of licensed vessels fishing in the EEZ. In the context of regulations applying to unlicensed foreign vessels, which are merely in transit through the zone, and have no access agreement or other licensing arrangement with the coastal State, the coastal State might be wise to take additional steps to ensure that the actions required from the vessel are clear and readily discoverable, particularly if the regulations apply to both fishing and fishing support vessels, and require active conduct (such as compliance with prior notification or routeing requirements) from the vessel. However, this issue has not yet arisen for consideration by an international court or tribunal, and in the cases involving the failure of unlicensed foreign fishing vessels to comply with prior notification requirements, no argument has been made that the vessel was unaware of—or unable to gain access to—the relevant laws and regulations of the coastal State. For example, in the *Camouco* case, the Master said that he had 'forgotten to declare the entry of the *Camouco* into the EEZ of the Crozet Islands to the Crozet authorities',[138] and in the *Monte Confurco* case, the Applicant said it was 'technically impossible for the Master to notify his entry into the [EEZ] or the tonnage of frozen fish carried on board, since the fax machine on board had broken down'.[139]

Another potential qualification on the coastal State's rights relates to the determination of what is 'reasonable' in the context of different types of fishing vessels. As Judge ad hoc Treves observed in the *Virginia G* case, 'the automatic application of all the rules applicable to fishing vessels to vessels engaged in bunkering fishing vessels is far from satisfactory', and a more nuanced approach, which establishes specific rules for fishing vessels and vessels engaged in fishing related activities, should be considered.[140] In particular, given the potential for bunkers and transhipment vessels to provide support services to both fishing vessels and other types of vessels navigating in the EEZ, a case-by-case approach may be needed to ensure that coastal State regulations retain their 'direct connection' to fishing,[141] and do not 'creep' further than they should.[142]

The variety of measures adopted—and seemingly accepted—in the widespread practice of coastal States demonstrates the 'functional' nature of jurisdiction in the EEZ. In order to make this functional jurisdiction effective, it is clear that some limits must be recognized on the 'freedom' of navigation that may be exercised by fishing vessels in the EEZ. In every instance, however, the 'reasonableness' of such

138 Cited in *Camouco* [32].
139 Cited in *Monte Confurco* [48].
140 *Virginia G* (Dec Treves) [11].
141 *Virginia G* [215].
142 In this regard, as Anderson has observed, '[b]unkering is a service: when it serves navigation, the rules on navigation apply, whereas, when it serves fishing in the EEZ the applicable rules are those on fishing': David Anderson, *Modern Law of the Sea: Selected Essays* (Martinus Nijhoff 2008) 227.

limits must be justified through an application of the balancing exercise required by the rule of due regard, undertaken in a way that acknowledges the difference between reasonable unilateral coastal State measures that relate to the conservation and management of living resources in the EEZ, and movements toward altering elements of the balance between the resource interests of coastal States and the navigational interests of flag States incorporated in the LOSC framework. The concepts of reasonableness and the balance of interests are also integral to the broader exercise of coastal State enforcement jurisdiction over foreign fishing vessels—licensed or unlicensed—under Article 73 of the LOSC, which is the focus of the next Chapter.

6
Enforcement Jurisdiction over Foreign Fishing in the EEZ

As the *Lotus* case famously confirmed, a State may not exercise enforcement jurisdiction beyond its territory except 'by virtue of a permissive rule derived from international custom or from a convention'.[1] Since the exclusive economic zone (EEZ) established in the United Nations Convention on the Law of the Sea (LOSC) is, by definition, beyond the territory and the sovereignty of the coastal State,[2] and the effective management of living resources is not possible without effective enforcement,[3] the LOSC includes a range of enforcement powers that can be exercised by coastal States in relation to foreign fishing vessels in the EEZ. As established in Article 73(1), in the exercise of its sovereign rights to explore, exploit, conserve, and manage the resources of the EEZ, a coastal State may 'take such measures, including boarding, inspection, arrest and judicial proceedings, as may be necessary to ensure compliance' with the laws and regulations adopted by it in conformity with the LOSC. In certain circumstances, these powers may also be exercised beyond the EEZ, pursuant to the right of hot pursuit in Article 111.[4]

Of course, the coastal State's enforcement jurisdiction is not unlimited. In order to protect the interests of flag States in ensuring continued navigational freedom for their vessels through the vast areas subjected to coastal State jurisdiction by the establishment of the EEZ, a number of important safeguards are included in the LOSC, which place both procedural and substantive limitations on the exercise of the coastal State's enforcement powers. These include the rules in Article 73 regarding the obligation of prompt release, the prohibition on imprisonment or any form of corporal punishment, and the requirement to promptly notify the flag State of actions taken and penalties imposed, which are collectively designed to ensure that the coastal State's enforcement measures do not limit the freedom of the persons involved or unduly jeopardize the rights of shipowners and the flag State, and to provide a basis for timely action by the flag State in response.[5] The interests of

1 *Lotus* 18–19.

2 LOSC art 55: 'the [EEZ] is an area beyond and adjacent to the territorial sea'; *Delimitation of the Maritime Boundary Between Guinea and Guinea-Bissau, Decision of 14 February 1985* (1985) XIX RIAA 149 [124]: 'neither the [EEZ] nor the continental shelf are areas of sovereignty'.

3 William T Burke, 'Exclusive Fisheries Zones and Freedom of Navigation' (1983) 20 SanDiegoLRev 595, 599.

4 On the right of hot pursuit, see Chapter 7.

5 *Juno Trader* (Sep Op Treves) [2].

Coastal State Jurisdiction over Living Resources in the Exclusive Economic Zone. Camille Goodman, Oxford University Press.
 DOI: 10.1093/oso/9780192896841.003.0006

the flag State are further safeguarded by the overriding requirement that the coastal State take only such measures as are 'necessary' to ensure compliance with its laws.[6]

Like the framework governing foreign access to living resources of the EEZ, these compromises were intended to strike a fair balance between the interests of coastal States in exercising sovereign rights over their resources and ensuring compliance with their laws and regulations, and the interests of flag States in protecting the navigational freedoms of their vessels. *Unlike* the framework established for foreign access to the living resources of the EEZ, the LOSC provisions on enforcement jurisdiction have been widely incorporated in the national legislation of coastal States.[7] However, enforcing fisheries regulations still remains a difficult—and sometimes almost impossible—task for coastal States.

First, fisheries enforcement is costly—even for the most prosperous developed coastal States, but particularly for developing coastal States with large maritime zones, or few resources to devote to fisheries enforcement, or both.[8] Second, even if the requisite resources are available, enforcement at sea is physically difficult,[9] and sometimes even dangerous, as several tragic accidents have demonstrated.[10] Third, the constant stream of new technology in the fishing sector and the highly adaptive capacity of illegal fishing operators present significant challenges to the establishment of adequate legal and policy frameworks and the acquisition and employment of relevant tools and techniques, making it hard for coastal States to respond swiftly and effectively to new types of illicit fishing activity.[11] And fourth, the very nature of fisheries offences makes their enforcement difficult; infringements can be hard to detect, particularly once they have been committed, let alone to prove. These difficulties are described in detail in the large body of literature on illegal, unreported, and unregulated (IUU) fishing,[12] which has estimated annual losses

[6] LOSC art 73(1).

[7] One notable exception is the prohibition on imprisonment as a penalty for fisheries offences, which has continued to feature in the regulations of a significant number of coastal States since the adoption and entry into force of the LOSC, despite the prohibition in art 73(3). See Section 6.3.2.1 and Table 6.2.

[8] In 2002, Australia estimated the cost of a fisheries patrol to be $5 million AUD per week ($5.78 million USD per week in 2020 figures): cited in *Volga* (Sep Op Cot) [9].

[9] The logistical difficulties of carrying out fisheries enforcement at sea are demonstrated in a number of cases involving vessels detected fishing illegally in Australia's EEZ in the Southern Ocean, including the *South Tomi* (pursued by Australian authorities for 3,300 nautical miles over fourteen days) and the *Viarsa I* (pursued for 3,900 nautical miles over twenty-one days): see Donald R Rothwell, 'Legal Challenges for Maritime Operations in the Southern Ocean' (2014) 28 OceanYB 423, 436–7.

[10] For example, the pursuit of Chinese vessels fishing without authorization in Palau's EEZ in 2012 resulted in the accidental death of a deckhand on one of the fishing vessels as well as the deaths of two Palauan policeman and an American pilot on board an aircraft sent to pursue the vessels, which became lost and ran out of fuel at sea: see Ian Urbina, *The Outlaw Ocean: Crime and Survival in the Last Untamed Frontier* (Penguin 2019) 57–9.

[11] See Anastasia Telesetsky, 'Laundering Fish in the Global Undercurrents: Illegal, Unreported, and Unregulated Fishing and Transnational Organized Crime' (2014) 41(4) ELQ 939, 950.

[12] See, eg, Rachel Baird, 'Illegal, Unreported and Unregulated Fishing: An Analysis of the Legal, Economic and Historical Factors Relevant to Its Development and Persistence' (2004) 5 MelbJIntlL 299;

of between 11 million and 26 million tonnes of fish—or $10 billion USD to $23.5 billion USD—from illegal fishing worldwide.[13]

Against this backdrop, it is relevant to ask whether in contemporary law and practice the balance between the interests of flag and coastal States has been (or should be) preserved as it was at the time the LOSC was negotiated, or whether—as Judge ad hoc Shearer suggested in his dissenting opinion in the *Volga* case—circumstances have changed, such that it is time for a new balance to be struck.[14] In particular, does the national legislation and practice of coastal (and flag) States merely 'fine-tune' the jurisdictional balance arrived at in 1982, or has there been a more dramatic alteration of this balance in the subsequent implementation of the LOSC? How are the developments in state practice reflected in, or consistent with, the way in which international courts and tribunals have interpreted and applied the safeguards established in the LOSC? And to what extent does the framework governing the conduct of fisheries enforcement qualify or limit the coastal State's discretion in the exercise of sovereign rights over living resources in the EEZ?

This Chapter explores these issues by examining the way in which coastal and flag State interests are balanced in the LOSC framework and the underlying issue of what constitutes a 'necessary' or 'reasonable' enforcement measure (Section 6.1). It considers how coastal States have exercised their discretion to take 'necessary' enforcement measures—including boarding, inspection, arrest, and judicial proceedings—against foreign fishing vessels under Article 73(1) (Section 6.2),[15] as well as the protections afforded flag States in the balance of Article 73, in particular the prompt release procedure and the limitations on the penalties that may be imposed by the coastal State (Section 6.3). Drawing on this analysis of law and practice, it concludes with a contemporary statement about how the balance of interests is struck in relation to enforcement jurisdiction in the law of the sea (Section 6.4).

Organization for Economic Cooperation and Development (OECD), *Fish Piracy: Combating Illegal, Unreported and Unregulated Fishing* (OECD 2004); Bertrand Le Gallic and Anthony Cox, 'An Economic Analysis of Illegal, Unreported and Unregulated (IUU) Fishing: Key Drivers and Possible Solutions' (2006) 30(6) MarPol 689.

[13] David J Agnew et al, 'Estimating the Worldwide Extent of Illegal Fishing' (2009) 4(2) PLOS ONE, available at <http://journals.plos.org/plosone/article?id=10.1371/journal.pone.0004570> accessed 29 November 2020.

[14] *Volga* (Diss Op Shearer) [19].

[15] This Chapter refers to the exercise of jurisdiction over 'fishing vessels' in the EEZ. However, as established in Chapter 3, coastal States can and do regulate a broad range of vessels engaged in both fishing and 'fishing related activities' in the EEZ, and enforcement jurisdiction may be asserted with respect to both fishing and fishing support vessels. The coastal State regulations referred to in this Chapter may be cross-referenced with the legislation set out in Table 3.1 in order to determine the vessels in relation to which enforcement powers are exercised by a particular coastal State.

6.1 The Balance of Interests under the LOSC Framework

As part of the EEZ regime, the framework for enforcement jurisdiction in Article 73 of the LOSC is directed at ensuring an effective balance between: 'the interest of the coastal State to take appropriate measures as may be necessary to ensure compliance with the laws and regulations adopted by it on the one hand and the interest of the flag State in securing a prompt release of its vessels and their crews from detention on the other. It strikes a fair balance between the two interests.'[16]

To effectively balance these interests, Article 73(1) provides that enforcement measures in relation to boarding, inspection, arrest, and judicial proceedings must be 'necessary', and Article 73(2) applies a requirement of 'reasonableness' to the bond or other security that may be set by a coastal State for the release of a foreign vessel and its crew. However, the jurisprudence of international courts and tribunals has made clear that every paragraph of Article 73 is to be read in the context of the Article as a whole—that a 'concern for fairness' is one of the purposes of this provision,[17] and that the concepts of 'necessity' and 'reasonableness' apply generally to enforcement measures under Article 73 of the LOSC.[18] Accordingly, any enforcement measure that is taken by a coastal State in relation to the activities of a foreign fishing vessel in the EEZ—whether boarding, inspection, arrest, or judicial proceedings, prompt release on deposit of a bond, or the imposition of penalties following conviction—must be both necessary *and* reasonable. Given the importance of these concepts in defining the balance of interests—and thus the extent of enforcement jurisdiction—in the EEZ, they deserve further consideration.

Although the term 'necessary' (or the concept of 'necessity') is a ubiquitous feature of contemporary international law, its meaning and effect is not always the same—not even within the LOSC, where it appears more than one hundred times in a wide variety of circumstances—and agreement on what constitutes a 'necessary' enforcement measure under Article 73(1) remains elusive (or at least, inconclusive). This uncertainty is clearly demonstrated in the *Virginia G* case, in which the majority found—without any explanation as to how the term 'necessary' should be interpreted—that Guinea-Bissau's boarding, inspection, and arrest of the *Virginia G* did *not* violate Article 73(1) of the LOSC, but that the subsequent confiscation of the vessel was not 'necessary' and therefore *did* violate Article 73(1).[19] While the majority's decision was subject to a significant number of strongly worded dissenting opinions setting out alternative approaches to this

[16] *Monte Confurco* [70]. As Judge Treves has observed, '[l]ooking more deeply into the way this balance is obtained, it appears that Article 73 sets out rights of the coastal State in paragraph 1, and rights of flag States in paragraphs 2, 3 and 4': *Juno Trader* (Sep Op Treves) [2].

[17] *Juno Trader* [77].

[18] *Virginia G* [270].

[19] Ibid [265]–[269].

issue,[20] perhaps the most helpful contribution was the Separate Opinion of Judge Paik (concurring with the majority), which set out a framework within which to consider what is 'necessary' under Article 73(1).[21]

Four key themes emerge from Judge Paik's decision. First, the extent to which something can be considered 'necessary' in any given situation is 'fact-intensive and circumstance-dependent'. As a result, the application of this term will always be to at least some extent subjective, or even speculative, and require assessment on a case-by-case basis.[22] Second, the term 'necessary' can be employed in both a positive and a negative sense; either as a 'positive obligation to be imposed on a State taking permissible measures', or as an 'exceptional condition to justify measures otherwise inconsistent with treaty obligations'.[23] While the term relates in both contexts to the relationship between the means used and the objective sought, there are some important differences, including differences of interpretation, depending on whether necessity is applied as a positive obligation or as a conditional exception, and differences in application, such as where the burden of proof lies in each circumstance. Third, while the ordinary meaning of 'necessary' is 'indispensable', 'vital', or 'essential',[24] when used in legal parlance it may have a weaker meaning, depending on where it is placed on the 'spectrum of compulsion or exigency'.[25] As such, it can be used to mean anything from 'indispensable' all the way down to 'making a contribution to'.[26] And fourth, in the context of international dispute settlement, the determination of what is 'necessary' will ultimately depend on the standard of review applied by the court or tribunal, including how intensively the measure is reviewed, and how much deference is granted to the State taking the measure.[27]

In applying these considerations to determine what is 'necessary' in the context of Article 73(1), Judge Paik concludes that:

- since the phrase 'as may be necessary' is employed in Article 73(1) to limit the broad enforcement powers positively afforded coastal States (rather than as an exception to something that is otherwise prohibited), it should be interpreted

[20] Ibid (Joint Diss Op Hoffman, Marotta Rangel, Chandrasekhara Rao, Kateka, Gao and Bouguetaia) [44]–[61], (Dec Gao) [14]–[17], (Diss Op Servulo Correia) [11]–[21], (Diss Op Jesus) [7]–[22], (Diss Op Ndiaye) [162]–[170].

[21] Ibid (Sep Op Paik) [8]–[38].

[22] Ibid [16].

[23] Ibid [15].

[24] *Oxford English Dictionary Online* (OUP December 2020), available at <http://www.oed.com> (accessed 18 January 2021).

[25] *Virginia G* (Sep Op Paik) [22], citing *Stroud's Judicial Dictionary of Words and Phrases Volume 2* (7th ed, Sweet and Maxwell 2006) 1753.

[26] James Harrison, 'Safeguards Against Excessive Enforcement Measures in the Exclusive Economic Zone—Law and Practice' in Henrik Ringbom (ed), *Jurisdiction over Ships: Post-UNCLOS Developments in the Law of the Sea* (Brill Nijhoff 2015) 220. See also *Virginia G* (Sep Op Paik) [25].

[27] Ibid [17]–[20].

in a way that is more flexible and less compulsory, and placed somewhere on the spectrum of compulsion between 'indispensable' and 'reasonable', 'desirable', 'useful', or 'conducive';[28]

- the term 'necessary' gives rise to a balancing test, involving consideration of the extent to which the measure contributes to the achievement of the objective sought by the coastal State, and the degree to which it encroaches upon the protected rights of other States (a measure does not need to be 'indispensable', but 'the greater the contribution and the less the encroachment, the more likely the measure will be considered necessary');[29] and
- although the LOSC does not specify a standard of review for assessing what is 'necessary' under Article 73(1), the standard applied by the Tribunal should be higher than a 'deferential review' but not as stringent as a '*de novo*' review.[30]

However, this review must not be undertaken in a vacuum. Since the concept of what is 'necessary' is, first and foremost, fact-specific and circumstance-dependent, the 'necessity' of coastal State enforcement measures must (like the regulation of unlicensed foreign fishing vessels) be considered on a case-by-case basis, taking into account: the availability of other (less onerous but equally effective) measures; the importance to the coastal State of taking the measure relative to the impact of the measure on the other State's protected rights; and the circumstances and manner in which the measure was taken.[31]

The question of what is 'reasonable' involves similar considerations—indeed, in the context of enforcement, reasonableness has been found to encompass the principles of necessity and proportionality.[32] In this regard, as discussed in Chapter 2:[33]

- reasonableness does not constitute a 'single standard', but must be approached on a case-by-case basis, in its factual and legal context (which, in the case of an enforcement measure includes reference not just to Article 73, but the scheme of the LOSC as a whole);[34]
- it 'requires State behaviour to be proportional to the aim legally pursued, with due regard to the rights and freedoms granted to another State';[35] and
- as 'an instrument for preserving the margin of appreciation of States and an instrument for courts to control the exercising of the discretionary power of

[28] Ibid [23].
[29] Ibid [24]–[25].
[30] Ibid [27].
[31] Ibid [28]–[29].
[32] *Duzgit Integrity Arbitration* [209] and [254]; *Arctic Sunrise Arbitration* [222].
[33] See Section 2.3.2.1 on the rule of due regard, Section 2.3.3.1 on the margin of appreciation, and Section 2.3.4.2 on 'necessary' enforcement measures. See also Sections 5.1.2 and 8.1.2.
[34] *Camouco* (Diss Op Anderson) [9].
[35] *Filleting in the Gulf of St Lawrence* [54]. See also *Volga* (Sep Op Cot) [21].

the State',[36] it raises similar questions to necessity regarding the standard of review that should be applied in its exercise.

Although the International Tribunal for the Law of the Sea (ITLOS) has been conscious of the need to accord a margin of appreciation to the coastal State in applying these principles—particularly in the context of Article 73—there have been significant differences of opinion between its members concerning the appropriate standard to be applied in order to maintain a proper balance between the interests of coastal and flag States.[37] Commentators have criticized ITLOS' approach in a number of cases as adopting an overly narrow approach, favouring flag State interests to the detriment of coastal States seeking to effectively enforce conservation and management measures in their EEZs, and failing to recognize the bigger picture of international concern regarding the serious impacts of illegal fishing—particularly in the application of the prompt release procedure.[38] As Harrison has observed, while the safeguards on EEZ enforcement powers are necessary in order to ensure that coastal States do not infringe upon the legitimate freedom of navigation, if they are interpreted too strictly the rights (and obligations) of the coastal State in the EEZ will be undermined.[39] Accordingly, it is important to examine the practice of coastal States in giving effect to the enforcement measures envisaged on the face of Article 73, in order to clarify the way in which the balance between coastal and flag State interests has been 'struck' in the implementation of the LOSC, and provide a basis for ensuring the uniform interpretation, application and effectiveness of this aspect of the Convention.[40]

6.2 Coastal State Interests: Boarding, Inspection, Arrest, and Judicial Proceedings (Article 73(1))

Article 73(1) provides coastal States with a broad discretion to take enforcement measures against foreign fishing vessels in the EEZ, including boarding, inspection, arrest, and judicial proceedings—limited, of course, by the requirement that any enforcement measures asserted by coastal States be necessary and

36 Ibid [18].

37 See *Camouco* (Diss Op Wolfrum) [11]–[12], (Diss Op Anderson) [50]; *Volga* (Sep Op Cot) [22]–[25], (Diss Op Anderson) [18]–[23].

38 See Donald R Rothwell and Tim Stephens, 'Illegal Southern Ocean Fishing and Prompt Release: Balancing Coastal and Flag State Rights and Interests' (2004) 53 ICLQ 171, 183–5; Rosemary Rayfuse, 'The Future of Compulsory Dispute Settlement under the Law of the Sea Convention' (2005) 36 VUWellLRev 683, 692–3; Robin Rolf Churchill, 'The Jurisprudence of the International Tribunal for the Law of the Sea Relating to Fisheries: Is There Much in the Net?' (2007) 22(3) IJMCL 383, 410; Harrison, 'Safeguards Against Excessive Enforcement Measures' (n 26) 248.

39 Ibid.

40 This Chapter primarily considers the jurisdictional rules permitting coastal States to exercise enforcement powers over foreign fishing vessels in the EEZ. For a more detailed examination of the operational rules governing maritime enforcement operations, see, eg, Douglas Guilfoyle, *Shipping Interdiction and the Law of the Sea* (CUP 2009) 265–338.

reasonable.[41] Coastal States have used this discretion to exercise not only the traditional forms of physical and judicial enforcement envisaged in Article 73(1), but an expanded range of modern and cooperative approaches which allow them to maximize the application and effectiveness of their jurisdiction in addressing the practical problems posed by illegal foreign fishing.

6.2.1 Traditional Enforcement: Boarding, Inspection, and Arrest

In practice, almost every coastal State has enacted legislation empowering authorized officers to board, inspect, and arrest foreign fishing vessels in the EEZ. In order to understand the effect of this practice on the interpretation of Article 73(1), it is necessary to consider what these measures involve, which vessels are subject to them, and under what circumstances.

6.2.1.1 What is 'Boarding, Inspection, and Arrest'?

In the context of fisheries enforcement, the term 'boarding' merely implies 'going on a vessel for enforcement purposes',[42] and is thus rarely used on its own.[43] Instead, it is routinely coupled with 'inspection', which is not defined or qualified in Article 73(1)[44] but can generally be interpreted in relation to fisheries enforcement as a power to search and examine all relevant areas of the vessel, its licence, gear, equipment, records, facilities, fish and fish products, and any relevant documents necessary to verify compliance with the coastal State's laws and regulations.[45] Inspection commonly includes requiring the master or crew to produce documents, open holds or containers for examination, answer questions or provide information about the registration, licence and activities of the vessel, but does not extend to further, coercive enforcement measures. However, such measures nonetheless come within the coastal State's broad powers of enforcement, which extend all the way to 'arrest'. The word 'arrest' is employed in two senses in Article 73(1)—both as the technical term from Anglo-American admiralty law for

[41] This is significantly broader than the enforcement powers in relation to pollution offences contained in art 220 (the only other provision in the LOSC to confer enforcement powers on coastal States in the EEZ), both in terms of the types of powers that may be exercised, and the circumstances in which they may be exercised.

[42] Satya Nandan and Shabtai Rosenne (eds), *United Nations Convention on the Law of the Sea 1982: A Commentary, Vol II* (Martinus Nijhoff 1993) 794.

[43] In the UNFSA, for example, arts 20, 21, and 22 refer to the act of 'boarding and inspection' (or the right to 'board and inspect'), but do not anywhere refer simply to the act of 'boarding' or the right to 'board'.

[44] In contrast, the 'physical inspection' of a vessel suspected of having violated marine pollution regulations is specifically 'limited to an examination of such certificates, records or other documents as the vessel is required to carry by generally accepted international rules and standards or of any similar documents which it is carrying': LOSC arts 220(2) and (5) and 226(1)(a).

[45] The term 'inspection' is used without definition or elaboration in both the UNFSA and the IPOA-IUU. However, guidance can be taken from the conservation and management measures adopted by regional fisheries management organizations (RFMOs) in relation to high seas boarding and inspection, and from Annex B of the Port State Measures Agreement.

initiating an action against a vessel *in rem,* and to describe the formal procedure for taking a suspect into custody.[46] In practice, however, the Article 73(1) power to 'arrest' a vessel generally manifests in national legislation as a power of 'seizure and detention', in that authorized officers are empowered to direct the master to take the vessel to port and, if he or she fails to comply, to seize the vessel (together with its catch, gear, equipment, stores and cargo, and any vessels, vehicles, or aircraft on board) and take it into port, where it is detained pending the outcome of the judicial proceedings.[47]

The conduct of all these measures is subject to the requirements of Article 225 of the LOSC, which seek to ensure that in taking enforcement measures against foreign vessels, port, and coastal States act with due regard for the safety of navigation, and the protection of the marine environment.[48] In addition, while the LOSC does not expressly deal with the use of physical force in the arrest of ships, it is generally accepted that the powers of the coastal State include the possibility of using force where it is unavoidable,[49] provided it does not go beyond 'what is necessary and reasonable in the circumstances'.[50] While the question of what is 'necessary and reasonable' will fall to be determined in the circumstances of each case, some guidance can be derived from the *Saiga (No 2)* case, in which ITLOS found that Guinean authorities used excessive force in boarding the *Saiga,* including by firing live ammunition directly at the *Saiga* from a fast-moving patrol boat without issuing any of the signals and warnings required by international law and practice, and by the indiscriminate use of firearms once on board the ship.[51]

6.2.1.2 Which Vessels may be Boarded, and under What Circumstances?

When is it 'necessary' for the coastal State to exercise these powers of boarding, inspection, and arrest? While there are a range of views about the vessels to which—and the circumstances in which—these measures can be applied,[52] the absence of any specific threshold in Article 73(1) has provided coastal States with a wide

[46] Nandan and Rosenne, *UNCLOS Commentary, Vol II* (n 42) 795.

[47] David Anderson, 'Investigation, Detention and Release of Foreign Vessels under the UN Convention on the Law of the Sea of 1982 and Other International Agreements' (1996) 11 IJMCL 165, 171.

[48] Since art 225 refers to the exercise of enforcement powers 'under the Convention', it should be observed by coastal States exercising fisheries enforcement jurisdiction under art 73 of the LOSC: *Virginia G* [373].

[49] In this context, the concept of 'use of force' equates broadly to the use of coercive enforcement (or 'police') measures, rather than to the use of armed force in the sense of art 2(4) of the Charter of the United Nations.

[50] *Saiga (No 2)* [155].

[51] Ibid [157]–[158]. These standards were applied again in *Virginia G,* in which ITLOS found that the coastal state (Guinea-Bissau) did not use excessive force in the course of boarding and inspection: *Virginia G* [362]. On the general international law requirements for the use of force at sea, see Guilfoyle, *Shipping Interdiction* (n 40) 277–93.

[52] See, eg, Bernard Oxman, 'The Third United Nations Conference on the Law of the Sea: The 1976 New York Sessions' (1977) AJIL 247, 264; Horace B Robertson 'Navigation in the Exclusive Economic Zone' (1984) VaJIntlL 865, 892–893; Harrison, 'Safeguards Against Excessive Enforcement Measures' (n 26) 221–2.

measure of discretion in this regard.[53] In practice, most coastal States simply distinguish between boarding and inspection—which may be undertaken with respect to any fishing vessel or fishing support vessel in the EEZ at any time—and seizure or detention—which may only be undertaken in circumstances where there are reasonable grounds to believe that there has been a violation of the fisheries laws and regulations of the coastal State.[54] For example, Gambia's *Fisheries Act 2007* provides that:

> 71(1) For the purposes of enforcing this Act, an authorized officer may, without a warrant—
>
> (a) stop, board and search any foreign fishing vessel within the fisheries waters and any locally-based foreign fishing vessel or local fishing vessel inside or outside the fisheries waters, and make any examination concerning that vessel, including its equipment, contents of holds and storage spaces, fishing gear, crew and fish or fishery products and any other cargo carried on board that vessel....
>
> 73(1) Where an authorized officer has reasonable grounds to believe that an offence has been committed under the prwovisions of this Act, he or she may, without a warrant—
>
> (c) seize any fishing vessel, including its fishing gear, equipment, stores and cargo, vehicle, aircraft, net or other fishing gear, which he or she has reasonable grounds to believe has been used in the commission of an offence, or in respect of which the offence has been committed....

In other words, as the Supreme Court of the Federated States of Micronesia has explained, '[w]hile the statutes pose no specific requirements as grounds for the search of a vessel, the power to seize is carefully conditioned upon illegal use of the vessel.'[55] This sort of approach is reflected with a remarkable degree of consistency in the national legislation of coastal States of all types, in all parts of the world, as demonstrated by the practice summarized in Table 6.1.

In light of the consistency in this practice, it is more useful to highlight the exceptions or variations—some of which broaden the application of the coastal State's enforcement measures, and others of which limit them. As depicted in Table 6.1:

[53] In contrast, a State must have 'reasonable grounds for suspecting' prohibited activity in order to board and inspect a vessel beyond the EEZ under art 110 or commence hot pursuit under art 111. This reflects the higher threshold that applies to non-flag State enforcement on board a vessel beyond the EEZ.

[54] This distinction is also made in arts 21 and 22 of the UNFSA, pursuant to which powers of boarding and inspection may be exercised unilaterally by the interdicting State on the high seas, but more extensive powers of investigation and enforcement (including securing evidence and directing the vessel to port) rest with the flag State.

[55] *Ishizawa v Pohnpei* [1985] FMSC 14 (15 August 1985), III(B).

Table 6.1 Coastal State approaches to boarding, inspection, arrest, and prompt release of foreign fishing vessels in the EEZ

	Board and inspect: any foreign fishing vessel (Any); on reasonable suspicion of fishing (RS) or of the actual or likely commission of an offence in the EEZ (Off)	Seize, arrest or order to port: a foreign fishing vessel on reasonable suspicion of actual or likely commission of an offence in the EEZ	Foreign fishing vessels: released on application and deposit of security (App); detained until fines paid (DF) or for investigation/evidence (DI)	Bond: 'reasonable' or 'sufficient' security (RS); by reference to maximum fine (F); value of vessel/gear/catch (V); costs of arrest/detention/repatriation/damage (C); method/amount prescribed (Presc) or discretionary (Disc); deposit in advance*	Relevant legislation and regulations
African Group					
Algeria	Off	X	DF	-	*Law 01-11 of 2001* arts 94, 97, 100
Angola	Any	X	App	FVC	*Law 6-A/04 of 2004* arts 223–5, 255
Benin	RS		App	FC	*Law 2014-19* arts 96, 102
Cameroon	Any			Disc	*Law 94/01* art 142
Cape Verde	Any	X		FVC	*Leg Dec 2/2020* arts 115, 116, 137
Comoros	Any	X	App	FVC	*Law 82-015* arts 9, 10, 17
Congo	Any	X	App	RS	*Law 2-2000* arts 64–8, 82
Cote d'Ivoire	Any	X		FC	*Law 2016-554* arts 70, 87, 98
Djibouti	Any	X		FC	*Law 187 of 2002* arts 21–2, 29–30
Egypt			DF	-	*Act 124 of 1983* art 53
Equatorial Guinea	Any	X			*Law 11/2017* art 118
Eritrea	Any	X		RS	*Proc 176/2014* arts 29, 34
Gabon	Any	X		Disc	*Law 15/2005* arts 76–80, 90, 95
Gambia	Any	X	App	FVC	*Act 2007* ss 71, 81
Ghana	Any	X	App	FVC*	*Act 2002* ss 68, 96, 106
Guinea	RS	X	App	FC	*Code 2015* arts 166, 182, 200–2, 224–5

Table 6.1 *Continued*

	Board and inspect: any foreign fishing vessel (Any); on reasonable suspicion of fishing (RS) or of the actual or likely commission of an offence in the EEZ (Off)	Seize, arrest or order to port: a foreign fishing vessel on reasonable suspicion of actual or likely commission of an offence in the EEZ	Foreign fishing vessels: released on application and deposit of security (App); detained until fines paid (DF) or for investigation/evidence (DI)	Bond: 'reasonable' or 'sufficient' security (RS); by reference to maximum fine (F); value of vessel/gear/catch (V); costs of arrest/detention/repatriation/damage (C); method/amount prescribed (Presc) or discretionary (Disc); deposit in advance*	Relevant legislation and regulations
Guinea-Bissau	Any	X	App	FC	*Dec Law 10/2011* arts 46, 50, 58–9
Kenya	Any	X	App	FVC*	*Act 2016* ss134, 140, 143, 162, 169(1)
Liberia	RS	X		RS*	*Law 2019* ss 5.4, 11.9
Libya	Any	X		*	*Law 14 of 1989* arts 2, 13(j)
Madagascar	Any	X	App	FC	*Code 2015* arts 65, 68–9, 76–7
Mauritania	Any	X		FVC	*Law 2015-017* arts 67, 70, 72–3, 95
Mauritius	Off	X		FVC	*Act 2007* arts 58, 65
Morocco	Any			RS	*Law 173255* arts 44–5, 48-1
Mozambique	Any	X	App	FV*	*Law 22/2013* arts 72, 94
Namibia	Any	X	App	FVC	*Act 2000* ss 5, 55
Nigeria	Any	X			*Act 1992* s 17
Sao Tome & Principe	Any	X		FC	*Law 9/2001* arts 49, 76
Senegal	RS	X	App	F	*Code 2015* arts 85, 91, 99, 101, 114–15
Seychelles	Any	X	App	FC	*Act 2014* ss 49, 53
Sierra Leone	Any	X		RS*	*Act 2018* ss 14, 23, 26; *Regs 2019* s 14(4)
Somalia	Any	X			*Law 2016* arts 26, 28

Continued

Table 6.1 *Continued*

	Board and inspect: any foreign fishing vessel (Any); on reasonable suspicion of fishing (RS) or of the actual or likely commission of an offence in the EEZ (Off)	Seize, arrest or order to port: a foreign fishing vessel on reasonable suspicion of actual or likely commission of an offence in the EEZ	Foreign fishing vessels: released on application and deposit of security (App); detained until fines paid (DF) or for investigation/evidence (DI)	Bond: 'reasonable' or 'sufficient' security (RS); by reference to maximum fine (F); value of vessel/gear/catch (V); costs of arrest/detention/repatriation/damage (C); method/amount prescribed (Presc) or discretionary (Disc); deposit in advance*	Relevant legislation and regulations
South Africa	Any	X	App	FVC	*Act 1998* ss 51, 62
Tanzania	Off	X		FVC*	*Act 2020* s 2 65–6, 68; *Regs 2009* s 10A; *Act 1989* s 14
Togo	RS	X	DF	-*	*Law 2016-026* arts 121–4, 127
Tunisia	Any	X			*Law 94-13* arts 27–30
Asia-Pacific Group					
Bahrain	Any				*Leg Dec 20 of 2002* art 31
Bangladesh	RS	X	App	*	*Act 2020* s 25, 33, 37; *Rules 1983* s 8(b)
Brunei	Off			FVC*	*Order 2009* ss 21, 41, 51
Cambodia	Any	X			*Law 2006* arts 75–76
China	Any			Disc	*Law 1998* art 12; *Prov Regs 1999* art 20
Chinese Taipei	Off	X			*Law 1998* art 16
Cook Islands	Any	X	App	FVC	*Act 2005* ss 46, 49, 55
Cyprus	Off	X			*Fisheries Law* art 7
Fiji	Any	X	App	FVC	*Dec 2012* ss 47, 50, 62
India	Any	X	App	Presc	*Act 1981* s 9 (bond not less than 50 per cent of property value)
Indonesia	Off	X	App	V	*Law 2004* art 69; *Act 1983* art 15 (bond includes proceeds)
Iran	Any	X	DF	-	*Law 1995* art 39

Table 6.1 *Continued*

	Board and inspect: any foreign fishing vessel (Any); on reasonable suspicion of fishing (RS) or of the actual or likely commission of an offence in the EEZ (Off)	Seize, arrest or order to port: a foreign fishing vessel on reasonable suspicion of actual or likely commission of an offence in the EEZ	Foreign fishing vessels: released on application and deposit of security (App); detained until fines paid (DF) or for investigation/evidence (DI)	Bond: 'reasonable' or 'sufficient' security (RS); by reference to maximum fine (F); value of vessel/gear/catch (V); costs of arrest/detention/repatriation/damage (C); method/amount prescribed (Presc) or discretionary (Disc); deposit in advance*	Relevant legislation and regulations
Japan	Any	X			*Act 1948* ss 17–18
Kiribati	Any	X		RS	*Act 2010* ss 23, 30
Korea	Off				*Fishing Act 1996* arts 6-2, 23
Kuwait	Any	X		Disc	*Law 1980* arts 10–11
Malaysia	Off			V	*Act 1985* ss 46, 50
Maldives	Any	X	App		*Act 2019* ss 60, 63–5 [rules for bonds to be prescribed]
Marshall Islands	Any	X	DI	FVC*	51 *MIRC* §§512, 566; *Regs 1998* s 17
Micronesia	Any	X	DI	FVC	24 *FSM Code* §§603, 806
Myanmar	Any	X		RS	*Law 1989* s 22
Nauru	Any	X	DI	FVC*	*Act 1997* ss 12B(2), 17, 21 (performance bond may be required in advance; shall be not less than $387,000 USD)
Niue	Off	X	App	FVC	*Act 1996* ss 39, 48
Oman	Any	X		F*	*Law 2019* arts 48, 57; *Res 4/94* art 11
Pakistan	Off	X			*Act 1975* arts 7–8
Palau	Any	X			27 *PNC* §188

Continued

Table 6.1 *Continued*

	Board and inspect: any foreign fishing vessel (Any); on reasonable suspicion of fishing (RS) or of the actual or likely commission of an offence in the EEZ (Off)	Seize, arrest or order to port: a foreign fishing vessel on reasonable suspicion of actual or likely commission of an offence in the EEZ	Foreign fishing vessels: released on application and deposit of security (App); detained until fines paid (DF) or for investigation/evidence (DI)	Bond: 'reasonable' or 'sufficient' security (RS); by reference to maximum fine (F); value of vessel/gear/catch (V); costs of arrest/detention/repatriation/damage (C); method/amount prescribed (Presc) or discretionary (Disc); deposit in advance*	Relevant legislation and regulations
Papua New Guinea	RS	X	DI	FVC*	*Act 1998* ss 49, 61(4); *Reg 2000* s 12
Philippines	Any	X			*Order 200 of 2000* ss 4–7
Qatar	Any	X		Disc	*Law 4 of 1983* arts 26–7
Samoa	Off	X	App	FVC	*Act 2016* ss 51–5, 57
Solomon Islands	Any		DI	FVC	*Act 2015* ss 58, 92
Sri Lanka	Any	X	App	FVC	*Act 1979* ss 13, 21; *Regs 1981* reg 8(b)
Thailand	Off	X			*Act BE 2482, 1939* ss 9–10
Timor-Leste	Any	X	App	FV*	*Dec Law 2004* arts 35, 141, 173; *Dec 5/2004* art 162
Tonga	Any	X	App	FVC	*Act 2002* ss 71, 80
Turkey					*Law 1380* art 33; *Reg 22223* art 33 (authorized officers may confiscate gear and equipment used in illegal fishing and submit them to the judicial authorities)
Tuvalu	Any	X		RS	*Act 2006* ss 47, 92
United Arab Emirates	Any	X			*Law 23 of 1999* art 57
Vanuatu	Any	X	DI	FVC	*Act 2014* ss 109, 125

Table 6.1 *Continued*

	Board and inspect: any foreign fishing vessel (Any); on reasonable suspicion of fishing (RS) or of the actual or likely commission of an offence in the EEZ (Off)	Seize, arrest or order to port: a foreign fishing vessel on reasonable suspicion of actual or likely commission of an offence in the EEZ	Foreign fishing vessels: released on application and deposit of security (App); detained until fines paid (DF) or for investigation/evidence (DI)	Bond: 'reasonable' or 'sufficient' security (RS); by reference to maximum fine (F); value of vessel/gear/catch (V); costs of arrest/detention/repatriation/damage (C); method/amount prescribed (Presc) or discretionary (Disc); deposit in advance*	Relevant legislation and regulations
Vietnam	Off	X			*Law 2017* art 88
Yemen					*Law 2 of 2006* art 61 (vessels breaching fisheries laws shall be detained for not more than fifteen days, during which time the Ministry shall try to arrive at a settlement with the owner)
Eastern Europe Group					
Albania	Any	X	DF	-	*Law 64/2012* arts 122–3, 128A(18)
Bulgaria				F	*Act 2001* art 53 (authorized officers may check licences, control compliance, seize and detain any items which are the subject of an offence or used in the commission of an offence); *Act 2000* art 124
Croatia					*Act 2017* arts 65, 66, 70 (authorized inspectors may carry out inspections, request and inspect documents, seize fish, equipment, gear, and other objects with which an offence was committed)
Estonia					*Act 2015* §§64–6 (authorized officers may supervise compliance with the requirements of the *Fisheries Act* pursuant to the measures and procedures in the *Law Enforcement Act*)

Continued

Table 6.1 *Continued*

	Board and inspect: any foreign fishing vessel (Any); on reasonable suspicion of fishing (RS) or of the actual or likely commission of an offence in the EEZ (Off)	Seize, arrest or order to port: a foreign fishing vessel on reasonable suspicion of actual or likely commission of an offence in the EEZ	Foreign fishing vessels: released on application and deposit of security (App); detained until fines paid (DF) or for investigation/evidence (DI)	Bond: 'reasonable' or 'sufficient' security (RS); by reference to maximum fine (F); value of vessel/gear/catch (V); costs of arrest/detention/repatriation/damage (C); method/amount prescribed (Presc) or discretionary (Disc); deposit in advance*	Relevant legislation and regulations
European Union					*Reg 1224/2009* arts 71–9, 83 (authorized officers shall conduct inspections, record suspected infringements in an inspection report, and in certain cases, require the vessel to proceed to port for a full investigation)
Latvia					*Law 1995* s 19 (authorized officers may perform fisheries inspections, draw up administrative reports, seize and confiscate fish and gear related to infringements of the regulations)
Lithuania	Any	X			*Law 2000* arts 50–1
Montenegro	Any	X			*Law 2009* arts 112, 114
Poland	Any	X			*Law 2014* arts 107–10
Romania				RS	*Ordinance 23/2008* arts 56–7 (authorized inspectors may access fishing vessels and gear to perform control and inspection functions, ascertain the commission of offences, and apply administrative sanctions); *Act 1990* art 42
Russia	RS	X		RS	*Act 1998* arts 36(1), 39(1)
Slovenia					*Act 2006* arts 44–5 (authorized officers may inspect vessels and gear, supervise vessel movement, and order the seizure of assets, gear, equipment, and catch)

Table 6.1 *Continued*

	Board and inspect: any foreign fishing vessel (Any); on reasonable suspicion of fishing (RS) or of the actual or likely commission of an offence in the EEZ (Off)	Seize, arrest or order to port: a foreign fishing vessel on reasonable suspicion of actual or likely commission of an offence in the EEZ	Foreign fishing vessels: released on application and deposit of security (App); detained until fines paid (DF) or for investigation/evidence (DI)	Bond: 'reasonable' or 'sufficient' security (RS); by reference to maximum fine (F); value of vessel/gear/catch (V); costs of arrest/detention/repatriation/damage (C); method/amount prescribed (Presc) or discretionary (Disc); deposit in advance*	Relevant legislation and regulations
Latin America and the Caribbean Group					
Antigua & Barbuda	Any	X	App	RS	*Act 2006* ss 62, 68
Argentina	Off	X		FC	*Res 396/2018* para 4; *Law 24.922 of 1998* art 54; *Dec 748/99* art 42
Bahamas	Any	X	DF	-	*Act 1977* ss 14, 16
Barbados	Any	X	App	RS	*Act 1993* ss 34, 39
Belize	Any	X		RS	*Act 2020* ss 44–6, 84(2)
Brazil					*Law 11.959 of 2009* art 31 (inspections cover fishing, cultivation, landing, transportation, processing, storage, and commercialization)
Chile	Any	X			*Law 1991* art 122
Colombia	Off	X			*Res 520/1999* arts 12–13
Costa Rica					*Dec 36.782* art 14 (authorized inspectors will have access to all fishing vessels to fulfil their functions, and will draw up a record reflecting the circumstances and results of their actions)
Cuba	RS				*Law 129/2019* art 28
Dominica	Any	X			*Act 1987* art 27

Continued

Table 6.1 *Continued*

	Board and inspect: any foreign fishing vessel (Any); on reasonable suspicion of fishing (RS) or of the actual or likely commission of an offence in the EEZ (Off)	**Seize, arrest or order to port: a foreign fishing vessel on reasonable suspicion of actual or likely commission of an offence in the EEZ**	**Foreign fishing vessels: released on application and deposit of security (App); detained until fines paid (DF) or for investigation/evidence (DI)**	**Bond: 'reasonable' or 'sufficient' security (RS); by reference to maximum fine (F); value of vessel/gear/catch (V); costs of arrest/detention/ repatriation/damage (C); method/amount prescribed (Presc) or discretionary (Disc); deposit in advance***	**Relevant legislation and regulations**
Dominican Republic				RS	*Law 307-04* arts 74–6 (authorized officers monitor compliance, record infractions and communicate them to the authorities); art 93(1)
Ecuador	RS	X			*Law 2020* arts 160, 197
El Salvador			DF	-	*Law 2001* art 84
Grenada	Any	X		RS	*Act 1986* ss 28, 33
Guatemala	Off	X	DF	-	*Dec 80-02* arts 81, 90
Guyana	Any	X	App	F*	*Act 2012* ss 18, 48, 57
Honduras		X	DF	-	*Dec 106-2015* art 113
Jamaica	RS	X		FV	*Act 2018* ss 72, 82
Mexico				Disc	*Law 2007* art 126 (inspections may be conducted on the basis of a written order setting out well-founded reasons and scope); *Reg 1999* art 157
Nicaragua		X		F	*Dec 9/2005* art 212; *Law 2004* art 123(21)
Peru					*Dec 012/2001/PE* arts 100–103 (authorized officers will ensure compliance with the law, including by carrying out inspections)
Saint Kitts & Nevis	Any	X	App	FVC	*Act 2016* ss 85–9, 110

Table 6.1 *Continued*

	Board and inspect: any foreign fishing vessel (Any); on reasonable suspicion of fishing (RS) or of the actual or likely commission of an offence in the EEZ (Off)	Seize, arrest or order to port: a foreign fishing vessel on reasonable suspicion of actual or likely commission of an offence in the EEZ	Foreign fishing vessels: released on application and deposit of security (App); detained until fines paid (DF) or for investigation/evidence (DI)	Bond: 'reasonable' or 'sufficient' security (RS); by reference to maximum fine (F); value of vessel/gear/catch (V); costs of arrest/detention/ repatriation/damage (C); method/amount prescribed (Presc) or discretionary (Disc); deposit in advance*	Relevant legislation and regulations
Saint Lucia	Any	X	App	RS	*Act 1984* ss 27, 32
Saint Vincent & Grenadines	Any	X		RS	*Act 1986* ss 33, 38
Trinidad & Tobago	Any	X		Presc	*Act 1986* s 28 (bond set at $37,000 USD)
Uruguay	Any	X			*Law 19.175* art 25 (authorized inspectors have free access to inspect foreign vessels and, if necessary, seize equipment, vehicles, goods, and gear used in the commission of an offence)
Venezuela	Any	X			*Dec Law 1,408 of 2014* arts 62–6 (authorized officers may order the modification, restriction, or cessation of fishing and related activities and detain fishing or fish transporting vessels)
Western Europe and Others Group					
Australia	Any	X		FVC	*Act 2013* ss 8, 18, 32–4, 88
Belgium	Any	X		F	*Law 1978* arts 4–5 (bond: up to max. fine plus 10 per cent)
Canada	Any	X		RS	*Act 1985* ss 7–9, 13
Denmark	Off			FVC	*Law 2017* §§120, 135
Finland	Any	X			*Act 379/2015* §§99–109; *Act 1188/ 2014* §12

Continued

Table 6.1 *Continued*

	Board and inspect: any foreign fishing vessel (Any); on reasonable suspicion of fishing (RS) or of the actual or likely commission of an offence in the EEZ (Off)	Seize, arrest or order to port: a foreign fishing vessel on reasonable suspicion of actual or likely commission of an offence in the EEZ	Foreign fishing vessels: released on application and deposit of security (App); detained until fines paid (DF) or for investigation/evidence (DI)	Bond: 'reasonable' or 'sufficient' security (RS); by reference to maximum fine (F); value of vessel/gear/catch (V); costs of arrest/detention/repatriation/damage (C); method/amount prescribed (Presc) or discretionary (Disc); deposit in advance*	Relevant legislation and regulations
France	Any	X	App	FVC	*Code* arts L942-5, 943-1, 943-5
France (Mayotte)	Any	X	App	FVC	*Code* arts L942-5, 943-1, 943-5 (per L951-1)
France (New Caledonia)	Any	X	App	FVC	*Code* arts L942-5, 943-1, 943-5 (per L957-3)
France (SAAT)	Any	X	App	FVC	*Code* arts L942-5, 943-1, 943-5 (per L958-2)
Germany	Any				*Law 2011* §§5, 16 (authorized officers may carry out seizures in accordance with the *Code of Criminal Procedure*; may only exercise powers to extent necessary to monitor compliance with fisheries regulations)
Iceland	Off	X		FVC	*Act 2006* s 9; *Act 1998* art 15
Ireland	Any	X		FVC	*Act 2006* ss 17–18, 21
Italy					Not determined.
Malta	Any	X		FC	*Act 2001* ss 19, 24
Netherlands	Any				*Act 1963* arts 58–62 (authorized officers may seize objects for confiscation, even without obvious commission of an offence)
New Zealand	Any	X			*Act 1996* ss 199–207
NZ (Tokelau)	Any	X	App	Presc	*Act 1977* s 12; *Regs 2012* ss 40, 41 (bond not less than vessel value)

Table 6.1 *Continued*

	Board and inspect: any foreign fishing vessel (Any); on reasonable suspicion of fishing (RS) or of the actual or likely commission of an offence in the EEZ (Off)	Seize, arrest or order to port: a foreign fishing vessel on reasonable suspicion of actual or likely commission of an offence in the EEZ	Foreign fishing vessels: released on application and deposit of security (App); detained until fines paid (DF) or for investigation/evidence (DI)	Bond: 'reasonable' or 'sufficient' security (RS); by reference to maximum fine (F); value of vessel/gear/catch (V); costs of arrest/detention/ repatriation/damage (C); method/amount prescribed (Presc) or discretionary (Disc); deposit in advance*	Relevant legislation and regulations
Norway	Any				*Act 2008* s 46 and *Act 1997* s 25
Portugal	Any			Presc	*Dec Law 35/2019* art 6 (authorized officers may board and inspect all vessels and direct them to an appropriate port or place for inspection); arts 22, 23 (bond one third of max. fine)
Spain	Any	X		F	*Dec 176/2003* arts 3–7; *Law 3/2001* art 98 (bond no more than maximum fine)
Sweden	Any	X			*Act 1993* §§34, 47
United Kingdom	Any	X			*Act 1968* s 8
UK (Falklands)	RS	X	App	FVC*	*Ordinance 2005* ss 5, 141, 157
UK (Montserrat)	Any	X	App	RS	*Act 2000* ss 47, 52
UK (Pitcairn)	Any	X	App	FV	*Ordinance 2016* ss 32–4
UK (SGSSI)	RS	X		FVC	*Ordinance 2000* ss 11–12, 14
UK (Turks & Caicos)					*Regs 1998* ss 37–9 (where there is reasonable cause to suspect that a vessel or gear has been used in connection with an offence, authorized officers may seize and hold it until proceedings can be brought)
United States	Any	X			16 *USC* §1861(b) and 14 *USC* §89(a)

Notes

a. The practice of EU member States is examined by reference to their national legislation, but relevant EU regulations are also included for information/comparison.

- some coastal States limit not only seizure and detention but boarding and inspection to situations where there are—at a minimum—reasonable grounds to believe that an offence has been, is being, or is about to be committed;
- some only authorize boarding and inspection when there are reasonable grounds to believe that the vessel is (or has been) engaged in fishing or a related activity; and
- some make no distinction between different levels of enforcement, authorizing not only the boarding and inspection but the seizure and detention of foreign fishing vessels in the EEZ, without the added requirement of 'reasonable grounds to believe' that an offence has been committed to justify the use of more extensive powers.

Some legislation provides additional enforcement opportunities, such as inspection powers extending beyond fisheries-related items to 'any other cargo carried on board',[56] requiring fishing vessels in transit to proceed, when directed, to a particular location for the purpose of carrying out inspections,[57] or authorizing use of the relevant powers in the port of another State (subject to agreement with that State).[58]

Clearly, the breadth of the coastal State's enforcement powers under Article 73(1) has enormous significance for ensuring compliance with laws and regulations relating to living resources, as well as for broader law enforcement and security purposes. For example, the possibility to board and inspect any foreign fishing vessel or fishing support vessel in the EEZ broadens the potential for discovery of both fisheries and non-fisheries related information, such as whether or not the vessel is carrying illicit cargo—ranging from narcotics and firearms to weapons of mass destruction—or is engaged in other transnational criminal activities like people smuggling or slavery. While the coastal State's fisheries enforcement jurisdiction under Article 73(1) does not provide a basis for taking any enforcement action on the basis of potential violation of a *non*-fisheries law, it may be possible to pursue such illicit activities on other jurisdictional bases or through other routes (including by seeking flag State authorization to take further action or sharing the information with the authorities of the vessel's next port of call). These possibilities are reflected in Article 21 of the *Agreement on Strengthening the Implementation of the Niue Treaty on Fisheries Surveillance and Law Enforcement in the South Pacific Region* (Niue Treaty Subsidiary Agreement),[59] which establishes a consent-based mechanism to facilitate the sharing of information provided under the Agreement with both non-Parties and inter-governmental organizations. This

[56] Gambia, *Act 2007* s 71.
[57] Canada, *Regs 2014* s 16.2(b).
[58] United Kingdom (Pitcairn Islands), *Ordinance 2016* s 35.
[59] (Opened for signature 2 November 2012, entered into force 30 July 2014) [2017] ATS 11.

could potentially include not only fisheries surveillance and enforcement partners, but regional law enforcement agencies and other relevant organizations such as the Pacific Islands Chiefs of Police, Interpol, or the Western and Central Pacific Fisheries Commission (WCPFC).

6.2.2 Modern Enforcement: Integrated Monitoring, Control and Surveillance, and the Use of Technology

Although the traditional enforcement powers of boarding, inspection, and arrest envisaged in Article 73(1) undeniably constitute an important part of the coastal State's jurisdiction, they are not the only—or necessarily the best or most cost-effective—method of ensuring compliance with fisheries laws and regulations. Even setting aside the difficulty and cost of physical patrols, the protection of fisheries may not be the main priority for a coastal State, whose limited enforcement assets may be deployed on other issues such as illegal migration, human trafficking, narcotics smuggling, piracy, or the protection of oil and gas installations. This is reflected in two clear developments in the implementation of the LOSC: first, the adoption of a broader policy framework for fisheries enforcement centring on the overarching concept of 'monitoring, control and surveillance', which emphasizes the use of preventive and deterrent measures to achieve compliance and enforcement; and second, the formal incorporation of an ever-increasing range of techniques and technologies for the 'remote' detection of fisheries offences in national, regional, and international law and practice.

6.2.2.1 Monitoring, Control, and Surveillance

The concept of monitoring, control, and surveillance (MCS), which has been described by the United Nations (UN) Food and Agriculture Organization (FAO) as 'the best hope for preventing, deterring and eliminating IUU fishing',[60] incorporates three elements:[61]

- monitoring—the collection, measurement, and analysis of fishing activity (effectively, 'data collection');
- control—specification of the terms and conditions under which the resources can be harvested (primarily through legislation and licensing); and

[60] FAO, 'Implementation of the International Plan of Action to Prevent, Deter and Eliminate Illegal, Unreported and Unregulated Fishing' *FAO Technical Guidelines for Responsible Fisheries No 9* (FAO 2002) [3.2.5].

[61] P Flewwelling et al, 'Recent Trends in Monitoring, Control and Surveillance Systems for Capture Fisheries' *FAO Fisheries Technical Paper 415* (FAO 2002) 7–8. While there is no single definition of MCS, the descriptions used by various regional and international organizations adopt similar terms and ideas.

- surveillance—the regulation and supervision of fishing activity to ensure that national legislation, terms and conditions of access, and management measures are observed (including components on land, at sea, in the air, and in space).

As these three elements suggest, in contrast to the separate allocations of prescriptive and enforcement jurisdiction set out in Part V of the LOSC, the concept of MCS involves a functional, holistic approach to the exercise of coastal State jurisdiction, in which policing and enforcement is integrated into the broader fisheries management process, and forms an integral and essential component of the coastal State's overall system to conserve and utilize marine resources, and maximize the economic returns from those resources. Accordingly, effective MCS does not relate simply to taking action against illegal fishing that is already underway,[62] but encompasses a wide range of tools aimed at prevention and deterrence, many of which were discussed in Chapter 4.[63]

Despite being essentially a policy concept (rather than a legal one) which does not appear in the LOSC, MCS is an integral aspect of contemporary international fisheries, featuring in the post-LOSC global fisheries instruments,[64] in regional fisheries management organizations (RFMOs),[65] in resolutions of the United Nations General Assembly (UNGA),[66] and in national law and practice.[67] While international instruments predominantly cast MCS in relation to—or as a method of—compliance and enforcement, this concept is not limited to the traditional measures of physical enforcement (such as boarding, inspection, arrest, and the imposition of penalties) but encompasses broader techniques, ranging from simple tools such as licensing, marking requirements, and vessel registers through to the establishment and operation of observer programmes, IUU vessel lists, and vessel monitoring systems (VMS).[68] This cross-cutting approach to regulation

[62] FAO, 'Implementation of the IPOA-IUU' (n 60) 19; Flewwelling et al, 'Recent Trends in MCS Systems' (n 61) 9.

[63] These include prescriptive measures adopted through licensing conditions, such as reporting requirements, the carriage of observers, and the installation and operation of a vessel monitoring system (VMS). See Sections 4.3.1 and 4.3.3.

[64] See UNFSA arts 5(l), 10(h) and 18(3)(g); Port State Measures Agreement art 21(4); IPOA-IUU [24]; FAO Code of Conduct arts 7.17 and 7.7.3; FAO Voluntary Guidelines [22] and Annex 2.

[65] MCS does not feature in the constituent instruments of older RFMOs but is common in those adopted (or amended) since 2000, and in the conservation and management measures adopted by all RFMOs.

[66] The term 'monitoring, control and surveillance' has appeared in the annual UNGA Resolution on Sustainable Fisheries since 2002. See, eg, UNGA Res 75/89 (8 December 2020) UN Doc A/75/89, Section V.

[67] Since MCS is essentially a policy framework, it is not implemented through a specific provision in national legislation, but through a combination of legislative, administrative, and enforcement activities. Its importance in the practice of coastal States is demonstrated in the way it is incorporated in the text of national plans of action adopted by coastal States pursuant to the IPOA-IUU.

[68] For example, the MCS measures addressed in Section V of UNGA Res 75/89 include: VMS; positive and negative vessel lists; the establishment of a global record of fishing vessels and a unique vessel identifier system; measures to improve traceability of fish and fish products; cooperative surveillance

enables coastal States to use a wide range of prescriptive, cost-effective, 'no force' measures to increase compliance, maximizing the application of their prescriptive jurisdiction, and minimizing the need for costly and difficult physical enforcement measures.

6.2.2.2 The Use of 'Remote' Detection Techniques

The use of 'no force' measures has also informed the adoption of 'remote' detection techniques, which enable fisheries surveillance to be conducted remotely using aerial and space-based mechanisms, rather than through physical boarding and inspections at sea. The development and application of new technologies—and the reduction in the costs of such technologies—has revolutionized the effectiveness and efficiency of coastal State surveillance and enforcement, which can now be conducted using not only VMS, but automatic identification systems (AIS),[69] satellite imagery,[70] and aerial and underwater drone technology.[71] This has been further assisted by the exchange and disclosure of fisheries surveillance information, including the decision of a number of coastal States to make their VMS data publicly available online via Global Fishing Watch.[72] By using state-of-the-art platforms and customizable computer algorithms to combine and analyse data from these sources (and integrate it with existing data on vessel registration, licensing, ownership, and historical involvement with IUU fishing) coastal States—often assisted by civil society and private sector collaborators—are able to monitor the activities of fishing vessels without requiring their cooperation, involvement, or even knowledge.[73] In this way, coastal states can detect vessel movements and patterns

and enforcement measures; and measures for the regulation of transhipment, in particular at-sea transhipment.

[69] AIS helps to ensure the safety of navigation by automatically providing information about ship movements to other ships and coastal authorities using very high frequency (VHF) radio. It is the least expensive and most transparent form of fisheries surveillance data and is transmitted with greater frequency than VMS data. For a useful discussion of AIS as a fisheries monitoring tool, see Solène Guggisberg, 'The Roles of Nongovernmental Actors in Improving Compliance with Fisheries Regulations' (2019) 28 RECIEL 314, 316–18.

[70] Satellite imagery can potentially detect all fishing vessels—including those without VMS or AIS units, and those with VMS or AIS units that are faulty or have been tampered with or switched off.

[71] Remotely operated aerial and underwater drones fitted with cameras and satellite positioning equipment have been used by a number of coastal States to detect illegal fishing and aid in prosecution. See, eg, Samantha Andrews, 'Drones: Keeping a Watchful Eye on Illegal Fishing' *The Fish Site*, 28 April 2016, available at <http://thefishsite.com/articles/drones-keeping-a-watchful-eye-on-illegal-fishing> accessed 21 January 2021; 'Intelligent Drones Crack down on Illegal Fishing in African Waters', 16 July 2018, available at <http://unenvironment.org/news-and-stories/story/intelligent-drones-crack-down-illegal-fishing-african-waters> accessed 18 January 2021.

[72] Global Fishing Watch, 'Ocean Sustainability through Transparency, Data-Sharing and Collaboration', available at <http://globalfishingwatch.org/wp-content/uploads/GFW-program-2020.pdf> accessed 19 January 2021. At the time of writing, the VMS data of Chile, Indonesia, Panama, and Peru was available online via Global Fishing Watch, and Brazil, Costa Rica, Ecuador, and Namibia had also made commitments to participate.

[73] Relevant platforms and initiatives include: 'Global Fishing Watch', developed in collaboration between civil society organization Oceana, with satellite technology expertise from Skytruth and data processing support from Google, available at <http://globalfishingwatch.org/about-us/> accessed 18

indicating suspicious or unauthorized behaviour in a fraction of the time (and at a fraction of the cost) of traditional enforcement methods, focus on the vessels or areas that pose the highest risk, and target their enforcement activities more efficiently and effectively.

Of course, using these technologies simply to deter or detect an instance of illegal fishing is not enough—the ultimate goal is not just surveillance but *enforcement*. There are three broad ways in which coastal States can use information gained through remote detection to enforce their fisheries laws and regulations. First, remote detection technologies enable coastal States to monitor the activities of fishing vessels in and around their waters in real-time, and then deploy carefully targeted aerial or at-sea patrols to intercept any vessels engaged in suspicious behaviour at the right time and place. While this is still a difficult and expensive exercise, it provides a much more selective and cost-effective approach to physical enforcement. In January 2015, for example, having used AIS data to detect the unlicensed Taiwanese-flagged fishing vessel *Shin Jyi Chuu 33* behaving suspiciously in Palau's 600,000 square kilometres EEZ, a data analyst was able to predict its course and remotely assist Palau's sole patrol boat to intercept and arrest the vessel just a few miles before it would have left Palau's jurisdiction and entered Indonesian waters.[74] The vessel, which was found to have 304 shark carcasses and several hundred shark fins on board, paid a fine of $100,000 USD and forfeited all of its catch.[75]

Second, even if it is not possible for the coastal State itself to physically inspect or arrest a vessel that is reasonably believed, on the basis of evidence derived from remote detection, to have engaged in unlawful fishing activities, such evidence can be provided to other States and organizations for further action, including:

- the flag State of the vessel, which is obliged to investigate and, where such allegations are established, take appropriate action with respect to unlawful activities by its fishing vessels;[76]
- other coastal States, including coastal States in the region who may wish to monitor the vessel's passage through or activities in their own waters, and coastal States in whose waters the vessel may be authorized to fish, where such

January 2021; 'Oversea Ocean Monitor' developed by the civil society organization Pew Charitable Trusts, in collaboration with technology company Satellite Applications Catapult and fisheries intelligence group Ocean Mind, available at <http://pewtrusts.org/en/research-and-analysis/fact-sheets/2017/11/oversea-ocean-monitor> accessed 18 January 2021.

[74] Urbina, *The Outlaw Ocean* (n 10) 48–50.

[75] Announcement by the Office of the President, Republic of Palau on *Facebook* (Business page) 19 March 2015, available at <http://facebook.com/permalink.php?story_fbid=465643860254385&id=167766706708770> accessed 19 January 2021. Pursuant to subsequent legislative amendments, similar conduct would now result in a significantly larger fine, between $500,000 USD and $1 million USD: Palau, 27 *PNC* §§181–2.

[76] *SRFC Advisory Opinion* [118]–[125]; UNFSA art 19; FAO Voluntary Guidelines for Flag State Responsibility [2(g)], [38], and [42].

evidence may provide a basis for the cancellation or suspension of the vessel's licence;

- port States, who may—and in some cases *must*—deny port entry to vessels reasonably believed to have engaged in illegal fishing activities, or undertake inspections and other enforcement actions when any such vessels enter their ports;[77] and
- any RFMO with responsibility for the area in which the vessel is operating, including by providing 'suitably documented' information to support the vessel being included on the organization's IUU vessel list.[78]

Third, remote detection techniques are increasingly being incorporated into coastal State legislation as a way of not only detecting but proving unlawful fishing activity. Given the difficulties of successfully prosecuting fisheries offences—which are committed at sea, beyond the direct observation of enforcement officers, where physical evidence is often unobtainable—such legislation can provide a crucial basis for securing convictions.[79] For example, some developing coastal States in Africa have specifically incorporated remote detection techniques into their enforcement process, in the form of a 'visual procedure' to be used where conditions do not allow physical boarding and inspection—whether due to poor weather, the suspect vessel's failure to comply with an order to stop, or the sheer number of fishing vessels in the area. Under these circumstances, offences can be detected remotely by technical means whose reliability is commonly accepted, including electronic surveillance, satellite surveillance, videos, and photographs, which are stated to constitute conclusive proof of the offence unless proven otherwise. The visual procedure may only be used to detect and record infringements relating to unauthorized fishing or fishing related activities, refusal to comply with an order to stop, and fishing in a closed area or during a closed period.[80]

Other coastal States have put the use of various technologies to detect and prove offences on a legislative basis. For example, Morocco provides for offences to be detected from a shore station, by an aircraft, or by any useful procedure, including aerospace detection and telecommunications;[81] the United States enables the use of 'commercial or governmental remote sensing technology to locate or identify

[77] See, eg, Port State Measures Agreement art 9; RFMO measures such as Southern Indian Ocean Fisheries Agreement (SIOFA) *CMM 2017/08 Conservation and Management Measure Establishing a Port Inspection Scheme* [9]–[10].

[78] IUU vessel lists are commonly compiled (in the first instance) on the basis of reports from members or cooperating non-members of the RFMO, trade, or statistical information obtained from the FAO, information from port States, and other 'suitably documented' information. See, eg, WCPFC, *CMM 2010-06 Conservation and Management Measure to Establish a List of Vessels Presumed to Have Carried Out Illegal, Unreported and Unregulated Fishing Activities in the WCPO* [2]. See further: Guggisberg, 'The Roles of Nongovernmental Actors in Improving Compliance' (n 69) 318–20.

[79] Flewwelling et al, 'Recent Trends in MCS Systems' (n 61) 26. See also IPOA-IUU [17].

[80] Guinea, *Code 2015* art 182; Mauritania, *Law 2015-017* art 70; Senegal, *Code 2015* art 91.

[81] Morocco, *Law 173255* art 45.

vessels engaged in [IUU] fishing on the high seas, including encroachments into the EEZ by fishing vessels of other nations';[82] and Palau's legislation states that 'credible technical data', which includes data from aerial surveillance, VMS, and satellite data, may be used as evidence of violations of fisheries law.[83] Perhaps the most comprehensive example is Section 24(3) of the Pitcairn Islands' *Marine Protected Area Ordinance 2016*, which provides that the means by which a fishing vessel may be found or observed to be engaged in unauthorized fishing 'include, but are not limited to:

(a) remote satellite technology;
(b) electronic monitoring by a VMS;
(c) an automated information system (AIS);
(d) unmanned aerial, surface, or underwater vehicle observations;
(e) video, radar, acoustical, and visual observations;
(f) any other means that can reasonably be used to determine vessel activity historically or in real time.'

The most common approach is simply to provide legislative confirmation of the evidentiary value of VMS data, which avoids the time and expense of using expert evidence to prove the validity and accuracy of information derived from a VMS.[84] For example, pursuant to Section 176(1) of Kenya's *Fisheries Management and Development Act 2016*, '[t]he readings of any mobile transceiver unit or other electronic location device integral to a [VMS] shall be admissible as evidence and may be used as prima facie evidence of the facts that they aver.' The legislation of many coastal States, particularly in Africa and Asia-Pacific, similarly includes provisions that:

- specify that certain machines or devices are 'notoriously accurate' so that courts can take judicial notice of evidence generated by them;[85]
- establish a category of 'observer devices' or 'designated machines' that are presumed to give accurate readings and provide prima facie evidence of the facts to which they relate;[86] or
- provide that the information from a VMS has 'full evidentiary value' or constitutes 'conclusive evidence' of the activities of fishing vessels unless proven otherwise.[87]

[82] United States, 16 *USC* §1829(b)(5).
[83] Palau, 27 *PNC* §191(a).
[84] Flewwelling et al, 'Recent Trends in MCS Systems' (n 61) 27–8. These provisions commonly also establish the accuracy of photographs, provided the date, time, and position was simultaneously superimposed on them.
[85] See, eg, Cook Islands, *Act 2005* s 62.
[86] See, eg, Kiribati, *Act 2010* ss 34–6.
[87] See, eg, Cape Verde, *Leg Dec 2/2020* art 133(2)(a); Guinea, *Code 2015* art 190.

Finally, in addition to those States who are sharing their VMS data publicly through Global Fishing Watch,[88] some coastal States have enacted provisions to enable their VMS data to be shared with the relevant authorities of other States for the purpose of cooperative MCS activities, or to discharge regional or international obligations, deter and eliminate illegal fishing, or maintain law and order.[89]

6.2.3 Cooperative Enforcement: Joint or Harmonized Surveillance and Enforcement Operations and Information Sharing

Another way to ensure compliance with fisheries laws and regulations is through cooperative enforcement. While there is no specific framework or mechanism for—or even reference to—cooperative enforcement in the fisheries provisions of the LOSC,[90] as Kaye has observed, it includes a 'continuum' of engagement between States, ranging from minimal forms of interaction (such as data exchange and the deployment of on-board observers) all the way through to situations where one State effectively steps into the shoes of another (such as the boarding and arrest of a foreign vessel by a third State on behalf of the coastal State).[91] In this regard, all the aspects of fisheries enforcement—from preventive 'no force' MCS measures to coercive enforcement activities—are mirrored and expanded through cooperation and collaboration, which is given effect through national legislation, bilateral and multilateral agreements and arrangements, and the practice of regional and sub-regional fisheries bodies. These cooperative approaches maximize the scope and effectiveness of each State's capacity for enforcement—both in terms of the legal capacity to assert jurisdiction, and the physical capacity to enforce that jurisdiction.

6.1.1.5 Forms of Cooperative Enforcement

At the minimal end of the engagement 'continuum', a wide range of MCS measures are given effect on a regional basis, including some of the prescriptive measures outlined in Chapters 4 and 5 (such as the collective application of compliance conditions through harmonized minimum terms and conditions, vessel registers, and reporting requirements) and the establishment and operation of regional observer programmes and VMS.[92] This is particularly evident in the practice of developing

[88] See n 72 and associated text.

[89] See, eg, Kiribati, *Regs 2014* s 18; Tonga, *Act 2002* s 17; Vanuatu, *Regs 2009* s 13; Albania, *Law 64/2012* art 73.

[90] Although there are numerous references to the 'duty to cooperate' in the provisions of Part V relating to fisheries management, cooperation is not mentioned in the only provision specifically relating to enforcement.

[91] Stuart Kaye, 'Enforcement Cooperation in Combating Illegal and Unauthorized Fishing: An Assessment of Contemporary Practice' (2014) 32 BerkeleyJIntlL 316, 317–18.

[92] See Sections 4.3.2 and 5.2.7.

coastal States, many of whom have adopted national legislation that specifically provides for the integration of domestic measures with a broader system of MCS at bilateral, sub-regional, regional, and international levels,[93] the exchange of information and evidentiary material relating to fishing,[94] or the establishment of cooperative agreements or arrangements for joint or harmonized surveillance and enforcement in respect of foreign fishing vessels.[95] These forms of cooperation are implemented through agreements and arrangements adopted under the auspices of regional fisheries bodies,[96] and in some cases through the establishment of a specialized regional fisheries surveillance centre or integrated taskforce.[97]

Several of these cooperative surveillance and enforcement arrangements specifically embrace and encourage the adoption of advanced tools and technologies to combat illegal fishing, and utilize the remote detection techniques discussed above on a regional basis to maximize the fisheries surveillance and enforcement information that is available to their members.[98] In the western and central Pacific, for example, the Regional Fisheries Surveillance Centre (RFSC) at the Pacific Island Forum Fisheries Agency (FFA) integrates the flow of VMS data from the FFA and WCPFC systems with publicly available AIS data, and then assesses it against each FFA Member's fishing licence list, the WCPFC IUU Vessel List, individual fishing vessel log entries, flag State catch and effort reports, and FFA Member boarding reports to generate a 'regional surveillance picture', which is overlaid with manually generated risk assessments, before a specific 'compliance index' is assigned to each vessel. Each FFA member has the right to access information pertaining to its own EEZ and the high seas, which allows them to prioritize and target physical enforcement to areas or vessels that pose the most risk, and cooperate with other coastal States in the region to investigate and respond to suspicious activity.

At the maximum end of the continuum, coastal States have adopted cooperative approaches to physical at-sea enforcement, reflected in the legislation[99] and agreements put in place to enable the conduct of:

[93] Kenya *Act 2016* s 20; Togo, *Law 2016-026* art 16; Papua New Guinea, *Act 1998* s 37; Samoa, *Act 2016* s 17; Saint Kitts and Nevis, *Act 2016* s 15.

[94] Timor-Leste *Dec Law 2004* art 115; Eritrea, *Proc 176/2014* art 10(8); Senegal, *Code 2015* art 92; Nauru, *Act 1997* s 7; Australia, *Act 1991* s 108B.

[95] Seychelles *Act 2014* s 57; Vanuatu, *Act 2014* s 58; Dominica, *Act 1987* s 6; Grenada, *Act 1986* s 6; Saint Lucia, *Act 1984* s 6; Saint Vincent and the Grenadines, *Act 1986* s 6; United Kingdom (Montserrat), *Act 2000* s 22.

[96] These include the Niue Treaty Subsidiary Agreement, FFA Harmonized MTCs, SRFC MCA Convention, FCWC MRA Convention, SWIOFC MTCs, and SADC Protocol. See also Section 4.3.2.

[97] For example, the FFA Regional Fisheries Surveillance Centre located in Honiara, Solomon Islands; the FISH-i Africa Taskforce, which includes individuals representing fisheries agencies from seven countries in the western Indian Ocean (Comoros, Kenya, Madagascar, Mauritius, Mozambique, Seychelles, and Tanzania); and the West Africa Task Force, which is facilitated by the Secretariat of the Fisheries Committee for the West Central Gulf of Guinea (FCWC).

[98] See, eg, SADC Protocol art 9(1)(e); Niue Treaty Subsidiary Agreement Preamble [4].

[99] Gambia *Act 2007* s 70(1); Cook Islands, *Act 2005* s 45; Fiji, *Dec 2012* s 46; Marshall Islands, 51 *MIRC* §511; Micronesia, 24 *FSM Code* §602; Niue, *Act 1996* s 38; Samoa, *Act 2016* s 9; Tonga, *Act 2002* s 70; Tuvalu, *Act 2006* s 46(4)(b); Vanuatu, *Act 2014* s 108; Antigua and Barbuda, *Act 2006* s 61; Dominica, *Act 1987* s 26; Grenada, *Act 1986* s 27; Guyana, *Act 2012* s 4(3); Saint Kitts and Nevis, *Act 2016* s 82; Saint

- joint or 'harmonized' surveillance and enforcement operations, undertaken by a coastal State in cooperation with another ('assisting') State or States;[100]
- surveillance and enforcement activities in the waters of the coastal State, using the enforcement assets of an assisting State, carrying an authorized officer from the coastal State as a 'ship-rider'[101] or 'controller';[102] and
- surveillance and enforcement activities by an assisting State on behalf of the coastal State, including through the designation of officers from the assisting State as 'authorized officers' of the coastal State.[103]

In addition, cooperation in physical surveillance and enforcement activities is (like the employment of remote detection techniques) no longer simply a State-to-State activity; in recent years, the inadequate physical enforcement capacity of coastal States—particularly developing coastal States—has been supplemented through collaboration with private security contractors[104] and, increasingly, non-government organizations (NGOs). In the past, the at-sea activities of NGOs have included some unilateral 'direct enforcement' actions in relation to both whaling and fishing (including violence against vessels and persons),[105] which have suffered from problems of legitimacy and legality.[106] However, this can be overcome—in the

Lucia, *Act 1984* s 26; Saint Vincent and the Grenadines, *Act 1986* s 32; Australia, *Act 2013* s 104(2) and *Act 1991* s 84B; United Kingdom (Montserrat), *Act 2000* s 46.

[100] See, eg, SRFC MCA Convention art 25; SADC Protocol art 9(1)(b); Niue Treaty Subsidiary Agreement art 9(1).

[101] See, eg, the 'Shiprider Agreements' entered into by the United States, such as the *Maritime Interdiction Agreement between the United States of America and Kiribati Concerning Cooperation in Maritime Surveillance Operations* (signed and entered into force 24 November 2008) TIAS 08-1124.

[102] See, eg, the *Agreement on Cooperative Enforcement of Fisheries Laws between the Government of Australia and the Government of the French Republic in the Maritime Areas Adjacent to the French Southern and Antarctic Territories, Heard Islands and the McDonald Islands* (Australia-France Cooperative Enforcement Agreement) (signed 8 January 2007, entered into force 7 January 2011) [2011] ATS 1.

[103] See, eg, SADC Protocol art 9(1)(c)–(d); Niue Treaty Subsidiary Agreement art 10; *Agreement establishing common fisheries surveillance zones of participating member States of the Organization of Eastern Caribbean States* (signed and entered into force 1 March 1991) LEX-FAOC001087.

[104] In the 1990s and 2000s, several West African countries entered into contracts with private security companies for fisheries protection services, including boarding, inspection, arrest, and levying fines against foreign vessels for fisheries violations in the EEZ. While these services reportedly produced some short-term success, they did not evolve from 'short-term bounty hunting operations into mature and sustainable MCS programs': Patrick Cullen, 'Africa: Fisheries under PSC Watch' *ISN Security Watch, Centre for Security Studies* (ETHzurich), 11 November 2008, available at <http://css.ethz.ch/en/services/digital-library/articles/article.html/93699> accessed 20 January 2021.

[105] On the law of the sea aspects of direct enforcement and direct action protest, see generally: G Plant, 'International Law and Direct Action Protests at Sea: Twenty Years on' (2002) 33 NYIL 75; Debra Doby, 'Whale Wars: How to End the Violence on the High Seas' (2013) 44 JMarL&Com 135.

[106] There is no 'private right' of enforcement under the LOSC: Donald K Anton, 'Protecting Whales by Hue and Cry: Is There a Role for Non-State Actors in the Enforcement of International Law?' (2011) 14(2) JIntlWildlifeL&Pol 137, 142–3. Accordingly, unilateral enforcement actions by NGOs have been criticized by governments, and given rise to charges of piracy and violence at sea, such as those considered in *Institute of Cetacean Research v Sea Shepherd Conservation Society* 708 F.3d 1099 (C.A.9 (Wash.) 2013).

EEZ, at least—through partnership with a coastal State, as reflected in the steady growth of cooperative enforcement operations undertaken between coastal States and NGOs over the last two decades, which have resulted in successful enforcement outcomes in relation to illegal foreign fishing in the EEZs of several coastal States.[107]

6.1.1.6 Formalities of Cooperative Enforcement

Since the LOSC does not directly address the conduct of cooperative fisheries law enforcement—whether through inter-State cooperation or public-private partnerships—it is, as ITLOS concluded in the *Virginia G* case, for the coastal State to decide which authorities will be responsible under its national law for exercising enforcement activities pursuant to Article 73(1).[108] However, ITLOS also found that 'general international law' requires that enforcement activities pursuant to Article 73(1) are exercised only by 'duly authorized identifiable officials of a coastal State' and that their vessels must be 'clearly marked as being on government service'.[109] While these requirements are specifically expressed to apply to some enforcement activities under the LOSC, they are not referred to in Article 73(1).[110] In practice, however, they seem both necessary and reasonable in the context of any form of enforcement at sea—whether or not relating to fisheries or carried out under Article 73(1)—and give effect to the idea that international law requires a clear and transparent delegation of authority.[111]

The requirement that powers only be exercised by 'duly authorized identifiable officials' ensures that coercive measures are only taken by those who are vested with the imprimatur of the coastal State and authorized to act on its behalf, whose actions can be properly attributed to the competent State.[112] The question of exactly *who* is duly authorized remains within the discretion of the coastal State, and there

[107] Since 2014, the Sea Shepherd Conservation Society and Greenpeace have been conducting fisheries surveillance and enforcement operations in cooperation with coastal States (including Benin, Gabon, Gambia, Guinea, Guinea-Bissau, Liberia, Namibia, Sao Tome and Principe, Senegal, Sierra Leone, Tanzania, and Timor-Leste) resulting in numerous inspections and arrests. See further Guggisberg, 'The Roles of Nongovernmental Actors in Improving Compliance' (n 69) 321; Valentin Schatz, 'Marine Fisheries Law Enforcement Partnerships in Waters under National Jurisdiction: The Legal Framework for Inter-State Cooperation and Public-Private Partnerships with Non-Governmental Organizations and Private Security Companies' (2018) 32 Ocean YB 329, 343–4.

[108] *Virginia G* [345].

[109] Ibid [342].

[110] In contrast, see the requirements for the conduct of enforcement activities in LOSC arts 107 (the seizure of pirate ships), 110 (the right of visit), 111 (hot pursuit), and 224 (enforcement of marine pollution measures). Like the threshold for boarding and inspection (discussed in n 53), this distinction is likely because the requirements for non-flag State enforcement beyond the EEZ (or within the EEZ where the coastal State is not enforcing 'sovereign rights') are more stringent than those for coastal State enforcement of sovereign rights in its EEZ.

[111] Andreas Fischer-Lescano and Lena Kreck, 'Piracy and Human Rights: Legal Issues in the Fight Against Piracy within the Context of the European Operation Atalanta' (2009) 52 GYIL 525, 548.

[112] See arts 2 and 4 of the 'Articles on the Responsibility of States for Internationally Wrongful Acts', *Report of the International Law Commission on the Work of its 53rd Session (23 April–1 June and 2 July–10 August 2001)* UN Doc A/56/589, 6.

is nothing to prevent coastal States from designating persons from other States or from private sector organizations or NGOs as 'authorized officials' under their national legislation for this purpose.

The requirement that vessels be clearly marked as being on government service is equally important, in order to avoid any incidents that might result from misunderstandings about the role or power of the vessel:[113] in short, 'it must be possible for the vessel being policed to ascertain without difficulty whether or not the vessel carrying out the policing activity is empowered to carry it out'.[114] Once again, the question of exactly how this is implemented remains within the discretion of the coastal State, provided that the vessel being targeted is able to easily ascertain from the vessel's markings that it is on government service and authorized to exercise the powers asserted in the circumstances of the case. As Schatz concludes, while the requirements established by ITLOS in the *Virginia G* case pose no 'insurmountable hurdles' to fisheries enforcement being undertaken through inter-State or public-private partnerships, 'scarce visual and other evidence available suggests that past activities of States and private actors alike possibly have fallen short of fulfilling the requirement in a number of cases'.[115] In light of the increasing incidence of arrests being undertaken in the context of cooperative enforcement operations, it seems likely that these issues will, at some point, come to be considered by a dispute settlement body.

6.2.4 Judicial Enforcement: Proving Fisheries Offences

The other aspect of enforcement directly addressed in Article 73(1) is judicial proceedings. While the LOSC does not specify any particular obligations of process or procedure in respect of the conduct of fisheries proceedings by a coastal State, ITLOS has emphasized in several cases that they must be consistent with 'international standards of due process' and 'elementary considerations of humanity'.[116] Although ITLOS has not given any indication as to the exact standards to be applied in this respect, it has been interpreted in the literature as a requirement to comply with human rights norms relating to the right to a fair trial,[117] which is

[113] For example, in the *Juno Trader* case, the master of the *Juno Trader* concluded that he was under pirate attack when approached by a speed boat with no distinctive markings of any kind, carrying one man in camouflage and four in civilian clothing. While this issue did not arise for consideration by ITLOS, the Applicant suggested that the Tribunal should 'recognize formally that vessels may not be boarded in the [EEZ] in just any way, by just anybody and using any means whatever': *ITLOS Pleadings, Minutes of Public Sittings and Documents* (2004) Vol 12 *"Juno Trader" (Saint Vincent and the Grenadines v Guinea-Bissau)* (Application of Saint Vincent and the Grenadines) [75]–[100].

[114] Tullio Treves, 'Navigation' in Rene-Jean Dupuy and Daniel Vignes (eds), *A Handbook on the New Law of the Sea, Vol II* (Martinus Nijhoff 1991) 900.

[115] Schatz, 'Marine Fisheries Law Enforcement Partnerships' (n 107) 365.

[116] *Juno Trader* [77]; *Tomimaru* [76] and [79]; *Virginia G* [254].

[117] Harrison, 'Safeguards Against Excessive Enforcement Measures' (n 26) 242.

generally accepted to include basic objective standards such as access to the courts, a fair and public hearing by a competent, independent, and impartial tribunal, the opportunity for the defendant to be fully informed of the charges and to state and defend his or her case, and the presumption of innocence.[118] As Harrison has noted, this indication that ITLOS may be willing to step into national courtrooms to assess whether or not domestic courts are complying with relevant standards of due process appears to introduce an additional safeguard on the exercise of coastal State powers, 'extending beyond the outcome of proceedings to the actual process itself'.[119]

6.2.4.1 The Use of Presumptions

While standards and procedures for proving an offence differ widely around the world, most legal systems require the prosecution to submit sufficient, reliable evidence to establish the elements of the offence with the requisite level of certainty.[120] However, since fisheries offences commonly involve facts that are very difficult to prove—including because of the difficulty and expense of gathering evidence in relation to activities at sea—coastal States have developed a range of carefully drafted evidentiary rules to help improve the chances of successfully prosecuting violations of their fisheries laws.[121] This includes the widespread employment of 'rebuttable presumptions' to shift the burden of proof from the prosecution to the defendant in relation to questions of fact that are difficult for the prosecution to prove (but easy for an innocent defendant to dis-prove). Such presumptions are used by coastal States in a wide range of practical situations, and particularly:

- where the coastal State seeks to exert a preventive or deterrent effect by making contingent assertions of jurisdiction through rebuttable presumption, such as the variety of presumptions that are used in relation to the transit of unlicensed foreign fishing vessels through the EEZ;[122] and
- where direct eyewitness evidence is not available or not sufficient, and expert evidence would otherwise be required to support the reliability of data or information derived by technical means such as VMS data, aerial or satellite photographs, or information from other devices that are recognized as 'notoriously accurate'.[123]

[118] See Human Rights Committee, *General Comment No.32—Article 14: Right to equality before courts and tribunals and to a fair trial* UN Doc. CCPR/C/GC/32 (2007).
[119] Harrison, 'Safeguards Against Excessive Enforcement Measures' (n 26) 242.
[120] Flewwelling et al, 'Recent Trends in MCS Systems' (n 61) 26.
[121] Ibid.
[122] See Table 5.1 and the discussion in Section 5.2.6 on the use of presumptions to regulate unlicensed vessels in transit.
[123] See nn 79–89 and associated text.

The legitimacy of using statutory presumptions in this way is demonstrated in the widespread practice of coastal States and confirmed in the literature,[124] and although there is no clear jurisprudence on this question, it has not been criticized by an international court or tribunal.[125]

However, a few notes of caution should be sounded. First, a rebuttable presumption should only be applied on the basis of perceived facts that make it reasonable.[126] In other words, while it is reasonable to employ presumptions in relation to situations where a vessel has done something that is prima facie illegal (such as failing to notify entry to the EEZ, or failing to stow gear), presumptions should not be applied to situations of mere fact that are not, of themselves and without more, illegal (such as the possession of fish).[127] Second, since presumptions constitute a reversal of the burden of proof—and, effectively, the presumption of innocence—they must be designed and drafted in a way that reasonably enables the defendant to use the information legitimately at his or her disposal to prove innocence. In this regard, if an offence is drafted in overly broad or vague terms, it may transfer an unreasonable burden of proof to the defendant, or remove the presumption of innocence entirely.[128] For example, if a statute were to provide that an offence will be presumed to have been committed by a vessel found in the EEZ of the coastal State unless it is acting 'in accordance with international law', the burden would transfer to the defendant to prove that the vessel was acting legally—that it was exercising a right conferred by international law—rather than the State being required to articulate the specific grounds of illegality or describe the elements of the offence.[129] Consideration of these issues should help to ensure that the offences established and enforced by coastal States meet both the test of 'reasonableness' under Article 73 of the LOSC, and the requirements of due process and a fair trial under general international law.

6.2.4.2 Civil and Administrative Proceedings

Of course, violations of fisheries law do not have to be dealt with through criminal—or even 'judicial'—proceedings. While there is no guidance in the LOSC

[124] William T Burke, 'Fisheries Regulations Under Extended Jurisdiction and International Law' *FAO Fisheries Technical Paper No 223* (FAO 1982) 15; David Freestone, 'The Burden of Proof in National Resources Legislation: Some Critical Issues for Fisheries Law' *FAO Legislative Study 63* (FAO 1998) 9.

[125] The Applicant questioned the legitimacy of the statutory presumptions underlying the factual scenarios in *Camouco* and *Monte Confurco*, but the question was not addressed by the Tribunal (although it was raised, to divergent effect, in dissenting opinions in *Monte Confurco*: (Diss Op Anderson) 131 ('rebuttable presumptions serve, in practice, to protect loaded fishing vessels in transit through an EEZ'); (Diss Op Laing) 135 (national laws are not in conformity with the LOSC 'if proof of their violation is adduced through legal presumptions').

[126] Burke, 'Fisheries Regulations Under Extended Jurisdiction' (n 124) 15.

[127] Flewwelling et al, 'Recent Trends in MCS Systems' (n 61) 27.

[128] Freestone, The Burden of Proof' (n 124) 9.

[129] As Freestone notes, it is 'highly debatable whether an individual can legitimately be required to prove that he is exercising a right conferred by international law' which would involve establishing the content of international law: ibid.

regarding the sort of proceedings that can or should be adopted by coastal States in dealing with fisheries offences (other than the requirements of 'necessity' and 'reasonableness' generally applied to Article 73), the IPOA-IUU notes that they 'may include the adoption of a civil sanction regime based on an administrative penalty scheme',[130] and in practice a growing number of States have shown interest in the alternative forms of enforcement that may be available.[131]

Some coastal States choose to avoid the difficulties and expense of a criminal trial by establishing civil or administrative penalties for fisheries violations. This typically involves details of the alleged violation being provided to the offender, along with an indication of the penalties likely to be imposed, leading to a civil or administrative hearing, or the negotiation of a settlement.[132] Another approach is to provide for the 'compounding' of offences (sometimes described in civil law countries as a 'transactional procedure'),[133] which entails vesting powers in an authorized person (usually the relevant Minister or chief executive of the fisheries department) who can decide to accept a specific sum of money from the offender if it is believed that an offence has been committed—usually not less than a specified minimum amount, or more than the maximum applicable fine.[134]

While civil and administrative hearings can provide flexibility in respect of evidentiary issues, lower the standard of proof, and expedite the time required to deal with fisheries offences,[135] due process requirements still apply, and as a minimum, 'the master of the vessel should be informed of the reasons for the detention and be given an opportunity to present an account of the circumstances before any further administrative decisions are taken.'[136]

6.3 Flag State Interests: Prompt Release, Penalties, and Notification (Article 73(2)–(4))

While the first paragraph of Article 73 establishes a broad array of enforcement measures that may be applied by the coastal State, paragraphs 2 to 4 protect the interests of the *flag State* through a range of safeguards designed to ensure that the coastal State's measures: 'will not have the effect of limiting the freedom of the

130 IPOA-IUU [21].

131 Phillippe Cacaud et al, 'Administrative Sanctions in Fisheries Law' *FAO Legislative Study* 82 (FAO 2003) 1.

132 On the use of civil and administrative penalties for fisheries offences, see Blaise Kuemlangan, 'National Legislative Options to Combat IUU Fishing' in *Report of and Papers Presented at the Expert Consultation on Illegal, Unreported and Unregulated Fishing, Sydney, Australia, 15-19 May 2000, FAO Fisheries Report 666* (FAO 2001) [48]–[58].

133 Cacaud et al, 'Administrative Sanctions' (n 131) 51.

134 The legal effects of 'compounding' an offence vary; they may preclude the institution of legal proceedings, constitute a 'defence' to relevant charges, or have the effect of an acquittal: ibid 52.

135 Kuemlangan, 'National Legislative Options' (n 132) [46].

136 David Anderson, *Modern Law of the Sea: Selected Essays* (Martinus Nijhoff 2008) 562.

persons involved (prompt release of the crew, prohibition of imprisonment as a penalty), and of unduly jeopardizing the rights of shipowners and of the flag State (prompt release of the vessel), while ensuring timely protective action by the flag State (obligation to notify in case of arrest and of the imposing of penalties).'[137] These safeguards are enhanced by the inclusion of a specific dispute settlement procedure in Article 292(1), which can be employed where a coastal State fails to comply with the substantive requirement for prompt release under Article 73(2).

In practice, the various aspects of Article 73 are closely connected and impact upon each other. For example, failure to notify the flag State of a vessel's arrest or detention as required by Article 73(4) can have a direct bearing on its ability to invoke the prompt release procedure under Article 73(2), and decisions by ITLOS under Article 292(1) regarding what constitutes a 'reasonable bond or other security' under Article 73(2) commonly involve consideration of the type and level of penalties that may be applied by coastal States consistent with Article 73(3) and the overriding requirements of reasonableness and necessity that apply to the whole of Article 73. Applications for the prompt release of vessels under Articles 73(2) and 292 have also proved to be one of the 'main attractions' of ITLOS[138] and one of the main sources of jurisprudence on Part V of the LOSC,[139] particularly given the limited circumstances in relation to which compulsory dispute settlement applies.[140]

6.3.1 Prompt Release on a Reasonable Bond (Article 73(2))

Once the coastal State has exercised its broad powers of arrest under Article 73(1) of the LOSC, Article 73(2) requires that arrested vessels and their crews be 'promptly released upon the posting of reasonable bond or other security'. As shown in Table 6.1, the fisheries legislation of most coastal States enables—or requires—the release of foreign fishing vessels and their crew on provision of an adequate bond or security.[141] However, in order to properly understand the nature and extent of coastal State jurisdiction, three issues must be considered. First, when and how does the

[137] *Juno Trader* (Sep Op Treves) [2].

[138] Erik Franckx, '"Reasonable Bond" in the Practice of the International Tribunal for the Law of the Sea' (2002) 32 CalWIntlLJ 303, 304.

[139] Nine of the twenty-nine cases so far brought before ITLOS have been prompt release cases instituted under art 292, all of which were (allegedly) founded on a failure to comply with art 73(2).

[140] Pursuant to art 298(1)(b) States may, by written declaration, exclude disputes concerning law enforcement activities relating to the exercise of sovereign rights with respect to living resources in the EEZ from compulsory settlement. However, if the dispute relates to allegations that a coastal State's law enforcement activity contravened the freedoms and rights of navigation in the EEZ as described in art 297(1)(a), compulsory dispute settlement does apply. On compulsory dispute settlement in relation to Part V, see Section 2.1.2.

[141] This book is focused on fisheries and maritime zone legislation, but criminal and procedural laws may also contain relevant provisions, particularly with respect to the release of crew.

obligation to release arise? Second, how is the 'reasonableness' of the bond to be determined? And third, to what extent does the practice and the jurisprudence on the interpretation and application of Article 73(2) maintain, develop, or alter the balance of interests between coastal and flag States in the EEZ?

6.3.1.1 The Obligation to Release

Very little has been written about the practical implementation of the prompt release requirement. On one view, the coastal State 'is under an obligation to set a bond'[142] and 'must offer to promptly release the vessels or crews'.[143] However, since the LOSC does not establish a precise procedure to be followed in giving effect to Article 73(2), it falls within the discretion of the coastal State to determine the most appropriate process in accordance with its national law, and practice varies.[144] The fisheries legislation of coastal States commonly provides for arrested foreign fishing vessels to be released upon 'application' or 'request' by the owner, operator, master, or local representative of the vessel, and following the provision of adequate security. For example, pursuant to Section 55 of Namibia's *Marine Resources Act 2000*:

> (4) The Minister may, upon application by the owner, the lessee, the charterer or the master of a foreign flag vessel seized under section 5(2)(b)(i), whether or not together with any fishing gear or marine resources on board of the vessel, direct that the vessel in question or all or any of the said property on board of it, or such vessel together with all or any of such property, be released to the owner, the lessee, the charterer or the master in question, subject to such conditions as the Minister may determine.
>
> (5) The Minister shall not exercise the power conferred by subsection (4) unless the owner, the lessee, the charterer or the master in question furnishes the Minister with a guarantee, approved by the Minister, securing the payment to the State, in accordance with subsection (6) (a) of an amount equal to the reasonable value, as the case may be, of the vessel or the fishing gear, marine resources or the vessel and such property, sought to be released.

Similar provisions are found in the legislation of coastal States in Africa, the Asia-Pacific, Latin America and the Caribbean, and the Western Europe and Others Group.[145] While this supports the conclusion that Article 73(2) does not require the coastal State to initiate the process for setting any bond required to release a vessel, the minimum extent of the coastal State's obligation must be to discuss and

[142] Harrison, 'Safeguards Against Excessive Enforcement Measures' (n 26) 232.

[143] James Harrison, 'Article 73' in Alexander Proelss (ed), *United Nations Convention on the Law of the Sea: A Commentary* (CH Beck 2017) 559.

[144] *Virginia G* [284]–[285].

[145] See Table 6.1.

set a bond if requested by the flag State, vessel owner, or other relevant party.[146] In this respect, although the bond must be set within a reasonable period of time,[147] the requirement of prompt release does not give rise to a 'precise time limit'.[148]

However, the fisheries legislation of some coastal States requires—or authorizes—the vessel to be detained until all proceedings have been concluded and all costs, penalties, and fines paid, or provide for an exception to the release of the vessel 'if it might be required as an exhibit in court proceedings, or is required for further investigations'.[149] Notwithstanding the way in which these provisions might be justified or categorized under the coastal State's national law, if they were relied on to deny the prompt release of a vessel, it is likely that an international court or tribunal would find them inconsistent with the direct duty of prompt release under Articles 73(2) and 292.[150]

6.3.1.2 The 'Reasonableness' of the Bond

In many instances, the question at issue in a prompt release application under Article 73(2) is not the coastal State's refusal to set a bond, but the flag State's view that the bond that has been set is not 'reasonable'.[151] While Articles 73(2) and 292(1) require that the bond or security fixed by the coastal State be 'reasonable', the LOSC does not give any further indications as to how this notion is to be applied or assessed in practice. Nor can additional guidance be gleaned from the ITLOS Rules, which simply refer back to Article 292.[152] Accordingly, while 'the reasonableness of a bond or other security can never be proved from an objective point of view',[153] it nonetheless falls to the competent international courts and tribunals to give 'concrete content' to the standard of reasonableness required by Article 73(2).[154]

ITLOS has outlined a range of factors to be taken into account in determining the reasonableness of a bond, which include the gravity of the offence, the penalties imposable under the laws of the coastal State, the value of the vessel and cargo (including fish and fishing gear), and the amount of the bond imposed and its form.[155] It is also clear that this is not a complete list of factors, there are no rigid rules as to

[146] The coastal State also has an obligation under art 73(4) to 'promptly notify' the flag State, through appropriate channels, of any action taken and of any penalties subsequently imposed.

[147] *'Hoshinmaru' (Japan v Russian Federation)* (Prompt Release, Judgment) (2005–2007) ITLOS Rep 18 [80] (*Hoshinmaru*).

[148] *Camouco* [54]. However, see Judge Tuerk's suggestion that a maximum period of one month would be reasonable: *Hoshinmaru* (Dec Tuerk) [3].

[149] See Table 6.1.

[150] See *Camouco* (Dec Laing) 41.

[151] This was the case in *Camouco*, *Monte Confurco*, *Volga*, and *Hoshinmaru*.

[152] *Rules of the Tribunal* (adopted 28 October 1997, last amended 25 September 2020) ITLOS/8, art 113.

[153] Shigeru Oda, 'Fisheries under the United Nations Convention on the Law of the Sea' (1983) 77 AJIL 739, 749.

[154] Bernard H Oxman, 'Observations on Vessel Release under the United Nations Convention on the Law of the Sea' (1996) 11 IJMCL 201, 309.

[155] *Camouco* [67].

the exact weight to be attached to each of them, and they must be assessed objectively, taking into account all information.[156] However, ITLOS has repeatedly emphasized that 'the amount of the bond should be proportionate to the gravity of the alleged offences',[157] established 'by reference to the penalties imposed or imposable under the laws of the detaining State'.[158]

ITLOS has also set down some rules regarding factors and forms that should *not* be used in setting a bond under Article 73(2). For example, notwithstanding the importance of penalties to determining the gravity of the offence, the bond 'should not be set on the basis of the maximum penalties which could be applicable',[159] and 'the value of the vessel alone may not be the controlling factor in the determination of the bond or other financial security.'[160] In addition, matters relating to the circumstances of the seizure of the vessel are not relevant to prompt release proceedings, and cannot be taken into account in determining the reasonableness of the bond.[161] Finally, ITLOS has found that the term 'bond or other security' in Article 73(2) should be interpreted as referring to 'a bond or security of a financial nature', and that non-financial conditions—or conditions intended as a 'good behaviour bond' to prevent future violations of the coastal State's laws—cannot be required.[162]

While it is clear that the reasonableness of a bond is to be assessed by reference to these components on a case-by-case basis, as Harrison has observed, it is less clear what standard of review the Tribunal is applying.[163] For example, despite having stated that it is 'not an appellate forum against a decision of a national court',[164] in some cases the Tribunal has disavowed findings of national judges,[165] and come 'perilously close' to entering into the merits of a case.[166] Moreover, having clearly established the factors to be considered in setting a bond, in practice the Tribunal has not indicated how the various factors have been weighed or applied in a particular case, but has simply substituted its own (lower) figure for that set by the coastal State without further explanation.[167] As such, the approach adopted by ITLOS has provided limited clarity for coastal States regarding the practical task of establishing a 'reasonable bond' under Article 73(2).[168]

[156] *Monte Confurco* [76]; *Juno Trader* [85].
[157] *Hoshinmaru* [88]. Similarly, *Monte Confurco* [73]; *Juno Trader* [89].
[158] Ibid; *Volga* [69].
[159] *Hoshinmaru* [93].
[160] *Camouco* [69].
[161] *Volga* [83]; *Juno Trader* [95].
[162] *Volga* [77] and [80].
[163] Harrison, 'Safeguards Against Excessive Enforcement Measures' (n 26) 234.
[164] *Monte Confurco* [72].
[165] Franckx, 'Reasonable Bond' (n 138) 32.
[166] *Monte Confurco* (Dec Mensah) [1].
[167] For example, in the *Camouco*, *Monte Confurco*, and *Hoshinmaru* cases, the Tribunal reduced the bonds set by the coastal State by between 30 per cent and 60 per cent.
[168] Franckx, 'Reasonable Bond' (n 138) 335 and fn 207, who notes that 'publicists and judges have repeatedly pointed to this lack of clarity' and cites a wide range of such criticisms.

Although it is difficult to examine the actual bonds set by coastal States for the release of foreign fishing vessels,[169] it is possible to examine the underlying legislation. While some States simply provide that foreign vessels and their crews shall be released upon posting a 'reasonable bond or other security',[170] most legislation establishes a framework within which bonds are to be determined by reference to the components established by ITLOS—namely, the gravity of the offence as reflected in the fine, and the value of the vessel and cargo. In the legislation of many States this framework also includes additional components, some of which appear to depart from the jurisprudence outlined above. In particular, as shown in Table 6.1:

- some States specify that the bond is to be calculated by having regard to[171]—or set at a figure not less than[172]—the maximum applicable fine for the offence or offences charged or likely to be charged;
- some States require that the bond include some or all of: the costs incurred in arresting and detaining the vessel and repatriating the crew; the costs likely to be recovered by the prosecution; and any damages and costs assessed as a consequence of the offence;[173] and
- some States specifically prescribe the amount of the bond in the legislation,[174] or direct the way in which it is to be calculated,[175] while others leave it completely to the discretion of the court or relevant authority.[176]

In addition, some of the provisions in national legislation appear to constitute pre-emptive measures that might, to a certain extent, overcome the limitations imposed by ITLOS in relation to prompt release. For example, a number of coastal States—particularly in Africa and the Asia-Pacific—require the deposit of a bond *in advance* of fishing activity, so that it can be used to defray the costs of fines, penalties or compensation in the event an offence is committed.[177] A potentially more controversial approach is taken in Libya, which requires various documents to be deposited with the coastal State prior to fishing, including the original vessel papers, and the passports of the master and crew.[178] These pre-emptive measures (or

[169] In many instances, the relevant Government official or Minister sets the bond within the framework established in the legislation and then advises the vessel owner or representative. Accordingly, the amount (or form) of the bond is often not made publicly available, unless it is challenged through administrative or judicial processes, which may not themselves be publicly reported.
[170] See Table 6.1.
[171] See, eg, Mauritius, *Act 2007* art 65(3).
[172] See, eg, South Africa, *Act 1998* s 62(2).
[173] See, eg, United Kingdom (Falkland Islands), *Ordinance 2005* s 157(1); Kenya, *Act 2016* s 169(1); Brunei, *Order 2009* s 51(2).
[174] See, eg, Trinidad and Tobago, *Act 1986* s 28.
[175] See, eg, Sri Lanka, *Act 1979* s 21.
[176] See, eg, Samoa, *Act 2016* s 57(2).
[177] See, eg, Liberia, *Law 2019* s 5.14.
[178] Libya, *Res 71 of 1990* arts 43 and 46.

'performance bonds') effectively allow the coastal State to set a bond in any form and at any level of its choosing—although of course they only apply in relation to vessels operating in the EEZ pursuant to a licence or access agreement with the coastal State.[179] In this respect, they demonstrate the possibility for coastal States to use their prescriptive jurisdiction under Article 62(4) innovatively in order to mitigate the limitations that may be imposed on their enforcement jurisdiction under Article 73.

Of course, it is also possible that a vessel owner (or a flag State) may not take issue with the reasonableness of a bond set by a coastal State, even if it falls outside some of the guidelines established in the jurisprudence, and the standards accepted by States may change over time. For example, ITLOS found in 2002 that Australia's requirement that the *Volga* carry a fully operational VMS until the conclusion of the legal proceedings was inconsistent with Article 73(2) on the basis that a bond could not include non-financial components.[180] However, since both flag and coastal States now generally require the carriage of such systems, a requirement of this sort might now be more acceptable, and other vessel owners (and their flag States) have subsequently accepted the imposition of such a condition as part of a bond.[181] There is nothing to prevent coastal States from seeking to include additional conditions as part of a bond for the release of a vessel—particularly in the context of broader or long standing relations with the relevant flag State as regards fisheries[182]—but the risk nonetheless remains that the other party will apply the prompt release procedure under Article 292 and seek to invoke the limitations previously applied by ITLOS.

6.3.1.3 The Balance of Interests

Regardless of which components are relied on by the coastal State in setting the amount and form of the bond, ITLOS has made clear that the guiding criterion in assessing its reasonableness is the 'balance of interests' emerging from Articles 73 and 292 of the LOSC.[183] In this respect, the Tribunal has found that the central objective is 'to reconcile the interest of the flag State to have its vessel and its crew released promptly with the interest of the detaining State to secure appearance in its court of the Master and the payment of penalties.'[184] However, this formulation

[179] See Chapter 4 n 40 and associated text.

[180] *Volga* [77] and [80].

[181] For example, in December 2016 the owners of the Papua New Guinea-flagged fishing vessel *CAPS 01* posted a bond for the return of their vessel on the condition that its location could be monitored by Australia's satellite-based tracking system: Australian Fisheries Management Authority, 'Record Penalties for Illegal Foreign Fisherman' 13 December 2016, available at <http://afma.gov.au/record-penalties-illegal-foreign-fisherman/> accessed 22 January 2021.

[182] As the majority observed in *Hoshinmaru*, 'between States that have long standing relations as regards fisheries, an agreed procedure for setting bonds in the event of the detention of fishing vessels may contribute to mutual confidence, help resolve misunderstandings and prevent disputes': *Hoshinmaru* [85]–[86].

[183] *Monte Confurco* [72].

[184] Ibid [71]. See also the interests identified in *Camouco* [57].

does not acknowledge the full range of interests that are implicitly affected—but not explicitly *balanced*—by the prompt release of vessels under Article 73(2).

First, it fails to recognize the broader interests and, importantly, *obligations* of the coastal State with respect to the conservation and management of the living resources of the EEZ, and thus risks creating a situation where the 'ceiling' imposed to limit the exercise of the coastal State's rights is lower than the 'floor' which it must meet to fulfil its obligations.[185] Second, a purely bilateral formulation of prompt release—cognisant only of the interests of the coastal State and flag State involved—fails to recognize the more complex range of interests affected by prompt release, which include the private rights of vessel owners,[186] and the common interests of the international community with respect to the protection of the marine environment and the conservation of living marine resources.[187] In particular, by failing to take account of the practical issues associated with IUU fishing, it risks interpreting Article 73(2) in a way that fails to take account of the broader 'mischief' that the LOSC seeks to address.[188]

In this respect, as Churchill has observed, 'while ITLOS pays lip service to the need to combat the evils of IUU fishing ... it does not always seem sufficiently aware of how some IUU fishing is conducted and thus what the appropriate penalties should be for those vessels that are caught.[189] This is reflected in the approach taken in the *Volga* case, in which the majority decision contained a mere two sentences giving the Tribunal's views on the importance of the factual circumstances underlying the case, stating simply that: 'The Tribunal takes note of the submissions of the Respondent. The Tribunal understands the international concerns about illegal, unregulated and unreported fishing and appreciates the objectives behind the measures taken by States, including the States Parties to CCAMLR, to deal with the problem.'[190]

However, as a number of judges pointed out in individual declarations or dissents,[191] Australia had put forward a significant amount of uncontested evidence

[185] Since the release of vessels and crews relates directly to law enforcement activities with regard to the exercise of the coastal State's sovereign rights, the question of prompt release 'cannot be an issue isolated from these fundamental questions, which relate to the competence of the coastal State with respect to fisheries in the [EEZ]': Shigeru Oda, 'Dispute Settlement Prospects in the Law of the Sea' (1995) 44 ICLQ 863, 866.

[186] Chester Brown, '"Reasonableness" in the Law of the Sea: The Prompt Release of the Volga' (2003) 16(3) LJIL 621, 629–30.

[187] Seline Trevisanut, 'Twenty Years of Prompt Release of Vessels: Admissibility, Jurisdiction, and Recent Trends' (2017) 48 ODIL 300, 302.

[188] Brown, '"Reasonableness" in the Law of the Sea' (n 186) 628.

[189] Robin Rolf Churchill, 'Dispute Settlement under the UN Convention on the Law of the Sea: Survey for 2007' (2008) 23 IJMCL 601, 610.

[190] *Volga* [68]. 'CCAMLR' (Commission on the Conservation of Antarctic Marine Living Resources) is a regional organization with responsibility for the conservation of marine living resources in the Antarctic.

[191] *Volga* (Diss Op Anderson) [22]–[23], (Dec Marsit) [2]–[3], (Diss Op Shearer) [17], (Sep Op Cot) [2]–[13].

about the factual circumstances of the case, which showed that: the risk of the *Volga* reoffending was real; that it was not acting alone, but was part of a broader fleet of vessels being actively directed by the vessel owners to conduct illegal fishing activities in the Australian EEZ; that the illegal fishing in question was of significant concern to the international community; and that it is difficult and expensive for coastal States to combat such activities. Notwithstanding this evidence, the Tribunal continued to apply the 'guiding criterion' of balancing the flag State's interest in the vessel's release with the coastal State's interest in securing its appearance in court, and found that the bond imposed by Australia was not 'reasonable'.

As the facts in *Volga* show, the 'balance of interests' performed in a prompt release case does not necessarily involve the interests of a flag State exercising responsibility for a vessel and crew with whom it has a genuine connection and effective control, but may effectively relate to the private claim of the vessel owner. In this respect, the stipulation in Article 292(2) that a prompt release application may be brought 'by or on behalf of' the flag State reflects the fact that it was originally drafted as a mechanism for 'the owner or operator of the vessel' to invoke the assistance of ITLOS.[192] This has been borne out in practice, with the majority of advocacy in prompt release cases being effected by private lawyers retained by vessel owners, rather than government lawyers from the flag State.[193]

In addition, while ITLOS has expressed the view that the coastal State's interest in the prompt release procedure is to enable it 'to secure appearance in its court of the Master and the payment of penalties',[194] in practice there is an inherent tension between the effective prosecution of illegal fishing and the possibility of using prompt release proceedings to enable a vessel to escape prosecution.[195] For example, of the eighteen fishing vessel masters arrested for illegal fishing in the French EEZ between 1997 and 2001, only one was able to be tried and punished, the rest having been released on bond and not returned for trial.[196]

ITLOS' approach to the balancing of coastal and flag State interests under Article 73(2)—and particularly its judgment in the *Volga* case—has been widely criticized as inappropriately favouring flag States, which arguably have limited practical interest in the outcome.[197] However, commentators have also argued that the binary 'balance of interests' approach employed by ITLOS is simply the 'product of compromise' between the rights of coastal and flag States under the LOSC, and is

[192] Satya Nandan and Shabtai Rosenne (eds), *United Nations Convention on the Law of the Sea 1982: A Commentary, Vol V* (Martinus Nijhoff 1989) 67.

[193] *Volga* (Diss Op Shearer) 72.

[194] *Monte Confurco* [71].

[195] Guilfoyle, *Shipping Interdiction* (n 40) 153.

[196] *ITLOS Pleadings, Minutes of Public Sittings and Documents, Vol 6* (2000) *Monte Confurco (Seychelles v France)* Verbatim Record of the Public Sitting held on 7 December 2000 at 3:15 pm, 6.

[197] See, eg, Brown, '"Reasonableness" in the Law of the Sea' (n 186) 630; Baird, 'IUU Fishing' (n 12) 321; Rothwell and Stephens, 'Illegal Southern Ocean Fishing and Prompt Release' (n 38) 183–4; Churchill, 'The Jurisprudence of ITLOS Relating to Fisheries' (n 38) 410. See also *Volga* (Diss Op Shearer) [19], (Diss Op Anderson) [63]–[64].

an appropriate counterbalance to the 'creeping jurisdiction' of coastal States.[198] On this view, prompt release is not intended to ensure the conservation and optimum utilization of the living resources of the EEZ or the effective enforcement of coastal State regulations, or address the problem of IUU fishing, but simply to secure the release of a vessel and crew on the posting of a reasonable bond.[199]

Of course, the standard for measuring what is 'necessary' or 'reasonable' always involves consideration of the balance of interests involved, and whether or how the actions of one party impair the freedoms of another. The key question is: are the right interests being balanced, and is it appropriate to balance them equally?[200] In this context, it is worth noting that all the existing jurisprudence on Article 73(2) prompt release dates from one ten year period, between 1997 and 2007.[201] While there has not been a prompt release case since 2007, there has been a significant amount of jurisprudence on other issues relating to the rights and responsibilities of both coastal and flag States, which might usefully inform consideration of the balance of interests in any future prompt release cases.

In particular, the balance of interests in prompt release could be informed by the standards of flag State responsibility established in the *SRFC Advisory Opinion*, in which ITLOS determined that the flag State 'has the obligation to take necessary measures, including those of enforcement, to ensure compliance by vessels flying its flag with the laws and regulations' of the coastal State and, where it is informed of illegal activities by its vessels must 'take any action necessary to remedy the situation as well as inform the reporting State of that action'.[202] Since a request for the prompt release of a vessel relies on the authority and standing of the flag State itself, ITLOS could take account of the flag State's actions with respect to the conduct of the vessel in order to confirm the legitimacy of its 'interest'—or even draw attention to the flag State's subsequent responsibility to take reasonable steps to ensure compliance with the terms of the bond, thus giving effect to the coastal State's 'interest'. For example, a flag State whose interests have been served by the prompt release of a vessel might reasonably be expected to exercise the authority required to ensure the fulfillment of the coastal State's interests with respect to the appearance in court of the vessel's master, owner, or operator, and the payment of penalties. This approach would more accurately reflect the underlying balance of the LOSC, in which the rights provided to flag States (such as the right to request

[198] Taisaku Ikeshima, 'The "Reasonableness" of Unreasonable Arguments in Prompt Release Cases in the ITLOS' (2009) 6 Waseda GlobalFor 107, 124.

[199] Ibid 123.

[200] For example, in *Monte Confurco*, which was brought on behalf of the flag State (the Seychelles) by legal representatives of the vessel and its master, Judge Anderson commented that 'the actual interests of the two sides in this case lie on entirely different planes': *Monte Confurco* (Diss Op Anderson) 130.

[201] The first prompt release case to be considered by ITLOS was the *Saiga* case in 1997, and (at the time of writing) the last was the *Tomimaru* case in 2007. While ITLOS has since ordered the release of vessels in other cases, these have involved the Tribunal's provisional measures jurisdiction rather than the prompt release mechanism in arts 73(2) and 292.

[202] *SRFC Advisory Opinion* [134]–[139].

prompt release) are inherently linked to correlative responsibilities (such as the obligation to effectively exercise jurisdiction and control with respect to the vessel released).

While Judge Cot found in *Volga* that attaching non-financial conditions to a bond in the way proposed by Australia would 'be tantamount to deflecting the Article 292 procedure from its purpose and distorting its meaning',[203] perhaps this would not be such a bad thing. Given the relationship between the rights and duties of coastal and flag States, it seems reasonable to conclude that, as suggested by Judge ad hoc Shearer (with whom Judge Anderson fully agreed),[204] it is time for a new 'balance' to be struck in the interpretation and implementation of Articles 73(2) and 292.[205] Prompt release under Article 73(2) needs to be understood not just by reference to Article 292 but in a broader context, taking into account the way that modern industrial fishing operates and the actors involved, and the value that the LOSC—and the international community—attaches to the conservation and management of living resources and the protection of the marine environment.[206] This would provide a basis to reconsider—even perhaps to 'distort'—the purpose and meaning of the Article 73(2) prompt release procedure in a way that more accurately reflects and balances the contemporary interests of coastal and flag States.[207]

6.3.2 Penalties for Violations of Fisheries Laws and Regulations (Article 73(3))

The determination of what is 'necessary' and 'reasonable'—and its effect on the balance between flag and coastal State interests—also dominates the jurisprudence about the penalties that coastal States may apply when foreign vessels violate their fisheries laws. In this respect, Article 73(3) of the LOSC establishes the outer limits of coastal State jurisdiction by restricting the penalties that may be imposed for foreign fishing offences (prohibiting corporal punishment and providing that imprisonment may only be imposed by agreement with the States concerned), but does not establish any positive requirements (or minimum obligations) for coastal States regarding the criminalization or punishment of illegal fishing.[208] Within the outer limits of Article 73(3), the LOSC thus confers significant discretion on coastal States regarding the type and magnitude of the penalties

[203] *Volga* (Sep Op Cot) [55]–[56].
[204] *Volga* (Diss Op Anderson) [65].
[205] *Volga* (Diss Op Shearer) [72].
[206] Trevisanut, 'Twenty Years of Prompt Release' (n 187) 302.
[207] Ibid.
[208] Some very general minimum requirements have been established in binding and non-binding global fisheries instruments adopted subsequent to the LOSC. See IPOA-IUU [21]; FAO Code of Conduct arts 7.7.2 and 8.1.9; UNFSA art 19.

that may be imposed for foreign fishing offences.[209] However, some additional restrictions have emerged from the jurisprudence—particularly the *Virginia G* case, in which ITLOS found that penalties imposed for fisheries offences are subject to the necessity test under Article 73(1). In *Virginia G*, the Tribunal applied this test through two limbs:[210] first, in the abstract, by considering whether the type of penalty imposed by the coastal State was objectively necessary to ensure compliance with the regulation concerned (having already established that the regulation had been adopted in conformity with the LOSC);[211] and second, in a concrete sense, by considering whether or not the penalty was necessary in the circumstances of the particular case.[212]

In considering the first limb of this test, the Tribunal determined that confiscation was a 'necessary' type of penalty, noting with approval that the laws of the coastal State (Guinea-Bissau) afforded the authorities 'flexibility' in the application of sanctions for violations of its fishing laws and regulations, and enabled the applicant to mount a legal challenge to confiscation.[213] However, in applying the second limb of its test, the Tribunal found that even though the vessel's actions constituted a 'serious violation' of the coastal State's laws, in the circumstances of the case, the confiscation of the vessel was 'not necessary either to sanction the violation committed or to deter the vessels or their operators from repeating this violation'.[214] In this respect, the Tribunal noted the existence of a number of 'mitigating factors', including that Guinea-Bissau was aware of the bunkering operation (even though the procedures had not been followed to secure the proper authorization), and that other vessels involved in the operation were not confiscated.[215]

In addition to the Article 73(1) 'necessity' test, the Tribunal stated that the principle of reasonableness applies generally to enforcement measures under Article 73 of the LOSC, and that 'in applying enforcement measures due regard has to be paid to the particular circumstances of the case and the gravity of the violation.'[216] On this basis, the Tribunal found that the confiscation of the *Virginia G* was 'not reasonable in light of the particular circumstances of this case'[217] but it did not provide any indication as to the content of the 'reasonableness' test, or acknowledge any margin of appreciation for the coastal State.[218]

This aspect of the decision—which was reached by a majority involving fourteen judges—was subject to significant criticism from members of the minority,

[209] Harrison, 'Article 73' (n 143) 562.
[210] Harrison, 'Safeguards Against Excessive Enforcement Measures' (n 26) 243.
[211] *Virginia G* [249]–[257].
[212] Ibid [258]–[269].
[213] Ibid [257].
[214] Ibid [269].
[215] Ibid [268].
[216] Ibid [270].
[217] Ibid.
[218] Harrison, 'Safeguards Against Excessive Enforcement Measures' (n 26) 245.

who considered that the Tribunal had overstepped its role in judicial review of the coastal State's exercise of enforcement jurisdiction, and functioned akin to an appellate court by substituting its own view for that of the local authorities.[219] The dissenting judges emphasized that the national courts and authorities of the coastal State are in a better position to appreciate all the questions of law and fact in the circumstances of the case, and should be given a broad 'margin of appreciation' in determining what enforcement measures are 'necessary' under Article 73(1).[220] In this respect, they noted that the exercise of sovereign rights by the coastal State in its EEZ should attract a 'degree of deference' from international courts and tribunals.[221]

The majority's decision on confiscation has also been subject to criticism in the literature, including on the basis that it 'tips the balance in favour of the interests of the flag state and it undermines the sovereign nature of the rights possessed by the coastal state',[222] and that the Tribunal used a non-textual principle of 'reasonableness' to annex to itself the power to overrule a coastal State's decision regarding the form of sanction imposed for an admittedly 'serious' violation of the laws implementing its sovereign rights.[223] However, the decision makes some positive contributions. For example, as Oxman and Coglianti-Bantz have observed: 'it went out of its way to uphold the law of Guinea-Bissau by finding that its statute affords the authorities and courts flexibility over whether or not to confiscate. Accordingly, it seems unlikely that reasoned determination of penalties by law enforcement professionals and municipal courts in light of the circumstances of the violation will be second-guessed.'[224]

In addition, the Tribunal emphasized that the necessity and reasonableness of a penalty must be assessed on a case-by-case basis, in light of the relevant circumstances, and noted that Article 73 must be interpreted in the light of the practice of coastal States on the sanctioning of violations of fishing laws and regulations.[225]

While it has not been possible in the course of this study to examine the penalties actually applied by courts and other authorities of coastal States in the particular circumstances of each case (the second limb of the 'necessity' test), this

[219] *Virginia G* (Joint Diss Op Hoffmann, Marotta Rangel, Chandrasekhara Rao, Kateka, Gao and Bouguetaia [50]–[56], (Diss Op Jesus) [9]–[22], (Diss Op Ndiaye) [163], (Diss Op Servulo Correia) [16]–[27].

[220] Ibid (Joint Diss Op Hoffmann, Marotta Rangel, Chandrasekhara Rao, Kateka, Gao and Bouguetaia) [50].

[221] Ibid [49]. On the margin of appreciation, see also Section 2.3.3.1.

[222] Harrison, 'Safeguards Against Excessive Enforcement Measures' (n 26) 245. Similarly, Zoe Scanlon, 'Upsetting the Balance? The Legality of Vessel Confiscation under the LOSC after the M/V Virginia G Case' (2018) 33(1) IJMCL 166, 198.

[223] Craig H Allen, 'Law Of The Sea Tribunal Implies A Principle Of Reasonableness In UNCLOS Article 73' *Opinio Juris Guest Blog*, 17 April 2014, available at <http://opiniojuris.org/2014/04/17/guest-post-law-sea-tribunal-implies-principle-reasonableness-unclos-article-73/> accessed 24 January 2021.

[224] Bernard H Oxman and Vincent P Coglianti-Bantz, 'The M/V Virginia G (Panama/Guinea Bissau)' (2014) 108(4) AJIL 769, 775.

[225] *Virginia G* [253].

Section instead considers the way in which the penalties that may potentially attach to fisheries offences are established in coastal State legislation. The treatment of fisheries offences varies widely between States. Some treat fisheries violations as criminal offences, and deal with them as a matter of criminal law, while others rely on a system of civil or administrative sanctions in place of—or in addition to—their criminal law enforcement mechanisms.[226] The approaches adopted by coastal States in relation to imprisonment, confiscation of vessels, gear and catch, and monetary penalties are summarized in Table 6.2 and addressed in detail in the discussion, together with other penalties such as fishing bans, blacklisting, and the burning or sinking of vessels.[227]

6.1.1.12 Imprisonment

Notwithstanding the prohibition in Article 73(3), the legislation of more than fifty coastal States provides for the possibility of imprisonment as a penalty for foreign fishing offences, as shown in Table 6.2. This is not a new trend.[228] Such provisions have previously been subject to formal protest from at least one flag State,[229] and criticized in the literature as inconsistent with the LOSC.[230] However, it is important to note that such provisions are not *of themselves* inconsistent with Article 73(3) of the LOSC; it is a question of the how they are applied in practice. In this respect, coastal States adopt a range of different techniques and approaches.

First, since Article 73(3) only prohibits imprisonment 'in the absence of agreements to the contrary by the States concerned', some coastal States specifically provide that imprisonment shall only be applied as a penalty with the agreement of the State of nationality.[231] For example, while imprisonment is included as a penalty for unauthorized foreign fishing under Section 125 of Kenya's *Fisheries Management and Development Act 2016*, Section 162 provides that: '[i]n the absence of any

[226] For a detailed discussion on administrative sanctions for fisheries offences, see Cacaud et al, 'Administrative Sanctions' (n 131).

[227] This book focuses primarily on determining the nature of the penalties for foreign fishing offences in the EEZ as established in the fisheries, natural resources, or maritime zone legislation of coastal States. While relevant offences and penalties may be contained in other legislation (such as the Criminal Code) or affected by general sentencing or criminal procedure laws, they are not comprehensively examined in this research.

[228] A 1983 FAO study noted that thirty-eight countries provided for imprisonment as a penalty for illegal foreign fishing: Gerald Moore, *Coastal State Requirements for Foreign Fishing* (Rev 1, FAO 1983) 19.

[229] 'Statement of the Ministry of Foreign Affairs of Thailand transmitted to the Secretary-General of the United Nations on 3 May 1993', reproduced in Division for Ocean Affairs and the Law of the Sea (DOALOS), *Law of the Sea Bulletin No 26* (UN 1994) 44. This position appears to be contradicted by Thailand's fisheries legislation, which provides for unauthorized fishing in the EEZ to be punished by a fine or a term of imprisonment not exceeding one year, and does not provide an exception or alternative for foreign fishers: Thailand, *Act BE 2482, 1939* s 11.

[230] See Francisco Orrego Vicuna, *The Exclusive Economic Zone* (CUP 1989) 159; Barbara Kwiatkowska, *The 200 Mile Exclusive Economic Zone in the New Law of the Sea* (Martinus Nijhoff 1989) 87.

[231] See Table 6.2.

Table 6.2 Coastal State approaches to penalties for foreign fishing offences in the EEZ

	Imprisonment for foreign fishing offences: explicitly excluded (N); included (Y); applies with agreement/reciprocity of relevant State (A); applies if fines not paid (F)	**Potential penalties for foreign fishing offences include confiscation of vessel (V), gear (G) and/or catch (C); confiscation applies automatically(*)**	**Fines for unauthorized foreign fishing (USD) (* doubled in case of recidivism)**	**Relevant legislation and regulations**
African Group				
Algeria		VGC*	37,500–60,000*	*Law 01-11 of 2001* arts 79, 98–9
Angola		VGC	Up to 100 x annual fishing fee*	*Law 6-A/04 of 2004* arts 233, 238, 241
Benin	Y		18,500–46,500*	*Law 2014-19* arts 110, 115–16
Cameroon		C	92,500–185,500	*Law 94/01* arts 148, 161
Cape Verde		VGC	331,000–6.623 million * (plus IUU listing)	*Leg Dec 2/2020* arts 119, 122–6
Comoros		VGC	18,500–148,500* (plus costs of detention and repatriation; vessel automatically confiscated for recidivism)	*Law 82-015* art 14
Congo			46,500–464,000*	*Law 2-2000* arts 86, 105
Cote d'Ivoire	A	VGC	371,000–1.855 million	*Law 2016-554* art 110
Djibouti			Up to 22,500	*Law 187 of 2002* art 41
Egypt			320–640	*Act 124 of 1983* art 53
Equatorial Guinea		GC	Vessel>36 m: 243,500–1.217 million (plus cost to restore any environmental damage)	*Law 11/2017* arts 163(1), 168(2)
Eritrea		VGC	33,500–66,500* (plus discretionary fine up to 3 x commercial value of catch)	*Proc 176/2014* arts 35–7
Gabon	Y	VGC	5,570–927,500* (plus market value of potential loading of ship)	*Law 15/2005* arts 99, 102–3

Table 6.2 *Continued*

	Imprisonment for foreign fishing offences: explicitly excluded (N); included (Y); applies with agreement/reciprocity of relevant State (A); applies if fines not paid (F)	Potential penalties for foreign fishing offences include confiscation of vessel (V), gear (G) and/or catch (C); confiscation applies automatically(*)	Fines for unauthorized foreign fishing (USD) (* doubled in case of recidivism)	Relevant legislation and regulations
Gambia	Y	VGC*	97,000–484,000*	*Act 2007* ss 39(9), 84(1), 101
Ghana		VGC*	250,000–2 million	*Act 2002* ss 62, 109
Guinea		GC*	Vessel >50 m: 1.217–2,434 million (plus detention of vessel for up to four months)	*Code 2015* art 264
Guinea-Bissau		VGC	185,500–464,000*	*Dec Law 10/2011* arts 63, 69–70, 72
Kenya	A	VGC	454,000	*Act 2016* ss 125, 162(3), 186
Liberia	A	VGC	Up to 1 million (plus costs of seizure, prosecution, and repatriation)	*Law 2019* ss 9.2, 12.1, 13.3, 15.4, 15.7
Libya	Y	VGC*	1,120–2,240	*Law 14 of 1989* arts 22–3
Madagascar	Y	VGC	300,000–700,000 (up to 900,000 if vessel fled to escape detection; vessel automatically confiscated for recidivism)	*Code 2015* arts 90–1
Mauritania		VGC*	Vessel >250 gross tonne (GT): 332,500	*Law 2015-017* art 83
Mauritius		VGC	1 million or 100 x licence fee for thirty days (whichever is higher)	*Act 2007* arts 70–1
Morocco	Y	VGC	Vessel >500 GT: $447,000–893,500	*Law 173255* arts 37, 39
Mozambique		VGC*	More than 1,150 times the minimum public service wage ($68,500)*	*Law 22/2013* arts 81, 98, 104

Continued

Table 6.2 *Continued*

	Imprisonment for foreign fishing offences: explicitly excluded (N); included (Y); applies with agreement/reciprocity of relevant State (A); applies if fines not paid (F)	Potential penalties for foreign fishing offences include confiscation of vessel (V), gear (G) and/or catch (C); confiscation applies automatically(*)	Fines for unauthorized foreign fishing (USD) (* doubled in case of recidivism)	Relevant legislation and regulations
Namibia	F	VGC	Up to $132,000 (plus 3 x likely profits)	*Act 2000* ss 52–4
Nigeria	Y	VC	$250,000 [currency unspecified]	*Act 1992* s 1(2)
Sao Tome & Principe		GC	$200,000–500,000*	*Law 9/2001* arts 60, 63
Senegal		VGC	$928,000–1.855 million* (vessel automatically confiscated for recidivism)	*Code 2015* arts 123, 135
Seychelles		VGC	Vessel >50m: $877,000–1.461 million	*Act 2014* ss 58, 70
Sierra Leone	A	VGC*	$2.5 million–3 million (plus costs of seizure, prosecution, repatriation)	*Act 2018* ss 38, 68, 70, 72; *Regs 2019* reg 11(1), Fourth Schedule
Somalia		VGC*	Vessel >101 Horsepower: $1 million–10 million	*Law 2016* arts 30–1
South Africa		VGC	Up to $330,000	*Act 1998* ss 58(3), 68
Tanzania		VGC	Up to $1 million (plus costs for loss or damage, seizure, and prosecution)	*Act 2020* ss 46(2), 71, 74, Schedule 2
Togo	Y	C	$190–9,280*	*Law 2015-10* arts 813, 818–19
Tunisia	Y	VGC*	$370–37,000*	*Law 94-13* arts 33, 37–42
Asia-Pacific Group				
Bahrain	Y	VGC	$800–2,660* (plus compensation for damage to marine resources)	*Leg Dec 20 of 2002* arts 33–4

Table 6.2 *Continued*

	Imprisonment for foreign fishing offences: explicitly excluded (N); included (Y); applies with agreement/reciprocity of relevant State (A); applies if fines not paid (F)	Potential penalties for foreign fishing offences include confiscation of vessel (V), gear (G) and/or catch (C); confiscation applies automatically(*)	Fines for unauthorized foreign fishing (USD) (* doubled in case of recidivism)	Relevant legislation and regulations
Bangladesh	Y	VGC*	Up to $590,000* (at least one-third of this amount)	*Act 2020* ss 24–5, 53
Brunei	Y	VGC	Up to $7,500	*Order 2009* ss 39–40, 53
Cambodia		C	Twice the market price of the evidence (plus costs for destruction and restoration of eco-system)	*Law 2006* arts 90, 94
China		V	Up to $77,000	*Law 2004* art 46
Chinese Taipei		VGC	$35,500–179,000	*Law 1998* art 20
Cook Islands		VGC	$72,000–720,000 (plus costs for loss or damage, seizure, and prosecution)	*Act 2005* ss 20, 66, 81
Cyprus	Y	VGC	Up to $243,500*	*Laws 2004 and 2014* s 7
Fiji		VGC	$490,000–980,500	*Dec 2012* ss 33, 99
India		VGC	Up to $1,370 (plus costs of detention)	*Act 1981* ss 10, 13, 16
Indonesia	Y	V	Up to $1.418 million	*Law 2004* arts 69(4), 93(2)
Iran	A	VGC	$50–2,500* (vessel automatically confiscated for recidivism)	*Law 1995* arts 44, 46, 49, 51
Japan	Y	VGC	Up to $96,500	*Act 2001* art 9; *Act 1996* arts 18, 20
Kiribati	F	VGC*	$38,500–772,000 (plus costs of arrest and prosecution)	*Act 2010* ss 8, 29, 42–3

Continued

Table 6.2 *Continued*

	Imprisonment for foreign fishing offences: explicitly excluded (N); included (Y); applies with agreement/reciprocity of relevant State (A); applies if fines not paid (F)	Potential penalties for foreign fishing offences include confiscation of vessel (V), gear (G) and/or catch (C); confiscation applies automatically(*)	Fines for unauthorized foreign fishing (USD) (* doubled in case of recidivism)	Relevant legislation and regulations
Korea		VGC	Up to $181,000	*Fishing Act 1996* arts 17, 21
Kuwait		VGC	$170–1,660 (plus double the licence fee)	*Law 1980* art 12
Malaysia		VGC*	Up to $247,500	*Act 1985* ss 25, 52
Maldives		VGC	Up to $519,500	*Act 2019* ss 67, 72–3
Marshall Islands		VGC	$100,000–1 million	51 *MIRC* §§425, 530
Micronesia		VGC	$100,000–1 million	24 *FSM Code* §§901, 907
Myanmar	F		$40–80	*Law 1989* s 38
Nauru		VGC	Up to $772,000 (plus costs of loss or damage and prosecution)	*Act 1997* ss 23, 33–5
Niue		VGC	Up to $500,000	*Act 1996* ss 18, 51
Oman		VGC	$130,000–1.3 million*	*Law 2019* arts 56, 60
Pakistan	Y	VGC	Up to $62,000	*Act 1975* s 9
Palau	Y	VGC	$500,000–1 million; or purse seine vessel $1 million–10 million (plus costs of restoration, replacement, compensation and 'response')	27 *PNC* §§181–2, 203, 207
Papua New Guinea	AF	VGC*	$2,260–226,000*; or purse seine vessel $56,500–564,500* (plus costs of seizure and prosecution)	*Act 1998* ss 46, 58, 62; *Reg 2000* Schedule 2
Philippines		VGC	$600,000–1.2 million (plus discretion for IUU listing and fines up to 5 x catch value)	*Code 1998* ss 91, 135
Qatar			$550* (vessel, gear and catch may be confiscated for a third offence)	*Law 4 of 1983* art 26

Table 6.2 *Continued*

	Imprisonment for foreign fishing offences: explicitly excluded (N); included (Y); applies with agreement/reciprocity of relevant State (A); applies if fines not paid (F)	Potential penalties for foreign fishing offences include confiscation of vessel (V), gear (G) and/or catch (C); confiscation applies automatically(*)	Fines for unauthorized foreign fishing (USD) (* doubled in case of recidivism)	Relevant legislation and regulations
Samoa		VGC	Up to $3.954 million (plus costs of loss or damage, seizure, and prosecution)	*Act 2016* ss 61, 74, 82, 85
Solomon Islands	A	VGC	Up to $1.494 million	*Act 2015* ss 37, 95, 103, Schedule 1
Sri Lanka		VGC*	Vessel >75m: up to $1.112 million (plus costs of detention and repatriation)	*Act 1979* ss 15B, 18, Schedule III
Thailand	Y	VGC	Vessel >150 GT: $200,000–1 million (plus discretion for IUU listing)	*Ordinance BE 2558, 2015* ss 113, 129, 169; *Act BE 2482, 1939* s 11
Timor-Leste	A	VGC*	$25,000–1.5 million* (taking into account damage to management and preservation of marine resources)	*Law 12/2004* arts 3, 5–6; *Dec Law 2004* arts 163–6
Tonga	Y	VGC	Up to $219,000	*Act 2002* ss 38, 68, 83
Turkey		VGC	$2,700–6,740	*Law 1380* art 36(a)
Tuvalu	N	VGC*	Not less than $3 million	*Act 2006* ss 13, 92
United Arab Emirates	Y	VG*	$13,500–27,000*	*Law 23 of 1999* art 51
Vanuatu	Y	VGC	Up to $9.207 million	*Act 2014* ss 53(6), 128
Vietnam		VGC	$34,500–$43,000 (fines can be doubled for legal entities)	*Dec 42/2019/ND-CP* arts 4, 20
Yemen	Y	VGC	$50,000–500,000	*Law 2 of 2006* art 55
Eastern Europe Group				
Albania		VGC	$197,000–443,500	*Law 64/2012* arts 128(18), 129

Continued

Table 6.2 *Continued*

	Imprisonment for foreign fishing offences: explicitly excluded (N); included (Y); applies with agreement/reciprocity of relevant State (A); applies if fines not paid (F)	Potential penalties for foreign fishing offences include confiscation of vessel (V), gear (G) and/or catch (C); confiscation applies automatically(*)	Fines for unauthorized foreign fishing (USD) (* doubled in case of recidivism)	Relevant legislation and regulations
Bulgaria			$310–310,500	*Act 2000* art 119(1)(2)
Croatia			$1,610–8,040	*Act 2017* art 77
Estonia		VGC	Up to $39,000	*Act 2015* §§75, 89
European Union		GC	At least 5 x value of products obtained (8 x for recidivism) taking account of damage to resources and the marine environment)	*Reg 1005/2008* arts 3, 42–6
Latvia	Y	GC	$160–850 (natural person); $1,700–17,000 (legal person) (plus compensation for losses to resource)	*Law 1995* ss 26, 30(8); *Law 1998* s 110
Lithuania		GC	2–5 x value of products obtained (5–8 x for recidivism) or 1–5 per cent of revenue (plus compensation for damage to stocks)	*Law 2000* arts 57, 60, 63
Montenegro		VGC*	$610–24,500	*Law 2009* arts 116, 120
Poland			$1,340–2,680 (11 x value of products obtained in case of recidivism)	*Law 2014* art 119(2); *Reg 2015* art 1(1)(4)(d)
Romania		VGC	$19.985–99.912 million (up to $374.659 million if committed repeatedly or cause significant consequences)	*Act 1990* arts 49–50
Russia	A	VGC	2–3 x value of products obtained	*Admin Code* art 8.17; *Act 1998* art 39(2); *Law 166-FZ of 2004* art 54
Slovenia		GC	$510–50,000	*Act 2006* arts 51, 53

Table 6.2 *Continued*

	Imprisonment for foreign fishing offences: explicitly excluded (N); included (Y); applies with agreement/reciprocity of relevant State (A); applies if fines not paid (F)	Potential penalties for foreign fishing offences include confiscation of vessel (V), gear (G) and/or catch (C); confiscation applies automatically(*)	Fines for unauthorized foreign fishing (USD) (* doubled in case of recidivism)	Relevant legislation and regulations
Latin America and the Caribbean Group				
Antigua & Barbuda		VGC	Up to $1.11 million	*Act 2006* ss 27(1), 69
Argentina		VGC	$58,000–116,000* (plus costs of arrest and detention)	*Law 24.922 of 1998* arts 51, 54, 58
Bahamas	Y	VC	$50,000*	*Act 1977* ss 20, 23
Barbados		VGC	Up to $250,000	*Act 1993* ss 8(7), 40
Belize	Y	VGC	$4,970–49,500	*Act 2020* ss 28, 38(4), 74
Brazil			$130–18,500	*Dec 6.514 of 2008* art 35
Chile		GC	$4,200–28,000 per GT of the vessel*	*Law 1991* art 115
Colombia		VGC	$10–$1 million	*Statute 13 of 1990* art 55
Costa Rica			$760–45,500 (or for tuna vessels, 25 per cent of vessel value)	*Law 8436 of 2005* art 136
Cuba		VGC	$190*	*Dec 1/2019* arts 32, 34
Dominica	F	VGC	$185,000	*Act 1987* ss 8, 32
Dominican Republic	Y	GC	$1,720–34,500*	*Law 307-04* arts 80–1, 87–8, 93
Ecuador		VGC*	$80,000–600,000	*Law 2020* arts 214(b), 215, 224
El Salvador		C	$20,000*	*Law 2001* arts 79(a), 83, 86
Grenada		VGC	$185,000	*Act 1986* ss 8, 34

Continued

Table 6.2 *Continued*

	Imprisonment for foreign fishing offences: explicitly excluded (N); included (Y); applies with agreement/reciprocity of relevant State (A); applies if fines not paid (F)	Potential penalties for foreign fishing offences include confiscation of vessel (V), gear (G) and/or catch (C); confiscation applies automatically(*)	Fines for unauthorized foreign fishing (USD) (* doubled in case of recidivism)	Relevant legislation and regulations
Guatemala			$103,000 (vessel, gear, catch confiscated in case of recidivism)	*Dec 80-02* art 81
Guyana		VGC*	Up to $48,000	*Act 2012* ss 18, 63
Honduras		GC	$205,000 (plus compensation for environmental damage)	*Dec 106-2015* arts 106, 112
Jamaica	Y	VGC	Up to $20,500	*Act 2018* ss 25(3), 84, 87, Fourth Schedule
Mexico		VGC	$70,500–211,500	*Law 2007* arts 132(X), 138, 142
Nicaragua		GC	$500 per GT of vessel* (vessel confiscated in case of recidivism)	*Law 2004* arts 123(21), 128
Panama		GC	Vessel >100 GT: $300,000–1 million or 3 x market value of catch (whichever is higher)	*Law 204 of 2021* arts 145–6
Peru		C*	Fines established in regulations for each fishery (determined considering damage caused and benefit illegally obtained)*	*Dec 012/2001/PE* arts 137, 140, 145
Saint Kitts & Nevis	A	VGC	Up to $999,000; tripled for a body corporate (plus costs of seizure, detention, repatriation, and aggravated penalty for damage to the environment)	*Act 2016* ss 63, 113, 118, 121–4
Saint Lucia		VGC	Up to $185,000	*Act 1984* ss 8, 33
Saint Vincent & Grenadines		VGC	Up to $185,000	*Act 1986* ss 8, 39
Trinidad & Tobago		VGC	$18,500	*Act 1986* ss 30

Table 6.2 *Continued*

	Imprisonment for foreign fishing offences: explicitly excluded (N); included (Y); applies with agreement/reciprocity of relevant State (A); applies if fines not paid (F)	Potential penalties for foreign fishing offences include confiscation of vessel (V), gear (G) and/or catch (C); confiscation applies automatically(*)	Fines for unauthorized foreign fishing (USD) (* doubled in case of recidivism)	Relevant legislation and regulations
Uruguay		GC	$5,000–100,000, but not more than 50 per cent of value of vessel and cargo (vessel confiscated for recidivism; environmental damage is an aggravating factor)	*Dec 540/971* art 18 (per *Dec 115/018* art 148); *Law 19.175 of 2013* art 81
Venezuela		GC*	$75,000–751,000	*Dec Law 1,408 of 2014* arts 86, 88, 113
Western Europe and Others Group				
Australia		VGC*	Vessel >24m: up to 1.214 million	*Act 1991* ss 101A, 106A
Belgium		GC	$50–3,000* (plus costs incurred, including relating to seizure of gear and catch)	*Law 1978* arts 4(3), 6(4)
Canada		VGC	Up to $588,500 (plus costs for berthing, security, maintenance and repatriation)	*Act 1985* ss 14, 18, 47
Denmark	Y	C	No legislated minimum or maximum	*Law 2017* §§130, 132
Finland			$2,430–121,500 or up to 5 x value of products obtained (8 x for recidivism)	*Act 1188/2014* §52
France	Y	VGC*	$91,000	*Code* arts L945-2(I)(3), L945-5
France (Mayotte)	Y	VGC*	$91,000	*Code* arts L945-2(I)(3), L945-5 (per L951-1)
France (New Caledonia)	Y	VGC*	$91,000	*Code* arts L945-2(I)(3), L945-5 (per L957-3)

Continued

Table 6.2 *Continued*

	Imprisonment for foreign fishing offences: explicitly excluded (N); included (Y); applies with agreement/reciprocity of relevant State (A); applies if fines not paid (F)	**Potential penalties for foreign fishing offences include confiscation of vessel (V), gear (G) and/or catch (C); confiscation applies automatically(*)**	**Fines for unauthorized foreign fishing (USD) (* doubled in case of recidivism)**	**Relevant legislation and regulations**
France (SAAT)	Y	VGC*	$91,000	*Code* arts L945-2(I)(3), L945-5 (per L958-2)
Germany	Y	VGC	Up to $121,500	*Law 2011* §§18(2)(3), 18(4), 18(7), 19
Greece			Fines calculated on the value of products obtained (at least 8 x value for recidivism)	*Circular 9354.1/1 of 5 December 2011* ss 92–5
Iceland		GC	$3,090–40,000 (maximum does not apply in case of major or repeated offences)	*Act 1998* arts 11–14
Ireland		GC*	Vessel >18m: up to $91,000	*Act 2006* ss 10(2), 28, Table 1
Malta		GC	$11,500–141,500*	*Act 2001* ss 10, 30
Netherlands	Y	VGC	Up to $105,000	*Act 1963* arts 5(1), 58(a); *Act 1950* arts 6–7; *Code* arts 23, 33a
New Zealand	A	VGC	Up to $359,500	*Act 1996* ss 252(2), 253, 255C
NZ (Tokelau)		VGC	Up to $72,000	*Regs 2012* ss 37, 44, 45
Norway	A	VGC	Up to $11,500	*Reg 1437* s 5; *Act 2008* ss 64–5
Portugal		GC	$910–303,500 (subsequent offences raised by one-third, then two-thirds, then 100 per cent)	*Dec Law 35/2019* arts 12–15
Spain		VGC	$73,000–728,500	*Law 3/2001* arts 101(e), 105–6

Table 6.2 *Continued*

	Imprisonment for foreign fishing offences: explicitly excluded (N); included (Y); applies with agreement/reciprocity of relevant State (A); applies if fines not paid (F)	Potential penalties for foreign fishing offences include confiscation of vessel (V), gear (G) and/or catch (C); confiscation applies automatically(*)	Fines for unauthorized foreign fishing (USD) (* doubled in case of recidivism)	Relevant legislation and regulations
Sweden		GC	Up to $60,500	*Act 1993* §§45, 50a, 51–5
United Kingdom		GC	Up to $13,500 (if financial gain is higher, referred for criminal prosecution and fines determined by the court)	*Act 2020* ss 12(3), 19; *Order 2011* art 3
UK (Falklands)	A	VGC*	Up to $854,000 (plus costs of pursuit and detention)	*Ordinance 2005* ss 167–8, 173, 201–4, Schedule 3
UK (Montserrat)		VGC	$3,700	*Act 2000* ss 9, 41, 53
UK (Pitcairn)	Y	VGC	Up to $1.078 million (plus up to 3 x value of any commercial gain)	*Ordinance 2016* ss 18–19, 26
UK (SGSSI)		C	Up to $683,000 (plus costs of prosecution)	*Ordinance 2000* ss 5(3), 19, 22
UK (Turks & Caicos)	Y	VGC	50,000	*Regs 1998* ss 5, 42
United States		VGC*	Up to $189,427 for each violation (each day is a separate offence)	16 *USC* §§1857, 1858(a), 1860(a)

Notes

a. The practice of EU member States is examined by reference to their national legislation, but relevant EU regulations are also noted for information/comparison.

b. To enable comparison, the fines in this Table have been converted from their original currency to United States dollars. Amounts less than $10,000 USD are rounded to the nearest $10; amounts between $10,000 USD and $1 million USD to the nearest $500 USD; amounts greater than $1 million USD to the nearest $1,000 USD. The figures were calculated in January 2021 using <xe.com>.

agreement to the contrary with the State of which the vessel or its crew are nationals, penalties for violations of this Act in the Kenya EEZ shall not include imprisonment or any form of corporal punishment.' Similar stipulations are included in the legislation of a number of other coastal States, and of course agreement could be sought from the State concerned prior to sentencing even if this is not stipulated in the legislation.[232]

Second, while Article 73(3) prohibits imprisonment for violations of fisheries laws and regulations, it does not rule out imprisonment completely, and coastal States have adopted a number of different techniques regarding the application of this penalty. Some provide for imprisonment to be applied in default of payment, in the case that an offender fails to pay a fine imposed for illegal fishing. In Kiribati, for example, fishing by an unlicensed vessel is punishable on conviction by a fine and, in default of payment, to imprisonment for ten years (for each of the master, fishing master, owner, and charterer of the vessel).[233] Similar provisions are included in the fisheries legislation of Namibia, Myanmar, and Papua New Guinea.[234] While such provisions have not been challenged before an international court or tribunal, their legitimacy requires consideration on a case-by-case basis in light of the domestic framework within which they are applied,[235] taking into account the need to ensure the proper functioning of the ordinary domestic process of enforcing compliance with domestic law, while recalling the intent and purpose of Article 73(3) and guarding against imprisonment 'through the back door'.[236]

[232] The majority of coastal States seem to treat the reference in art 73(3) to 'States concerned' as referring to the State of nationality. One notable exception is Norway, which prohibits imprisonment in relation to offences committed by foreign vessels outside the territorial sea unless 'this follows from an agreement with a foreign state *or if the vessel is stateless*' (emphasis added), thus implying that the relevant State is the flag State of the vessel, rather than the offender's State of nationality: Norway, *Act 2008* s 64.

[233] Kiribati, *Act 2010* s 8. This was affirmed in *Republic v Jong Kim* [1999] KIHC 13 (applying similar provisions in earlier legislation), in which the court noted that under Kiribati law 'imprisonment in default of payment of a fine terminates whenever the fine is paid'.

[234] Table 6.2. Terms of imprisonment may also arise through the operation of other (non-fisheries) legislation. For example, while Australia's fisheries legislation does not include imprisonment as a penalty for foreign fishing offences, failure to pay a fine within a specified timeframe can give rise to imprisonment in default pursuant to the operation of criminal law statutes.

[235] For example, the Australian courts have stated in this context that 'any imprisonment suffered is not by way of the imposition of a penalty but by way of the ordinary process of providing sanctions to enforce compliance with the law': *Aruli v Mitchell* [1999] WASCA 1042 (Unreported, Kennedy, Pidgeon, and Murray JJ, 31 March 1999) 14. However, the Australian courts have emphasized that 'where imprisonment is not an available sentencing option, a fine and an immediate default period of imprisonment is not to be imposed on the basis that the offence merits imprisonment and the default period represents what would be an appropriate term of imprisonment for the offence': *Djou v Commonwealth Department of Fisheries* (2004) 29 WAR 216 [48].

[236] *Aruli v Mitchell* (n 235) (Pidgeon J) 10. For further discussion of this issue, see Rachel Baird, 'Foreign Fisheries Enforcement: Do Not Pass Go, Proceed Slowly to Jail—Is Australia Playing by the Rules?' (2007) 30 UNSWLJ 1, 5–7.

In addition, penalties of imprisonment may be imposed in other ways, or in relation to other offences. Some coastal States impose 'good behaviour bonds' in relation to fisheries offences—particularly in situations where the offender is unlikely to be able to pay a fine—and any breach of that good behaviour bond (such as the commission of another fisheries offence) results in a sentence of imprisonment. This approach has been used in relation to illegal fishing in Australia's EEZ by small vessels from nearby countries such as Indonesia, Papua New Guinea, and Vietnam.[237] Terms of imprisonment are also imposed by some coastal States for offences relating to conduct that, although committed in the context of fishing or on a fishing vessel, is not directly an offence against the fisheries laws and regulations of the coastal State, but comprises a different form of wrongdoing or interferes with the coastal State's exercise of its sovereign rights. This includes offences that are committed against authorized officers or fisheries observers, or involve obstruction or interference with the performance of their duties,[238] offences that involve a weapon,[239] or the offence of having on board a person who has been banned from going or remaining on board a fishing vessel in the EEZ.[240] In addition, penalties of imprisonment are widely expressed to apply in relation to offences involving destructive fishing practices (using poisons or other noxious substances or explosives), without any distinction being made in their application to foreign nationals.

6.3.2.2 Monetary Penalties

The most common penalty for a foreign fishing offence is monetary. In this respect, the LOSC does not contain anything that would limit the coastal State's discretion as to the appropriate level of a fine, and 'no rules exist in international law that suggest a universal standard' in this respect.[241] This has been confirmed in the separate and dissenting opinions of several members of ITLOS, who have noted that the LOSC does not limit the size of fines, that coastal States may specify whatever monetary penalties they consider appropriate, and that fines may legitimately include deterrence.[242]

While the type and magnitude of the penalties applied by coastal States for foreign fishing offences may differ, the underlying objective is generally the same: to

[237] See, eg, Joint Press Release by Australian Fisheries Management Authority and Australian Border Force, 'Illegal Foreign Fishers Convicted', 2 December 2016, available at <http://newsroom.abf.gov.au/releases/illegal-foreign-fishers-convicted> accessed 28 January 2021.

[238] Senegal, *Code 2015* arts 131–2; Seychelles, *Act 2014* s 63; Niue, *Act 1996* s 44; Samoa, *Act 2016* s12; Saint Lucia, *Act 1984* s 30; Australia, *Act 1991* s 108(1); Canada, *Act 1985* s 18(4). Once again, relevant provisions may also be contained in non-fisheries legislation.

[239] United States, 16 *USC* §309.

[240] Ghana, *Act 2002* s 127(2); Sierra Leone, *Act 2018* s 72(2); Samoa, *Act 2016* s 85(2).

[241] Shigeru Oda, 'Fisheries under the United Nations Convention on the Law of the Sea' (1983) 77 AJIL 739, 747–9.

[242] See *Camouco* (Diss Op Wolfrum) [6]; *Monte Confurco* (Diss Op Anderson) 129; *Volga* (Sep Op Cot) [11] and [13].

ensure that penalties are of 'sufficient severity to effectively prevent, deter and eliminate IUU fishing and to deprive offenders of the benefits accruing from such fishing'.[243] Accordingly, within the framework adopted by each coastal State, the courts or other authorities imposing penalties are commonly directed to take into account not only the circumstances of the offence—including matters such as the gravity of the offence, the degree of guilt, the prior offending history, and whether or not the vessel sought to evade arrest—but the need to maintain adequate deterrence against the commission of such offences, having regard to the difficulties inherent in detecting and prosecuting fisheries offences.[244] The importance of deterrence in determining the penalties to be applied for foreign fishing has been recognized in the decisions of national courts and tribunals.[245]

Beyond this, the actual penalties established in national legislation vary widely, including with respect to the particular offence in question. In order to provide a consistent basis for comparison, this book examines the minimum and maximum fines established in the national legislation of all coastal States in relation to just one offence: that of unauthorized—or 'unlicensed'—commercial fishing in the EEZ, whether by natural or legal persons, or the owner, master, operator, or charterer. As the summary in Table 6.2 demonstrates, while the level of fines that may be applied in relation to unauthorized fishing varies enormously both within and between coastal States, there is a noticeable trend toward the establishment of high maximum fines, which are commonly expressed to apply to each of the owner, charterer, master, and operator of the vessel, and doubled in case of recidivism. More than twenty-five coastal States have set the maximum fine for unauthorized fishing by a foreign vessel in the EEZ at or above $1 million USD, and some have also established high minimum fines, reflecting the gravity with which the conduct is to be treated, regardless of the amount of catch resulting from the offence.[246]

In addition, a number of coastal States provide for the imposition of additional financial penalties over and above the fines specified for the particular offence. Some specifically require the court to include a component relating to compensation or restitution in relation to the damage caused to marine living resources or

[243] IPOA-IUU [21].

[244] See, eg, Papua New Guinea, *Act 1998* s 58(11): in determining the penalty, a court 'may have regard to the need to ensure that any penalty imposed should be adequate in severity to discourage further offences, and where possible should deprive the offenders of the benefits accruing from their unlawful activity'; New Zealand, *Act 1996* s 254: the court shall take into account the purpose of the Act and shall have regard to: '(a) the difficulties inherent in detecting fisheries offences; and (b) the need to maintain adequate deterrents against the commission of such offences'.

[245] See, eg, *Golden Key Petroleum P/L & Anor v Republic* Crt App No 1 of 1991 (Kiribati Court of Appeal), cited in *Republic v Jong Kim* (n 233): 'The loss caused to the Republic by illegal fishing within the fishery limits is likely to be great. Offences of this kind are difficult to detect and warrant a severe penalty in the hope of deterring others from committing similar offences.' Similarly, the High Court of Australia has noted that: 'The difficulty of enforcing compliance along the length of the Australian coastline called for a stern deterrent if observance of the provisions was to take place': *Cheatley v The Queen* (1972) 127 CLR 291, 310.

[246] See Table 6.2.

the marine environment,[247] or a punitive sum calculated by reference to the 'economic benefit' that the offender had sought or expected to receive through commission of the offence.[248] In addition, the total financial penalties sought from the offender may include the recovery of costs associated with pursuing, seizing, and detaining the vessel, and repatriating the crew.[249]

While the LOSC does not place any specific restrictions on the level of financial penalties imposed for foreign fishing offences, by emphasizing that the 'gravity' of an offence is to be established by reference to the penalties imposable under the legislation of the coastal State, ITLOS has inextricably linked the level of fines with the level of the bond that can 'reasonably' be set by the coastal State under Article 73(2) for the prompt release of a vessel charged with such offences.[250] That is, by raising the level of fines for foreign fishing offences, a coastal State can raise the level of an appropriate bond while remaining within the parameters of 'reasonableness' established by ITLOS. Noting the Tribunal's history of reducing the bonds set by the coastal State, and its statement that bonds should not be set by reference to the maximum applicable penalty, it might be thought that setting high penalties for foreign fishing offences provides coastal States with 'a way of securing the aim of deterrence without transgressing the limitations drawn by the ITLOS'.[251]

6.3.2.3 Confiscation of Vessels and Gear

In practice, however, even significant fines have not proved sufficient to effectively deter illegal fishing, and many coastal States have resorted to additional (non-monetary) penalties, including the confiscation of vessels, gear, and catch. Like monetary penalties, these measures are not mentioned in the text of the LOSC, and thus fall within the discretion of the coastal State in taking the measures necessary to ensure compliance with its laws and regulations. As ITLOS has noted, such measures are not *per se* inconsistent with Article 73(1), and 'many coastal States provide for measures of confiscation of fishing vessels as a sanction' for the violation of fisheries laws and regulations.[252]

[247] See, eg, Cambodia, *Law 2006* art 90: 'Any person committing a fishery offence leading to damage of the fishery eco-system in the fishery domain must pay the cost of destruction and restoration to its original condition.'

[248] See, eg, Namibia, *Act 2000* s 53: 'If a person is convicted of an offence under this Act, the court shall summarily enquire into and determine the monetary value of any advantage or potential advantage which such person has or could have gained in consequence of that offence, and, in addition to any other penalty that may be imposed in respect of that offence, impose a fine equal to three times the value so determined, which fine may be recovered as a civil judgment.'

[249] See, eg, Liberia, *Law 2019* s 13.5: The owner or charterer shall bear the costs incurred in connection with: 'a. the seizure of a fishing vessel, vehicle or aircraft or other item for an offence against this Act, including any relevant costs of pursuit of a vessel, vehicle or aircraft; b. the prosecution for an offence in accordance with this Act; and c. the repatriation of the master or crew of any vessel seized under this Act.'

[250] See nn 155–9 and associated text.

[251] Alan Vaughan Lowe, 'The International Tribunal for the Law of the Sea: Survey for 2002' (2003) 18(4) IJMCL 447, 454.

[252] *Tomimaru* [72]; *Virginia G* [253].

The breadth of this practice is reflected in Table 6.2, which shows that the overwhelming majority of coastal States provide for forfeiture of the vessel involved in the offence, as well as the gear and catch on board. The legislation commonly provides explicit guidance about the full extent of the property to be confiscated. For example, Section 52(1) of Malaysia's *Fisheries Act 1985* provides that where any person is found guilty of the offence of unauthorized foreign fishing under Section 15(1):

> the court shall, in addition to any other penalty that may be imposed—
> (i) order that the vessel (including its equipment, furniture, appurtenances, stores, cargo and fishing appliance), vehicle, article or thing used in the commission of such offence or in relation to which such offence has been committed be forfeited; and
> (ii) order that any fish caught in the commission of such offence or the proceeds of the sale of any fish or other article of a perishable nature referred to in section 48, and any explosive, poison, pollutant, apparatus or prohibited gear used or intended to be used in the commission of such offence be forfeited.

Similar provisions—expressed with varying amounts of detail—are found in the legislation of coastal States in every region of the world and from every legal tradition.[253]

However, the legitimacy of these measures depends on the way in which they are applied and the extent to which they are necessary and reasonable in the circumstances of the case.[254] In addition, the question of forfeiture is inherently linked to the operation of the prompt release procedure under Article 73(2). In this context, it is clear that while finalized—or 'definitive'—forfeiture proceedings giving rise to a change of ownership of the vessel can bar the jurisdiction of ITLOS under Article 292,[255] 'confiscation of a fishing vessel must not be used in such a manner as to upset the balance of the interests of the flag State and of the coastal State' under the LOSC.[256] In this regard, a decision by the coastal State to confiscate a vessel: 'should not be taken in such a way as to prevent the shipowner from having recourse to available domestic judicial remedies, or as to prevent the flag State from resorting to the prompt release procedure set forth in the Convention; nor should it be taken through proceedings inconsistent with international standards of due process of law. In particular, a confiscation decided in unjustified haste would jeopardise the operation of Article 292 of the Convention.'[257]

[253] See Table 6.2.
[254] See nn 208–25 and associated text.
[255] *Juno Trader* [63]; *Tomimaru* [78]–[79].
[256] Ibid [75].
[257] Ibid [76].

Accordingly, it appears that even in the case of a definitive confiscation, ITLOS would be willing to review the process undertaken by the coastal State to ascertain its consistency with international standards of due process.[258]

With this jurisprudence in mind, it is relevant to ask whether national legislation that provides for the 'automatic' forfeiture of foreign fishing vessels is consistent with the requirements established by ITLOS, including the need to apply forfeiture provisions 'flexibly' and allow the applicant to challenge the forfeiture,[259] and to respect international due process standards.[260] As Table 6.2 shows, coastal States approach the forfeiture of foreign fishing vessels, gear, and catch in a variety of ways:

- some provide that an illegal foreign fishing offence automatically results in the forfeiture of the vessel used to commit the offence (either on its own or together with its gear and/or catch);[261]
- some (particularly EU member States) provide only for the confiscation of the gear and catch (and not the vessel);[262] and
- some provide for automatic forfeiture of the vessel (and/or the gear and catch) upon the commission of a second or subsequent offence.[263]

Automatic forfeiture provisions have generated significant discussion in the literature, particularly in Australia, where the *Fisheries Management Act 1991* (Cth) provides for the automatic transfer of title from a foreign fishing vessel owner to the Government of Australia at the time the offence is committed, without requiring a conviction or judicial decision ordering the forfeiture.[264] These provisions have been upheld by domestic courts,[265] but questioned by commentators.[266] The legitimacy of measures taken pursuant to provisions of this sort will depend (perhaps even more than the other types of enforcement measures considered in this Section) on the particular circumstances of the case,

[258] Guilfoyle, *Shipping Interdiction* (n 40) 154; Harrison, 'Article 73', (n 143) 562.
[259] *Virginia G* [257].
[260] *Tomimaru* [76].
[261] See, eg, Gambia, *Act 2007* s 84(1).
[262] See, eg, EU, *Reg 1005/2008* arts 45–6; Ireland, *Act 2006* s 28.
[263] See, eg, Madagascar, *Code 2015* art 90(6).
[264] These provisions were introduced into Australia's fisheries legislation following the 1999 *Alizia Glacial* case, in which the vessel's owners went bankrupt shortly after it was arrested for foreign fishing offences in the Australian EEZ, and the court ordered that the vessel be sold and the proceeds transferred to the Norwegian mortgagee: Rachel Baird, 'Testing the Waters: Fine Tuning the Provisions of the Fisheries Management Act 1991 (Cth)' (2004) 32 UWALRev 63, 73–5.
[265] *Olbers v Commonwealth of Australia (No 4)* [2004] 205 ALR 432, applied in *R v Amoedo and Dominguez* [2006] NSWDC 187.
[266] See Warwick Gullett, 'Developments in Australian Fisheries Law: Setting the Law of the Sea Convention Adrift?' (2004) 21(3) Env&Planning LJ 169; Rachel Baird, 'Australia's Response to Illegal Foreign Fishing: A Case of Winning the Battle but Losing the Law?' (2008) 23 IJMCL 95; Michael White and Rosemary Gibson, 'Fisheries and Automatic Forfeiture of Vessels: Draconian Commonwealth Laws' (2010) 84 ALJ 319.

and on the detailed legal framework within which they operate—in particular, the extent to which they are able to be challenged by the vessel owner before a relevant domestic forum.[267]

A final issue of relevance is the practice of burning and sinking foreign vessels that have engaged in illegal fishing in the EEZ. In recent years, press releases and media reports have noted the burning and sinking of illegal foreign fishing vessels by a wide range of coastal States in the Asia-Pacific, including Australia, Indonesia, Malaysia, Micronesia, Palau, Papua New Guinea, and the Solomon Islands. While the consistency of this practice with the LOSC has been questioned,[268] it once again depends on the circumstances of the case. For example, if the fishing offences were committed in the territorial sea, the vessel is subject to the sovereignty of the coastal State and the limitations of Article 73 do not apply.[269] If they were committed by a vessel without nationality (or with more than one nationality),[270] the prompt release procedure is not available,[271] and the vessel itself is not protected under international law.[272] In addition, following the 'definitive' forfeiture of a foreign fishing vessel under the circumstances discussed above, the method of disposing of such a vessel is entirely within the discretion of the coastal State—from selling it, to re-purposing it as a patrol or training vessel, sinking it to create an artificial reef, or simply scuttling it on safety grounds or to reduce fishing capacity. Some countries have noted that by burning illegal foreign fishing vessels at sea rather than simply sinking them, they are seeking to send a clear and visible message that illegal fishing will not be tolerated.[273]

The national legislation of some coastal States provides for the possibility of scuttling an illegal foreign fishing vessel at sea without bringing it to port, in light of issues such as the condition of the vessel, navigational safety, dangerous weather, public health, or biosecurity risks. For example, Section 106D(1) of the Australian *Fisheries Management Act 1991* (Cth) provides for a vessel to be disposed of before the period for challenging forfeiture has expired, in situations where the authorities are satisfied that: '(a) the boat is unseaworthy; or (b) the

[267] The Australian legislation provides for the confiscation to be contested in a court of law: *Act 1991* ss 106E–106G; *Olbers v Commonwealth of Australia* (n 265) [89]–[94].

[268] Mary-Ann Palma-Robles, 'Fisheries Enforcement and the Concepts of Compliance and Monitoring, Control and Surveillance' in Robin Warner and Stuart Kaye (eds), *Routledge Handbook of Maritime Regulation and Enforcement* (Routledge 2016) 139, 146.

[269] LOSC arts 2(1) and 19(2)(i).

[270] Ibid art 92(2).

[271] An application for prompt release under art 292 can only be brought 'by or on behalf of the flag State' of the vessel. If the vessel does not have a flag State at the time the application is made, the Tribunal will not have jurisdiction to consider it: *The 'Grand Prince' Case (Belize v France)* (Prompt Release, Judgment) (2001) ITLOS Rep 17 [80]–[94].

[272] Satya Nandan and Shabtai Rosenne (eds), *United Nations Convention on the Law of the Sea 1982: A Commentary, Vol III* (Martinus Nijhoff 1995) 127.

[273] See Prashanth Parameswaran, 'Why Did Malaysia Just Burn an Illegal Fishing Vessel?' *The Diplomat*, 1 September 2017, available at <http://thediplomat.com/2017/09/why-did-malaysia-just-burn-an-illegal-fishing-vessel/> accessed 29 January 2021.

boat poses a serious risk to safety or public health; or (ba) the boat poses an unacceptable level of biosecurity risk ... ; or (c) the boat poses a serious risk of damage to other property or the environment; or (d) the expenses of custody and maintenance of the boat between its seizure and condemnation are likely to be greater than its value.'

A similar approach is evident in Section 69(4) of Indonesia's *Law on Fisheries No 31 of 2004*, which provides for authorized fisheries officers to burn or sink foreign fishing vessels at sea where there is 'adequate preliminary evidence'[274] that they have engaged in fishing or transporting fish in Indonesian waters without a licence and under specified circumstances (such as threats to navigational safety or poor weather, quarantine concerns, unseaworthiness of the vessel, or the difficulty or cost of escorting large numbers of vessels to port).[275] Similarly, French legislation provides that a judge may order the destruction of a vessel if it presents a risk for the safety of persons or the environment.[276]

While such measures are not specifically permitted under the LOSC, they are not prohibited and—consistent with the *Lotus* rule—may constitute a legitimate exercise of coastal State jurisdiction, provided they comply with the standards of necessity and reasonableness generally applicable to enforcement measures under Article 73. They might in some cases be considered necessary to give effect to Article 225 of the LOSC, which requires that in the exercise of enforcement powers against foreign vessels in the EEZ, coastal States do not 'endanger the safety of navigation or otherwise create any hazard to a vessel, or bring a vessel to an unsafe port or anchorage, or expose the marine environment to an unreasonable risk'.[277] On the other hand, they might upset the 'balance of interests' established in the LOSC, by precluding the flag State having recourse to the prompt release procedure under Article 292.[278] In practice, such measures are most likely to be applied to small-scale vessels that are not of sufficient value to be the subject of a prompt release application, and are in any case not registered with a flag State or operated by owners who would instigate such an application.[279] This is reinforced by the fact that while

[274] In this context, 'adequate preliminary evidence' is considered to mean 'initial evidence to allege any criminal act' by a foreign fishing vessel in the EEZ: Indonesia, *Elucidation on Law No 45 of 2009 regarding amendment to Law No 41 of 2004 regarding Fisheries* Point 29 (Article 69(4)).

[275] Zaki Mubarok Busro, 'Burning And/or Sinking Foreign Fishing Vessels Conducting Illegal Fishing in Indonesia: Some Obligations and Loopholes' (2017) 2 APacJOceanL&Pol 174, 176–8. Vessels may also be destroyed on the order of a court, as the instrument of a fisheries crime: Indonesia, *Law 2004* art 76A.

[276] France, *Code* art L-943-6.

[277] See n 48.

[278] *Tomimaru* [75]–[76].

[279] For example, the Vietnamese Government has expressed doubt that the large fleets of 'blue boats' arrested and destroyed for illegal fishing in the waters of coastal States around the western and central Pacific are Vietnamese (despite being crewed by Vietnamese citizens and coming from Vietnamese ports): PNA Media Release, 'Illegal Fishing by "Blue Boats" Criticized by PNA Member at Tuna Commission' 7 December 2016, available at <http://pnatuna.com/node/382> accessed 29 January 2021.

large numbers of vessels have been disposed of by sinking and burning in recent years, no steps have been taken by flag States to formally assert that such actions are illegitimate.[280] Accordingly, it seems that both coastal and flag States accept that such actions may constitute reasonable and necessary enforcement measures in certain situations or with respect to certain vessels.

6.3.2.4 Bans and Blacklisting

A final category of penalties relates to measures that restrict the ability of fishing vessels—and their owners, operators, and masters—to engage in fishing activities, by providing for the suspension or revocation of fishing licences, vessel licences, and fishing rights, and placing restrictions on the issuance of new licences. For example, pursuant to Section 40 of the Barbados *Fisheries Act 1993*: 'Where any person is convicted of an offence under this Act, the court, in addition to any other penalty imposed: … (c) may order that any fishing licence issued under this Act be cancelled or suspended and that no new fishing licence be issued to the person convicted of the offence for such period of time as the court may specify.'

Provisions relating to forfeiture or cancellation of licences are included in the legislation of a large number of coastal States. In some legislation, the forfeiture or cancellation of licences is included as a mandatory part of the minimum penalty,[281] while in others it is provided as an ancillary penalty that applies at the discretion of the court,[282] or applies automatically upon the accumulation of a certain number of penalty 'points' as a result of fishing offences.[283] Alternatively—or additionally—some coastal States provide for the suspension or revocation of relevant licences in the case of recidivism or the commission of multiple offences.[284]

The national legislation of some coastal States goes further, banning a person not only from holding a licence, but from going on or remaining aboard a vessel in the EEZ, or engaging in fishing or related activities in the EEZ for a specified period—whether on their own behalf or as an employee of another. Such legislation generally also prohibits having a banned person on board a fishing vessel, with potentially significant penalties for both the master and the banned person. For example, pursuant to Section 80 of the Cook Islands *Marine Resources Act 2005*:

[280] Between October 2014 and August 2018, Indonesia destroyed 488 vessels flagged to Vietnam, the Philippines, Thailand, Malaysia, China, Papua New Guinea, and Belize: Dita Liliansa, 'The Necessity of Indonesia's Measures to Sink Vessels for IUU Fishing in the Exclusive Economic Zone' (2020) 10 Asian JIntlL 125, 130. While 'several Southeast Asian countries' have reportedly discussed this issue with Indonesia, they have not publicly made any formal allegations about the legality of destroying vessels. See, eg, P Parameswaran, 'Vietnam "Deeply Concerned" by Indonesia's War on Illegal Fishing' *The Diplomat*, 21 August 2015, available at <http://thediplomat.com/2015/08/vietnam-deeply-concerned-by-indonesias-war-on-illegal-fishing>> accessed 31 January 2021.

[281] See, eg, Malaysia, *Act 1985* s 33(1).

[282] See, eg, Namibia, *Act 2000* s 54(1).

[283] See, eg, EU, *Reg 1224/2009* art 92.

[284] See, eg, New Zealand, *Act 1996* s 257(1).

> (1) Where any person who is convicted of an offence against this Act or any regulation made under this Act and within 7 years from the date of that conviction is convicted on another occasion of the same or any other offence against this Act or any regulation made under this Act, the Court may, in addition to any other fine or penalty provided under this Act, make an order prohibiting that person from engaging in—(a) fishing; (b) fishing related activities; (c) any other activity as may be provided for under this Act; for a period of up to 3 years from the date of conviction.
>
> (2) Any person who contravenes an order made under subsection (1) or the master of a fishing vessel who has aboard a person he knows is banned under subsection (1) commits an offence and shall be liable on conviction to a fine not exceeding $250,000 [NZD].

Similar provisions are established in the legislation of a number of other coastal States.[285] This approach is applied on an even broader basis in the fisheries legislation of Mozambique, which provides that a master, owner, or operator who has used or consented to the use of a fishing vessel to which they are connected for the transport, smuggling, or illegal trafficking of persons, toxic drugs, narcotics, psychotropic substances, firearms, armaments, or other products prohibited by law is banned from fishing or any other fishing related activities for a period of ten years.[286]

In addition to bans relating to the conduct of fishing activity in the EEZ, there are other ways in which coastal States can impose bans or 'blacklist' vessels in response to illegal fishing offences—whether by denying access to their ports, nominating vessels for inclusion on the IUU vessel list of an RFMO, or seeking to revoke the vessel's good standing with a regional fisheries body. Moreover, noting that it is people (not vessels) who are the source of IUU fishing, the members of the FFA are seeking to broaden the application of such measures to focus not only on illegal vessels but on the 'drivers, controllers and operators of rogue vessels'.[287] The FFA is considering ways to ensure that relevant information on 'persons of interest' is included in national or regional databases or IUU lists, including potentially through the establishment of a 'unique personal identifier' allowing unique identification details, such as passport details, to be connected to each master's name and

[285] Ghana, *Act 2002* s 127; Liberia, *Law 2019* s 15.7; Seychelles, *Act 2014* s 70(c); Samoa, *Act 2016* s 85; Vanuatu, *Act 2014* ss 133–4; Marshall Islands, 51 *MIRC* §530; Saint Kitts and Nevis, *Act 2016* s 125; United Kingdom (Falkland Islands) *Ordinance 2005* s 166.

[286] Mozambique, *Law 22/2013* art 109.

[287] Fatu Tauafiafi, 'Legal Weapon: The Potential Breakthrough to Bring down Illegal Tuna Fishers in Pacific Waters' *FFA's Tuna Pacific: Fisheries News and Views*, 15 December 2016, available at <http://tunapacific.org/2016/12/15/legal-weapon-the-potential-breakthrough-to-bring-down-illegal-tuna-fishers-in-pacific-waters/> accessed 31 January 2021.

nationality.[288] In future, such developments may provide coastal States with additional options for adopting and enforcing bans and blacklisting measures against those convicted of fishing offences, and even help to extend the effectiveness of such measures beyond the coastal State's EEZ.

6.4 Conclusion

The ultimate objective of fisheries enforcement jurisdiction is identical to that of prescriptive jurisdiction: ensuring a credible fisheries management system that can deliver the expected benefits.[289] Enforcement is a crucial part of balancing this equation—in order to maintain credibility, departures from the prescribed rules must be penalized, and thus 'absent effective enforcement, credibility declines, the management system itself may be threatened, and potential benefits are reduced'.[290] Accordingly, the regime of the EEZ established in Part V of the LOSC gives the coastal State specific powers to enforce its fisheries laws against foreign vessels. At the same time, it is important to safeguard the freedom of navigation by the vessels of other States in the vast areas of ocean subject to the fisheries enforcement jurisdiction of coastal States—including with respect to the 'particularly sensitive' issue of arrest and detention.[291] In this respect, Article 73 protects the interests of both coastal and flag States by providing the coastal State with enforcement powers, but placing conditions on the way in which they may be exercised.[292] However, it is important to ensure that these conditions are not interpreted and applied so narrowly as to restrict the coastal State's ability to effectively enforce its laws, since this would undermine not only the credibility and benefits of the coastal State's fishery management system and the exercise of its sovereign rights, but the balance of interests that is at the heart of the *sui generis* framework for the EEZ.

While the responsibility to strike this balance falls initially to the coastal State in the way it exercises its enforcement jurisdiction under Article 73, there is also an important role for courts and tribunals in maintaining it, by reviewing the innovations and interpretations advanced by coastal States, and ensuring that their jurisdiction does not 'creep' further than it should.[293] Notwithstanding the limitations on compulsory settlement of disputes concerning fisheries and law enforcement activities, Article 73 is one of the most commonly litigated provisions in the

[288] WCPFC, *Summary Report of the 13th Regular Session, Denarau Island, Fiji, 5–9 December 2016* [212], available at < https://meetings.wcpfc.int/meetings/wcpfc13> accessed 1 August 2021.
[289] Burke, 'Exclusive Fisheries Zones' (n 3) 598.
[290] Ibid 598–9.
[291] Oxman, 'Observations on Vessel Release under the LOSC' (n 154) 202.
[292] Harrison, 'Safeguards Against Excessive Enforcement Measures' (n 26) 217.
[293] Ibid 218.

LOSC.[294] As the cases examined in this Chapter show, ITLOS has generally taken a narrow and literal approach to the interpretation of Article 73, and has sought to constrain what it views as excessive assertions of coastal State enforcement jurisdiction.[295]

ITLOS' jurisprudence has given rise to a number of additional restrictions on the exercise of coastal State enforcement jurisdiction, some of which go beyond the requirements of Article 73 and have deprived coastal States of measures that could enable them to more effectively address illegal fishing. These include, for example:

- the requirement that all enforcement measures taken by the coastal State under Article 73 are both 'necessary' and 'reasonable';[296]
- the application of the Article 224 rule—that enforcement activities can be exercised only by duly authorized identifiable officials of a coastal State and that their vessels must be clearly marked as being on government service—to the conduct of enforcement under Article 73;[297]
- the finding that the bond set by the coastal State for the prompt release of a vessel under Article 73(2) may not include any non-financial conditions;[298] and
- the establishment of a number of other limitations on the issues that may legitimately be considered in establishing the level of the bond.[299]

Moreover, the approach that ITLOS has taken in reviewing the fisheries enforcement measures of coastal States—which has included reducing the bonds set by the coastal State without explaining how the new amounts have been calculated, and determining the 'reasonableness' of the coastal State's penalties at both an objective and subjective level—has given rise to a 'broad and imprecise principle that allows the ITLOS to interfere with individual enforcement measures [and] leaves coastal States with great legal uncertainty'.[300]

In addition, while the importance of the 'balance of interests' is widely referred to in the literature and jurisprudence on enforcement, in many cases its application seems perfunctory, constituting a routine statement or acknowledgement of the accepted wisdom rather than a meaningful examination of its content in the particular circumstances of the case. For example, while the 'balance of interests'

[294] Scanlon, 'Upsetting the Balance?' (n 222) 167.

[295] Tim Stephens and Donald R Rothwell, 'The LOSC Framework for Maritime Jurisdiction and Enforcement 30 Years On' (2012) 27 IJMCL 701, 705.

[296] *Virginia G* [270].

[297] Ibid [342].

[298] *Volga* [77] and [80].

[299] See the issues discussed in Section 6.3.1, in particular nn 159–68 and associated text.

[300] Valentin Schatz, 'Combating Illegal Fishing in the Exclusive Economic Zone—Flag State Obligations in the Context of the Primary Responsibility of the Coastal State' (2016) 7(2) GoettingenJIntlLaw 383, 394.

is the 'guiding criterion' in the context of prompt release under Article 73(2), it is determined by reference to Article 292—which does not include any such requirement—and is based on a narrowly constructed binary equation involving the interest of the flag State in having its vessel and crew released promptly, and the interest of the coastal State in ensuring compliance with its laws and regulations by securing appearance in its court of the Master and the payment of penalties.[301] However, as the discussion in this Chapter has shown, the outcome of these decisions might be vastly different if prompt release cases under Article 73(2) were determined in the context of Part V and by reference to the 'balance of interests' sought to be achieved in the EEZ, which involves broader considerations of freedom of navigation and the exercise of sovereign rights over living resources.

Ideally, the interpretation of the coastal State's enforcement powers under Article 73 would take into account the overall scheme of the LOSC and consider not only the rights but also the responsibilities of the coastal State, as well as those of flag States. In this respect, it is encouraging that recent jurisprudence has addressed the broader framework governing living resources in the EEZ, specifically recognizing the responsibilities of both coastal States (which have the 'primary responsibility for taking the necessary measures to prevent, deter and eliminate IUU fishing')[302] and those of flag States (which 'are obliged to take the necessary measures to ensure that their nationals and vessels flying their flag are not engaged in IUU fishing activities').[303] However, it remains to be seen how—or whether—this broader framework is taken into account when ITLOS is again called upon to consider the exercise of coastal State enforcement jurisdiction under Article 73 and to balance the rights and interests of coastal and flag States in the EEZ.

While courts and tribunals may have taken a narrow approach to the interpretation of enforcement measures under the LOSC, the same cannot be said of coastal States. Faced with not only legal but practical and financial difficulties in enforcing their fisheries laws through the physical enforcement measures envisaged in Article 73, coastal States have developed a range of alternative approaches to achieve the same result. These approaches—which have remained within the general framework of Part V—include a variety of prescriptive and pre-emptive techniques that are used within a broader system of MCS measures to prevent and deter illegal fishing activity, as well as the use of remote detection technologies to detect and monitor the activities of foreign fishing vessels, and to prove fishing offences in court.

Indeed, the incorporation of modern technology into fisheries surveillance and enforcement operations has provided fertile ground for the adoption of innovative and cost-effective approaches to the exercise of 'no-force' coastal State enforcement

[301] *Monte Confurco* [71]; *Camouco* [57].
[302] *SRFC Advisory Opinion* [106].
[303] Ibid [124].

jurisdiction, and—in contrast to some other aspects of the LOSC—has even been supported by international courts and tribunals in some recent cases. For example, coastal States may find some comfort in Judge Lucky's view that: 'Since 1982, technology has advanced and therefore ... judges must take a robust approach and apply the law in a legal but pragmatic way.... I am of the view that there is a presumption that a rational construction ought to be given where circumstances have changed and technology has advanced.'[304]

A similar approach was adopted by the *Arctic Sunrise Arbitration* Tribunal in the context of hot pursuit under Article 111.[305] Notwithstanding the historical tendency of international courts and tribunals to take a literal or textual interpretation in respect of issues associated with enforcement jurisdiction, it seems inevitable that modern technology will come to play an increasingly important role in the conduct of fisheries enforcement operations, and may result in quite different challenges with respect to the type of interests to be balanced in the interpretation and application of Article 73.

In addition, coastal States have recognized that the effectiveness of all their fisheries enforcement measures—including traditional physical enforcement activities such as at-sea boarding and inspection, as well as modern 'no-force' MCS measures, and remote detection techniques—can be enhanced through the collective action of two or more coastal States. The ways in which coastal States employ co-operative approaches to enforcement are constantly expanding and are applied in collaboration not only with other coastal States, but with port States and flag States, as well as RFMOs and regional fisheries bodies, and private sector and civil society organizations. As this increasingly networked approach to cooperation demonstrates, enforcement is no longer the sole prerogative of the coastal State in whose EEZ an offence occurs; in many cases, it is more effective (both generally and in terms of cost) for a coastal State to employ modern technologies in the remote detection of offences, and then collaborate with other actors and jurisdictions (which may include other coastal States in the region, the flag State of the vessel, the port State at which it next calls, and RFMOs in which it fishes) to ensure that appropriate enforcement action is taken.

As Judge Paik has observed, enforcement in the EEZ is a 'highly delicate matter', in which the balance between the interests of the coastal State and those of other States should be preserved to the full extent.[306] However, the practical context in which this balance must be preserved is constantly evolving—both in terms of the way in which the fishing industry operates, and the way in which fisheries enforcement is conducted. While the coastal State's acquisition of sovereign rights over

[304] *SRFC Advisory Opinion* (Sep Op Lucky) [18]–[19]. See also *Juno Trader* (Sep Op Lucky) [41] (noting that: 'Law is dynamic, not static, and, as such, the law or statute should be given a broad interpretation to suit changing circumstances. The law must advance as technology advances').

[305] *Arctic Sunrise Arbitration* [260].

[306] *Virginia G* (Sep Op Paik) [38].

the resources of the EEZ originally appeared to be a 'triumph of unilateralism over collectivism',[307] cooperative approaches to the enforcement of fisheries laws are becoming an increasingly important component of contemporary State practice, together with a recognition of the broader community interest in—and responsibility for—preventing, deterring, and eliminating illegal fishing wherever it occurs. Maintaining an equitable balance between the conflicting interests at play in the EEZ will be crucial to the ongoing effectiveness of the regime for this 'zone of tension' established in Part V of the LOSC. However, it is important to recognize that this balance (and these interests) are not static and will change over time. In order to maintain the equilibrium of the EEZ, it is necessary to take a clear-eyed approach to the question of whose interests are being balanced in the conduct of particular enforcement activities, what those interests are, and whether they should be 'balanced' equally. These considerations are also relevant to the exercise of coastal State enforcement jurisdiction beyond the EEZ, following the conduct of hot pursuit, which will be the focus of Chapter 7.

[307] DP O'Connell, *The International Law of the Sea, Vol I* (OUP 1982) 552.

7
Hot Pursuit and the Exercise of Enforcement Jurisdiction beyond the EEZ

In addition to enforcement jurisdiction within the exclusive economic zone (EEZ) under Article 73 of the United Nations Convention on the Law of the Sea (LOSC), the right of hot pursuit established in Article 111 constitutes an extraordinary grant of enforcement jurisdiction that may be exercised by coastal States *beyond* that zone. Since the right of hot pursuit operates as an exception to the freedom of navigation and the generally exclusive jurisdiction of flag States on the high seas, the balance of interests protected through Article 111 is different from that in Article 73. It involves, on the one hand, the coastal State's interests in the enforcement of its laws and the effective protection of its sovereign rights, and on the other, the community interest in the uninterrupted freedom of navigation on the high seas. In order to ensure this balance is maintained, the right of hot pursuit is subject to a number of significant—and cumulative—procedural limitations set out in Article 111, each of which must be satisfied for the legitimate conduct of hot pursuit under the LOSC.[1]

While the general framework for hot pursuit is clear, its substantive content and operation is less clear, particularly in situations that do not fall neatly within the black and white terms of that framework.[2] For example, some of the key terms used in the LOSC have not been defined—such as when a pursuit has been 'interrupted' or what constitutes a 'good reason to believe' that a vessel has violated the coastal State's laws and regulations. Others have been defined—such as the method for signalling a vessel or maintaining pursuit—but may not meet current law enforcement needs, particularly in the face of illegal, unreported, and unregulated (IUU) fishing.[3] These challenges are exacerbated by the cumulative nature of the conditions for hot pursuit, which provide significant latitude for the validity of individual elements of a pursuit to be challenged before domestic and international courts and tribunals.[4] In this respect, flexible interpretations of some of the procedural

[1] *Saiga (No 2)* [146]; *Arctic Sunrise Arbitration* [246].
[2] Robert C Reuland, 'The Customary Right of Hot Pursuit Onto the High Seas: Annotations to Article 111 of the Law of the Sea' (1993) 33 VaJIntlL 557, 557.
[3] Rachel Baird, 'Illegal, Unreported and Unregulated Fishing: An Analysis of the Legal, Economic and Historical Factors Relevant to Its Development and Persistence' (2004) 5 MelbJIntlL 299, 327–30.
[4] Ibid 330.

Coastal State Jurisdiction over Living Resources in the Exclusive Economic Zone. Camille Goodman, Oxford University Press.
 DOI: 10.1093/oso/9780192896841.003.0007

limitations on hot pursuit have been recommended by commentators[5]—and, in some instances, endorsed by international courts and tribunals[6]—in light of practical and policy imperatives such as technological advances and the difficulties of combating particular forms of illicit activities.

With these challenges in mind, this Chapter will examine the framework for hot pursuit established in the LOSC, particularly as it applies in relation to fisheries offences in the EEZ. It will consider the key challenges to this framework identified in the existing literature and jurisprudence (Section 7.1) and identify the extent to which—and the ways in which—States have implemented, developed, or departed from this framework in practice (Section 7.2). While not all of the case-law or commentary examined in this Chapter relates specifically to the hot pursuit of vessels involved in the commission of fisheries offences in the EEZ, the principles established in Article 111 apply to the violation of any 'laws and regulations' of the coastal State applicable in its maritime zones consistent with the LOSC. Accordingly, even where they arise in other factual contexts, the principles and arguments relating to hot pursuit that are identified in this Chapter apply equally in relation to offences against coastal State fisheries laws.

7.1 The LOSC Framework for Hot Pursuit

Hot pursuit evolved in the customary international law of the sea for more than a century before its codification in Article 23 of the 1958 Convention on the High Seas[7] and subsequently in Article 111 of the LOSC, which is generally accepted to constitute a reasonable—if more detailed—corollary of the customary rule.[8] Accordingly, in the modern law of the sea, the right of hot pursuit exists

[5] See, eg, RR Churchill and AV Lowe, *The Law of the Sea* (3rd ed, MUP 1999) 216; David Anderson, 'Freedoms of the High Seas in the Modern Law of the Sea' in David Freestone, Richard Barnes, and David Ong (eds), *The Law of the Sea: Progress and Prospects* (OUP 2006) 343–4.

[6] Such as the *Arctic Sunrise Arbitration,* in which the Arbitral Tribunal applied a flexible interpretation to some of the requirements for hot pursuit under Article 111, including the method used for signalling the vessel, the standard to be applied for determining the location of the vessel at the time pursuit is commenced, and the marking and identification of the government ships or aircraft involved in the pursuit: *Arctic Sunrise Arbitration* [100]–[101], [260] and [267].

[7] Art 111 of the LOSC is closely based on art 23 of the 1958 Convention on the High Seas, adapted to recognize the application of hot pursuit to archipelagic waters, the EEZ, and the continental shelf. Art 23 in turn reflected the earlier rule on hot pursuit in the International Law Commission's (ILC) 1956 Articles on the Law of the Sea, which was, in the main, taken from the draft prepared by the Hague Codification Conference in 1930: ILC, 'Articles Concerning the Law of the Sea with Commentaries' *Yearbook of the International Law Commission (1956) Vol II*, UN Doc A/CN.4/SER.A/1956/Add.l 265, 285.

[8] DP O'Connell, *The International Law of the Sea, Volume II* (OUP 1984) 1079; Douglas Guilfoyle, 'Article 111' in Alexander Proelss (ed), *United Nations Convention on the Law of the Sea: A Commentary* (CH Beck 2017) 775. See also the unreported 1995 Canadian case of *R v Mills and Others*, in which the judge found that the rule on hot pursuit in art 23 of the 1958 Convention on the High Seas constituted a codification of pre-existing customary international law: cited in William C Gilmore, 'Hot Pursuit: The Case of R v Mills and Others' (1995) 44 ICLQ 927, 953–4.

simultaneously as a rule of both conventional and customary international law, and regardless of the basis upon which it is asserted, the basic framework for its exercise can be understood by considering when the right of hot pursuit arises, how it must be exercised, who may exercise it, and when the right terminates.

7.1.1 When Does the Right of Hot Pursuit Arise?

The first prerequisite for the legitimate exercise of the right of hot pursuit, set out in Article 111(1), is that the 'competent authorities' must have 'good reason to believe' that the vessel being pursued has violated the laws and regulations of that State. A few practical observations can be made about this requirement. First, while the term 'competent authorities' is not defined, it is likely to include the coast guard and fisheries agency, as well as the navy, customs, police, or other maritime or law enforcement authorities of the coastal State.[9] Second, while the 'laws and regulations' in question must be applicable to the pursued vessel under the LOSC in the relevant maritime zone, there is no requirement that they relate to offences of any particular level of severity nor that any particular punishment or consequence be foreseen for their violation.[10] In practice, however, in light of the resources involved, the seriousness of intruding on the freedom of navigation, and questions of international comity, hot pursuit tends to be reserved for more serious offences.[11] Third, there must be some tangible evidence or reasonable basis upon which the coastal State can be said to have 'good reason to believe' that such laws and regulations have been violated.[12]

In the latter respect, while the International Tribunal for the Law of the Sea (ITLOS) has indicated that information that could give rise to 'no more than a suspicion' is not enough,[13] it is generally accepted that the coastal State is not required to have actual knowledge of an infringement.[14] In practice, a wide variety of factual circumstances may give the coastal State 'good reason to believe' that there has been a violation of its laws and regulations. In Australia's pursuit of the *Viarsa*, for example, circumstantial evidence to support a reasonable belief included the

[9] Guilfoyle, 'Article 111' (n 8) 776.

[10] O'Connell, *The International Law of the Sea* (n 8) 1080; Reuland, 'The Customary Right of Hot Pursuit' (n 2) 566–8; Natalie Klein, *Maritime Security and the Law of the Sea* (OUP 2011) 121–2.

[11] For example, the *Arctic Sunrise Arbitration* Tribunal found that whether any consequence or punishment was foreseen under Russian law for a violation of the prohibition was not relevant: *Arctic Sunrise Arbitration* [249]–[251].

[12] Satya Nandan and Shabtai Rosenne (eds), *United Nations Convention on the Law of the Sea 1982: A Commentary, Vol III* (Martinus Nijhoff 1995) 256.

[13] *Saiga (No 2)* [147].

[14] See, eg, Nicholas M Poulantzas, *The Right of Hot Pursuit in International Law* (2nd ed, Kluwer Law International 2002) 156–7 ('reasonable suspicion'); Rachel Baird, 'Arrests in a Cold Climate (Part 2)—Shaping Hot Pursuit through State Practice' (2009) 13 Ant&SthnOcean L&Pol OccPap 1, 6–7 (belief 'founded upon strong indications and not upon mere suspicion or suppositions').

presence of an unlicensed foreign fishing vessel in poor weather in a remote area of Australia's EEZ nearly 4,000 kilometres from port, the jettisoning of nets and fish by the vessel on approach from the coastal State authorities, and the obscuring of the vessel's identification by blacking out its name and number.[15] Moreover, as Reuland observes, States are unlikely to take unfair advantage of the imprecision of the standard in Article 111(1) because of the 'twin constraints of comity and the requirement that States compensate the victims of unjustified hot pursuit' as provided in Article 111(8).[16]

7.1.2 How Must the Right of Hot Pursuit be Exercised?

Article 111 places three important conditions on the way in which the right of hot pursuit is exercised, relating to: where hot pursuit is commenced; how it is commenced; and for how long it may be continued. Collectively, the object of these conditions is to ensure: that the vessel is in fact subject to boarding by the coastal State at the time when pursuit is commenced; that it has notice of the coastal State's attempt to board it; and that there is no chance the vessel will be subsequently mis-identified (which could result in interference with the freedom of navigation of an innocent vessel).[17] While these conditions apply regardless of the maritime zone in which the originating offence is committed, this discussion will focus on offences against the coastal State's laws and regulations in the EEZ.

Pursuant to Article 111(4), hot pursuit must be commenced while the foreign vessel (or one of its boats) is within the EEZ.[18] The pursuing ship or aircraft need not itself be inside the zone,[19] but must have 'satisfied itself by such practical means as may be available' that the vessel is within the EEZ. This subjective formulation acknowledges the practical difficulty of accurately pinpointing the location of the pursued vessel, and suggests that the lawfulness of the pursuit will not necessarily be affected if it is subsequently determined that the vessel was just outside the zone.[20] This flexible approach has been endorsed in the jurisprudence, which indicates that the location of the vessel 'should not be evaluated with the full benefit of hindsight, but rather looked at from the perspective of the pursuing

15 Ibid 7.

16 Reuland, 'The Customary Right of Hot Pursuit' (n 2) 569 fn 65.

17 Craig H Allen, 'Doctrine of Hot Pursuit: A Functional Interpretation Adaptable to Emerging Maritime Law Enforcement Technologies and Practices' (1989) 20(4) ODIL 309, 318.

18 Under the doctrine of 'constructive presence', the right of hot pursuit can be extended to cover the activities of 'mother ships' that hover outside the relevant maritime zone, working in association with other ships that commit offences within the zone.

19 ILC, 'Articles Concerning the Law of the Sea' (n 7) 285 (art 47, Comment 1(i)).

20 Klein, *Maritime Security* (n 10) 110. However, this does not preclude review of the pursuing vessel's determination: Myres S McDougal and William T Burke, *The Public Order of the Oceans: A Contemporary International Law of the Sea* (New Haven Press 1985) 916–17.

ship',[21] and affords the coastal State some margin of appreciation in making this determination.[22]

Having satisfied itself that the pursued vessel is within the EEZ, the coastal state must give the appropriate signal in order to commence the pursuit. In this respect, Article 111(4) provides that 'the pursuit may only be commenced after a visual or auditory signal to stop has been given at a distance which enables it to be seen or heard by the foreign ship.' In its 1956 commentaries, the ILC indicated that in order to prevent abuse, this condition was intended to exclude 'signals given at a great distance and transmitted by wireless'.[23] However, it was also noted during the course of the ILC's discussions that the 'important point was the fundamental right to give the order to stop and to undertake hot pursuit, not the specific means by which the right was exercised',[24] and in practice this requirement has been interpreted more flexibly to include, at a minimum, radio communications. For example, in Australia's pursuits of the *South Tomi* and the *Volga*, the signal to stop was given by radio and was not challenged by the flag States (Togo and Russia, respectively).[25] This approach has been widely accepted in the literature,[26] and was confirmed in the *Arctic Sunrise Arbitration,* in which the Tribunal found that the coastal State—which had used very high frequency (VHF) radio to signal the *Arctic Sunrise*—had complied with the conditions for giving a signal to stop.[27]

Once a hot pursuit has been validly commenced under Article 111(4), it may only be continued outside the EEZ if it has not been 'interrupted'.[28] The rationale underpinning this rule is twofold: first, continuity of pursuit is required to maintain the 'jurisdictional link' between the coastal State and the vessel pursued; and second, it ensures that enforcement action is not taken against the wrong vessel.[29] While the LOSC does not define what constitutes 'interruption' for these purposes, it has been observed that 'this rule must be applied with some flexibility',[30] and the literature and jurisprudence has provided some guidance as to what should (and should not) be considered to constitute an interruption to the continuity of hot pursuit.

[21] *Arctic Sunrise Arbitration* [267].

[22] James Harrison, 'The Arctic Sunrise Arbitration (Netherlands v. Russia)' (2016) 31(1) IJMCL 145, 152.

[23] ILC, 'Articles Concerning the Law of the Sea' (n 7) 285 (art 47, Comment 1(iii)).

[24] ILC, 'Summary Records of the Eighth Session, 23 April–4 July 1956' *Yearbook of the International Law Commission (1956) Vol I*, UN Doc A/CN.4/SER.A/1956/Add.l, 54.

[25] Baird, 'IUU Fishing' (n 3) 328.

[26] See, eg, McDougal and Burke, *The Public Order of the Oceans* (n 20) 897; Allen, 'Doctrine of Hot Pursuit' (n 17) 319; Poulantzas, *The Right of Hot Pursuit* (n 14) xv and xviii; Klein, *Maritime Security* (n 10) 110.

[27] *Arctic Sunrise Arbitration* [260]. See also the earlier case of *R v Mills and Others*, in which the court found that messages sent by VHF radio 'comply with the preconditions of the [LOSC] to the exercise of the right of hot pursuit': cited in Gilmore, 'Hot Pursuit' (n 8) 956–7.

[28] LOSC art 111(1).

[29] Allen, 'Doctrine of Hot Pursuit' (n 17) 319.

[30] O'Connell, *The International Law of the Sea, Vol II* (n 8) 1093–4.

For example, there are a number of circumstances that might give rise to short gaps in pursuit—such as where the pursuing vessel stops to pick up evidence of the offence or temporarily loses sight of the vessel due to poor weather, horizon distance, or darkness—but would not affect its continuity provided the pursuing vessel remains in pursuit and can positively identify the fleeing vessel.[31] In contrast, a more substantial intervention, such as the recall of the pursuing vessel, would constitute an interruption of the pursuit. This was the case in the *Saiga* pursuit, in which the coastal State (Guinea) recalled the patrol vessel when there was evidence that the *Saiga* had changed course, which ITLOS concluded 'constituted a clear interruption of any pursuit'.[32] Diverting a patrol vessel from hot pursuit to respond to a distress call would also amount to an interruption, but there is potential for this to be used as a diversionary tactic—as demonstrated by Australia's 2001 pursuit of the *Lena*, which was discontinued when the patrol vessel was forced to break off pursuit to respond to a nearby distress call that proved to be a false alarm, with no vessel in distress in the vicinity.[33]

While a 'preliminary but incomplete' boarding of the pursued vessel[34] or a 'mere pause in an attempt to actively arrest a vessel'[35] would not preclude the resumption of pursuit, a protracted period of merely monitoring the vessel without active attempts at enforcement is likely to constitute an interruption. This was the case in the *Arctic Sunrise Arbitration*, in which the Tribunal found that while the coastal State's initial actions in pursuit of the vessel were consistent with the notion of hot pursuit, its later actions (which included unloading its gun mounts and shadowing the vessel for thirty-three hours without attempting to issue any orders to it) were not consistent with continuous pursuit, the final objective of which would have been to board the *Arctic Sunrise* as soon as possible.[36] Accordingly, the Tribunal considered that the pursuit had been interrupted. Finally, Article 111(6) makes clear that pursuit may validly be continued by 'relay', with one pursuing vessel or aircraft taking over from another—so the vessel that finally makes the arrest may not be the one that began the pursuit.

7.1.3 Who may Exercise the Right of Hot Pursuit?

Pursuant to Article 111(5), hot pursuit may only be carried out by 'warships or military aircraft, or other ships or aircraft clearly marked and identifiable as being

[31] Allen, 'Doctrine of Hot Pursuit' (n 17) 319–20.
[32] *Saiga (No 2)* [147].
[33] Baird, 'Arrests in a Cold Climate' (n 14) 12.
[34] Poulantzas, *The Right of Hot Pursuit* (n 14) 213–14, relying on the *SS "I'm Alone" (Canada v United States)* (1935) III RIAA 1609, in which officers from the pursuing vessel were allowed to board the vessel but not to examine its papers or search it, and then resumed pursuit.
[35] Harrison, 'The Arctic Sunrise Arbitration' (n 22) 53.
[36] *Arctic Sunrise Arbitration* [270]–[275].

on government service and authorized to that effect'.[37] This requirement is generally accepted to include police patrol boats, coast guard and customs vessels, and fisheries inspection vessels.[38] However, it is not clear how strictly (or flexibly) this requirement is applied in practice, or how it might be interpreted by international courts and tribunals. In the *Arctic Sunrise Arbitration*, for example, while the vessel used to pursue the *Arctic Sunrise* was clearly marked as a coastguard patrol vessel, the helicopter from which the arrest was ultimately effected was unmarked save for a red star on its underside, and 'the men descending from it did not, in the recollection of the crew of the *Arctic Sunrise*, identify themselves.'[39] Nonetheless, the Tribunal simply stated that it was 'satisfied, in context, that the vessel was boarded by Russian officials', and did not make any reference to the requirement of Article 111(5).[40]

It remains to be seen whether the flexible and contextual approach applied in *Arctic Sunrise* would support the use of a private sector or civil society vessel or aircraft, such as those sometimes used in cooperative enforcement within the EEZ,[41] in the conduct of enforcement following hot pursuit onto the high seas. In this respect, it is within the subjective purview of the coastal State to decide which ships and aircraft are 'on government service and authorized to that effect', and to authorize the conduct of hot pursuit by such ships and aircraft in individual circumstances.[42] However, the question of whether such ships and aircraft are 'clearly marked and identifiable' as being on government service should be objectively determined, in order to avoid misunderstandings about the powers exercisable by the ship or aircraft, and ensure that the vessel being pursued can ascertain without difficulty whether or not the ship or aircraft carrying out the pursuit is legitimately empowered to do so.

[37] This is consistent with the requirements established in arts 107 and 110 for non-flag State enforcement on the high seas with respect to other issues (seizure of pirate ships and the right of visit), and those in art 224 for enforcement of measures relating to the protection and preservation of the marine environment in the EEZ (see also Chapter 6 n 110 and associated text.)

[38] Nandan and Rosenne, *UNCLOS Commentary, Vol III* (n 12) 258; Guilfoyle, 'Article 111' (n 8) 776;

[39] *Arctic Sunrise Arbitration* [100]–[101].

[40] Ibid [101].

[41] See the discussion in Section 6.2.3.2.

[42] Poulantzas makes a distinction between 'warships and military aircraft', which he concludes need no 'special authorization' to conduct hot pursuit, and 'other ships or aircraft on government service', including customs and fisheries inspection vessels, which should be 'specially authorized to exercise the right of hot pursuit against foreign infringing vessels': Poulantzas, *The Right of Hot Pursuit* (n 14) 196–7. See also Reuland, 'The Customary Right of Hot Pursuit' (n 2) 562. While such a distinction is not evident in practice, the underlying objective—of preventing unlawful interference with foreign-flagged vessels or breaches of international law by unauthorized or irresponsible ships or aircraft—remains important.

7.1.4 When Does the Right of Hot Pursuit Terminate?

In addition to the rule on interruption, pursuant to Article 111(3) 'the right of hot pursuit ceases as soon as the ship pursued enters the territorial sea of its own State or of a third State.' While this limitation is not discussed in the commentaries to the 1956 Articles on the Law of the Sea, it is generally accepted to reflect coastal State sovereignty in the territorial sea, and more broadly to provide a pragmatic balance between the pursuing State's interests in the enforcement of its laws, the community interest in the freedom of navigation, and the importance of preserving territorial integrity. However, this limitation can have significant practical impacts for the pursuing State—particularly if used by a pursued vessel to evade the consequences of its actions and be 'washed clean of its sins by the territorial waters of a third State.'[43] For example, evidence uncovered by the Australian authorities following the hot pursuit and arrest of both the *Lena* and the *South Tomi* in the Southern Ocean suggests that, during the course of those pursuits, the vessels received instructions as to how pursuit might be evaded by entering the territorial sea of France.[44] In this respect, a number of more flexible interpretations have been offered in order to address the situation where a pursued vessel deliberately enters the territorial sea to avoid apprehension.

First, a number of commentators endorse the view that 'a short stay or passage of the pursued vessel through the territorial waters of a State, obviously taken with the intention of evading the law, does not preclude resumption of pursuit.'[45] The basis for this argument is that since the pursued vessel is seeking to take unjustifiable advantage of a situation laid down in law, the activity should be deprived of its legal consequences. While this approach would enable the continuation of hot pursuit without offending the sovereignty of the third State, it has been criticized on the basis that it breaks the 'jurisdictional' link on which the pursuit is based, and upsets the balance struck in the hot pursuit doctrine 'precariously against the sovereign rights of the flag State.'[46] Alternatively, it has been suggested that upon entry to its territorial sea, the third State could 'take over' the hot pursuit of the vessel from the pursuing State.[47] In this scenario, however, the third State would presumably need to assert a breach of its own laws relating to innocent passage, rather than seeking

[43] Reuland, 'The Customary Right of Hot Pursuit' (n 2) 581.

[44] Baird, 'Arrests in a Cold Climate' (n 14) 13.

[45] Poulantzas, *The Right of Hot Pursuit* (n 14) 231. See also McDougal and Burke, *The Public Order of the Oceans* (n 20) 898; Allen, 'Doctrine of Hot Pursuit' (n 17) 320.

[46] Reuland, 'The Customary Right of Hot Pursuit' (n 2) 581. Similarly, Colombos argues that the rule requiring cessation of hot pursuit is to prevent the pursuing State from prolonging a right which, since it is exceptional, should give rise only to a narrow derogation from the flag State's exclusive jurisdiction: C Colombos, *The International Law of the Sea* (Longmans 1967) 169–70.

[47] Warwick Gullett and Clive Schofield, 'Pushing the Limits of the Law of the Sea Convention: Australian and French Cooperative Surveillance and Enforcement in the Southern Ocean' (2007) 22 IJMCL 545, 568.

to enforce the alleged breach of the pursuing State's laws on which the original pursuit was based.[48]

Another way of closing this loophole is for the third State to grant consent to the continuation of hot pursuit—or the exercise of enforcement powers—by the pursuing State in its territorial sea. While this approach has not been tested before an international court or tribunal, it has received significant support in the contemporary literature.[49] It maintains the jurisdictional link underpinning the pursuit, and does not infringe the third State's sovereignty or the right of innocent passage (since the vessel's intent in entering the territorial sea is not 'innocent').[50] It has been suggested that the legality of an arrest made under these circumstances could be successfully challenged, since an agreement between (in this case) a pursuing State and a third State should not affect or modify the rights of the flag State under the LOSC.[51] However, in light of the flexible interpretations that have been taken in relation to other elements of hot pursuit, there seems to be potential for international courts and tribunals to take a broader, more purposive approach to the balance of interests to be struck under Article 111, which recognizes the increase in the capacity and sophistication of illegal maritime activity and the need for a correlative adjustment in the principles relating to hot pursuit.[52] In this respect, State practice can play an important role.

7.2 State Practice in Relation to Hot Pursuit

In a 2004 speech commemorating ten years since the entry into force of the LOSC, the then Australian Foreign Minister noted that 'the international law of the sea, like all other branches of international law, cannot stand still and it must develop to meet the challenges of the modern era and be updated in light of developments in technology.'[53] In this context, he stated that Australia was working towards 'a 21st

[48] Ibid.

[49] See, eg, Allen, 'Doctrine of Hot Pursuit' (n 17) 320; Baird, 'Arrests in a Cold Climate' (n 14) 13; Erik Jaap Molenaar, 'Multilateral Hot Pursuit and Illegal Fishing in the Southern Ocean: The Pursuits of the Viarsa 1 and the South Tomi' (2004) 19 IJMCL 19, 29; Mincai Yu, 'The Implementation of the Right of Hot Pursuit and China's Maritime Law Enforcement' (2005) 1 China Oceans LRev 385, 398–9; Rothwell and Stephens, *The International Law of the Sea* (2nd ed, Hart 2016) 451; Jacqueline Espenilla 'Expanding the Right of Hot Pursuit: Challenges for Cooperative Maritime Law Enforcement Between the Philippines and Indonesia' (2017) 9 IntlJMarAff&Fish 1, 8; Guilfoyle, 'Article 111' (n 8) 776.

[50] LOSC art 19(2)(1): passage is not innocent if the ship engages in any activity 'not having a direct bearing on passage'.

[51] Klein, *Maritime Security* (n 10) 111–12, invoking art 311 of the LOSC. See also Gullett and Schofield, 'Pushing the Limits of the LOSC' (n 47) 567, who note that the pursuing State would need to argue for a purposive interpretation of art 111, but express doubt that the LOSC provides a firm foundation for such an interpretation.

[52] Dale Stephens, 'The Role of Courts and Tribunals in Maritime Regulation and Enforcement' in Robin Warner and Stuart Kaye (eds), *Routledge Handbook of Maritime Regulation and Enforcement* (Routledge 2016) 122, 132–3.

[53] Alexander Downer, 'The United Nations Convention on the Law of the Sea: Ten Years of Benefits for Australia', Speech to *Strategic Directions for Australia and the Law of the Sea Symposium, Canberra,*

century definition' of hot pursuit.[54] Australia has not been alone in this endeavour; in addition to a wide range of commentators who have endorsed the adoption of a more liberal, flexible, and functional approach to the interpretation of modern hot pursuit,[55] the implementation of this doctrine in the contemporary practice of coastal States also reveals some significant developments in this direction. This is demonstrated in the way that hot pursuit is generally reflected in domestic law and policy, as well as by the adoption of measures that develop or depart from the traditional procedural limitations imposed by Article 111, particularly with respect to the use of modern technology, and the adoption of cooperative approaches to hot pursuit.

7.2.1 The Domestic Legal Basis for Hot Pursuit

It is difficult to comprehensively examine the way in which maritime hot pursuit is approached by coastal States—even the domestic legal basis for its conduct is often hard to determine. Hot pursuit can arise from the violation of a wide range of laws and regulations in various maritime zones, and a range of maritime and law enforcement agencies may be authorized by the coastal State to conduct hot pursuit, including both military and civilian services. As a result, provisions relating to hot pursuit may be found in laws relating to the powers of different agencies (including defence, customs, police, and coastguard) and laws regulating different subject matters (from general criminal laws to legislation specifically relating to fisheries, narcotics, piracy, security, and transnational crimes).

In addition, while some coastal States *explicitly* implement the right of hot pursuit in legislation or establish specific procedures for its conduct, others treat it *implicitly* as part of their right to exercise powers with respect to foreign-flagged vessels in and beyond the EEZ.[56] For example, while broad powers of maritime enforcement are established in the legislation of the United States,[57] there is no explicit mention of the conduct of hot pursuit. Nonetheless, it is clear that the right

16 November 2004, reproduced in Jennifer Cavenagh, 'Australian Practice in International Law 2004' (2006) 25 AustYBIL 463, 496.

[54] Ibid 486.

[55] See, eg, Allen, 'Doctrine of Hot Pursuit' (n 17) 321–2; Churchill and Lowe, *The Law of the Sea* (n 5) 216; Vasilios Tasikas, 'Unmanned Aerial Vehicles and the Doctrine of Hot Pursuit: A New Era of Coast Guard Maritime Law Enforcement Operations' (2004) 29 TulMarLJ 59, 80; Baird, 'Arrests in a Cold Climate' (n 14) 16; Klein, *Maritime Security* (n 10) 109; Stephens, 'The Role of Courts and Tribunals' (n 52) 132–3.

[56] As Poulantzas observes: '[t]he right of hot pursuit may be implied when it is deemed as accompanying the right of the littoral states to control, visit and search every ship in the waters under their jurisdiction. These rights are in many cases ineffective if not accompanied by the right of hot pursuit': Poulantzas, *The Right of Hot Pursuit* (n 14) 93 and fn 87.

[57] 46 *USC* §70502(c)(1)(E) and 16 *USC* §§1861 and 1826(g).

of hot pursuit exists and is exercised under United States law.[58] In the context of maritime enforcement of narcotics laws, the *implicit* power to conduct hot pursuit can be contrasted with the *explicit* provision for the exercise of powers in the territorial sea of a third State, which states that vessels 'subject to the jurisdiction of the United States' include 'a vessel in the territorial waters of a foreign nation if the nation consents to the enforcement of United States law by the United States'.[59]

For some coastal States, hot pursuit may be exercised as a common law right or directly as a rule of customary international law. For example, the Canadian courts have stated: '[a]lthough a treaty requires domestic legislation to enforce its specific provisions against another signatory this does not apply when generally accepted principles of international law exist. The domestic legislation which would permit enforcement within territorial boundaries is simply extended by these principles to cover situations where it is necessary to pursue and return the offender.'[60]

Moreover, like procedures for the use of force, the detailed procedures governing the conduct of hot pursuit are commonly established in manuals and handbooks developed for the use of maritime law enforcement authorities, rather than spelt out in primary or secondary legislation. For example, while the United States has not put procedures for the conduct of hot pursuit on a legislative footing, the Department of Navy has issued detailed instructions on how it is to be initiated and conducted.[61]

An overview of the domestic legal basis for conducting hot pursuit in relation to fisheries offences is set out in Table 7.1, which predominantly reflects fisheries and maritime zone legislation, as well as relevant policies and procedures. Given the variety of ways in which the right of hot pursuit may arise and be exercised, it is also likely to be governed by other sources of domestic law and practice not included in Table 7.1, and there are a number of coastal States (particularly in Eastern Europe and Latin America) for which no relevant provisions were identified in the legislation examined. However, it nonetheless provides a useful overview of the contemporary approach taken by coastal States to the question of hot pursuit in the specific context of fisheries. Table 7.1 also indicates the States that are party to, or participants in, agreements or arrangements that envision the continuation of hot pursuit into the territorial sea with coastal State consent as discussed in Section 7.2.3.2—not only in relation to fisheries but in the context of general maritime law enforcement, narcotics, migrants, security, and piracy.

The most obvious feature of this practice is the general tendency of coastal States to define the conduct of hot pursuit by reference to international law generally,

[58] *United States v F/V Taiyo Maru* [395AD] F.Supp 413 (D.Me.1975).

[59] 46 *USC* §70502(c)(1)(E).

[60] *Regina v Sunila and Solayman* (1986) 28 (4th) Dom. Law Rep. 450, 456. See also the earlier decision of the Supreme Court of Canada in *The Ship 'North' v The King* (1906) 37 SCR 385.

[61] See United States Navy, *The Commander's Handbook on the Law of Naval Operations* (August 2017) 3.11.2.2.4.

Table 7.1 Coastal State approaches to hot pursuit

Party/Participant to agreement/arrangement allowing hot pursuit to continue into territorial sea with consent in relation to enforcement for: Fisheries (F); General maritime law enforcement (G); Narcotics (N); Migrants (M); Security (S); Piracy (P)			
Legislation provides that hot pursuit ends on entry to territorial sea (E) or may continue with coastal State consent (C)			
	Relevant legislation and regulations		
African Group			
Algeria	*Law 01-11 of 2001* art 95: a vessel may be stopped beyond the EEZ, provided the pursuit started inside the zone. The right of pursuit stops when the pursued vessel enters the territorial sea of its flag or a third State.	E	
Angola	*Law 6-A/04 of 2004* art 229: a foreign vessel may be pursued beyond the EEZ if there is good reason to believe it has violated fishing laws and regulations in Angolan waters. Pursuit ceases when the vessel enters the territorial sea of its flag State or a third State. Exercise of the right of hot pursuit is defined in regulations, in accordance with the LOSC.	E	FP
Benin	Not determined.		P
Cameroon	Not determined.		P
Cape Verde	Not determined.		FP
Comoros	*Law 82-015* art 12: when a foreign fishing vessel is pursued beyond the limits of the EEZ as a result of an infringement of the legislation in force, authorized officers may exercise powers in accordance with the rules laid down by international law.		P
Congo	Not determined.		P
Cote d'Ivoire	Not determined.		P
Djibouti	Not determined.		P
Egypt	Not determined.		P
Equatorial Guinea	*Law 11/2017* arts 1, 119, 151: hot pursuit begins in the jurisdictional waters of the coastal State and ends with the entry of the offending ship into the territorial sea of another State. Powers may be exercised by authorized officers beyond the jurisdictional waters of Equatorial Guinea in the case of a hot pursuit that started in those waters. The Government will sign cooperation agreements with neighbouring countries for hot pursuit, including of industrial vessels that are practising IUU fishing in Equatorial Guinea's waters and flee to a neighbouring country.		P

Table 7.1 *Continued*

Party/Participant to agreement/arrangement allowing hot pursuit to continue into territorial sea with consent in relation to enforcement for: Fisheries (F); General maritime law enforcement (G); Narcotics (N); Migrants (M); Security (S); Piracy (P)			
Legislation provides that hot pursuit ends on entry to territorial sea (E) or may continue with coastal State consent (C)			
	Relevant legislation and regulations		
Eritrea	*Proc 176/2014* art 30: where a vessel is pursued beyond Eritrean waters after committing an offence, powers are exercisable by authorized officers in circumstances and to the extent recognized by international law or any applicable bilateral or regional agreements.		P
Gabon	*Law 15/2005* arts 82–3: if a vessel absconds, the authorized officer may, on the basis of cooperation agreements, pursue it into the national waters of States Parties to those agreements, including the flag State of the vessel.	C	P
Gambia	*Act 2007* s 72: if there are reasonable grounds to believe a fishing vessel has committed an offence under the Act, it may be pursued beyond the EEZ 'to the extent recognized by international law'. Pursuit is not taken to be terminated or substantially interrupted if only sight of the vessel (including output from a radar or other sensing device) is lost.		FGP
Ghana	*Act 2002* ss 96–7: if there are reasonable grounds to believe that an offence under the Act has been or is being committed, authorized officers may follow a foreign vessel in hot pursuit and exercise powers beyond the EEZ in accordance with international law.		P
Guinea	*Code 2015* art 187: the right of pursuit is exercised in accordance with international law, in particular the provisions of Article 111 of the LOSC, and shall cease when the vessel enters the territorial sea of its flag State or a third State. This provision is without prejudice to the specific modalities of the right of hot pursuit within the framework of bilateral or subregional international agreements.	EC	FP
Guinea-Bissau	*Dec Law 10/2011* art 54: a foreign fishing vessel may be boarded beyond the EEZ if the pursuit was initiated within the zone and there is strong evidence to presume it has infringed the fisheries laws. The right of pursuit shall be exercised in accordance with international law and ceases when the vessel enters the territorial sea of its flag State or a third State. This is without prejudice to the rules of international agreements that may provide for the possibility of Guinea-Bissau inspection vessels exercising the right of pursuit within waters under the jurisdiction of other States.	EC	FP

Continued

Table 7.1 *Continued*

Party/Participant to agreement/arrangement allowing hot pursuit to continue into territorial sea with consent in relation to enforcement for: Fisheries (F); General maritime law enforcement (G); Narcotics (N); Migrants (M); Security (S); Piracy (P)			
Legislation provides that hot pursuit ends on entry to territorial sea (E) or may continue with coastal State consent (C)			
	Relevant legislation and regulations		
Kenya	*Act 2016* s 139: authorised officers may stop, board, and inspect any vessel in Kenya's EEZ in performance of functions under the Act, and may order the vessel to port if they believe that it has been used in contravention of the Act or its licence.		P
Liberia	*Law 2019* s 11.7: following hot pursuit commenced within the fisheries waters and continued outside it in accordance with international law, authorized officers may exercise powers in relation to any vessel which they have reasonable grounds to believe has been used in the commission of an offence.		P
Madagascar	Not determined.		P
Mauritania	*Law 2015-017* art 75: the right of hot pursuit is exercised in accordance with international law and ceases when the vessel enters the territorial sea of its flag State or a third State, without prejudice to any bilateral, subregional, or international agreements that might otherwise provide.	EC	F
Mauritius	*Act 2007* art 62: authorized officers may exercise powers beyond the EEZ following hot pursuit in accordance with international law as reflected in Article 111 of the LOSC in relation to a foreign vessel which they have reason to believe was used in the commission of an offence. These powers shall cease when the vessel enters the territorial sea of another State.	E	FP
Mozambique	*Law 22/2013* art 91: when authorized officers have reasonable grounds to believe that a fishing vessel has violated fishing laws and regulations, they may exercise the right of hot pursuit in accordance with international law.		FGP
Namibia	*Act 2000* s 5(3): authorized inspectors may exercise their powers with respect to foreign flag vessels outside Namibian waters to the extent authorized by international agreements to which Namibia is a party.		FP
Nigeria	*Act 2007* s 23: authorized officers have the power to exercise the right of hot pursuit.		
Sao Tome & Principe	Not determined.		P

Table 7.1 *Continued*

Party/Participant to agreement/arrangement allowing hot pursuit to continue into territorial sea with consent in relation to enforcement for: Fisheries (F); General maritime law enforcement (G); Narcotics (N); Migrants (M); Security (S); Piracy (P)			
Legislation provides that hot pursuit ends on entry to territorial sea (E) or may continue with coastal State consent (C)			
	Relevant legislation and regulations		
Senegal	*Code 2015* art 88: the right of hot pursuit is exercised in accordance with international law, in particular the provisions of Article 111 of the LOSC and ceases when the vessel enters the territorial sea of its flag State or a third State. However, this is without prejudice to any special modalities of hot pursuit within the framework of international agreements concluded at the bilateral or regional level.	EC	FP
Seychelles	*Act 2014* s 50: authorized officers may exercise powers in relation to a foreign fishing vessel beyond the EEZ following hot pursuit in accordance with international law as referred to in Article 111 of the LOSC.		P
Sierra Leone	*Act 2018* s 2: the fisheries law applies in areas beyond the jurisdiction of Sierra Leone following hot pursuit conducted in accordance with international law.		FP
Somalia	Not determined.		P
South Africa	*Act 1998* s 52: following hot pursuit in accordance with international law as reflected in Article 111 of the LOSC, authorized officers may exercise powers beyond the EEZ with respect to foreign fishing vessels that they have reasonable grounds to believe were used to commit an offence within the zone. *Defence Act 2002* s 22(3)(a): enforcement may not take place in the territorial sea of a foreign State except on board a South African ship or pursuant to an agreement on law enforcement co-operation with that State.		FG
Tanzania	*Act 2020* s 64: authorized officers have the power to pursue a vessel beyond the EEZ based on evidence from a VMS, GPS, aerial photography, satellite system, or any other 'accepted international technological communication system'. In the exercise of hot pursuit, authorized inspectors shall take into consideration any relevant bilateral, regional, or international instruments to which Tanzania is a party.		FG
Togo	Not determined.		P

Continued

Table 7.1 *Continued*

Party/Participant to agreement/arrangement allowing hot pursuit to continue into territorial sea with consent in relation to enforcement for: Fisheries (F); General maritime law enforcement (G); Narcotics (N); Migrants (M); Security (S); Piracy (P)			
Legislation provides that hot pursuit ends on entry to territorial sea (E) or may continue with coastal State consent (C)			
	Relevant legislation and regulations		
Asia-Pacific Group			
Bangladesh	*Act 2020* s 35: authorized officers may give the signal to stop by means of any international signal, code, or other recognized means. If the vessel fails to stop, it may be pursued and detained beyond the EEZ.		
China	*Code of Practice for Fishery Patrols,* Chapter 4(IV): authorized officers may exercise the right of hot pursuit if there is good reason to believe that a foreign vessel has violated the laws and regulations in the EEZ. Hot pursuit terminates when the vessel reaches the territorial sea of another State.	E	
Chinese Taipei	*Law 1998* arts 16 and 110: authorized officers may conduct hot pursuit where a person has engaged in any activity violating the laws and regulations of Chinese Taipei, in accordance with the rules for hot pursuit in Article 111 of the LOSC.		
Cook Islands	*Act 2005* s 52: authorized officers may exercise powers with respect to a foreign fishing vessel beyond the EEZ if they believe on reasonable grounds that a person on board the vessel committed an offence within the EEZ and they are in hot pursuit of (or have freshly pursued) the vessel and commenced that pursuit in the EEZ.		FG
Fiji	*Dec 2012* ss (1), 53: authorized officers may exercise their powers in respect of a foreign fishing vessel beyond the EEZ if they believe on reasonable grounds that a person on the vessel committed an offence in Fijian waters and are in hot pursuit of or have recently pursued the vessel, having commenced that pursuit within Fijian waters (as defined by reference to the right of hot pursuit in Article 111 of the LOSC).		F
India	*Act 1981* s 9(5): authorized officers may exercise powers over foreign vessels pursued beyond the limits of the EEZ in the circumstances and to the extent recognized by international law and practice.		
Indonesia	*Act 1983* Explanatory Note to art 4(1): Indonesia has the right under international law to undertake a hot pursuit of any foreign ships committing a violation of a provision of Indonesia's statutory regulations in the EEZ.		S

Table 7.1 *Continued*

			Party/Participant to agreement/arrangement allowing hot pursuit to continue into territorial sea with consent in relation to enforcement for: Fisheries (F); General maritime law enforcement (G); Narcotics (N); Migrants (M); Security (S); Piracy (P)
		Legislation provides that hot pursuit ends on entry to territorial sea (E) or may continue with coastal State consent (C)	
	Relevant legislation and regulations		
Iran	*Law 1995* art 40: foreign fishing vessels may be arrested outside the EEZ provided that the pursuit started within Iranian waters and has been exercised according to the principles of international law. The right of pursuit ceases upon entry into the territorial sea of another State, unless otherwise specified by the provisions of international agreements.	EC	
Japan	*Act 1996* art 1(4): hot pursuit may be undertaken in accordance with Article 111 of the LOSC.		
Kiribati	*Act 2010* ss 23(2), 24: if they have reasonable grounds to believe that an offence is being or has been committed in the EEZ, authorized officers may exercise hot pursuit in accordance with international law and may exercise their powers beyond the EEZ in accordance with international law.		F
Korea	*EEZ Act 1996* art 5(3): Where it is suspected that the laws and regulations of the EEZ have been violated, the authorities may take necessary measures of enforcement including the exercise of hot pursuit as provided for in Article 111 of the LOSC.		
Malaysia	*Act 1984* s 25(3): authorized officers may undertake hot pursuit if they have reason to believe a vessel has contravened any provision of the Act or applicable law and may exercise powers beyond the EEZ to the extent allowed by international law. The right of hot pursuit ceases when the vessel enters the territorial sea or EEZ of its own State or a third State, except as otherwise provided by a regional or bilateral agreement to which Malaysia is party.	C	S
Marshall Islands	51 *MIRC* §512(d): following hot pursuit in accordance with international law commenced within the EEZ, authorized officers may stop, board, and search any fishing vessel outside the EEZ which they have reasonable grounds to believe has been used in the commission of an offence.		F
Micronesia	24 *FSM Code* §603: following hot pursuit in accordance with international law commenced within the EEZ, authorized officers may stop, board, and search any fishing vessel outside the EEZ which they have reasonable grounds to believe has been used in the commission of an offence.		F

Continued

Table 7.1 *Continued*

Party/Participant to agreement/arrangement allowing hot pursuit to continue into territorial sea with consent in relation to enforcement for: Fisheries (F); General maritime law enforcement (G); Narcotics (N); Migrants (M); Security (S); Piracy (P)			
Legislation provides that hot pursuit ends on entry to territorial sea (E) or may continue with coastal State consent (C)			
	Relevant legislation and regulations		
Myanmar	*Law 2017* s 26: the right of hot pursuit may be exercised in relation to a foreign ship which violates or is believed to have violated relevant laws. Such right ceases if a foreign ship pursued enters its territorial sea or the territorial sea of a third State. *Law 1989* §22: after pursuing and seizing it in accordance with international law, authorized officers may return to Burmese waters a foreign fishing vessel which has contravened any provisions of this law.	E	
Nauru	*Act 1997* s 17: authorized officers may, following hot pursuit carried out in accordance with international law and commenced within the EEZ, exercise powers with respect to a foreign fishing vessel outside the EEZ.		F
Niue	*Act 1996* ss 39(2)(c), 40(1): following hot pursuit in accordance with international law and commenced within the fisheries waters, authorized officers may exercise powers with respect to a vessel beyond the EEZ if they have reasonable grounds to believe that it has been used in the commission of an offence within the zone.		F
Oman	Not determined.		P
Palau	27 *PNC* §204: hot pursuit may be undertaken if there is good reason to believe that the vessel has violated the laws and regulations of Palau. It must be commenced when the foreign vessel is in the internal waters, territorial sea, archipelagic waters, or contiguous zone, and may only be continued outside if it has not been interrupted.		F
Philippines	Not determined.		S
Papua New Guinea	*Act 1998* s 49: following hot pursuit outside the EEZ in accordance with international law and commenced within the zone, authorized officers may exercise powers with respect to any vessel which they have reasonable grounds to believe were used in the commission of an offence.		F
Samoa	*Act 2016* s 2(2): hot pursuit means the pursuit of a vessel under Article 111 of the LOSC.		F
Solomon Islands	*Regs 2017* s 23: the master and crew of a fishing vessel must allow access by authorized officers following a hot pursuit that commenced in fisheries waters.		F

Table 7.1 *Continued*

Party/Participant to agreement/arrangement allowing hot pursuit to continue into territorial sea with consent in relation to enforcement for: Fisheries (F); General maritime law enforcement (G); Narcotics (N); Migrants (M); Security (S); Piracy (P)			
Legislation provides that hot pursuit ends on entry to territorial sea (E) or may continue with coastal State consent (C)			
	Relevant legislation and regulations		
Sri Lanka	*Act 1979* ss 15B, 18: where a foreign fishing boat is pursued beyond the limits of Sri Lankan waters following the commission of an offence within those waters, authorized officers may exercise their powers beyond the waters in the circumstances, and to the extent, recognized by international law.		
Thailand	Not determined.		S
Timor-Leste	*Dec Law 2004* art 152: authorized officers may pursue a foreign vessel if there are well-founded reasons to believe that it violated fishing laws and regulations in the fisheries waters. The pursuit must commence within those waters and be continuous, but ceases when the pursued vessel enters the territorial sea of the flag State or a third State. The requirements, procedures, and powers in the exercise of the right of pursuit shall be defined by regulation in accordance with the LOSC.		E
Tonga	*Act 2002* s 73: a vessel may be pursued beyond the EEZ and powers exercised by authorized officers in circumstances and to the extent recognized by international law, provided that the pursuit was not terminated or interrupted at any time. A pursuit is not taken to be terminated or interrupted only because the authorised officers lose sight of the vessel (which includes a reference to output from a radar or other sensing device).		F
Tuvalu	*Act 2006* s 47: if an authorized officer has reasonable grounds to believe that an offence has been committed in the EEZ, they may exercise powers over a vessel outside the fishery waters following hot pursuit in accordance with international law and commenced within the fishery waters.		F
United Arab Emirates	Not determined.		P
Vanuatu	*Act 2014* ss 109(2)(c), 110(1): if an authorized officer has reasonable grounds to believe that an offence against the Act has been committed, they may follow in hot pursuit in accordance with international law. If pursuit has commenced within Vanuatu waters, officers may exercise powers outside Vanuatu waters in accordance with international law.		F

Continued

Table 7.1 *Continued*

Party/Participant to agreement/arrangement allowing hot pursuit to continue into territorial sea with consent in relation to enforcement for: Fisheries (F); General maritime law enforcement (G); Narcotics (N); Migrants (M); Security (S); Piracy (P)			
Legislation provides that hot pursuit ends on entry to territorial sea (E) or may continue with coastal State consent (C)			
	Relevant legislation and regulations		
Vietnam	*Law 2012* art 41: the right of hot pursuit is exercised after the patrol and surveillance forces have transmitted signals requesting the violating vessel or suspected violating vessel to stop for inspection and such vessel does not cooperate. The pursuit may be continued if it has not been interrupted and terminates when the vessel pursued enters the territorial sea of another State.	E	
Yemen	Not determined.		P
Eastern Europe Group			
Bulgaria	*Act 2000* art 67: hot pursuit shall be exercised by government vessels and aircraft authorized for the purpose and bearing the appropriate insignia and shall continue until the ship pursued enters the territorial sea of its own or of another State.	E	
Croatia	*Code 1994* art 47: hot pursuit can be continued in the open sea, the EEZ or the contiguous zone of a foreign country if the pursuit has not been interrupted, until the ship has entered the territorial sea of its own or of a third state.		E
Montenegro	*Law 2009* art 115: authorized inspectors may exercise powers over a foreign vessel beyond the EEZ within the authority laid down by ratified international agreement.		
Romania	*Act 1990* arts 26–7: hot pursuit of a foreign ship beyond the EEZ may be continued without interruption until the pursued ship enters the territorial sea of its own State or of a third State.		E
Russia	*Act 1998* art 36(1)(iii): authorized officers may engage in hot pursuit and detain ships which are violating the fisheries law and take them to the nearest port.		
Slovenia	*Code* art 22: hot pursuit may be initiated in the internal waters or territorial sea and may continue in accordance with the generally recognized rules of international law, until the ship enters the territorial sea of its own or another country, provided that it has not been suspended.		E

Table 7.1 *Continued*

Party/Participant to agreement/arrangement allowing hot pursuit to continue into territorial sea with consent in relation to enforcement for: Fisheries (F); General maritime law enforcement (G); Narcotics (N); Migrants (M); Security (S); Piracy (P)			
Legislation provides that hot pursuit ends on entry to territorial sea (E) or may continue with coastal State consent (C)			
	Relevant legislation and regulations		
Latin America and the Caribbean Group			
Antigua & Barbuda	*Act 2006* s 52: if a foreign fishing vessel that has committed an offence under the Act is pursued beyond the limits of Antigua and Barbuda waters, authorized officers may exercise powers in circumstances and to the extent recognized by international law.		G
Bahamas	Not determined.		NM
Barbados	*Act 1993* s 34(4): if a foreign fishing vessel that has committed an offence is pursued beyond the limits of the waters of Barbados, the powers conferred on an authorized officer are exercisable beyond the limits of the waters of Barbados in the circumstances and to the extent recognized by international law.		GN
Belize	Not determined.		N
Costa Rica	Not determined.		N
Dominica	*Act 1987* s 27(4): where, following the commission of an offence under this Act, a foreign fishing vessel is pursued beyond the limits of the fishery waters, the powers of authorized officers shall be exercisable in the circumstances and to the extent recognized by international law.		G
Dominican Republic	Not determined.		M
Grenada	*Act 1986* s 28(4): where, following the commission of an offence under this Act, a foreign fishing vessel is pursued beyond the limits of the fishery waters, the powers of authorized officers shall be exercisable in the circumstances and to the extent recognized by international law.		G
Guatemala	Not determined.		N

Continued

Table 7.1 *Continued*

Party/Participant to agreement/arrangement allowing hot pursuit to continue into territorial sea with consent in relation to enforcement for: Fisheries (F); General maritime law enforcement (G); Narcotics (N); Migrants (M); Security (S); Piracy (P)			
Legislation provides that hot pursuit ends on entry to territorial sea (E) or may continue with coastal State consent (C)			
	Relevant legislation and regulations		
Guyana	*Act 2012* s 49(10): where, following the commission of an offence, a foreign fishing vessel is pursued beyond the limits of the fisheries waters in circumstances and to the extent recognized by international law, the powers conferred on authorized officers under this Act shall be exercisable beyond the limits of national jurisdiction in accordance with international law.		N
Haiti	Not determined.		N
Honduras	Not determined.		N
Jamaica	Not determined.		N
Nicaragua	*Dec 9/2005* art 211: the pursuit of foreign fishing vessels shall cease when the pursued vessel enters the territorial sea of its flag State or a third State.		N
Panama	Not determined.		G
Saint Kitts & Nevis	*Act 2016* s 3(i): the Act applies to and in relation to following in hot pursuit conducted in accordance with international law.		G
Saint Lucia	*Act 1984* s 27(4): where, following the commission of an offence under this Act, a foreign fishing vessel is pursued beyond the limits of the fishery waters, the powers of authorized officers may be exercised in the circumstances and to the extent recognized by international law.		G
Saint Vincent & Grenadines	*Act 1986* s 33(4): where, following the commission of an offence under this Act, a foreign fishing vessel is pursued beyond the limits of the fishery waters, the powers of authorized officers may be exercised in the circumstances and to the extent recognized by international law.		G
Suriname	Not determined.		N
Trinidad & Tobago	Not determined.		N

Table 7.1 *Continued*

Party/Participant to agreement/arrangement allowing hot pursuit to continue into territorial sea with consent in relation to enforcement for: Fisheries (F); General maritime law enforcement (G); Narcotics (N); Migrants (M); Security (S); Piracy (P)			
Legislation provides that hot pursuit ends on entry to territorial sea (E) or may continue with coastal State consent (C)			
	Relevant legislation and regulations		
Uruguay	*Act 17.033 of 1998* art 20: monitoring and supervision of the maritime areas may be extended beyond those areas in exercise of the right of hot pursuit, in accordance with Article 111 of the Convention.		
Venezuela	*Dec 1,446 of 2014* art 41: the hot pursuit of a foreign ship may be undertaken in accordance with international norms, when there are substantial grounds for believing that the foreign ship is violating or has violated national or international law.		
Western Europe and Others Group			
Australia	*Act 2013* ss 40, 41(1)(i), 42: powers may be exercised outside Australian waters in relation to a foreign vessel if it has been chased without interruption. The chase is not 'interrupted' only because: it is continued by another officer; it is begun or taken over by another vessel or aircraft (including a vessel or aircraft of a foreign country); if the chase is continued by a vessel or aircraft of a foreign country—there is no maritime officer on board; the vessel is out of sight of any or all maritime officers, or officers of a foreign country, involved in the chase; or the vessel cannot be tracked by remote means, including radio, radar, satellite, or sonar. Enforcement powers may be exercised in the territorial sea of another country at the request or with the agreement of that country.	C	F
Canada	*Act 1985* s 18.2(1): where pursuit has been commenced, authorized officers may exercise their powers with respect to foreign fishing vessels at any place on the seas other than in the territorial sea or internal waters of another State.	E	
France	*Defence Code* art L1521-6: authorized officers may exercise the right of hot pursuit of a foreign vessel under the conditions provided for by international law. (Applies in relation to overseas territories per art L1521-1.)		FN

Continued

Table 7.1 *Continued*

Party/Participant to agreement/arrangement allowing hot pursuit to continue into territorial sea with consent in relation to enforcement for: Fisheries (F); General maritime law enforcement (G); Narcotics (N); Migrants (M); Security (S); Piracy (P)			
Legislation provides that hot pursuit ends on entry to territorial sea (E) or may continue with coastal State consent (C)			
	Relevant legislation and regulations		
Malta	*Act 1972* art 8: hot pursuit may be continued into the high seas provided that it has not been interrupted and shall cease where the suspect vessel enters the territorial sea of its own State or of a third State.	E	
Netherlands	Not determined.		N
New Zealand	*Act 1996* s 215: authorized officers may exercise their powers beyond New Zealand fisheries waters if there are reasonable grounds to believe that an offence was committed in New Zealand waters and the officers are 'in fresh pursuit of' or 'have freshly pursued' the vessel and the pursuit commenced in New Zealand waters.		F
NZ (Tokelau)	Not determined.		F
Portugal	*Law 34/2006* art 16(3): if a vessel does not comply with an order to stop, pursuit may be undertaken under the terms of international law.		
Spain	*Law 14/2014* art 48: hot pursuit shall be exercised for the causes and in the manner in which it is established in the LOSC and other applicable international conventions.		
United Kingdom	Not determined.		N
UK (Falklands)	*Ordinance 2005* s 156: authorized officers may exercise powers with respect to a vessel pursued beyond the fisheries waters, but not within the territorial sea of another country and provided that: prior to commencing pursuit a visual or auditory signal to stop was given at a distance which enabled it to be seen or heard at a place within the fisheries waters; the officers have pursued the vessel from the place where the order to stop was given to the place where the powers are exercised; and the pursuit was not interrupted at any time. The pursuit is not taken to be interrupted only because visual or non-visual contact was interrupted temporarily.	E	

Table 7.1 *Continued*

			Party/Participant to agreement/arrangement allowing hot pursuit to continue into territorial sea with consent in relation to enforcement for: Fisheries (F); General maritime law enforcement (G); Narcotics (N); Migrants (M); Security (S); Piracy (P)
		Legislation provides that hot pursuit ends on entry to territorial sea (E) or may continue with coastal State consent (C)	
	Relevant legislation and regulations		
UK (Montserrat)	*Act 2000* s 47(4): where, following the commission of an offence, a foreign fishing vessel is pursued beyond the limits of the fishery waters, the powers of authorized officers shall be exercisable beyond the limits of the fishery waters in the circumstances and to the extent recognized by international law.		N
UK (SGSSI)	*Ordinance 2005* s 11(2): the powers of authorized officers may be exercised outside the fishing waters so far as is in accord with international law and practice.		
United States	*The Commander's Handbook on the Law of Naval Operations* (2017) para 3.11.2.2.4: once successfully initiated, hot pursuit must be continued without interruption, either visually or through electronic means. The right of hot pursuit ceases as soon as the ship pursued enters the territorial sea of its own State or of a third State, unless the coastal State concerned permits the pursuit to continue.	C	GN

rather than Article 111 or the LOSC specifically. For example, as Table 7.1 shows, although some coastal States specifically refer to the conduct of hot pursuit in accordance with international law 'as referred to in Article 111' of the LOSC (or similar),[62] the legislation of most coastal States examined either refers simply to hot pursuit 'in accordance with international law' without making any reference or link to the LOSC,[63] or just provides a right for authorized officers to conduct hot pursuit—or to exercise powers beyond the EEZ following hot pursuit—without reference to any particular source or rule.[64] In addition, some countries (particularly

[62] See Table 7.1: Guinea, Mauritius, Senegal, Seychelles, South Africa, Chinese Taipei, Fiji, Japan, Korea, Samoa, Timor-Leste, Uruguay, Spain.

[63] Ibid: Comoros, Eritrea, Gambia, Ghana, Guinea-Bissau, Liberia, Mauritania, Mozambique, Sierra Leone, India, Indonesia, Iran, Malaysia, Marshall Islands, Micronesia, Nauru, Niue, Papua New Guinea, Sri Lanka, Tonga, Tuvalu, Vanuatu, Slovenia, Antigua and Barbuda, Dominica, Grenada, Guyana, Saint Kitts and Nevis, Saint Lucia, Saint Vincent and the Grenadines, Venezuela, France (including Mayotte, New Caledonia, the Southern and Antarctic Territories (SAAT)), Portugal, United Kingdom (Montserrat, South Georgia, and the South Sandwich Islands (SGSSI)).

[64] Ibid: Equatorial Guinea, Bangladesh, Cook Islands, Palau, Solomon Islands, Vietnam, Russia, Australia, Canada, New Zealand, United Kingdom (Falkland Islands).

in Africa) contemplate the conduct of hot pursuit being regulated through 'other applicable agreements or arrangements',[65] or specify that hot pursuit is exercised in accordance with Article 111 but 'without prejudice' to any other agreements concluded bilaterally or sub-regionally.[66]

As this practice shows, a significant number of coastal States do not express the rule on hot pursuit by reference to the treaty-based standards in the LOSC, but instead specifically contemplate that the procedures for hot pursuit may be established in agreements or arrangements outside the LOSC, or by reference to 'international law' generally. This gives rise to some complex questions about the legal effect of State practice in relation to the conduct of hot pursuit. For instance, if hot pursuit is conducted in accordance with—or to the extent permitted by—'international law' rather than pursuant to the procedures in the LOSC, this would likely not constitute subsequent practice in the interpretation of the LOSC but, depending on the intention of the States in question, might be relevant to establishing the state of the customary international law rule on hot pursuit.[67] In this respect, it is useful to consider whether—and how—the procedures used by coastal States in the conduct of hot pursuit depart from or develop the existing rules in Article 111 of the LOSC (which also represent customary international law), by reference to two trends that feature prominently in contemporary State practice: the use of modern technology in hot pursuit, and cooperative approaches to the conduct of hot pursuit.

7.2.2 The Use of Modern Technology

The increased focus in State practice on the effective use of modern technologies in fisheries enforcement has already been discussed in the context of Article 73, including with respect to the use of 'remote detection' techniques such as vessel monitoring systems (VMS), automatic identification systems (AIS), satellite-based radar, infrared and photographic imagery, and aerial and underwater drone technology.[68] These tools and technologies are also becoming increasingly common in the context of hot pursuit, and have the potential to significantly change the way that hot pursuit is conducted, including with respect to:

- detecting the offence (giving the coastal State 'good reason to believe' that an offence has been committed within the EEZ);[69]

65 Ibid: Eritrea, Namibia, Tanzania.
66 Ibid: Guinea-Bissau, Senegal.
67 The legal effect of State practice on the interpretation of treaties and the development of customary international law is discussed in Section 1.2.
68 See Section 6.2.2.
69 LOSC art 111(1).

- locating the pursued vessel (allowing the coastal State to satisfy itself 'by such practical means as may be available' that the vessel is within the EEZ at the time the pursuit is commenced);[70]
- notifying the vessel of the commencement of hot pursuit (as a means for giving the vessel a signal to stop);[71] and
- continuing hot pursuit (as a way of maintaining continuous observation of the vessel and ensuring that the pursuit is not 'interrupted').[72]

This approach was endorsed in *Arctic Sunrise,* in which the Tribunal stated that '[t]he parameters of the right of hot pursuit must be interpreted in the light of their object and purpose, having regard to the modern use of technology.'[73] While the Tribunal's decision related specifically to the method used by the coastal State to give the notification to stop, this logic can be applied equally to the requirements of detection, location, and continuation. Nonetheless, since each of these actions constitutes an independent element of the cumulative conditions that are required for the conduct of hot pursuit under the LOSC and customary international law, they are all vulnerable to challenge by a flag State and thus bear individual examination.

7.2.2.1 Detection of the Offence and Location of the Vessel

The use of modern technology to fulfill the first two elements of hot pursuit—detecting the offence and locating the pursued vessel within the EEZ—has not been challenged by any flag State and should be uncontroversial. This is confirmed by the history of Article 111(4) of the LOSC, which as originally drafted in Article 47(3) of the 1956 Articles on the Law of the Sea would have required the pursuing vessel to satisfy itself of the location of the pursued vessel 'by bearings, sextant angles or other like means'.[74] Fortunately, this was replaced during the negotiation of the 1958 Convention on the High Seas with the current text ('such practicable means as may be available') in order to 'allow all practical methods to be used for ascertaining the position of the ship pursued',[75] which was replicated in Article 111(4) of the LOSC. Accordingly, it can be understood as including 'every technical instrument at the disposal of a competent vessel of the coastal State for the detection and establishment of the position of infringing ships.'[76] In this respect, as

[70] Ibid art 111(4).
[71] Ibid.
[72] Ibid art 111(1).
[73] *Arctic Sunrise Arbitration* [259].
[74] This text was originally adopted during the 1930 Hague Codification Conference, and was maintained by the ILC in its 1956 Articles on the Law of the Sea: Poulantzas, *The Right of Hot Pursuit* (n 14) 200–1.
[75] United Nations (UN), *Official Records of the United Nations Conference on the Law of the Sea, Geneva, 24 February to 27 April 1958, Vol IV (Summary Records, Plenary, General Committee, First, Second and Third Committees, as well as Documents of the Conference, Third Session (Geneva, 17 March to 9 May 1975))* UN Doc A/CONF.62/36, 82.
[76] Poulantzas, *The Right of Hot Pursuit* (n 14) 202.

Klein has observed, the margin of error afforded the coastal State should diminish as the technology used to detect offences and locate vessels becomes more sophisticated, accurate, and widespread.[77]

7.2.2.2 Notification to Stop

The use of modern technology to give effect to the third element—notification to stop—is also fairly uncontroversial. This issue was addressed (albeit in the context of offences relating to non-living resources on the continental shelf rather than fisheries in the EEZ) in the *Arctic Sunrise Arbitration,* in which the coastal State used modern technology (in the form of VHF radio) to fulfil the requirement that a 'visual or auditory signal to stop has been given at a distance which enables it to be seen or heard by the foreign ship'. This form of notification was challenged by the flag State,[78] but accepted by the Tribunal.[79] Highlighting the need to interpret Article 111(4) in light of its object and purpose, the Tribunal noted that the principal object of the rule requiring a signal to be given at the commencement of hot pursuit is to ensure that the pursued ship is made aware of the pursuit—which was clearly the case since at least some of the messages were received and acknowledged.[80] In addition, the Tribunal noted that VHF messages are the standard means of communication between ships at sea, and that the 1974 *International Convention for the Safety of Life at Sea*[81] requires ships to constantly monitor an international VHF distress channel.[82] Finally, the Tribunal commented that the ILC's concern (expressed in 1956) to 'prevent abuse' of the hot pursuit rule by excluding signals given by wireless and at great distance does not carry the same weight today, in light of the extended areas of maritime jurisdiction established in the LOSC, and that: 'given the large areas that now must be policed by coastal States and the availability of more reliable advanced technology (sea-bed sensors, satellite surveillance, over-the-horizon radar, unmanned aerial vehicles), it would not make sense to limit valid orders to stop to those given by an enforcement craft within the proximity required for an audio or visual signal that makes no use of radio communication.'[83]

The *Arctic Sunrise* decision clearly rejects a narrow understanding of the notification requirement, and while it does not specify exactly what modern

[77] Klein, *Maritime Security* (n 10) 110.

[78] The Netherlands argued that the words 'visual or auditory signal' exclude the use of radio messages, by reference to the drafting history of art 111 and the commentary to the 1956 Articles on the Law of the Sea: *Arctic Sunrise Arbitration* (Memorial of the Kingdom of the Netherlands) [278].

[79] *Arctic Sunrise Arbitration* [260].

[80] Ibid [259].

[81] (Concluded 1 November 1974, entered into force 25 May 1980) 1184 UNTS 2.

[82] *Arctic Sunrise Arbitration* [259].

[83] Ibid [260]. Similarly, Allen (writing in 1989) noted that vessel operators universally communicate by radio and many by satellite comunications, and routinely maintain a continuous listening watch on at least one of the maritime distress and calling frequencies: Allen, 'Doctrine of Hot Pursuit' (n 17) 323.

technologies (other than VHF radio) may be used to give the requisite signal, there a number of options that could be used which would also satisfy the underlying objective of ensuring (and proving) that the pursued vessel is aware of the pursuit. This could potentially include technologies ranging from satellite phone, email, or fax, to internet-based communication platforms or messaging applications, provided they show evidence that a message is not only sent and received, but is actually read or heard by the pursued vessel.

7.2.2.3 Continuation of the Pursuit

While the *Arctic Sunrise* decision only strictly applies to the question of notification, its logic can also be applied to the use of technology as a means of fulfilling the fourth element of the hot pursuit framework—the requirement that the hot pursuit is continued without interruption. In this respect, as McDougal and Burke have observed: 'There seems to be no good reason for requiring either that the pursuing vessel maintain visual observation of the fleeing ship or that companion ships refrain from participating in the chase in relays. Radar permits continual observation without close proximity and its use should not be denied without good reason. No such reason appears to exist.'[84]

This approach is also reflected in the practice of coastal States, which—as noted in relation to Article 73(1)—anticipates the use of a wide range of credible and reliable modern technologies to detect and monitor illegal fishing vessels.

In addition to the wide range of national laws providing for the use of remote detection technology in the general context of fisheries enforcement,[85] some coastal States have enacted legislative provisions specifically underpinning the use of technology in hot pursuit. For example, Tanzania's legislation provides that vessels may be pursued beyond the EEZ based on evidence from a VMS, global positioning system, aerial photography, satellite system, or any other 'accepted international technological communication system'.[86] Gambia, Tonga, and the United States specifically recognize the use of technology in ensuring the continual observation of a vessel,[87] and Australia's legislation provides that the chase is not 'interrupted' only because the vessel is out of sight of any or all officers involved in the chase, or the vessel cannot be tracked by remote means, including radio, radar, satellite, or sonar.[88]

The use of modern technologies in continuing hot pursuit is also envisaged in bilateral and regional agreements on fisheries surveillance and cooperation between coastal States in the western and central Pacific Ocean and the Southern

84 McDougal and Burke, *The Public Order of the Oceans* (n 20) 897.
85 See Section 6.2.2.
86 Tanzania, *Act 2020* s 64.
87 Gambia, *Act 2007* s 72; Tonga, *Act 2002* s 73; United States Navy, *Commander's Handbook* (n 61) 3.11.2.2.4.2.
88 Australia, *Act 2013* ss 2(2)(d) and (e).

Ocean. For example, Article 4 of the Australia-France Cooperative Enforcement Agreement provides that in the context of hot pursuit, continual positive identification, and tracking of a vessel may be maintained on the basis of direct visual contact or 'evidence obtained by or on behalf of the authorized vessel by technical means'.[89] While 'technical means' is not defined, it would likely include VMS, satellite images or radar, or any other forms of reliable technology that may be developed, such as unmanned aerial vehicles or marine autonomous vessels, for example.[90]

Remote detection and tracking technologies are likely to become increasingly accepted and employed in the conduct of hot pursuit—particularly since they can significantly enhance the coastal State's enforcement capacity and reduce the need for costly and often dangerous at-sea enforcement operations. However, it is important that the functional procedural requirements established in Article 111 are nonetheless observed, in order to ensure that the underlying objectives of the hot pursuit doctrine are fulfilled and the balance between high seas freedoms and coastal State jurisdiction is maintained.[91] In particular, coastal States will need to ensure that:

- regardless of the method used to give a signal to stop at the commencement of hot pursuit, the notification is actually received (seen, read, or heard) by the vessel;
- where continuous pursuit is maintained through remote tracking technology, regular contact is maintained with the vessel, in order to ensure that it is aware of the continued tracking and pursuit, and avoid any implication that the pursuit has been discontinued or abandoned; and
- the technology is generally accepted as credible and reliable, is well maintained and functions accurately, and is operated with skill and accuracy.

However, not every coastal State will have the technology or know-how required to successfully use these techniques without assistance. Moreover, merely detecting, identifying, and tracking vessels will not be enough to effectively enforce the coastal State's fisheries laws: at the end of a hot pursuit, they need to be subject to enforcement action. This is where cooperative approaches to hot pursuit come in.

[89] See also Niue Treaty Subsidiary Agreement art 13(5).

[90] See Vasilios Tasikas, 'Unmanned Aerial Vehicles and the Doctrine of Hot Pursuit: A New Era of Coast Guard Maritime Law Enforcement Operations' (2004) 29 TulMarLJ 59, 79; Natalie Klein, 'Maritime Autonomous Vehicles within the International Law Framework to Enhance Maritime Security' (2019) 95 IntlLSt 244, 253–5.

[91] Allen, 'Doctrine of Hot Pursuit' (n 17) 325.

7.2.3 Cooperative Approaches to Hot Pursuit

As Chapter 6 demonstrated, the reach and effectiveness of almost any unilateral measure of enforcement can be multiplied exponentially—and in some cases can only be concluded successfully—through cooperation with other States. This is particularly true with respect to enforcement beyond the EEZ following hot pursuit, where the coastal State may require cooperation from other States in order to secure the technical or physical resources required to continue or conclude the pursuit, or to secure the jurisdictional basis for exercising enforcement powers.

7.2.3.1 Multilateral Hot Pursuit

While Article 111 of the LOSC does not specifically envisage the coastal State being assisted by another State (or States) in the hot pursuit of a foreign vessel, cooperative approaches to hot pursuit have emerged in State practice as a way of addressing some of the practical challenges faced in conducting at-sea enforcement operations. As a result, cooperative hot pursuit—or 'multilateral hot pursuit'[92]—is a functional concept, which does not have a fixed form, but refers generally to the involvement of vessels, aircraft, and officials from more than one State in the hot pursuit of a vessel.[93] In this context, multilateral hot pursuit can be seen not as a departure from, or radical application of, the hot pursuit doctrine, but simply another form of cooperative enforcement, which, as discussed in Chapter 6,[94] can include:

- joint enforcement operations undertaken in cooperation between the coastal State and an assisting State;
- the embarkation of authorized officials from the coastal State as 'ship-riders' on board a vessel or aircraft of the assisting State; and
- the authorization (or 'cross-vesting') of officials and assets from the assisting State with the power to conduct enforcement on behalf of the coastal State.

The most well-known examples of multilateral hot pursuit are those conducted by Australia in the Southern Ocean: the 2001 pursuit of the Togo-flagged vessel *South Tomi*, which lasted fourteen days before the *South Tomi* was arrested with the aid of South Africa; and the 2003 pursuit of the Uruguayan-flagged vessel *Viarsa I*, which was arrested after twenty-one days with the help of British and South African vessels.[95] Despite the very public and formal aftermath of these hot pursuits, their

[92] The term 'multilateral hot pursuit' first appeared in a 2004 article about Australia's pursuits of the *South Tomi* and the *Viarsa I*, which noted that '[t]he concept of multilateral hot pursuit is, as far as the author is aware, not an existing concept': Molenaar, 'Multilateral Hot Pursuit' (n 49) 31. Of course, since multiple States can (individually or together) undertake a 'unilateral act', there is nothing 'scientific' in the use of the term 'multilateral' in this context; it simply refers to the involvement of multiple States in the conduct of a single hot pursuit.

[93] Ibid 20.

[94] Chapter 6 nn 99–107 and associated text.

[95] For a detailed description of these pursuits see Molenaar, 'Multilateral Hot Pursuit' (n 49) 20–3.

multilateral nature was not challenged by the flag State of either vessel, or criticized by the broader international community,[96] and the legitimacy of taking cooperative approaches to the exercise of enforcement powers beyond the EEZ in the context of hot pursuit has been widely accepted in the literature.[97]

Cooperative approaches to hot pursuit beyond the EEZ are logically no different to cooperative approaches to fisheries enforcement within the EEZ and can be conducted within the existing framework for hot pursuit under Article 111; provided the requirements for the exercise of the coastal State's enforcement powers are met, there is nothing to prevent those powers being exercised by appropriately authorized resources from another State. Accordingly, while the Australian patrol vessel *Southern Supporter* was in continuous pursuit of both the *South Tomi* and the *Viarsa I*, and only required assistance in order to stop the vessels and make the arrest, the requirements of Article 111 could also be satisfied if the continuous pursuit of the vessel involved a vessel or aircraft from a third State, provided this had been authorized by the coastal State[98]—constituting, in effect, hot pursuit by multilateral 'relay' under Article 111(6)(b).

This is reflected in the establishment of formal arrangements allowing for the conduct of multilateral hot pursuit in coastal State legislation[99] and in bilateral and regional agreements and arrangements.[100] In the western and central Pacific region, for example, Article 13(5) of the Niue Treaty Subsidiary Agreement provides

[96] In both cases, forfeiture notices were issued by the Australian Government pursuant to the regime described in Chapter 6 nn 264–7 and associated text. While the owners of the *Viarsa I* challenged the forfeiture order, the courts ultimately dismissed the application and confirmed the forfeiture: Laurence Blakely, 'The End of the Viarsa Saga and the Legality of Australia's Vessel Forfeiture Penalty for Illegal Fishing in Its Exclusive Economic Zone' (2008) 17(3) PacRim L&PolJ 677, 678. The owners' challenge to the forfeiture of *South Tomi* was withdrawn, and the forfeiture notice became binding: Rachel Baird, 'Coastal State Fisheries Management: A Review of Australian Enforcement Action in the Heard and McDonald Islands Australian Fishing Zone' (2004) 9(1) DeakinLRev 91, 105. In neither case did the owners challenge the multilateral nature of the hot pursuit. In addition, Australia provided details of the arrests to the 2001 and 2003 annual meetings of the Commission for the Conservation of Antarctic Marine Living Resources (CCAMLR), where no complaints about the 'multilateral' nature of the pursuit were raised by the flag States or any other State.

[97] See, eg, Molenaar, 'Multilateral Hot Pursuit' (n 49) 40–1; Gullett and Schofield, 'Pushing the Limits of the LOSC' (n 47) 569; Baird, 'Arrests in a Cold Climate' (n 14) 14–15; Klein, *Maritime Security* (n 10) 113; Guilfoyle, 'Article 111' (n 8) 778.

[98] While Molenaar suggests that it would be preferable if an official from the coastal State were on board to formally apprehend or arrest the pursued vessel, there is no reason that an official from an assisting State could not perform this function, provided they were appropriately authorized to exercise enforcement powers on behalf of the coastal State: Molenaar, 'Multilateral Hot Pursuit' (n 49) 40–1.

[99] See, eg, Australia, *Act 2013* s 42(2): 'the chase is not interrupted only because: (b) it is begun, or taken over, by a vessel or aircraft (including a vessel or aircraft of a foreign country) other than the vessel from which the requirement was made; or (c) if the chase is continued by a vessel or aircraft of a foreign country—there is no maritime officer on board the vessel or aircraft'. See also South Africa, *Defence Act 2002* s 29 and *Customs and Excise Act 1964* s 4C(3).

[100] While the bilateral agreements between Australia and France in the Southern Ocean are the most commonly cited examples, numerous agreements and arrangements provide for cooperative approaches to hot pursuit, including those discussed in the context of cooperative fisheries enforcement within the EEZ (Chapter 6 nn 100–7) and in the context of consent to the continuation of hot pursuit into the territorial sea (Section 7.2.3.2).

that: 'Hot pursuit shall be deemed to have continued without interruption provided that positive tracking and identification of the pursued vessel is maintained by resources authorized under this Agreement by the Party in whose waters the vessel was detected, whether by:

(a) direct visual contact; or
(b) reliable technical means.'

Given the broad possibilities envisaged in the Niue Treaty Subsidiary Agreement with respect to both the forms of cooperation and the types of technology that may be used in fisheries surveillance and law enforcement, the 'resources authorized under this Agreement' could potentially include personnel from any other Party or even officials from the Pacific Islands Forum Fisheries Agency (FFA) in the Regional Fisheries and Surveillance Centre in Honiara,[101] provided they are appropriately 'authorized' by the Party in whose waters the vessel was detected.[102]

7.2.3.2 Consent to Continue Hot Pursuit into the Territorial Sea

Another important avenue for cooperation arises when the pursued vessel flees into the territorial sea of a third State. While Article 111(3) provides that 'the right of hot pursuit ceases as soon as the ship pursued enters the territorial sea of its own State or a third State', it is possible that this limitation could be overcome by the third State consenting to the continuation of pursuit—or the exercise of enforcement powers—in its territorial sea. This approach has the advantage of ensuring respect for the sovereignty of the third State, while closing down a significant loophole in the traditional doctrine of hot pursuit, particularly 'in a remote environment where suspect vessels in one party's EEZ may attempt to break pursuit by entering the other's territorial sea.'[103] While this approach is widely supported in the literature,[104] most of the commentary refers only to a few common examples, and there has not been any comprehensive assessment of State practice in relation to this issue. In order to reach a more convincing conclusion, it is necessary to examine whether the contemporary practice of coastal States still reflects a narrow interpretation of Article 111(3), or whether it indicates that the hot pursuit doctrine has developed—or is developing—to incorporate the concept that hot pursuit may be continued into the territorial sea of a third State with its consent.

[101] Art 10(6) provides that Parties 'may elect to authorize or request support from personnel of the Forum Fisheries Agency to assist in the implementation and operation of this Agreement'.
[102] Arts 10 and 11 establish specific requirements intended to ensure the proper authorization and identification of personnel and assets participating in cooperative surveillance and enforcement activities.
[103] Douglas Guilfoyle, *Shipping Interdiction and the Law of the Sea* (CUP 2009) 145.
[104] See nn 49–52.

As depicted in Table 7.1, the legislation of some coastal States specifically states that hot pursuit ceases when the ship pursued enters the territorial sea of its own State or a third State.[105] However, there are also a number of coastal States who specifically provide that hot pursuit may be continued into the territorial sea with the consent of the coastal State, or pursuant to a bilateral or regional agreement or arrangement. For example, in Australia, pursuant to Section 40(1)(a) of the *Maritime Powers Act 2013* (Cth), powers may be exercised 'at a place in another country'[106] provided they are exercised 'at the request or with the agreement of the other country'.[107] This agreement need not be in writing and includes a standing request or agreement, or a request or agreement that relates to particular circumstances or covers a particular period of time. It may be made or given by the head of State or head of government, the minister responsible for foreign affairs or defence, or any official or body that has, or could be expected to have, authority to make or give such a request or agreement.[108] Similarly, the United States *Commander's Handbook on the Law of Naval Operations* provides that: 'The right of hot pursuit ceases as soon as the ship pursued enters the territorial sea of its own State or of a third State, unless the coastal State concerned permits the pursuit to continue.'[109]

The legislation of a number of coastal States in Africa and the Asia-Pacific envisages such consent being provided through agreements or arrangements. For example, pursuant to Article 54 of Guinea-Bissau's *Decree Law No 10/2011 approving the Basic Fishing Legislation:*

> 1. The boarding of a fishing vessel may take place beyond the boundaries of the waters under the jurisdiction of Guinea-Bissau if its pursuit has been initiated within those waters and there is strong evidence to presume that it has infringed the fisheries laws of Guinea-Bissau.
> 2. The right of enforcement referred to in the preceding paragraph shall be exercised in accordance with international law and shall cease when the fishing vessel enters the territorial sea of the State of its flag or of a third State.
> 3. The provisions of the preceding paragraph shall be without prejudice to the rules of international agreements, which may provide for the possibility of Guinea-Bissau inspection vessels exercising the right of enforcement within waters under the jurisdiction of other States.

[105] See Table 7.1: Algeria, Angola, Mauritius, China, Myanmar, Timor-Leste, Vietnam, Bulgaria, Croatia, Romania, Slovenia, Nicaragua, Canada, Malta, United Kingdom (Falkland Islands).

[106] Pursuant to s 8, the term 'country', when used in a geographical sense, includes 'the territorial sea, and any archipelagic waters, of the country'.

[107] Australia, *Act 2013* s 48(1)–(2).

[108] Ibid.

[109] (n 61) 3.11.2.2.4.3. This aligns with the United States *Maritime Drug Law Enforcement Act*, which provides, in the context of maritime drug law enforcement, that vessels 'subject to the jurisdiction of the United States' include 'a vessel in the territorial waters of a foreign nation if the nation consents to the enforcement of United States law by the United States': 46 *USC* §70502(c)(1)(E).

Similar provisions are included in the legislation of Gabon, Guinea, Mauritania, Senegal, Iran, and Malaysia.[110]

A significant number of coastal States have entered into bilateral or regional agreements or arrangements providing for the continuation of hot pursuit into the territorial sea on the basis of consent. Some directly provide the coastal State's consent to the continuation of hot pursuit into the territorial sea by other Parties or Participants in relevant circumstances (such as during the course of a joint enforcement operation, or upon notice to the coastal State), while others establish a framework within which such consent can be provided, or simply contemplate the provision of consent. While many of these agreements and arrangements relate to hot pursuit arising in the context of fisheries offences, others address different forms of maritime law enforcement, including piracy, drug trafficking, migrant smuggling, and other types of maritime crime.

In west Africa, for example, the *Convention on Sub-Regional Cooperation in the Exercise of Maritime Hot Pursuit* was adopted by the members of the Sub-Regional Fisheries Commission (SRFC) in 1993 to define the general principles governing the right of hot pursuit in situations where the pursued vessel seeks refuge in the waters of a neighbouring State,[111] and provides for its Parties to adopt bilateral and multilateral protocols establishing procedures for the continuation of pursuit into their territorial sea.[112] All SRFC members have reportedly adopted such protocols on a bilateral basis with one or more other members.[113] Consent to continue hot pursuit into the territorial sea is also provided in a bilateral agreement between

[110] See Table 7.1.

[111] (Signed and entered into force 1 September 1993) art 3: 'Any vessel carrying out fishing activities in the waters under the jurisdiction of one of the States Parties to the present Convention may be pursued and arrested by a vessel or aircraft of that State, when, after unsuccessful signals to stop, that vessel tries to escape the control of the pursuing State, beyond its maritime boundary. The right of hot pursuit must not be interrupted: (1) without limit beyond the territorial sea; (2) within the limits of the territorial sea, in accordance with the limits agreed upon by the States through the protocol.'.

[112] Art 9 provides: 'This Convention shall be implemented by bilateral and multilateral protocols among the Parties.' It is supplemented by the *Protocol on the Practical Modalities for the Coordination of Surveillance Operations within the Member States of the Sub-Regional Fisheries Commission* (signed and entered into force 1 September 1993), which (somewhat circularly) provides in art 9: 'The right of hot pursuit shall be applied in accordance with the agreement on sub-regional cooperation in the right of hot pursuit and the application protocols concluded between the Parties.'

[113] These include: Cape Verde/Mauritania (*Protocol of agreement relative to the coordination of surveillance operations and hot pursuit, and protocol on its application*, 25 April 2000); Cape Verde/Senegal (*Protocol on coordination of surveillance and on hot pursuit*, 17 November 1994); Guinea/Guinea-Bissau (*Protocol and regulation on coordination of surveillance activities and on hot pursuit*, 7 June 1996); Mauritania/Senegal (*Hot pursuit protocol*, 14 January 2000); and Sierra Leone/Guinea, cited in: Daniel Owen, 'Legal and Institutional Aspects of Management Arrangements for Shared Stocks with Reference to Small Pelagics in Northwest Africa' *FAO Fisheries Circular No 988* (FAO 2003) 41–2; and Kieran Kelleher, 'Robbers, Reefers and Ramasseurs. A Review of Fisheries Monitoring, Control and Surveillance in Seven West African Countries' *Report for the Sub-Regional Fisheries Commission, Project FAO/GCP/INT/722/LUX (ARF/013)* (2002) 50 and 100, available at <http://researchgate.net/profile/Kieran_Kelleher/publication/278785493_Robbers_Reefers_and_Ramasseurs_A_review_of_fisheries_Monitoring_Control_and_Surveillance_in_seven_West_African_countries/links/5585e47008aeb0cdaddf7016/Robbers-Reefers-and-Ramasseu> accessed 14 December 2020.

Gambia and the United States relating to cooperation in the suppression of illicit transnational maritime activity, including illegal fishing.[114]

A similar framework seems to be envisaged in southern Africa, where the South African Development Community (SADC) Protocol on Fisheries provides in Article 8(3) that 'State Parties shall establish appropriate arrangements to enable co-operation on hot pursuit of vessels that violate the laws of one Party and enter the jurisdiction of another State Party.'[115] This approach has been implemented in an agreement between South Africa and Namibia on curbing illegal fishing, which provides that 'upon notification, through the normal diplomatic channels, each of our Governments will grant to the other the right to pursue and apprehend such vessels if and when they escape into its fishing waters.'[116] In addition, a bilateral agreement between South Africa and France relating to cooperation in the maritime areas adjacent to their territories in the Southern Ocean states that one Party may continue hot pursuit 'through the territorial waters of the other Party, provided that the other Party is informed, and without taking physical law enforcement or other coercive action against the vessel pursued during the phase of the hot pursuit'.[117] And in a broader context, a trilateral arrangement between South Africa, Tanzania, and Mozambique on maritime security cooperation provides that each country is authorized to 'patrol, search, arrest, seize and undertake hot pursuit operations on any piracy or maritime crime suspect in the international waters and territorial waters of each respective country in keeping with the international law principles of hot pursuit'.[118]

In the context of piracy, following a series of United Nations Security Council (UNSC) Resolutions authorizing other States to pursue vessels into Somalia's territorial sea in order to repress acts of piracy and armed robbery (passed with Somalia's consent),[119] a number of arrangements have been developed that

[114] *Agreement Between the Government of the United States of America and the Government of the Republic of the Gambia Concerning Cooperation to Suppress Illicit Transnational Maritime Activity* (signed and entered into force 10 October 2011) TIAS 11-1010, art 6(2).

[115] The Parties to the SADC Protocol are Angola, Botswana, Lesotho, Malawi, Mauritius, Mozambique, Namibia, South Africa, Swaziland, Tanzania, Zambia, Zimbabwe.

[116] *Agreement between the Government of South Africa and the Government of Namibia Relating to Mutual Assistance in Curbing and Preventing Illegal Fishing* (signed and entered into force 22 March 1991) (1991) 311 *South Africa Government Gazette* 13239, 2–3.

[117] *Agreement between the Government of the Republic of South Africa and the Government of the French Republic on Cooperation in the Maritime Areas Adjacent to the French Southern and Antarctic Territories (TAAF) and the South African Territory of Marion Island* (signed 11 July 2016, not yet in force) art 6.

[118] *Memorandum of Understanding Between the Government of the Republic of Mozambique, the Government of the Republic of South Africa and the Government of the United Republic of Tanzania on Maritime Security Cooperation* (adopted and entered into force 13 December 2011) art 4(6).

[119] UNSC Res 1816 (2 June 2008) UN Doc S/RES/1816 (2008) [7]; UNSC Res 1846 (2 December 2008) S/RES/1846 (2008) [10]; UNSC Res 1897 (30 November 2009) UN Doc S/RES/1897 (2009) [7]; UNSC Res 1950 (23 November 2010) UN Doc S/RES/1950 (2010) [7]. The authorization provided by these Resolutions applied only to States named by the UN Secretary-General as 'co-operating' with Somalia's Transitional Federal Government and for limited periods (six or twelve months).

contemplate the consent-based pursuit of vessels into the territorial sea. For example, both the 2009 Djibouti Code of Conduct[120] and the 2013 Yaoundé Code of Conduct[121] specify that: 'Any pursuit of a ship, where there are reasonable grounds to suspect that the ship is engaged in piracy, extending in and over the territorial sea of a Participant is subject to the authority of that Participant. No Participant should pursue such a ship in or over the territory or territorial sea of any coastal State without the permission of that State.'

This negative prohibition (specifying that pursuit cannot continue without consent) necessarily implies that pursuit *can* continue if consent is obtained. Interestingly, this provision is not included in the equivalent maritime security agreement in the Asia-Pacific region.[122] However, Malaysia, Singapore, Indonesia, and Thailand have reportedly agreed on measures to enable the continuation of hot pursuit into each other's territorial seas in order to address problems of maritime hijacking, kidnapping, and piracy in the Malacca Straits (although there is no publicly available information about the extent to which such measures have been used).[123] Malaysia, Singapore, and the Philippines have reportedly agreed to establish similar arrangements for the Sulu-Sulawesi Seas.[124]

In the western and central Pacific, hot pursuit is addressed primarily in the context of fisheries, rather than piracy or security. Article VI(1) of the Niue Treaty, adopted in 1992 by the members of the FFA, envisions subsidiary agreements between its Parties, allowing one Party 'to permit another Party to extend its fisheries surveillance and law enforcement activities to the territorial sea and archipelagic waters of that Party'.[125] While the Niue Treaty itself does not specifically refer to

[120] *Code of Conduct Concerning the Repression of Piracy and Armed Robbery Against Ships in the Western Indian Ocean and the Gulf of Aden* (adopted 29 January 2009). The signatories are Comoros, Djibouti, Egypt, Eritrea, Ethiopia, Jordan, Kenya, Madagascar, Maldives, Mauritius, Mozambique, Oman, Saudi Arabia, Seychelles, Somalia, South Africa, Sudan, Tanzania, the United Arab Emirates, and Yemen.

[121] *Code of Conduct Concerning the Repression of Piracy, Armed Robbery Against Ships, and Illicit Maritime Activity in West and Central Africa* (opened for signature 25 June 2013). The signatories are Angola, Benin, Burkina Faso, Burundi, Cameroon, Cape Verde, the Central African Republic, Chad, Congo, Cote d'Ivoire, the Democratic Republic of the Congo, Equatorial Guinea, Gabon, the Gambia, Ghana, Guinea, Guinea-Bissau, Liberia, Mali, Niger, Nigeria, Sao Tome e Principe, Senegal, Sierra Leone, and Togo.

[122] *Regional Cooperation Agreement on Combating Piracy and Armed Robbery against Ships in Asia* (adopted 11 November 2004, entered into force 4 September 2006) 2398 UNTS 199.

[123] Hadyu Ikrami, 'Sulu-Sulawesi Seas Patrol: Lessons from the Malacca Straits Patrol and Other Similar Cooperative Frameworks' (2018) 33 IJMCL 1, 21. See also Robert Beckman, 'Combatting Piracy and Armed Robbery Against Ships in Southeast Asia: The Way Forward' (2002) 33 ODIL 317, 330.

[124] Ikrami, 'Sulu-Sulawesi Seas Patrol' (n 125) 21; Zachary Abuza, 'Trilateral Maritime Patrols in the Sulu Sea: Asymmetry in Need, Capability and Political Will' *Centre for International Maritime Security* 6 July 2016, available at <http://cimsec.org/trilateral-maritime-patrols-sulu-sea-asymmetry-need-capability-political-will/26251> accessed 3 February 2021.

[125] The Parties to the Niue Treaty are Australia, Cook Islands, Fiji, Kiribati, Marshall Islands, Micronesia, Nauru, New Zealand, Niue, Palau, Papua New Guinea, Samoa, Solomon Islands, Tokelau, Tonga, Tuvalu, and Vanuatu.

the continuation of hot pursuit into the territorial sea,[126] this is provided for in a number of bilateral and trilateral subsidiary agreements between the Parties[127] and on a multilateral basis through the Niue Treaty Subsidiary Agreement, which provides in Article 13(2) that: 'Hot pursuit may be continued into the territorial sea of a Party with the consent of that Party. Each Party shall notify the Administrator, through a hot pursuit notification, of:

(a) whether it consents to hot pursuit being continued into its territorial sea and to which Party or Parties this consent applies; and
(b) any conditions associated with the continuation of hot pursuit into its territorial sea, including any notification or reporting requirements.'[128]

Outside the framework of the Niue Treaty, consent to the continuation of hot pursuit is included in a number of bilateral treaties in both the Pacific and the Southern Ocean. The most well-known of these is a 2005 bilateral agreement between Australia and France relating to cooperative surveillance in the maritime zones of their adjacent Southern Ocean territories, which provides that hot pursuit by a vessel 'authorized by one of the Parties may continue through the territorial sea of the other Party, provided that the other Party is informed, and without taking physical law enforcement or other coercive action against the vessel pursued during this phase of the hot pursuit'.[129] The adoption of this agreement followed Australia's pursuit of the Russian-flagged vessel *Lena* in December 2001, during the course of which France provided ad hoc consent for Australia to continue the

[126] Aqorau, who was involved in drafting the Niue Treaty, explains that Article VI is intended to allow hot pursuit into the territorial sea of the other Parties to the treaty, and refers to the original text of art VI, which provided that 'each Party shall permit access to its territorial sea or archipelagic waters by a vessel of another party for the purposes of maintaining the continuous hot pursuit of a foreign fishing vessel, being a hot pursuit commenced in waters in which the other Party claims jurisdiction for fisheries purposes, seizing that vessel, and escorting it back to the waters of the other Party': Transform Aqorau, *Analysis of the Responses of the Pacific Island States to the Fisheries Provisions of the Law of the Sea Convention* (DPhil thesis, University of Wollongong 1998) 238. This interpretation is supported by the development of subsidiary agreements to this effect.

[127] See, eg, *Agreement between the Governments of the Cook Islands and the Independent State of Samoa on Cooperation in Fisheries Surveillance and Law Enforcement* (signed and entered into force 27 June 2008); *Agreement among the Governments of the Federated States of Micronesia, the Republic of the Marshall Islands and the Republic of Palau on Cooperation in Fisheries Surveillance and Law Enforcement* (signed and entered into force 7 February 2002) (copies on file with author). Art 4 of both Agreements provides: 'The parties agree that the continuation of hot pursuit of a foreign fishing vessel into each other's territorial sea is permitted and that reasonable effort shall be made to promptly notify the National Authority of the Party whose territorial waters the hot pursuit is entering pursuant to Article 2 of the Agreement. Every effort must be made to seek the cooperation of the Flag State of the vessel being pursued.'

[128] All FFA members are party to the Niue Treaty Subsidiary Agreement except Fiji, Kiribati, Papua New Guinea, and Tokelau (which have signed but not ratified the Agreement).

[129] *Treaty between the Government of Australia and the Government of the French Republic on Cooperation in the Maritime Areas Adjacent to the French Southern and Antarctic Territories (TAAF), Heard Island and the McDonald Islands* (signed 24 November 2003, entered into force 1 February 2005) [2005] ATS 6, art 4.

pursuit into the territorial sea around the Kerguelen Islands. Russia did not protest Australia's continuation of the hot pursuit through the territorial sea of France—although it might be argued that this was unnecessary since the pursuit did not result in an arrest or the exercise of any further enforcement powers.[130] Consent for continuing hot pursuit into the territorial sea is also envisaged in a bilateral agreement on general maritime law enforcement cooperation between Vanuatu and the United States, which provides that designated officials embarked as 'ship-riders' on a law enforcement vessel of the other Party may '[a]uthorize the pursuit, by the law enforcement vessel on which they are embarked, of suspect vessels fleeing into the territory of the ship-rider's State'.[131]

Consent to the continuation of hot pursuit into the territorial sea is also encompassed in treaties between coastal States in Latin America and the Caribbean. For example, the *Treaty Establishing the Regional Security System*,[132] adopted in 1996 by the Organization of Eastern Caribbean States in order to promote cooperation in the prevention and interdiction of maritime security issues (including fisheries protection), provides that '[t]he interests of one Member State are the interests of the others; and accordingly the Member States shall have the right of "hot pursuit" within each other's territorial sea and [EEZ].' In addition, a multilateral agreement for the suppression of drug trafficking in the Caribbean region adopted in 2003 provides that the law enforcement vessel of one Party may 'follow a suspect vessel into the waters of another Party and take actions to prevent the escape of the vessel, board the vessel and secure the vessel and persons on board awaiting an expeditious response from the other Party', if either they have received authorization from the other Party, or on notice to the other Party.[133]

There are also a number of bilateral agreements between the United States and various countries in Latin America and the Caribbean that provide for the continuation of hot pursuit into the territorial sea. While there is some variation among them, these agreements most commonly provide that:

[130] The *Lena* was not ultimately arrested during this pursuit which was broken off when the Australian vessel was called away to attend a nearby distress call, which proved to be a false alarm. However, the *Lena* was subsequently boarded and arrested by Australia in February 2002 (having been repainted and renamed the *Ana*): Baird, 'Arrests in a Cold Climate' (n 14) 16.

[131] *Agreement between the United States of America and the Republic of Vanuatu Concerning Counter Illicit Transnational Maritime Activity Operations* (signed and entered into force 31 October 2016) TIAS 16-1031, art III(2)(b). The Agreement relates to 'illicit transnational maritime activity', which is defined in art II(4) to include 'IUU fishing' as well as a range of other maritime crimes.

[132] (Signed 5 March 1996) art 4(3). The Parties are Antigua and Barbuda, Barbados, Dominica, Grenada, Saint Kitts and Nevis, Saint Lucia, and Saint Vincent and the Grenadines.

[133] *Agreement Concerning Cooperation in Suppressing Illicit Maritime and Air Trafficking in Narcotic Drugs and Psychotropic Substances in the Caribbean Region* (concluded 10 April 2003, entered into force 18 September 2008) TIAS, art 12. The 'waters of a Party' is defined in art 1 to mean the territorial sea and archipelagic waters of that Party. The Parties are Belize, Costa Rica, the Dominican Republic, France, Guatemala, the Netherlands, Nicaragua, and the United States.

- authorized officials (or 'ship-riders') of one Party, embarked on law enforcement vessels of the other Party, may authorize the pursuit of suspect vessels and aircraft fleeing into the territorial sea of the Party by which they are authorized; and
- even in the absence of an embarked official from the other Party, each Party is authorized to pursue a suspect vessel into the other Party's territorial sea, subject to prompt notification to that Party.[134]

Some of these agreements apply in the context of maritime drug law enforcement—such as those with Barbados,[135] Costa Rica,[136] Jamaica,[137] Guatemala,[138] Guyana,[139] Haiti,[140] Honduras,[141] Nicaragua,[142] Panama,[143] Suriname,[144] Trinidad and Tobago,[145] and the United Kingdom (including in respect of Montserrat and the Turks and Caicos Islands).[146] Some apply in respect of maritime migration law

[134] Some of these agreements provide reciprocal authorization, allowing the law enforcement vessels of each Party to enter the territorial sea of the other in pursuit of a suspect vessel; in other cases authorization is given for law enforcement vessels of the United States to enter the territorial sea of the other Party (but not vice versa). On the operation of these agreements, see further Guilfoyle, *Shipping Interdiction* (n 103) 89–94.

[135] *Narcotic Drugs Shiprider Agreement Between the United States of America and Barbados* (signed 25 June 1997, entered into force 11 October 1998) TIAS 12872, art 6(1).

[136] *Agreement between the United States of America and Costa Rica Concerning Cooperation to Suppress Illicit Traffic* (signed 1 December 1998, entered into force 19 November 1999) and *Amending Protocol* (signed 2 July 1999, entered into force 19 November 1999) TIAS 13005, arts 7, 8, and 10.

[137] *Agreement between the United States of America and Jamaica Concerning Cooperation in Suppressing Illicit Maritime Trafficking* (signed 6 May 1997, entered into force 10 March 1998) and *Amending Protocol* (signed and entered into force 6 February 2004) TIAS 98-310, art IV(2)(b).

[138] *Agreement between the United States of America and Guatemala Concerning Cooperation to Suppress Illicit Traffic in Narcotic Drugs and Psychotropic Substances by Sea and Air* (signed 19 June 2003, entered into force 10 October 2003) TIAS 04-116, art 6(2).

[139] *Agreement between the Government of the United States of America and the Government of the Co-operative Republic of Guyana concerning cooperation to suppress illicit traffic by sea and air* (signed at Georgetown 10 April 2001, entered into force 21 September 2020) TIAS, arts 4(2)(b) and 6(2)(b).

[140] *Agreement between the United States of America and Haiti Concerning Cooperation to Suppress Illicit Maritime Drug Traffic* (signed 17 October 1997, entered into force 5 September 2002) 2002 WL 31504914, arts 5 and 6.

[141] *Agreement between the United States of America and Honduras Concerning Cooperation for the Suppression of Illicit Maritime Traffic in Narcotic Drugs and Psychotropic Substances and Implementing Agreement* (signed 29 March 2000, entered into force 30 January 2001) TIAS 13088, art IV(2)(b).

[142] *Agreement between the United States of America and Nicaragua Concerning Cooperation to Suppress Illicit Traffic by Sea and Air* (signed 1 June 2001, entered into force 15 November 2001) TIAS 13153, arts 4(2)(b) and (3)(b) and 6(2)(b).

[143] *Supplementary Arrangement between the Government of the United States of America and the Government of Panama to the Arrangement between the Government of the United States and the Government of Panama for Support and Assistance from the US Coast Guard for the National Maritime Service of the Ministry of Government and Justice* (signed and entered into force 5 February 2002) TIAS 02-205.1, arts IV(2)(b) and VI.

[144] *Agreement Between the United States of America and Suriname Concerning Cooperation in Maritime Law Enforcement* (signed 31 December 1998, entered into force 26 August 1999) TIAS 13016, arts 3(3)(b) and 6(2)(b).

[145] *Agreement between the United States of America and Trinidad and Tobago Concerning Maritime Counter-Drug Operations* (signed and entered into force 4 March 1996) TIAS 12732, arts 5(b) and 8.

[146] *Agreement between the Government of the United States of America and the Government of the United Kingdom of Great Britain and Northern Ireland concerning maritime and aerial operations to*

enforcement—such as the agreement with Dominican Republic.[147] Some—such as the agreement with the Bahamas—apply to both.[148]

As these various examples demonstrate, the concept of continuing hot pursuit into the territorial sea on the basis of consent has been given effect by States from almost every region of the world, with the exception of Eastern Europe. This includes States from the Western Europe and Others Group with significant coastal State interests in different regions of the world—and in some cases significant flag State interests as well—including Australia, France, the Netherlands, New Zealand, the United Kingdom, and the United States.

Of course, these agreements and arrangements only provide for the continuation of hot pursuit by certain States, in certain circumstances: some relate to hot pursuit in order to enforce fisheries offences, and some apply in a broader context of maritime enforcement or regional security, or in relation to specific areas of cooperation such as piracy, migrant smuggling, or narcotics. This is to be expected: the maritime enforcement priorities and objectives of coastal States reflect a wide range of geographic circumstances, practical challenges, and policy priorities. While illegal fishing vessels fleeing pursuit into the territorial sea of another State may be a systemic problem for some coastal States—particularly those with remote and co-located areas of maritime jurisdiction—others are more affected by narcotic trafficking or maritime security issues. Regardless of the subject matter or the States by or to whom consent is granted, the underlying principle is the same: hot pursuit may continue into the territorial sea of a third State on the basis of consent by that State.

As this discussion shows, the contemporary practice of States demonstrates a widespread acceptance of this principle. But what is the legal effect of this practice? Should it be seen as subsequent practice in the interpretation of Article 111(3) of the LOSC, or does it relate to the customary international law rule of hot pursuit? Perhaps the best approach is to recognize that the conventional and customary rules on hot pursuit are developing in parallel, and that rather than departing from the established framework for hot pursuit, this principle simply clarifies or interprets it. In this respect, it is clear that the cessation of the 'right' of hot pursuit does not relate to the balance of interests between the coastal State and the flag State in relation to the pursuit itself, but is necessary to preserve the sovereignty of the third State. Accordingly, the balance of interests between the coastal State and the flag

suppress illicit trafficking by sea in waters of the Caribbean and Bermuda (signed 13 July 1998, entered into force 30 October 2000) TIAS 00-1030, arts 4(2) and (3) and 6(1).

[147] *Agreement between the United States of America and the Dominican Republic Concerning Cooperation in Maritime Migration Law Enforcement* (signed and entered into force 20 May 2003) TIAS 03-520, arts 4(2)(b) and 5(2).

[148] *Agreement between the United States of America and the Bahamas Concerning Cooperation in Maritime Law Enforcement* (signed and entered into force 29 June 2004) TIAS 04-629, art 6(2).

State is unaffected if the third State, in an exercise of its sovereignty, consents to the coastal State's continuation of the pursuit through its territorial sea. As such, both the existing customary law rule and Article 111(3) can logically be interpreted as allowing for the continuation of hot pursuit through the territorial sea on the basis of consent, without jeopardizing the overall framework of hot pursuit.

7.3 Conclusion

As this Chapter has demonstrated, while Article 111 of the LOSC is generally accepted as reflecting the customary international law rule on hot pursuit, it remains 'both inevitable and desirable that the conditions for the exercise of the right of pursuit be given a flexible interpretation in order to permit effective exercise of police powers on the high seas.'[149] At the same time, this flexibility is inherently limited by the 'exceptional' nature of the enforcement jurisdiction enabled by the right of hot pursuit, and the need to preserve the freedom of navigation by innocent vessels on the high seas. Once again, this requires a careful balance to be struck, taking into account the relevant interests. Although the rule on hot pursuit is generally described as striking a balance between the rights of the coastal State in ensuring compliance with its laws and regulations, and the exclusive jurisdiction of the flag State over its vessels on the high seas, there is also a broader community interest on both sides of this equation—in ensuring the effective conservation and management of living resources, and in preserving the freedom of navigation. Accordingly, the balance of interests could more accurately and effectively be assured by taking a functional approach to the interpretation of hot pursuit, which 'would render illegitimate only those actions that violate an innocent vessel's freedom of navigation on the high seas'.[150]

In practice, this functional approach to hot pursuit has been—and continues to be—implemented within the existing framework of the hot pursuit doctrine, which has proved to be at once flexible and remarkably enduring. While the general framework of the doctrine has remained almost the same for nearly a century,[151] the technical and functional details have evolved and adapted to reflect the changing practical and legal circumstances in the law of the sea: from the use of sextant angles and loudhailers to a variety of 'reliable technical means'; from pursuit by vessels, to aircraft, to remote technologies; and from offences committed in the internal waters and the territorial sea to those in the EEZ. Indeed, it appears

[149] Churchill and Lowe, *The Law of the Sea* (n 5) 216.

[150] Allen, 'Doctrine of Hot Pursuit' (n 17) 322.

[151] See, eg, the rule on hot pursuit proposed in art 11 of the Annex on 'The Legal Status of the Territorial Sea' developed by the Committee on the Territorial Sea at the 1930 Hague Codification Conference: 'Official Documents of the Conference for the Codification of International Law, Held at the Hague in March-April, 1930' (1930) 24 AJIL Sup 169, 186–187.

that the adoption of evolutionary and innovative approaches to the conduct of hot pursuit in recent years—in particular, the adoption of modern technologies and cooperative approaches to address new environmental and logistical challenges—might have breathed new life into an increasingly outdated enforcement tool.

However, the legitimacy of this '21st century' hot pursuit relies on coastal States continuing to ensure that their innovations remain within the established framework, and do not impinge on flag State jurisdiction, community interests, or third State sovereignty. In this respect, it is vital to ensure that the 'who', 'what', 'where', and 'why' are clearly established and give effect to the key objectives underlying the various elements of hot pursuit. In particular, it is important to ensure:

- that any officials or assets purporting to exercise enforcement powers on behalf of the coastal State beyond its EEZ are appropriately authorized and identified;
- that the powers that may be exercised by or on behalf of the coastal State in particular areas are clearly understood (and that the use of terms such as 'fisheries waters' does not lead to confusion); and
- that modern tools and technologies are employed in a way that is credible and reliable, and provides clarity and transparency regarding the basis upon which hot pursuit is commenced and continued.

8
Conclusion

Writing almost forty years ago, shortly after the adoption of the United Nations Convention on the Law of the Sea (LOSC), Allot observed that:

> The Convention's main structural feature is its comprehensiveness. It is comprehensive in dealing with the whole non-land area of the world. It is also legally comprehensive. It has a rule for everything. The rule may be a permissive rule. It may be an obligation. It may confer an explicit freedom or leave a residual liberty by not specifying a right or a duty. But a Flying Dutchman wandering the sea areas of the world, carrying his copy of the Convention, would always be able to answer in legal terms the questions: who am I? who is that over there? where am I? what may I do now? what must I do now? The Convention would never fail him.[1]

Although this description is legally accurate, the reality is more complex. While the text of the LOSC would provide an answer to the hypothetical Flying Dutchman's questions in legal terms—by specifying the basic 'power' of each actor (in the form of an obligation, freedom, discretion, right, duty, or residual liberty) in each situation—the real effect or content of such powers can only be established through a much broader enquiry, taking into account their relationship with other powers, the variety of 'mediating concepts' in the LOSC that allow for the accommodation of changing interests and novel issues, and other developments that have influenced its interpretation. In this respect, as Allott noted a decade later, the LOSC can also be seen as 'a half-formed new structural uniqueness, full of painful ambiguities and exciting possibilities'.[2] This is particularly true for the exclusive economic zone (EEZ), one of the 'real inventions' of the Third United Nations Conference on the Law of the Sea, whose practical implementation, operation and future development was far from clear at the time the LOSC was adopted.[3]

The objective of this book was to consider these ambiguities and possibilities in the specific context of coastal State jurisdiction over living resources in the EEZ—to identify both the contemporary 'extent' of coastal State jurisdiction over living resources in the EEZ and the broader 'nature' of that jurisdiction, in order

[1] Philip Allott, 'Power Sharing in the Law of the Sea' (1983) 77 AJIL 1, 8. In maritime legend, the *Flying Dutchman* is a ghost ship doomed to sail the seas for eternity.
[2] Philip Allott, 'Mare Nostrum: A New International Law of the Sea' (1992) 86 AJIL 764, 765–766.
[3] Alexander Proelss, 'The Law on the EEZ in Perspective: Legal Status and Resolution of User Conflicts Revisited' (2012) 26 OceanYB 87, 87.

Coastal State Jurisdiction over Living Resources in the Exclusive Economic Zone. Camille Goodman, Oxford University Press.
 DOI: 10.1093/oso/9780192896841.003.0008

to provide a more predictable framework within which to understand and resolve current and future jurisdictional issues. This concluding Chapter draws on the cumulative analysis in the book to address both aspects of this question. It examines the 'nature' of coastal State jurisdiction over living resources in the EEZ and how the key principles underlying this jurisdiction inform the 'continuum' that govern its exercise (Section 8.1) and considers how the interpretation and implementation of the LOSC has affected the 'extent' of coastal State jurisdiction over living resources and the balance of interests at the heart of the EEZ regime in Part V of the LOSC (Section 8.2).

8.1 The Nature of Coastal State Jurisdiction over Living Resources in the EEZ

From the wide range of law and practice examined in this book, it is clear that the nature of coastal State jurisdiction over the living resources of the EEZ is best described as a broad discretion constrained by functional limits, which are determined on the basis of reasonableness and by reference to the balance of interests reflected in the EEZ regime. The strong but flexible nature of this formulation provides both certainty and adaptability; while the basic parameters of the 'jurisdictional continuum' are clearly established in both conventional and customary international law, its limits and application can be adjusted over time, taking into account relevant developments in law—and in life—in order to maintain the effectiveness of the compromise between inclusive and exclusive interests that is embedded in the concept of the EEZ. The vitality of this formulation is reflected in—and dictated by—the broader context of the LOSC, which is intended at once to be a comprehensive framework that settles all matters related to the law of the sea and allocates jurisdiction at sea,[4] and a 'living instrument' that evolves and adapts in response to changing circumstances and requirements.[5]

The implications of this formulation are revealed by interrogating its components. First, in order to understand the effect of the coastal State's broad discretion and its 'functional limits', it is necessary to ask: what is the legal status of the coastal State's 'sovereign rights' over living resources in the EEZ, how are they different from 'sovereignty', and what is the content of 'functional' jurisdiction? And second,

[4] LOSC Preamble [1].

[5] The concept of the LOSC as a 'living instrument' is referred to in literature, jurisprudence, and State practice. See, eg, Michael Wood, 'Reflections on the United Nations Convention on the Law of the Sea: A Living Instrument' in Jill Barrett and Richard Barnes (eds), *Law of the Sea: UNCLOS as a Living Treaty* (BIICL, 2016) lxxvii; Maria Gavouneli, *Functional Jurisdiction in the Law of the Sea* (Martinus Nijhoff 2007) 156; *SRFC Advisory Opinion* (Sep Op Judge Lucky) [18]; *Pleadings, Minutes of Public Sittings and Documents* (2015) Vol 22 *Request for an Advisory Opinion Submitted by the Sub-Regional Fisheries Commission* (Advisory Opinion) Written Statement by the Federal Republic of Germany, 18 November 2013 [8].

in order to properly understand the 'continuum' governing the exercise of this jurisdiction and establish the minimum obligations and maximum rights of the coastal State, it is important to consider: what is the role of 'reasonableness' in limiting the coastal State's jurisdiction, and how is the balance of interests determined and applied in this context?

8.1.1 A Broad Discretion Exercisable within Functional Limits

While the coastal State's 'sovereign rights' to explore and exploit, conserve and manage the living resources of the EEZ give rise to a broad discretion, this must be balanced against the rights and duties of other States.[6] Since the EEZ is beyond the territorial sovereignty of any State, this 'balancing' inevitably produces a tension between the exclusive rights of coastal States and the inclusive rights of other States. While such tension is inherent in the extraterritorial nature of jurisdiction at sea (where power cannot be plenary, as it is intra-territorially), no simple formula is available to determine its nature and extent since, as O'Connell has observed, 'the jurists have been unsuccessful in their search for a touchstone of the exercise of governmental authority outside the boundaries of national territory.'[7] Nonetheless, in order to understand the nature of the jurisdiction that flows from the coastal State's sovereign rights over living resources in the EEZ, it is necessary to examine the contemporary relationship between sovereignty and effective power in the law of the sea.

8.1.1.1 Sovereignty and 'Sovereign Rights'

As discussed in Chapter 1, the development of the law of the sea has been characterized by an ongoing struggle between sovereignty and freedom; the question of whether the oceans are freely open to all (*mare liberum*) or subject to the influence and occupation of individual States (*mare clausum*).[8] Historically, this dichotomy was underpinned by a deeper struggle between the concepts of '*dominium*' (sovereignty or ownership) and '*imperium*' (jurisdiction or power to control), and the issue of whether the power to rule relied on sovereignty or ownership of the maritime domain, or could be exercised independently of such ownership.[9] Put simply, the question was: must the oceans be entirely either *mare clausum* or *mare liberum*, or can the concepts of ownership of ocean space and control over ocean activities be separated?[10]

[6] LOSC art 56(2).
[7] DP O'Connell, *The International Law of the Sea, Vol I* (OUP 1982) 14.
[8] See Chapter 1 nn 40–2 and associated text.
[9] O'Connell, *The International Law of the Sea, Vol I* (n 7) 14–15.
[10] David Bederman, 'The Sea' in Bardo Fassbender and Anne Peters (eds), *The Oxford Handbook of the History of International Law* (OUP 2012) 363.

This question was answered by the International Law Commission's (ILC) 1956 Articles Concerning the Law of the Sea, which proposed that the coastal State should be recognized as exercising 'sovereign rights' over the continental shelf, and introduced an important distinction between the concepts of 'sovereignty' and 'sovereign rights' over different areas of the sea.[11] In using the term 'sovereign rights' rather than 'sovereignty', the ILC specifically rejected the notion that 'occupation' of the seabed was required in order to exercise rights and control over its resources,[12] dissolving the conjunction between *dominium* and *imperium* that had dominated juristic thought since 1700,[13] and paving the way for the development of a more divisible, differentiated concept of jurisdiction at sea. This differentiated approach was incorporated in Article 2(3) of the 1958 Convention on the Continental Shelf, and confirmed and developed in the LOSC, which distinguishes between 'sovereignty', 'sovereign rights', and 'jurisdiction' in relation to different areas and activities in the ocean.

Relevantly, the LOSC makes a clear distinction between:

- the 'sovereignty' of the coastal State, which (beyond its land territory) only applies in the internal waters, archipelagic waters, and territorial sea;[14]
- the 'sovereign rights' afforded to the coastal State for the purposes of 'exploring and exploiting, conserving and managing' the natural resources of the EEZ (and 'exploring' the continental shelf beyond the outer limits of the EEZ and 'exploiting' its resources);[15] and
- the rights of 'jurisdiction' of the coastal State in relation to other activities in the EEZ (the establishment and use of artificial islands, installations and structures, marine scientific research, and the protection and preservation of the marine environment).[16]

Clearly, the nature of the jurisdiction that may be exercised by the coastal State on the basis of its 'sovereign rights' in the EEZ is not intended to be equivalent to that which may be exercised on the basis of its 'sovereignty' in the territorial sea and archipelagic waters, nor to that which applies in relation to the other (non-resource related) activities in the EEZ. As discussed in Chapter 3, the notion of sovereign rights is widely accepted to constitute a 'functionally-limited variation' of the comprehensive concept of sovereignty, which has been extended to the EEZ for the limited purposes specified in Article 56(1)(a).[17] What then is the nature of the

[11] ILC, 'Articles Concerning the Law of the Sea with Commentaries' in *Yearbook of the International Law Commission (1956) Volume II*, UN Doc A/CN.4/SER.A/1956/Add.l, 265, art 68.

[12] ILC, 'Report of the International Law Commission to the General Assembly' in *Yearbook of the International Law Commission (1951) Volume II*, UN Doc A/CN.4/SER.A/1951/Add.l, 142.

[13] See O'Connell, *The International Law of the Sea, Vol I* (n 7) 15.

[14] LOSC art 2.

[15] LOSC arts 56(1)(a) and 77(1).

[16] LOSC art 56(1)(b).

[17] See Section 3.1.

'functional jurisdiction' that may be exercised on the basis of these sovereign rights and the broad discretion that they generate?

The legal effect of the coastal State's sovereign rights has been described in a variety of ways. At one end of the spectrum are those who conclude that, notwithstanding the clear textual distinctions made in the LOSC, the practical effect of sovereign rights is nonetheless similar to sovereignty. For example, O'Connell has observed that 'a claim to sovereign rights, however framed on paper, is inherently a claim to dominion, and there is no limit to the extent of the claim short of the faculties of sovereignty',[18] and Judge Oda has suggested that 'the 200-mile [EEZ] will eventually be assimilated to the territorial sea.'[19] Similar logic is evident in Dupuy's statement that '[t]he internal logic of sovereignty, a naturally indivisible concept, makes it reconstitute itself after the attempts to dismember it in the name of the theory of the [EEZ] in order to render it more acceptable to the major maritime powers and the land-locked countries.'[20] This approach is also reflected in the work of Verhoeven, who states that while the notion of sovereign rights denotes something less than full sovereignty, '[o]ne can only be hesitant to admit it, so artificial is the supposedly established distinction between "sovereign" rights and "sovereignty".'[21]

In contemporary practice, evidence for this approach can be found in the effectively unrestricted way that coastal States may exercise their prescriptive jurisdiction over living resources,[22] and in the broad range of vessels that may be subject to regulation or boarding and inspection by coastal States.[23] However, the specific limits on coastal State enforcement powers, which clearly recognize the concurrent rights and interests of other States,[24] together with the requirement that coastal State regulation be based on a 'direct connection' to fishing,[25] nonetheless ensure that the practical effect of the coastal State's 'sovereign rights' over living resources remains a functionally-limited variation of sovereignty, and not sovereignty itself.

At the other end of the spectrum, some authors argue that the way in which the coastal State's sovereign rights are framed by Part V of the LOSC place it in a position of 'custodianship' or 'stewardship' rather than 'ownership' with respect to the living resources of the EEZ. For example, Lowe relies on a textual interpretation of Part V of the LOSC to argue that: 'The coastal State here is not a proprietor, free to

[18] O'Connell, *The International Law of the Sea, Vol I* (n 7) 15.

[19] Shigeru Oda, *International Law of the Resources of the Sea* (Sijthoff & Noordhoff International 1979) 39–40.

[20] Rene-Jean Dupuy, 'The Sea Under National Competence' in Rene-Jean Dupuy and and Daniel Vignes (eds), *A Handbook on the New Law of the Sea* (Dordrecht 1991) 276.

[21] Joe Verhoeven, *Droit International Public* (Larcier, 2000) 550 (translated from the original French text: 'On ne peut qu'hésiter à l'admettre, tant paraît artificielle la distinction prétendument établie entre les droits "souverains" et une "souveraineté" ').

[22] See generally Chapters 3 and 4.

[23] See Chapter 5 and Section 6.2.1.

[24] As discussed in Section 6.3 and Chapter 7.

[25] *Virginia G* [215].

do with those resources what it will. It is a custodian, a steward, which must pursue management policies laid down by international law and designed to advance the specified interests of other States, and not simply of the coastal State itself.'[26]

The concept of stewardship is endorsed by Allott, who proposes a conceptual understanding of the LOSC pursuant to which the legal regime of the EEZ is one 'not of possession but of participation', which transcends 'traditional property relations' and should be understood as establishing a new form of progressive, participatory social development.[27] Similarly, Barnes concludes that 'strong forms of exclusive ownership or access control will not be compatible with the [LOSC]', although he also notes that the inclusion of economic considerations in Articles 61 and 62 of the LOSC may justify 'a more efficient private property-based management regime'.[28] Notwithstanding the theoretical attraction of this approach, under the broad and ambiguous framework of the LOSC, the coastal State's largely unfettered authority with respect to living resources in the EEZ is more akin to 'ownership' than 'stewardship'—at least in so far as defining the value to be optimized from its resources, and prescribing the conditions for access to and exploitation of those resources, is concerned.[29]

8.1.1.2 Functional Jurisdiction

In practice, the nature of the jurisdiction that is generated by the coastal State's sovereign rights over the living resources of the EEZ is neither that of sovereignty nor that of stewardship. Rather, it is a *sui generis* form of 'functional' jurisdiction,[30] pursuant to which the jurisdiction exercisable by the coastal State is not determined 'mechanically', by reference to its geographic location or specific procedural rules to be followed in its exercise, but 'functionally', by reference to the policy goals it is intended to fulfill—specifically, by its connection to the conservation, management, exploration, or exploitation of the living resources of the EEZ.[31] The substantive effect of this jurisdiction is characterized by two key principles: exclusivity and functionality.

[26] AV Lowe, 'Reflections on the Waters: Changing Conceptions of Property Rights in the Law of the Sea' (1986) 1 IJECL 1, 9. See also LDM Nelson, 'The Patrimonial Sea' (1973) 22 ICLQ 668, 680–2.

[27] Allott, 'Mare Nostrum' (n 2) 773 and 784–5.

[28] Richard Barnes, *Sovereignty, Property and Maritime Zones* (Hart 2018) 306.

[29] See Section 4.4. The leading proponent of the 'ownership approach' is Burke: William T Burke, '1982 Convention on the Law of the Sea Provisions on Conditions of Access to Fisheries Subject to National Jurisdiction' (1984) 63 OrLRev 73.

[30] See, eg, Gavouneli, *Functional Jurisdiction* (n 5) 68; Barnes, *Sovereignty, Property and Maritime Zones,* (n 28) 296; *Pleadings, Minutes of Public Sittings and Documents* (2013) Vol 20 *Arctic Sunrise (Netherlands v Russia)* (Provisional Measures) Verbatim Record of the Public Sitting held on 6 November 2012 at 10am, 19.

[31] See, eg, Craig H Allen, 'Doctrine of Hot Pursuit: A Functional Interpretation Adaptable to Emerging Maritime Law Enforcement Technologies and Practices' (1989) 20(4) ODIL 309, 322; Gavouneli, *Functional Jurisdiction* (n 5) 69; Barnes, *Sovereignty, Property and Maritime Zones* (n 28) 297.

First, as the ILC made clear in relation to the continental shelf, the coastal State's sovereign rights over the living resources of the EEZ are 'exclusive', in the sense that, if the coastal State does not exploit those resources, no one else may do so without the coastal State's consent.[32] Absent the physical possession or 'effective occupation' that accompanies territorial sovereignty, such exclusivity of jurisdiction is necessary not only to allow the coastal State to fully enjoy its sovereign rights by alienating other interests, but to ensure 'international recognition of marketable title' to the resources of the EEZ.[33] In this context, as Brilmayer and Klein point out, it is in the interests of each State to respect the exclusivity of such jurisdiction, in order to create a system of reciprocity allowing for the stable exploitation of resources.[34] The breadth of the discretion generated by this exclusivity is clearly demonstrated in the wide variety of issues that are regulated—and objectives that are pursued—by coastal States on the basis of their prescriptive jurisdiction over foreign fishing vessels.[35]

Second, the 'functionality' of the coastal State's sovereign rights dictates that they must be 'extensively interpreted to include whatever powers are needed to ensure that the coastal State is able to enjoy its rights in full'.[36] The functional nature of this jurisdiction is evident in State practice: it underpins the exercise of coastal State jurisdiction over not only fishing but fishing related activities in the EEZ,[37] enables the coastal State to apply regulations to not only licensed vessels but unlicensed vessels in transit through the EEZ,[38] and allows the coastal State to board and inspect any fishing or fishing support vessel in the EEZ at any time.[39] As these examples make clear, the determinant of 'functionality' in this context is not the activity of fishing *per se*, but its connection with the *resources* over which the coastal State has sovereign rights.[40]

Clarifying the functional application of the coastal State's jurisdiction in this way—by reference to resources, rather than activities—makes very clear that, notwithstanding the description of the EEZ as an exclusive 'economic' zone, the coastal

[32] ILC, 'Articles Concerning the Law of the Sea' (n 11) 297.

[33] Lea Brilmayer and Natalie Klein, 'Land and Sea: Two Sovereignty Regimes In Search of a Common Denominator' (2001) 33 NYUJIntlL&Pol 703, 736.

[34] Ibid.

[35] See the substantive conclusions on the extent of the coastal State's prescriptive jurisdiction over foreign fishing vessels in Section 4.4.

[36] Edward Duncan Brown, *The International Law of the Sea: Vol 1* (Dartmouth 1994) 220.

[37] See Chapter 3.

[38] See Chapter 5.

[39] See Sections 5.1.1 and 6.2.1.

[40] A distinction between the regulation of 'resources' and 'activities' was suggested—although with a different effect—by Riphagen during the negotiation of the LOSC. Reflecting on the juridical regime for the territorial sea established in the 1958 Convention on the Territorial Sea, Riphagen suggested that the concept that the fish in the territorial sea belonged to the coastal State constituted a shift from 'activity' to 'resource'; and that in contrast, the proposal being discussed in the LOSC negotiations to afford the coastal State exclusive rights in the EEZ to the extent that its nationals had the capacity to catch, constituted a shift from 'resource' to 'activity': W Riphagen, 'Some Reflections on "Functional Sovereignty"' (1975) 6 NYIL 121, 138–9.

State does not, as has sometimes been asserted, have 'economic sovereignty' in the EEZ.[41] Nor, as the International Tribunal for the Law of the Sea (ITLOS) made clear in the *Saiga (No 2)* case, does the coastal State have jurisdiction over activities in the EEZ on an 'economic' or 'public interest' basis.[42] Rather, the jurisdiction that flows from the coastal State's sovereign rights over living resources is enlivened on a functional basis, by connection with those resources—in terms of the regulation of both the resources themselves, and activities related to those resources.

Importantly, the functional nature of this jurisdiction has not only an 'enabling' but also a 'limiting' effect: it simultaneously extends the coastal State's jurisdiction as far as is necessary to enable the coastal State to enjoy its rights over living resources in full (such as by applying regulations to prevent illegal fishing by unlicensed foreign fishing vessels in transit through the EEZ), and constrains the coastal State's exercise of jurisdiction to activities that are based on and directed towards those resources (such as by precluding the application of similar regulations to other (non-fishing) vessels in transit through the EEZ). In this respect, as Allen observes, the employment of a 'functional' approach to jurisdiction seeks to strike a workable balance between discretion and the rule of law, by writing flexible rules that fix the limits within which discretion may be exercised.[43] It is thus necessary to consider how these limits are to be determined.

8.1.2 Determined on the Basis of Reasonableness and the Balance of Interests

Sovereign rights—like sovereignty itself—are not absolute, but must be exercised in accordance with any restrictions imposed by international law.[44] Accordingly, notwithstanding the exclusive and functional nature of the coastal State's sovereign rights over living resources, they are inherently subject to limits. These limits are determined on the basis of reasonableness, which necessarily involves reference to the balance of rights and interests embedded in the EEZ regime.

8.1.2.1 The Requirement of Reasonableness

The concept of reasonableness is one of the underlying objectives of jurisdiction, and operates as a restraint on the exercise of arbitrary or exorbitant jurisdiction.[45]

[41] See, eg, Reynaldo Galindo Pohl, 'The Exclusive Economic Zone in the Light of Negotiations of the Third United Nations Conference on the Law of the Sea' in Francisco Orrego Vicuna (ed), *The Exclusive Economic Zone: A Latin American Perspective* (Westview Press 1984) 45.

[42] *Saiga (No 2)* [127]–[131].

[43] Allen, 'Doctrine of Hot Pursuit' (n 31) 322.

[44] *Nuclear Weapons Advisory Opinion* (Diss Op Shahabudeen) 393. On the inherent limits of sovereignty, see Chapter 1 nn 25–7 and associated text.

[45] FA Mann, 'The Doctrine of International Jurisdiction Revisited After Twenty Years' (1984) 186(III) RdC 9, 28–9.

It is embodied in the generally accepted rule that any exercise of extraterritorial jurisdiction must be based on a reasonable, legitimate connection between the State and the factual situation it is seeking to regulate.[46] Reasonableness also enables international law to effectively take account of diverse interests, by providing a mechanism for normative standards to be adjusted and applied taking into account the reality of concrete circumstances, and allowing for flexibility and compromise in the application of universal rules while modulating the discretionary powers of States.[47] In this respect, while States commonly use the term 'reasonable' in legal instruments in order to introduce a degree of flexibility, tribunals have also been known to 'reformulate' a treaty provision by introducing the notion of reasonableness despite its absence from the original text.[48]

In the law of the sea, the requirement of 'reasonableness' is relied upon—whether explicitly or implicitly—to play an important role in determining the limit of all aspects of coastal State jurisdiction. In the context of the EEZ, the concept of reasonableness:

- is an integral element in applying the rule of 'reciprocal due regard' set out in Articles 56 and 58;[49]
- is an implied aspect of the standard for resolving conflicts over the attribution of residual rights under Article 59;[50]
- is used to determine whether laws and regulations applied by the coastal State under Article 62 are 'consistent with' the LOSC;[51]
- is explicitly included as a test for establishing the legitimacy of a bond in Article 73(2), and has been interpreted to apply generally to coastal State enforcement measures under Article 73;[52] and
- provides the basic standard for determining whether a coastal State had a 'good reason to believe' that its laws and regulations had been violated such as to justify the commencement of a hot pursuit under Article 111.[53]

In each of these cases, the rule of reasonableness 'requires State behaviour to be proportional to the aim legally pursued, with due regard to the rights and freedoms

[46] See Chapter 1 nn 28–33 and associated text. Ryngaert takes this further, suggesting a rule of reasonableness as a method for resolving problems of concurrent jurisdiction in international law: Cedric Ryngaert *Jurisdiction in International Law* (2nd ed, OUP 2015).

[47] See, eg, Olivier Corten, 'The Notion of "Reasonable" in International Law: Legal Discourse, Reason and Contradictions' (1999) 48(3) ICLQ 613, 615–20.

[48] Ibid 615. In *Virginia G*, for example, notwithstanding the fact that the concept of 'reasonableness' appears only in paragraph 2 of art 73, the Tribunal stated that 'the principle of reasonableness applies generally to enforcement measures under Article 73 of the [LOSC]': *Virginia G* [270].

[49] See Sections 2.3.2.1 and 5.1.2.

[50] See Section 3.1.3.

[51] See Section 4.3.3.

[52] See Section 6.1.

[53] See Section 7.1.1.

granted to another State'.[54] As such, determining the 'reasonable' extent of the coastal State's jurisdiction necessarily involves considering the balance between the rights and interests of coastal and other States under the *sui generis* legal regime of the EEZ.

8.1.2.2 The Balance of Interests

The LOSC establishes an intricate mechanism for balancing the interests of coastal and other States in the EEZ. The pivot of this mechanism is found in Articles 56 and 58, which, together, provide a framework for accommodating the 'rights and duties' of all interested parties.[55] However, in order to properly understand the effect of this framework, it is necessary to recall that jurisdiction is not simply a question of rights versus duties, but 'a mixture of discretionary, mandatory and prohibitive elements'.[56] As such, the legal framework for coastal State jurisdiction under the LOSC—like that under general international law—does not consist in a binary weighing of rights and duties, but exists as a continuum of prohibitions, rights, and duties, pursuant to which a State may be obliged, authorized but not required, or prohibited from exercising jurisdiction in relation to a person or activity. In this respect, the concept of jurisdictional 'obligations' is an important feature of the EEZ regime—and the LOSC framework generally—and is reflected in the shift from traditional reliance on the 'rights' and 'powers' of States to recognition of their 'duties' and 'obligations', and from a focus on the exclusive rights of the coastal State to the inclusive rights of other (or all) States.[57]

As set out in the well-known analysis of Hohfeld, legal relationships are traditionally categorized as either 'correlative' or 'opposite': 'rights' and 'duties' are correlative (such that when a right is invaded, a duty is violated), while the opposite of 'rights' is considered to be 'no-rights'.[58] Although the LOSC extensively employs Hohfeldian terms to allocate powers at sea—including rights, duties, privileges, powers, immunities, and liabilities—the legal relationships described by these terms are layered and limited by critical power modifiers,[59] such as 'in accordance with', having 'due regard to', 'subject to', 'in so far as they are not incompatible with', 'taking into account', 'appropriate', 'necessary', and 'reasonable'. Accordingly, the legal relationships between States in the EEZ are more 'corresponding'—or in some instances 'competing'—than 'correlative', and in many instances may in fact involve multiple 'corresponding' or 'competing' considerations.[60]

[54] *Filleting in the Gulf of St Lawrence* [54].
[55] David Joseph Attard, *The EEZ in International Law* (Clarendon Press 1987) 293.
[56] Alex Mills, 'Rethinking Jurisdiction in International Law' (2014) 84(1) BYIL 187, 212–13.
[57] Barbara Kwiatkowska, *The 200 Mile Exclusive Economic Zone in the New Law of the Sea* (Martinus Nijhoff 1989) 5–6. See also Chapter 1 nn 34–8 and associated text.
[58] Wesley Newcomb Hohfeld, 'Some Fundamental Legal Conceptions as Applied in Judicial Reasoning' (1913) 23 YaleLJ 16, 30–2.
[59] Allott, 'Power Sharing in the Law of the Sea' (n 1) 9–11.
[60] As Pound observes, 'Hohfeld's scheme presupposes that there can only be one opposite and one correlative and that there must be an opposite and a correlative. But there may be many contrasts and

ITLOS has noted that 'while the [LOSC] approaches the issue of conservation and management of living resources from the perspective of *obligations* of the coastal State, these obligations entail corresponding *rights*',[61] and Kwiatkowska states that for every right in the LOSC, a countervailing obligation can be found.[62] While both of these things are true, the situation is actually more three-dimensional. For example, the coastal State's sovereign rights to explore, exploit, conserve, and manage living resources in the EEZ involve multiple corresponding obligations: in addition to the obligation to have 'due regard' to the rights and duties of other States,[63] there are also a wide range of additional duties associated with the conservation and management of the living resources of the zone—including the specific obligations set out in Part V of the LOSC,[64] and the general obligation to protect and preserve the marine environment under Part XII[65]—the combined effect of which is to give the coastal State primary responsibility for taking the necessary measures to prevent, deter, and eliminate illegal, unreported, and unregulated (IUU) fishing in the EEZ.[66] A similar analysis can be undertaken for other States: the right to navigate freely through the EEZ is subject not only to the specific duty to have 'due regard' to the rights and interests of the coastal State, but to the flag State obligations in Part VII[67] and the general obligations to protect and preserve the marine environment in Part XII, which apply 'in all maritime areas regulated by the [LOSC], including the [EEZ] of the coastal State'.[68]

At its theoretical apogee, assessing the balance of 'rights and duties' in the EEZ thus involves a three-step, multi-dimensional approach. First, it is necessary to consider the relationship between the coastal State's own rights and duties, in order to ensure that the 'ceiling' on the coastal State's rights is interpreted in a way that keeps it above the 'floor' of the coastal State's obligations[69]—in other words, that the coastal State's rights are not interpreted so restrictively as to impede the fulfilment of its obligations, and vice versa. Second, a similar exercise must be undertaken with respect to any relevant rights and duties of other States—to ensure that their duties are not interpreted so onerously as to prevent the enjoyment of their rights (and vice versa). Finally, the outcome of these two considerations must be

there are sometimes two correlatives': Roscoe Pound, 'Fifty Years of Jurisprudence' (1937) 50 HarvLRev 557, 573.

61 *SRFC Advisory Opinion* [205] (emphasis added).
62 Kwiatkowska, *The 200 Mile EEZ* (n 57) 6 (emphasis added).
63 LOSC art 56(2).
64 LOSC arts 61–7 and 73. In addition, ITLOS has made clear that in the context of an application for prompt release of a vessel under art 73(2), the balance of interests includes reference to art 292 (see Section 6.3.1.3).
65 LOSC arts 192 and 194. See Sections 2.1.5 and 2.3.1.
66 *SRFC Advisory Opinion* [106].
67 LOSC arts 91, 92, and 94.
68 *SRFC Advisory Opinion* [111].
69 Mills, 'Rethinking Jurisdiction in International Law' (n 56) 209–10.

balanced against each other—and, in some cases, against the interests of the international community as a whole—in order to preserve the compromise embedded in the *sui generis* regime for the EEZ.

For example, as discussed in Chapter 6, in considering the 'balance of interests' in an application for prompt release, there are strong grounds for including the broader context; considering not only the rights and interests of the coastal and flag State, but taking into account the way that modern industrial fishing operates and the actors involved, and the community interest in the conservation and management of living resources and the protection of the marine environment. Similarly, as discussed in Chapter 7, while the rule on hot pursuit balances the rights of the coastal State in ensuring compliance with its laws and regulations with the exclusive jurisdiction of the flag State over its vessels on the high seas, there is also a broader community interest in both of these issues (with respect to ensuring the conservation and management of living resources, and with respect to preserving the freedom of navigation).

The way in which the various corresponding (or competing) rights and duties of both coastal and other States are balanced ultimately determines the minimum duties and maximum prohibitions of the 'jurisdictional continuum' that governs the extent of coastal State jurisdiction over living resources in the EEZ. However, since this continuum is implemented and effected primarily through the actions and decisions of the coastal State, the dominant characteristic in this regime remains the substantial discretion enjoyed by the coastal State to explore, exploit, conserve, and manage the living resources of the EEZ.

8.2 The Extent of Coastal State Jurisdiction over Living Resources in the EEZ

Over the last forty years, coastal States have developed innovative ways to exercise their rights and fulfil their responsibilities with respect to the living resources of the EEZ, 'optimize' the utilization of those resources, and enforce their jurisdiction as coastal States. The approaches adopted by coastal States in the exercise of their jurisdiction in relation to different issues and activities—and the effect of this practice on the substantive 'extent' of such jurisdiction—are described in detail in Chapters 3 to 7. Those Chapters demonstrate some clear themes regarding the extent of coastal State jurisdiction over living resources under the LOSC, including:

- the breadth of regulation that is enabled by coastal State discretion, and the jurisdictional 'opportunities' that result from ambiguity in the LOSC;
- the adoption of measures to respond to evolutions in technology and society, and the regulation of issues or activities to address practical imperatives not envisaged in the LOSC; and

- the development of alternative legal, policy, or regulatory approaches to overcome limits on jurisdiction.

In addition, they show how coastal States use a variety of tools and techniques to maximize the extent of their jurisdiction, including approaches that 'thicken' their jurisdiction within the EEZ, 'project' their jurisdiction beyond the EEZ, expand the effect of their jurisdiction through cooperation and collective action, and enhance the application of their jurisdiction through the use of technology.

With these themes, tools, and techniques in mind, it is worth returning to some broader issues relating to the 'extent' of coastal State jurisdiction that were raised in Chapter 1: the role of state practice in the interpretation and implementation of coastal State jurisdiction in the EEZ under the LOSC; and the extent to which this practice confirms assertions that the 'creeping jurisdiction' of coastal States will upset the balance of rights and interests in the EEZ.

8.2.1 The Role of Implementation and Interpretation

Of course, the jurisdiction asserted by each coastal State varies widely, since it is influenced by—and implemented under—vastly differing circumstances, from the realities of maritime geography, stock distribution, and biological factors, to resource constraints, scientific and policy challenges, development priorities, and political, social, economic, security, and environmental interests. In particular, States seek to achieve different objectives through regulating the living resources of the EEZ—whether to ensure food security, maximize economic benefit, generate jobs and investment, enhance environmental protections, or advance policies on issues ranging from human rights and industrial relations to transnational crime and security.

In the context of coastal State jurisdiction over living resources in the EEZ, while state practice in the implementation of the LOSC has in some respects departed from its exact terms, direct challenges to the basic jurisdictional scheme it establishes are rare.[70] This is reflected, for example, in the way that coastal States have addressed limitations on the exercise of jurisdiction by finding alternative approaches that respect the jurisdictional allocations established in the LOSC—such as by obtaining consent from the relevant flag State or State of nationality before imposing a term of imprisonment in relation to a foreign fishing offence,[71]

[70] Ringbom endorses the application of this conclusion at a more general level (beyond jurisdiction over living resources in the EEZ), noting that 'evolutions in jurisdictional balance do not usually take the form of outright confrontations with the law of the sea': Henrik Ringbom, 'Introduction' in Henrik Ringbom (ed) *Jurisdiction over Ships: Post-UNCLOS Developments in the Law of the Sea* (Brill Nijhoff 2015) 11.

[71] See Section 6.3.2.1 and Table 6.2.

or seeking consent from the relevant coastal State to continue hot pursuit into its territorial sea.[72] In addition, since the LOSC establishes a broad framework for the allocation of jurisdiction at sea, it necessarily relies on interpretation and implementation to give substance and detail to the general rights and obligations of both coastal and other States—particularly in relation to the *sui generis* regime of the EEZ. As such, even though not all the exercises of coastal State jurisdiction examined in this book are directly envisaged or specifically enabled by the LOSC, they can nonetheless generally be seen as developing or adding detail to—rather than derogating or departing from—the framework that is established in Part V of the LOSC.

Importantly, while not all coastal States have adopted the same approaches to implementing their rights and obligations relating to the living resources of the EEZ, there is a high level of acceptance of coastal State regulation in this area.[73] There are relatively few instances in which formal protests have been recorded about the exercise of coastal State jurisdiction in relation to foreign fishing (or foreign fishing vessels) in the EEZ, and in some cases, such protests have in any case been followed by the adoption or acceptance of similar regulations by the protesting State. And while the compulsory dispute settlement system (although otherwise rather restricted in its application to the EEZ)[74] allows for challenges to be brought in situations where a coastal State is alleged to have contravened the freedom of navigation of other States in its EEZ, there are—with the exception of cases relating to the prompt release rule[75]—very few instances in which the legitimacy of regulations applied by a coastal State in relation to living resources has been formally challenged by other States on this basis.[76] Moreover, flag States have implicitly endorsed a wide range of coastal State regulations through the act of continuing to authorize their vessels and nationals to fish in the waters of coastal States.[77] Under these circumstances, much of the practice of coastal States in implementing the LOSC can be seen as constituting objective evidence of the understanding of the Parties as to the meaning of its provisions, to which recourse can be had as an authentic means of interpretation under Article 31(3)(b) of the Vienna Convention on the Law of Treaties (VCLT).

State practice also demonstrates the widespread adoption of an evolutionary approach to the interpretation of the LOSC—from the regulation of modern 'fishing related activities' to the use of technology in the conduct of hot pursuit.[78] In this

[72] See Section 7.2.3.2 and Table 7.1.
[73] On the standards for assessing the effect of subsequent practice, see Sections 1.2.2 and 1.2.3.
[74] See Section 2.1.2.
[75] See Section 6.3.1.
[76] Of all the contentious cases submitted to resolution under Part XV of the LOSC, the only case involving substantive issues relating to coastal State jurisdiction over living resources to have been resolved on the merits is *Virginia G*.
[77] See Chapter 4 nn 189–91 and associated text.
[78] See Chapter 2 nn 206–14 and associated text.

regard, the legitimacy—indeed, necessity—of taking an evolutionary approach to the interpretation of the LOSC is not only an inherent consequence of its widely accepted role as a 'constitution for the oceans',[79] but is embedded in the LOSC itself, which includes a range of evolutionary provisions,[80] and introduces concepts that necessarily involve questions of social policy and other changing standards—such as 'optimum utilization' and 'national interest'—as well as important 'mediating concepts' that allow for the accommodation of changing interests over time—such as 'due regard' and 'reasonableness'.

In practice, both of these approaches—interpreting the LOSC by adopting an evolutionary approach, or by reference to the subsequent agreement and subsequent practice of States in its implementation—can produce similar results, and ensure that the LOSC can survive and adapt to contemporary priorities and realities. While both approaches rely on the intention of the Parties, they operate by different mechanisms: the former looks to the *original* intention of the Parties, and the latter to their *subsequent* intention.[81] In this respect, an evolutionary interpretation based on the original intentions of the Parties might be confirmed by reference to their subsequent intentions as expressed in practice—as in the case of the rule on hot pursuit, for example. Ultimately, however, both approaches must be applied consistently with, and in order to achieve, a good faith interpretation of the LOSC in light of its object and purpose, pursuant to Article 31(1) and (2) of the VCLT—and thus the balance of rights and interests embedded in the *sui generis* regime for the EEZ.

8.2.2 The Question of 'Creeping Jurisdiction'

Given the complex web of rights and obligations of coastal and other States that must be balanced in the EEZ—and the possibility for the jurisdictional balance to evolve through implementation and interpretation of the LOSC—the ultimate question about the 'extent' of coastal State jurisdiction over living resources is whether, 'in pursuit of the final goal, the exercise of one of the parallel and contradictory rights may well be wholly obliterated.'[82] This raises the vexed issue of 'creeping jurisdiction'.

Expanded unilateral assertions of jurisdiction by coastal States have long prompted fears of the 'territorialization of the oceans' by the 'creeping jurisdiction'

[79] See 'A Constitution for the Oceans', Statement of Ambassador Tommy T B Koh, President of the Third United Nations Conference on the Law of the Sea, at its final session in Montego Bay, Jamaica, 10 December 1982, reproduced in *The Law of the Sea: Official Text of the United Nations Convention on the Law of the Sea* (UN 1983) xxxiii.
[80] See Chapter 1 nn 115–18 and associated text.
[81] Irina Buga, *Modification of Treaties by Subsequent Practice* (OUP 2018) 93.
[82] Gavouneli, *Functional Jurisdiction* (n 5) 69.

of coastal States.[83] In its original form, the concept of creeping jurisdiction related to the geographic expansion of coastal State authority in pursuit of ocean resources (both real and potential) and economic security.[84] While the adoption of the LOSC—and the establishment of maritime zones—was intended to freeze the expansion of coastal State authority and provide stability and predictability in the exercise of jurisdiction at sea,[85] the concept of 'creeping jurisdiction' has not disappeared. Instead, it now relates primarily to substantive expansions of coastal State authority, primarily in pursuit of military and environmental security, and protection of the geographic authority already secured (and the resources contained within it).[86] This is understandable: a State which has jurisdiction for some purposes feels the need to extend it 'in order to safeguard what it has, or because it seems reasonable to do so and there appears to be no reason not to do so'.[87] But does it constitute a renewed attempt at 'territorialization' of the EEZ that threatens to upset the substantive balance of rights and interests achieved in the LOSC and render the traditional freedoms of the sea 'mere exceptions to coastal State sovereignty'?[88] Or is it merely a question of how existing rights and interests are interpreted, and where the balance between them is struck at different times and in response to different challenges?

The trend toward further, substantive, expansions of jurisdiction is clearly evident in contemporary assertions of authority by coastal States over a wide range of activities with respect to which the LOSC does not assign them jurisdiction in the EEZ—in particular, attempts to prohibit or restrict military activities and hydrographic surveys by foreign-flagged vessels, and regulate issues such as customs, underwater cultural heritage, the laying of cables and pipelines, and the carriage of hazardous materials. However, some argue that 'creeping jurisdiction' is also reflected in various exercises of coastal State jurisdiction with respect to living resources, such as the extension of coastal State regulations to unlicensed fishing (and fishing support) vessels in transit through the EEZ, the boarding and inspection of foreign fishing vessels in the EEZ, and the application of licence conditions that apply beyond the outer limits of the EEZ (in particular, those which prohibit fishing in certain areas of the high seas).[89] But as the principles and practice

[83] See Chapter 1 n 45.

[84] John A Knauss, 'Creeping Jurisdiction and Customary International Law' (1985) 15(2) ODIL 209, 211.

[85] Bernard H Oxman, 'The Territorial Temptation: A Siren Song at Sea' (2006) 100 AJIL 830, 835.

[86] Sophia Kopela, 'The "Territorialization" of the Exclusive Economic Zone: Implications for Maritime Jurisdiction' in *20th Anniversary Conference of the International Boundary Research Unit on 'The State of Sovereignty, 1–3 April 2009'* 14–15, available at <http://dur.ac.uk/resources/ibru/conferences/sos/s_kopela_paper.pdf> accessed 20 February 2021.

[87] Ram Prakash Anand, *Legal Regime of the Sea-Bed and the Developing Countries* (AW Sijthoff 1976) 111.

[88] Helmut Tuerk, *Reflections on the Contemporary Law of the Sea* (Martinus Nijhoff 2012) 161.

[89] See, eg, Jon M Van Dyke, 'The Disappearing Right to Navigational Freedom in the Exclusive Economic Zone' (2005) 29 MarPol 107, 108–9; Erik Franckx, 'The 200-Mile Limit: Between Creeping Jurisdiction and Creeping Common Heritage?' (2007) 39 GWashIntlLRev 467, 484–5 and

examined in this book have shown, these assertions do not constitute illegitimate jurisdictional 'creep', but are merely an exercise of the coastal State's sovereign rights over living resources in its EEZ, falling within the contemporary interpretation and implementation of its jurisdiction under Part V of the LOSC.

Franckx suggests that the concept of 'creeping' jurisdiction refers to 'the idea of unilateral action directed at upsetting a legal framework adhered to by the majority of other States'.[90] While coastal States have interpreted and implemented their sovereign rights over living resources in a number of new and novel ways, this is enabled by the broad jurisdictional framework of the LOSC, within which jurisdiction can legitimately 'creep' in ways that, despite being significant in substantive terms, do not threaten the overall jurisdictional balance of the LOSC, or the certainty and stability of the framework.[91] Moreover, even if the legitimacy of jurisdiction over these activities were considered by reference to the 'residual rights' formula in Article 59 of the LOSC,[92] it is widely agreed that, given the functional nature of the EEZ, this formula would normally favour the coastal State where interests or activities relating to sovereign rights over their resources are concerned.[93]

Accordingly, provided coastal State jurisdiction remains within the 'functional' limits discussed in this book, it is not likely to constitute 'creeping' jurisdiction, properly defined. For example, in relation to the functional limits which would be likely to apply in relation to the 'expansions' of coastal State jurisdiction discussed above:[94]

- while regulations may be applied to fishing and fishing support vessels in transit through the EEZ on the basis of the coastal State's sovereign rights over living resources, this would not extend to their application to other sorts of vessels;[95]
- while the coastal State may board and inspect any fishing vessel or fishing support vessel in the EEZ at any time, additional forms of enforcement (such as

490–2; Niquole Esters, 'Impacts of Language: Creeping Jurisdiction and Its Challenges to the Equal Implementation of the Law of the Sea Convention' in *Paper presented at the 5th Advisory Board on the Law of the Sea Conference on the Difficulties in Implementing the Provisions of UNCLOS, Monaco, 15–17 October 2008* 14–16, available at <http://legacy.iho.int/mtg_docs/com_wg/ABLOS/ABLOS_Conf5/Papers/Session5-Paper1-Esters.pdf> accessed 20 February 2021.

[90] Franckx, 'The 200-Mile Limit' (n 89) 487.
[91] Ringbom, 'Introduction' (n 70) 14.
[92] Section 3.1.3.
[93] See, eg, Satya Nandan and Shabtai Rosenne (eds), *United Nations Convention on the Law of the Sea 1982: A Commentary, Vol II* (Martinus Nijhoff 1993) 569; Donald R Rothwell and Tim Stephens, *The International Law of the Sea* (2nd ed, Hart Publishing 2016) 91; Alexander Proelss, 'Article 59' in Alexander Proelss (ed), *United Nations Convention on the Law of the Sea: A Commentary* (CH Beck 2017) 461.
[94] See n 89 and associated text.
[95] See Section 5.3.

seizure or detention) may only be undertaken in circumstances where there are 'reasonable grounds to believe' that there has been a violation of the fisheries laws and regulations of the coastal State;[96] and
- the application of coastal State fisheries laws and regulations beyond the outer limits of the EEZ must be legitimately linked to the sovereign rights of the coastal State within the EEZ.[97]

Nor is this formulation of jurisdiction likely to upset the balance of interests in the EEZ, which, like the freedom of the seas, is 'neither absolute nor static: it embodies the balance of jurisdictional functions among States which at any time best serve the community of nations and its content is subject to constant modification as that community adjusts itself to the solution of new problems.'[98]

8.3 Conclusion: Striking the Right Balance

Pursuant to the framework established by the LOSC, the 'nature' of coastal State jurisdiction over living resources in the EEZ is flexible, but functional—consisting of a broad discretion, exercisable within functional limits that are determined on the basis of reasonableness and by reference to the balance of rights and interests in the EEZ. Similarly, the minimum duties and maximum obligations of the jurisdictional continuum that governs the 'extent' of coastal State jurisdiction over living resources in the EEZ are determined by the way in which the various corresponding (or competing) rights and duties of coastal and other States are balanced.

Since this jurisdictional continuum is implemented and effected primarily through the actions and decisions of the coastal State, the dominant characteristic of this regime remains the substantial discretion enjoyed by the coastal State—characterized by exclusivity and functionality—to explore, exploit, conserve, and manage the living resources of the EEZ. While this provides significant scope for ongoing innovation and development by coastal States, the continued effectiveness of this framework will depend on how the rights and obligations of States in the zone are interpreted—how the balance is struck between the rights and duties of coastal and other States in the EEZ.

This balance will need to be struck repeatedly and not always in the same place, since the law of the sea is continually developing as social, economic, political, and geographic change, and advances in scientific knowledge and technology, affect the needs and the practice of States. While it remains important for coastal States to recognize—and regulate within—the limits of the existing legal framework, it

[96] See Section 6.3.1
[97] See Section 4.3.3
[98] DP O'Connell, *The International Law of the Sea, Vol II* (OUP 1984) 796–7.

is equally important to recognize that those limits are not static, but must be interpreted with appropriate reference to State practice, consideration of all relevant interests, and in an evolutionary and purposive way that allows coastal States—and other States—to give effect to the object and purpose of the LOSC regime and effectively and innovatively address the challenges of contemporary international fisheries governance.

Select Bibliography

Books

Anderson, David, 'The Regulation of Fishing and Related Activities in Exclusive Economic Zones' in Erik Franckx and Philippe Gauthier (eds), *The Exclusive Economic Zone and the United Nations Convention on the Law of the Sea, 1982–2000: A Preliminary Assessment of State Practice* (Bruylant 2003) 31–49

Anderson, David, 'Freedoms of the High Seas in the Modern Law of the Sea' in David Freestone, Richard Barnes, and David Ong (eds), *The Law of the Sea: Progress and Prospects* (OUP 2006) 327–46

Anderson, David, *Modern Law of the Sea: Selected Essays* (Martinus Nijhoff 2008)

Anderson, David, 'Coastal State Jurisdiction and High Seas Freedoms in the EEZ in the Light of the Saiga Case' in Clive R Symmons (ed), *Selected Contemporary Issues in the Law of the Sea* (Brill Nijhoff 2011) 105–15

Andreone, Gemma, 'The Exclusive Economic Zone' in Donald R Rothwell et al (eds), *The Oxford Handbook of the Law of the Sea* (OUP 2015) 159–80

Attard, David Joseph, *The Exclusive Economic Zone in International Law* (Clarendon Press 1987)

Barnes, Richard A, 'The Continuing Vitality of UNCLOS' in J Barrett and Barnes R (eds), *Law of the Sea: UNCLOS as a Living Treaty* (BIICL 2016) 459–89

Barnes, Richard, *Sovereignty, Property and Maritime Zones* (Hart 2018)

Bernhardt, Rudolf, 'Custom and Treaty in the Law of the Sea' (1987) 205 RdC 255

Brown, Edward Duncan, *The International Law of the Sea: Vol 1* (Dartmouth 1994)

Buga, Irina, 'Between Stability and Change in the Law of the Sea Convention: Subsequent Practice, Treaty Modification and Regime Interaction' in Donald R Rothwell et al (eds), *The Oxford Handbook of the Law of the Sea* (OUP 2015) 46–68

Burke, William T, *The New International Law of Fisheries* (Clarendon Press 1994)

Castaneda, Jorge, 'Negotiations on the Exclusive Economic Zone at the Third United Nations Conference on the Law of the Sea' in Jerzy Makarczyk (ed), *Essays in International Law in Honor of Judge Manfred Lachs* (Brill 1984) 605–23

Christie, Donna R, 'The Conservation and Management of Stocks Located Solely Within the Exclusive Economic Zone' in Ellen Hey (ed), *Developments in International Fisheries Law* (Kluwer 1999) 395–419

Churchill RR and AV Lowe, *The Law of the Sea* (3rd ed, MUP 1999)

Churchill, Robin and Daniel Owen, *The EC Common Fisheries Policy* (OUP 2010)

Churchill, Robin R, 'The 1982 United Nations Convention on the Law of the Sea' in Donald R Rothwell et al (eds), *The Oxford Handbook of the Law of the Sea* (OUP 2015) 24–45

Cot, Jean-Pierre, 'The Law of the Sea and the Margin of Appreciation' in Tafsir Malick Ndiaye and Rüdiger Wolfrum (eds), *Law of the Sea, Environmental Law and Settlement of Disputes: Liber Amicorum Judge Thomas A Mensah* (Martinus Nijhoff 2007) 389–403

Dahmani, Mohamed, *The Fisheries Regime of the Exclusive Economic Zone* (Martinus Nijhoff 1987)

Dupuy, Rene-Jean, 'The Sea Under National Competence' in Rene-Jean Dupuy and and Daniel Vignes (eds), *A Handbook on the New Law of the Sea, Vol 1* (Martinus Nijhoff 1991) 247–315

Galindo Pohl, Reynaldo, 'The Exclusive Economic Zone in the Light of Negotiations of the Third United Nations Conference on the Law of the Sea' in Francisco Orrego Vicuna (ed), *The Exclusive Economic Zone: A Latin American Perspective* (Westview Press 1984) 31–59

Gavouneli, Maria, *Functional Jurisdiction in the Law of the Sea* (Martinus Nijhoff 2007)

Guilfoyle, Douglas, *Shipping Interdiction and the Law of the Sea* (CUP 2009)

Guilfoyle, Douglas, 'Article 111' in Alexander Proelss (ed), *United Nations Convention on the Law of the Sea: A Commentary* (CH Beck 2017) 772–9

Guilfoyle, Douglas, 'SS Lotus' in Eirik Bjorge and Cameron Miles (eds), *Landmark Cases in Public International Law* (Hart 2017) 89–109

Harrison, James, *Making the Law of the Sea* (CUP 2011)

Harrison, James, 'Safeguards Against Excessive Enforcement Measures in the Exclusive Economic Zone—Law and Practice' in Henrik Ringbom (ed), *Jurisdiction over Ships: Post-UNCLOS Developments in the Law of the Sea* (Brill Nijhoff 2015) 217–48

Harrison, James, 'Article 73' in Alexander Proelss (ed), *United Nations Convention on the Law of the Sea: A Commentary* (CH Beck 2017) 556–63

Harrison, James and Elisa Morgera, 'Article 62' in Alexander Proelss (ed), *United Nations Convention on the Law of the Sea: A Commentary* (CH Beck 2017) 493–506

Kaye, Stuart, 'Freedom of Navigation in a Post 9/11 World: Security and Creeping Jurisdiction' in David Freestone, Richard Barnes, and David Ong (eds), *The Law of the Sea: Progress and Prospects* (OUP 2006) 347–64

Klein, Natalie, *Maritime Security and the Law of the Sea* (OUP 2011)

Kwiatkowska, Barbara, 'Conservation and Optimum Utilization of Living Resources' in Thomas A Clingan (ed), *The Law of the Sea: What Lies Ahead? Proceedings of the 20th Annual Conference of the Law of the Sea Institute, July 21–24, 1986* (Law of the Sea Institute 1988) 245–75

Kwiatkowska, Barbara, *The 200 Mile Exclusive Economic Zone in the New Law of the Sea* (Martinus Nijhoff 1989)

Lagoni, Rainer, 'Offshore Bunkering in the Exclusive Economic Zone' in Tafsir Malick Ndiaye and Rüdiger Wolfrum (eds), *Law of the Sea, Environmental Law and Settlement of Disputes: Liber Amicorum Judge Thomas A Mensah* (Martinus Nijhoff 2007) 613–27

Markowski, Marion, *The International Law of EEZ Fisheries* (Europa Law 2010)

McDougal, Myres S and William T Burke, *The Public Order of the Oceans: A Contemporary International Law of the Sea* (New Haven Press 1985)

Nandan, Satya and Shabtai Rosenne (eds), *United Nations Convention on the Law of the Sea 1982: A Commentary, Vol II* (Martinus Nijhoff 1993) and *Vol III* (Martinus Nijhoff 1995)

O'Connell, DP, *The International Law of the Sea, Vol I* (OUP 1982) and *Vol II* (OUP 1984)

Oda, Shigeru, *International Law of the Resources of the Sea* (Sijthoff & Noordhoff International 1979)

Orrego Vicuna, Francisco, *The Exclusive Economic Zone* (CUP 1989)

Poulantzas, Nicholas M, *The Right of Hot Pursuit in International Law* (2nd ed, Kluwer Law International 2002)

Proelss, Alexander, 'Article 56', 'Article 58', and 'Article 59' in Alexander Proelss (ed), *United Nations Convention on the Law of the Sea: A Commentary* (CH Beck 2017) 418–63

Roach, J. Ashley, *Excessive Maritime Claims* (4th ed, Brill Nijhoff 2020)

Rothwell, Donald R and Tim Stephens, *The International Law of the Sea* (2nd ed, Hart 2016)

Ryngaert, Cedric, 'Jurisdiction: Towards a Reasonableness Test' in Malcolm Langford et al (eds), *Global Justice, State Duties. The Extraterritorial Scope of Economic, Social and Cultural Rights in International Law* (CUP 2013) 192–211

Ryngaert, Cedric, *Jurisdiction in International Law* (2nd ed, OUP 2015)

Treves, Tullio, 'Some International Law Aspects of the Use of Vessel Monitoring Systems for Preventing Illegal Unreported and Unregulated Fishing' in Tafsir Malick Ndiaye and Rüdiger Wolfrum (eds), *Law of the Sea, Environmental Law and Settlement of Disputes: Liber Amicorum Judge Thomas A Mensah* (Martinus Nijhoff 2007) 811–20

Treves, Tullio, 'Jurisdiction over Vessels in the Areas of Pollution and Fisheries: General Report' in Erik Franckx and Philippe Gautier (eds), *The Exercise of Jurisdiction Over Vessels: New Developments in the Fields of Pollution, Fisheries, Crimes and Sea and Trafficking of Weapons of Mass Destruction* (Bruylant 2011) 1–28

Tuerk, Helmut, *Reflections on the Contemporary Law of the Sea* (Martinus Nijhoff 2012)

van der Marel, Eva, 'Problems and Progress in Combatting IUU Fishing' in Erik Jaap Molenaar and Richard Caddell (eds), *Strengthening International Fisheries Law in an Era of Changing Oceans* (Hart 2018) 291–318

Xue, Guifang, *China and International Fisheries Law and Policy* (Martinus Nijhoff 2005)

Journal Articles

Agnew, David J et al, 'Estimating the Worldwide Extent of Illegal Fishing' (2009) 4(2) PLOS ONE e4570, available at <http://journals.plos.org/plosone/article?id=10.1371/journal.pone.0004570> accessed 29 November 2020

Allen, Craig H, 'Doctrine of Hot Pursuit: A Functional Interpretation Adaptable to Emerging Maritime Law Enforcement Technologies and Practices' (1989) 20(4) ODIL 309

Allott, Philip, 'Power Sharing in the Law of the Sea' (1983) 77 AJIL 1

Allott, Philip, 'Mare Nostrum: A New International Law of the Sea' (1992) 86 AJIL 764

Anand, RP, '"Tyranny" of the Freedom-of-the-Seas Doctrine' (1973) 12(3) IntSt 416

Baird, Rachel, 'Illegal, Unreported and Unregulated Fishing: An Analysis of the Legal, Economic and Historical Factors Relevant to Its Development and Persistence' (2004) 5 MelbJIntlLaw 299

Baird, Rachel, 'Arrests in a Cold Climate (Part 2)—Shaping Hot Pursuit through State Practice' (2009) 13 Ant&SthnOcean L&Pol OccPap 1

Brilmayer, Lea and Natalie Klein, 'Land and Sea: Two Sovereignty Regimes In Search of a Common Denominator' (2001) 33 NYUJIntlL&Pol 703

Brown, Chester, '"Reasonableness" in the Law of the Sea: The Prompt Release of the Volga' (2003) 16(3) LJIL 621

Brown, Edward Duncan, 'The Exclusive Economic Zone: Criteria and Machinery for the Resolution of International Conflicts between Different Users of the EEZ' (1977) 4 MarPolManagement 325

Burke, William T, 'Exclusive Fisheries Zones and Freedom of Navigation' (1983) 20 SanDiegoLRev 595

Burke, William T, '1982 Convention on the Law of the Sea Provisions on Conditions of Access to Fisheries Subject to National Jurisdiction' (1984) 63 OrLRev 73

Burke, William T, 'Coastal State Fishery Regulation Under International Law: A Comment on the La Bretagne Award of July 17, 1986 (The Arbitration Between Canada and France)' (1988) 25 SanDiegoLRev 495

Butler, William E, 'Custom, Treaty, State Practice and the 1982 Convention' (1987) 81 ProcAnnMtg (ASIL) 84
Caddell, Richard, 'Platforms, Protestors and Provisional Measures: The Arctic Sunrise Dispute and Environmental Activism at Sea' (2014) 45 NYIL 359
Caminos, Hugo and Michael R Molitor, 'Progressive Development of International Law and the Package Deal' (1985) 79(4) AJIL 871
Christie, Donna R, 'It Don't Come EEZ: The Failure and Future of Coastal State Fisheries Management' (2004) 14 JTransnatLawPol 1
Churchill, Robin Rolf, 'The Barents Sea Loophole Agreement: A "Coastal State" Solution to a Straddling Stock Problem' (1999) 14 IJMCL 467
Churchill, Robin Rolf, 'The Jurisprudence of the International Tribunal for the Law of the Sea Relating to Fisheries: Is There Much in the Net?' (2007) 22(3) IJMCL 383
Corten, Olivier, 'The Notion of "Reasonable" in International Law: Legal Discourse, Reason and Contradictions' (1999) 48(3) ICLQ 613
Edeson, William, 'Closing the Gap: The Role of "Soft" International Instruments to Control Fishing' (1999) 20 AustYBIL 83
Franckx, Erik, '"Reasonable Bond" in the Practice of the International Tribunal for the Law of the Sea' (2002) 32 CalWIntlLJ 303
Franckx, Eric, 'The 200-Mile Limit: Between Creeping Jurisdiction and Creeping Common Heritage?' (2007) 39 GWashIntlLRev 467
Gilmore, William C, 'Hot Pursuit: The Case of R v Mills and Others' (1995) 44 ICLQ 927
Guggisberg, Solène, 'The Roles of Nongovernmental Actors in Improving Compliance with Fisheries Regulations' (2019) 28 RECIEL 314
Guilfoyle, Douglas and Cameron A Miles, 'Provisional Measures and the MV Arctic Sunrise' (2014) 108 AJIL 271
Gullett, Warwick and Clive Schofield, 'Pushing the Limits of the Law of the Sea Convention: Australian and French Cooperative Surveillance and Enforcement in the Southern Ocean' (2007) 22 IJMCL 545
Hanich, Quentin et al, 'Sovereignty and Cooperation in Regional Pacific Tuna Fisheries Management: Politics, Economics, Conservation and the Vessel Day Scheme' (2010) 2(1) AustJMar&OceanAff 2
Harrison, James, 'The Arctic Sunrise Arbitration (Netherlands v. Russia)' (2016) 31 IJMCL 145
Havice, Elizabeth, 'The Structure of Tuna Access Agreements in the Western and Central Pacific Ocean: Lessons for Vessel Day Scheme Planning' (2010) 34(5) MarPol 979
Havice, Elizabeth, 'Rights-Based Management in the Western and Central Pacific Ocean Tuna Fishery: Economic and Environmental Change under the Vessel Day Scheme' (2013) 42 MarPol 259
Hohfeld, Wesley Newcomb, 'Some Fundamental Legal Conceptions as Applied in Judicial Reasoning' (1913) 23 YaleLJ 16
Ikeshima, Taisaku, 'The "Reasonableness" of Unreasonable Arguments in Prompt Release Cases in the ITLOS' (2009) 6 Waseda GlobalFor 107
Kaye, Stuart, 'Enforcement Cooperation in Combating Illegal and Unauthorized Fishing: An Assessment of Contemporary Practice' (2014) 32 BerkeleyJIntlL 316
Klein, Natalie, 'Maritime Autonomous Vehicles within the International Law Framework to Enhance Maritime Security' (2019) 95 IntlLSt 244
Knauss, John A, 'Creeping Jurisdiction and Customary International Law' (1985) 15(2) ODIL 209

Le Gallic, Bertrand and Anthony Cox, 'An Economic Analysis of Illegal, Unreported and Unregulated (IUU) Fishing: Key Drivers and Possible Solutions' (2006) 30(6) MarPol 689
Lowe, AV, 'Reflections on the Waters: Changing Conceptions of Property Rights in the Law of the Sea' (1986) 1 IJECL 1
Mills, Alex, 'Rethinking Jurisdiction in International Law' (2014) 84(1) BYIL 187
Molenaar, Erik Jaap and Martin Tsamenyi, 'Satellite-Based Vessel Monitoring Systems for Fisheries Management: International Legal Aspects' (2000) 15 IJMCL 65
Molenaar, Erik Jaap, 'Multilateral Hot Pursuit and Illegal Fishing in the Southern Ocean: The Pursuits of the Viarsa 1 and the South Tomi' (2004) 19 IJMCL 19
Mossop, Joanna, 'Protests against Oil Exploration at Sea: Lessons from the Arctic Sunrise Arbitration' (2016) 31(1) IJMCL 60
Ndiaye, Tafsir Malick, 'Illegal, Unreported and Unregulated Fishing: Responses in General and in West Africa' (2011) 10 ChineseJIntlL 373
Nichols, Rachel et al, 'Fishing Access Agreements and Harvesting Decisions of Host and Distant Water Fishing Nations' (2015) 54 MarPol 77
Oda, Shigeru, 'Fisheries under the United Nations Convention on the Law of the Sea' (1983) 77 AJIL 739
Oda, Shigeru, 'Dispute Settlement Prospects in the Law of the Sea' (1995) 44 ICLQ 863
Oxman, Bernard H, 'Observations on Vessel Release under the United Nations Convention on the Law of the Sea' (1996) 11 IJMCL 201
Oxman, Bernard H and Vincent Bantz, 'The M/V "Saiga" (No 2) (Saint Vincent and the Grenadines v Guinea), Judgment (ITLOS Case No 2)' (2000) 94(1) AJIL 140
Oxman, Bernard, 'The Territorial Temptation: A Siren Song at Sea' (2006) 100 AJIL 830
Oxman, Bernard H and Vincent P Coglianti-Bantz, 'The M/V Virginia G (Panama/Guinea Bissau)' (2014) 108(4) AJIL 769
Petersen, Elizabeth, 'The Catch in Trading Fishing Access for Foreign Aid' (2003) 27(3) MarPol 219
Plant, G, 'International Law and Direct Action Protests at Sea: Twenty Years on' (2002) 33 NYIL 75
Proelss, Alexander, 'The Law on the Exclusive Economic Zone in Perspective: Legal Status and Resolution of User Conflicts Revisited' (2012) 26 OceanYB 87
Rayfuse, Rosemary, 'The Future of Compulsory Dispute Settlement under the Law of the Sea Convention' (2005) 36 VUWellLRev 683
Reuland, Robert C, 'The Customary Right of Hot Pursuit Onto the High Seas: Annotations to Article 111 of the Law of the Sea' (1993) 33 VaJIntlL 557
Riphagen, W, 'Some Reflections on "Functional Sovereignty"' (1975) 6 NYIL 121
Roach, J Ashley, 'Today's Customary International Law of the Sea' (2014) 45(3) ODIL 239
Robertson, Horace B, 'Navigation in the Exclusive Economic Zone' (1984) 24 VaJIntlL 865
Rothwell, Donald R, 'Navigational Rights and Freedoms in the Asia Pacific Following Entry Into Force of the Law of the Sea Convention' (1995) 35 VaJIntlL 587
Rothwell, Donald R and Tim Stephens, 'Illegal Southern Ocean Fishing and Prompt Release: Balancing Coastal and Flag State Rights and Interests' (2004) 53 ICLQ 171
Rothwell, Donald R, 'Legal Challenges for Maritime Operations in the Southern Ocean' (2014) 28 OceanYB 423
Schatz, Valentin, 'Combating Illegal Fishing in the Exclusive Economic Zone—Flag State Obligations in the Context of the Primary Responsibility of the Coastal State' (2016) 7(2) GoettingenJIntlLaw 383
Schatz, Valentin, 'Fishing for Interpretation: The ITLOS Advisory Opinion on Flag State Responsibility for Illegal Fishing in the EEZ' (2016) 47(4) ODIL 327

Schatz, Valentin, 'The Contribution of Fisheries Access Agreements to Flag State Responsibility' (2017) 84 MarPol 313

Schatz, Valentin, 'Marine Fisheries Law Enforcement Partnerships in Waters under National Jurisdiction: The Legal Framework for Inter-State Cooperation and Public-Private Partnerships with Non-Governmental Organizations and Private Security Companies' (2018) 32 Ocean YB 329

Shearer, Ivan, 'Problems of Jurisdiction and Law Enforcement Against Delinquent Vessels' (1986) 35 ICLQ 320

Stephens, Tim and Donald R Rothwell, 'The LOSC Framework for Maritime Jurisdiction and Enforcement 30 Years On' (2012) 27 IJMCL 701

Telesetsky, Anastasia, 'Laundering Fish in the Global Undercurrents: Illegal, Unreported, and Unregulated Fishing and Transnational Organised Crime' (2014) 41(4) ELQ 939

Theilen, Jens T, 'What's in a Name? The Illegality of Illegal, Unreported and Unregulated Fishing' (2013) 28 IJMCL 533

Treves, Tullio, 'Coastal States' Rights in the Maritime Areas under UNCLOS' (2015) 12(1) BrazilJIntlLaw 39

Trevisanut, Seline, 'Twenty Years of Prompt Release of Vessels: Admissibility, Jurisdiction, and Recent Trends' (2017) 48 ODIL 300

Van Dyke, Jon M, 'The Disappearing Right to Navigational Freedom in the Exclusive Economic Zone' (2005) 29 MarPol 107

Yeeting, Agnes D et al, 'Implications of New Economic Policy Instruments for Tuna Management in the Western and Central Pacific' (2016) 63 MarPol 45

Other Materials

Burke, William T, 'Fisheries Regulations Under Extended Jurisdiction and International Law' *FAO Fisheries Technical Paper No 223* (FAO 1982)

Cacaud, Phillippe et al, 'Administrative Sanctions in Fisheries Law' *FAO Legislative Study 82* (FAO 2003)

Carroz, Jean and Michel Savini, 'The Practice of Coastal States Regarding Foreign Access to Fishery Resources (An Analysis of Bilateral Agreements)' in *Report of the Expert Consultation on the Conditions of Access to the Fish Resources of the Exclusive Economic Zones* (FAO 1983) Annex 2, 43–72

Christy, LC and Gerald Moore, 'Forms of Foreign Participation in Fisheries: Coastal State Practice' in *Report of the Expert Consultation on the Conditions of Access to the Fish Resources of the Exclusive Economic Zones* (FAO 1983) Annex 6, 95–9

Clark, Les, 'Case Study on Foreign Fishing Agreements in the Western Pacific' in *Trade in Fishing Services: Emerging Perspectives on Foreign Fishing Arrangements* (World Bank 2014) Appendix B, 61–70

FAO, Regional Fisheries Body Map Viewer, available at <http://www.fao.org/figis/geoserver/factsheets/rfbs.html>

FAO, *The State of World Fisheries and Aquaculture 2020: Sustainability in Action* (FAO 2020)

FAO, *Yearbook of Fishery and Aquaculture Statistics 2018* (FAO 2020)

FAO Legal Office, *Coastal State Requirements for Foreign Fishing* (Rev 4, FAO 1993)

FAO, FAOLEX Database, available at <http://www.fao.org/faolex/country-profiles/en/>

Flanders Marine Institute Maritime Boundaries Geodatabase, *Maritime Boundaries and Exclusive Economic Zones* (200NM) (Version 11, 2019), available at <http://www.marineregions.org/>

Flewwelling, P, *An Introduction to Monitoring, Control and Surveillance Systems for Capture Fisheries* (FAO 1994)

Flewwelling, P et al, 'Recent Trends in Monitoring, Control and Surveillance Systems for Capture Fisheries' *FAO Fisheries Technical Paper 415* (FAO 2002)

Freestone, David, *The Burden of Proof in National Resources Legislation: Some Critical Issues for Fisheries Law* (FAO 1998)

International Law Commission, 'Articles Concerning the Law of the Sea with Commentaries' *Yearbook of the International Law Commission (1956) Volume II*, UN Doc A/CN.4/SER.A/1956/Add.l 265 265–301

International Law Commission, 'Text of the Draft Conclusions on the Identification of Customary International Law', *Report of the International Law Commission on the Work of its 68th Session (2 May–10 June and 4 July–12 August 2016)* UN Doc A/71/10 76–117

International Law Commission, 'Text of the Draft Conclusions on Subsequent Agreements and Subsequent Practice in Relation to the Interpretation of Treaties', *Report of the International Law Commission on the Work of its 68th Session (2 May–10 June and 4 July–12 August 2016)* UN Doc A/71/10) 120–240

Mangatalle, Danielle, *Legislation on Coastal State Requirements for Foreign Fishing* (6th ed, FAO 1996)

Martin, Will et al, *A Handbook for Negotiating Fishing Access Agreements* (World Wildlife Fund 2001)

Mbithi Mwikya, Stephen, *Fisheries Access Agreements: Trade and Development Issues* (International Centre for Trade and Sustainable Development 2006)

Moore, Gerald, *Coastal State Requirements for Foreign Fishing* (Rev 1, FAO 1983)

Moore, Gerald, *Coastal State Requirements for Foreign Fishing* (Rev 2, FAO 1985)

Moore, Gerald, *Coastal State Requirements for Foreign Fishing* (Rev 3, FAO 1988)

Munro, Gordon, 'The Legal and Economic Principles Underlying Foreign Fishing Arrangements' in *Trade in Fishing Services: Emerging Perspectives on Foreign Fishing Arrangements* (World Bank 2014)

Natural Earth, Vector and Raster Map Data, available at <http://naturalearthdata.com>

Orellana, Marcos *Towards Sustainable Fisheries Access Agreements* (United Nations Environment Programme 2008)

Robb, Dean, 'Access Conditions and Compliance Control' in *Report of the Expert Consultation on the Conditions of Access to the Fish Resources of the Exclusive Economic Zones* (FAO 1983)

World Bank, *Trade in Fishing Services: Emerging Perspectives on Foreign Fishing Arrangements*, World Bank Report No 92622 (World Bank 2014),

Index

For the benefit of digital users, indexed terms that span two pages (e.g., 52–53) may, on occasion, appear on only one of those pages.

Tables and figures are indicated by *t* and *f* following the page number